PRIVACY, INFORMATION, AND TECHNOLOGY

D1500507

ASPEN ELECTIVES SERIES

PRIVACY, INFORMATION, AND TECHNOLOGY

Third Edition

Daniel J. Solove
John Marshall Harlan Research Professor of Law
George Washington University Law School

Paul M. Schwartz
Faculty Director, Berkeley Center for Law & Technology
Professor of Law
U.C. Berkeley Law School

Wolters Kluwer
Law & Business

Printed in the United States of America.

1 2 3 4 5 6 7 8 9 0

ISBN 978-0-7355-1042-5

Library of Congress Cataloging-in-Publication Data

Solove, Daniel J. 1972-
   Privacy, information, and technology/Daniel J. Solove, Paul M. Schwartz — 3rd ed.
   p. cm — (Aspen elective series)
   Includes bibliographical references and index.
   ISBN 978-0-7355-1042-5 (alk. paper)
   1. Privacy, Right of—United States. 2. Data protection—Law and legislation—
United States.   I. Schwartz, Paul M., 1959- II.   Title.
   KF 1262.S66 2011
   342.7308'58—dc23

                                                                    2011043911

About Wolters Kluwer Law & Business

Wolters Kluwer Law & Business is a leading global provider of intelligent information and digital solutions for legal and business professionals in key specialty areas, and respected educational resources for professors and law students. Wolters Kluwer Law & Business connects legal and business professionals as well as those in the education market with timely, specialized authoritative content and information-enabled solutions to support success through productivity, accuracy and mobility.

Serving customers worldwide, Wolters Kluwer Law & Business products include those under the Aspen Publishers, CCH, Kluwer Law International, Loislaw, Best Case, ftwilliam.com and MediRegs family of products.

CCH products have been a trusted resource since 1913, and are highly regarded resources for legal, securities, antitrust and trade regulation, government contracting, banking, pension, payroll, employment and labor, and healthcare reimbursement and compliance professionals.

Aspen Publishers products provide essential information to attorneys, business professionals and law students. Written by preeminent authorities, the product line offers analytical and practical information in a range of specialty practice areas from securities law and intellectual property to mergers and acquisitions and pension/benefits. Aspen's trusted legal education resources provide professors and students with high-quality, up-to-date and effective resources for successful instruction and study in all areas of the law.

Kluwer Law International products provide the global business community with reliable international legal information in English. Legal practitioners, corporate counsel and business executives around the world rely on Kluwer Law journals, looseleafs, books, and electronic products for comprehensive information in many areas of international legal practice.

Loislaw is a comprehensive online legal research product providing legal content to law firm practitioners of various specializations. Loislaw provides attorneys with the ability to quickly and efficiently find the necessary legal information they need, when and where they need it, by facilitating access to primary law as well as state-specific law, records, forms and treatises.

Best Case Solutions is the leading bankruptcy software product to the bankruptcy industry. It provides software and workflow tools to flawlessly streamline petition preparation and the electronic filing process, while timely incorporating ever-changing court requirements.

ftwilliam.com offers employee benefits professionals the highest quality plan documents (retirement, welfare and non-qualified) and government forms (5500/PBGC, 1099 and IRS) software at highly competitive prices.

MediRegs products provide integrated health care compliance content and software solutions for professionals in healthcare, higher education and life sciences, including professionals in accounting, law and consulting.

Wolters Kluwer Law & Business, a division of Wolters Kluwer, is headquartered in New York. Wolters Kluwer is a market-leading global information services company focused on professionals.

To my parents and grandparents—DJS

To Steffie, Clara, and Leo—PMS

SUMMARY OF CONTENTS

CONTENTS

3 PRIVACY AND GOVERNMENT RECORDS AND DATABASES

4 PRIVACY OF FINANCIAL AND COMMERCIAL DATA   383

PREFACE

The rapid growth of the Internet, coupled with new business practices and new efforts by government to deploy technology for law enforcement and the administration of programs, has raised far-reaching questions about the future of privacy.

Central to many of these debates is the role of law. To what extent can the law safeguard the right of privacy in an era of rapidly evolving technology? What competing interests must be considered? What is the appropriate role of the courts and the legislatures? These questions are not new, but they have acquired greater urgency as the law is asked to evaluate an increasingly complex array of privacy matters.

For lawyers, this rapid growth has raised both new challenges and new opportunities. In the private sector, attorneys now routinely advise business clients about the development of privacy policies, compliance with privacy statutes, and privacy regulations in new markets. Attorneys litigate on behalf of clients who believe that their privacy has been violated, while others defend against these allegations. State attorneys general have become leading champions of privacy rights. Policymakers in government evaluate new legislative proposals both to expand and to limit privacy claims. Legal advisors on trade policy, technology development, consumer protection, and national security all consider privacy issues in the course of their work. Clearly, information privacy has emerged as one of the critical legal subjects in the modern era.

This text aims to provide a comprehensive and accessible introduction to the legal, social, and political issues involving information privacy. The text begins with a broad introduction to the conceptual underpinnings of information privacy. It sets forth clearly and concisely the range of laws that address information privacy, and it discusses the basic policy issues that inhabit the field. The text then examines the legal and policy implications of the growing accumulation and use of personal information by the government and by businesses. We have included extensive notes and commentary, and have integrated cases and statutes with theoretical and policy perspectives. To facilitate discussion and debate, we have included excerpts from commentators with a wide range of viewpoints. Technical terms are clearly explained.

When selecting cases, we have included the leading cases as well as endeavoured to provide a solid historical background and a timely and fresh perspective on the major privacy issues facing lawyers in the twenty-first century. Important majority opinions are followed by equally important dissents. The text includes extensive notes and commentary, and it integrates cases and statutes with theoretical and policy perspectives. To facilitate discussion and debate, we have included excerpts from commentators with a wide range of viewpoints. Technical terms are clearly explained.

A Note on the Casebook Website. We strive to keep the book up to date between editions, and we maintain a web page for the book with downloadable updates and other useful information. We invite you to visit the website:

> http://informationprivacylaw.com

A Note on New Changes to the Book. We made many changes and updates to the book but have retained its basic organizational structure and pedagogical style. Specific changes and additions to the book are documented in the Teacher's Manual.

A Note on Privacy Law Fundamentals. Students may find our short volume, *Privacy Law Fundamentals,* to be a useful companion to the casebook. *Privacy Law Fundamentals* is designed to be a distilled overview of information privacy law for both practitioners and students. More information about this book can be found at http://informationprivacylaw.com.

A Note on the Editing. We have deleted many citations and footnotes from the cases to facilitate readability. The footnotes that have been retained in the cases have been renumbered. When discussing books, articles, and other materials in the notes and commentary, we have included full citations in footnotes in order to make the text easier to read. We have also included many citations to additional works in the footnotes that may be of interest to the reader.

Daniel J. Solove
Paul M. Schwartz

November 2011

ACKNOWLEDGMENTS

Daniel J. Solove: I would like to thank Carl Coleman, Scott Forbes, Susan Freiwald, Tomás Gómez-Arostegui, Stephen Gottlieb, Marcia Hofmann, Chris Hoofnagle, John Jacobi, Orin Kerr, Raymond Ku, Peter Raven-Hansen, Joel Reidenberg, Neil Richards, Michael Risinger, Lior Strahilevitz, Peter Swire, William Thompson, and Peter Winn for helpful comments and suggestions. Charlie Sullivan and Jake Barnes provided indispensable advice about how to bring this project to fruition. Special thanks to Richard Mixter at Aspen Publishers for his encouragement and faith in this project. Thanks as well to the other folks at Aspen who have contributed greatly to the editing and development of this book: John Devins, Christine Hannan, Carmen Reid, Jessica Barmack, John Burdeaux, and Sandra Doherty. I would like to thank my research assistants Peter Choy, Monica Contreras, Carly Grey, Maeve Miller, James Murphy, Poornima Ravishankar, Sheerin Shahinpoor, John Spaccarotella, Tiffany Stedman, Eli Weiss, and Kate Yannitte. I would also like to thank Dean Fred Lawrence for providing the resources I needed.

Paul M. Schwartz: For their suggestions, encouragement, and insights into information privacy law, I would like to thank Ken Bamberger, Fred Cate, Malcolm Crompton, Christopher Gulotta, Andrew Guzman, Chris Hoofnagle, Ted Janger, Ronald D. Lee, Lance Liebman, Steven McDonald, Viktor Mayer-Schönberger, Deirdre Mulligan, Karl-Nikolaus Peifer, Joel Reidenberg, Ira Rubinstein, Pam Samuelson, Lior Strahilevitz, Peter Swire, William M. Treanor, and Peter Winn. I benefited as well from the help of my talented research assistants: Cesar Alvarez, Benedikt Burger, Kai-Dieter Classen, Leah Duranti, Alpa Patel, Karl Saddlemire, Brian St. John, Laura Sullivan, and Sebastian Zimmeck. Many thanks to my co-author, Daniel Solove. Many thanks as well to my mother, Nancy Schwartz, and to Laura Schwartz and Ed Holden; David Schwartz and Kathy Smith; and Daniel Schwartz.

A profound debt is owed Spiros Simitis. My interest in the subject of information privacy began in 1985 with his suggestion that I visit his office of the Hessian Data Protection Commissioner in Wiesbaden and sit in on meetings there. Through his scholarship, example, and friendship, Professor Simitis has provided essential guidance during the decades since that initial trip to Wiesbaden. My portion of the book is dedicated to Steffie, Clara, and Leo, with my gratitude and love.

Finally, both of us would like to thank Marc Rotenberg, who helped us shape the book in its first two editions and provided invaluable input.

We are grateful to the following sources for their permission to reprint excerpts of their scholarship:

Anita L. Allen, *Coercing Privacy*, 40 William & Mary L. Rev. 723 (1999). Used by permission. © 1999 by William & Mary Law Review and Anita L. Allen.

William C. Banks & M.E. Bowman, *Executive Authority For National Security Surveillance*, 50 Am. U. L. Rev. 1 (2000). Reprinted with permission.

Fred H. Cate, *The Privacy Problem: A Broader View of Information Privacy and the Costs and Consequences of Protecting It*, 4 First Reports 1 (March 2003). Reprinted with permission.

Julie E. Cohen, *Examined Lives: Informational Privacy*, 52 Stan. L. Rev. 1371 (2000). © 2000. Reprinted by permission of the Stanford Law Review in the format textbook via Copyright Clearance Center and Julie Cohen.

Julie E. Cohen, *A Right to Read Anonymously: A Closer Look at "Copyright Management" in Cyberspace*, 28 Conn. L. Rev. 981 (1996). © 1996 by Connecticut Law Review and Julie E. Cohen. Reprinted with permission.

Mary DeRosa, *Data Mining and Data Analysis for Counterterrorism*, Center for Strategic and International Studies 6-8 (CSIS) (2004). Reprinted with permission.

Eric Goldman, *The Privacy Hoax*, Forbes (Oct. 14, 2002) available at http:// www.ericgoldman.org/Articles/privacyhoax.htm. Reprinted with permission. Lawrence O. Gostin, Health Information Privacy, 80 Cornell L. Rev. 451 (1995). Reprinted with permission.

Steven Hetcher, *The FTC as Internet Privacy Norm Entrepreneur*, 53 Vand. L. Rev. 2041 (2000). Reprinted with the permission of Steven Hetcher.

Edward Janger & Paul M. Schwartz, *The Gramm-Leach-Bliley Act, Information Privacy, and the Limits of Default Rules*, 86 Minn. L. Rev. 1219 (2002). Reprinted with permission.

Orin S. Kerr, *A User's Guide to the Stored Communications Act — and a Legislator's Guide to Amending It*, 72 Geo. Wash. L. Rev. 1208 (2004). Reprinted with permission.

Orin S. Kerr, *Internet Surveillance Law After the USA PATRIOT Act: The Big Brother That Isn't*, 97 Nw. U. L. Rev. 607 (2003). Reprinted with permission.

Catharine A. MacKinnon, Toward a Feminist Theory of the State 190-193 (1989). © 1989 by Harvard University Press. Reprinted with permission.

Richard A. Posner, *The Right of Privacy*, 12 Ga. L. Rev. 393 (1978). Reprinted with permission.

Marc Rotenberg, *Fair Information Practices and the Architecture of Privacy (What Larry Doesn't Get)*, 2001 Stan. Tech. L. Rev. 1, 43 (2001). Reprinted with permission.

Paul M. Schwartz, *Privacy and Democracy in Cyberspace*, 52 Vand. L. Rev. 1609 (1999). Reprinted with the permission of Paul Schwartz.

Reva B. Seigel, *The Rule of Love: Wife Beating as Prerogative of Privacy*, 105 Yale L.J. 2117 (1996). Reprinted by permission of the *Yale Law Journal* Company and the William S. Hein Company, from the *Yale Law Journal*, vol. 105, pages 2117-2207.

Spiros Simitis, *Reviewing Privacy in an Informational Society*, 135 U. Pa. L. Rev. 707, 709-710, 724-726, 732-738, 746 (1987). © 1987 by the University of Pennsylvania Law Review. Reprinted by permission of the University of Pennsylvania Law Review and Spiros Simitis.

Daniel J. Solove, *Conceptualizing Privacy*, 90 California Law Review 1087 (2002). © 2002 by the California Law Review.

Daniel J. Solove, *Reconstructing Electronic Surveillance Law*, 72 George Washington Law Review 1264 (2004). © 2004 by Daniel J. Solove.

Daniel J. Solove, *The Virtues of Knowing Less: Justifying Privacy Protections Against Disclosure*, 53 Duke Law Journal 967 (2003). © 2003 by Daniel J. Solove.

Jeff Sovern, *Opting In, Opting Out, or No Options at All: The Fight for Control of Personal Information*, 74 Wash. L. Rev. 1033 (1999). Reprinted with permission.

Michael E. Staten & Fred H. Cate, *The Impact of Opt-In Privacy Rules on Retail Markets: A Case Study of MBNA*, 52 Duke L.J. 745 (2003). Reprinted with permission.

Alan Westin, Privacy and Freedom 7, 31-38 (1967). A study sponsored by the Association of the Bar of the City of New York. Reprinted with permission.

Peter A. Winn, *Online Court Records: Balancing Judicial Accountability and Privacy in an Age of Electronic Information*, 79 Wash. L. Rev. 307 (2004). Reprinted with permission.

PRIVACY, INFORMATION, AND TECHNOLOGY

CHAPTER 1

INTRODUCTION

A. INFORMATION PRIVACY, TECHNOLOGY, AND THE LAW

We live in a world shaped by technology and fueled by information. Technological devices — such as mobile phones, video and audio recording devices, computers, and the Internet — have revolutionized our ability to capture information about the world and to communicate with each other. Information is the lifeblood of today's society. Increasingly, our everyday activities involve the transfer and recording of information. The government collects vast quantities of personal information in records pertaining to an individual's birth, marriage, divorce, property, court proceedings, motor vehicles, voting activities, criminal transgressions, professional licensing, and other activities. Private sector entities also amass gigantic databases of personal information for marketing purposes or to prepare credit histories. Wherever we go, whatever we do, we could easily leave behind a trail of data that is recorded and gathered together.

These new technologies, coupled with the increasing use of personal information by business and government, pose new challenges for the protection of privacy. This book is about the law's response to new challenges to privacy. A significant amount of law regulates information privacy in the United States and around the world. Is this law responsive to the present and future dangers to privacy? Can information privacy itself endanger other important values? What duties and responsibilities must corporations, government agencies, and other private and public sector entities have with regard to personal data? What rights do individuals have to prevent and redress invasions to their privacy? When and how should privacy rights be limited? Does the war on terrorism require less privacy and more sharing of information? How should the law respond to an age of rapid technological change? Has the meaning of privacy changed in the age of social media and powerful search engines? These are some of the questions that this text will address.

This book's topic is information privacy law. Information privacy concerns the collection, use, and disclosure of personal information. Information privacy is often contrasted with "decisional privacy," which concerns the freedom to make decisions about one's body and family. Decisional privacy involves matters such as contraception, procreation, abortion, and child rearing, and is at the center of a series of Supreme Court cases often referred to as "substantive due process" or "the constitutional right to privacy." But information privacy increasingly incorporates elements of decisional privacy as the use of data both expands and limits individual autonomy.

Information privacy law is an interrelated web of tort law, federal and state constitutional law, federal and state statutory law, evidentiary privileges, property law, contract law, and criminal law. Information privacy law is relatively new, although its roots reach far back. It is developing coherence as privacy doctrines in one area are being used to inform and structure legal responses in other areas. Information privacy law raises a related set of political, policy, and philosophical questions: What is privacy? Why is privacy important? What is the impact of technology on privacy? How does privacy affect the efforts of law enforcement and national security agencies to protect the public? What is the role of the courts, the legislatures, and the law in safeguarding, or in placing limits on, privacy?

Furthermore, one might wonder: Why study information privacy law? There are a number of answers to this question. First, in today's Information Age, privacy is an issue of paramount significance for freedom, democracy, and security. One of the central issues of information privacy concerns the power of commercial and government entities over individual autonomy and decision making. Privacy also concerns the drawing of rules that may limit this autonomy and decision making by necessarily permitting commercial and government entities access to personal information. Understood broadly, information privacy plays an important role in the society we are constructing in today's Information Age.

Second, information privacy is an issue of growing public concern. Information privacy has become a priority on the legislative agenda of Congress and many state legislatures. Information privacy problems are also timely, frequently in the news, and often the subject of litigation.

Third, there are many new laws and legal developments regarding information privacy. It is a growth area in the law. Increased litigation, legislation, regulation, as well as public concern over privacy are spurring corporations in a variety of businesses to address privacy. Lawyers are drafting privacy policies, litigating privacy issues, and developing ways for dot-com companies, corporations, hospitals, insurers, and banks to conform to privacy regulations. A new position, the Chief Privacy Officer, is a mainstay at most corporations. The leading organization of these officers, the International Association of Privacy Professionals (IAPP), boasts thousands of members. Attorneys increasingly are grappling with privacy issues — either through litigation of privacy violations or through measures to comply with privacy regulations and to prevent litigation. All of these developments demand lawyers who are well-versed in the grand scheme and subtle nuances of information privacy law.

Fourth, information privacy law is an engaging and fascinating topic. The issues are controversial, complex, relevant, and current. Few areas of law are more closely intertwined with our world of rapid technological innovation. Moreover, concerns regarding information privacy play an important role in debates regarding security in post 9/11 America. The study of privacy law also helps us understand how our legal institutions respond to change and may help prepare us for other challenges ahead.

SIDIS V. F-R PUBLISHING CORP.

113 F.2d 806 (2d Cir. 1940)

[William James Sidis (1898–1944) was perhaps the most famous child prodigy of his day. According to Amy Wallace's biography of Sidis, *The Prodigy*, he was able to read the *New York Times* at the age of 18 months.[1] By the time he was three, William had learned to operate a typewriter and used it to compose a letter to Macy's to order toys. At that age, he also learned Latin "as a birthday present for his father." That year, after his father taught him the Greek alphabet, he taught himself to read Homer with the aid of a Greek primer. By the time he started elementary school, at the age of six, he could speak and read at least eight languages. At the age of five, he had already devised a method for calculating the day of the week on which any given date occurred, and when he was seven years old, he wrote a book about calendars. At that time, he had already prepared manuscripts about anatomy, astronomy, grammar, linguistics, and mathematics. At the age of eight, he created a new table of logarithms, which used a base of twelve instead of the conventional ten. From early childhood on, Sidis was also passionately interested in politics and world events. According to Wallace, Sidis was one of the few child prodigies in world history whose talents were not limited to a single field.

In 1909, Harvard University permitted Sidis to enroll in it; he was 11 years old and the youngest student in the history of Harvard. Sidis also made the front pages of newspapers around the nation when on January 5, 1910, he delivered a two-hour lecture to the Harvard Mathematics Club. The *New York Times* featured Sidis on its front page of October 11, 1909, as "Harvard's Child Prodigy."[2]

Boris Sidis, William's father, was a distinguished physician, early pioneer of American psychology (and opponent of Sigmund Freud), and prolific author. In 1911, Boris published a book about his educational theories and his virulent opposition to the educational institutions of the day. At the time of the publication of this book, *Philistine and Genius*, William was 13, and in Wallace's description, "teetering on the edge of his endurance to public exposure." Although the book did not mention his son by name, it did discuss him and his accomplishments, which brought William additional publicity. Sarah Sidis, William's mother and herself a physician, had a domineering and deeply troubled relationship with her son. Neither she nor Boris did anything to shelter William from the great publicity that followed him from an early age and the tremendous stress that it created in his life.

When he graduated from Harvard at age 16, William told reporters: "I want to live the perfect life. The only way to live the perfect life is to live it in seclusion. I have always hated crowds." After graduating from college, Sidis

---

[1] Amy Wallace, *The Prodigy* (1986).
[2] *Harvard's Child Prodigy: All Amazed at Mathematical Grasp of Youngest Matriculate, Aged 13 Years*, N.Y. Times (Oct. 10, 1909), at A1.

accepted a teaching position at the Rice University in Houston. After a difficult eight months as a professor of mathematics there, William returned to Boston and enrolled in Harvard Law School in 1916. He left the law school in his last semester there without taking a degree.

From 1918 until a *New Yorker* article about him in 1937, Sidis engaged in socialist and other radical politics, published numerous newsletters, lived an active social life, addressed a monthly study group, wrote a treatise about the classification of streetcar transfers, and financed his life through a series of modest clerical jobs and sales of his patented "perpetual calendar." During this period, in 1925, Sidis also published *The Animate and the Inanimate*. In Wallace's view, this book is the first work on the subject of "black holes" in space as well as an extraordinary work in the field of cosmogony, or the study of the origins of the universe. The book did not receive a single review at the time and was ignored by academia.

Before 1937, Sidis had done an excellent job of avoiding publicity for a decade. In that year, however, a local paper, the *Boston Sunday Advertiser*, published an article about him. This was followed by the August 14, 1937, issue of the *New Yorker*, which contained a brief biographical sketch about Sidis, his life following his graduation from Harvard, and the subsequent decades during which he lived in obscurity.[3] The article was part of a regular feature of the magazine called "Where Are They Now?," which provided brief updates on the lives of famous figures of the past. The article was printed under the subtitle *April Fool*, a reference to the fact that Sidis was born on April Fool's Day. The article recounted the history of Sidis's life and his current whereabouts: "William James Sidis lives today, at the age of thirty-nine, in a hall bedroom of Boston's shabby south end." The article also contained numerous errors about Sidis's life.

A mystery still exists regarding the interview at the basis of this article. According to Wallace, Sidis's contemporary biographer, a member of the monthly study group, whom she refers to only as "John," had brought along a friend to one meeting. Several members of this group suspected that this woman, who was the daughter of a publisher at a large company, served as the basis for the *New Yorker*'s report. Yet, the mystery remains as this individual did not interview Sidis at the time of the monthly meeting. Wallace writes: "William always maintained that the entire article was a combination of imagination and old stories about him, and no strangers had gained access to his room." Another possibility is that Sidis spoke to someone without knowing that she was a reporter, which seems unlikely due to his aversion to publicity.

The *New Yorker* article described Sidis's famous childhood and then recounted his subsequent career as an insignificant clerk: "He seems to get a great and ironic enjoyment out of leading a life of wandering irresponsibility after a childhood of scrupulous regimentation." Sidis never remained at one job for too long because "his employers or fellow-workers [would] soon find out that he is the famous boy wonder, and he can't tolerate a position after that." According to Sidis: "The every sight of a mathematical formula makes me physically ill. . . . All I want to do is run an adding machine, but they won't let

---

[3] J.L. Manley, *Where Are They Now?: April Fool!*, New Yorker 22 (Aug. 14, 1937).

me alone." The article also described Sidis's dwelling, a small bedroom in a poor part of Boston and his personal activities, interests, and habits.

In his legal action against the *Boston Sunday Advertiser*, Sidis won a settlement of $375. Sidis also sued F-R Publishing Corporation, the publisher of the *New Yorker*. Among his claims were a violation of his privacy rights under §§ 50-51 of the N.Y. Civil Rights Law.]

CLARK, C.J. . . . It is not contended that any of the matter printed is untrue. Nor is the manner of the author unfriendly; Sidis today is described as having "a certain childlike charm." But the article is merciless in its dissection of intimate details of its subject's personal life, and this in company with elaborate accounts of Sidis' passion for privacy and the pitiable lengths to which he has gone in order to avoid public scrutiny. The work possesses great reader interest, for it is both amusing and instructive; but it may be fairly described as a ruthless exposure of a once public character, who has since sought and has now been deprived of the seclusion of private life.

The article of December 25, 1937, was a biographical sketch of another former child prodigy, in the course of which William James Sidis and the recent account of him were mentioned. The advertisement published in the New York World-Telegram of August 13, 1937, read: "Out Today. Harvard Prodigy. Biography of the man who astonished Harvard at age 11. Where are they now? by J.L. Manley. Page 22. The New Yorker."

The complaint contains a general allegation, repeated for all the claims, of publication by the defendant of *The New Yorker*, "a weekly magazine of wide circulation throughout the United States." Then each separate "cause" contains an allegation that the defendant publicly circulated the articles or caused them to be circulated in the particular states upon whose law that cause is assumed to be founded. Circulation of the New York World-Telegram advertisement is, however, alleged only with respect to the second "cause," for asserted violation of New York law.

Under the first "cause of action" we are asked to declare that this exposure transgresses upon plaintiff's right of privacy, as recognized in California, Georgia, Kansas, Kentucky, and Missouri. Each of these states except California grants to the individual a common law right, and California a constitutional right, to be let alone to a certain extent. The decisions have been carefully analyzed by the court below, and we need not examine them further. None of the cited rulings goes so far as to prevent a newspaper or magazine from publishing the truth about a person, however intimate, revealing, or harmful the truth may be. Nor are there any decided cases that confer such a privilege upon the press. . . .

It must be conceded that under the strict standards suggested by [Warren and Brandeis in their article, *The Right to Privacy*] plaintiff's right of privacy has been invaded. Sidis today is neither politician, public administrator, nor statesman. Even if he were, some of the personal details revealed were of the sort that Warren and Brandeis believed "all men alike are entitled to keep from popular curiosity."

But despite eminent opinion to the contrary, we are not yet disposed to afford to all of the intimate details of private life an absolute immunity from the prying of the press. Everyone will agree that at some point the public interest in obtaining information becomes dominant over the individual's desire for privacy. Warren and Brandeis were willing to lift the veil somewhat in the case of public officers. We would go further, though we are not yet prepared to say how far. At least we would permit limited scrutiny of the "private" life of any person who has achieved, or has had thrust upon him, the questionable and indefinable status of a "public figure."

William James Sidis was once a public figure. As a child prodigy, he excited both admiration and curiosity. Of him great deeds were expected. In 1910, he was a person about whom the newspapers might display a legitimate intellectual interest, in the sense meant by Warren and Brandeis, as distinguished from a trivial and unseemly curiosity. But the precise motives of the press we regard as unimportant. And even if Sidis had loathed public attention at that time, we think his uncommon achievements and personality would have made the attention permissible. Since then Sidis has cloaked himself in obscurity, but his subsequent history, containing as it did the answer to the question of whether or not he had fulfilled his early promise, was still a matter of public concern. The article in *The New Yorker* sketched the life of an unusual personality, and it possessed considerable popular news interest.

We express no comment on whether or not the newsworthiness of the matter printed will always constitute a complete defense. Revelations may be so intimate and so unwarranted in view of the victim's position as to outrage the community's notions of decency. But when focused upon public characters, truthful comments upon dress, speech, habits, and the ordinary aspects of personality will usually not transgress this line. Regrettably or not, the misfortunes and frailties of neighbors and "public figures" are subjects of considerable interest and discussion to the rest of the population. And when such are the mores of the community, it would be unwise for a court to bar their expression in the newspapers, books, and magazines of the day.

Plaintiff in his first "cause of action" charged actual malice in the publication, and now claims that an order of dismissal was improper in the face of such an allegation. We cannot agree. If plaintiff's right of privacy was not invaded by the article, the existence of actual malice in its publication would not change that result. Unless made so by statute, a truthful and therefore non-libelous statement will not become libelous when uttered maliciously. A similar rule should prevail on invasions of the right of privacy. "Personal ill-will is not an ingredient of the offence, any more than in an ordinary case of trespass to person or to property." Warren and Brandeis, supra at page 218. Nor does the malice give rise to an independent wrong based on an intentional invasion of the plaintiff's interest in mental and emotional tranquility.

If the article appearing in the issue of August 14, 1937, does not furnish grounds for action, then it is clear that the brief and incidental reference to it contained in the article of December 25, 1937, is not actionable. . . .

[The court concluded that the second cause of action under N.Y. Civil Rights Law was properly dismissed as well. The second cause of action charged invasion of the rights conferred on plaintiff by §§ 50 and 51 of the N.Y. Civil Rights Law. Section 50 states: "A person, firm or corporation that uses for advertising purposes, or for the purposes of trade, the name, portrait or picture of any living person without having first obtained the written consent of such person, or if a minor of his or her parent or guardian, is guilty of a misdemeanor." Section 51 gives the injured person an injunction remedy and damages. The court found: "Though a publisher sells a commodity, and expects to profit from the sale of his product, he is immune from the interdict of Secs. 50 and 51 so long as he confines himself to the unembroidered dissemination of facts. . . . *The New Yorker* articles limit themselves to the unvarnished, unfictionalized truth."]

NOTES & QUESTIONS

1. ***Involuntary Public Figures.*** After losing his privacy suit against the *New Yorker,* Sidis sued it for libel for the false information in the story. Among his charges, he claimed that a reader of the article would think that he was a reprehensible character, disloyal to his country, a loathsome and filthy person in personal habits, suffered a mental breakdown, and was a fool, who lived in misery and poverty. The *New Yorker* settled this case out of court for a small amount of money, which Wallace estimates in her biography of Sidis at between $500 and $600.

   Sidis suffered from high blood pressure, and, approximately three months after receiving the settlement from the *New Yorker*, on July 17, 1944, he died from a cerebral hemorrhage and pneumonia. He was 46 years old and had $652.81 in his bank account.

   The life of William Sidis illustrates a man profoundly disturbed by being thrust by his parents into the limelight as a child and by the media hounding him. He tried to spend his adult life fleeing from being the focus of any public attention. If he had been an involuntary public figure in the past, should this affect whether he should be able to retreat from the public eye in the future? Does it matter that he became a public figure as a child, that is, that he did not voluntarily choose this status as an adult?

   The *Sidis* case suggests the principle that once one is a public figure, one is always a public figure. Can people who were once famous ever retreat into obscurity?

2. ***Who Was J.L. Manley? What Did He Try to Convey in His Article?*** The Sidis article was written by a "J.L. Manley." In a biography of James Thurber, the famous American humorist, Burton Bernstein reveals that Thurber used Jared L. Manley as a pseudonym.[4] Under this signature, Thurber wrote 24 profiles of onetime celebrities, including the Sidis piece. All pieces were

---

[4] *See* Burton Bernstein, *Thurber* 261 (1975). Bernstein writes:

> For all the distractions of city life and his sleepless schedule, Thurber was getting a lot of good work done. In early 1936, he began to write (really rewrite, since some of the New Yorker's best reporters, like Eugene Kinkead, were doing the research) a number of short, retrospective Profiles. His nonfiction craft rose to a new high in these excellent pieces, which lent themselves to his human approach.

Id. Bernstein also reveals that Jared L. Manley was a name that Thurber cobbled together when writing his first piece about an old boxer based on the initials of the boxer John L. Sullivan and "Manley" based on "the manly art of self-defense."

based on the research of other reporters at the *New Yorker*, including the unnamed reporter who actually interviewed Sidis.

In Thurber's own account of his time at the *New Yorker*, he faulted the *Sidis* court on one matter: "[N]owhere was there any indication of what I thought had stood out all through my story, implicit though it was — my feeling that the piece would help to curb the great American thrusting of talented children into the glare of fame or notoriety, a procedure in so many cases disastrous to the later career and happiness of the exploited youngsters."[5]

3. ***J.D. Salinger's Letters.*** In 1998, Joyce Maynard wrote an autobiography, *At Home in the World*, that describes her romance with J.D. Salinger in the 1970s. J.D. Salinger, an acclaimed author who wrote *The Catcher in the Rye*, had long ago completely retreated from public life and adopted a highly secluded existence in New Hampshire. In 1999, Maynard auctioned the letters J.D. Salinger wrote to her. She received $156,500 for the letters from the auction at Sotheby's. CNN reported at that time, "California philanthropist Peter Norton, who bought the letters, said he plans to return them to Salinger." Should Salinger have a right to privacy in the disclosure of the letters? Copyright law does create a copyright interest in unpublished letters — which prevents not only the publication of the entire contents of the letters, but a paraphrase of the letters that is too close to the actual text of the letters. *See Salinger v. Random House, Inc.*, 811 F.2d 90 (2d Cir. 1987). Should privacy law provide Salinger with the right to sue over the writing of Maynard's book?

4. ***Girls Gone Wild.*** A company markets videotapes of young college women at spring break or Mardi Gras flashing and undressing. The women, often intoxicated, reveal their nudity in public and give their permission to use the video footage on the company's videotapes, which are called "Girls Gone Wild." Later on, when sober, some of the women regret their decision to be in the video. Have they waived all privacy rights to their nude images on the video if they sign a consent form? Or should they be entitled to have some time to reconsider? Should they not be able to sign away these rights even when sober? Others have sued claiming that they were just filmed in public without signing a consent form. Do they have a valid privacy claim even when they exposed themselves in public?

5. ***Privacy Inalienability.*** Do we care whether or not Sidis knew he was talking to a reporter as opposed to a new neighbor? Can we assume that anyone who talks to a reporter has abandoned a privacy interest in the information that she shares with the journalist? More broadly, to what extent should privacy interests be tradable, waiveable, or otherwise alienable?[6]

6. ***Googleization.*** The Internet makes the preservation and dissemination of information much easier. Information about a person can be easily discovered

---

[5] James Thurber, *My Years with Ross* (1959).

[6] Paul M. Schwartz, *Property, Privacy, and Personal Data*, 117 Harv. L. Rev. 2055, 2074 (2004).

by "Googling" them — running a search on their name with the Internet search engine Google. Google will pull up dozens, sometimes hundreds of thousands, of information fragments about a person. It is becoming increasingly difficult for people to hide their personal information, which used to fade into obscurity but is now preserved forever on the Internet. Youthful indiscretions become permanent baggage. Consider the plight of one Michael, who was briefly imprisoned as a minor. The information comes up on a Google search, and Michael finds that it is inhibiting his ability to date, since many of the women he dates inquire about his time in prison. They have obviously Googled him:

> "When you meet someone," Michael says, "you don't say, 'I had an affair one time,' or 'I was arrested for DUI once,' or 'I cheated on my taxes in 1984.'"... [W]hat Michael finds most disturbing are the sudden silences. "Instead of thinking, 'Was I curt last week?' or 'Did I insult this political party or that belief?' I have to think about what happened when I was 17."[7]

Is Sidis's claim to privacy quaint by today's standards? How do we protect privacy in a post-Google world?

7. ***The* Star Wars *Kid and the* Numa Numa *Dance.*** An overweight, awkward 15-year-old kid videotaped himself pretending to be a character from a *Star Wars* movie.[8] He swung around a golf ball retriever pretending that it was a light saber and made his own sound effects. Somebody found the video, digitized it, and posted it on the Internet. The video created a buzz on the Internet, and it was downloaded millions of times around the world. Versions of the video with music and special effects were soon posted. People made fun of the kid in various discussions throughout the Internet.

In December 2005, Gary Brolsma placed on the Internet a clip of himself lip-synching and dancing in a chair to a Romanian pop song.[9] He called his performance the "Numa Numa Dance." The video was featured on newsgrounds.com, a website devoted to animation and videos, as well as elsewhere on the Internet. Newsgrounds.com alone soon received almost two million hits for the "Numa Numa Dance." Brolsma appeared on Good Morning America, and CNN and VH1 showed his clip.

Suddenly, however, he decided that he disliked the attention. The *New York Times* reported that Brolsma "has now sought refuge from his fame in his family's small house on a gritty street in Saddle Brook." The article added: "According to his relatives, he mopes around the house. . . . He is distraught, embarrassed." His grandmother quoted him as saying: "I just want this to end."

---

[7] Neil Swidey, *A Nation of Voyeurs: How the Internet Search Engine Google Is Changing What We Can Find Out About Each Other and Raising Questions About Whether We Should,* Boston Globe Mag., Feb. 2, 2003, at 10.

[8] Amy Harmon, *Fame Is No Laughing Matter for the "Star Wars" Kid,* N.Y. Times, May 19, 2003, at C3.

[9] Alan Feuer & Jason George, *Internet Fame Is Cruel Mistress for Dancer of the Numa Numa,* N.Y. Times, Feb. 26, 2005, at A1.

Is this simply life in the Internet Age? Does it matter that the parents of the "*Star Wars* kid" alleged that the clip of their son was placed online without his permission? In contrast, Brolsma posted the video of his dance himself. Is there something that the law can do to protect people like the *Star Wars* kid or Numa Numa dancer? If so, what?

As an update to the story of the Numa Numa Dance, Brolsma has moved beyond any anguish at his fame or notoriety. In September 2006, he released a second video, "New Numa" with corporate sponsorship at newnuma.com. The new video features Brolsma and members of a rock band, the Nowadays, and a new song. The video was released along a promotion that allowed the public to submit their own videos and win a share of $45,000 in prizes. Brolsma also offered a selection of t-shirts and a coffee mug for sale to the public. In 2008, he started a website, the Numa Network, which has grown to include a YouTube channel and a Facebook presence.

B. INFORMATION PRIVACY LAW: ORIGINS AND TYPES

Information privacy law is a wide-ranging body of law, encompassing common law, constitutional law, statutory law, and international law. This section will provide a brief introduction to the various strands of information privacy law that will be covered throughout this book. It begins by looking in detail at the most important article ever written about privacy.

1. COMMON LAW

(a) The Warren and Brandeis Article

The common law's development of tort remedies to protect privacy is one of the most significant chapters in the history of privacy law. In the late nineteenth century, considerable concerns about privacy captured the public's attention, ultimately resulting in the 1890 publication of Samuel Warren and Louis Brandeis's pathbreaking article, *The Right to Privacy*.[10] According to Roscoe Pound, the article did "nothing less than add a chapter to our law."[11] Harry Kalven even hailed it as the "most influential law review article of all."[12] The clearest indication of the article's ongoing vitality can be found in the Supreme Court's decision *Kyllo v. United States*, 533 U.S. 27 (2001). The Brandeis and Warren article is cited by the majority, those in concurrence, and even those in dissent.

Several developments in the late nineteenth century created a growing interest in privacy. First, the press became increasingly sensationalistic. Prior to the Civil War, wide-circulation newspapers were rare. However, the development

---

[10] Samuel Warren & Louis Brandeis, *The Right to Privacy*, 4 Harv. L. Rev. 193 (1890).

[11] Quoted in Alpheus Mason, *Brandeis: A Free Man's Life* 70 (1946).

[12] Harry Kalven, Jr., *Privacy in Tort Law — Were Warren and Brandeis Wrong?*, 31 L. & Contemp. Probs. 326, 327 (1966).

of a new form of sensationalistic journalism, known as "yellow journalism," made newspapers wildly successful. In 1833, Benjamin Day began publishing a newspaper called the *Sun* patterned after the "penny presses" in London (so named because they sold for a penny). The *Sun* contained news of scandals, such as family squabbles, public drunkenness, and petty crimes. In about four months, the *Sun* had a circulation of 4,000, almost the same as the existing New York daily papers. Just two months later, the *Sun* was reaching 8,000 in circulation. Other penny press papers soon followed. In reporting on his travels in America, Charles Dickens observed that New York newspapers were "pulling off the roofs of private houses."[13] In his great novel of 1844, *The Life and Adventures of Martin Chuzzlewit*, he listed (imaginary) New York newspapers called *The Sewer, The Stabber, The Family Spy, The Private Listener, The Peeper, The Plunderer,* and *The Keyhole Reporter.*[14]

Between 1850 and 1890, newspaper circulation increased about 1,000 percent — from 100 papers with 800,000 readers to 900 papers with more than 8 million readers. Joseph Pulitzer and William Randolph Hearst became the leading rivals in the newspaper business, each amassing newspaper empires. Their highly sensationalistic journalism became the paradigm for yellow journalism.[15]

Second, technological developments caused great alarm for privacy. In their article, Warren and Brandeis pointed to the invention of "instantaneous photography" as a new challenge to privacy. Photography had been around for many years before Warren and Brandeis penned their article. However, the equipment was expensive, cumbersome, and complicated to use. In 1884, the Eastman Kodak Company introduced the "snap camera," a handheld camera that was small and cheap enough for use by the general public. The snap camera allowed people to take candid photographs in public places for the first time. In the late nineteenth century, few daily newspapers even printed drawings, let alone photographs. Warren and Brandeis, however, astutely recognized the potential for the new technology of cameras to be used by the sensationalistic press.

The question of the origin of Warren and Brandeis's article has led to considerable debate. Some scholars suggest that Warren and Brandeis were strongly influenced by an article written in 1890 by E.L. Godkin, a famous social commentator in his day.[16] In the article, Godkin observed:

> . . . Privacy is a distinctly modern product, one of the luxuries of civilization, which is not only unsought for but unknown in primitive or barbarous societies. . . .
>
> The chief enemy of privacy in modern life is that interest in other people and their affairs known as curiosity, which in the days before newspapers

---

[13] Charles Dickens, *American Notes* (1842).

[14] Charles Dickens, *The Life and Adventures of Martin Chuzzlewit* (1844).

[15] For more information about yellow journalism, *see generally* Gini Graham Scott, *Mind Your Own Business: The Battle for Personal Privacy* 37-38 (1995); Robert Ellis Smith, *Ben Franklin's Web Site: Privacy and Curiosity from Plymouth Rock to the Internet* 102-20 (2000).

[16] *See* Elbridge L. Adams, *The Right to Privacy and Its Relation to the Law of Libel*, 39 Am. L. Rev. 37 (1905); Dorothy J. Glancy, *The Invention of the Right to Privacy*, 21 Ariz. L. Rev. 1 (1979).

created personal gossip. . . . [A]s long as gossip was oral, it spread, as regarded any one individual, over a very small area, and was confined to the immediate circle of his acquaintances. It did not reach, or but rarely reached, those who knew nothing of him. It did not make his name, or his walk, or his conversation familiar to strangers. . . . [G]ossip about private individuals is now printed, and makes its victim, with all his imperfections on his head, known to hundreds or thousands miles away from his place of abode; and, what is worst of all, brings to his knowledge exactly what is said about him, with all its details. It thus inflicts what is, to many men, the great pain of believing that everybody he meets in the street is perfectly familiar with some folly, or misfortune, or indiscretion, or weakness, which he had previously supposed had never got beyond his domestic circle. . . .

In truth, there is only one remedy for the violations of the right to privacy within the reach of the American public, and that is but an imperfect one. It is to be found in attaching social discredit to invasions of it on the part of conductors of the press. At present this check can hardly be said to exist. It is to a large extent nullified by the fact that the offence is often pecuniarily profitable.[17]

Warren and Brandeis referred to Godkin's essay, and their article does bear some similarities to his work. One difference is that Godkin, although recognizing the growing threats to privacy, remained cynical about the possibility of a solution, expressing only the hope that attitudes would change to be more respectful of privacy. Warren and Brandeis had a different view. In their judgment, the law could and should provide protection for privacy.

Another theory suggests that incursions by journalists into the privacy of Samuel Warren inspired the article. Warren, a wealthy and powerful attorney in Boston, practiced law with Louis Brandeis, who later went on to become a U.S. Supreme Court Justice. In 1883, Samuel Warren married Mabel Bayard, the daughter of a prominent senator from Delaware, and set up house in Boston's Back Bay. The Warrens were among the Boston elite and were frequently reported on in the *Saturday Evening Gazette*, "which specialized in 'blue blood items,'" and "reported their activities in lurid detail."[18]

According to William Prosser, Warren was motivated to write the article because reporters intruded upon his daughter's wedding. However, this certainly could not have been the reason because in 1890, Warren's oldest daughter was not even ten years old![19] Most likely, the impetus for writing the article was Warren's displeasure about a number of stories in the *Gazette* about his dinner parties.[20]

---

[17] E.L. Godkin, *The Rights of the Citizen: To His Own Reputation*, Scribner's Mag. (1890); *see also* E.L. Godkin, *The Right to Privacy*, The Nation (Dec. 25, 1890).

[18] Mason, *Brandeis, supra*, at 46.

[19] *See* James H. Barron, *Warren and Brandeis*, The Right to Privacy, 4 Harv. L. Rev. 193 (1890): *Demystifying a Landmark Citation*, 13 Suffolk L. Rev. 875 (1979).

[20] *See* Smith, *Ben Franklin's Web Site, supra*, at 118-19. For further discussion of the circumstances surrounding the publication of the article, see Martin Burgess Green, *The Mount Vernon Street Warrens: A Boston Story, 1860–1910* (1989); Morris L. Ernst & Alan U. Schwartz, *Privacy: The Right to Be Let Alone* 45-46 (1962); Philippa Strum, *Brandeis: Beyond Progressivism* (1993); Lewis J. Paper, *Brandeis* (1983); Irwin R. Kramer, *The Birth of Privacy Law: A Century Since Warren and Brandeis*, 39 Cath. U. L. Rev. 703 (1990); Dorothy Glancy, *The Invention of the*

Whatever inspired them to write, Warren and Brandeis published an article that profoundly shaped the development of the law of privacy.

SAMUEL D. WARREN AND LOUIS D. BRANDEIS, *THE RIGHT TO PRIVACY*

4 Harv. L. Rev. 193 (1890)

It could be done only on principles of private justice, moral fitness, and public convenience, which, when applied to a new subject, make common law without a precedent; much more when received and approved by usage.

— Willes, J., in *Millar v. Taylor,* 4 Burr. 2303, 2312

That the individual shall have full protection in person and in property is a principle as old as the common law; but it has been found necessary from time to time to define anew the exact nature and extent of such protection. Political, social, and economic changes entail the recognition of new rights, and the common law, in its eternal youth, grows to meet the demands of society. Thus, in very early times, the law gave a remedy only for physical interference with life and property, for trespasses *vi et armis.*[21] Then the "right to life" served only to protect the subject from battery in its various forms; liberty meant freedom from actual restraint; and the right to property secured to the individual his lands and his cattle. Later, there came a recognition of man's spiritual nature, of his feelings and his intellect. Gradually the scope of these legal rights broadened; and now the right to life has come to mean the right to enjoy life, — the right to be let alone; the right to liberty secures the exercise of extensive civil privileges; and the term "property" has grown to comprise every form of possession — intangible, as well as tangible.

Thus, with the recognition of the legal value of sensations, the protection against actual bodily injury was extended to prohibit mere attempts to do such injury; that is, the putting another in fear of such injury. From the action of battery grew that of assault. Much later there came a qualified protection of the individual against offensive noises and odors, against dust and smoke, and excessive vibration. The law of nuisance was developed. So regard for human emotions soon extended the scope of personal immunity beyond the body of the individual. His reputation, the standing among his fellow-men, was considered, and the law of slander and libel arose. Man's family relations became a part of the legal conception of his life, and the alienation of a wife's affections was held remediable. Occasionally the law halted, — as in its refusal to recognize the intrusion by seduction upon the honor of the family. But even here the demands of society were met. A mean fiction, the action *per quod servitium amisit,*[22] was resorted to, and by allowing damages for injury to the parents' feelings, an adequate remedy was ordinarily afforded. Similar to the expansion of the right to life was the growth of the legal conception of property. From corporeal property

---

Right to Privacy, 21 Ariz. L. Rev. 1, 25-27 (1979); Symposium, *The Right to Privacy One Hundred Years Later*, 41 Case W. Res. L. Rev. 643-928 (1991).

[21] Editors' Note: Latin — By or with force and arms.

[22] Editors' Note: Latin — Whereby he lost the services (of his servant).

arose the incorporeal rights issuing out of it; and then there opened the wide realm of intangible property, in the products and processes of the mind, as works of literature and art, goodwill, trade secrets, and trademarks.

This development of the law was inevitable. The intense intellectual and emotional life, and the heightening of sensations which came with the advance of civilization, made it clear to men that only a part of the pain, pleasure, and profit of life lay in physical things. Thoughts, emotions, and sensations demanded legal recognition, and the beautiful capacity for growth which characterizes the common law enabled the judges to afford the requisite protection, without the interposition of the legislature.

Recent inventions and business methods call attention to the next step which must be taken for the protection of the person, and for securing to the individual what Judge Cooley calls the right "to be let alone."[23] Instantaneous photographs and newspaper enterprise have invaded the sacred precincts of private and domestic life; and numerous mechanical devices threaten to make good the prediction that "what is whispered in the closet shall be proclaimed from the house-tops." For years there has been a feeling that the law must afford some remedy for the unauthorized circulation of portraits of private persons; and the evil of invasion of privacy by the newspapers, long keenly felt, has been but recently discussed by an able writer. The alleged facts of a somewhat notorious case brought before an inferior tribunal in New York a few months ago, directly involved the consideration of the right of circulating portraits; and the question whether our law will recognize and protect the right to privacy in this and in other respects must soon come before our courts for consideration.

Of the desirability — indeed of the necessity — of some such protection, there can, it is believed, be no doubt. The press is overstepping in every direction the obvious bounds of propriety and of decency. Gossip is no longer the resource of the idle and of the vicious, but has become a trade, which is pursued with industry as well as effrontery. To satisfy a prurient taste the details of sexual relations are spread broadcast in the columns of the daily papers. To occupy the indolent, column upon column is filled with idle gossip, which can only be procured by intrusion upon the domestic circle. The intensity and complexity of life, attendant upon advancing civilization, have rendered necessary some retreat from the world, and man, under the refining influence of culture, has become more sensitive to publicity, so that solitude and privacy have become more essential to the individual; but modern enterprise and invention have, through invasions upon his privacy, subjected him to mental pain and distress, far greater than could be inflicted by mere bodily injury. Nor is the harm wrought by such invasions confined to the suffering of those who may be made the subjects of journalistic or other enterprise. In this, as in other branches of commerce, the supply creates the demand. Each crop of unseemly gossip, thus harvested, becomes the seed of more, and, in direct proportion to its circulation, results in a lowering of social standards and of morality. Even gossip apparently harmless, when widely and persistently circulated, is potent for evil. It both belittles and perverts. It belittles by inverting the relative importance of things, thus dwarfing the thoughts and aspirations of a people. When personal gossip attains the dignity

---

[23] Cooley on Torts, 2d ed., p. 29.

of print, and crowds the space available for matters of real interest to the community, what wonder that the ignorant and thoughtless mistake its relative importance. Easy of comprehension, appealing to that weak side of human nature which is never wholly cast down by the misfortunes and frailties of our neighbors, no one can be surprised that it usurps the place of interest in brains capable of other things. Triviality destroys at once robustness of thought and delicacy of feeling. No enthusiasm can flourish, no generous impulse can survive under its blighting influence.

It is our purpose to consider whether the existing law affords a principle which can properly be invoked to protect the privacy of the individual; and, if it does, what the nature and extent of such protection is.

Owing to the nature of the instruments by which privacy is invaded, the injury inflicted bears a superficial resemblance to the wrongs dealt with by the law of slander and of libel, while a legal remedy for such injury seems to involve the treatment of mere wounded feelings, as a substantive cause of action. The principle on which the law of defamation rests, covers, however, a radically different class of effects from those for which attention is now asked. It deals only with damage to reputation, with the injury done to the individual in his external relations to the community, by lowering him in the estimation of his fellows. The matter published of him, however widely circulated, and however unsuited to publicity, must, in order to be actionable, have a direct tendency to injure him in his intercourse with others, and even if in writing or in print, must subject him to the hatred, ridicule, or contempt of his fellow-men, — the effect of the publication upon his estimate of himself and upon his own feelings not forming an essential element in the cause of action. In short, the wrongs and correlative rights recognized by the law of slander and libel are in their nature material rather than spiritual. That branch of the law simply extends the protection surrounding physical property to certain of the conditions necessary or helpful to worldly prosperity. On the other hand, our law recognizes no principle upon which compensation can be granted for mere injury to the feelings. However painful the mental effects upon another of an act, though purely wanton or even malicious, yet if the act itself is otherwise lawful, the suffering inflicted is *damnum absque injuria*.[24] Injury of feelings may indeed be taken account of in ascertaining the amount of damages when attending what is recognized as a legal injury; but our system, unlike the Roman law, does not afford a remedy even for mental suffering which results from mere contumely and insult, from an intentional and unwarranted violation of the "honor" of another.

It is not however necessary, in order to sustain the view that the common law recognizes and upholds a principle applicable to cases of invasion of privacy, to invoke the analogy, which is but superficial, to injuries sustained, either by an attack upon reputation or by what the civilians called a violation of honor; for the legal doctrines relating to infractions of what is ordinarily termed the common-law right to intellectual and artistic property are, it is believed, but instances and applications of a general right to privacy, which properly understood afford a remedy for the evils under consideration.

---

[24] Editors' Note: Latin — Loss or harm from something other than a wrongful act and which occasions no legal remedy.

The common law secures to each individual the right of determining, ordinarily, to what extent his thoughts, sentiments, and emotions shall be communicated to others. Under our system of government, he can never be compelled to express them (except when upon the witness-stand); and even if he has chosen to give them expression, he generally retains the power to fix the limits of the publicity which shall be given them. The existence of this right does not depend upon the particular method of expression adopted. It is immaterial whether it be by word or by signs, in painting, by sculpture, or in music. Neither does the existence of the right depend upon the nature or value of the thought or emotion, nor upon the excellence of the means of expression. The same protection is accorded to a casual letter or an entry in a diary and to the most valuable poem or essay, to a botch or daub and to a masterpiece. In every such case the individual is entitled to decide whether that which is his shall be given to the public. No other has the right to publish his productions in any form, without his consent. This right is wholly independent of the material on which, or the means by which, the thought, sentiment, or emotion is expressed. It may exist independently of any corporeal being, as in words spoken, a song sung, a drama acted. Or if expressed on any material, as in a poem in writing, the author may have parted with the paper, without forfeiting any proprietary right in the composition itself. The right is lost only when the author himself communicates his production to the public, — in other words, publishes it. It is entirely independent of the copyright laws, and their extension into the domain of art. The aim of those statutes is to secure to the author, composer, or artist the entire profits arising from publication; but the common-law protection enables him to control absolutely the act of publication, and in the exercise of his own discretion, to decide whether there shall be any publication at all. The statutory right is of no value, *unless* there is a publication; the common-law right is lost *as soon as* there is a publication.

What is the nature, the basis, of this right to prevent the publication of manuscripts or works of art? It is stated to be the enforcement of a right of property; and no difficulty arises in accepting this view, so long as we have only to deal with the reproduction of literary and artistic compositions. They certainly possess many of the attributes of ordinary property: they are transferable; they have a value; and publication or reproduction is a use by which that value is realized. But where the value of the production is found not in the right to take the profits arising from publication, but in the peace of mind or the relief afforded by the ability to prevent any publication at all, it is difficult to regard the right as one of property, in the common acceptation of that term. A man records in a letter to his son, or in his diary, that he did not dine with his wife on a certain day. No one into whose hands those papers fall could publish them to the world, even if possession of the documents had been obtained rightfully; and the prohibition would not be confined to the publication of a copy of the letter itself, or of the diary entry; the restraint extends also to a publication of the contents. What is the thing which is protected? Surely, not the intellectual act of recording the fact that the husband did not dine with his wife, but that fact itself. It is not the intellectual product, but the domestic occurrence. A man writes a dozen letters to different people. No person would be permitted to publish a list of the letters written. If the letters or the contents of the diary were protected as literary compositions, the scope of the protection afforded should be the same secured to a published writing under the copyright law. But the copyright law would not prevent an enumeration of the letters, or the publication of some of the facts contained therein. The copyright of a series of paintings or etchings would prevent a reproduction of the paintings as pictures; but it would not prevent a publication of list or even a description of them. Yet in the famous case of *Prince Albert v. Strange*, the court held that the common-law rule prohibited not merely the reproduction of the etchings which the plaintiff and Queen Victoria had made for their own pleasure, but also "the publishing (at least by printing or writing), though not by copy or resemblance, a description of them, whether more or less limited or summary, whether in the form of a catalogue or otherwise." Likewise, an unpublished collection of news possessing no element of a literary nature is protected from piracy.

That this protection cannot rest upon the right to literary or artistic property in any exact sense, appears the more clearly when the subject-matter for which protection is invoked is not even in the form of intellectual property, but has the attributes of ordinary tangible property. Suppose a man has a collection of gems or curiosities which he keeps private: it would hardly be contended that any person could publish a catalogue of them, and yet the articles enumerated are certainly not intellectual property in the legal sense, any more than a collection of stoves or of chairs.

The belief that the idea of property in its narrow sense was the basis of the protection of unpublished manuscripts led an able court to refuse, in several cases, injunctions against the publication of private letters, on the ground that "letters not possessing the attributes of literary compositions are not property entitled to protection;" and that it was "evident the plaintiff could not have considered the letters as of any value whatever as literary productions, for a letter cannot be considered of value to the author which he never would consent to have published." But those decisions have not been followed, and it may now be considered settled that the protection afforded by the common law to the author of any writing is entirely independent of its pecuniary value, its intrinsic merits, or of any intention to publish the same and, of course, also, wholly independent of the material, if any, upon which, or the mode in which, the thought or sentiment was expressed.

Although the courts have asserted that they rested their decisions on the narrow grounds of protection to property, yet there are recognitions of a more liberal doctrine. Thus in the case of *Prince Albert v. Strange*, already referred to, the opinions both of the Vice-Chancellor and of the Lord Chancellor, on appeal, show a more or less clearly defined perception of a principle broader than those which were mainly discussed, and on which they both placed their chief reliance. Vice-Chancellor Knight Bruce referred to publishing of a man that he had "written to particular persons or on particular subjects" as an instance of possibly injurious disclosures as to private matters, that the courts would in a proper case prevent; yet it is difficult to perceive how, in such a case, any right of privacy, in the narrow sense, would be drawn in question, or why, if such a publication would be restrained when it threatened to expose the victim not merely to sarcasm, but to ruin, it should not equally be enjoined, if it threatened to embitter his life. To deprive a man of the potential profits to be realized by publishing a catalogue of his gems cannot *per se* be a wrong to him. The possibility of future profits is not a right of property which the law ordinarily recognizes; it must, therefore, be an infraction of other rights which constitutes the wrongful act, and that infraction is equally wrongful, whether its results are to forestall the profits that the individual himself might secure by giving the matter a publicity obnoxious to him, or to gain an advantage at the expense of his mental pain and suffering. . . .

These considerations lead to the conclusion that the protection afforded to thoughts, sentiments, and emotions, expressed through the medium of writing or of the arts, so far as it consists in preventing publication, is merely an instance of the enforcement of the more general right of the individual to be let alone. It is like the right not be assaulted or beaten, the right not be imprisoned, the right not to be maliciously prosecuted, the right not to be defamed. In each of these rights, as indeed in all other rights recognized by the law, there inheres the quality of being owned or possessed — and (as that is the distinguishing attribute of property) there may be some propriety in speaking of those rights as property. But, obviously, they bear little resemblance to what is ordinarily comprehended under that term. The principle which protects personal writings and all other personal productions, not against theft and physical appropriation, but against publication in any form, is in reality not the principle of private property, but that of an inviolate personality.

If we are correct in this conclusion, the existing law affords a principle which may be invoked to protect the privacy of the individual from invasion either by the too enterprising press, the photographer, or the possessor of any other modern device for recording or reproducing scenes or sounds. For the protection afforded is not confined by the authorities to those cases where any particular medium or form of expression has been adopted, not to products of the intellect. The same protection is afforded to emotions and sensations expressed in a musical composition or other work of art as to a literary composition; and words spoken, a pantomime acted, a sonata performed, is no less entitled to protection than if each had been reduced to writing. The circumstance that a thought or emotion has been recorded in a permanent form renders its identification easier, and hence may be important from the point of view of evidence, but it has no significance as a matter of substantive right. If, then, the decisions indicate a general right to privacy for thoughts, emotions, and sensations, these should receive the same protection, whether expressed in writing, or in conduct, in conversation, in attitudes, or in facial expression.

It may be urged that a distinction should be taken between the deliberate expression of thoughts and emotions in literary or artistic compositions and the casual and often involuntary expression given to them in the ordinary conduct of life. In other words, it may be contended that the protection afforded is granted to the conscious products of labor, perhaps as an encouragement to effort. This contention, however plausible, has, in fact, little to recommend it. If the amount of labor involved be adopted as the test, we might well find that the effort to conduct one's self properly in business and in domestic relations had been far greater than that involved in painting a picture or writing a book; one would find that it was far easier to express lofty sentiments in a diary than in the conduct of a noble life. If the test of deliberateness of the act be adopted, much casual correspondence which is now accorded full protection would be excluded from the beneficent operation of existing rules. After the decisions denying the distinction attempted to be made between those literary productions which it was intended to publish and those which it was not, all considerations of the amount of labor involved, the degree of deliberation, the value of the product, and the intention of publishing must be abandoned, and no basis is discerned upon which the right to restrain publication and reproduction of such so-called literary and artistic works can be rested, except the right to privacy, as a part of the more general right to the immunity of the person, — the right to one's personality.

It should be stated that, in some instances where protection has been afforded against wrongful publication, the jurisdiction has been asserted, not on the ground of property, or at least not wholly on that ground, but upon the ground of an alleged breach of an implied contract or of a trust or confidence. . . .

This process of implying a term in a contract, or of implying a trust (particularly where the contract is written, and where there is no established usage or custom), is nothing more nor less than a judicial declaration that public morality, private justice, and general convenience demand the recognition of such a rule, and that the publication under similar circumstances would be considered an intolerable abuse. So long as these circumstances happen to present a contract upon which such a term can be engrafted by the judicial mind, or to supply relations upon which a trust or confidence can be erected, there may be no objection to working out the desired protection through the doctrines of contract or of trust. But the court can hardly stop there. The narrower doctrine may have satisfied the demands of society at a time when the abuse to be guarded against could rarely have arisen without violating a contract or a special confidence; but now that modern devices afford abundant opportunities for the perpetration of such wrongs without any participation by the injured party, the protection granted by the law must be placed upon a broader foundation. While, for instance, the state of the photographic art was such that one's picture could seldom be taken without his consciously "sitting" for the purpose, the law of contract or of trust might afford the prudent man sufficient safeguards against the improper circulation of his portrait; but since the latest advances in photographic art have rendered it possible to take pictures surreptitiously, the doctrines of contract and of trust are inadequate to support the required protection, and the law of tort must be resorted to. The right of property in its widest sense, including all possession, including all rights and privileges, and hence embracing the right to an inviolate personality, affords alone that broad basis upon which the protection which the individual demands can be rested.

Thus, the courts, in searching for some principle upon which the publication of private letters could be enjoined, naturally came upon the ideas of a breach of confidence, and of an implied contract; but it required little consideration to discern that this doctrine could not afford all the protection required, since it would not support the court in granting a remedy against a stranger; and so the theory of property in the contents of letters was adopted. Indeed, it is difficult to conceive on what theory of the law the casual recipient of a letter, who proceeds to publish it, is guilty of a breach of contract, express or implied, or of any breach of trust, in the ordinary acceptation of that term. Suppose a letter has been addressed to him without his solicitation. He opens it, and reads. Surely, he has not made any contract; he has not accepted any trust. He cannot, by opening and reading the letter, have come under any obligation save what the law declares; and, however expressed, that obligation is simply to observe the legal right of the sender, whatever it may be, and whether it be called his right or property in the contents of the letter, or his right to privacy. . . .

We must therefore conclude that the rights, so protected, whatever their exact nature, are not rights arising from contract or from special trust, but are rights as against the world; and, as above stated, the principle which has been applied to protect these rights is in reality not the principle of private property, unless that word be used in an extended and unusual sense. The principle which protects personal writings and any other productions of the intellect of or the emotions, is the right to privacy, and the law has no new principle to formulate when it extends this protection to the personal appearance, sayings, acts, and to personal relation, domestic or otherwise.

If the invasion of privacy constitutes a legal *injuria*, the elements for demanding redress exist, since already the value of mental suffering, caused by an act wrongful in itself, is recognized as a basis for compensation.

The right of one who has remained a private individual, to prevent his public portraiture, presents the simplest case for such extension; the right to protect one's self from pen portraiture, from a discussion by the press of one's private affairs, would be a more important and far-reaching one. If casual and unimportant statements in a letter, if handiwork, however inartistic and valueless, if possessions of all sorts are protected not only against reproduction, but against description and enumeration, how much more should the acts and sayings of a man in his social and domestic relations be guarded from ruthless publicity. If you may not reproduce a woman's face photographically without her consent, how much less should be tolerated the reproduction of her face, her form, and her actions, by graphic descriptions colored to suit a gross and depraved imagination.

The right to privacy, limited as such right must necessarily be, has already found expression in the law of France.

It remains to consider what are the limitations of this right to privacy, and what remedies may be granted for the enforcement of the right. To determine in advance of experience the exact line at which the dignity and convenience of the individual must yield to the demands of the public welfare or of private justice would be a difficult task; but the more general rules are furnished by the legal analogies already developed in the law of slander and libel, and in the law of literary and artistic property.

1. The right to privacy does not prohibit any publication of matter which is of public or general interest.

In determining the scope of this rule, aid would be afforded by the analogy, in the law of libel and slander, of cases which deal with the qualified privilege of comment and criticism on matters of public and general interest. There are of course difficulties in applying such a rule; but they are inherent in the subject-matter, and are certainly no greater than those which exist in many other branches of the law, — for instance, in that large class of cases in which the reasonableness or unreasonableness of an act is made the test of liability. The design of the law must be to protect those persons with whose affairs the community has no legitimate concern, from being dragged into an undesirable and undesired publicity and to protect all persons, whatsoever; their position or station, from having matters which they may properly prefer to keep private, made public against their will. It is the unwarranted invasion of individual privacy which is reprehended, and to be, so far as possible, prevented. The distinction, however, noted in the above statement is obvious and fundamental. There are persons who may reasonably claim as a right, protection from the notoriety entailed by being made the victims of journalistic enterprise. There are others who, in varying degrees, have renounced the right to live their lives screened from public observation. Matters which men of the first class may justly contend, concern themselves alone, may in those of the second be the subject of legitimate interest to their fellow-citizens. Peculiarities of manner and person, which in the ordinary individual should be free from comment, may acquire a public importance, if found in a candidate for public office. Some further discrimination is necessary, therefore, than to class facts or deeds as public or private according to a standard to be applied to the fact or deed *per se*. To publish of a modest and retiring individual that he suffers from an impediment in his speech or that he cannot spell correctly, is an unwarranted, if not an unexampled, infringement of his rights, while to state and comment on the same characteristics found in a would-be congressman could not be regarded as beyond the pale of propriety.

The general object in view is to protect the privacy of private life, and to whatever degree and in whatever connection a man's life has ceased to be private, before the publication under consideration has been made, to that extent the protection is to be withdrawn. Since, then, the propriety of publishing the very same facts may depend wholly upon the person concerning whom they are published, no fixed formula can be used to prohibit obnoxious publications. Any rule of liability adopted must have in it an elasticity which shall take account of the varying circumstances of each case, — a necessity which unfortunately renders such a doctrine not only more difficult of application, but also to a certain extent uncertain in its operation and easily rendered abortive. Besides, it is only the more flagrant breaches of decency and propriety that could in practice be reached, and it is not perhaps desirable even to attempt to repress everything which the nicest taste and keenest sense of the respect due to private life would condemn.

In general, then, the matters of which the publication should be repressed may be described as those which concern the private life, habits, acts, and relations of an individual, and have no legitimate connection with his fitness for a public office which he seeks or for which he is suggested, or for any public or quasi public position which he seeks or for which he is suggested, and have no legitimate relation to or bearing upon any act done by him in a public or quasi public capacity. The foregoing is not designed as a wholly accurate or exhaustive definition, since that which must ultimately in a vast number of cases become a question of individual judgment and opinion is incapable of such definition; but it is an attempt to indicate broadly the class of matters referred to. Some things all men alike are entitled to keep from popular curiosity, whether in public life or not, while others are only private because the persons concerned have not assumed a position which makes their doings legitimate matters of public investigation.

2. The right to privacy does not prohibit the communication of any matter, though in its nature private, when the publication is made under circumstances which would render it a privileged communication according to the law of slander and libel.

Under this rule, the right to privacy is not invaded by any publication made in a court of justice, in legislative bodies, or the committees of those bodies; in municipal assemblies, or the committees of such assemblies, or practically by any communication made in any other public body, municipal or parochial, or in any body quasi public, like the large voluntary associations formed for almost every purpose of benevolence, business, or other general interest; and (at least in many jurisdictions) reports of any such proceedings would in some measure be accorded a like privilege. Nor would the rule prohibit any publication made by one in the discharge of some public or private duty, whether legal or moral, or in conduct of one's own affairs, in matters where his own interest is concerned.

3. The law would probably not grant any redress for the invasion of privacy by oral publication in the absence of special damage.

The same reasons exist for distinguishing between oral and written publications of private matters, as is afforded in the law of defamation by the restricted liability for slander as compared with the liability for libel. The injury resulting from such oral communications would ordinarily be so trifling that the law might well, in the interest of free speech, disregard it altogether.

4. The right to privacy ceases upon the publication of the facts by the individual, or with his consent.

This is but another application of the rule which has become familiar in the law of literary and artistic property. The cases there decided establish also what should be deemed a publication, — the important principle in this connection being that a private communication of circulation for a restricted purpose is not a publication within the meaning of the law.

5. The truth of the matter published does not afford a defence. Obviously this branch of the law should have no concern with the truth or falsehood of the matters published. It is not for injury to the individual's character that redress or prevention is sought, but for injury to the right of privacy. For the former, the law of slander and libel provides perhaps a sufficient safeguard. The latter implies the right not merely to prevent inaccurate portrayal of private life, but to prevent its being depicted at all.

6. The absence of "malice" in the publisher does not afford a defence.

Personal ill-will is not an ingredient of the offence, any more than in an ordinary case of trespass to person or to property. Such malice is never necessary to be shown in an action for libel or slander at common law, except in rebuttal of some defence, *e.g.*, that the occasion rendered the communication privileged, or, under the statutes in this State and elsewhere, that the statement complained of was true. The invasion of the privacy that is to be protected is equally complete and equally injurious, whether the motives by which the speaker or writer was actuated are, taken by themselves, culpable or not; just as the damage to character, and to some extent the tendency to provoke a breach of the peace, is equally the result of defamation without regard to the motives leading to its publication. Viewed as a wrong to the individual, this rule is the same pervading the whole law of torts, by which one is held responsible for his intentional acts, even though they are committed with no sinister intent; and viewed as a wrong to society, it is the same principle adopted in a large category of statutory offences.

The remedies for an invasion of the right of privacy are also suggested by those administered in the law of defamation, and in the law of literary and artistic property, namely: —

1. An action of tort for damages in all cases. Even in the absence of special damages, substantial compensation could be allowed for injury to feelings as in the action of slander and libel.

2. An injunction, in perhaps a very limited class of cases.

It would doubtless be desirable that the privacy of the individual should receive the added protection of the criminal law, but for this, legislation would be required. Perhaps it would be deemed proper to bring the criminal liability for such publication within narrower limits; but that the community has an interest in preventing such invasions of privacy, sufficiently strong to justify the introduction of such a remedy, cannot be doubted. Still, the protection of society must come mainly through a recognition of the rights of the individual. Each man is responsible for his own acts and omissions only. If he condones what he reprobates, with a weapon at hand equal to his defence, he is responsible for the results. If he resists, public opinion will rally to his support. Has he then such a weapon? It is believed that the common law provides him with one, forged in the slow fire of the centuries, and to-day fitly tempered to his hand. The common law has always recognized a man's house as his castle, impregnable, often, even to its own officers engaged in the execution of its command. Shall the courts thus close the front entrance to constituted authority, and open wide the back door to idle or prurient curiosity?

NOTES & QUESTIONS

1. *The Need for a New Right.* The article argued for the creation of a new right — the right to privacy. Why did the authors believe that other legal claims were inadequate? For example, why does the law of defamation or the law of contracts not provide a sufficient remedy for the harm described by the authors? Why do Warren and Brandeis reject property rights and copyright as tools to protect privacy?

2. *Deriving a Right to Privacy in the Common Law.* How do Warren and Brandeis derive a right to privacy from the common law? Under what principle do they locate this right? In a footnote in the article, Warren and Brandeis observe:

> The application of an existing principle to a new state of facts is not judicial legislation. To call it such is to assert that the existing body of law consists practically of the statutes and decided cases, and to deny that the principles (of which these cases are ordinarily said to be evidence) exist at all. It is not the application of an existing principle to new cases, but the introduction of a new principle, which is properly termed judicial legislation.
>
> But even the fact that a certain decision would involve judicial legislation should not be taken against the property of making it. This power has been commonly exercised by our judges, when applying to a new subject

principles of private justice, moral fitness, and public convenience. Indeed, the elasticity of our law, its adaptability to new conditions, the capacity for growth, which has enabled it to meet the wants of an ever changing society and to apply immediate relief for every recognized wrong, have been its greatest boast. . . .

Why do they include this footnote? Do you agree with their argument?

3. ***Inviolate Personality in the United States and Germany.*** The authors describe privacy as not "the principle of private property but that of inviolate personality." What does that mean? James Whitman traces the idea of the personality right from Warren and Brandeis back to nineteenth-century German legal philosophy:

> . . . [N]ineteenth-century Germans often thought of "freedom" as opposed primarily to determinism. To be free was, in the first instance, not to be free from government control, nor to be free to engage in market transactions. Instead, to be free was to exercise free will, and the defining characteristic of creatures with free will was that they were unpredictably individual, creatures whom no science of mechanics or biology could ever capture in their full richness. For Germans who thought of things in this way, the purpose of "freedom" was to allow each individual fully to realize his potential as an individual: to give full expression to his peculiar capacities and powers.[25]

Although the Warren and Brandeis article has been highly influential, their concept of a personality right has failed to gain traction in U.S. privacy law. Nonetheless, the idea of a personality right has formed the basis of modern German information privacy law. As Paul Schwartz and Karl-Nikolaus Peifer state, it is "a 'source right' that has proven a fertile source for the creation of a related series of legal rights" in Germany.[26] More specifically, they note that "the right has been used to protect honor and reputation, privacy in a spatial sense (a '*Privatsphäre*,' or a private area), individuality, and commercial uses of personality." Why do you think the concept of a "right of personality" has been unsuccessful as a legal concept for privacy in the United States?

4. ***"The Right to Be Let Alone."*** Warren and Brandeis refer to privacy as "the right to be let alone." This phrase was coined by Judge Thomas Cooley earlier in his famous treatise on torts.[27] Do Warren and Brandeis define what privacy is or elaborate upon what being "let alone" consists of? If so, what do they say privacy is? Is this a good account of what constitutes privacy?

5. ***The Scope of the Right to Privacy.*** Brandeis and Warren were careful not to describe privacy as an absolute right. They set out six limitations on the right to privacy. Consider the first limitation and the relationship between the right to privacy and the need for publication on matters of public concern. What conclusions do the authors reach about these competing claims? According to

[25] James Q. Whitman, *The Two Western Cultures of Privacy: Dignity Versus Liberty*, 113 Yale L.J. 1151, 1181 (2004).

[26] Paul M. Schwartz & Karl-Nikolaus Peifer, *Prosser's Privacy and the German Right of Personality*, 98 Cal. L. Rev. 1925, 1952 (2010).

[27] Thomas M. Cooley, *Law of Torts* 29 (2d ed. 1888).

Warren and Brandeis, would the reporting that a public official engaged in illegal business practices be protected by a right to privacy? What about illicit sexual activity? Consider the holding of the *Sidis* court regarding a person who was once of public interest due to his great achievements. Do you think that Warren and Brandeis would agree with the conclusion of *Sidis*?

6. *The Nature of the Injury Caused by Privacy Invasions.* Warren and Brandeis argue that privacy invasions are more harmful than bodily injuries. Do you agree? Warren and Brandeis characterize the injury caused by the violation of privacy as an injury to the feelings. Do you agree? Or do you think that the injury extends beyond an injury to the feelings?

7. *Remedies.* Brandeis and Warren suggest two remedies for an invasion of privacy — an action in tort and injunction. These remedies are similar to those in defamation and copyright. What do the authors say about a criminal remedy?

8. *Criticisms.* Some have argued that the article is a defense of bourgeois values, i.e., the freedom of an elite group to avoid public scrutiny.[28] Which aspects of the article support this view? Do parts of the article suggest otherwise? Is privacy, as described in the Warren and Brandeis article, a class-based right?

9. *Did Brandeis Change His Mind?* Neil Richards argues that Brandeis's views about the importance of publicity and free speech eventually eclipsed the views he set forth in his article with Warren. According to Richards, the First Amendment views that Brandeis developed in the 1920s are "inconsistent with many aspects of the right to privacy that he called for in 1890." As a further matter, Richard contends that "to the extent [Brandeis] retained a belief in tort privacy to the end of his life, it was a narrow category subordinated to the interests of publicity and free speech." At a normative level, Richards builds on Brandeis to develop a "concept of intellectual privacy" — a more focused concept that views privacy as a paramount value when it "is relevant to the activities of thinking, reading, and discussing safeguarded by the First Amendment."[29]

(b) The Recognition of Warren and Brandeis's Privacy Torts

Warren and Brandeis's 1890 article suggested that the existing causes of action under the common law did not adequately protect privacy but that the legal concepts in the common law could be modified to achieve the task. As early as 1903, courts and legislatures responded to the Warren and Brandeis article by creating a number of privacy torts to redress the harms that Warren and Brandeis had noted. In *Roberson v. Rochester Folding Box Co.*, 64 N.E. 442 (N.Y. 1902), the New York Court of Appeals refused to recognize a common law tort action for privacy invasions. Franklin Mills Flour displayed a lithograph of Abigail Roberson (a teenager) on 25,000 advertisement flyers without her consent. The lithograph printed her photograph with the advertising pun: "Flour of the

---

[28] *See* Donald R. Pember, *Privacy and the Press* (1972).

[29] Neil Richards, *The Puzzle of Brandeis, Privacy, and Speech*, 63 Vand. L. Rev. 1295, 1312 (2010).

Family." Roberson claimed that the use of her image on the flyer caused her great humiliation and resulted in illness requiring medical help. The court, however, concluded:

> . . . There is no precedent for such an action to be found in the decisions of this court. . . . Mention of such a right is not to be found in Blackstone, Kent, or any other of the great commentators upon the law; nor, so far as the learning of counsel or the courts in this case have been able to discover, does its existence seem to have been asserted prior to about the year 1890. . . .
>
> The legislative body could very well interfere and arbitrarily provide that no one should be permitted for his own selfish purpose to use the picture or the name of another for advertising purposes without his general consent. In such event no embarrassment would result to the general body of law, for the law would be applicable only to cases provided for by statute. The courts, however, being without authority to legislate, are required to decide cases upon principle, and so are necessarily embarrassed by precedents created by an extreme, and therefore unjustifiable, application of an old principle. . . . [W]hile justice in a given case may be worked out by a decision of the court according to the notions of right which govern the individual judge or body of judges comprising the court, the mischief which will finally result may be almost incalculable under our system, which makes a decision in one case a precedent for decisions in all future cases which are akin to it in the essential facts. . . .

Shortly after the decision, a note in the *Yale Law Journal* criticized the *Roberson* decision because it enabled the press "to pry into and grossly display before the public matters of the most private and personal concern."[30] One of the judges in the majority defended the opinion in the *Columbia Law Review*.[31]

In 1903, the New York legislature responded to the explicit invitation in *Roberson* to legislate by creating a privacy tort action by statute. *See* N.Y. Civ. Rights Act § 51. This statute is still in use today. As you will see again later on in this text, courts are frequently engaged in a dialogue with legislatures about the scope of privacy rights.

In the 1905 case *Pavesich v. New England Life Insurance Co.*, 50 S.E. 68 (Ga. 1905), Georgia became the first state to recognize a common law tort action for privacy invasions. There, a newspaper published a life insurance advertisement with a photograph of the plaintiff without the plaintiff's consent. The court held:

> . . . The right of privacy has its foundation in the instincts of nature. It is recognized intuitively, consciousness being the witness that can be called to establish its existence. Any person whose intellect is in a normal condition recognizes at once that as to each individual member of society there are matters private, and there are matters public so far as the individual is concerned. Each individual as instinctively resents any encroachment by the public upon his rights which are of a private nature as he does the withdrawal of those of his rights which are of a public nature. A right of privacy in matters purely private is therefore derived from natural law. . . .

---

[30] *An Actionable Right to Privacy?*, 12 Yale L.J. 34 (1902).
[31] Denis O'Brien, *The Right to Privacy*, 2 Colum. L. Rev. 486 (1902).

All will admit that the individual who desires to live a life of seclusion cannot be compelled against his consent, to exhibit his person in any public place, unless such exhibition is demanded by the law of the land. He may be required to come from his place of seclusion to perform public duties — to serve as a juror and to testify as a witness and the like; but, when the public duty is once performed, if he exercises his liberty to go again into seclusion, no one can deny him the right. One who desires to live a life of partial seclusion has a right to choose the times, places, and manner in which and at which he will submit himself to the public gaze. Subject to the limitation above referred to, the body of a person cannot be put on exhibition at any time or at any place without his consent. . . .

It therefore follows from what has been said that a violation of the right of privacy is a direct invasion of a legal right of the individual. . . .

In 1960, Dean William Prosser wrote his famous article, *Privacy*, examining the over 300 privacy tort cases decided in the 70 years since the Warren and Brandeis article.

WILLIAM PROSSER, *PRIVACY*

48 Cal. L. Rev. 383 (1960)

. . . The law of privacy comprises four distinct kinds of invasion of four different interests of the plaintiff, which are tied together by the common name, but otherwise have almost nothing in common except that each represents an interference with the right of the plaintiff, in the phrase coined by Judge Cooley, "to be let alone." Without any attempt at exact definition, these four torts may be described as follows:

1. Intrusion upon the plaintiff's seclusion or solitude, or into his private affairs.
2. Public disclosure of embarrassing private facts about the plaintiff.
3. Publicity which places the plaintiff in a false light in the public eye.
4. Appropriation, for the defendant's advantage, of the plaintiff's name or likeness. . . .

Judge Briggs has described the present state of the law of privacy as "still that of a haystack in a hurricane." Disarray there certainly is; but almost all of the confusion is due to a failure to separate and distinguish these four forms of invasion and to realize that they call for different things. . . .

Taking them in order — intrusion, disclosure, false light, and appropriation — the first and second require the invasion of something secret, secluded or private pertaining to the plaintiff; the third and fourth do not. The second and third depend upon publicity, while the first does not, nor does the fourth, although it usually involves it. The third requires falsity or fiction; the other three do not. The fourth involves a use for the defendant's advantage, which is not true of the rest. Obviously this is an area in which one must tread warily and be on the lookout for bogs. Nor is the difficulty decreased by the fact that quite often two or more of these forms of invasion may be found in the same case, and quite conceivably in all four.

NOTES & QUESTIONS

1. ***The Restatement of Torts.*** Prosser's analytical framework imposed order and clarity on the jumbled line of cases that followed the Warren and Brandeis article. The Restatement of Torts recognizes the four torts Prosser described in his article. These torts are known collectively as "invasion of privacy." The torts are: (1) intrusion upon seclusion, (2) public disclosure of private facts, (3) false light, and (4) appropriation.

2. ***The Interests Protected by the Privacy Torts.*** In response to Prosser's assertion that the privacy torts have almost "nothing in common," Edward Bloustein replied that "what provoked Warren and Brandeis to write their article was a fear that a rampant press feeding on the stuff of private life would destroy individual dignity and integrity and emasculate individual freedom and independence." This underlying principle is a protection of "human dignity" and "personality."[32]

   In contrast to Bloustein, Robert Post contends that the privacy torts do "not simply uphold the interests of individuals against the demands of the community, but instead safeguard[ ] rules of civility that in some significant measure constitute both individuals and community." Post argues that the torts establish boundaries between people, which when violated create strife. The privacy torts promote "forms of respect [for other people] by which we maintain a community."[33]

3. ***Prosser's Privacy at 50.*** In 2010, the California Law Review held a symposium at Berkeley Law School to celebrate the fiftieth anniversary of the publication of Prosser's *Privacy*. The verdict on the momentous article is mixed. Lior Strahilevitz advocates abandoning the Prosser categories and replacing them with a unitary tort for invasion of privacy. The key under the recast privacy tort would simply be whether "the gravity of the harm to the plaintiff's privacy interest [is] outweighed by a privacy policy interest."[34]

   Along similar negative lines, Neil Richards and Daniel Solove concluded that Prosser's view of the privacy tort has been "rigid and ossifying." Dean Prosser "stunted [privacy law's] development in ways that have limited its ability to adapt to the problems of the Information Age." The authors conclude that tort law should look beyond the narrow categories Prosser proposed in order for it to "regain the creative spirit it once possessed." One way for tort law to do so, in their view, would be to adopt the English approach to the tort of confidentiality.[35]

   In contrast, Paul Schwartz and Karl-Nikolaus Peifer praised Prosser: "Prosser pragmatically assessed the kind and amount of privacy that the American legal system was willing to accommodate." In their summary,

---

[32] Edward J. Bloustein, *Privacy as an Aspect of Human Dignity: An Answer to Dean Prosser*, 39 N.Y.U. L. Rev. 962, 974, 1000-01 (1964).

[33] Robert C. Post, *The Social Foundations of Privacy: Community and Self in the Common Law Tort*, 77 Cal. L. Rev. 957 (1989).

[34] Lior Strahilevitz, *Reunifying Privacy Law*, 98 Cal. L. Rev. 2007 (2010).

[35] Neil Richards & Daniel Solove, *Prosser's Privacy Law: A Mixed Legacy*, 98 Cal. L. Rev. 1887, 1924 (2010).

"Prosser's contribution generated useful doctrinal categories where previously had been unclassified cases and a lingering air of skepticism towards the tort."[36]

Would it be useful to extend the four privacy torts as Richards and Solove propose? Or would a better approach be to replace Prosser's four torts with pure balancing as Strahilevitz advocates? Or do Prosser's categories adequately capture the various privacy interests that should be addressed by tort law?

LAKE V. WAL-MART STORES, INC.

582 N.W.2d 231 (Minn. 1998)

BLATZ, C.J. . . . Elli Lake and Melissa Weber appeal from a dismissal of their complaint for failure to state a claim upon which relief may be granted. The district court and court of appeals held that Lake and Weber's complaint alleging intrusion upon seclusion, appropriation, publication of private facts, and false light publicity could not proceed because Minnesota does not recognize a common law tort action for invasion of privacy. We reverse as to the claims of intrusion upon seclusion, appropriation, and publication of private facts, but affirm as to false light publicity.

Nineteen-year-old Elli Lake and 20-year-old Melissa Weber vacationed in Mexico in March 1995 with Weber's sister. During the vacation, Weber's sister took a photograph of Lake and Weber naked in the shower together. After their vacation, Lake and Weber brought five rolls of film to the Dilworth, Minnesota Wal-Mart store and photo lab. When they received their developed photographs along with the negatives, an enclosed written notice stated that one or more of the photographs had not been printed because of their "nature."

In July 1995, an acquaintance of Lake and Weber alluded to the photograph and questioned their sexual orientation. Again, in December 1995, another friend told Lake and Weber that a Wal-Mart employee had shown her a copy of the photograph. By February 1996, Lake was informed that one or more copies of the photograph were circulating in the community.

Lake and Weber filed a complaint against Wal-Mart Stores, Inc. and one or more as-yet unidentified Wal-Mart employees on February 23, 1996, alleging the four traditional invasion of privacy torts — intrusion upon seclusion, appropriation, publication of private facts, and false light publicity. . . . The district court granted Wal-Mart's motion to dismiss, explaining that Minnesota has not recognized any of the four invasion of privacy torts. The court of appeals affirmed.

Whether Minnesota should recognize any or all of the invasion of privacy causes of action is a question of first impression in Minnesota. . . .

This court has the power to recognize and abolish common law doctrines. The common law is not composed of firmly fixed rules. Rather, as we have long recognized, the common law:

---

[36] Paul M. Schwartz & Karl-Nikolaus Peifer, *Prosser's Privacy and the German Right of Personality*, 98 Cal. L. Rev. 1925, 1982 (2010).

is the embodiment of broad and comprehensive unwritten principles, inspired by natural reason, an innate sense of justice, adopted by common consent for the regulation and government of the affairs of men. It is the growth of ages, and an examination of many of its principles, as enunciated and discussed in the books, discloses a constant improvement and development in keeping with advancing civilization and new conditions of society. Its guiding star has always been the rule of right and wrong, and in this country its principles demonstrate that there is in fact, as well as in theory, a remedy for all wrongs.

As society changes over time, the common law must also evolve:

It must be remembered that the common law is the result of growth, and that its development has been determined by the social needs of the community which it governs. It is the resultant of conflicting social forces, and those forces which are for the time dominant leave their impress upon the law. It is of judicial origin, and seeks to establish doctrines and rules for the determination, protection, and enforcement of legal rights. Manifestly it must change as society changes and new rights are recognized. To be an efficient instrument, and not a mere abstraction, it must gradually adapt itself to changed conditions.

To determine the common law, we look to other states as well as to England.

The tort of invasion of privacy is rooted in a common law right to privacy first described in an 1890 law review article by Samuel Warren and Louis Brandeis. The article posited that the common law has always protected an individual's person and property, with the extent and nature of that protection changing over time. The fundamental right to privacy is both reflected in those protections and grows out of them:

Thus, in the very early times, the law gave a remedy only for physical interference with life and property, for trespass vi et armis. Then the "right to life" served only to protect the subject from battery in its various forms; liberty meant freedom from actual restraint; and the right to property secured to the individual his lands and his cattle. Later, there came a recognition of a man's spiritual nature, of his feelings and his intellect. Gradually the scope of these legal rights broadened; and now the right to life has come to mean the right to enjoy life, — the right to be let alone; the right to liberty secures the exercise of extensive civil privileges; and the term "property" has grown to comprise every form of possession — intangible, as well as tangible.

Although no English cases explicitly articulated a "right to privacy," several cases decided under theories of property, contract, or breach of confidence also included invasion of privacy as a basis for protecting personal violations. The article encouraged recognition of the common law right to privacy, as the strength of our legal system lies in its elasticity, adaptability, capacity for growth, and ability "to meet the wants of an ever changing society and to apply immediate relief for every recognized wrong.". . .

Today, the vast majority of jurisdictions now recognize some form of the right to privacy. Only Minnesota, North Dakota, and Wyoming have not yet recognized any of the four privacy torts. Although New York and Nebraska courts have declined to recognize a common law basis for the right to privacy and instead provide statutory protection, we reject the proposition that only the legislature may establish new causes of action. The right to privacy is inherent in the English protections of individual property and contract rights and the "right to be let alone" is recognized as part of the common law across this country. Thus, it is within the province of the judiciary to establish privacy torts in this jurisdiction.

Today we join the majority of jurisdictions and recognize the tort of invasion of privacy. The right to privacy is an integral part of our humanity; one has a public persona, exposed and active, and a private persona, guarded and preserved. The heart of our liberty is choosing which parts of our lives shall become public and which parts we shall hold close. . . .

We decline to recognize the tort of false light publicity at this time. We are concerned that claims under false light are similar to claims of defamation, and to the extent that false light is more expansive than defamation, tension between this tort and the First Amendment is increased.

False light is the most widely criticized of the four privacy torts and has been rejected by several jurisdictions. . . .

Thus we recognize a right to privacy present in the common law of Minnesota, including causes of action in tort for intrusion upon seclusion, appropriation, and publication of private facts, but we decline to recognize the tort of false light publicity. . . .

TOMLJANOVICH, J. dissenting. I would not recognize a cause of action for intrusion upon seclusion, appropriation or publication of private facts. . . .

An action for an invasion of the right to privacy is not rooted in the Constitution. "[T]he Fourth Amendment cannot be translated into a general constitutional 'right to privacy.'" *Katz v. United States*, 389 U.S. 347, 350 (1967). Those privacy rights that have their origin in the Constitution are much more fundamental rights of privacy — marriage and reproduction. *See Griswold v. Connecticut*, 381 U.S. 479, 485 (1965) (penumbral rights of privacy and repose protect notions of privacy surrounding the marriage relationship and reproduction).

We have become a much more litigious society since 1975 when we acknowledged that we have never recognized a cause of action for invasion of privacy. We should be even more reluctant now to recognize a new tort.

In the absence of a constitutional basis, I would leave to the legislature the decision to create a new tort for invasion of privacy.

NOTES & QUESTIONS

1. *Other Remedies?* If the Minnesota Supreme Court had rejected the privacy tort, what other legal remedies might be available to Elli Lake?

2. *Postscript.* What happened in *Lake* after the Minnesota Supreme Court's decision? In response to a query from the casebook authors, the lead attorney for the *Lake* plaintiff, Keith L. Miller of Miller, Norman & Associates, Ltd., explained that his client lost at the trial that followed the remand. He writes: "The jury found that an invasion of Ms. Lake's privacy had occurred, but that it did not happen 'in the course and scope' of a Wal-Mart worker's employment." In other words, tort notions of agency were found to apply, and

a privacy tort violation could be attributed to Wal-Mart only if the employee had carried out the tort in the course and scope of employment. Miller added: "Our proof was problematic because, expectedly, no employee could specifically be identified as the culprit. It was all circumstantial." Finally, he summarized his experience litigating this case: "Gratifying? Certainly. Remunerative? Not so much."

3. *Legislatures vs. Courts.* The dissent in *Lake* contends, in a similar way as *Roberson*, that it should be the legislature, not the courts, that recognize new tort actions to protect privacy. In New York, the statute passed in response to *Roberson* remains the state's source for privacy tort remedies. Like New York, some states have recognized the privacy torts legislatively; other states, like Georgia in *Pavesich* and Minnesota in *Lake*, have recognized them judicially. Which means of recognizing the torts do you believe to be most justifiable? Why? Does the legislature have expertise that courts lack? Are courts more or less sensitive to civil rights issues, such as privacy?

(c) Privacy Protection in Tort Law

The Privacy Torts. Prosser's classification of these torts survives to this day. The Restatement (Second) of Torts recognizes four privacy torts:

(1) *Public Disclosure of Private Facts.* This tort creates a cause of action for one who publicly discloses a private matter that is "highly offensive to a reasonable person" and "is not of legitimate concern to the public." Restatement (Second) of Torts § 652D (1977).

(2) *Intrusion upon Seclusion.* This tort provides a remedy when one intrudes "upon the solitude or seclusion of another or his private affairs or concerns" if the intrusion is "highly offensive to a reasonable person." Restatement (Second) of Torts § 652B (1977).

(3) *False Light.* This tort creates a cause of action when one publicly discloses a matter that places a person "in a false light" that is "highly offensive to a reasonable person." Restatement (Second) of Torts § 652E (1977).

(4) *Appropriation.* Under this tort, a plaintiff has a remedy against one "who appropriates to his own use or benefit the name or likeness" of the plaintiff. Restatement (Second) of Torts § 652C (1977).

Today, most states recognize some or all of these torts.

Breach of Confidentiality. The tort of breach of confidentiality provides a remedy when a professional (i.e., doctor, lawyer, banker) divulges a patient or client's confidential information.

Defamation. The law of defamation existed long before Warren and Brandeis's article. Defamation law, consisting of the torts of libel and slander, creates liability when one makes a false statement about a person that harms the person's reputation. The Supreme Court has held that the First Amendment places certain limits on defamation law.

Infliction of Emotional Distress. The tort of intentional infliction of emotional distress can also serve as a remedy for certain privacy invasions. This tort provides a remedy when one "by extreme and outrageous conduct intentionally or recklessly causes severe emotional distress to another." Restatement (Second) of Torts § 46 (1977). Since privacy invasions can often result in severe emotional distress, this tort may provide a remedy. However, it is limited by the requirement of "extreme and outrageous conduct."

(d) Privacy Protection in Evidence Law

The law of evidence has long recognized privacy as an important goal that can override the truth-seeking function of the trial. Under the common law, certain communications are privileged, and hence cannot be inquired into during a legal proceeding. The law of evidence has recognized the importance of protecting the privacy of communications between attorney and client, priest and penitent, husband and wife, physician and patient, and psychotherapist and patient.

(e) Privacy Protection via Property Rights

Property Rights. Although there are few property laws specifically governing privacy, these laws often implicate privacy. The appropriation tort is akin to a property right, and some commentators suggest that personal information should be viewed as a form of property.[37] If personal information is understood as a form of property, the tort of conversion might apply to those who collect and use a person's private data. Take a look at the *Moore* case in the section on genetic privacy in Chapter 4. Recall, however, that Warren and Brandeis rejected property as an adequate protection for privacy. What kind of market structures might be needed if personal data is to be traded or sold?

Trespass. The law of trespass, which provides tort remedies and criminal penalties for the unauthorized entry onto another's land, can protect privacy. There is some overlap between the torts of intrusion and trespass, as many forms of intrusion involve a trespass as well.

(f) Privacy Protection in Contract Law

Sometimes specific contractual provisions protect against the collection, use, or disclosure of personal information. In certain contexts, courts have entertained actions for breach of implied contract or tort actions based on implicit duties once certain relationships are established, such as physician-patient relationships, which have been analogized to fiduciary relationships. Privacy policies as well as terms of service containing privacy provisions can sometimes be analogized to a contract.

---

[37] *See, e.g.,* Alan Westin, *Privacy and Freedom* 324 (1967); *see also* Richard S. Murphy, *Property Rights in Personal Information: An Economic Defense of Privacy*, 84 Geo. L.J. 2381 (1996); Richard A. Posner, *The Economics of Justice* (1981); Lawrence Lessig, *Code and Other Laws of Cyberspace* 154-62 (1999); Paul M. Schwartz, *Property, Privacy, and Personal Data*, 117 Harv. L. Rev. 2055 (2004).

Contract often functions as a way of sidestepping state and federal privacy laws. Many employers make employees consent to drug testing as well as e-mail and workplace surveillance in their employment contracts.

Some commentators advocate a contractual approach to privacy, such as Jerry Kang, who suggests a contractual default rule that limits the way personal information can be used but that can be contracted around by parties who do not desire to be governed by the rule.[38]

(g) Privacy Protection in Criminal Law

Warren and Brandeis noted that under certain circumstances, criminal law would be appropriate to protect privacy. The criminal law protects bodily invasions, such as assault, battery, and rape. The privacy of one's home is also protected by criminal sanctions for trespass. Stalking and harassing can give rise to criminal culpability. The crime of blackmail prohibits coercing an individual by threatening to expose her personal secrets. Many of the statutes protecting privacy also contain criminal penalties, such as the statutes pertaining to wiretapping and identity theft.

2. CONSTITUTIONAL LAW

Federal Constitutional Law. Although the United States Constitution does not specifically mention privacy, it has a number of provisions that protect privacy, and it has been interpreted as providing a right to privacy. In some instances the First Amendment serves to safeguard privacy. For example, the First Amendment protects the right to speak anonymously. *See McIntyre v. Ohio Election Comm'n*, 514 U.S. 334 (1995). The First Amendment's freedom of association clause protects individuals from being compelled to disclose the groups to which they belong or contribute. Under the First Amendment "Congress shall make no law . . . abridging . . . the right of the people peaceably to assemble. . . ." For example, the Court has struck down the compulsory disclosure of the names and addresses of an organization's members, *see NAACP v. Alabama*, 357 U.S. 449 (1958), as well as a law requiring public teachers to list all organizations to which they belong or contribute. *See Shelton v. Tucker*, 364 U.S. 479 (1960).

The Third Amendment protects the privacy of the home by preventing the government from requiring soldiers to reside in people's homes: "No Soldier shall, in time of peace be quartered in any house, without the consent of the Owner, nor in time of war, but in a manner to be prescribed by law."

The Fourth Amendment provides that people have the right "to be secure in their persons, houses, papers, and effects, against unreasonable searches and seizures. . . ." Almost 40 years after writing *The Right to Privacy*, Brandeis, then a Supreme Court Justice, wrote a dissent that has had a significant influence on Fourth Amendment law. The case was *Olmstead v. United States*, 277 U.S. 438 (1928), where the Court held that wiretapping was not an invasion of privacy under the Fourth Amendment because it was not a physical trespass into the

---

[38] *See* Jerry Kang, *Information Privacy in Cyberspace Transactions*, 50 Stan. L. Rev. 1193 (1998).

home. Justice Brandeis dissented, contending that the central interest protected by the Fourth Amendment was not property but the "right to be let alone":

> The protection guaranteed by the amendments is much broader in scope. The makers of our Constitution undertook to secure conditions favorable to the pursuit of happiness. They recognized the significance of man's spiritual nature, of his feelings and of his intellect. They knew that only a part of the pain, pleasure and satisfactions of life are to be found in material things. They sought to protect Americans in their beliefs, their thoughts, their emotions and their sensations. They conferred, as against the government, the right to be let alone — the most comprehensive of rights and the right most valued by civilized men. To protect that right, every unjustifiable intrusion by the government upon the privacy of the individual, whatever the means employed, must be deemed a violation of the Fourth Amendment.

Brandeis's dissent demonstrated that the "right to be let alone" did not merely have common law roots (as he had argued in *The Right to Privacy*) but also had constitutional roots as well in the Fourth Amendment.

Modern Fourth Amendment law incorporates much of Brandeis's view. In *Katz v. United States*, 389 U.S. 347 (1967), the Court held that the Fourth Amendment "protects people, not places" and said that the police must obtain a warrant when a search takes place in a public pay phone on a public street. The Court currently determines a person's right to privacy by the "reasonable expectations of privacy" test, a standard articulated in Justice Harlan's concurrence to *Katz*. First, a person must "have exhibited an actual (subjective) expectation of privacy" and, second, "the expectation [must] be one that society is prepared to recognize as 'reasonable.' "

The Fifth Amendment guarantees that: "No person . . . shall be compelled in any criminal case to be a witness against himself. . . ." This right, commonly referred to as the "privilege against self-incrimination," protects privacy by restricting the ability of the government to force individuals to divulge certain information about themselves.

In the landmark 1965 case *Griswold v. Connecticut*, 318 U.S. 479 (1965), the Court declared that an individual has a constitutional right to privacy. The Court located this right within the "penumbras" or "zones" of freedom created by an expansive interpretation of the Bill of Rights. Subsequently, the Court has handed down a line of cases protecting certain fundamental life choices such as abortion and aspects of one's intimate sexual life.

In *Whalen v. Roe*, 433 U.S. 425 (1977), the Court extended its substantive due process privacy protection to information privacy, holding that the "zone of privacy" protected by the Constitution encompasses the "individual interest in avoiding disclosure of personal matters." This offshoot of the right to privacy has become known as the "constitutional right to information privacy."

State Constitutional Law. A number of states have directly provided for the protection of privacy in their constitutions. For example, the Alaska Constitution provides: "The right of the people to privacy is recognized and shall not be infringed." Alaska Const. art. I, § 22. According to the California Constitution: "All people are by their nature free and independent and have inalienable rights.

Among these are enjoying and defending life and liberty, acquiring, possessing, and protecting property, and pursuing and obtaining safety, happiness, and privacy." Cal. Const. art. I, § 1. Unlike most state constitutional provisions, the California constitutional right to privacy applies not only to state actors but also to private parties. *See, e.g., Hill v. NCAA*, 865 P.2d 638 (Cal. 1994). The Florida Constitution provides: "Every natural person has the right to be let alone and free from governmental intrusion into his private life except as otherwise provided herein." Fla. Const. art. I, § 23.[39]

3. STATUTORY LAW

Federal Statutory Law. From the mid-1960s to the mid-1970s, privacy emerged as a central political and social concern. In tune with the heightened attention to privacy, philosophers, legal scholars, and others turned their focus on privacy, raising public awareness about the growing threats to privacy from technology.[40]

In the mid-1960s electronic eavesdropping erupted into a substantial public issue, spawning numerous television news documentaries as well as receiving significant attention in major newspapers. A proposal for a National Data Center in 1965 triggered public protest and congressional hearings. At this time, the computer was a new and unexplored technological tool that raised risks of unprecedented data collection about individuals, with potentially devastating effects on privacy. Indeed, toward the end of the 1960s, the issue of the collection of personal information in databases had become one of the defining social issues of American society.

During this time the Supreme Court announced landmark decisions regarding the right to privacy, including *Griswold v. Connecticut* in 1965 and *Roe v. Wade* in 1973, which were landmark decisions regarding the right to deci-sional/reproductive privacy and autonomy. The famous reasonable expectations of privacy test in Fourth Amendment jurisprudence emerged in 1967 with *Katz v. United States*.

Due to growing fears about the ability of computers to store and search personal information, Congress devoted increasing attention to the issue of privacy. As Priscilla Regan observes:

> In 1965, a new problem was placed on the congressional agenda by subcommittee chairs in both the House and the Senate. The problem was defined as the

---

[39] For more examples, see Ariz. Const. art. II, § 8; Mont. Const. art. II, § 10; Haw. Const. art. I, § 6; Ill. Const. art. I, §§ 6, 12; La. Const. art. I, § 5; S.C. Const. art. I, § 10; Wash. Const. art. I, § 7. For a further discussion of state constitutional protections of privacy, see Timothy O. Lenz, *"Rights Talk" about Privacy in State Courts*, 60 Alb. L. Rev. 1613 (1997); Mark Silverstein, Note, *Privacy Rights in State Constitutions: Models for Illinois?*, 1989 U. Ill. L. Rev. 215.

[40] *See, e.g.,* Vance Packard, *The Naked Society* (1964); Myron Brenton, *The Privacy Invaders* (1964); Alan Westin, *Privacy and Freedom* (1967); Arthur Miller, *The Assault on Privacy* (1971); *Nomos XII: Privacy* (J. Ronald Pennock & J.W. Chapman eds., 1971); Alan Westin & Michael A. Baker, *Databanks in a Free Society: Computers, Record-Keeping and Privacy* (1972); Aryeh Neier, *The Secret Files They Keep on You* (1975); Kenneth L. Karst, *"The Files": Legal Controls over the Accuracy and Accessibility of Stored Personal Data*, 31 L. & Contemp. Probs. 342 (1966); Symposium, *Computers, Data Banks, and Individual Privacy*, 53 Minn. L. Rev. 211-45 (1968); Symposium, *Privacy*, 31 L. & Contemp. Probs. 251-435 (1966).

invasion of privacy by computers and evoked images of *1984*, the "Computerized Man," and a dossier society. Press interest was high, public concern was generated and resulted in numerous letters being sent to members of Congress, and almost thirty days of congressional hearings were held in the late 1960s and early 1970s.[41]

In 1973, in a highly influential report, the United States Department of Health, Education, and Welfare (HEW) undertook an extensive review of data processing in the United States. Among many recommendations, the HEW report proposed that a Code of Fair Information Practices be established. The Fair Information Practices consist of a number of basic information privacy principles that allocate rights and responsibilities in the collection and use of personal information:

- There must be no personal-data record-keeping systems whose very existence is secret.

- There must be a way for an individual to find out what information about him is in a record and how it is used.

- There must be a way for an individual to prevent information about him obtained for one purpose from being used or made available for other purposes without his consent.

- There must be a way for an individual to correct or amend a record of identifiable information about him.

- Any organization creating, maintaining, using, or disseminating records of identifiable personal data must ensure the reliability of the data for their intended use and must take reasonable precautions to prevent misuse of the data.[42]

As Marc Rotenberg observes, the Fair Information Practices have "played a significant role in framing privacy laws in the United States."[43]

Beginning in the 1970s, Congress has passed a number of laws protecting privacy in various sectors of the information economy:

- Fair Credit Reporting Act of 1970, Pub. L. No. 90-32, 15 U.S.C. §§ 1681 et seq. — provides citizens with rights regarding the use and disclosure of their personal information by credit reporting agencies.

- Privacy Act of 1974, Pub. L. No. 93-579, 5 U.S.C. § 552a — provides individuals with a number of rights concerning their personal information maintained in government record systems, such as the right to see one's records and to ensure that the information in them is accurate.

- Family Educational Rights and Privacy Act of 1974, Pub. L. No. 93-380, 20 U.S.C. §§ 1221 note, 1232g — protects the privacy of school records.

---

[41] Priscilla M. Regan, *Legislating Privacy: Technology, Social Values, and Public Policy* 82 (1995).

[42] *See* U.S. Dep't of Health, Education, and Welfare, *Secretary's Advisory Committee on Automated Personal Data Systems, Records, Computers, and Rights of Citizens* viii (1973).

[43] Marc Rotenberg, *Fair Information Practices and the Architecture of Privacy (What Larry Doesn't Get)*, Stan. Tech. L. Rev. 1, 44 (2001).

- Right to Financial Privacy Act of 1978, Pub. L. No. 95-630, 12 U.S.C. §§ 3401–3422 — requires a subpoena or search warrant for law enforcement officials to obtain financial records.

- Foreign Intelligence Surveillance Act of 1978, Pub. L. No. 95-511, 15 U.S.C. §§ 1801-1811 — regulates foreign intelligence gathering within the U.S.

- Privacy Protection Act of 1980, Pub. L. No. 96-440, 42 U.S.C. § 2000aa — restricts the government's ability to search and seize the work product of the press and the media.

- Cable Communications Policy Act of 1984, Pub. L. No. 98-549, 47 U.S.C. § 551 — mandates privacy protection for records maintained by cable companies.

- Electronic Communications Privacy Act of 1986, Pub. L. No. 99-508 and Pub. L. No. 103-414, 18 U.S.C §§ 2510–2522, 2701–2709 — updates federal electronic surveillance law to respond to the new developments in technology.

- Computer Matching and Privacy Protection Act of 1988, Pub. L. No. 100-503, 5 U.S.C. §§ 552a — regulates automated investigations conducted by government agencies comparing computer files.

- Employee Polygraph Protection Act of 1988, Pub. L. No. 100-347, 29 U.S.C. §§ 2001–2009 — governs the use of polygraphs by employers.

- Video Privacy Protection Act of 1988, Pub. L. No. 100-618, 18 U.S.C. §§ 2710–2711 — protects the privacy of videotape rental information.

- Telephone Consumer Protection Act of 1991, Pub. L. No. 102-243, 47 U.S.C. § 227 — provides certain remedies from repeat telephone calls by telemarketers.

- Driver's Privacy Protection Act of 1994, Pub. L. No. 103-322, 18 U.S.C. §§ 2721–2725 — restricts the states from disclosing or selling personal information in their motor vehicle records.

- Health Insurance Portability and Accountability Act of 1996, Pub. L. No. 104-191 — gives the Department of Health and Human Services (HHS) the authority to promulgate regulations governing the privacy of medical records.

- Identity Theft and Assumption Deterrence Act of 1998, Pub. L. No. 105-318, 18 U.S.C. § 1028 — criminalizes the transfer or use of fraudulent identification with the intent to commit unlawful activity.

- Children's Online Privacy Protection Act of 1998, Pub. L. No. 106-170, 15 U.S.C. §§ 6501–6506 — restricts the use of information gathered from children under age 13 by Internet websites.

- Gramm-Leach-Bliley Act of 1999, Pub. L. No. 106-102, 15 U.S.C. §§ 6801–6809 — requires privacy notices and provides opt-out rights when financial institutions seek to disclose personal data to other companies.

- CAN-SPAM Act of 2003, Pub. L. No. 108-187 — provides penalties for the transmission of unsolicited e-mail.

- Fair and Accurate Credit Transactions Act of 2003, Pub. L. No. 108-159 — amends and updates the Fair Credit Reporting Act, providing (among other things) additional protections against identity theft.

- Video Voyeurism Prevention Act of 2004, Pub. L. No. 108-495, 18 U.S.C. § 1801 — criminalizes the capturing of nude images of people (when on federal property) under circumstances where they have a reasonable expectation of privacy.

Not all of Congress's legislation regarding privacy has been protective of privacy. A number of statutes have mandated the government collection of sensitive personal data or facilitated government investigation techniques:

- Bank Secrecy Act of 1970, Pub. L. No. 91-508 — requires banks to maintain reports of people's financial transactions to assist in government white collar investigations.

- Communications Assistance for Law Enforcement Act of 1994, Pub. L. No. 103-414 — requires telecommunication providers to help facilitate government interceptions of communications and surveillance.

- Personal Responsibility and Work Opportunity Reconciliation Act of 1996, Pub. L. No. 104-193 — requires the collection of personal information (including Social Security numbers, addresses, and wages) of all people who obtain a new job anywhere in the nation, which will be placed into a national database to help track down deadbeat parents.

- USA-PATRIOT Act of 2001, Pub. L. No. 107-56 — amends a number of electronic surveillance statutes and other statutes to facilitate law enforcement investigations and access to information.

State Statutory Law. The states have passed statutes protecting privacy in many contexts, regulating both the public and private sectors. These laws cover a wide range of subjects, from employment records and medical records to library records and student records. However, less than a third have enacted a general privacy law akin to the Privacy Act.[44] As Paul Schwartz observes, most states lack "omnibus data protection laws."[45]

4. INTERNATIONAL LAW

Privacy is a global concern. International law, and more precisely, the privacy laws of other countries and international privacy norms, implicate privacy interests in the United States. For example, commercial firms in the United States must comply with the various standards for global commerce. The Organization of Economic Cooperation and Development (OECD) developed an extensive series of privacy guidelines in 1980 that formed the basis for privacy laws in North America, Europe, and East Asia. In 1995, the European Union issued the *European Community Directive on Data Protection*, which outlines

---

[44] *See* Smith, *Ben Franklin's Web Site, supra*, at 333.
[45] Paul M. Schwartz, *Privacy and Participation: Personal Information and Public Sector Regulation in the United States*, 80 Iowa L. Rev. 553, 605 (1995).

the basic principles for privacy legislation for European Union member countries.[46] The Directive became effective on October 25, 1998. In November 2004, an Asian-Pacific Economic Cooperative (APEC) Privacy Framework was endorsed by the ministers of the APEC countries. The APEC countries are more than 20 nations, mostly in Asia, but also including the United States.

C. PERSPECTIVES ON PRIVACY

1. THE PHILOSOPHICAL DISCOURSE ABOUT PRIVACY

(a) The Concept of Privacy and the Right to Privacy

At the outset, it is important to distinguish between the concept of privacy and the right of privacy. As Hyman Gross observed, "[t]he law does not determine what privacy is, but only what situations of privacy will be afforded legal protection."[47] Privacy as a concept involves what privacy entails and how it is to be valued. Privacy as a right involves the extent to which privacy is (and should be) legally protected.

While instructive and illuminative, law cannot be the exclusive material for constructing a concept of privacy. Law is the product of the weighing of competing values, and it sometimes embodies difficult trade-offs. In order to determine what the law *should* protect, we cannot merely look to what the law *does* protect.

(b) The Public and Private Spheres

A long-standing distinction in philosophical discourse is between the public and private spheres. Some form of boundary between public and private has been maintained throughout the history of Western civilization.[48]

Generally, the public sphere is the realm of life experienced in the open, in the community, and in the world of politics. The private sphere is the realm of life where one retreats to isolation or to one's family. At its core is the world of the home. The private sphere, observes Edward Shils, is a realm where the individual "is not bound by the rules that govern public life. . . . The 'private life' is a secluded life, a life separated from the compelling burdens of public authority."[49]

---

[46] *See* Directive of the European Parliament and the Council of Europe on the Protection of Individuals with Regard to the Processing of Personal Data and on the Free Movement of Such Data (1996). For more information about the EU Data Directive, see Paul M. Schwartz & Joel R. Reidenberg, *Data Privacy Law* (1996); Peter P. Swire & Robert E. Litan, *None of Your Business: World Data Flows, Electronic Commerce, and the European Privacy Directive* (1998); Colin J. Bennett, *Regulating Privacy: Data Protection of Public Policy in Europe and the United States* (1992); David H. Flaherty, *Protecting Privacy in Surveillance Societies* (1989).

[47] Hyman Gross, *The Concept of Privacy*, 42 N.Y.U. L. Rev. 34, 36 (1967).

[48] *See* Georges Duby, *Foreword*, in *A History of the Private Life I: From Pagan Rome to Byzantium* viii (Paul Veyne ed. & Arthur Goldhammer trans., 1987); *see also* Jürgen Habermas, *The Structural Transformation of the Public Sphere* (Thomas Burger trans., 1991).

[49] Edward Shils, *Privacy: Its Constitution and Vicissitudes*, 31 L. & Contemp. Probs. 281, 283 (1966).

According to Hannah Arendt, both spheres are essential dimensions of human life:

> . . . In ancient feeling, the privative trait of privacy, indicated in the word itself, was all-important; it meant literally a state of being deprived of something, and even of the highest and most human of man's capacities. A man who lived only a private life, who like the slave was not permitted to enter the public realm, or like the barbarian had chosen not to establish such a realm, was not fully human. We no longer think primarily of deprivation when we use the word "privacy," and this is partly due to the enormous enrichment of the private sphere through modern individualism. . . .
>
> To live an entirely private life means above all to be deprived of things essential to a truly human life: to be deprived of the reality that comes from being seen and heard by others, to be deprived of an "objective" relationship with them that comes from being related to and separated from them through the intermediary of a common world of things, to be deprived of the possibility of achieving something more permanent than life itself. . . .
>
> . . . [T]he four walls of one's private property offer the only reliable hiding place from the common public world, not only from everything that goes on in it but also from its very publicity, from being seen and being heard. A life spent entirely in public, in the presence of others, becomes, as we would say, shallow. While it retains visibility, it loses the quality of rising into sight from some darker ground which must remain hidden if it is not to lose its depth in a very real, non-subjective sense. . . . [50]

John Stuart Mill relied upon a notion of the public/private dichotomy to determine when society should regulate individual conduct. Mill contended that there was a realm where people had social responsibilities and where society could properly restrain people from acting or punish them for their deeds. This realm consisted in acts that were hurtful to others or to which people "may rightfully be compelled to perform; such as to give evidence in a court of justice; to bear his fair share in the common defence, or in any other joint work necessary to the interest of the society of which he enjoys the protection." However, "there is a sphere of action in which society, as distinguished from the individual, has, if any, only an indirect interest; comprehending all that portion of a person's life and conduct which affects only himself, or if it also affects others, only with their free, voluntary, and undeceived consent and participation." Conduct within this sphere consists of "self-regarding" acts, and society should not interfere with such acts. As Mill further elaborated:

> . . . I fully admit that the mischief which a person does to himself may seriously affect, both through their sympathies and their interests, those nearly connected with him and, in a minor degree, society at large. When, by conduct of this sort, a person is led to violate a distinct and assignable obligation to any other person or persons, the case is taken out of the self-regarding class, and becomes amenable to moral disapprobation in the proper sense of the term. . . . Whenever, in short, there is a definite damage, or a definite risk of damage, either to an individual or to the public, the case is taken out of the province of liberty, and placed in that of morality or law.

---

[50] Hannah Arendt, *The Human Condition* (1958).

But with regard to the merely contingent, or, as it may be called, constructive injury which a person causes to society, by conduct which neither violates any specific duty to the public, nor occasions perceptible hurt to any assignable individual except himself; the inconvenience is one which society can afford to bear, for the sake of the greater good of human freedom. . . . [51]

2. THE DEFINITION AND THE VALUE OF PRIVACY

The following excerpts explore the definition and value of privacy. Those who attempt to define privacy seek to describe what privacy constitutes. Over the past four decades, academics have defined privacy as a right of personhood, intimacy, secrecy, limited access to the self, and control over information. However, defining privacy has proven to be quite complicated, and many commentators have expressed great difficulty in defining precisely what privacy is. In the words of one commentator, "even the most strenuous advocate of a right to privacy must confess that there are serious problems of defining the essence and scope of this right."[52] According to Robert Post, "[p]rivacy is a value so complex, so entangled in competing and contradictory dimensions, so engorged with various and distinct meanings, that I sometimes despair whether it can be usefully addressed at all."[53]

Conceptualizing privacy not only involves defining privacy but articulating the value of privacy. The value of privacy concerns its importance — how privacy is to be weighed relative to other interests and values. The excerpts that follow attempt to grapple with the complicated task of defining privacy and explaining why privacy is worth protecting.

ALAN WESTIN, *PRIVACY AND FREEDOM*

(1967)

. . . Privacy is the claim of individuals, groups, or institutions to determine for themselves when, how, and to what extent information about them is communicated to others. Viewed in terms of the relation of the individual to social participation, privacy is the voluntary and temporary withdrawal of a person from the general society through physical or psychological means, either in a state of solitude or small-group intimacy or, when among larger groups, in a condition of anonymity or reserve. The individual's desire for privacy is never absolute, since participation in society is an equally powerful desire. Thus each individual is continually engaged in a personal adjustment process in which he balances the desire for privacy with the desire for disclosure and communication of himself to others, in light of the environmental conditions and social norms set by the society in which he lives. The individual does so in the face of pressures from the curiosity of others and from the processes of surveillance that every society sets in order to enforce its social norms. . . .

---

[51] John Stuart Mill, *On Liberty* 12, 13, 74-75 (1859).

[52] William M. Beaney, *The Right to Privacy and American Law*, 31 L. & Contemp. Probs. 253, 255 (1966).

[53] Robert C. Post, *Three Concepts of Privacy*, 89 Geo. L.J. 2087, 2087 (2001).

Recognizing the differences that political and sensory cultures make in setting norms of privacy among modern societies, it is still possible to describe the general functions that privacy performs for individuals and groups in Western democratic nations. Before describing these, it is helpful to explain in somewhat greater detail the four basic states of individual privacy [which are solitude, intimacy, anonymity, and reserve.] . . .

The first state of privacy is solitude; here the individual is separated from the group and freed from the observation of other persons. He may be subjected to jarring physical stimuli, such as noise, odors, and vibrations. His peace of mind may continue to be disturbed by physical sensations of heat, cold, itching, and pain. He may believe that he is being observed by God or some supernatural force, or fear that some authority is secretly watching him. Finally, in solitude he will be especially subject to that familiar dialogue with the mind or conscience. But, despite all these physical or psychological intrusions, solitude is the most complete state of privacy that individuals can achieve.

In the second state of privacy, the individual is acting as part of a small unit that claims and is allowed to exercise corporate seclusion so that it may achieve a close, relaxed, and frank relationship between two or more individuals. Typical units of intimacy are husband and wife, the family, a friendship circle, or a work clique. Whether close contact brings relaxed relations or abrasive hostility depends on the personal interaction of the members, but without intimacy a basic need of human contact would not be met.

The third state of privacy, anonymity, occurs when the individual is in public places or performing public acts but still seeks, and finds, freedom from identification and surveillance. He may be riding a subway, attending a ball game, or walking the streets; he is among people and knows that he is being observed; but unless he is a well-known celebrity, he does not expect to be personally identified and held to the full rules of behavior and role that would operate if he were known to those observing him. In this state the individual is able to merge into the "situational landscape." Knowledge or fear that one is under systematic observation in public places destroys the sense of relaxation and freedom that men seek in open spaces and public arenas. . . .

Still another kind of anonymity is the publication of ideas anonymously. Here the individual wants to present some idea publicly to the community or to a segment of it, but does not want to be universally identified at once as the author — especially not by the authorities, who may be forced to take action if they "know" the perpetrator. The core of each of these types of anonymous action is the desire of individuals for times of "public privacy."

Reserve, the fourth and most subtle state of privacy, is the creation of a psychological barrier against unwanted intrusion; this occurs when the individual's need to limit communication about himself is protected by the willing discretion of those surrounding him. Most of our lives are spent not in solitude or anonymity but in situations of intimacy and in group settings where we are known to others. Even in the most intimate relations, communication of self to others is always incomplete and is based on the need to hold back some parts of one's self as either too personal and sacred or too shameful and profane to express. This circumstance gives rise to what Simmel called "reciprocal reserve and indifference," the relation that creates "mental distance" to protect the personality. This creation of mental distance—a variant of the concept of "social distance" — takes place in every sort of relationship under rules of social etiquette; it expresses the individual's choice to withhold or disclose information — the choice that is the dynamic aspect of privacy in daily interpersonal relations. . . .

This analysis of the various states of privacy is useful in discussing the basic question of the functions privacy performs for individuals in democratic societies. These can also be grouped conveniently under four headings — personal autonomy, emotional release, self-evaluation, and limited and protected communication. . . .

Personal Autonomy. . . . Each person is aware of the gap between what he wants to be and what he actually is, between what the world sees of him and what he knows to be his much more complex reality. In addition, there are aspects of himself that the individual does not fully understand but is slowly exploring and shaping as he develops. Every individual lives behind a mask in this manner; indeed, the first etymological meaning of the word "person" was "mask," indicating both the conscious and expressive presentation of the self to a social audience. If this mask is torn off and the individual's real self bared to a world in which everyone else still wears his mask and believes in masked performances, the individual can be seared by the hot light of selective, forced exposure. . . .

The autonomy that privacy protects is also vital to the development of individuality and consciousness of individual choice in life. . . . This development of individuality is particularly important in democratic societies, since qualities of independent thought, diversity of views, and non-conformity are considered desirable traits for individuals. Such independence requires time for sheltered experimentation and testing of ideas, for preparation and practice in thought and conduct, without fear of ridicule or penalty, and for the opportunity to alter opinions before making them public. The individual's sense that it is he who decides when to "go public" is a crucial aspect of his feeling of autonomy. Without such time for incubation and growth, through privacy, many ideas and positions would be launched into the world with dangerous prematurity. . . .

Emotional Release. Life in society generates such tensions for the individual that both physical and psychological health demand periods of privacy for various types of emotional release. At one level, such relaxation is required from the pressure of playing social roles. Social scientists agree that each person constantly plays a series of varied and multiple roles, depending on his audience and behavioral situation. On any given day a man may move through the roles of stern father, loving husband, car-pool comedian, skilled lathe operator, union steward, water-cooler flirt, and American Legion committee chairman — all psychologically different roles that he adopts as he moves from scene to scene on the social stage. Like actors on the dramatic stage, Goffman has noted, individuals can sustain roles only for reasonable periods of time, and no individual can play indefinitely, without relief, the variety of roles that life demands. There have to be moments "off stage" when the individual can be "himself": tender, angry, irritable, lustful, or dream-filled. . . .

Another form of emotional release is provided by the protection privacy gives to minor non-compliance with social norms. Some norms are formally adopted — perhaps as law — which society really expects many persons to break. This ambivalence produces a situation in which almost everyone does break some social or institutional norms — for example, violating traffic laws, breaking sexual mores, cheating on expense accounts, overstating income-tax deductions, or smoking in rest rooms when this is prohibited. Although society will usually punish the most flagrant abuses, it tolerates the great bulk of the violations as "permissible" deviations. If there were no privacy to permit society to ignore these deviations — if all transgressions were known — most persons in society would be under organizational discipline or in jail, or could be manipulated by threats of such action. The firm expectation of having privacy for permissible deviations is a distinguishing characteristic of life in a free society. At a lesser but still important level, privacy also allows individuals to deviate temporarily from social etiquette when alone or among intimates, as by putting feet on desks, cursing, letting one's face go slack, or scratching wherever one itches.

Another aspect of release is the "safety-valve" function afforded by privacy. Most persons need to give vent to their anger at "the system," "city hall," "the boss," and various others who exercise authority over them, and to do this in the intimacy of family or friendship circles, or in private papers, without fear of being held responsible for such comments. . . . Without the aid of such release in accommodating the daily abrasions with authorities, most people would experience serious emotional pressure. . . .

Limited and Protected Communication. The greatest threat to civilized social life would be a situation in which each individual was utterly candid in his communications with others, saying exactly what he knew or felt at all times. The havoc done to interpersonal relations by children, saints, mental patients, and adult "innocents" is legendary. . . .

Privacy for limited and protected communication has two general aspects. First, it provides the individual with the opportunities he needs for sharing confidences and intimacies with those he trusts — spouse, "the family," personal friends, and close associates at work. The individual discloses because he knows that his confidences will be held, and because he knows that breach of confidence violates social norms in a civilized society. "A friend," said Emerson, "is someone before . . . [whom] I can think aloud." In addition, the individual often wants to secure counsel from persons with whom he does not have to live daily after disclosing his confidences. He seeks professionally objective advice from persons whose status in society promises that they will not later use his distress to take advantage of him. To protect freedom of limited communication, such relationships — with doctors, lawyers, ministers, psychiatrists, psychologists, and others — are given varying but important degrees of legal privilege against forced disclosure. . . .

NOTES & QUESTIONS

1. *Privacy as Control over Information.* A number of theorists, including Westin, conceive of privacy as a form of control over personal information.[54] Consider Charles Fried's definition of privacy:

> At first approximation, privacy seems to be related to secrecy, to limiting the knowledge of others about oneself. This notion must be refined. It is not true, for instance, that the less that is known about us the more privacy we have. Privacy is not simply an absence of information about what is in the minds of others; rather it is the *control* we have over information about ourselves.
>
> To refer for instance to the privacy of a lonely man on a desert island would be to engage in irony. The person who enjoys privacy is able to grant or deny access to others. . . .
>
> Privacy, thus, is control over knowledge about oneself. But it is not simply control over the quantity of information abroad; there are modulations in the quality of the knowledge as well. We may not mind that a person knows a general fact about us, and yet feel our privacy invaded if he knows the details.[55]

Is this a compelling definition of privacy?

2. *Privacy as Limited Access to the Self.* Another group of theorists view privacy as a form of limited access to the self. Consider Ruth Gavison:

> . . . Our interest in privacy . . . is related to our concern over our accessibility to others: the extent to which we are known to others, the extent to which others have physical access to us, and the extent to which we are the subject of others' attention. This concept of privacy as concern for limited accessibility enables us to identify when losses of privacy occur. Furthermore, the reasons for which we claim privacy in different situations are similar. They are related to the functions privacy has in our lives: the promotion of liberty, autonomy, selfhood, and human relations, and furthering the existence of a free society. . . .
>
> The concept of privacy suggested here is a complex of these three independent and irreducible elements: secrecy, anonymity, and solitude. Each is independent in the sense that a loss of privacy may occur through a change in any one of the three, without a necessary loss in either of the other two. The concept is nevertheless coherent because the three elements are all part of the same notion of accessibility, and are related in many important ways.[56]

---

[54] *See* Adam Carlyle Breckenridge, *The Right to Privacy* 1 (1970); Randall P. Bezanson, *The Right to Privacy Revisited: Privacy, News, and Social Change, 1810–1990*, 80 Cal. L. Rev. 1133 (1992). For a critique of privacy as control, see Anita L. Allen, *Privacy as Data Control: Conceptual, Practical, and Moral Limits of the Paradigm*, 32 Conn. L. Rev. 861 (2000).

[55] Charles Fried, *Privacy*, 77 Yale L.J. 475 (1968).

[56] Ruth Gavison, *Privacy and the Limits of Law*, 89 Yale L.J. 421 (1980); *see also* Edward Shils, *Privacy: Its Constitution and Vicissitudes*, 31 L. & Contemp. Probs. 281, 281 (1996); Sissela Bok, *Secrets: On the Ethics of Concealment and Revelation* 10-11 (1982); Ernest Van Den Haag, *On Privacy*, in *Nomos XII: Privacy* 149 (J. Ronald Pennock & J.W. Chapman eds., 1971); Sidney M. Jourard, *Some Psychological Aspects of Privacy*, 31 L. & Contemp. Probs. 307, 307 (1966); David O'Brien, *Privacy, Law, and Public Policy* 16 (1979); Hyman Gross, *The Concept of Privacy*, 42 N.Y.U. L. Rev. 34 (1967).

How does this theory of privacy differ from the notion of privacy as "the right to be let alone"? How does it differ from privacy as control over information? How much control should individuals have over access to themselves? Should the decision depend upon each particular person's desires? Or should there be an objective standard — a reasonable degree of control over access?

3. *Privacy as Intimacy.* A number of theorists argue that "intimacy" appropriately defines what information or matters are private. For example, Julie Inness argues that "intimacy" is the common denominator in all the matters that people claim to be private. Privacy is "the state of the agent having control over decisions concerning matters that draw their meaning and value from the agent's love, caring, or liking. These decisions cover choices on the agent's part about access to herself, the dissemination of information about herself, and her actions."[57]

Jeffrey Rosen adopts a similar view when he writes:

> . . . Privacy protects us from being misdefined and judged out of context in a world of short attention spans, a world in which information can easily be confused with knowledge. True knowledge of another person is the culmination of a slow process of mutual revelation. It requires the gradual setting aside of social masks, the incremental building of trust, which leads to the exchange of personal disclosures. It cannot be rushed; this is why, after intemperate self-revelation in the heat of passion, one may feel something close to self-betrayal. True knowledge of another person, in all of his or her complexity, can be achieved only with a handful of friends, lovers, or family members. In order to flourish, the intimate relationships on which true knowledge of another person depends need space as well as time: sanctuaries from the gaze of the crowd in which slow mutual self-disclosure is possible.
>
> When intimate personal information circulates among a small group of people who know us well, its significance can be weighed against other aspects of our personality and character. By contrast, when intimate information is removed from its original context and revealed to strangers, we are vulnerable to being misjudged on the basis of our most embarrassing, and therefore most memorable, tastes and preferences. . . . In a world in which citizens are bombarded with information, people form impressions quickly, based on sound bites, and these impressions are likely to oversimplify and misrepresent our complicated and often contradictory characters.[58]

Does "intimacy" adequately separate private matters from public ones? Can something be private but not intimate? Can something be intimate but not private?

In reaction to Rosen's views on privacy, Lawrence Lessig restates the problem of short attention spans in this fashion: "Privacy, the argument goes,

---

[57] Julie C. Inness, *Privacy, Intimacy, and Isolation* 56, 58, 63, 64, 67 (1992). For other proponents of privacy as intimacy, see Robert S. Gerstein, *Intimacy and Privacy*, in *Philosophical Dimensions of Privacy: An Anthology* 265, 265 (Ferdinand David Schoeman ed., 1984); James Rachels, *Why Privacy Is Important*, in *Philosophical Dimensions of Privacy: An Anthology* 290, 292 (Ferdinand David Schoeman ed., 1984); Tom Gerety, *Redefining Privacy*, 12 Harv. C.R.-C.L. L. Rev. 233 (1977).

[58] Jeffrey Rosen, *The Unwanted Gaze: The Destruction of Privacy in America* 8-9 (2000).

would remedy such a problem by concealing those things that would not be understood with the given attention span. Privacy's function . . . is not to protect the presumptively innocent from true but damaging information, but rather to protect the actually innocent from damaging conclusions drawn from misunderstood information."[59] Lessig notes his skepticism regarding this approach: privacy will not alone solve the problem with the information market. Moreover, there "are possible solutions to this problem of attention span. But what should be clear is that there is no guarantee that a particular problem of attention span will have any solution at all."

JULIE E. COHEN, EXAMINED LIVES: INFORMATIONAL PRIVACY AND THE SUBJECT AS OBJECT

52 Stan. L. Rev. 1373 (2000)

Prevailing market-based approaches to data privacy policy — including "solutions" in the form of tradable privacy rights or heightened disclosure requirements before consent — treat preferences for informational privacy as a matter of individual taste, entitled to no more (and often much less) weight than preferences for black shoes over brown or red wine over white. But the values of informational privacy are far more fundamental. A degree of freedom from scrutiny and categorization by others promotes important noninstrumental values, and serves vital individual and collective ends.

First, informational autonomy comports with important values concerning the fair and just treatment of individuals within society. From Kant to Rawls, a central strand of Western philosophical tradition emphasizes respect for the fundamental dignity of persons, and a concomitant commitment to egalitarianism in both principle and practice. Advocates of strong data privacy protection argue that these principles have clear and very specific implications for the treatment of personally-identified data: They require that we forbid data-processing practices that treat individuals as mere conglomerations of transactional data, or that rank people as prospective customers, tenants, neighbors, employees, or insureds based on their financial or genetic desirability. . . .

Autonomous individuals do not spring full-blown from the womb. We must learn to process information and to draw our own conclusions about the world around us. We must learn to choose, and must learn something before we can choose anything. Here, though, information theory suggests a paradox: "Autonomy" connotes an essential independence of critical faculty and an imperviousness to influence. But to the extent that information shapes behavior, autonomy is radically contingent upon environment and circumstance. . . . Autonomy in a contingent world requires a zone of relative insulation from outside scrutiny and interference — a field of operation within which to engage in the conscious construction of self. The solution to the paradox of contingent autonomy, in other words, lies in a second paradox: To exist in fact as well as in theory, autonomy must be nurtured.

---

[59] Lawrence Lessig, *Privacy and Attention Span*, 89 Geo. L. J. 2063, 2065 (2001).

A realm of autonomous, unmonitored choice, in turn, promotes a vital diversity of speech and behavior. The recognition that anonymity shelters constitutionally-protected decisions about speech, belief, and political and intellectual association — decisions that otherwise might be chilled by unpopularity or simple difference — is part of our constitutional tradition. . . .

The benefits of informational privacy are related to, but distinct from, those afforded by seclusion from visual monitoring. It is well-recognized that respite from visual scrutiny affords individuals an important measure of psychological repose. Within our society, at least, we are accustomed to physical spaces within which we can be unobserved, and intrusion into those spaces is experienced as violating the boundaries of self. But the scrutiny, and the repose, can be informational as well as visual, and this does not depend entirely on whether the behavior takes place "in private." The injury, here, does not lie in the exposure of formerly private behaviors to public view, but in the dissolution of the boundaries that insulate different spheres of behavior from one another. The universe of all information about all record-generating behaviors generates a "picture" that, in some respects, is more detailed and intimate than that produced by visual observation, and that picture is accessible, in theory and often in reality, to just about anyone who wants to see it. In such a world, we all may be more cautious.

The point is not that people will not learn under conditions of no-privacy, but that they will learn differently, and that the experience of being watched will constrain, ex ante, the acceptable spectrum of belief and behavior. Pervasive monitoring of every first move or false start will, at the margin, incline choices toward the bland and the mainstream. The result will be a subtle yet fundamental shift in the content of our character, a blunting and blurring of rough edges and sharp lines. . . . The condition of no-privacy threatens not only to chill the expression of eccentric individuality, but also, gradually, to dampen the force of our aspirations to it. . . .

. . . [T]he insulation provided by informational privacy also plays a subtler, more conservative role in reinforcing the existing social fabric. Sociologist Erving Goffman demonstrated that the construction of social facades to mediate between self and community is both instinctive and expected. Alan Westin describes this social dimension of privacy as "reserve." This characterization, though, seems incomplete. On Goffman's account, the construction of social personae isn't just about withholding information that we don't want others to have. It is about defining the parameters of social interaction in ways that maximize social ease, and thus is about collective as well as individual comfort. We do not need, or even want, to know each other that well. Less information makes routine interactions easier; we are then free to choose, consensually and without embarrassment, the interactions that we wish to treat as less routine. Informational privacy, in short, is a constitutive element of a civil society in the broadest sense of that term. . . .

NOTES & QUESTIONS

1. *Privacy and Respect for Persons.* Julie Cohen's theory locates the purpose of privacy as promoting the development of autonomous individuals and, more broadly, civil society. Compare her theory to the following theory by Stanley Benn:

> Finding oneself an object of scrutiny, as the focus of another's attention, brings one to a new consciousness of oneself, as something seen through another's eyes. According to [Jean-Paul] Sartre, indeed, it is a necessary condition for knowing oneself as anything at all that one should conceive oneself as an object of scrutiny. It is only through the regard of the other that the observed becomes aware of himself as an object, knowable, having a determinate character, in principle predictable. His consciousness of pure freedom as subject, as originator and chooser, is at once assailed by it; he is fixed as *something* — with limited probabilities rather than infinite, indeterminate possibilities. . . .
>
> The underpinning of a claim not to be watched without leave will be more general if it can be grounded in this way on the principle of respect for persons than on a utilitarian duty to avoid inflicting suffering. . . . But respect for persons will sustain an objection even to secret watching, which may do no actual harm at all. Covert observation — spying — is objectionable because it deliberately deceives a person about his world, thwarting, for reasons that *cannot* be his reasons, his attempts to make a rational choice. One cannot be said to respect a man as engaged on an enterprise worthy of consideration if one knowingly and deliberately alters his conditions of action, concealing the fact from him. . . .[60]

How is Cohen's theory similar to and/or different from Benn's?

Benn argues that privacy is a form of respect for persons. By being watched, Benn contends, the observed becomes "fixed as *something* — with limited probabilities rather than infinite indeterminate possibilities." Does Benn adequately capture why surveillance is harmful? Is Benn really concerned about the negative consequences of surveillance on a person's behavior? Or is Benn more concerned about the violation of respect for another?

2. *Privacy as an Individual Right and as a Social Value.* Consider the following argument from Priscilla Regan:

> . . . [The] emphasis of privacy as an individual right or an individual interest provides a weak basis for formulating policy to protect privacy. When privacy is defined as an individual right, policy formulation entails a balancing of the individual right to privacy against a competing interest or right. In general, the competing interest is recognized as a social interest. . . . It is also assumed that the individual has a stake in these societal interests. As a result, privacy has been on the defensive, with those alleging a privacy invasion bearing the burden of proving that a certain activity does indeed invade privacy and that the "social" benefit to be gained from the privacy invasion is less important than the individual harm incurred. . . .

---

[60] Stanley I. Benn, *Privacy, Freedom, and Respect for Persons,* from *Nomos XIII: Privacy* (J. Ronald Pennock & J.W. Chapman eds., 1971).

Privacy is a *common value* in that all individuals value some degree of privacy and have some common perceptions about privacy. Privacy is also a *public value* in that it has value not just to the individual as an individual or to all individuals in common but also to the democratic political system. . . .

A public value of privacy derives not only from its protection of the individual as an individual but also from its usefulness as a restraint on the government or on the use of power. . . .[61]

DANIEL J. SOLOVE, *CONCEPTUALIZING PRIVACY*

90 Cal. L. Rev. 1087 (2002)

Despite what appears to be a welter of different conceptions of privacy, I argue that they can be dealt with under six general headings, which capture the recurrent ideas in the discourse. These headings include: (1) the right to be let alone — Samuel Warren and Louis Brandeis's famous formulation for the right to privacy; (2) limited access to the self — the ability to shield oneself from unwanted access by others; (3) secrecy — the concealment of certain matters from others; (4) control over personal information — the ability to exercise control over information about oneself; (5) personhood — the protection of one's personality, individuality, and dignity; and (6) intimacy — control over, or limited access to, one's intimate relationships or aspects of life. Some of the conceptions concentrate on means to achieve privacy; others focus on the ends or goals of privacy. Further, there is overlap between conceptions, and the conceptions discussed under different headings are by no means independent from each other. For example, control over personal information can be seen as a subset of limited access to the self, which in turn bears significant similarities to the right to be let alone. . . .

The most prevalent problem with the conceptions is that they are either too narrow or too broad. The conceptions are often too narrow because they fail to include the aspects of life that we typically view as private, and are often too broad because they fail to exclude matters that we do not deem private. Often, the same conceptions can suffer from being both too narrow and too broad. I contend that these problems stem from the way that the discourse goes about the task of conceptualizing privacy. . . .

Most attempts to conceptualize privacy thus far have followed the traditional method of conceptualizing. The majority of theorists conceptualize privacy by defining it *per genus et differentiam*. In other words, theorists look for a common set of necessary and sufficient elements that single out privacy as unique from other conceptions. . . .

[Philosopher Ludwig] Wittgenstein suggests that certain concepts might not share one common characteristic; rather they draw from a common pool of similar characteristics, "a complicated network of similarities overlapping and criss-crossing: sometimes overall similarities, sometimes similarities of detail." . . .

---

[61] Priscilla M. Regan, *Legislating Privacy: Technology, Social Values, and Public Policy* 213, 225 (1995).

Wittgenstein uses the term "family resemblances," analogizing to the overlapping and crisscrossing characteristics that exist between members of a family, such as "build, features, colour of eyes, gait, temperament, etc." For example, in a family, each child has certain features similar to each parent; and the children share similar features with each other; but they may not all resemble each other in the same way. Nevertheless, they all bear a resemblance to each other. . . .

When we state that we are protecting "privacy," we are claiming to guard against disruptions to certain practices. Privacy invasions disrupt and sometimes completely annihilate certain practices. Practices can be disrupted in certain ways, such as interference with peace of mind and tranquility, invasion of solitude, breach of confidentiality, loss of control over facts about oneself, searches of one's person and property, threats to or violations of personal security, destruction of reputation, surveillance, and so on.

There are certain similarities in particular types of disruptions as well as in the practices that they disrupt; but there are differences as well. We should conceptualize privacy by focusing on the specific types of disruption and the specific practices disrupted rather than looking for the common denominator that links all of them. If privacy is conceptualized as a web of interconnected types of disruption of specific practices, then the act of conceptualizing privacy should consist of mapping the typography of the web. . . .

It is reductive to carve the world of social practices into two spheres, public and private, and then attempt to determine what matters belong in each sphere. First, the matters we consider private change over time. While some form of dichotomy between public and private has been maintained throughout the history of Western civilization, the matters that have been considered public and private have metamorphosed throughout history due to changing attitudes, institutions, living conditions, and technology. The matters we consider to be private are shaped by culture and history, and have differed across cultures and historical epochs.

Second, although certain matters have moved from being public to being private and vice versa, the change often has been more subtle than a complete transformation from public to private. Particular matters have long remained private but in different ways; they have been understood as private but because of different attributes; or they have been regarded as private for some people or groups but not for others. In other words, to say simply that something is public or private is to make a rather general claim; what it means for something to be private is the central question. We consider our Social Security number, our sexual behavior, our diary, and our home private, but we do not consider them private in the same way. A number of aspects of life have commonly been viewed as private: the family, body, and home to name a few. To say simply that these things are private is imprecise because what it means for them to be private is different today than it was in the past. . . .

. . . [P]rivacy is not simply an empirical and historical question that measures the collective sense in any given society of what is and has long been considered to be private. Without a normative component, a conception of privacy can only provide a status report on existing privacy norms rather than guide us toward shaping privacy law and policy in the future. If we focus simply on people's current expectations of privacy, our conception of privacy would continually shrink given the increasing surveillance in the modern world. Similarly, the government could gradually condition people to accept wiretapping or other privacy incursions, thus altering society's expectations of privacy. On the other hand, if we merely seek to preserve those activities and matters that have historically been considered private, then we fail to adapt to the changing realities of the modern world. . . .

NOTES & QUESTIONS

1. *Core Characteristics vs. Family Resemblances.* Is there a core characteristic common in all the things we understand as being "private"? If so, what do you think it is? Can privacy be more adequately conceptualized by shifting away from the quest to find the common core characteristics of privacy?

2. *Context.* Solove contends that the meaning of privacy depends upon context, that there is no common denominator to all things we refer to as "privacy." Does this make privacy too amorphous a concept?

    Consider Helen Nissenbaum:

    Specifically, whether a particular action is determined a violation of privacy is a function of several variables, including the nature of the situation, or context; the nature of the information in relation to that context; the roles of agents receiving information; their relationships to information subjects; on what terms the information is shared by the subject; and the terms of further dissemination. . . .

    [N]orms of privacy in fact vary considerably from place to place, culture to culture, period to period; this theory not only incorporates this reality but systematically pinpoints the sources of variation. A second consequence is that, because questions about whether particular restrictions on flow are acceptable call for investigation into the relevant contextual details, protecting privacy will be a messy task, requiring a grasp of concepts and social institutions as well as knowledge of facts of the matter.[62]

3. *Revising the Prosser Taxonomy.* Daniel Solove contends that the taxonomy of four privacy interests identified by William Prosser, *supra,* must be revised as well as expanded beyond tort law. Solove identifies 16 different kinds of activity that create privacy harms or problems:

    The first group of activities that affect privacy involve information collection. *Surveillance* is the watching, listening to, or recording of an individual's activities. *Interrogation* consists of various forms of questioning or probing for information.

    A second group of activities involves the way information is stored, manipulated, and used — what I refer to collectively as "information processing." *Aggregation* involves the combination of various pieces of data about a person. *Identification* is linking information to particular individuals. *Insecurity* involves carelessness in protecting stored information from being leaked or improperly accessed. *Secondary use* is the use of information collected for one

---

[62] Helen Nissenbaum, *Privacy as Contextual Integrity,* 79 Wash. L. Rev. 119, 155-56 (2004). For a more complete account of Nissenbaum's theory, see Helen Nissenbaum, *Privacy in Context: Technology, Policy, and the Integrity of Social Life* (2010).

purpose for a different purpose without a person's consent. *Exclusion* concerns the failure to allow people to know about the data that others have about them and participate in its handling and use. These activities do not involve the gathering of data, since it has already been collected. Instead, these activities involve the way data is maintained and used.

The third group of activities involves the dissemination of information. *Breach of confidentiality* is breaking the promise to keep a person's information confidential. *Disclosure* involves the revelation of truthful information about a person which impacts the way others judge that person's character. *Exposure* involves revealing another's nudity, grief, or bodily functions. *Increased accessibility* is amplifying the accessibility of information. *Blackmail* is the threat to disclose personal information. *Appropriation* involves the use of another's identity to serve the aims and interests of another. *Distortion* consists of the dissemination of false or misleading information about individuals. Information dissemination activities all involve the spreading or transfer of personal data — or the threat to do so.

The fourth and final group of activities involves invasions into people's private affairs. Invasion, unlike the other groupings, need not involve personal information (although in numerous instances, it does). *Intrusion* concerns invasive acts that disturb one's tranquility or solitude. *Decisional interference* involves the government's incursion into people's decisions regarding their private affairs.[63]

4. *Reductionists.* Some theorists, referred to as "reductionists," assert that privacy can be reduced to other concepts and rights. For example, Judith Jarvis Thomson contends that there is nothing particularly distinctive about privacy and to talk about things as violating the "right to privacy" is not all that useful. Privacy is really a cluster of other rights, such as the right to liberty, property rights, and the right not to be injured: "[T]he right to privacy is everywhere overlapped by other rights."[64] Is there something distinctive about privacy? Or can privacy be explained in terms of other, more primary rights and interests? What does privacy capture that these other rights and interests (autonomy, property, liberty, etc.) do not?

ANITA L. ALLEN, *COERCING PRIVACY*

40 Wm. & Mary L. Rev. 723 (1999)

. . . The final decades of the twentieth century could be remembered for the rapid erosion of expectations of personal privacy and of the taste for personal privacy in the United States. . . . I sense that people expect increasingly little physical, informational, and proprietary privacy, and that people seem to prefer less of these types of privacy relative to other goods. . . .

One way to address the erosion would be to stop the avalanche of technology and commercial opportunity responsible for the erosion. We could stop the avalanche of technology, but we will not, if the past is any indication. . . . In the

---

[63] Daniel J. Solove, *A Taxonomy of Privacy,* 154 U. Pa. L. Rev. 477 (2006). For a more complete account of Solove's theory, see Daniel J. Solove, *Understanding Privacy* (2008).

[64] Judith Jarvis Thomson, *The Right to Privacy,* 4 Phil. & Pub. Aff. 295 (1975).

United States, with a few exceptions like government-funded human cloning and fetal tissue research, the rule is that technology marches on.

We could stop the avalanche of commercial opportunity by intervening in the market for privacy; that is, we could (some way or another) increase the costs of consuming other people's privacy and lower the profits of voluntarily giving up one's own privacy. The problem with this suggested strategy is that, even without the details of implementation, it raises the specter of censorship, repression, paternalism, and bureaucracy. Privacy is something we think people are supposed to want; if it turns out that they do not, perhaps third parties should not force it on them, decreasing both their utility and that of those who enjoy disclosure, revelation, and exposure.

Of course, we force privacy on people all the time. Our elected officials criminalize public nudity, even to the point of discouraging breastfeeding. . . . It is one thing, the argument might go, to force privacy on someone by criminalizing nude sun-bathing and topless dancing. These activities have pernicious third-party effects and attract vice. It would be wrong, the argument might continue, to force privacy on someone, in the absence of harm to others, solely on the grounds that one ought not say too much about one's thoughts, feelings, and experiences; one ought not reveal in detail how one spends one's time at home; and one ought not live constantly on display. Paternalistic laws against extremes of factual and physical self-revelation seem utterly inconsistent with liberal self-expression, and yet such laws are suggested by the strong claims liberal theorists make about the value of privacy. Liberal theorists claim that we need privacy to be persons, independent thinkers, free political actors, and citizens of a tolerant democracy. . . .

For people under forty-five who understand that they do not, and cannot, expect to have many secrets, informational privacy may now seem less important. As a culture, we seem to be learning how to be happy and productive — even spiritual — knowing that we are like open books, our houses made of glass. Our parents may appear on the television shows of Oprah Winfrey or Jerry Springer to discuss incest, homosexuality, miscegenation, adultery, transvestitism, and cruelty in the family. Our adopted children may go on television to be reunited with their birth parents. Our law students may compete with their peers for a spot on the MTV program The Real World, and a chance to live with television cameras for months on end and be viewed by mass audiences. Our ten-year-olds may aspire to have their summer camp experiences — snits, fights, fun, and all — chronicled by camera crews and broadcast as entertainment for others on the Disney Channel.

Should we worry about any of this? What values are at stake? Scholars and other commentators associate privacy with several important clusters of value. Privacy has value relative to normative conceptions of spiritual personality, political freedom, health and welfare, human dignity, and autonomy. . . .

To speak of "coercing" privacy is to call attention to privacy as a foundation, a precondition of a liberal egalitarian society. Privacy is not an optional good, like a second home or an investment account. . . .

A hard task seems to lay before us — namely, deciding which forms of privacy are so critical that they should become matters of coercion. . . .

As liberals, we should not want people to sell all their freedom, and, as liberals, we should not want people to sell all their privacy and capacities for private choices. This is, in part, because the liberal conceptions of private choice as freedom from governmental and other outside interference with decisionmaking closely link privacy and freedom. The liberal conception of privacy as freedom from unwanted disclosures, publicity, and loss of control of personality also closely links privacy to freedom. . . .

Government will have to intervene in private lives for the sake of privacy and values associated with it. . . . The threat to liberalism is not that individuals sometimes expose their naked bodies in public places, display affection with same-sex partners in public, or broadcast personal information on national television. The threat to liberalism is that in an increasing variety of ways our lives are being emptied of privacy on a daily basis, especially physical and informational privacy. . . .

NOTES & QUESTIONS

1. ***Should Privacy Be an Inalienable Right?*** Allen argues that people regularly surrender their privacy and that we should "coerce" privacy. In other words, privacy must be seen as an inalienable right, one that people cannot give away. What if a person wants to live in the spotlight or to give away her personal information? Why shouldn't she be allowed to do so? Recall those who defined privacy as control over information. One aspect of control is that an individual can decide for herself how much privacy she desires. What would Allen say about such a definition of privacy?

2. ***Privacy and Publicity.*** Consider also whether a desire for publicity and a desire for privacy can coexist. Does the person who "tells it all" on the Jerry Springer talk show have any less expectation of privacy when she returns home to be with her family and friends or picks up the telephone to make a private call?

3. ***Eroding Expectations of Privacy and Privacy Paternalism.*** Allen contends that our society is changing by becoming more exhibitionistic and voyeuristic. The result is that expectations of privacy are eroding. In 2011, Allen further develops these themes in a book, *Unpopular Privacy*. She argues that "privacy is so important and so neglected in contemporary life that democratic states, though liberal and feminist, could be justified in undertaking a rescue mission that includes enacting paternalistic privacy laws for the benefit of uneager beneficiaries."[65]

  If people no longer expect privacy in many situations, then why should the law continue to protect it? If people no longer desire privacy, should the law force privacy upon them? Under what circumstances?

---

[65] Anita L. Allen, *Unpopular Privacy* (2011).

PAUL M. SCHWARTZ, *PRIVACY AND DEMOCRACY IN CYBERSPACE*

52 Vand. L. Rev. 1609 (1999)

. . . Self-determination is a capacity that is embodied and developed through social forms and practices. The threat to this quality arises when private or government action interferes with a person's control of her reasoning process. . . . [P]erfected surveillance of naked thought's digital expression short-circuits the individual's own process of decisionmaking. . . .

The maintenance of a democratic order requires both deliberative democracy and an individual capacity for self-determination. . . . [T]he emerging pattern of information use in cyberspace poses a risk to these two essential values. Our task now is to develop privacy standards that are capable of structuring the right kind of information use. . . .

Most scholars, and much of the law in this area, work around a liberal paradigm that we can term "privacy-control." From the age of computer mainframes in the 1960s to the current reign of the Internet's decentralized networks, academics and the law have gravitated towards the idea of privacy as a personal right to control the use of one's data. . . .

. . . [One flaw with the "privacy-control" paradigm is the "autonomy trap."] [T]he organization of information privacy through individual control of personal data rests on a view of autonomy as a given, preexisting quality. . . .

As a policy cornerstone, however, the idea of privacy-control falls straight into the "autonomy trap." The difficulty with privacy-control in the Information Age is that individual self-determination is itself shaped by the processing of personal data. . . .

To give an example of an autonomy trap in cyberspace, the act of clicking through a "consent" screen on a Web site may be considered by some observers to be an exercise of self-reliant choice. Yet, this screen can contain boilerplate language that permits all further processing and transmission of one's personal data. Even without a consent screen, some Web sites place consent boilerplate within a "privacy statement" on their home page or elsewhere on their site. For example, the online version of one New York newspaper states, "By using this site, you agree to the Privacy Policy of the New York Post." This language presents the conditions for data processing on a take-it-or-leave-it basis. It seeks to create the legal fiction that all who visit this Web site have expressed informed consent to its data processing practices. An even more extreme manifestation of the "consent trap" is a belief that an initial decision to surf the Web itself is a self-reliant choice to accept all further use of one's personal data generated by this activity. . . .

The liberal ideal views autonomous individuals as able to interact freely and equally so long as the government or public does not interfere. The reality is, however, that individuals can be trapped when such glorification of freedom of action neglects the actual conditions of choice. Here, another problem arises with self-governance through information-control: the "data seclusion deception." The idea of privacy as data seclusion is easy to explain: unless the individual wishes to surrender her personal information, she is to be free to use her privacy right as a trump to keep it confidential or to subject its release to conditions that she alone wishes to set. The individual is to be at the center of shaping data anonymity. Yet, this right to keep data isolated quickly proves illusory because of the demands of the Information Age. . . .

NOTES & QUESTIONS

1. ***Privacy and Personhood.*** Like Schwartz, a number of theorists argue that privacy is essential for self-development. According to Jeffrey Reiman, privacy "protects the individual's interest in becoming, being, and remaining a person."[66] The notion that privacy protects personhood or identity is captured in Warren and Brandeis's notion of "inviolate personality." How does privacy promote self-development?

   Consider the following: "Every acceptance of a public role entails the repression, channelizing, and deflection of 'private' or personal attention, motives, and demands upon the self in order to address oneself to the expectations of others."[67] Can we really be ourselves in the public sphere? Is our "public self" any less part of our persona than our "private self"?

2. ***Privacy and Democracy.*** Schwartz views privacy as essential for a democratic society. Why is privacy important for political participation?

3. ***Privacy and Role Playing.*** Recall Westin's view of selfhood:

   > Each person is aware of the gap between what he wants to be and what he actually is, between what the world sees of him and what he knows to be his much more complex reality. In addition, there are aspects of himself that the individual does not fully understand but is slowly exploring and shaping as he develops. Every individual lives behind a mask in this manner; indeed, the first etymological meaning of the word "person" was "mask," indicating both the conscious and expressive presentation of the self to a social audience. If this mask is torn off and the individual's real self bared to a world in which everyone else still wears his mask and believes in masked performances, the individual can be seared by the hot light of selective, forced exposure.

   Is there a "true" or "core" or "authentic" self? Or do we perform many roles and perhaps have multiple selves? Is there a self beneath the roles that we play?

   Daniel Solove contends that "[s]ociety accepts that public reputations will be groomed to some degree. . . . Society protects privacy because it wants to provide individuals with some degree of influence over how they are judged in the public arena."[68] To what extent should the law allow people to promote a polished public image and hide the dirt in private?

4. ***Individual Autonomy, Democratic Order, and Data Trade.*** In a later article, Schwartz argues from the premise that "[p]ersonal information is an important

---

[66] Jeffrey H. Reiman, *Privacy, Intimacy, and Personhood*, in *Philosophical Dimensions of Privacy: An Anthology* 300, 308 (Ferdinand David Schoeman ed., 1984).

[67] Joseph Bensman & Robert Lilienfeld, *Between Public and Private: Lost Boundaries of the Self* 174 (1979).

[68] Daniel J. Solove, *The Virtues of Knowing Less: Justifying Privacy Protections Against Disclosure,* 53 Duke L.J. 957 (2003).

currency in the new millennium."[69] He rejects arguments that opposed propertization of personal data, and developed a model to permit data trade consistent with individual autonomy and the maintenance of a democratic order. A key concept in this model is that of the "privacy commons," where privacy is viewed "as a social and not merely an individual good." As a result, Schwartz states, "If sound rules for the use of personal data are not established and enforced, society as a whole will suffer because people will decline to engage in a range of different social interactions due to concerns about use of personal information. A public good—the privacy commons— will be degraded." Do you think that property is a sound concept for building a public goods approach to information privacy?

SPIROS SIMITIS, *REVIEWING PRIVACY IN AN INFORMATION SOCIETY*

135 U. Pa. L. Rev. 707 (1987)

. . . . The increased access to personal information resulting from modern, sophisticated techniques of automated processing has sharpened the need to abandon the search for a "neutral" concept in favor of an understanding free of abstractions and fully aware of the political and societal background of all privacy debates. Modern forms of data collection have altered the privacy discussion in three principal ways. First, privacy considerations no longer arise out of particular individual problems; rather, they express conflicts affecting everyone. The course of the privacy debate is neither determined by the caricature of a prominent golfer with a chocolate packet protruding out of his pocket, nor by the hints at the use of a sexual stimulant by a respected university professor, but by the intensive retrieval of personal data of virtually every employee, taxpayer, patient, bank customer, welfare recipient, or car driver. Second, smart cards and videotex make it possible to record and reconstruct individual activities in minute detail.[70] Surveillance has thereby lost its exceptional character and has become a more and more routine practice. Finally, personal information is increasingly used to enforce standards of behavior. Information processing is developing, therefore, into an essential element of long-term strategies of manipulation intended to mold and adjust individual conduct. . . .

. . . [B]ecause of both the broad availability of personal data and the elaborate matching procedures, individual activities can be accurately reconstructed through automated processing. Surveillance becomes the order of the day. Significantly enough, security agencies were among the first to discover the advantages of automated retrieval. They not only quickly computerized their own data

---

[69] Paul M. Schwartz, *Property, Privacy, and Personal Data*, 117 Harv. L. Rev. 2055 (2004).

[70] Editors' Note: Smart cards are also known as "chip cards" or "integrated circuit cards." These devices, generally the size of a credit card, feature an embedded circuit for the processing of data. A precursor of the Internet, Videotex enjoyed its heyday from the late 1970s to mid-1980s. Videotex was typically deployed through a centralized system with one provider of information and involved the display of text on a television screen or dedicated terminal. France Telecom's Minitel was the most successful videotext system in the world.

collections but also sought and obtained access to state and private data banks. Entirely new investigation techniques, such as computer profiling, were developed, enabling the agencies to trace wanted persons by matching a presumptive pattern of consumption habits against, for instance, the records of utility companies. The successful attempts at computer-based voice and picture identification will probably influence the work of security agencies even more. . . .

Both the quest for greater transparency and the defense of free speech are legitimated by the goal of allowing the individual to understand social reality better and thus to form a personal opinion on its decisive factors as well as on possible changes. The citizen's right to be "a participator in the government of affairs," to use Jefferson's terms, reflects a profoundly rational process. It presupposes individuals who not only disperse the necessary information but also have the capacity to transform the accessible data into policy expectations. Transparency is, in other words, a basic element of competent communicative action and consequently remains indispensable as long as social discourse is to be promoted, not inhibited.

Inhibition, however, tends to be the rule once automated processing of personal data becomes a normal tool of both government and private enterprises. The price for an undoubted improvement in transparency is a no less evident loss in competence of communication. Habits, activities, and preferences are compiled, registered, and retrieved to facilitate better adjustment, not to improve the individual's capacity to act and to decide. Whatever the original incentive for computerization may have been, processing increasingly appears as the ideal means to adapt an individual to a predetermined, standardized behavior that aims at the highest possible degree of compliance with the model patient, consumer, taxpayer, employee, or citizen. Furthermore, interactive systems do not, despite all contrary assertions, restore a long lost individuality by correcting the effects of mass production in a mass society. On the contrary, the telematic integration forces the individual once more into a preset scheme. The media supplier dictates the conditions under which communication takes place, fixes the possible subjects of the dialogue, and, due to the personal data collected, is in an increasingly better position to influence the subscriber's behavior. Interactive systems, therefore, suggest individual activity where in fact no more than stereotyped reactions occur.

In short, the transparency achieved through automated processing creates possibly the best conditions for colonization of the individual's lifeworld.[71] Accurate, constantly updated knowledge of her personal history is systematically incorporated into policies that deliberately structure her behavior. The more routinized automated processing augments the transparency, however, the more privacy proves to be a prerequisite to the capacity to participate in social discourse. Where privacy is dismantled, both the chance for personal assessment of the political and societal process and the opportunity to develop and maintain a particular style of life fade. . . .

---

[71] For both the colonization process and the impact of the individual's lifeworld on communicative action, see Jürgen Habermas, 1 *The Theory of Communicative Action* 70-71 (1983) (defining "lifeworld" as shared understandings about what will be treated as a fact, valid norms, and subjective experience). . . .

The processing of personal data is not unique to a particular society. On the contrary, the attractiveness of information technology transcends political boundaries, particularly because of the opportunity to guide the individual's behavior. For a democratic society, however, the risks are high: labeling of individuals, manipulative tendencies, magnification of errors, and strengthening of social control threaten the very fabric of democracy. Yet, despite the incontestable importance of its technical aspects, informatization, like industrialization, is primarily a political and social challenge. When the relationship between information processing and democracy is understood, it becomes clear that the protection of privacy is the price necessary to secure the individual's ability to communicate and participate. Regulations that create precisely specified conditions for personal data processing are the decisive test for discerning whether society is aware of this price and willing to pay it. If the signs of experience are correct, this payment can be delayed no further. There is, in fact, no alternative to the advice of Horace: Seize the day, put not trust in the morrow. . . .

NOTES & QUESTIONS

1. *Privacy and Democracy.* As Simitis and other authors in this section observe, privacy is an issue about social structure. What is the relationship between privacy and democracy according to Simitis?

2. *Privacy Law and Information Flow.* Generally, one would assume that greater information flow facilitates democracy — it enables more expression, more political discourse, more information about the workings of government. Simitis, however, contends that privacy is "necessary to secure the individual's ability to communicate and participate." How are these two notions about information flow to be reconciled? Consider Joel Reidenberg:

> Data privacy rules are often cast as a balance between two basic liberties: fundamental human rights on one side and the free flow of information on the other side. Yet, because societies differ on how and when personal information should be available for private and public sector needs, the treatment and interaction of these liberties will express a specific delineation between the state, civil society, and the citizen.[72]

Privacy, according to Reidenberg, involves establishing a balance between protecting the rights of individuals and enabling information flow. Do you think these interests always exist in opposition? Consider financial services, communications networks, and medical care. Does privacy impair or enable information flow?[73]

---

[72] Joel R. Reidenberg, *Resolving Conflicting International Data Privacy Rules in Cyberspace,* 52 Stan. L. Rev. 1315 (2000).

[73] For additional reading about philosophical theories of privacy, see Judith W. DeCew, *In Pursuit of Privacy: Law, Ethics, and the Rise of Technology* (1997) (surveying and critiquing various theories of privacy); Anita L. Allen, *Uneasy Access: Privacy for Women in a Free Society* (1988) (same); Ferdinand David Schoeman, ed., *Philosophical Dimensions of Privacy* (1984) (anthology of articles about the concept of privacy).

3. CRITICS OF PRIVACY

RICHARD A. POSNER, *THE RIGHT OF PRIVACY*

12 Ga. L. Rev. 393 (1978)

People invariably possess information, including facts about themselves and contents of communications, that they will incur costs to conceal. Sometimes such information is of value to others: that is, others will incur costs to discover it. Thus we have two economic goods, "privacy" and "prying." . . . .

[M]uch of the casual prying (a term used here without any pejorative connotation) into the private lives of friends and colleagues that is so common a feature of social life is also motivated, to a greater extent than we may realize, by rational considerations of self-interest. Prying enables one to form a more accurate picture of a friend or colleague, and the knowledge gained is useful in one's social or professional dealings with him. For example, in choosing a friend one legitimately wants to know whether he will be discreet or indiscreet, selfish or generous, and these qualities are not always apparent on initial acquaintance. Even a pure altruist needs to know the (approximate) wealth of any prospective beneficiary of his altruism in order to be able to gauge the value of a transfer to him.

The other side of the coin is that social, like business, dealings present opportunities for exploitation through misrepresentation. Psychologists and sociologists have pointed out that even in every day life people try to manipulate by misrepresentation other people's opinion of them. As one psychologist has written, the "wish for privacy expresses a desire . . . to control others' perceptions and beliefs vis-à-vis the self-concealing person." Even the strongest defenders of privacy describe the individual's right to privacy as the right to "control the flow of information about him." A seldom remarked corollary to a right to misrepresent one's character is that others have a legitimate interest in unmasking the deception.

Yet some of the demand for private information about other people is not self-protection in the foregoing sense but seems mysteriously disinterested — for example, that of the readers of newspaper gossip columns, whose "idle curiosity" Warren and Brandeis deplored, groundlessly in my opinion. Gossip columns recount the personal lives of wealthy and successful people whose tastes and habits offer models — that is, yield information — to the ordinary person in making consumption, career, and other decisions. . . . Gossip columns open people's eyes to opportunities and dangers; they are genuinely informational. . . .

Warren and Brandeis attributed the rise of curiosity about people's lives to the excesses of the press. The economist does not believe, however, that supply creates demand. A more persuasive explanation for the rise of the gossip column is the secular increase in personal incomes. There is apparently very little privacy in poor societies, where, consequently, people can easily observe at first hand the intimate lives of others. Personal surveillance is costlier in wealthier societies both because people live in conditions that give them greater privacy from such observation and because the value (and hence opportunity cost) of time is greater—too great to make a generous allotment of time to watching neighbors worthwhile. People in wealthier societies sought an alternative method of informing themselves about how others live and the press provided it. A legitimate and important function of the press is to provide specialization in prying in societies where the costs of obtaining information have become too great for the Nosey Parker. . . .

Transaction-cost considerations may also militate against the assignment of a property right to the possessor of a secret. . . . Consider, for example, . . . whether the law should allow a magazine to sell its subscriber list to another magazine without obtaining the subscribers' consent. . . . [T]he costs of obtaining subscriber approval would be high relative to the value of the list. If, therefore, we believe that these lists are generally worth more to the purchasers than being shielded from possible unwanted solicitations is worth to the subscribers, we should assign the property right to the magazine; and the law does this. . . .

Much of the demand for privacy . . . concerns discreditable information, often information concerning past or present criminal activity or moral conduct at variance with a person's professed moral standards. And often the motive for concealment is, as suggested earlier, to mislead those with whom he transacts. Other private information that people wish to conceal, while not strictly discreditable, would if revealed correct misapprehensions that the individual is trying to exploit, as when a worker conceals a serious health problem from his employer or a prospective husband conceals his sterility from his fiancée. It is not clear why society should assign the property right in such information to the individual to whom it pertains; and the common law, as we shall see, generally does not. . . .

We think it wrong (and inefficient) that the law should permit a seller in hawking his wares to make false or incomplete representations as to their quality. But people "sell" themselves as well as their goods. They profess high standards of behavior in order to induce others to engage in social or business dealings with them from which they derive an advantage but at the same time they conceal some of the facts that these acquaintances would find useful in forming an accurate picture of their character. There are practical reasons for not imposing a general legal duty of full and frank disclosure of one's material. . . .

. . . [E]veryone should be allowed to protect himself from disadvantageous transactions by ferreting out concealed facts about individuals which are material to the representations (implicit or explicit) that those individuals make concerning their moral qualities.

It is no answer that such individuals have "the right to be let alone." Very few people want to be let alone. They want to manipulate the world around them by selective disclosure of facts about themselves. Why should others be asked to take their self-serving claims at face value and be prevented from obtaining the information necessary to verify or disprove these claims?

NOTES & QUESTIONS

1. *Posner's Conception of Privacy.* What is Posner's definition of privacy? How does Posner determine the value of privacy (i.e., how it should be weighed relative to other interests and values)? In what circumstances is Posner likely to defend a privacy claim?

2. *Irrational Judgments.* One economic argument for privacy is that sometimes people form irrational judgments based upon learning certain information about others. For example, an employer may not hire certain people based on their political views or associations, sexual orientation, mental illness, and prior criminal convictions — even though these facts may have no relevance to a potential employee's abilities to do the job. These judgments decrease efficiency. In *The Economics of Justice*, Posner offers a response:

> This objection overlooks the opportunity costs of shunning people for stupid reasons, or, stated otherwise, the gains from dealing with someone whom others shun irrationally. If ex-convicts are good workers but most employers do not know this, employers who do know will be able to hire them at a below-average wage because of their depressed job opportunities and will thereby obtain a competitive advantage over the bigots. In a diverse, decentralized, and competitive society, irrational shunning will be weeded out over time. . . [74]

Will the market be able to eradicate irrational judgments?

3. *The Dangers of the "Masquerade Ball."* Consider Dennis Bailey:

> . . . [I]t is interesting to consider the ways in which the world has become like a giant masquerade ball. Far removed from the tight knit social fabric of the village of the past, we've lost the ability to recognize the people we pass on the street. People might as well be wearing masks because we are likely to know very little about them. In other words, these strangers are anonymous to us, anonymous in the sense that not only their names, but their entire identities, are unknown to us — the intimate details of who they are, where they have come from, and how they have lived their lives. . . .
>
> [A]nonymity has become one of the central vulnerabilities of an open society. Freedom may have allowed [9/11 terrorists] al-Mihdhar and al-Hamzi to rent an apartment, use a cell phone, meet with terrorists overseas, and take flying lessons in preparation for 9/11, but anonymity kept hidden the manner in which these individual actions fit together into a larger mosaic of death. [75]

Are we living in a "masquerade ball"? Businesses and the government have unprecedented new technologies to engage in surveillance and gather information. Should the law facilitate or restrict anonymity?

Also consider Steven Nock:

> Any method of social control depends, immediately, on information about individuals. . . . There can be no social control without such information. . . .
>
> Modern Americans enjoy vastly more privacy than did their forebears because ever and ever larger numbers of strangers in our lives are legitimately denied access to our personal affairs. . . . Privacy, however, makes it difficult to form reliable opinions of one another. Legitimately shielded from other's

---

[74] Richard A. Posner, *The Economics of Justice* (1981). Posner further develops his theories about privacy in Richard A. Posner, *Overcoming Law* 531-51 (1995). Posner first set out his views on privacy in Richard A. Posner, *An Economic Theory of Privacy*, Regulations (May/June 1978).

[75] Dennis Bailey, *The Open Society Paradox* 26-27 (2004).

regular scrutiny, we are thereby more immune to the routine monitoring that once formed the basis of our individual reputations.[76]

Does too much privacy erode trust and lessen social control in detrimental ways?

4. *Information Dissemination and Economic Efficiency.* Does economic theory necessarily lead to the conclusion that more personal information is generally preferable? Consider the following critique of Posner by Edward Bloustein:

> We must remember that Posner stated in *Economic Analysis of Law* that economics "cannot prescribe social change"; it can only tell us about the economic costs of managing it one way or another. . . . [Posner's] characterization of the privacy of personal information as a species of commercial fraud . . . [is an] extension[ ] of a social value judgment rather than implications or conclusions of economic theory. . . .Our society, in fact, places a very high value on maintaining individual privacy, even to the extent of concealing "discreditable" information. . . .[77]

Also consider Richard Murphy's critique of Posner:

> [D]emarcating a relatively large sphere for the private self creates an opportunity for discovery or actualization of a "true" nature, which may have a value beyond the utility of satisfying preferences. . . . As Roger Rosenblatt put it, "Out of our private gropings and self-inspections grow our imaginative values — private language, imagery, memory. In the caves of the mind one bats about to discover a light entirely of one's own which, though it should turn out to be dim, is still worth a life." Unless a person can investigate without risk of reproach what his own preferences are, he will not be able to maximize his own happiness.[78]

When can the circulation of less personal information be more economically efficient than greater information flow?

5. *Why Don't Individuals Protect Their Privacy?* Empirical studies frequently report on growing privacy concerns across the United States. Yet, individuals seem willing to exchange privacy for services or small rewards and generally fail to adopt technologies and techniques that would protect their privacy. If people are willing to sell their privacy for very little in return, isn't this evidence that they do not really value privacy as much as they say they do?

Alessandro Acqusiti and Jens Grossklags have pointed to a number of reasons for this divergence between stated privacy preferences and actual behavior:

> First, incomplete information affects privacy decision making because of externalities (when third parties share personal information about an individual, they might affect that individual without his being part of the

---

[76] Steven L. Nock, *The Costs of Privacy: Surveillance and Reputation in America* (1993).

[77] Edward J. Bloustein, *Privacy Is Dear at Any Price: A Response to Professor Posner's Economic Theory*, 12 Ga. L. Rev. 429, 441 (1978). For another critique of Posner's approach, see Kim Lane Scheppele, *Legal Secrets: Equality and Efficiency in the Common Law* (1988).

[78] Richard S. Murphy, *Property Rights in Personal Information: An Economic Defense of Privacy,* 84 Geo. L.J. 2381 (1996).

transaction between those parties), information asymmetries (information relevant to the privacy decision process — for example, how personal information will be used — might be known only to a subset of the parties making decisions), risk (most privacy related payoffs are not deterministic), and uncertainties (payoffs might not only be stochastic, but dependent on unknown random distributions). Benefits and costs associated with privacy intrusions and protection are complex, multifaceted, and context-specific. They are frequently bundled with other products and services (for example, a search engine query can prompt the desired result but can also give observers information about the searcher's interests), and they are often recognized only after privacy violations have taken place. They can be monetary but also immaterial and, thus, difficult to quantify.

Second, even if individuals had access to complete information, they would be unable to process and act optimally on vast amounts of data. Especially in the presence of complex, ramified consequences associated with the protection or release of personal information, our innate bounded rationality limits our ability to acquire, memorize and process all relevant information, and it makes us rely on simplified mental models, approximate strategies, and heuristics. These strategies replace theoretical quantitative approaches with qualitative evaluations and "aspirational" solutions that stop short of perfect (numerical) optimization. Bounded problem solving is usually neither unreasonable nor irrational, and it needs not be inferior to rational utility maximization. However, even marginal deviations by several individuals from their optimal strategies can substantially impact the market outcome.

Third, even if individuals had access to complete information and could successfully calculate optimization strategies for their privacy sensitive decisions, they might still deviate from the rational strategy. A vast body of economic and psychological literature has revealed several forms of systematic psychological deviations from rationality that affect individual decision making. . . . Research in psychology . . . documents how individuals mispredict their own future preferences or draw inaccurate conclusions from past choices. In addition, individuals often suffer from self-control problems — in particular, the tendency to trade off costs and benefits in ways that damage their future utility in favor of immediate gratification. Individuals' behavior can also be guided by social preferences or norms, such as fairness or altruism. Many of these deviations apply naturally to privacy-sensitive scenarios.[79]

FRED H. CATE, *PRINCIPLES OF INTERNET PRIVACY*

32 Conn. L. Rev. 877 (2000)

Perhaps the most important consideration when balancing restrictions on information is the historical importance of the free flow of information. The free flow concept is one that is not only enshrined in the First Amendment, but frankly in any form of democratic or market economy. In the United States, we have placed extraordinary importance on the open flow of information. As the Federal Reserve Board noted in its report to Congress on data protection in

---

[79] Alessandro Acquisti & Jens Grossklags, *Privacy and Rationality in Decision Making*, IEEE, Security and Privacy 24 (2005).

financial institutions, "it is the freedom to speak, supported by the availability of information and the free-flow of data, that is the cornerstone of a democratic society and market economy."

The significance of open data flows is reflected in the constitutional provisions not only for freedom of expression, but for copyrights — to promote the creation and dissemination of expression, and for a post office — to deliver the mail and the news. Federal regulations demonstrate a sweeping preference for openness, reflected in the Freedom of Information Act, Government in the Sunshine Act, and dozens of other laws applicable to the government. There are even more laws requiring disclosure by private industry, such as the regulatory disclosures required by securities and commodities laws, banking and insurance laws, and many others. This is a very basic tenet of the society in which we live. Laws that restrict that free flow almost always conflict with this basic principle. That does not mean that such laws are never upheld, but merely that they face a considerable constitutional hurdle.

This is done with good reason. Open information flows are not only essential to self-governance; they have also generated significant, practical benefits. The ready availability of personal information helps businesses "deliver the right products and services to the right customers, at the right time, more effectively and at lower cost," Fred Smith, founder and President of the Competitive Enterprise Institute, has written. Federal Reserve Board Governor Edward Gramlich testified before Congress in July 1999 that "[i]nformation about individuals' needs and preferences is the cornerstone of any system that allocates goods and services within an economy." The more such information is available, he continued, "the more accurately and efficiently will the economy meet those needs and preferences."

Federal Reserve Board Chairman Alan Greenspan has been perhaps the most articulate spokesperson for the extraordinary value of accessible personal information. In 1998, he wrote to Congressman Ed Markey (D-Mass.):

> A critical component of our ever more finely hewn competitive market system has been the plethora of information on the characteristics of customers both businesses and individuals. Such information has enabled producers and marketers to fine tune production schedules to the ever greater demands of our consuming public for diversity and individuality of products and services. Newly devised derivative products, for example, have enabled financial institutions to unbundle risk in a manner that enables those desirous of taking on that risk (and potential reward) to do so, and those that chose otherwise, to be risk averse. It has enabled financial institutions to offer a wide variety of customized insurance and other products.
>
> Detailed data obtained from consumers as they seek credit or make product choices help engender the whole set of sensitive price signals that are so essential to the functioning of an advanced information based economy such as ours. . . .

In a recent report on public record information, Richard Varn, Chief Information Officer of the State of Iowa, and I examined the critical roles played by public record information in our economy and society. We concluded that such information constitutes part of this nation's "essential infrastructure," the benefits of which are "so numerous and diverse that they impact virtually every facet of American life. . . ." The ready availability of public record data "facilitates a vibrant economy, improves efficiency, reduces costs, creates jobs, and provides valuable products and services that people want."

Perhaps most importantly, widely accessible personal information has helped to create a democratization of opportunity in the United States. Anyone can go almost anywhere, make purchases from vendors they will never see, maintain accounts with banks they will never visit, and obtain credit far from home all because of open information flows. Americans can take advantage of opportunities based on their records, on what they have done rather than who they know, because access to consumer information makes it possible for distant companies and creditors to make rational decisions about doing business with individuals. The open flow of information gives consumers real choice. This is what the open flow of information principle reflects, not just the constitutional importance of information flows, but their significant economic and social benefits as well.

NOTES & QUESTIONS

1. ***The Pros and Cons of the Free Flow of Information.*** In a striking passage, Cate points out that free flows of information create a "democratization of opportunity in the United States." With this phrase, he reminds us that part of the equality at the basis of American life concerns economic opportunity, and that, in his view, a certain kind of flow of personal information will contribute to this goal. While privacy can be problematic, can open access to information also raise difficulties? How should one establish a baseline for open access or restricted access to personal information?

2. ***The Costs of Privacy.*** Can you think of some of the other important values with which privacy might conflict and the costs that privacy can impose? What should the baseline be in measuring costs?

3. ***The Business of Data Trade.*** The trade in personal information is now a valuable part of the U.S. economy. As a single example, Google reached an agreement on April 14, 2007, to purchase DoubleClick, an online advertising company, for $3.1 billion. The deal was driven by Google's interest in behavioral advertising, in which companies use digital data collection techniques to track individuals around the Internet and serve them targeted ads. Should consumers be allowed to sign up for a National Do Not Track List?

4. ***The Benefits of Information Collection and Use.*** Consider Kent Walker:

   > Having some information about yourself out there in the world offers real convenience that goes beyond dollars and cents. Many people benefit from warehousing information — billing and shipping addresses, credit card numbers, individual preferences, and the like — with trustworthy third parties. Such storage of information can dramatically simplify the purchasing experience, ensure that you get a nonsmoking room, or automate the task of ordering a kiddie meal every time your child boards a plane. Likewise, most people prefer to use a credit card rather than a debit card, trading confidentiality of purchases for the convenience of deferred payment. . . .

While there's often little individual incentive to participate in the aggregation of information about people, a great collective good results from the default participation of most people. The aggregation of information often requires a critical mass to be worth doing, or for the results to be worth using. (A phone book with only one out of ten numbers would hardly be worth using, let alone printing.) . . .

Another example is Caller ID, which pits different privacy claims against one another. Many people like the notion of an electronic peephole, letting them know who's at the electronic door before they decide whether to pick up the phone. Yet many people block transmission of their own numbers, valuing protection of their privacy. Neither choice is necessarily right, but it's worth recognizing that the assertion of the privacy claim affects the contending desires of others. The classic Tragedy of the Commons aspects are clear. From my selfish perspective, I want access to information about everyone else — the identity of who's calling me, their listed phone number, etc. I want to be able to intrude on others without their knowing who I am (which I can accomplish by blocking Caller ID), and don't want others to be able to intrude on me unbidden (which I can accomplish by unlisting my phone number). The gain in privacy makes it harder to find the people you want to reach, and harder to know who's calling you.[80]

5. *Privacy as the "Cheshire Cat of Values"?* Many commentators have noted that although people express concern over privacy, their behavior indicates that they do not care very much about privacy. As Jonathan Franzen, the novelist, writes:

> The panic about privacy has all the finger-pointing and paranoia of a good old American scare, but it's missing one vital ingredient: a genuinely alarmed public. Americans care about privacy in the abstract. . . .
>
> On closer examination . . . privacy proves to be the Cheshire cat of values: not much substance, but a very winning smile.
>
> Legally, the concept is a mess. Privacy violation is the emotional core of many crimes, from stalking and rape to Peeping Tommery and trespass, but no criminal statute forbids it in the abstract. . . .
>
> When Americans do genuinely sacrifice privacy . . . they do so for tangible gains in health or safety or efficiency. Most legalized infringements — HIV notification, airport X-rays, Megan's Law, Breathalyzer roadblocks, the drug-testing of student athletes, . . . remote monitoring of automobile emissions . . . are essentially public health measures. I resent the security cameras in Washington Square, but I appreciate the ones on a subway platform. The risk that someone is abusing my E-ZPass toll records seems to me comfortably low in comparison with my gain in convenience. Ditto the risk that some gossip rag will make me a victim of the First Amendment; with two hundred and seventy million people in the country, any individual's chances of being nationally exposed are next to nil.[81]

Do arguments about bounded rationality, as developed in the earlier section, answer Franzen's concerns?

---

[80] Kent Walker, *Where Everybody Knows Your Name: A Pragmatic Look at the Costs of Privacy and the Benefits of Information Exchange,* 2000 Stan. Tech. L. Rev. 2, 39, 46, 48 (2000).

[81] Jonathan Franzen, *How to Be Alone: Essays* 42, 45-46 (2003).

4. THE FEMINIST PERSPECTIVE ON PRIVACY

Has the legal concept of privacy hurt or helped women throughout history? What is the impact of privacy on women today?

STATE V. RHODES

1868 WL 1278 (N.C. 1868)

[The defendant was indicted for an assault and battery upon his wife, Elizabeth Rhodes. The jury returned the following special verdict: "We find that the defendant struck Elizabeth Rhodes, his wife, three licks, with a switch about the size of one of his fingers (but not as large as a man's thumb) without any provocation except some words uttered by her and not recollected by the witness." The lower court found that the defendant "had a right to whip his wife with a switch no larger than his thumb, and that upon the facts found in the special verdict he was not guilty in law." Judgment in favor of the defendant was entered from which the State appealed.]

The laws of this State do not recognize *the right of the husband to whip his wife,* but our Courts will not interfere to punish him for moderate correction of her, even if there had been no provocation for it.

Family government being in its nature as complete in itself as the State government is in itself, the Courts will not attempt to control, or interfere with it, in favor of either party, except in cases where permanent or malicious injury is inflicted or threatened, or the condition of the party is intolerable.

In determining whether the husband has been guilty of an indictable assault and battery upon his wife, the criterion is the *effect produced,* and not the manner of producing it or the instrument used. . . .

READE J. The violence complained of would without question have constituted a battery if the subject of it had not been the defendant's wife. The question is how far that fact affects the case.

The courts have been loath to take cognizance of trivial complaints arising out of the domestic relations — such as master and apprentice, teacher and pupil, parent and child, husband and wife. Not because those relations are not subject to the law, but because the evil of publicity would be greater than the evil involved in the trifles complained of; and because they ought to be left to family government. . . .

In this case no provocation worth the name was proved. The fact found was that it was "without any provocation except some words which were not recollected by the witness." The words must have been of the slightest import to have made no impression on the memory. We must therefore, consider the violence as unprovoked. The question is therefore plainly presented, whether the court will allow a conviction of the husband for moderate correction of the wife without provocation.

Our divorce laws do not compel a separation of husband and wife, unless the conduct of the husband be so cruel as to render the wife's condition intolerable, or her life burdensome. What sort of conduct on the part of the husband, would be allowed to have that effect, has been repeatedly considered. And it has not been found easy to lay down any iron rule upon the subject. In some cases it has been held that actual and repeated violence to the person, was not sufficient. In others that insults, indignities and neglect without any actual violence, were quite sufficient. So much does each case depend upon its peculiar surroundings.

We have sought the aid of the experience and wisdom of other times, and of other countries.

Blackstone says "that the husband, by the old law, might give the wife moderate correction, for as he was to answer for her misbehavior, he ought to have the power to control her; but that in the polite reign of Charles the Second, this power of correction began to be doubted." . . . The old law of moderate correction has been questioned even in England, and has been repudiated in Ireland and Scotland. The old rule is approved in Mississippi, but it has met with but little favor elsewhere in the United States. In looking into the discussions of the other States we find but little uniformity. . . .

Our conclusion is that family government is recognized by law as being as complete in itself as the State government is in itself, and yet subordinate to it; and that we will not interfere with or attempt to control it, in favor of either husband or wife, unless in cases where permanent or malicious injury is inflicted or threatened, or the condition of the party is intolerable. For, however great are the evils of ill temper, quarrels, and even personal conflicts inflicting only temporary pain, they are not comparable with the evils which would result from raising the curtain, and exposing to public curiosity and criticism, the nursery and the bed chamber. Every household has and must have, a government of its own, modeled to suit the temper, disposition and condition of its inmates. Mere ebullitions of passion, impulsive violence, and temporary pain, affection will soon forget and forgive; and each member will find excuse for the other in his own frailties. But when trifles are taken hold of by the public, and the parties are exposed and disgraced, and each endeavors to justify himself or herself by criminating the other, that which ought to be forgotten in a day, will be remembered for life.

It is urged in this case, that as there was no provocation the violence was of course excessive and malicious; that every one in whatever relation of life should be able to purchase immunity from pain, by obedience to authority and faithfulness in duty. . . . Take the case before us. The witness said, there was no provocation except some slight words. But then who can tell what significance the trifling words may have had to the husband? Who can tell what had happened an hour before, and every hour for a week? To him they may have been sharper than a sword. And so in every case, it might be impossible for the court to appreciate what might be offered as an excuse, or no excuse might appear at all, when a complete justification exists. Or, suppose the provocation could in every case be known, and the court should undertake to weigh the provocation in every trifling family broil, what would be the standard? Suppose a case coming up to us from a hovel, where neither delicacy of sentiment nor refinement of manners is appreciated or known. The parties themselves would be amazed, if they were to be held responsible for rudeness or trifling violence. What do they care for insults and indignities? In such cases what end would be gained by investigation or punishment? Take a case from the middle class, where modesty and purity have their abode but nevertheless have not immunity from the frailties of nature, and are sometimes moved by the mysteries of passion. What could be more harassing to them, or injurious to society, than to draw a crowd around their seclusion. Or take a case from the higher ranks, where education and culture have so refined nature, that a look cuts like a knife, and a word strikes like a hammer; where the most delicate attention gives pleasure, and the slightest neglect pain; where an indignity is disgrace and exposure is ruin. Bring all these cases into court side by side, with the same offence charged and the same proof made; and what conceivable charge of the court to the jury would be alike appropriate to all the cases, except, That they all have domestic government, which they have formed for themselves, suited to their own peculiar conditions, and that those governments are supreme, and from them there is no appeal except in cases of great importance requiring the strong arm of the law, and that to those governments they must submit themselves.

It will be observed that the ground upon which we have put this decision, is not, that the husband has the *right* to whip his wife much or little; but that we will not interfere with family government in trifling cases. We will no more interfere where the husband whips the wife, than where the wife whips the husband; and yet we would hardly be supposed to hold, that a wife has a *right* to whip her husband. We will not inflict upon society the greater evil of raising the curtain upon domestic privacy, to punish the lesser evil of trifling violence. Two boys under fourteen years of age fight upon the play-ground, and yet the courts will take no notice of it, not for the reason that boys have the *right* to fight, but because the interests of society require that they should be left to the more appropriate discipline of the school room and of home. . . . The standard is the *effect produced,* and not the manner of producing it, or the instrument used.

Because our opinion is not in unison with the decisions of some of the sister States, or with the philosophy of some very respectable law writers, and could not be in unison with all, because of their contrariety, — a decent respect for the opinions of others has induced us to be very full in stating the reasons for our conclusion.

REVA B. SIEGEL, *"THE RULE OF LOVE": WIFE BEATING AS PREROGATIVE AND PRIVACY*

105 Yale L.J. 2117 (1996)

. . . The Anglo-American common law originally provided that a husband, as master of his household, could subject his wife to corporal punishment or "chastisement" so long as he did not inflict permanent injury upon her. During the nineteenth century, an era of feminist agitation for reform of marriage law, authorities in England and the United States declared that a husband no longer had the right to chastise his wife. Yet, for a century after courts repudiated the right of chastisement, the American legal system continued to treat wife beating differently from other cases of assault and battery. While authorities denied that a husband had the right to beat his wife, they intervened only intermittently in cases of marital violence: Men who assaulted their wives were often granted formal and informal immunities from prosecution, in order to protect the privacy of the family and to promote "domestic harmony." In the late 1970s, the feminist movement began to challenge the concept of family privacy that shielded wife abuse, and since then, it has secured many reforms designed to protect women from marital violence. . . .

Until the late nineteenth century, Anglo-American common law structured marriage to give a husband superiority over his wife in most aspects of the relationship. By law, a husband acquired rights to his wife's person, the value of her paid and unpaid labor, and most property she brought into the marriage. A wife was obliged to obey and serve her husband, and the husband was subject to a reciprocal duty to support his wife and represent her within the legal system. . . .

As master of the household, a husband could command his wife's obedience, and subject her to corporal punishment or "chastisement" if she defied his authority. In his treatise on the English common law, Blackstone explained that a husband could "give his wife moderate correction." . . .

During the 1850s, woman's rights advocates organized numerous conventions throughout the Northeast and Midwest, published newspapers, and conducted petition campaigns seeking for women the right to vote and demanding various reforms of marriage law. And in time the movement did elicit a response. Legislatures and courts began to modify the common law of marital status — first giving wives the right to hold property in marriage, and then the right to their earnings and the rudiments of legal agency: the right to file suit in their own names and to claim contract and tort damages. . . .

. . . By the 1880s, prominent members of the American Bar Association advocated punishing wife beaters at the whipping post, and campaigned vigorously for legislation authorizing the penalty. Between 1876 and 1906, twelve states and the District of Columbia considered enacting legislation that provided for the punishment of wife beaters at the whipping post. The bills were enacted in Maryland (1882), Delaware (1901), and Oregon (1906). . . .

We are left with a striking portrait of legal change. Jurists and lawmakers emphatically repudiated the doctrine of marital chastisement, yet responded to marital violence erratically — often condoning it, and condemning it in circumstances suggesting little interest in the plight of battered wives. Given this record, how are we to make sense of chastisement's demise? . . .

A key concept in the doctrinal regime that emerged from chastisement's demise was the notion of marital privacy. During the antebellum era, courts began to invoke marital privacy as a supplementary rationale for chastisement, in order to justify the common law doctrine within the discourse of companionate marriage, when rationales rooted in authority-based discourses of marriage had begun to lose their persuasive power. . . .

To quote a North Carolina chastisement opinion:

> We know that a slap on the cheek, let it be as light as it may, indeed any touching of the person of another in a rude or angry manner — is in law an assault and battery. In the nature of things it cannot apply to persons in the marriage state, it would break down the great principle of mutual confidence and dependence; throw open the bedroom to the gaze of the public; and spread discord and misery, contention and strife, where peace and concord ought to reign. It must be remembered that rules of law are intended to act in all classes of society. . . .

In *Rhodes*, the defendant whipped his wife "three licks, with a switch about the size of one of his fingers (but not as large as a man's thumb)"; the trial court ruled that a husband had the right to chastise his wife and so was not guilty of assault and battery. On appeal, the North Carolina Supreme Court upheld the verdict but justified it on different grounds. Opening its opinion with the blunt observation that "[t]he violence complained of would without question have constituted a battery if the subject of it had not been the defendant's wife," the court explained why it would not find the defendant guilty:

> The courts have been loath to take cognizance of trivial complaints arising out of the domestic relations — such as master and apprentice, teacher and pupil, parent and child, husband and wife. Not because those relations are not subject to law, but because the evil of publicity would be greater than the evil involved in the trifles complained of; and because they ought to be left to family government. . . .

. . . By now it should be clear enough how privacy talk was deployed in the domestic violence context to enforce and preserve authority relations between man and wife. . . .

. . . By the early twentieth century, numerous state supreme courts had barred wives from suing their husbands for intentional torts — typically on the grounds that "the tranquility of family relations" would be "disturb[ed]." . . .

It was not until the late 1970s that the contemporary women's rights movement mounted an effective challenge to this regime. Today, after numerous protest activities and law suits, there are shelters for battered women and their children, new arrest procedures for police departments across the country, and even federal legislation making gender-motivated assaults a civil rights violation. . . .

There is remarkably little scholarship on the social history of privacy discourses; consequently, we know very little about the ways in which conceptions of privacy shaped popular understandings of marriage, or marital violence, in the nineteenth century. But there is no reason to assume that, before demise of the chastisement prerogative, married persons understood a traditional prerogative of marriage, rooted in notions of a husband's authority as master and head of his household, in a framework of "privacy" and "domestic harmony." It seems just as likely that legal elites devised the story linking "privacy" and "domestic harmony" to wife beating in the wake of chastisement's demise (or in anticipation of it). . . .

CATHARINE A. MACKINNON, *TOWARD A FEMINIST THEORY OF THE STATE*

(1989)

The liberal ideal of the private holds that, as long as the public does not interfere, autonomous individuals interact freely and equally. Privacy is the ultimate value of the negative state. Conceptually, this private is hermetic. It means that which is inaccessible to, unaccountable to, unconstructed by, anything beyond itself. By definition, it is not part of or conditioned by anything systematic outside it. It is personal, intimate, autonomous, particular, individual, the original source and final outpost of the self, gender neutral. It is defined by everything that feminism reveals women have never been allowed to be or to have, and by everything that women have been equated with and defined in terms of men's ability to have. To complain in public of inequality within the private contradicts the liberal definition of the private. . . . Its inviolability by the state, framed as an individual right, presupposes that the private is not already an arm of the state. In this scheme, intimacy is implicitly thought to guarantee symmetry of power. Injuries arise through violation of the private sphere, not within and by and because of it.

In private, consent tends to be presumed. Showing coercion is supposed to avoid this presumption. But the problem is getting anything private to be perceived as coercive. This is an epistemic problem of major dimensions and explains why privacy doctrine is most at home at home, the place women experience the most force, in the family, and why it centers on sex. Why a person would "allow" force in private (the "why doesn't she leave" question raised to battered women) is a question given its insult by the social meaning of the private as a sphere of choice. For women the measure of the intimacy has been the measure of oppression. This is why feminism has seen the personal as the political. The private is public for those for whom the personal is political. In this sense, for women there is no private, either normatively or empirically. Feminism confronts the fact that women have no privacy to lose or to guarantee. Women are not inviolable. Women's sexuality is not only violable, it is — hence, women are — seen in and as their violation. To confront the fact that women have no privacy is to confront the intimate degradation of women as the public order. . . .

When the law of privacy restricts intrusions into intimacy, it bars changes in control over that intimacy through law. The existing distribution of power and resources within the private sphere are precisely what the law of privacy exists to protect. . . . [T]he legal concept of privacy can and has shielded the place of battery, marital rape, and women's exploited domestic labor. It has preserved the central institutions whereby women are deprived of identity, autonomy, control, and self-definition. It has protected a primary activity through which male supremacy is expressed and enforced. . . .

This right to privacy is a right of men "to be let alone" to oppress women one at a time. . . .

ANITA L. ALLEN, *UNEASY ACCESS: PRIVACY FOR WOMEN IN A FREE SOCIETY*

(1988)

Critiques of privacy such as MacKinnon's go wrong at the point where the historic unequal treatment of women and the misuse of the private household to further women's domination is taken as grounds for rejecting either the condition of privacy itself or the long-overdue legal rights to effective decisionmaking that promote and protect that condition. Privacy, here broadly defined as the inaccessibility of persons, their mental states, or information about them to the senses and surveillance devices of others . . . does not pose an inherent threat to women. Nor do sex, love, marriage, and children any longer presume the total abrogation of the forms of privacy a woman might otherwise enjoy. On the contrary, women today are finally in a position to expect, experience, and exploit real privacy within the home and within heterosexual relationships. The women's movement, education, access to affordable birth control, liberalized divorce laws, and the larger role for women in politics, government, and the economy have expanded women's opinions and contributed to the erosion of oppressively nonegalitarian styles of home life. These advances have enhanced the capacity of American men and women, but especially and for the first time women, to secure conditions of adequate and meaningful privacy at home paramount to moral personhood and responsible participation in families and larger segments of society. Instead of rejecting privacy as "male ideology" and subjugation, women can and ought to embrace opportunities for privacy and the exercise of reproductive liberty in their private lives.

NOTES & QUESTIONS

1. *Privacy and Gender.* As the *Rhodes* court stated in 1868: "We will not interfere with family government in trifling cases. We will no more interfere where the husband whips the wife, than where the wife whips the husband; and yet we would hardly be supposed to hold, that a wife has a *right* to whip her husband." Is this decision really a neutral one? Does the right to privacy described by Warren and Brandeis apply equally to men and women?[82]

2. *The Uses of the Public/Private Distinction.* Reva Siegel points out the troubling use of privacy to protect the oppression of women in the home, which Catharine MacKinnon has discussed at length elsewhere. Is MacKinnon's negative response to the public/private distinction justifiable given the prior uses of this distinction? Or do you agree with Anita Allen that privacy can and should not be abandoned as a value despite its checkered past?[83]

3. *To What Extent Can Law Change Social Practices?* According to Frances Olsen, "The notion of noninterference in the family depends upon some shared conception of proper family roles, and 'neutrality' [of the State] can be understood only with reference to such roles."[84] This idea suggests that privacy, within or without the family, might also depend on shared views as to proper social roles. Do you agree?

   Olsen also notes: "The theory of the private family, like free market theory, includes the assertion that particularized adjustments of seemingly unfair or inhumane results will not actually serve anybody's long run interests." Specifically, "it is claimed that state intervention to protect the weaker family members from abuse by the stronger is ineffective because powerful, underlying 'real' relations between family members will inevitably reassert

---

[82] For a feminist critique of the Warren and Brandeis article, see Anita L. Allen & Erin Mack, *How Privacy Got Its Gender*, 10 N. Ill. U. L. Rev. 441 (1990).

[83] For an overview of the feminist critique of privacy, see generally Judith W. DeCew, *In Pursuit of Privacy: Law, Ethics, and the Rise of Technology* 81-94 (1997); Patricia Boling, *Privacy and the Politics of Intimate Life* (1996); Frances Olsen, *Constitutional Law: Feminist Critiques of the Public/Private Distinction*, 10 Const. Commentary 327 (1993); Ruth Gavison, *Feminism and the Public/Private Distinction*, 45 Stan. L. Rev. 21 (1992).

[84] Frances Olsen, *The Family and the Market: A Study of Ideology and Legal Reform*, 96 Harv. L. Rev. 1497, 1506 (1983).

themselves." This argument, which one might term the argument from futility, was rejected in the course of the twentieth century by the powerful social movement to stop spousal abuse and mistreatment of children. Are similar arguments from futility being made today about the "inevitable" erosion of privacy?

CHAPTER 2

PRIVACY AND LAW ENFORCEMENT

A. THE FOURTH AMENDMENT AND EMERGING TECHNOLOGY

1. INTRODUCTION

(a) Privacy and Security

One of the central tensions in information privacy law is between privacy and security. Security involves society's interest in protecting its citizens from crimes, including physical and monetary threats. One way that government promotes security is by investigating and punishing crimes. To do this, law enforcement officials must gather information about suspected individuals. Monitoring and information gathering pose substantial threats to privacy. At the same time, however, monitoring and information gathering offer the potential of increasing security. Throughout the twentieth century, technology provided the government significantly greater ability to probe into the private lives of individuals.

The prevailing metaphor for the threat to privacy caused by law enforcement surveillance techniques is George Orwell's novel *Nineteen Eighty-Four*. Written in 1949, the novel depicted an all-powerful and omniscient government called "Big Brother" that monitored and controlled every facet of individuals' lives:

> Outside, even through the shut window-pane, the world looked cold. Down in the street little eddies of wind were whirling dust and torn paper into spirals, and though the sun was shining and the sky a harsh blue, there seemed to be no colour in anything, except the posters that were plastered everywhere. The black moustachio'd face gazed down from every commanding corner. There was one on the house-front immediately opposite. BIG BROTHER IS WATCHING YOU, the caption said, while the dark eyes looked deep into Winston's own. Down at streetlevel another poster, torn at one corner, flapped fitfully in the wind, alternately covering and uncovering the single word INGSOC. In the far distance a helicopter skimmed down between the roofs, hovered for an instant like a bluebottle, and darted away again with a curving flight. It was the police patrol, snooping into people's windows. The patrols did not matter, however. Only the Thought Police mattered.

> Behind Winston's back the voice from the telescreen was still babbling away about pig-iron and the overfulfilment of the Ninth Three-Year Plan. The telescreen received and transmitted simultaneously. Any sound that Winston made, above the level of a very low whisper, would be picked up by it, moreover, so long as he remained within the field of vision which the metal plaque commanded, he could be seen as well as heard. There was of course no way of knowing whether you were being watched at any given moment. How often, or on what system, the Thought Police plugged in on any individual wire was guesswork. It was even conceivable that they watched everybody all the time. But at any rate they could plug in your wire whenever they wanted to. You had to live — did live, from habit that became instinct — in the assumption that every sound you made was overheard, and, except in darkness, every movement scrutinized.[1]

Orwell's harrowing portrait of a police state illustrates the importance of limiting the power of the government to monitor its citizens. But consider the reverse as well: Will overly restrictive limitations on the power of the police restrict their ability to protect the public?

Although privacy and security may at times be viewed in conflict, consider the opening words of the Fourth Amendment: "The right of the people to be *secure* in their persons, houses, papers, and effects . . ." (emphasis added). Are the interests in public security and privacy fated to be always at odds? Are there times when the opposition between security and privacy proves a false dichotomy?

(b) The Fourth and Fifth Amendments

In the United States, policing is predominantly carried out by local governments. The Constitution, however, provides a national regulatory regime for police conduct. The Fourth and Fifth Amendments significantly limit the government's power to gather information. The Fourth Amendment provides:

> The right of the people to be secure in their persons, houses, papers, and effects, against unreasonable searches and seizures, shall not be violated, and no warrants shall issue, but upon probable cause, supported by oath or affirmation, and particularly describing the place to be searched, and the persons or things to be seized.

As the Supreme Court has recognized, "[t]he overriding function of the Fourth Amendment is to protect personal privacy and dignity against unwarranted intrusion by the State." *Schmerber v. California*, 384 U.S. 757 (1966).[2]

The Fifth Amendment guarantees that "[n]o person . . . shall be compelled in any criminal case to be a witness against himself. . . ." The Fifth Amendment establishes a "privilege against self-incrimination," and it prohibits the government from compelling individuals to disclose inculpatory information about themselves.

---

[1] George Orwell, *Nineteen Eighty-Four* 3-4 (1949).

[2] For a comprehensive historical account of the origins of the Fourth Amendment, see William J. Cuddihy, *The Fourth Amendment: Origins and Original Meaning* 602-1791 (2009).

The Fifth Amendment does not apply to all incriminating statements, but to information that is compelled. Further, the information must be "testimonial" in nature, and the Court has held that the Fifth Amendment does not apply to fingerprinting, photographing, taking measurements, writing or speaking for identification purposes, and having blood or bodily fluids drawn and tested. *See Schmerber v. California,* 384 U.S. 757 (1966). Finally, the Fifth Amendment does not protect broadly against prying into private secrets; it is limited to information that is incriminating.[3]

(c) Privacy of the Mail

In *Ex Parte Jackson,* 96 U.S. 727 (1877), one of its earliest Fourth Amendment cases, the Supreme Court held that the Fourth Amendment required a warrant to search sealed letters sent via the U.S. Postal Service:

> The constitutional guaranty of the right of the people to be secure in their persons against unreasonable searches and seizures extends to their papers, thus closed against inspection, wherever they may be. Whilst in the mail, they can only be opened and examined under like warrant, issued upon similar oath or affirmation, particularly describing the thing to be seized, as is required when papers are subjected to search in one's own household.

Although the Fourth Amendment protects the contents of a sealed letter, it does not protect the outside of letters, where addressing of information is typically located. As the Court noted in *Ex Parte Jackson,* "the outward form and weight" of letters and sealed packages are unprotected by the Fourth Amendment. Modern caselaw follows this distinction.

Today, federal law also restricts the government's ability to search people's mail. Pursuant to 39 U.S.C. §3623(d):

> No letter of such a class of domestic origin shall be opened except under authority of a search warrant authorized by law, or by an officer or employee of the Postal Service for the sole purpose of determining an address at which the letter can be delivered, or pursuant to the authorization of the addressee.

However, the government can search letters sent from abroad. *See United States v. Various Articles of Obscene Merchandise, Schedule No. 1213,* 395 F. Supp. 791 (S.D.N.Y. 1975), *aff'd,* 538 F.2d 317.

(d) Privacy of Papers and Documents

In *Boyd v. United States,* 116 U.S. 616 (1886), one of the foundational cases defining the meaning of the Fourth and Fifth Amendments, the government issued a subpoena to compel Boyd, a merchant, to produce invoices on cases of

---

[3] For more background about the Fifth Amendment, see R. Kent Greenawalt, *Silence as a Moral and Constitutional Right,* 23 Wm. & Mary L. Rev. 15 (1981); Stephen J. Schulhofer, *Some Kind Words for the Privilege Against Self-Incrimination,* 26 Val. U. L. Rev. 311 (1991); William J. Stuntz, *Self-Incrimination and Excuse,* 99 Colum. L. Rev. 1227 (1988); David Donlinko, *Is There a Rationale for the Privilege Against Self-Incrimination?,* 33 UCLA L. Rev. 1063 (1986); Donald A. Dripps, *Self-Incrimination and Self-Preservation: A Skeptical View,* 1991 U. Ill. L. Rev. 329; Michael Dann, *The Fifth Amendment Privilege Against Self-Incrimination: Extorting Evidence from a Suspect,* 43 S. Cal. L. Rev. 597 (1970).

imported glass for use in a civil forfeiture proceeding. The Court held that the subpoena violated the Fourth and Fifth Amendments:

> . . . [B]y the proceeding now under consideration, the court attempts to extort from the party his private books and papers to make him liable for a penalty or to forfeit his property. . . .
>
> . . . It is not the breaking of his doors, and the rummaging of his drawers, that constitutes the essence of the offence; but it is the invasion of his indefeasible right to personal security, personal liberty and private property, where the right has never been forfeited by his conviction of some public offence. . . . Breaking into a house and opening boxes and drawers are circumstances of aggravation; but any forcible and compulsory extortion of a man's own testimony or of his private papers to be used as evidence to convict him of crime or to forfeit his goods, is within the condemnation of that judgment. In this regard the Fourth and Fifth Amendments run almost into each other.

In *Gouled v. United States*, 255 U.S. 298 (1921), the Court held that law enforcement officials could not use search warrants to search a person's "house or office or papers" to obtain evidence to use against her in a criminal proceeding. The holdings of *Boyd* and *Gouled* became known as the "mere evidence" rule — the government could only seize papers if they were instrumentalities of a crime, fruits of a crime, or illegal contraband. This idea was based on a property-based approach to the Fourth Amendment.

The holding in *Boyd* has been significantly cut back. In *Warden v. Hayden*, 387 U.S. 294 (1967), the Court abolished the mere evidence rule. As the Court currently interprets the Fifth Amendment, the government can require a person to produce papers and records. *See Shapiro v. United States*, 335 U.S. 1 (1948). The Fifth Amendment also does not protect against subpoenas for a person's records and papers held by third parties. In *Couch v. United States*, 409 U.S. 322 (1973), the Court upheld a subpoena to a person's accountant for documents because "the Fifth Amendment privilege is a personal privilege: it adheres basically to the person, not to information that may incriminate him." The Fifth Amendment, the Court reasoned, only prevents "[i]nquisitorial pressure or coercion against a potentially accused person, compelling her, against her will, to utter self-condemning words or produce incriminating documents." Similarly, in *Fisher v. United States*, 425 U.S. 391 (1976), the Court upheld a subpoena to a person's attorney for documents pertaining to that person. The Fifth Amendment is not a "general protector of privacy" but protects against the "compelled self-incrimination."

(e) The Applicability of the Fourth Amendment

The Fourth Amendment governs the investigatory power of government officials. It applies every time a government official (not just police) conducts a "search" or the "seizure" of an object or document. Some examples of "searches" include peeking into one's pockets or searching one's person; entering into and looking around one's house, apartment, office, hotel room, or private property; and opening up and examining the contents of one's luggage or parcels. A "seizure" is a taking away of items by the police. A seizure can be of physical things or of persons (arrests). There must be a search or seizure to invoke the protection of the Fourth Amendment.

The Fourth Amendment does not apply simply when the police happen to observe something in "plain view." Whatever law enforcement officials see in plain view is not covered by the protection of the Fourth Amendment. Thus, the initial issue in Fourth Amendment analysis is whether the Amendment applies in the first place.[4]

(f) Reasonable Searches and Seizures

If the Fourth Amendment applies, then it requires that the search be "reasonable." Generally, a search is reasonable if the police have obtained a valid search warrant. To obtain a warrant, the police must go before a judge or magistrate and demonstrate that they have "probable cause" to conduct a search or seizure. Probable cause requires that government officials have "reasonably trustworthy information" that is sufficient to "warrant a man of reasonable caution in the belief that an offense has been or is being committed" or that evidence will be found in the place to be searched. *Brinegar v. United States*, 338 U.S. 160 (1949). Probable cause is more than "bare suspicion." Probable cause must be measured on a case-by-case basis, via the facts of particular cases. *See Wong Sun v. United States*, 371 U.S. 471 (1963). The purpose of a warrant is to have an independent party (judges) ensure that police really do have probable cause to conduct a search.

A search is valid if the warrant is supported by probable cause and the search is within the scope of the warrant. A warrantless search is generally considered to be per se unreasonable; however, there are a number of exceptions to this rule. Under these exceptions, a search is valid even if a warrant was not obtained as long as there was probable cause. For example, a search is not unreasonable if consent is obtained. When exigent circumstances make obtaining a warrant impractical, certain warrantless searches are reasonable.

Even with a warrant, certain searches are unreasonable. For example, in *Winston v. Lee*, 470 U.S. 753 (1985), the removal of a bullet lodged deep in the accused's chest was deemed unreasonable. However, the Court concluded that the taking of blood from a suspect constituted a reasonable search. *See Schmerber v. California*, 384 U.S. 757 (1966).[5]

(g) The "Special Needs" Doctrine

Under certain circumstances, the Fourth Amendment does not require government officials to have a warrant or probable cause to conduct a search. Pur-

---

[4] There have been extensive writings about the Fourth Amendment's function of protecting privacy. For some background, see Christopher Slobogin, *The World Without a Fourth Amendment*, 39 UCLA L. Rev. 1 (1991); Silas J. Wasserstrom & Louis Michael Seidman, *The Fourth Amendment as Constitutional Theory*, 77 Geo. L.J. 19, 34 (1988); William J. Stuntz, *Privacy's Problem and the Law of Criminal Procedure*, 93 Mich. L. Rev. 1016 (1995); Scott E. Sundby, *"Everyman's" Fourth Amendment: Privacy or Mutual Trust Between Government and Citizen?*, 94 Colum. L. Rev. 1751 (1994); John Kent Walker, Jr., Note, *Covert Searches*, 39 Stan. L. Rev. 545 (1987).

[5] For more background about the Fourth Amendment's requirement of "reasonableness," see Sherry F. Colb, *The Qualitative Dimension of Fourth Amendment "Reasonableness,"* 98 Colum. L. Rev. 1642 (1998); Tracey Maclin, *Constructing Fourth Amendment Principles from the Government Perspective: Whose Amendment Is It, Anyway?*, 25 Am. Crim. L. Rev. 669 (1988).

suant to the "special needs" doctrine, searches and seizures are reasonable without a warrant or probable cause if "special needs, beyond the normal need for law enforcement, make the warrant and probable-cause requirement impracticable." *Griffin v. Wisconsin*, 483 U.S. 868 (1987). "The validity of a search is judged by the standard of 'reasonableness . . . under all the circumstances.'" *O'Connor v. Ortega*, 480 U.S. 709 (1987).

The special needs doctrine applies to searches in schools, government workplaces, and certain highly regulated businesses. As an example, the Supreme Court has upheld random drug tests for high school students participating in any competitive extracurricular activities, including academic extracurricular activities. *Board of Education v. Earls*, 536 U.S. 822 (2002). The special needs doctrine applies only when a search is not for a law enforcement purpose. Thus, in *New Jersey v. T.L.O.*, the Court upheld a search of a student's purse by school officials and noted that the search was "carried out by school authorities acting alone and on their own authority" as opposed to searches that might be conducted "in conjunction with or at the behest of law enforcement officials." *New Jersey v. T.L.O*, 469 U.S. 337 (1985).

(h) Administrative Searches

Generally, the need to inspect homes for health and safety violations is outweighed by the individual's privacy interest. *See Camara v. Municipal Court*, 387 U.S. 523 (1967) (holding that warrantless inspections of residences for housing code violations were unreasonable); *see v. City of Seattle*, 387 U.S. 541 (1967) (holding that search of a warehouse for fire code violations was unreasonable).

(i) Checkpoints

The police cannot randomly stop cars to check license and registration. *See Delaware v. Prouse*, 440 U.S. 648 (1979). However, fixed sobriety checkpoints are constitutional. *See Michigan Dep't of State Police v. Sitz*, 496 U.S. 444 (1990). Such a checkpoint search does not require "particularized suspicion." On the other hand, in *Indianapolis v. Edmond*, 531 U.S. 32 (2000), the Court held that checkpoints established to investigate possible drug violations were indistinguishable from a general purpose crime control search and were therefore unconstitutional:

> We have never approved a checkpoint program whose primary purpose was to detect evidence of ordinary criminal wrongdoing. Rather, our checkpoint cases have recognized only limited exceptions to the general rule that a seizure must be accompanied by some measure of individualized suspicion. We suggested in *Prouse* that we would not credit the "general interest in crime control" as justification for a regime of suspicionless stops. Consistent with this suggestion, each of the checkpoint programs that we have approved was designed primarily to serve purposes closely related to the problems of policing the border or the necessity of ensuring roadway safety. Because the primary purpose of the Indianapolis narcotics checkpoint program is to uncover evidence of ordinary criminal wrongdoing, the program contravenes the Fourth Amendment. . . .

The Supreme Court in *Illinois v. Lidster*, 540 U.S. 419 (2004), upheld the constitutionality of so-called "information-seeking highway stops." Following a hit-and-run accident that killed a 70-year-old bicyclist, the police in Lombard, Illinois set up a checkpoint at the approximate scene of the accident. The police stopped vehicles, asked the occupants of the car whether they had seen anything the previous weekend, and gave each driver a flyer that described the fatal accident and asked for assistance in identifying the vehicle and driver in the accident. The Supreme Court found that "special law enforcement concerns will sometimes justify highway stops without individualized suspicion." It also found that the stop in question was reasonable as well as constitutional. First, the "relevant public concern was grave," involving police investigation of a human death. Second, the stop advanced the grave public concern to a significant degree. "The police appropriately tailored their checkpoint stops to fit important criminal investigatory needs." Third, and "[m]ost importantly, the stops interfered only minimally with liberty of the sort the Fourth Amendment seeks to protect." As the *Lidster* Court concluded: "Viewed objectively each stop required only a brief wait in line — a very few minutes at most. Contact with the police lasted only a few seconds. . . . Viewed subjectively, the contact provided little reason for anxiety or alarm."

In *MacWade v. Kelly*, 460 F.3d 260 (2d Cir. 2006), the New York Police Department instituted a random search program in the subways following a bombing on a subway in London. Police searched people's bags and other items as they entered subway stations. Those wishing not to be searched could leave the station. The court upheld the program under a Fourth Amendment challenge:

> Although a subway rider enjoys a full privacy expectation in the contents of his baggage, the kind of search at issue here minimally intrudes upon that interest. Several uncontested facts establish that the Program is narrowly tailored to achieve its purpose: (1) passengers receive notice of the searches and may decline to be searched so long as they leave the subway; (2) police search only those containers capable of concealing explosives, inspect eligible containers only to determine whether they contain explosives, inspect the containers visually unless it is necessary to manipulate their contents, and do not read printed or written material or request personal information; (3) a typical search lasts only for a matter of seconds; (4) uniformed personnel conduct the searches out in the open, which reduces the fear and stigma that removal to a hidden area can cause; and (5) police exercise no discretion in selecting whom to search, but rather employ a formula that ensures they do not arbitrarily exercise their authority. . . . .
>
> [W]e need only determine whether the Program is "a reasonably effective means of addressing" the government interest in deterring and detecting a terrorist attack on the subway system.
>
> We will not peruse, parse, or extrapolate four months' worth of data in an attempt to divine how many checkpoints the City ought to deploy in the exercise of its day-to-day police power. Counter-terrorism experts and politically accountable officials have undertaken the delicate and esoteric task of deciding how best to marshal their available resources in light of the conditions prevailing on any given day.

(j) *Terry* Stops

In *Terry v. Ohio,* 392 U.S. 1 (1968), the Court carved out another exception to warrants and probable cause. The Court held that a police officer can "stop" an individual if the officer has "reasonable suspicion" that criminal activity is afoot. "Reasonable suspicion" is a standard that is lower than probable cause. A stop must be brief or temporary. If it lasts too long, it becomes a seizure, which requires probable cause. During the stop, the officer may "frisk" an individual for weapons if the officer has reasonable suspicion that the person is armed and dangerous. A frisk is not a full search. The officer cannot search the person for other items — only weapons. If, in the course of searching a person for weapons, the officer finds evidence of a crime, it will still be admissible if it was found within the scope of a valid frisk. For example, in *Minnesota v. Dickerson,* 508 U.S. 366 (1993), a police officer was searching a suspect for weapons and felt an object in the suspect's pocket. The officer did not believe it to be a weapon, but continued to inspect it. The Court concluded that this was an invalid search that extended beyond the limited confines of a frisk.

(k) The Enforcement of the Fourth Amendment

When law enforcement officials violate an individual's Fourth Amendment rights, the individual can seek at least two forms of redress. First, if the individual is a defendant in a criminal trial, she can move to have the evidence obtained in violation of the Fourth Amendment suppressed. This is known as the "exclusionary rule." In *Weeks v. United States,* 232 U.S. 383 (1914), the Court established the exclusionary rule as the way to enforce the Fourth Amendment on federal officials. Later, in *Mapp v. Ohio,* 367 U.S. 643 (1961), the Court held that the exclusionary rule applies to all government searches, whether state or federal. The purpose of the exclusionary rule is to deter law enforcement officials from violating the Constitution.

If the police illegally search or seize evidence in violation of the Constitution, not only is that evidence suppressed but all other evidence derived from the illegally obtained evidence is also suppressed. This is known as the "fruit of the poisonous tree" doctrine. For example, suppose the police illegally search a person's luggage and find evidence that the person is a drug trafficker. Armed with that evidence, the police obtain a warrant to search the person's home, where they uncover new evidence of drug-trafficking along with a weapon used in a murder. The person is charged with drug trafficking and murder. Under the Fourth Amendment, the evidence found in the person's luggage will be suppressed. Additionally, since the search warrant could not have been obtained but for the evidence turned up in the illegal search, the evidence found at the house, including the additional drug trafficking evidence as well as the murder evidence, will be suppressed. However, if the police obtained a warrant or located evidence by an "independent source," then the fruit of the poisonous tree doctrine does not apply. *See Silverthorne Lumber Co. v. United States,* 251 U.S. 385 (1920). Returning to the example above, if the police had evidence supplied from the person's cohort that the person was engaged in drug trafficking out of his home and had murdered somebody, this evidence may suffice to give the police probable cause to have a warrant issued to search the person's house. This evidence is independent from the illegal search, and it is admissible.[6]

The second form of redress for a violation of the Fourth Amendment is a civil remedy. A person, whether a criminal defendant or anybody else, can obtain civil damages for a Fourth Amendment violation by way of 42 U.S.C. § 1983.

2. WIRETAPPING, BUGGING, AND BEYOND

At common law, eavesdropping was considered a nuisance. "Eavesdropping" as William Blackstone defined it, meant to "listen under walls or window, or the eaves of a house, to hearken after discourse, and thereupon to frame slanderous and mischievous tales."[7] Before the advent of electronic communication, people could easily avoid eavesdroppers by ensuring that nobody else was around during their conversations.

The invention of the telegraph in 1844 followed by the telephone in 1876 substantially altered the way people communicated with each other. Today, the telephone has become an essential part of everyday communications. The advent of electronic communications was soon followed by the invention of recording and transmitting devices that enabled new and more sophisticated forms of eavesdropping than overhearing a conversation with the naked ear. One feature of electronic surveillance is that unlike the unsealing of letters, the interception of communications is undetectable. Some of the current forms of electronic surveillance technology include wiretaps, bugs, and parabolic microphones. New legal questions are raised by modern technology such as a cell phone, which can provide information about the physical location of the person using it.

A "wiretap" is a device used to intercept telephone (or telegraph) communications. Wiretapping began before the invention of the telephone. Wiretapping was used to intercept telegraph communications during the Civil War and became very prevalent after the invention of the telephone. The first police wiretap occurred in the early 1890s. In the first half of the twentieth century, wiretaps proliferated due to law enforcement attempts to monitor protests over bad industrial working conditions, social unrest caused by World War I, and the smuggling of alcohol during the Prohibition Years.[8]

A "bug" is a device, often quite miniature in size, that can be hidden on a person or in a place that can transmit conversations in a room to a remote receiving device, where the conversation can be listened to.

---

[6] The exclusionary rule has received significant scholarly attention. A number of scholars question its efficacy and advocate that the Fourth Amendment be enforced through other mechanisms such as civil sanctions. *See* Akhil Reed Amar, *The Constitution and Criminal Procedure* 28 (1997); Christopher Slobogin, *Why Liberals Should Chuck the Exclusionary Rule*, 1999 U. Ill. L. Rev. 363, 400-01 (1999). Other commentators contend that civil sanctions will be ineffective. *See* Arnold H. Loewy, *The Fourth Amendment as a Device for Protecting the Innocent*, 81 Mich. L. Rev. 1229, 1266 (1983); Tracey Maclin, *When the Cure for the Fourth Amendment Is Worse Than the Disease*, 68 S. Cal. L. Rev. 1, 62 (1994).

[7] 4 Blackstone, *Commentaries* 168 (1769).

[8] For more background on the history of wiretapping, see generally Robert Ellis Smith, *Ben Franklin's Web Site: Privacy and Curiosity from Plymouth Rock to the Internet* (2000); Priscilla M. Regan, *Legislating Privacy: Technology, Social Values, and Public Policy* (1995); James G. Carr, *The Law of Electronic Surveillance* (1994); Whitfield Diffie & Susan Landau, *Privacy on the Line: The Politics of Wiretapping and Encryption* (1998).

A "parabolic microphone" can pick up a conversation from a distance. Typically, a small dish behind the microphone enables the amplification of sound far away from the microphone itself.

Electronic surveillance devices were not in existence at the time that the Fourth Amendment was drafted. How, then, should the Fourth Amendment regulate these devices? In 1928, the Supreme Court attempted to answer this question in *Olmstead v. United States*, the first electronic surveillance case to come before the Court.

OLMSTEAD V. UNITED STATES
277 U.S. 438 (1928)

TAFT, C.J. The petitioners were convicted in the District Court for the Western District of Washington of a conspiracy to violate the National Prohibition Act by unlawfully possessing, transporting and importing intoxicating liquors and maintaining nuisances, and by selling intoxicating liquors. Seventy-two others, in addition to the petitioners, were indicted. Some were not apprehended, some were acquitted, and others pleaded guilty. . . .

The information which led to the discovery of the conspiracy and its nature and extent was largely obtained by intercepting messages on the telephones of the conspirators by four federal prohibition officers. Small wires were inserted along the ordinary telephone wires from the residences of four of the petitioners and those leading from the chief office. The insertions were made without trespass upon any property of the defendants. They were made in the basement of the large office building. The taps from house lines were made in the streets near the houses. . . .

The well-known historical purpose of the Fourth Amendment, directed against general warrants and writs of assistance, was to prevent the use of governmental force to search a man's house, his person, his papers, and his effects, and to prevent their seizure against his will. This phase of the misuse of governmental power of compulsion is the emphasis of the opinion of the court in the *Boyd* Case. . . .

. . . The Fourth Amendment may have proper application to a sealed letter in the mail, because of the constitutional provision for the Post Office Department and the relations between the government and those who pay to secure protection of their sealed letters. . . . It is plainly within the words of the amendment to say that the unlawful rifling by a government agent of a sealed letter is a search and seizure of the sender's papers or effects. The letter is a paper, an effect, and in the custody of a government that forbids carriage, except under its protection.

The United States takes no such care of telegraph or telephone messages as of mailed sealed letters. The amendment does not forbid what was done here. There was no searching. There was no seizure. The evidence was secured by the use of the sense of hearing and that only. There was no entry of the houses or offices of the defendants. . . .

The language of the amendment cannot be extended and expanded to include telephone wires, reaching to the whole world from the defendant's house or office. The intervening wires are not part of his house or office, any more than are the highways along which they are stretched. . . .

Congress may, of course, protect the secrecy of telephone messages by making them, when intercepted, inadmissible in evidence in federal criminal trials, by direct legislation, and thus depart from the common law of evidence. But the courts may not adopt such a policy by attributing an enlarged and unusual meaning to the Fourth Amendment. The reasonable view is that one who installs in his house a telephone instrument with connecting wires intends to project his voice to those quite outside, and that the wires beyond his house, and messages while passing over them, are not within the protection of the Fourth Amendment. Here those who intercepted the projected voices were not in the house of either party to the conversation. . . .

BRANDEIS, J. dissenting. The government makes no attempt to defend the methods employed by its officers. Indeed, it concedes that, if wire tapping can be deemed a search and seizure within the Fourth Amendment, such wire tapping as was practiced in the case at bar was an unreasonable search and seizure, and that the evidence thus obtained was inadmissible. But it relies on the language of the amendment, and it claims that the protection given thereby cannot properly be held to include a telephone conversation.

"We must never forget," said Mr. Chief Justice Marshall in *McCulloch v. Maryland*, "that it is a Constitution we are expounding." Since then this court has repeatedly sustained the exercise of power by Congress, under various clauses of that instrument, over objects of which the fathers could not have dreamed. We have likewise held that general limitations on the powers of government, like those embodied in the due process clauses of the Fifth and Fourteenth Amendments, do not forbid the United States or the states from meeting modern conditions by regulations which "a century ago, or even half a century ago, probably would have been rejected as arbitrary and oppressive." Clauses guaranteeing to the individual protection against specific abuses of power, must have a similar capacity of adaptation to a changing world. It was with reference to such a clause that this court said in *Weems v. United States*, 217 U.S. 349, 373:

> Legislation, both statutory and constitutional, is enacted, it is true, from an experience of evils, but its general language should not, therefore, be necessarily confined to the form that evil had theretofore taken. Time works changes, brings into existence new conditions and purposes. Therefore a principle to be vital must be capable of wider application than the mischief which gave it birth. This is peculiarly true of Constitutions. They are not ephemeral enactments, designed to meet passing occasions. They are, to use the words of Chief Justice Marshall, "designed to approach immortality as nearly as human institutions can approach it." The future is their care and provision for events of good and bad tendencies of which no prophecy can be made. In the application of a Constitution, therefore, our contemplation cannot be only of what has been but of what may be. Under any other rule a Constitution would indeed be as easy of application as it would be deficient in efficacy and power. Its general principles would have little value and be converted by precedent into impotent and lifeless formulas. Rights declared in words might be lost in reality.

When the Fourth and Fifth Amendments were adopted, "the form that evil had theretofore taken" had been necessarily simple. Force and violence were then the only means known to man by which a government could directly effect self-incrimination. It could compel the individual to testify — a compulsion effected, if need be, by torture. It could secure possession of his papers and other articles incident to his private life — a seizure effected, if need be, by breaking and entry. Protection against such invasion of "the sanctities of a man's home and the privacies of life" was provided in the Fourth and Fifth Amendments by specific language. *Boyd v. United States*, 116 U.S. 616 (1886). But "time works changes, brings into existence new conditions and purposes." Subtler and more far-reaching means of invading privacy have become available to the government. Discovery and invention have made it possible for the government, by means far more effective than stretching upon the rack, to obtain disclosure in court of what is whispered in the closet.

Moreover, "in the application of a Constitution, our contemplation cannot be only of what has been, but of what may be." The progress of science in furnishing the government with means of espionage is not likely to stop with wire tapping. Ways may some day be developed by which the government, without removing papers from secret drawers, can reproduce them in court, and by which it will be enabled to expose to a jury the most intimate occurrences of the home. Advances in the psychic and related sciences may bring means of exploring unexpressed beliefs, thoughts and emotions. "That places the liberty of every man in the hands of every petty officer" was said by James Otis of much lesser intrusions than these. To Lord Camden a far slighter intrusion seemed "subversive of all the comforts of society." Can it be that the Constitution affords no protection against such invasions of individual security?

A sufficient answer is found in *Boyd v. United States*, 116 U.S. 616 (1886), a case that will be remembered as long as civil liberty lives in the United States. This court there reviewed the history that lay behind the Fourth and Fifth Amendments. We said with reference to Lord Camden's judgment in *Entick v. Carrington*, 19 Howell's State Trials, 1030:

> The principles laid down in this opinion affect the very essence of constitutional liberty and security. They reach farther than the concrete form of the case there before the court, with its adventitious circumstances; they apply to all invasions on the part of the government and its employees of the sanctities of a man's home and the privacies of life. It is not the breaking of his doors, and the rummaging of his drawers, that constitutes the essence of the offense; but it is the invasion of his indefeasible right of personal security, personal liberty and private property, where that right has never been forfeited by his conviction of some public offense — it is the invasion of this sacred right which underlies and constitutes the essence of Lord Camden's judgment. Breaking into a house and opening boxes and drawers are circumstances of aggravation; but any forcible and compulsory extortion of a man's own testimony or of his private papers to be used as evidence of a crime or to forfeit his goods, is within the condemnation of that judgment. In this regard the Fourth and Fifth Amendments run almost into each other.

In *Ex parte Jackson*, 96 U.S. 727 (1877), it was held that a sealed letter entrusted to the mail is protected by the amendments. The mail is a public service furnished by the government. The telephone is a public service furnished by its authority. There is, in essence, no difference between the sealed letter and the private telephone message. . . .

The evil incident to invasion of the privacy of the telephone is far greater than that involved in tampering with the mails. Whenever a telephone line is tapped, the privacy of the persons at both ends of the line is invaded, and all conversations between them upon any subject, and although proper, confidential, and privileged, may be overheard. Moreover, the tapping of one man's telephone line involves the tapping of the telephone of every other person whom he may call, or who may call him. As a means of espionage, writs of assistance and general warrants are but puny instruments of tyranny and oppression when compared with wire tapping.

Time and again this court, in giving effect to the principle underlying the Fourth Amendment, has refused to place an unduly literal construction upon it. . . .

The protection guaranteed by the amendments is much broader in scope. The makers of our Constitution undertook to secure conditions favorable to the pursuit of happiness. They recognized the significance of man's spiritual nature, of his feelings and of his intellect. They knew that only a part of the pain, pleasure and satisfactions of life are to be found in material things. They sought to protect Americans in their beliefs, their thoughts, their emotions and their sensations. They conferred, as against the government, the right to be let alone — the most comprehensive of rights and the right most valued by civilized men. To protect that right, every unjustifiable intrusion by the government upon the privacy of the individual, whatever the means employed, must be deemed a violation of the Fourth Amendment. And the use, as evidence in a criminal proceeding, of facts ascertained by such intrusion must be deemed a violation of the Fifth.

Applying to the Fourth and Fifth Amendments the established rule of construction, the defendants' objections to the evidence obtained by wire tapping must, in my opinion, be sustained. It is, of course, immaterial where the physical connection with the telephone wires leading into the defendants' premises was made. And it is also immaterial that the intrusion was in aid of law enforcement. Experience should teach us to be most on our guard to protect liberty when the government's purposes are beneficent. Men born to freedom are naturally alert to repel invasion of their liberty by evil-minded rulers. The greatest dangers to liberty lurk in insidious encroachment by men of zeal, well-meaning but without understanding. . . .

NOTES & QUESTIONS

1. *Background and Epilogue.* Roy Olmstead, known as the "King of Bootleggers," ran a gigantic illegal alcohol distribution operation on the Pacific Coast during Prohibition. Formerly a police officer, Olmstead had long avoided trouble with state police by bribing them, but federal officials soon caught up with him. The federal investigators, led by Roy Lyle, Director

of Prohibition, were wiretapping all of the telephones in Olmstead's home for around five months. The case was widely followed in the press, and it was dubbed "the case of the whispering wires." Olmstead was careful not to leave evidence in his very large home; when the agents searched it, they turned up no evidence. Most of the evidence in the case came from the wiretaps. Olmstead knew he was being wiretapped; he had been tipped off by a freelance wiretapper the government had hired. But Olmstead believed that because wiretapping was illegal in the state of Washington, the wiretap evidence could not be used against him at trial. He was wrong. At trial, Olmstead was convicted and sentenced to four years in prison. He was later pardoned by President Roosevelt in 1935. In an ironic twist, while Olmstead was in prison, Roy Lyle was arrested for conspiring with rumrunners. Olmstead testified against Lyle at Lyle's trial. While in prison, Olmstead became a Christian Scientist, and after his release, he repudiated alcohol as one of the ills of society.[9]

2. *The Physical Trespass Doctrine, Detectaphones, and "Spike Mikes."* In *Olmstead,* the Supreme Court concluded that Fourth Amendment protections are triggered only when there is a physical trespass. The Court followed this approach for nearly 40 years. In *Goldman v. United States,* 316 U.S. 129 (1942), the police placed a device called a "detectaphone" next to a wall adjacent to a person's office. The device enabled the police to listen in on conversations inside the office. The Court concluded that since there was no trespass, there was no Fourth Amendment violation.

In *Silverman v. United States,* 365 U.S. 505 (1961), the police used a device called a "spike mike" to listen in from a vacant row house to conversations in an adjoining row house. The device consisted of a microphone with a spike of about a foot in length attached to it. The spike was inserted into a baseboard of the vacant row house on the wall adjoining the row house next door. The spike hit the heating duct serving the next door row house, which transformed the heating system into a sound conductor. The Court held that the use of the "spike mike" violated the Fourth Amendment because it constituted an "unauthorized physical encroachment" into the adjoining row house. The Court distinguished *Olmstead* and *Goldman* because those cases did not involve any "physical invasion" or "trespass" onto the defendant's property, whereas the "spike mike" "usurp[ed] part of the [defendant's] house or office." Do you agree with the Court's distinction between *Goldman/Olmstead* and *Silverman* — between surveillance involving physical intrusion (however slight) and surveillance not involving any trespassing on the premises?

3. *Brandeis's Dissent and the Warren and Brandeis Article.* Justice Brandeis's dissent is one of the most famous dissents in Supreme Court history. Note the similarities between Brandeis's 1890 article, *The Right to Privacy,* and his

---

[9] Samuel Dash, *The Intruders: Unreasonable Searches and Seizures from King John to John Ashcroft* 74-78 (2004); Robert C. Post, *Federalism, Positive Law, and the Emergence of the American Administrative State: Prohibition in the Taft Court Era,* 48 Wm. & Mary L. Rev. 1, 139-50 (2006).

dissent nearly 40 years later in *Olmstead*. What themes are repeated? Recall that *The Right to Privacy* concerned locating common law roots for privacy protection. What is Brandeis saying about the roots of constitutional protection of privacy?

4. ***Changing Technology and the Constitution.*** Brandeis contends that the Constitution should keep pace with changing technology. But given the rapid pace of technological change and the fact that the Constitution must serve as the stable foundation for our society, can the Constitution keep pace? How adaptable should the Constitution be?

5. ***Wiretapping vs. Mail Tampering.*** Brandeis contends that wiretapping is more insidious than tampering with the mail. Why? How would you compare wiretapping with intercepting e-mail or instant messages?

6. ***State Wiretapping Law.*** In the state of Washington, where the wiretapping in *Olmstead* took place, wiretapping was a criminal act, and the officers had thus violated the law. In a separate dissenting opinion, Justice Holmes noted that:

> . . . [A]part from the Constitution the government ought not to use evidence obtained and only obtainable by a criminal act. . . . It is desirable that criminals should be detected, and to that end that all available evidence should be used. It also is desirable that the government should not itself foster and pay for other crimes, when they are the means by which the evidence is to be obtained. If it pays its officers for having got evidence by crime I do not see why it may not as well pay them for getting it in the same way, and I can attach no importance to protestations of disapproval if it knowingly accepts and pays and announces that in future it will pay for the fruits. We have to choose, and for my part I think it a less evil that some criminals should escape than that the government should play an ignoble part.

Should it matter in Fourth Amendment analysis whether particular federal law enforcement surveillance tactics are illegal under state law?

7. ***The Birth of Federal Electronic Surveillance Law.*** The *Olmstead* decision was not well received by the public. In 1934, Congress responded to *Olmstead* by enacting § 605 of the Federal Communications Act, making wiretapping a federal crime. This statute will be discussed later in the part on electronic surveillance law.

8. ***Secret Agents and Misplaced Trust.*** In *Hoffa v. United States*, 385 U.S. 293 (1966), an undercover informant, Edward Partin, befriended James Hoffa and elicited statements from him about his plans to bribe jurors in a criminal trial in which Hoffa was a defendant. According to the Court:

> In the present case . . . it is evident that no interest legitimately protected by the Fourth Amendment is involved. It is obvious that the petitioner was not relying on the security of his hotel suite when he made the incriminating statements to Partin or in Partin's presence. Partin did not enter the suite by force or by stealth. He was not a surreptitious eavesdropper. Partin was in the suite by invitation, and every conversation which he heard was either directed to him or knowingly carried on in his presence. The petitioner, in a word, was not relying on the security of the hotel room; he was relying upon his misplaced confidence that Partin would not reveal his wrongdoing.

Likewise, in *Lewis v. United States*, 385 U.S. 206 (1966), the defendant sold drugs to an undercover agent in his house. The Court held:

> In the instant case . . . the petitioner invited the undercover agent to his home for the specific purpose of executing a felonious sale of narcotics. Petitioner's only concern was whether the agent was a willing purchaser who could pay the agreed price. . . . During neither of his visits to petitioner's home did the agent see, hear, or take anything that was not contemplated, and in fact intended, by petitioner as a necessary part of his illegal business. Were we to hold the deceptions of the agent in this case constitutionally prohibited, we would come near to a rule that the use of undercover agents in any manner is virtually unconstitutional per se. Such a rule would, for example, severely hamper the Government in ferreting out those organized criminal activities that are characterized by covert dealings with victims who either cannot or do not protest. A prime example is provided by the narcotics traffic. . . .

Hoffa and *Lewis* establish that a person does not have a privacy interest in the loyalty of her friends. The government may deceive a person by sending in secret agents to befriend her. Is it problematic that government is permitted to use spies and deception as a law enforcement technique? Consider the following observation by Anthony Amsterdam:

> I can see no significant difference between police spies . . . and electronic surveillance, either in their uses or abuses. Both have long been asserted by law enforcement officers to be indispensable tools in investigating crime, particularly victimless and political crime, precisely because they both search out privacies that government could not otherwise invade. Both tend to repress crime in the same way, by making people distrustful and unwilling to talk to one another. The only difference is that under electronic surveillance you are afraid to talk to anybody in your office or over the phone, while under a spy system you are afraid to talk to anybody at all.[10]

9. ***Bugs, Transmitters, and Recording Devices.*** In *On Lee v. United States*, 343 U.S. 747 (1952), Chin Poy, a government informant with a concealed transmitter, engaged On Lee in conversation for the purpose of eliciting that On Lee was a drug dealer. The conversation was transmitted to a law enforcement agent, who later testified at trial about the content of the conversation. The Court held that the Fourth Amendment did not apply:

> Petitioner was talking confidentially and indiscreetly with one he trusted, and he was overheard. This was due to aid from a transmitter and receiver, to be sure, but with the same effect on his privacy as if agent Lee had been eavesdropping outside an open window. The use of bifocals, field glasses or the telescope to magnify the object of a witness' vision is not a forbidden search or seizure, even if they focus without his knowledge or consent upon what one supposes to be private indiscretions. It would be a dubious service to the genuine liberties protected by the Fourth Amendment to make them bedfellows with spurious liberties improvised by farfetched analogies which

---

[10] Anthony G. Amsterdam, *Perspectives on the Fourth Amendment*, 58 Minn. L. Rev. 349, 407 (1974). For a detailed analysis of undercover agents, see Gary T. Marx, *Under Cover: Police Surveillance in America* (1988).

would liken eavesdropping on a conversation, with the connivance of one of the parties, to an unreasonable search or seizure. We find no violation of the Fourth Amendment here.

Does the use of electronic devices distinguish *On Lee* from *Hoffa* and *Lewis* in a material way?

LOPEZ V. UNITED STATES
373 U.S. 427 (1963)

[The petitioner, German S. Lopez, was tried in a federal court on a four-count indictment charging him with attempted bribery of an Internal Revenue agent, Roger S. Davis. The evidence against him had been obtained by a series of meetings between him and Davis. The last meeting was recorded by Davis with a pocket wire recorder. Prior to trial, Lopez moved to suppress the recorded conversation.]

HARLAN, J. . . . [Petitioner's] argument is primarily addressed to the recording of the conversation, which he claims was obtained in violation of his rights under the Fourth Amendment. Recognizing the weakness of this position if Davis was properly permitted to testify about the same conversation, petitioner now challenges that testimony as well, although he failed to do so at the trial. . . .

Once it is plain that Davis could properly testify about his conversation with Lopez, the constitutional claim relating to the recording of that conversation emerges in proper perspective. The Court has in the past sustained instances of "electronic eavesdropping" against constitutional challenge, when devices have been used to enable government agents to overhear conversations which would have been beyond the reach of the human ear. *See, e.g., Olmstead v. United States.* It has been insisted only that the electronic device not be planted by an unlawful physical invasion of a constitutionally protected area. . . . Indeed this case involves no "eavesdropping" whatever in any proper sense of that term. The Government did not use an electronic device to listen in on conversations it could not otherwise have heard. Instead, the device was used only to obtain the most reliable evidence possible of a conversation in which the Government's own agent was a participant and which that agent was fully entitled to disclose. And the device was not planted by means of an unlawful physical invasion of petitioner's premises under circumstances which would violate the Fourth Amendment. It was carried in and out by an agent who was there with petitioner's assent, and it neither saw nor heard more than the agent himself. . . .

Stripped to its essentials, petitioner's argument amounts to saying that he has a constitutional right to rely on possible flaws in the agent's memory, or to challenge the agent's credibility without being beset by corroborating evidence that is not susceptible of impeachment. For no other argument can justify excluding an accurate version of a conversation that the agent could testify to from memory. We think the risk that petitioner took in offering a bribe to Davis fairly included the risk that the offer would be accurately reproduced in court, whether by faultless memory or mechanical recording. . . .

WARREN, C.J. concurring. I also share the opinion of Mr. Justice Brennan that the fantastic advances in the field of electronic communication constitute a great danger to the privacy of the individual; that indiscriminate use of such devices in law enforcement raises grave constitutional questions under the Fourth and Fifth Amendments; and that these considerations impose a heavier responsibility on this Court in its supervision of the fairness of procedures in the federal court system. However, I do not believe that, as a result, all uses of such devices should be proscribed either as unconstitutional or as unfair law enforcement methods. One of the lines I would draw would be between this case and *On Lee*. . . .

The use and purpose of the transmitter in *On Lee* was substantially different from the use of the recorder here. Its advantage was not to corroborate the testimony of Chin Poy, but rather, to obviate the need to put him on the stand. The Court in *On Lee* itself stated:

> We can only speculate on the reasons why Chin Poy was not called. It seems a not unlikely assumption that the very defects of character and blemishes of record which made On Lee trust him with confidences would make a jury distrust his testimony. Chin Poy was close enough to the underworld to serve as bait, near enough the criminal design so that petitioner would embrace him as a confidante, but too close to it for the Government to vouch for him as a witness. Instead, the Government called agent Lee.

However, there were further advantages in not using Chin Poy. Had Chin Poy been available for cross-examination, counsel for On Lee could have explored the nature of Chin Poy's friendship with On Lee, the possibility of other unmonitored conversations and appeals to friendship, the possibility of entrapments, police pressure brought to bear to persuade Chin Poy to turn informer, and Chin Poy's own recollection of the contents of the conversation. . . .

Thus while I join the Court in permitting the use of electronic devices to corroborate an agent under the particular facts of this case, I cannot sanction by implication the use of these same devices to radically shift the pattern of presentation of evidence in the criminal trial, a shift that may be used to conceal substantial factual and legal issues concerning the rights of the accused and the administration of criminal justice.

BRENNAN, J. joined by DOUGLAS and GOLDBERG, JJ. dissenting. . . . [T]he Government's argument is that Lopez surrendered his right of privacy when he communicated his "secret thoughts" to Agent Davis. The assumption, manifestly untenable, is that the Fourth Amendment is only designed to protect secrecy. If a person commits his secret thoughts to paper, that is no license for the police to seize the paper; if a person communicates his secret thoughts verbally to another, that is no license for the police to record the words. *On Lee* certainly rested on no such theory of waiver. The right of privacy would mean little if it were limited to a person's solitary thoughts, and so fostered secretiveness. It must embrace a concept of the liberty of one's communications, and historically it has. "The common law secures to each individual the right of determining, ordinarily, to what extent his thoughts, sentiments, and emotions shall be communicated to others . . . and even if he has chosen to give them expression, he generally retains the power to fix the limits of the publicity which shall be given them." Warren and Brandeis, *The Right to Privacy*, 4 Harv. L. Rev. 193, 198 (1890).

That is not to say that all communications are privileged. On Lee assumed the risk that his acquaintance would divulge their conversation; Lopez assumed the same risk vis-à-vis Davis. The risk inheres in all communications which are not in the sight of the law privileged. It is not an undue risk to ask persons to assume, for it does no more than compel them to use discretion in choosing their auditors, to make damaging disclosures only to persons whose character and motives may be trusted. But the risk which both *On Lee* and today's decision impose is of a different order. It is the risk that third parties, whether mechanical auditors like the Minifon or human transcribers of mechanical transmissions as in *On Lee* — third parties who cannot be shut out of a conversation as conventional eavesdroppers can be, merely by a lowering of voices, or withdrawing to a private place — may give independent evidence of any conversation. There is only one way to guard against such a risk, and that is to keep one's mouth shut on all occasions. . . .

The risk of being overheard by an eavesdropper or betrayed by an informer or deceived as to the identity of one with whom one deals is probably inherent in the conditions of human society. It is the kind of risk we necessarily assume whenever we speak. But as soon as electronic surveillance comes into play, the risk changes crucially. There is no security from that kind of eavesdropping, no way of mitigating the risk, and so not even a residuum of true privacy. . . .

NOTES & QUESTIONS

1. *Is Electronic Surveillance Different?* Should electronic surveillance be treated similarly or differently than regular eavesdropping? Is it consistent to agree that Davis could testify as to what Lopez said via his memory but cannot introduce a recording of what Lopez said?

Katz v. United States
389 U.S. 347 (1967)

STEWART, J. The petitioner was convicted in the District Court for the Southern District of California under an eight-count indictment charging him with transmitting wagering information by telephone from Los Angeles to Miami and Boston in violation of a federal statute. At trial the Government was permitted, over the petitioner's objection, to introduce evidence of the petitioner's end of telephone conversations, overheard by FBI agents who had attached an electronic listening and recording device to the outside of the public telephone booth from which he had placed his calls. In affirming his conviction, the Court of Appeals rejected the contention that the recordings had been obtained in violation of the Fourth Amendment, because "[t]here was no physical entrance into the area occupied by, (the petitioner)." We granted certiorari in order to consider the constitutional questions thus presented.

The petitioner had phrased those questions as follows:

A. Whether a public telephone booth is a constitutionally protected area so that evidence obtained by attaching an electronic listening recording device to the top of such a booth is obtained in violation of the right to privacy of the user of the booth.
B. Whether physical penetration of a constitutionally protected area is necessary before a search and seizure can be said to be violative of the Fourth Amendment to the United States Constitution.

We decline to adopt this formulation of the issues. In the first place the correct solution of Fourth Amendment problems is not necessarily promoted by incantation of the phrase "constitutionally protected area." Secondly, the Fourth Amendment cannot be translated into a general constitutional "right to privacy." That Amendment protects individual privacy against certain kinds of governmental intrusion, but its protections go further, and often have nothing to do with privacy at all. Other provisions of the Constitution protect personal privacy from other forms of governmental invasion. But the protection of a person's general right to privacy — his right to be let alone by other people — is, like the protection of his property and of his very life, left largely to the law of the individual States.

Because of the misleading way the issues have been formulated, the parties have attached great significance to the characterization of the telephone booth from which the petitioner placed his calls. The petitioner has strenuously argued that the booth was a "constitutionally protected area." The Government has maintained with equal vigor that it was not. But this effort to decide whether or not a given "area," viewed in the abstract, is "constitutionally protected" deflects attention from the problem presented by this case. For the Fourth Amendment protects people, not places. What a person knowingly exposes to the public, even in his own home or office, is not a subject of Fourth Amendment protection. But what he seeks to preserve as private, even in an area accessible to the public, may be constitutionally protected.

The Government stresses the fact that the telephone booth from which the petitioner made his calls was constructed partly of glass, so that he was as visible after he entered it as he would have been if he had remained outside. But what he sought to exclude when he entered the booth was not the intruding eye — it was the uninvited ear. He did not shed his right to do so simply because he made his calls from a place where he might be seen. No less than an individual in a business office, in a friend's apartment, or in a taxicab, a person in a telephone booth may rely upon the protection of the Fourth Amendment. One who occupies it, shuts the door behind him, and pays the toll that permits him to place a call is surely entitled to assume that the words he utters into the mouthpiece will not be broadcast to the world. To read the Constitution more narrowly is to ignore the vital role that the public telephone has come to play in private communication.

The Government contends, however, that the activities of its agents in this case should not be tested by Fourth Amendment requirements, for the surveillance technique they employed involved no physical penetration of the telephone booth from which the petitioner placed his calls. It is true that the absence of such penetration was at one time thought to foreclose further Fourth

Amendment inquiry, *Olmstead v. United States, Goldman v. United States,* for that Amendment was thought to limit only searches and seizures of tangible property. But "[t]he premise that property interests control the right of the Government to search and seize has been discredited." . . . [O]nce this much is acknowledged, and once it is recognized that the Fourth Amendment protects people — and not simply "areas" — against unreasonable searches and seizures it becomes clear that the reach of that Amendment cannot turn upon the presence or absence of a physical intrusion into any given enclosure.

We conclude that the underpinnings of *Olmstead* and *Goldman* have been so eroded by our subsequent decisions that the "trespass" doctrine there enunciated can no longer be regarded as controlling. . . .

The question remaining for decision, then, is whether the search and seizure conducted in this case complied with constitutional standards. In that regard, the Government's position is that its agents acted in an entirely defensible manner: They did not begin their electronic surveillance until investigation of the petitioner's activities had established a strong probability that he was using the telephone in question to transmit gambling information to persons in other States, in violation of federal law. Moreover, the surveillance was limited, both in scope and in duration, to the specific purpose of establishing the contents of the petitioner's unlawful telephonic communications. The agents confined their surveillance to the brief periods during which he used the telephone booth, and they took great care to overhear only the conversations of the petitioner himself. . . .

. . . It is apparent that the agents in this case acted with restraint. Yet the inescapable fact is that this restraint was imposed by the agents themselves, not by a judicial officer. They were not required, before commencing the search, to present their estimate of probable cause for detached scrutiny by a neutral magistrate. They were not compelled, during the conduct of the search itself, to observe precise limits established in advance by a specific court order. Nor were they directed, after the search had been completed, to notify the authorizing magistrate in detail of all that had been seized. In the absence of such safeguards, this Court has never sustained a search upon the sole ground that officers reasonably expected to find evidence of a particular crime and voluntarily confined their activities to the least intrusive means consistent with that end. Searches conducted without warrants have been held unlawful "notwithstanding facts unquestionably showing probable cause." . . . "Over and again this Court has emphasized that the mandate of the [Fourth] Amendment requires adherence to judicial processes," and that searches conducted outside the judicial process, without prior approval by judge or magistrate, are per se unreasonable under the Fourth Amendment — subject only to a few specifically established and well-delineated exceptions. . . .

HARLAN, J. concurring. . . . As the Court's opinion states, "the Fourth Amendment protects people, not places." The question, however, is what protection it affords to those people. Generally, as here, the answer to that question requires reference to a "place." My understanding of the rule that has emerged from prior decisions is that there is a twofold requirement, first that a person have exhibited an actual (subjective) expectation of privacy and, second, that the expectation be one that society is prepared to recognize as "reasonable."

Thus a man's home is, for most purposes, a place where he expects privacy, but objects, activities, or statements that he exposes to the "plain view" of outsiders are not "protected" because no intention to keep them to himself has been exhibited. On the other hand, conversations in the open would not be protected against being overheard, for the expectation of privacy under the circumstances would be unreasonable.

The critical fact in this case is that "(o)ne who occupies it, (a telephone booth) shuts the door behind him, and pays the toll that permits him to place a call is surely entitled to assume" that his conversation is not being intercepted. The point is not that the booth is "accessible to the public" at other times, but that it is a temporarily private place whose momentary occupants' expectations of freedom from intrusion are recognized as reasonable.

BLACK, J. dissenting. . . . My basic objection is twofold: (1) I do not believe that the words of the Amendment will bear the meaning given them by today's decision, and (2) I do not believe that it is the proper role of this Court to rewrite the Amendment in order "to bring it into harmony with the times" and thus reach a result that many people believe to be desirable.

While I realize that an argument based on the meaning of words lacks the scope, and no doubt the appeal, of broad policy discussions and philosophical discourses on such nebulous subjects as privacy, for me the language of the Amendment is the crucial place to look in construing a written document such as our Constitution. The Fourth Amendment says that

> The right of the people to be secure in their persons, houses, papers, and effects, against unreasonable searches and seizures, shall not be violated, and no Warrants shall issue, but upon probable cause, supported by Oath or affirmation, and particularly describing the place to be searched, and the persons or things to be seized.

The first clause protects "persons, houses, papers, and effects, against unreasonable searches and seizures. . . ." These words connote the idea of tangible things with size, form, and weight, things capable of being searched, seized, or both. The second clause of the Amendment still further establishes its Framers' purpose to limit its protection to tangible things by providing that no warrants shall issue but those "particularly describing the place to be searched, and the persons or things to be seized." A conversation overheard by eavesdropping, whether by plain snooping or wiretapping, is not tangible and, under the normally accepted meanings of the words, can neither be searched nor seized. . . .

NOTES & QUESTIONS

1. *Who Was Charlie Katz?* David Sklansky describes the background to *Katz*:

> Charlie Katz was a Damon Runyon character plopped into 1960s Los Angeles. Katz was a professional bettor . . . Katz wagered on sports events, sometimes for himself and sometimes on commission for others. He specialized in basketball games, and he had his own, elaborate system for

ranking teams and predicting outcomes. In February 1965, he was living in a poolside hotel room on the Sunset Strip.[11]

Sklanksy describes how the FBI would observe Katz leaving his hotel to place his bets from the telephone booth. An agent stationed outside would radio the news to another agent near the booth. This second agent would turn on a tape recorder placed on top of the telephone booth, observe Katz making his calls, and once Katz was finished and left the telephone booth, turn the recorder off and take it down from the top of the booth.

2. **The Reasonable Expectation of Privacy Test.** The *Katz* decision established a widely cited test for whether the Fourth Amendment is applicable in a given situation. That test was articulated not in the majority opinion but in the concurring opinion by Justice Harlan. The rule as articulated in Justice Harlan's concurrence has become known as the "reasonable expectation of privacy test." Under the test, (1) a person must exhibit an "actual (subjective) expectation of privacy" and (2) "the expectation [must] be one that society is prepared to recognize as 'reasonable.'"

According to Christopher Slobogin and Joseph Schumacher:

> For the most part, the Court has been content with fleshing out the meaning of the phrase[] "reasonable expectations of privacy" . . . through [its] application to specific cases. But the Court has also provided two significant guidelines as to how [this phrase] should be interpreted. The first guideline came in *Rakas v. Illinois*, where the majority opinion, by then-Associate Justice Rehnquist, stated that "legitimation of expectations of privacy by law must have a source outside of the Fourth Amendment, either by reference to concepts of real or personal property law or to understandings that are recognized and permitted by society." Most important for present purposes is the last clause of this excerpt, which indicates the Court's willingness to rely on societal understandings in defining "reasonable expectations of privacy." Although this language appeared in a footnote, and was directed solely toward defining the standing concept, it has since been relied upon in the text of several other cases involving the "search" issue, often rephrased in terms of expectations of privacy "society is prepared to recognize as 'reasonable.'"
>
> The second guideline came from the same footnote in *Rakas*. According to the Court, the use of the word "legitimate" or "reasonable" before "expectations of privacy" is meant to convey "more than a subjective expectation of not being discovered." As the Court explained,
>
> > [a] burglar plying his trade in a summer cabin during the off season may have a thoroughly justified subjective expectation of privacy, but it is not one which the law recognizes as "legitimate." His presence . . . is "wrongful"; his expectation is not "one that society is prepared to recognize as 'reasonable.'"
>
> In short, the Fourth Amendment does not protect expectations of privacy that only a criminal would have.[12]

[11] David A. Sklansky, *Katz v. United States*, in *Criminal Procedure Stories* (Carol S. Steiker, ed., 2006).
[12] Christopher Slobogin & Joseph E. Schumacher, *Reasonable Expectations of Privacy and Autonomy in Fourth Amendment Cases: An Empirical Look at "Understandings Recognized and Permitted by Society,"* 42 Duke L.J. 727, 731-32 (1993).

3. ***Variations on* Katz.** What if the door to the telephone booth in *Katz* had been open? Would the Court still have concluded that the Fourth Amendment applied? What if the cop stood outside the booth, and Katz spoke loud enough for the cop to hear? Suppose the police placed a sound recording device outside the phone booth, and the device could pick up Katz's voice, which would be inaudible to the naked ear outside the phone booth. Would this be a violation of the Fourth Amendment?

4. ***"Conditioned" Expectations of Privacy.*** Before *Katz*, police sometimes tapped phones. How would this behavior affect a person's expectations of privacy when speaking on the phone? Consider the following observation by the Court in *Smith v. Maryland*, 442 U.S. 735, 741 n.5 (1979):

> Situations can be imagined, of course, in which Katz' two-pronged inquiry would provide an inadequate index of Fourth Amendment protection. For example, if the Government were suddenly to announce on nationwide television that all homes henceforth would be subject to warrantless entry, individuals thereafter might not in fact entertain any actual expectation or privacy regarding their homes, papers, and effects. Similarly, if a refugee from a totalitarian country, unaware of this Nation's traditions, erroneously assumed that police were continuously monitoring his telephone conversations, a subjective expectation of privacy regarding the contents of his calls might be lacking as well. In such circumstances, where an individual's subjective expectations had been "conditioned" by influences alien to well-recognized Fourth Amendment freedoms, those subjective expectations obviously could play no meaningful role in ascertaining what the scope of Fourth Amendment protection was. In determining whether a "legitimate expectation of privacy" existed in such cases, a normative inquiry would be proper.

5. **Berger v. New York.** *Berger v. New York*, 388 U.S. 41 (1967), is an important Fourth Amendment case decided after the Supreme Court agreed to hear *Katz* but before it heard oral arguments in that case. In *Berger*, the Court struck down portions of New York's eavesdropping statute as violating the Fourth Amendment. The New York law authorized the installation of electronic surveillance devices for 60 days, and it allowed the surveillance to be extended beyond the 60 days without a showing of present probable cause to continue the eavesdrop. The Court held:

> . . . The Fourth Amendment commands that a warrant issue not only upon probable cause supported by oath or affirmation, but also "particularly describing the place to be searched, and the persons or things to be seized." New York's statute lacks this particularization. It merely says that a warrant may issue on reasonable ground to believe that evidence of crime may be obtained by the eavesdrop. It lays down no requirement for particularity in the warrant as to what specific crime has been or is being committed, nor "the place to be searched," or "the persons or things to be seized" as specifically required by the Fourth Amendment. The need for particularity and evidence of reliability in the showing required when judicial authorization of a search is sought is especially great in the case of eavesdropping. By its very nature eavesdropping involves an intrusion on privacy that is broad in scope. . . .

. . . New York's statute . . . lays down no . . . "precise and discriminate" requirements. . . . New York's broadside authorization rather than being "carefully circumscribed" so as to prevent unauthorized invasions of privacy actually permits general searches by electronic devices, the truly offensive character of which was first condemned in *Entick v. Carrington*, 19 How. St. Tr. 1029, and which were then known as "general warrants." The use of the latter was a motivating factor behind the Declaration of Independence. In view of the many cases commenting on the practice it is sufficient here to point out that under these "general warrants" customs officials were given blanket authority to conduct general searches for goods imported to the Colonies in violation of the tax laws of the Crown. The Fourth Amendment's requirement that a warrant "particularly describ(e) the place to be searched, and the persons or things to be seized," repudiated these general warrants and "makes general searches . . . impossible and prevents the seizure of one thing under a warrant describing another. As to what is to be taken, nothing is left to the discretion of the officer executing the warrant."

We believe the statute here is equally offensive. First, as we have mentioned, eavesdropping is authorized without requiring belief that any particular offense has been or is being committed; nor that the "property" sought, the conversations, be particularly described. The purpose of the probable cause requirement of the Fourth Amendment, to keep the state out of constitutionally protected areas until it has reason to believe that a specific crime has been or is being committed, is thereby wholly aborted. Likewise the statute's failure to describe with particularity the conversations sought gives the officer a roving commission to "seize" any and all conversations. . . . As with general warrants this leaves too much to the discretion of the officer executing the order. Secondly, authorization of eavesdropping for a two-month period is the equivalent of a series of intrusions, searches, and seizures pursuant to a single showing of probable cause. Prompt execution is also avoided. During such a long and continuous (24 hours a day) period the conversations of any and all persons coming into the area covered by the device will be seized indiscriminately and without regard to their connection with the crime under investigation. Moreover, the statute permits, and there were authorized here, extensions of the original two-month period — presumably for two months each — on a mere showing that such extension is "in the public interest." Apparently the original grounds on which the eavesdrop order was initially issued also form the basis of the renewal. This we believe insufficient without a showing of present probable cause for the continuance of the eavesdrop. Third, the statute places no termination date on the eavesdrop once the conversation sought is seized. This is left entirely in the discretion of the officer. Finally, the statute's procedure, necessarily because its success depends on secrecy, has no requirement for notice as do conventional warrants, nor does it overcome this defect by requiring some showing of special facts. On the contrary, it permits uncontested entry without any showing of exigent circumstances. . . . In short, the statute's blanket grant of permission to eavesdrop is without adequate judicial supervision or protective procedures. . . .

As Sklansky points out, the effect of *Berger* combined with two other cases decided immediately before *Katz* — *Warren v. Hayden*, 387 U.S. 294 (1967) and *Camara v. Municipal Court*, 387 U.S. 523 (1967) — was to underscore the "centrality of the warrant requirement to the Fourth Amendment."[13]

UNITED STATES V. WHITE

401 U.S. 745 (1971)

WHITE, J. In 1966, respondent James A. White was tried and convicted under two consolidated indictments charging various illegal transactions in narcotics. . . . He was fined and sentenced as a second offender to 25-year concurrent sentences. The issue before us is whether the Fourth Amendment bars from evidence the testimony of governmental agents who related certain conversations which had occurred between defendant White and a government informant, Harvey Jackson, and which the agents overheard by monitoring the frequency of a radio transmitter carried by Jackson and concealed on his person. On four occasions the conversations took place in Jackson's home; each of these conversations was overheard by an agent concealed in a kitchen closet with Jackson's consent and by a second agent outside the house using a radio receiver. Four other conversations — one in respondent's home, one in a restaurant, and two in Jackson's car — were overheard by the use of radio equipment. The prosecution was unable to locate and produce Jackson at the trial and the trial court overruled objections to the testimony of the agents who conducted the electronic surveillance. The jury returned a guilty verdict and defendant appealed. . . .

Concededly a police agent who conceals his police connections may write down for official use his conversations with a defendant and testify concerning them, without a warrant authorizing his encounters with the defendant and without otherwise violating the latter's Fourth Amendment rights. For constitutional purposes, no different result is required if the agent instead of immediately reporting and transcribing his conversations with defendant, either (1) simultaneously records them with electronic equipment which he is carrying on his person, *Lopez v. United States*; (2) or carries radio equipment which simultaneously transmits the conversations either to recording equipment located elsewhere or to other agents monitoring the transmitting frequency. *On Lee v. United States*. If the conduct and revelations of an agent operating without electronic equipment do not invade the defendant's constitutionally justifiable expectations of privacy, neither does a simultaneous recording of the same conversations made by the agent or by others from transmissions received from the agent to whom the defendant is talking and whose trustworthiness the defendant necessarily risks.

Our problem is not what the privacy expectations of particular defendants in particular situations may be or the extent to which they may in fact have relied on the discretion of their companions. Very probably, individual defendants neither know nor suspect that their colleagues have gone or will go to the police or are

---

[13] David A. Sklansky, *Katz v. United States*, in *Criminal Procedure Stories* (Carol S. Steiker, ed., 2006).

carrying recorders or transmitters. Otherwise, conversation would cease and our problem with these encounters would be nonexistent or far different from those now before us. Our problem, in terms of the principles announced in *Katz*, is what expectations of privacy are constitutionally "justifiable" — what expectations the Fourth Amendment will protect in the absence of a warrant. So far, the law permits the frustration of actual expectations of privacy by permitting authorities to use the testimony of those associates who for one reason or another have determined to turn to the police, as well as by authorizing the use of informants in the manner exemplified by *Hoffa* and *Lewis*. If the law gives no protection to the wrongdoer whose trusted accomplice is or becomes a police agent, neither should it protect him when that same agent has recorded or transmitted the conversations which are later offered in evidence to prove the State's case.

Inescapably, one contemplating illegal activities must realize and risk that his companions may be reporting to the police. If he sufficiently doubts their trustworthiness, the association will very probably end or never materialize. But if he has no doubts, or allays them, or risks what doubt he has, the risk is his. In terms of what his course will be, what he will or will not do or say, we are unpersuaded that he would distinguish between probably informers on the one hand and probable informers with transmitters on the other. . . .

Nor should we be too ready to erect constitutional barriers to relevant and probative evidence which is also accurate and reliable. An electronic recording will many times produce a more reliable rendition of what a defendant has said than will the unaided memory of a police agent. It may also be that with the recording in existence it is less likely that the informant will change his mind, less chance that threat or injury will suppress unfavorable evidence and less chance that cross-examination will confound the testimony. Considerations like these obviously do not favor the defendant, but we are not prepared to hold that a defendant who has no constitutional right to exclude the informer's unaided testimony nevertheless has a Fourth Amendment privilege against a more accurate version of the events in question. . . .

HARLAN, J. dissenting. . . . Since it is the task of the law to form and project, as well as mirror and reflect, we should not, as judges, merely recite the expectations and risks without examining the desirability of saddling them upon society. The critical question, therefore, is whether under our system of government, as reflected in the Constitution, we should impose on our citizens the risks of the electronic listener or observer without at least the protection of a warrant requirement.

This question must, in my view, be answered by assessing the nature of a particular practice and the likely extent of its impact on the individual's sense of security balanced against the utility of the conduct as a technique of law enforcement. For those more extensive intrusions that significantly jeopardize the sense of security which is the paramount concern of Fourth Amendment liberties, I am of the view that more than self-restraint by law enforcement officials is required and at the least warrants should be necessary. The impact of the practice of third-party bugging, must, I think, be considered such as to undermine that confidence and sense of security in dealing with one another that is characteristic of individual relationships between citizens in a free society. It goes beyond the impact on privacy occasioned by the ordinary type of "informer" investigation upheld in *Lewis* and *Hoffa*. The argument of the plurality opinion, to the effect that it is irrelevant whether secrets are revealed by the mere tattletale or the transistor, ignores the differences occasioned by third-party monitoring and recording which insures full and accurate disclosure of all that is said, free of the possibility of error and oversight that inheres in human reporting.

Authority is hardly required to support the proposition that words would be measured a good deal more carefully and communication inhibited if one suspected his conversations were being transmitted and transcribed. Were third-party bugging a prevalent practice, it might well smother that spontaneity — reflected in frivolous, impetuous, sacrilegious, and defiant discourse — that liberates daily life. Much offhand exchange is easily forgotten and one may count on the obscurity of his remarks, protected by the very fact of a limited audience, and the likelihood that the listener will either overlook or forget what is said, as well as the listener's inability to reformulate a conversation without having to contend with a documented record. All these values are sacrificed by a rule of law that permits official monitoring of private discourse limited only by the need to locate a willing assistant. . . .

Interposition of a warrant requirement is designed not to shield "wrong-doers," but to secure a measure of privacy and a sense of personal security throughout our society. The Fourth Amendment does, of course, leave room for the employment of modern technology in criminal law enforcement, but in the stream of current developments in Fourth Amendment law I think it must be held that third-party electronic monitoring, subject only to the self-restraint of law enforcement officials, has no place in our society.

DOUGLAS, J. dissenting. . . . *On Lee* and *Lopez* are of a vintage opposed to *Berger* and *Katz*. However they may be explained, they are products of the old common-law notions of trespass. *Katz*, on the other hand, emphasized that with few exceptions "searches conducted outside the judicial process, without prior approval by judge or magistrate, are per se unreasonable under the Fourth Amendment.". . .

Monitoring, if prevalent, certainly kills free discourse and spontaneous utterances. Free discourse — a First Amendment value — may be frivolous or serious, humble or defiant, reactionary or revolutionary, profane or in good taste; but it is not free if there is surveillance. . . .

Now that the discredited decisions in *On Lee* and *Lopez* are resuscitated and revived, must everyone live in fear that every word he speaks may be transmitted or recorded and later repeated to the entire world? I can imagine nothing that has a more chilling effect on people speaking their minds and expressing their views on important matters. The advocates of that regime should spend some time in totalitarian countries and learn firsthand the kind of regime they are creating here. . . .

NOTES & QUESTIONS

1. **White *vs.* Katz.** Is this case more akin to the bugging in *On Lee* and *Lopez* rather than the wiretapping of *Katz*? Does it matter whether the police heard the conversation simultaneously? Suppose the conversation had been recorded by a hidden recorder and then handed over later to the police.

2. *Covert Agents and the Misplaced Trust Doctrine. White* suggests that the misplaced trust doctrine in *Hoffa, Lewis, Lopez,* and *On Lee* survives after *Katz.* Under the misplaced trust doctrine, people place their trust in others at their own peril and must assume the risk of betrayal. But should the misplaced trust doctrine survive after *Katz*? Do we have a reasonable expectation that our friends aren't government agents in disguise?

   In a comparative study of how the United States and Germany regulate undercover policing, Jacqueline Ross identifies numerous differences in the two legal systems.[14] She argues:

   > In Germany, undercover policing is a necessary evil in that it harms targets by invading their constitutionally protected right to privacy, along with other fundamental rights. . . . German law responds to these concerns through legislation that carves out special limitations on the most intrusive covert tactics, namely long-term deep cover operations. Viewing covert policing as an invasion of privacy assimilates it to other police powers, like searches and seizures. While these tactics burden civil liberties, they do so permissibly, through police compliance with procedural constraints such as warrant requirements. Because civil liberties may lawfully be compromised in the name of security, thinking of covert surveillance as invasions of privacy allows the legal system to justify the burdens that covert policing imposes on rights. This regulatory approach also entails the use of procedural constraints on how covert tactics may be authorized, alongside substantive limits on what undercover operatives may do.
   >
   > German privacy law protects dignitary interests, while American conceptions of privacy emphasize physical privacy in the home along with decisional privacy or autonomy. Germany's concern with individual dignity is part of the German Constitution's concern with safeguarding the "free development of personality," in direct reaction to the totalitarian oppression and violations of personal dignity under the Nazi regime. Invasions of privacy also have special salience for residents of the five new eastern states who remember the encompassing surveillance practiced more recently in the GDR [German Democratic Republic, also known as East Germany]. Given these concerns, police infiltration is deeply problematic. It interferes with the rights of all persons to control the face they present to the world; it reveals too much about the intimate details of a person's life; and it disrupts personal relationships. Giving constitutional status to these harms means that the government must satisfy certain requirements before inflicting them. Constitutional protection entails a warrant procedure, a showing of need, and statutory limits on the crimes that the government may target in this way.
   >
   > By contrast, the United States legal system does not treat undercover policing as an intrinsic invasion of privacy rights. Undercover policing is not

---

[14] Jacqueline E. Ross, *The Place of Covert Surveillance in Democratic Societies: A Comparative Study of the United States and Germany*, 55 Am. J. Comp. L. 493 (2007).

recognized as a search or seizure under the Fourth Amendment. Because they have no Fourth Amendment significance, undercover investigations require no warrant and no showing of probable cause or even reasonable suspicion as a matter of constitutional law. . . .

Conceiving of covert policing as a threat to privacy creates other problems for the legitimacy of these tactics. Framing the discourse in terms of constitutional rights (like the right to privacy) invites critics to identify other constitutional rights that may be at risk. Accordingly, German courts (unlike their American counterparts) have accepted defense arguments that the use of jail-house informers to squeeze admissions out of prisoners infringes on prisoners' autonomy, by taking advantage of targets' "psychological compulsion to unburden themselves." Critics also raise special objections to those sting operations by which undercover agents befriend and wring confessions from persons suspected of long-ago, unsolved crimes, arguing that these undercover contacts unfairly circumvent suspects' rights to counsel and their right not to incriminate themselves.

What would be the impact on law enforcement if *White* came out the other way after *Katz*? In other words, suppose that *Katz* eliminated the misplaced trust doctrine. How would the Fourth Amendment apply to covert agents or informers? Would this unduly hamper police investigations of drug rings, mafia activity, and terrorist cells?

3. ***Electronic Surveillance and the First Amendment.*** Justice Douglas contends that electronic surveillance impinges upon and chills freedom of expression for all individuals in society. Is electronic surveillance without a warrant consistent with the First Amendment? What kind of process should be required to make use of the warrant consistent with the First Amendment?

3. THE REASONABLE EXPECTATION OF PRIVACY TEST AND EMERGING TECHNOLOGY

(a) Applying the Reasonable Expectation of Privacy Test

SMITH V. MARYLAND

442 U.S. 735 (1979)

BLACKMUN, J. This case presents the question whether the installation and use of a pen register[15] constitutes a "search" within the meaning of the Fourth Amendment, made applicable to the States through the Fourteenth Amendment.

On March 5, 1976, in Baltimore, Md., Patricia McDonough was robbed. She gave the police a description of the robber and of a 1975 Monte Carlo automobile she had observed near the scene of the crime. After the robbery, McDonough began receiving threatening and obscene phone calls from a man identifying

---

[15] "A pen register is a mechanical device that records the numbers dialed on a telephone by monitoring the electrical impulses caused when the dial on the telephone is released. It does not overhear oral communications and does not indicate whether calls are actually completed." A pen register is "usually installed at a central telephone facility [and] records on a paper tape all numbers dialed from [the] line" to which it is attached.

himself as the robber. On one occasion, the caller asked that she step out on her front porch; she did so, and saw the 1975 Monte Carlo she had earlier described to police moving slowly past her home. On March 16, police spotted a man who met McDonough's description driving a 1975 Monte Carlo in her neighborhood. By tracing the license plate number, police learned that the car was registered in the name of petitioner, Michael Lee Smith.

The next day, the telephone company, at police request, installed a pen register at its central offices to record the numbers dialed from the telephone at petitioner's home. The police did not get a warrant or court order before having the pen register installed. The register revealed that on March 17 a call was placed from petitioner's home to McDonough's phone. On the basis of this and other evidence, the police obtained a warrant to search petitioner's residence. [A search of Smith's home revealed more evidence that Smith was the robber. Smith moved to suppress all evidence obtained from (and derived from) the pen register. The trial court denied his motion, and Smith was convicted and sentenced to six years' imprisonment.] . . .

The Fourth Amendment guarantees "[t]he right of the people to be secure in their persons, houses, papers, and effects, against unreasonable searches and seizures." In determining whether a particular form of government-initiated electronic surveillance is a "search" within the meaning of the Fourth Amendment,[16] our lodestar is *Katz v. United States*, 389 U.S. 347 (1967). . . .

Consistently with *Katz,* this Court uniformly has held that the application of the Fourth Amendment depends on whether the person invoking its protection can claim a "justifiable," a "reasonable," or a "legitimate expectation of privacy" that has been invaded by government action. This inquiry, as Mr. Justice Harlan aptly noted in his *Katz* concurrence, normally embraces two discrete questions. The first is whether the individual, by his conduct, has "exhibited an actual (subjective) expectation of privacy," — whether, in the words of the *Katz* majority, the individual has shown that "he seeks to preserve [something] as private." The second question is whether the individual's subjective expectation of privacy is "one that society is prepared to recognize as 'reasonable,' — whether, in the words of the *Katz* majority, the individual's expectation, viewed objectively, is "justifiable" under the circumstances.[17]

---

[16] In this case, the pen register was installed, and the numbers dialed were recorded, by the telephone company. The telephone company, however, acted at police request. In view of this, respondent appears to concede that the company is to be deemed an "agent" of the police for purposes of this case, so as to render the installation and use of the pen register "state action" under the Fourth and Fourteenth Amendments. We may assume that "state action" was present here.

[17] Situations can be imagined, of course, in which *Katz*'s two-pronged inquiry would provide an inadequate index of Fourth Amendment protection. For example, if the Government were suddenly to announce on nationwide television that all homes henceforth would be subject to warrantless entry, individuals thereafter might not in fact entertain any actual expectation or privacy regarding their homes, papers, and effects. Similarly, if a refugee from a totalitarian country, unaware of this Nation's traditions, erroneously assumed that police were continuously monitoring his telephone conversations, a subjective expectation of privacy regarding the contents of his calls might be lacking as well. In such circumstances, where an individual's subjective expectations had been "conditioned" by influences alien to well-recognized Fourth Amendment freedoms, those subjective expectations obviously could play no meaningful role in ascertaining what the scope of Fourth Amendment protection was. In determining whether a "legitimate expectation of privacy" existed in such cases, a normative inquiry would be proper.

In applying the *Katz* analysis to this case, it is important to begin by specifying precisely the nature of the state activity that is challenged. The activity here took the form of installing and using a pen register. Since the pen register was installed on telephone company property at the telephone company's central offices, petitioner obviously cannot claim that his "property" was invaded or that police intruded into a "constitutionally protected area." Petitioner's claim, rather, is that, notwithstanding the absence of a trespass, the State, as did the Government in *Katz*, infringed a "legitimate expectation of privacy" that petitioner held. Yet a pen register differs significantly from the listening device employed in *Katz*, for pen registers do not acquire the contents of communications. This Court recently noted:

> Indeed, a law enforcement official could not even determine from the use of a pen register whether a communication existed. These devices do not hear sound. They disclose only the telephone numbers that have been dialed — a means of establishing communication. Neither the purport of any communication between the caller and the recipient of the call, their identities, nor whether the call was even completed is disclosed by pen registers. *United States v. New York Tel. Co.*, 434 U.S. 159, 167 (1977).

Given a pen register's limited capabilities, therefore, petitioner's argument that its installation and use constituted a "search" necessarily rests upon a claim that he had a "legitimate expectation of privacy" regarding the numbers he dialed on his phone.

This claim must be rejected. First, we doubt that people in general entertain any actual expectation of privacy in the numbers they dial. All telephone users realize that they must "convey" phone numbers to the telephone company, since it is through telephone company switching equipment that their calls are completed. All subscribers realize, moreover, that the phone company has facilities for making permanent records of the numbers they dial, for they see a list of their long-distance (toll) calls on their monthly bills. In fact, pen registers and similar devices are routinely used by telephone companies "for the purposes of checking billing operations, detecting fraud and preventing violations of law." Electronic equipment is used not only to keep billing records of toll calls, but also "to keep a record of all calls dialed from a telephone which is subject to a special rate structure." Pen registers are regularly employed "to determine whether a home phone is being used to conduct a business, to check for a defective dial, or to check for overbilling." Although most people may be oblivious to a pen register's esoteric functions, they presumably have some awareness of one common use: to aid in the identification of persons making annoying or obscene calls. Most phone books tell subscribers, on a page entitled "Consumer Information," that the company "can frequently help in identifying to the authorities the origin of unwelcome and troublesome calls." Telephone users, in sum, typically know that they must convey numerical information to the phone company; that the phone company has facilities for recording this information; and that the phone company does in fact record this information for a variety of legitimate business purposes. Although subjective expectations cannot be scientifically gauged, it is too much to believe that telephone subscribers, under these circumstances, harbor any general expectation that the numbers they dial will remain secret.

Petitioner argues, however, that, whatever the expectations of telephone users in general, he demonstrated an expectation of privacy by his own conduct here, since he "us[ed] the telephone *in his house* to the exclusion of all others." But the site of the call is immaterial for purposes of analysis in this case. Although petitioner's conduct may have been calculated to keep the *contents* of his conversation private, his conduct was not and could not have been calculated to preserve the privacy of the number he dialed. Regardless of his location, petitioner had to convey that number to the telephone company in precisely the same way if he wished to complete his call. The fact that he dialed the number on his home phone rather than on some other phone could make no conceivable difference, nor could any subscriber rationally think that it would. Second, even if petitioner did harbor some subjective expectation that the phone numbers he dialed would remain private, this expectation is not "one that society is prepared to recognize as 'reasonable.'" This Court consistently has held that a person has no legitimate expectation of privacy in information he voluntarily turns over to third parties. In [*United States v.*] *Miller*, for example, the Court held that a bank depositor has no "legitimate 'expectation of privacy'" in financial information "voluntarily conveyed to . . . banks and exposed to their employees in the ordinary course of business." The Court explained:

> The depositor takes the risk, in revealing his affairs to another, that the information will be conveyed by that person to the Government. . . . This Court has held repeatedly that the Fourth Amendment does not prohibit the obtaining of information revealed to a third party and conveyed by him to Government authorities, even if the information is revealed on the assumption that it will be used only for a limited purpose and the confidence placed in the third party will not be betrayed.

Because the depositor "assumed the risk" of disclosure, the Court held that it would be unreasonable for him to expect his financial records to remain private.

This analysis dictates that petitioner can claim no legitimate expectation of privacy here. When he used his phone, petitioner voluntarily conveyed numerical information to the telephone company and "exposed" that information to its equipment in the ordinary course of business. In so doing, petitioner assumed the risk that the company would reveal to police the numbers he dialed. The switching equipment that processed those numbers is merely the modern counterpart of the operator who, in an earlier day, personally completed calls for the subscriber. Petitioner concedes that if he had placed his calls through an operator, he could claim no legitimate expectation of privacy. We are not inclined to hold that a different constitutional result is required because the telephone company has decided to automate.

Petitioner argues, however, that automatic switching equipment differs from a live operator in one pertinent respect. An operator, in theory at least, is capable of remembering every number that is conveyed to him by callers. Electronic equipment, by contrast can "remember" only those numbers it is programmed to record, and telephone companies, in view of their present billing practices, usually do not record local calls. Since petitioner, in calling McDonough, was making a local call, his expectation of privacy as to her number, on this theory, would be "legitimate."

This argument does not withstand scrutiny. The fortuity of whether or not the phone company in fact elects to make a quasi-permanent record of a particular number dialed does not in our view, make any constitutional difference. Regardless of the phone company's election, petitioner voluntarily conveyed to it information that it had facilities for recording and that it was free to record. In these circumstances, petitioner assumed the risk that the information would be divulged to police. . . .

STEWART, J. joined by BRENNAN, J. dissenting. . . . The numbers dialed from a private telephone — although certainly more prosaic than the conversation itself — are not without "content." Most private telephone subscribers may have their own numbers listed in a publicly distributed directory, but I doubt there are any who would be happy to have broadcast to the world a list of the local or long distance numbers they have called. This is not because such a list might in some sense be incriminating, but because it easily could reveal the identities of the persons and the places called, and thus reveal the most intimate details of a person's life.

MARSHALL, J. joined by BRENNAN, J. dissenting. . . . Privacy is not a discrete commodity, possessed absolutely or not at all. Those who disclose certain facts to a bank or phone company for a limited business purpose need not assume that this information will be released to other persons for other purposes.

The crux of the Court's holding, however, is that whatever expectation of privacy petitioner may in fact have entertained regarding his calls, it is not one "society is prepared to recognize as 'reasonable.'" In so ruling, the Court determines that individuals who convey information to third parties have "assumed the risk" of disclosure to the government. This analysis is misconceived in two critical respects.

Implicit in the concept of assumption of risk is some notion of choice. At least in the third-party consensual surveillance cases, which first incorporated risk analysis into Fourth Amendment doctrine, the defendant presumably had exercised some discretion in deciding who should enjoy his confidential communications. By contrast here, unless a person is prepared to forgo use of what for many has become a personal or professional necessity, he cannot help but accept the risk of surveillance. It is idle to speak of "assuming" risks in contexts where, as a practical matter, individuals have no realistic alternative.

More fundamentally, to make risk analysis dispositive in assessing the reasonableness of privacy expectations would allow the government to define the scope of Fourth Amendment protections. For example, law enforcement officials, simply by announcing their intent to monitor the content of random samples of first-class mail or private phone conversations, could put the public on notice of the risks they would thereafter assume in such communications. . . .

In my view, whether privacy expectations are legitimate within the meaning of *Katz* depends not on the risks an individual can be presumed to accept when imparting information to third parties, but on the risks he should be forced to assume in a free and open society. . . .

The use of pen registers, I believe, constitutes such an extensive intrusion. To hold otherwise ignores the vital role telephonic communication plays in our personal and professional relationships, as well as the First and Fourth Amendment interests implicated by unfettered official surveillance. Privacy in placing calls is of value not only to those engaged in criminal activity. The prospect of unregulated governmental monitoring will undoubtedly prove disturbing even to those with nothing illicit to hide. Many individuals, including members of unpopular political organizations or journalists with confidential sources, may legitimately wish to avoid disclosure of their personal contacts. Permitting governmental access to telephone records on less than probable cause may thus impede certain forms of political affiliation and journalistic endeavor that are the hallmark of a truly free society. Particularly given the Government's previous reliance on warrantless telephonic surveillance to trace reporters' sources and monitor protected political activity, I am unwilling to insulate use of pen registers from independent judicial review. . . .

NOTES & QUESTIONS

1. *Pen Registers and Trap and Trace Devices.* A pen register records outgoing telephone calls. Another device, known as a trap and trace device, records all incoming calls. In *Smith v. Maryland*, the Supreme Court ruled that a use of pen registers or trap and trace devices was not a form of wiretap (akin to that in *Katz*). What are the critical differences between the pen register and trap and device, on the one hand, and the wiretap, on the other?

2. *Critiques of the* Smith *Decision.* Consider the following observation by Laurence Tribe about *Smith*:

> The "assumption of risk" — more aptly, "assumption of broadcast" — notion underling the holding in *Smith* . . . reveals alarming tendencies in the Supreme Court's understanding of what privacy means and ought to mean. The Court treats privacy almost as if it were "a discrete commodity, possessed absolutely or not at all" [quoting Justice Marshall's dissent]. Yet what could be more commonplace than the idea that it is up to the *individual* to *measure out information* about herself *selectively* — to whomever she chooses?[18]

Patricia Bellia contends that *Smith* conflicts with *Katz*: "In *Katz*, the phone company necessarily carried the defendant's telephone call, and the phone company no doubt had the technical ability to hear the contents of that call. That technical ability, however, was no impediment to the Court's conclusion that Katz had an expectation of privacy in the conversation."[19] Likewise, Susan Freiwald contends: "The *Smith* court ignored the lesson of *Katz*: We do not lose privacy in communications merely because they may be intercepted." She goes on to argue that the Court in *Smith* "avoided normative analysis and failed to consider how much privacy the law should actually grant to

---

[18] Laurence Tribe, *American Constitutional Law* 1391 (2d ed. 1988). For another critique of *Smith v. Maryland*, see Daniel J. Solove, *Digital Dossiers and the Dissipation*, 75 S. Cal. L. Rev. 1083 (2002).

[19] Patricia Bellia, *Surveillance Law Through Cyberlaw's Lens*, 72 Geo. Wash. L. Rev. 1375, 1405 (2004).

information. If the law treats information as private, then it will not be acceptable to acquire it, even when it possible to do so."[20]

Deirdre Mulligan explains that the Court addressed the discrepancies between *Katz* and *Smith* by discussing in *Smith* "at some length the limited information that can be gleaned from a phone number, contrasting it with what may be revealed from a telephone conversation."[21] Does the holding of *Smith* rest on the fact that the numbers were exposed to a third party or on the fact that the numbers revealed limited information about a person or on both of these factors?

3. **State Constitutional Law.** Some states have rejected the *Smith* holding under their constitutions. For example, in *State v. Hunt*, 450 A.2d 952 (N.J. 1982), the New Jersey Supreme Court rejected *Smith* and held that under the New Jersey Constitution, there is a reasonable expectation of privacy in telephone records:

> The telephone has become an essential instrument in carrying on our personal affairs. It has become part and parcel of the home. When a telephone call is made, it is as if two people are having a private conversation in the sanctity of their living room. . . .
>
> The telephone caller is . . . entitled to assume that the numbers he dials in the privacy of his home will be recorded solely for the telephone company's business purposes. From the viewpoint of the customer, all the information which he furnishes with respect to a particular call is private. The numbers dialed are private. . . .
>
> It is unrealistic to say that the cloak of privacy has been shed because the telephone company and some of its employees are aware of this information. Telephone calls cannot be made except through the telephone company's property and without payment to it for the service. This disclosure has been necessitated because of the nature of the instrumentality, but more significantly the disclosure has been made for a limited business purpose and not for release to other persons for other reasons. . . .

In an analysis of state constitutional law, Stephen Henderson concludes that 11 states have rejected the third party doctrine. Ten more states have not explicitly rejected the third party doctrine, but have case law suggesting that they might do so in the future.[22]

4. **Federal Statutory Law.** Sometimes when the Court fails to identify a privacy interest involving some aspect of the collection of personal information, Congress responds by enacting legislation that provides protection by statutory means. That happened after *Smith* with the Pen Register Act, 18 U.S.C. §§ 3121–3127. This statute requires that the government obtain a court order by certifying that the use of a pen register is "relevant to an ongoing

---

[20] Susan Freiwald, *Online Surveillance: Remembering the Lessons of the Wiretap Act,* 56 Ala. L. Rev. 9, 40, 66 (2004).

[21] Deirdre K. Mulligan, *Reasonable Expectations in Electronic Communications: A Critical Perspective on the Electronic Communications Privacy Act,* 72 Geo. Wash. L. Rev. 1557, 1581 (2004).

[22] Stephen E. Henderson, *Learning from All Fifty States: How to Apply the Fourth Amendment and Its State Analogues to Protect Third Party Information from Unreasonable Seizure,* 55 Cath. U. L. Rev. 373, 395 (2006).

investigation." This standard, however, is significantly less stringent than the probable cause required to obtain a Fourth Amendment warrant.

5. ***Critiques and Defenses of the Third Party Doctrine.*** Susan Brenner and Leo Clark argue that the third party doctrine is flawed because it assumes that a "disclosure to a trusted, reputable [third party] is the same as indiscriminate disclosure to the public." If we disclose information on a public website, "we have clearly demonstrated our lack of interest in controlling access to the information in question." In contrast, when we share information with third parties, these are "controlled disclosures, in that they represent the limited, focused sharing of information with a [third party] as an integral part of a legitimate transaction."[23]

Daniel Solove contends that "the third party doctrine is one of the greatest threats to privacy in our times." He argues that because so much of our information is now in the hands of third parties, the third party doctrine will eviscerate Fourth Amendment protection. He further contends:

> According to the third party doctrine . . . even a written contract isn't enough to give people an expectation of privacy. But promises and contracts are the foundation of modern civil society. If people couldn't reply on them, business and commerce would grind to a halt. Yet when it comes to privacy, the U.S. Supreme Court thinks that promises and contracts don't matter.[24]

Taking a different approach, Thomas Crocker contrasts the third party doctrine with the Supreme Court's protection of interpersonal relations in *Lawrence v. Texas,* 539 U.S. 558 (2003), where it invalidated a Texas state statute criminalizing homosexual sodomy. While the *Lawrence* Court protected "conduct important to interpersonal relations," the third party doctrine leads to a view that "privacy protects only what we keep to ourselves."[25]

Orin Kerr defends the third party doctrine. In his view, it "ensures technological neutrality in Fourth Amendment rules." He argues that

> criminals could use third-party agents to fully enshroud their criminal enterprises in Fourth Amendment protection. A criminal could plot and execute his entire crime from home knowing that the police could not send in undercover agents, record the fact of his phone calls, or watch any aspect of his Internet usage without first obtaining a warrant. He could use third parties to create a bubble of Fourth Amendment protection around the entirety of his criminal activity.

Kerr concludes that the "third-party doctrine blocks such efforts, resulting in a rough equivalence in the overall amount of privacy for criminals acting

---

[23] Susan W. Brenner & Leo L. Clarke, *Fourth Amendment Protection for Shared Privacy Rights in Stored Transactional Data*, 14 J.L. & Pol'y 211, 258 (2006). For another critique of the third party doctrine, see Stephen E. Henderson, Beyond the (Current) Fourth Amendment: Protecting Third-Party Information, Third Parties, and the Rest of Us Too, 34 Pepp. L. Rev. 975 (2007).

[24] Daniel J. Solove, *Nothing to Hide: The False Tradeoff Between Privacy and Security* 13, 108-09 (2011).

[25] Thomas P. Crocker, *From Privacy to Liberty: The Fourth Amendment After* Lawrence, 57 UCLA L. Rev. 1 (2009).

alone and the amount of privacy for those using third parties."[26] Does modern technology make detecting crime more difficult as Kerr contends? It can also make investigating crime easier. How should the Fourth Amendment respond when new technology affects the way crimes are committed and investigated?

6. *The First Amendment and Pen Register Information.* Daniel Solove argues that the First Amendment should be understood as a source of criminal procedure and should protect pen register information:

> Although the Supreme Court has focused on the Fourth Amendment, obtaining pen register data without a warrant potentially violates the First Amendment. A log of incoming and outgoing calls can be used to trace channels of communication. It is relatively easy to link a phone number to a person or organization. Pen registers can reveal associational ties, since association in contemporary times often occurs by way of telephone or e-mail. As David Cole argues, modern communications technology has made association possible without physical assembly. For example, if the government scrutinized the phone logs of the main office of the Communist Party, it might discover many of the Party's members. The information would not be equivalent to a membership list, but it would probably include identifying data about countless individuals who would not want the government to discover their connection to the Communist Party. If the government were to examine the phone logs or e-mail headers of a particular individual, it might discover that the individual contacted particular organizations that the individual wants to keep private. The pen register information, therefore, implicates First Amendment values.[27]

Solove contends that government access to pen register information can violate the First Amendment, and he goes on to argue that the First Amendment should require a warrant before the government can obtain such information. Does pen register information implicate the First Amendment? If so, what kind of protections should the First Amendment require?

Neil Richards also contends that the First Amendment protects what he calls "intellectual privacy." According to Richards:

> Intellectual privacy is the ability, whether protected by law or social circumstances, to develop ideas and beliefs away from the unwanted gaze or interference of others. Surveillance or interference can warp the integrity of our freedom of thought and can skew the way we think, with clear repercussions for the content of our subsequent speech or writing. The ability to freely make up our minds and to develop new ideas thus depends upon a substantial measure of intellectual privacy. In this way, intellectual privacy is a cornerstone of meaningful First Amendment liberties.

---

[26] Orin S. Kerr, *The Case for the Third-Party Doctrine*, 107 Mich. L. Rev. 561, 575-76 (2009). For a critique of Kerr's article, see Richard A. Epstein, *Privacy and the Third Hand: Lessons from the Common Law of Reasonable Expectations*, 24 Berkeley Tech. L.J. 1199 (2009); Erin Murphy, *The Case Against the Case for the Third Party Doctrine: A Response to Epstein and Kerr*, 24 Berkeley Tech. L.J. 1239 (2009).

[27] Daniel J. Solove, *The First Amendment as Criminal Procedure*, 82 N.Y.U. L. Rev. 112, 169 (2007).

According to Richards, the government can implicate intellectual privacy when it

> seeks to secretly obtain from third parties intellectual records such as book purchases, library records, Web-use histories, and search-engine queries. Such records reveal not just reading habits but intellectual interests, and in the case of search-engine records come very close to being a transcript of the operation of a human mind. As such, they threaten both the freedom of thought and the freedom of intellectual exploration.[28]

Richards argues that when intellectual privacy is involved, heightened constitutional protections should be required. How would Richards's notion of intellectual privacy apply to pen registers?

UNITED STATES V. PLACE

462 U.S. 696 (1983)

O'CONNOR, J. The Fourth Amendment "protects people from unreasonable government intrusions into their legitimate expectations of privacy." We have affirmed that a person possesses a privacy interest in the contents of personal luggage that is protected by the Fourth Amendment. A "canine sniff" by a well-trained narcotics detection dog, however, does not require opening the luggage. It does not expose noncontraband items that otherwise would remain hidden from public view, as does, for example, an officer's rummaging through the contents of the luggage. Thus, the manner in which information is obtained through this investigative technique is much less intrusive than a typical search. Moreover, the sniff discloses only the presence or absence of narcotics, a contraband item. Thus, despite the fact that the sniff tells the authorities something about the contents of the luggage, the information obtained is limited. This limited disclosure also ensures that the owner of the property is not subjected to the embarrassment and inconvenience entailed in less discriminate and more intrusive investigative methods.

In these respects, the canine sniff is *sui generis*. We are aware of no other investigative procedure that is so limited both in the manner in which the information is obtained and in the content of the information revealed by the procedure. Therefore, we conclude that the particular course of investigation that the agents intended to pursue here — exposure of respondent's luggage, which was located in a public place, to a trained canine — did not constitute a "search" within the meaning of the Fourth Amendment. . . .

---

[28] Neil M. Richards, *Intellectual Privacy,* 87 Tex. L. Rev. 387, 389, 439 (2008).

ILLINOIS V. CABALLES

543 U.S. 405 (2005)

STEVENS, J. Illinois State Trooper Daniel Gillette stopped respondent for speeding on an interstate highway. When Gillette radioed the police dispatcher to report the stop, a second trooper, Craig Graham, a member of the Illinois State Police Drug Interdiction Team, overheard the transmission and immediately headed for the scene with his narcotics-detection dog. When they arrived, respondent's car was on the shoulder of the road and respondent was in Gillette's vehicle. While Gillette was in the process of writing a warning ticket, Graham walked his dog around respondent's car. The dog alerted at the trunk. Based on that alert, the officers searched the trunk, found marijuana, and arrested respondent. The entire incident lasted less than 10 minutes.

Respondent was convicted of a narcotics offense and sentenced to 12 years' imprisonment and a $256,136 fine. . . .

The question on which we granted certiorari is narrow: "Whether the Fourth Amendment requires reasonable, articulable suspicion to justify using a drug-detection dog to sniff a vehicle during a legitimate traffic stop." Thus, we proceed on the assumption that the officer conducting the dog sniff had no information about respondent except that he had been stopped for speeding; accordingly, we have omitted any reference to facts about respondent that might have triggered a modicum of suspicion. . . .

In our view, conducting a dog sniff would not change the character of a traffic stop that is lawful at its inception and otherwise executed in a reasonable manner, unless the dog sniff itself infringed respondent's constitutionally protected interest in privacy. Our cases hold that it did not.

Official conduct that does not "compromise any legitimate interest in privacy" is not a search subject to the Fourth Amendment. We have held that any interest in possessing contraband cannot be deemed "legitimate," and thus, governmental conduct that *only* reveals the possession of contraband "compromises no legitimate privacy interest." This is because the expectation "that certain facts will not come to the attention of the authorities" is not the same as an interest in "privacy that society is prepared to consider reasonable." In *United States v. Place,* 462 U.S. 696 (1983), we treated a canine sniff by a well-trained narcotics-detection dog as "*sui generis*" because it "discloses only the presence or absence of narcotics, a contraband item." Respondent likewise concedes that "drug sniffs are designed, and if properly conducted are generally likely, to reveal only the presence of contraband." Although respondent argues that the error rates, particularly the existence of false positives, call into question the premise that drug-detection dogs alert only to contraband, the record contains no evidence or findings that support his argument. Moreover, respondent does not suggest that an erroneous alert, in and of itself, reveals any legitimate private information, and, in this case, the trial judge found that the dog sniff was sufficiently reliable to establish probable cause to conduct a full-blown search of the trunk.

Accordingly, the use of a well-trained narcotics-detection dog—one that "does not expose noncontraband items that otherwise would remain hidden from public view," *Place,* 462 U.S., at 707, during a lawful traffic stop, generally does not implicate legitimate privacy interests. In this case, the dog sniff was performed on the exterior of respondent's car while he was lawfully seized for a traffic violation. Any intrusion on respondent's privacy expectations does not rise to the level of a constitutionally cognizable infringement.

SOUTER, J., dissenting. I would hold that using the dog for the purposes of determining the presence of marijuana in the car's trunk was a search unauthorized as an incident of the speeding stop and unjustified on any other ground. I would accordingly affirm the judgment of the Supreme Court of Illinois, and I respectfully dissent.

At the heart both of *Place* and the Court's opinion today is the proposition that sniffs by a trained dog are *sui generis* because a reaction by the dog in going alert is a response to nothing but the presence of contraband.[29] Hence, the argument goes, because the sniff can only reveal the presence of items devoid of any legal use, the sniff "does not implicate legitimate privacy interests" and is not to be treated as a search.

The infallible dog, however, is a creature of legal fiction. Although the Supreme Court of Illinois did not get into the sniffing averages of drug dogs, their supposed infallibility is belied by judicial opinions describing well-trained animals sniffing and alerting with less than perfect accuracy, whether owing to errors by their handlers, the limitations of the dogs themselves, or even the pervasive contamination of currency by cocaine. *See, e.g., United States v. Kennedy,* 131 F.3d 1371, 1378 (C.A.10 1997) (describing a dog that had a 71% accuracy rate); *United States v. Scarborough,* 128 F.3d 1373, 1378, n. 3 (C.A.10 1997) (describing a dog that erroneously alerted 4 times out of 19 while working for the postal service and 8% of the time over its entire career); *United States v. Limares,* 269 F.3d 794, 797 (C.A.7 2001) (accepting as reliable a dog that gave false positives between 7 and 38% of the time); *Laime v. State,* 347 Ark. 142, 159, 60 S.W.3d 464, 476 (2001) (speaking of a dog that made between 10 and 50 errors); *United States v. $242,484.00,* 351 F.3d 499, 511 (C.A.11 2003) (noting that because as much as 80% of all currency in circulation contains drug residue, a dog alert "is of little value"). . . . Indeed, a study cited by Illinois in this case for the proposition that dog sniffs are "generally reliable" shows that dogs in artificial testing situations return false positives anywhere from 12.5 to 60% of the time, depending on the length of the search. In practical terms, the evidence is clear that the dog that alerts hundreds of times will be wrong dozens of times.

Once the dog's fallibility is recognized, however, that ends the justification claimed in *Place* for treating the sniff as *sui generis* under the Fourth Amendment: the sniff alert does not necessarily signal hidden contraband, and opening the container or enclosed space whose emanations the dog has sensed will not necessarily reveal contraband or any other evidence of crime. This is not, of course, to deny that a dog's reaction may provide reasonable suspicion, or

---

[29] Another proffered justification for *sui generis* status is that a dog sniff is a particularly nonintrusive procedure. *United States v. Place,* 462 U.S. 696, 707 (1983). I agree with Justice Ginsburg that the introduction of a dog to a traffic stop (let alone an encounter with someone walking down the street) can in fact be quite intrusive.

probable cause, to search the container or enclosure; the Fourth Amendment does not demand certainty of success to justify a search for evidence or contraband. The point is simply that the sniff and alert cannot claim the certainty that *Place* assumed, both in treating the deliberate use of sniffing dogs as *sui generis* and then taking that characterization as a reason to say they are not searches subject to Fourth Amendment scrutiny. And when that aura of uniqueness disappears, there is no basis in *Place*'s reasoning, and no good reason otherwise, to ignore the actual function that dog sniffs perform. They are conducted to obtain information about the contents of private spaces beyond anything that human senses could perceive, even when conventionally enhanced. The information is not provided by independent third parties beyond the reach of constitutional limitations, but gathered by the government's own officers in order to justify searches of the traditional sort, which may or may not reveal evidence of crime but will disclose anything meant to be kept private in the area searched. Thus in practice the government's use of a trained narcotics dog functions as a limited search to reveal undisclosed facts about private enclosures, to be used to justify a further and complete search of the enclosed area. And given the fallibility of the dog, the sniff is the first step in a process that may disclose "intimate details" without revealing contraband. . . .

GINSBURG and SOUTER, JJ., dissenting. . . . In *Terry v. Ohio,* the Court upheld the stop and subsequent frisk of an individual based on an officer's observation of suspicious behavior and his reasonable belief that the suspect was armed. . . . In a *Terry*-type investigatory stop, "the officer's action [must be] justified at its inception, and . . . reasonably related in scope to the circumstances which justified the interference in the first place." In applying *Terry,* the Court has several times indicated that the limitation on "scope" is not confined to the duration of the seizure; it also encompasses the manner in which the seizure is conducted. . . .

Terry, it merits repetition, instructs that any investigation must be "reasonably related in *scope* to the circumstances which justified the interference in the first place" (emphasis added). The unwarranted and nonconsensual expansion of the seizure here from a routine traffic stop to a drug investigation broadened the scope of the investigation in a manner that, in my judgment, runs afoul of the Fourth Amendment. . . .

A drug-detection dog is an intimidating animal. Injecting such an animal into a routine traffic stop changes the character of the encounter between the police and the motorist. The stop becomes broader, more adversarial, and (in at least some cases) longer. Caballes — who, as far as Troopers Gillette and Graham knew, was guilty solely of driving six miles per hour over the speed limit—was exposed to the embarrassment and intimidation of being investigated, on a public thoroughfare, for drugs.

NOTES & QUESTIONS

1. ***Detecting Only Illegal Contraband.*** Suppose the police had used a special x-ray machine to examine the contents of the bag. Would this be a Fourth Amendment violation under *Caballes*? Why or why not? Suppose that an x-ray device could be developed that would only detect illegal items, such as drugs, child pornography, weapons, or stolen items. Would the use of such a device to examine the contents of a person's bag or home constitute a search?

2. ***Is the Fourth Amendment Primarily Protective of the Individual or Society?*** Consider the following observation by Anthony Amsterdam:

> [Should the Fourth Amendment] be viewed as a collection of protections of atomistic spheres of interest of individual citizens or as a regulation of governmental conduct[?] Does it safeguard *my* person and *your* house and *her* papers and *his* effects against unreasonable searches and seizures; or is it essentially a regulatory canon requiring government to order its law enforcement procedures in a fashion that keeps us collectively secure in our persons, houses, papers, and effects, against unreasonable searches and seizures?[30]

> Under what view does the Supreme Court seem to be operating? Which view do you think is the most appropriate?

3. ***Is Government Observation Different from Observation by Others?*** Amsterdam also argues that one's privacy may be violated by being observed by the police but may not be violated by the very same observation from others:

> [I]f you live in a cheap hotel or in a ghetto flat, your neighbors can hear you breathing quietly even in temperate weather when it is possible to keep the windows and doors closed. For the tenement dweller, the difference between observation by neighbors and visitors who ordinarily use the common hallways and observation by policemen who come into hallways to "check up" or "look around" is the difference between all the privacy that his condition allows and none. Is that small difference too unimportant to claim [F]ourth [A]mendment protection?[31]

> Do you agree that our expectations of privacy turn on who is watching rather than simply whether we are being watched? Should the "reasonable expectation of privacy" test be changed to the "reasonable expectation of what the police can observe or search" test?

4. ***Bomb Detection vs. Drug Detection?*** The dissents of both Justice Souter and Justice Ginsburg in *Caballes* distinguish a canine search for drugs from one for bombs. Justice Souter argued in a footnote of his dissent that he reserved judgment concerning "a possible case significantly unlike this one":

---

[30] Anthony G. Amsterdam, *Perspectives on the Fourth Amendment*, 58 Minn. L. Rev. 349, 367 (1974). For an additional critique of the reasonable expectation of privacy test, see Andrew E. Taslitz, *The Fourth Amendment in the Twenty-First Century: Technology, Privacy, and Human Emotions,* 65 Law & Contemp. Probs. 125 (2002).

[31] Amsterdam, *Fourth Amendment, supra,* at 404.

All of us are concerned not to prejudge a claim of authority to detect explosives and dangerous chemical or biological weapons that might be carried by a terrorist who prompts no individualized suspicion. Suffice it to say here that what is a reasonable search depends in part on demonstrated risk. Unreasonable sniff searches for marijuana are not necessarily unreasonable sniff searches for destructive or deadly material if suicide bombs are a societal risk.

For Justice Ginsburg, the use of a bomb-detection dog to check vehicles would be closer to sobriety checkpoints that the Supreme Court has upheld. *Michigan Dep't of State Police v. Sitz*, 496 U.S. 444 (1990). Do you agree with these attempts to distinguish dogs that detect bombs from those that detect drugs?

CALIFORNIA V. GREENWOOD
486 U.S. 35 (1988)

[Police investigators searched the plastic garbage bags that Greenwood left on the curb in front of his house to be picked up by the trash collector. The officers found indications of drug use from the search of Greenwood's trash and obtained a warrant to search the house, where they uncovered more evidence of drug trafficking. Greenwood was arrested.]

WHITE, J. . . . The warrantless search and seizure of the garbage bags left at the curb outside the Greenwood house would violate the Fourth Amendment only if respondents manifested a subjective expectation of privacy in their garbage that society accepts as objectively reasonable.

. . . [The Greenwoods] assert . . . that they had, and exhibited, an expectation of privacy with respect to the trash that was searched by the police: The trash, which was placed on the street for collection at a fixed time, was contained in opaque plastic bags, which the garbage collector was expected to pick up, mingle with the trash of others, and deposit at the garbage dump. The trash was only temporarily on the street, and there was little likelihood that it would be inspected by anyone.

It may well be that respondents did not expect that the contents of their garbage bags would become known to the police or other members of the public. An expectation of privacy does not give rise to Fourth Amendment protection, however, unless society is prepared to accept that expectation as objectively reasonable.

Here, we conclude that respondents exposed their garbage to the public sufficiently to defeat their claim to Fourth Amendment protection. It is common knowledge that plastic garbage bags left on or at the side of a public street are readily accessible to animals, children, scavengers, snoops, and other members of the public. Moreover, respondents placed their refuse at the curb for the express purpose of conveying it to a third party, the trash collector, who might himself have sorted through respondents' trash or permitted others, such as the police, to do so. Accordingly, having deposited their garbage "in an area particularly suited for public inspection and, in a manner of speaking, public consumption, for the express purpose of having strangers take it," respondents could have had no reasonable expectation of privacy in the inculpatory items that they discarded. . .

BRENNAN, J. joined by MARSHALL, J. dissenting. . . . Scrutiny of another's trash is contrary to commonly accepted notions of civilized behavior. I suspect, therefore, that members of our society will be shocked to learn that the Court, the ultimate guarantor of liberty, deems unreasonable our expectation that the aspects of our private lives that are concealed safely in a trash bag will not become public.

"A container which can support a reasonable expectation of privacy may not be searched, even on probable cause, without a warrant." *United States v. Jacobsen*, 466 U.S. 109, 120, n.17 (1984) (citations omitted). Thus, as the Court observes, if Greenwood had a reasonable expectation that the contents of the bags that he placed on the curb would remain private, the warrantless search of those bags violated the Fourth Amendment. . . .

Our precedent, therefore, leaves no room to doubt that had respondents been carrying their personal effects in opaque, sealed plastic bags — identical to the ones they placed on the curb — their privacy would have been protected from warrantless police intrusion. . . .

Respondents deserve no less protection just because Greenwood used the bags to discard rather than to transport his personal effects. Their contents are not inherently any less private, and Greenwood's decision to discard them, at least in the manner in which he did, does not diminish his expectation of privacy.

A trash bag, like any of the above-mentioned containers, "is a common repository for one's personal effects" and, even more than many of them, is "therefore . . . inevitably associated with the expectation of privacy." "[A]lmost every human activity ultimately manifests itself in waste products. . . ." *Smith v. State*, 510 P.2d 793, 798 (Alaska 1973). A single bag of trash testifies eloquently to the eating, reading, and recreational habits of the person who produced it. A search of trash, like a search of the bedroom, can relate intimate details about sexual practices, health, and personal hygiene. Like rifling through desk drawers or intercepting phone calls, rummaging through trash can divulge the target's financial and professional status, political affiliations and inclinations, private thoughts, personal relationships, and romantic interests. It cannot be doubted that a sealed trash bag harbors telling evidence of the "intimate activity associated with the 'sanctity of a man's home and the privacies of life,'" which the Fourth Amendment is designed to protect. . . .

. . . Most of us, I believe, would be incensed to discover a meddler — whether a neighbor, a reporter, or a detective — scrutinizing our sealed trash containers to discover some detail of our personal lives. . . .

The mere possibility that unwelcome meddlers might open and rummage through the containers does not negate the expectation of privacy in their contents any more than the possibility of a burglary negates an expectation of privacy in the home; or the possibility of a private intrusion negates an expectation of privacy in an unopened package; or the possibility that an operator will listen in on a telephone conversation negates an expectation of privacy in the words spoken on the telephone. "What a person . . . seeks to preserve as private, even in an area accessible to the public, may be constitutionally protected." *Katz*, 389 U.S. at 351-52. . . .

NOTES & QUESTIONS

1. *Recycling and Surveillance of Garbage.* In dissent in *Greenwood*, Justice Brennan states, "Scrutiny of another's trash is contrary to commonly accepted notions of civilized behavior." The Supreme Court decided *Greenwood* in 1988. In the twenty-first century, however, an increasing number of communities have imposed recycling obligations on their citizens. Sanitation departments sometimes oversee the recycling by routinely checking people's trash, and, in the case of noncompliance, imposing fines. Does this development alter the extent of any reasonable expectation of privacy in one's trash vis-à-vis the police?

2. *Surveillance 24/7.* In addition to searching through Greenwood's trash, the police were staking out his home, watching who came and went from his house. Does the Fourth Amendment protect against such surveillance? Imagine that for one year, the police were to stake out a person's home and follow the person wherever he or she went throughout the day. The person would be under 24-hour surveillance, seven days a week. Assume that the police would simply observe the person anytime he or she was in public. Is this more invasive to privacy than a one-time search of particular items, such as one's luggage? Does the Fourth Amendment provide any limitation on the police activities described above?

3. *State Courts and State Constitutions.* In examining the same issue as *Greenwood*, some state supreme courts have come to a different conclusion in interpreting their state constitutions. For example, the Supreme Court of Vermont declared that "the Vermont Constitution protects persons from warrantless police searches into the contents of secured opaque trash bags left at curbside for garbage collection and disposal." *State of Vermont v. Morris*, 680 A.2d 90 (Vt. 1996). It observed that the California, Hawaii, New Jersey, and Washington state supreme courts had already declined to follow the *Greenwood* analysis. The court argued that "the mere possibility that unwelcome animals or persons might rummage through one's garbage bags does not negate the expectation of privacy in the contents of those bags any more than the possibility of a burglary or break-in negates an expectation of privacy in one's home or car, or the possibility that a cleaning person or house guest will exceed the scope of a visit negates an expectation of privacy in a hotel room or home." Is one or more of these comparisons more convincing than the other?

PLAIN VIEW, OPEN FIELDS, AND CURTILAGE

"[I]t has long been settled that objects falling in the plain view of an officer who has a right to be in the position to have that view are subject to seizure and may be introduced in evidence." *Harris v. United States*, 390 U.S. 234, 236 (1968).

This has become known as the "plain view" doctrine. If it is possible for something to be seen or heard from a public vantage point, there can be no reasonable expectation of privacy.

An extension of the plain view rule is the "open fields" doctrine. An individual does not have a reasonable expectation of privacy in the open fields that she owns. In *Oliver v. United States*, 466 U.S. 170 (1984), the defendant placed "No Trespassing" signs throughout his farm and maintained a locked gate around the farm's entrance. The fields could not be seen from any public vantage point. The police trespassed onto the fields and found marijuana. The Court held, however, that there is no reasonable expectation of privacy in open fields, and the defendant's attempt to keep them secluded and shielded from public view was irrelevant.

An exception to the open fields doctrine is the legal treatment of a house's so-called "curtilage." Under the curtilage doctrine, parts of one's property immediately outside one's home do not fall within the open fields rule. This exception does not mean that the curtilage is automatically afforded Fourth Amendment protection; a reasonable expectation of privacy analysis still must be performed. The question of whether an area constitutes a curtilage depends upon "whether the area in question is so intimately tied to the home itself that it should be placed within the home's 'umbrella' of Fourth Amendment protection." *United States v. Dunn*, 480 U.S. 294, 301 (1987).

FLORIDA V. RILEY

488 U.S. 445 (1989)

WHITE, J. . . . Respondent Riley lived in a mobile home located on five acres of rural property. A greenhouse was located 10 to 20 feet behind the mobile home. Two sides of the greenhouse were enclosed. The other two sides were not enclosed but the contents of the greenhouse were obscured from view from surrounding property by trees, shrubs, and the mobile home. The greenhouse was covered by corrugated roofing panels, some translucent and some opaque. At the time relevant to this case, two of the panels, amounting to approximately 10% of the roof area, were missing. A wire fence surrounded the mobile home and the greenhouse, and the property was posted with a "DO NOT ENTER" sign.

This case originated with an anonymous tip to the Pasco County Sheriff's office that marijuana was being grown on respondent's property. When an investigating officer discovered that he could not see the contents of the greenhouse from the road, he circled twice over respondent's property in a helicopter at the height of 400 feet. With his naked eye, he was able to see through the openings in the roof and one or more of the open sides of the greenhouse and to identify what he thought was marijuana growing in the structure. A warrant was obtained based on these observations, and the ensuing search revealed marijuana growing in the greenhouse. Respondent was charged with possession of marijuana under Florida law. . . .

We agree with the State's submission that our decision in *California v. Ciraolo*, 476 U.S. 207 (1986), controls this case. There, acting on a tip, the police inspected the back-yard of a particular house while flying in a fixed-wing aircraft at 1,000 feet. With the naked eye the officers saw what they concluded was marijuana growing in the yard. A search warrant was obtained on the strength of this airborne inspection, and marijuana plants were found. The trial court refused to suppress this evidence, but a state appellate court held that the inspection violated the Fourth and Fourteenth Amendments to the United States Constitution, and that the warrant was therefore invalid. We in turn reversed, holding that the inspection was not a search subject to the Fourth Amendment. We recognized that the yard was within the curtilage of the house, that a fence shielded the yard from observation from the street, and that the occupant had a subjective expectation of privacy. We held, however, that such an expectation was not reasonable and not one "that society is prepared to honor." Our reasoning was that the home and its curtilage are not necessarily protected from inspection that involves no physical invasion. "'What a person knowingly exposes to the public, even in his own home or office, is not a subject of Fourth Amendment protection.'" As a general proposition, the police may see what may be seen "from a public vantage point where [they have] a right to be." Thus the police, like the public, would have been free to inspect the backyard garden from the street if their view had been unobstructed. They were likewise free to inspect the yard from the vantage point of an aircraft flying in the navigable airspace as this plane was. "In an age where private and commercial flight in the public airways is routine, it is unreasonable for respondent to expect that his marijuana plants were constitutionally protected from being observed with the naked eye from an altitude of 1,000 feet. The Fourth Amendment simply does not require the police traveling in the public airways at this altitude to obtain a warrant in order to observe what is visible to the naked eye."

We arrive at the same conclusion in the present case. In this case, as in *Ciraolo*, the property surveyed was within the curtilage of respondent's home. Riley no doubt intended and expected that his greenhouse would not be open to public inspection, and the precautions he took protected against ground-level observation. Because the sides and roof of his greenhouse were left partially open, however, what was growing in the greenhouse was subject to viewing from the air. Under the holding in *Ciraolo*, Riley could not reasonably have expected the contents of his greenhouse to be immune from examination by an officer seated in a fixed-wing aircraft flying in navigable airspace at an altitude of 1,000 feet or, as the Florida Supreme Court seemed to recognize, at an altitude of 500 feet, the lower limit of the navigable airspace for such an aircraft. Here, the inspection was made from a helicopter, but as is the case with fixed-wing planes, "private and commercial flight [by helicopter] in the public airways is routine" in this country, and there is no indication that such flights are unheard of in Pasco County, Florida. Riley could not reasonably have expected that his greenhouse was protected from public or official observation from a helicopter had it been flying within the navigable airspace for fixed-wing aircraft.

Nor on the facts before us, does it make a difference for Fourth Amendment purposes that the helicopter was flying at 400 feet when the officer saw what was growing in the greenhouse through the partially open roof and sides of the structure. We would have a different case if flying at that altitude had been contrary to law or regulation. But helicopters are not bound by the lower limits of the navigable airspace allowed to other aircraft.[32] Any member of the public could legally have been flying over Riley's property in a helicopter at the altitude of 400 feet and could have observed Riley's greenhouse. The police officer did no more. . . . As far as this record reveals, no intimate details connected with the use of the home or curtilage were observed, and there was no undue noise, and no wind, dust, or threat of injury. In these circumstances, there was no violation of the Fourth Amendment.

O'CONNOR, J. concurring in the judgment. Ciraolo's expectation of privacy was unreasonable not because the airplane was operating where it had a "right to be," but because public air travel at 1,000 feet is a sufficiently routine part of modern life that it is unreasonable for persons on the ground to expect that their curtilage will not be observed from the air at that altitude. Although "helicopters are not bound by the lower limits of the navigable airspace allowed to other aircraft," there is no reason to assume that compliance with FAA regulations alone determines "'whether the government's intrusion infringes upon the personal and societal values protected by the Fourth Amendment.'" Because the FAA has decided that helicopters can lawfully operate at virtually any altitude so long as they pose no safety hazard, it does not follow that the expectations of privacy "society is prepared to recognize as 'reasonable'" simply mirror the FAA's safety concerns. . . .

. . . However, if the public can generally be expected to travel over residential backyards at an altitude of 400 feet, Riley cannot reasonably expect his curtilage from such aerial observation. In my view, the defendant must bear the burden of proving that his expectation of privacy was a reasonable one, and thus that a "search" within the meaning of the Fourth Amendment even took place.

Because there is reason to believe that there is considerable public use of airspace at altitudes of 400 feet and above, and because Riley introduced no evidence to the contrary before the Florida courts, I conclude that Riley's expectation that his curtilage was protected from naked-eye aerial observation from that altitude was not a reasonable one. However, public use of altitudes lower than that — particularly public observations from helicopters circling over the curtilage of a home — may be sufficiently rare that public surveillance from such altitudes would violate reasonable expectations of privacy, despite compliance with FAA air safety regulations.

BRENNAN, J. joined by MARSHALL and STEVENS, JJ. dissenting. Under the plurality's exceedingly grudging Fourth Amendment theory, the expectation of privacy is defeated if a single member of the public could conceivably position herself to see into the area in question without doing anything illegal. It is defeated whatever the difficulty a person would have in so positioning herself,

---

[32] While Federal Aviation Administration regulations permit fixed-wing-aircraft to be operated at an altitude of 1,000 feet while flying over congested areas and at an altitude of 500 feet above the surface in other than congested areas, helicopters may be operated at less than the minimums for fixed-wing-aircraft "if the operation is conducted without hazard to persons or property on the surface. In addition, each person operating a helicopter shall comply with routes or altitudes specifically prescribed for helicopters by the [FAA] Administrator." 14 CFR § 91.79 (1988).

and however infrequently anyone would in fact do so. In taking this view the plurality ignores the very essence of *Katz*. The reason why there is no reasonable expectation of privacy in an area that is exposed to the public is that little diminution in "the amount of privacy and freedom remaining to citizens" will result from police surveillance of something that any passerby readily sees. To pretend, as the plurality opinion does, that the same is true when the police use a helicopter to peer over high fences is, at best, disingenuous. . . .

It is a curious notion that the reach of the Fourth Amendment can be so largely defined by administrative regulations issued for purposes of flight safety.[33] It is more curious still that the plurality relies to such an extent on the legality of the officer's act, when we have consistently refused to equate police violation of the law with infringement of the Fourth Amendment.

The police officer positioned 400 feet above Riley's backyard was not, however, standing on a public road. The vantage point he enjoyed was not one any citizen could readily share. His ability to see over Riley's fence depended on his use of a very expensive and sophisticated piece of machinery to which few ordinary citizens have access. In such circumstances it makes no more sense to rely on the legality of the officer's position in the skies than it would to judge the constitutionality of the wiretap in *Katz* by the legality of the officer's position outside the telephone booth. The simple inquiry whether the police officer had the legal right to be in the position from which he made his observations cannot suffice, for we cannot assume that Riley's curtilage was so open to the observations of passersby in the skies that he retained little privacy or personal security to be lost to police surveillance. The question before us must be not whether the police were where they had a right to be, but whether public observation of Riley's curtilage was so commonplace that Riley's expectation of privacy in his backyard could not be considered reasonable. . . .

. . . The Fourth Amendment demands that we temper our efforts to apprehend criminals with a concern for the impact on our fundamental liberties of the methods we use. I hope it will be a matter of concern to my colleagues that the police surveillance methods they would sanction were among those described 40 years ago in George Orwell's dread vision of life in the 1980's:

> The black-mustachio'd face gazed down from every commanding corner. There was one on the house front immediately opposite. BIG BROTHER IS WATCHING YOU, the caption said. . . . In the far distance a helicopter skimmed down between the roofs, hovered for an instant like a bluebottle, and darted away again with a curving flight. It was the Police Patrol, snooping into people's windows.

Who can read this passage without a shudder, and without the instinctive reaction that it depicts life in some country other than ours? I respectfully dissent.

---

[33] The plurality's use of the FAA regulations as a means for determining whether Riley enjoyed a reasonable expectation of privacy produces an incredible result. Fixed-wing aircraft may not be operated below 500 feet (1,000 feet over congested areas), while helicopters may be operated below those levels. Therefore, whether Riley's expectation of privacy is reasonable turns on whether the police officer at 400 feet above his curtilage is seated in an airplane or a helicopter. This cannot be the law.

NOTES & QUESTIONS

1. *Privacy in Public.* The court quotes from *Katz v. United States* that "[w]hat a person knowingly exposes to the public . . . is not a subject of Fourth Amendment protection." How far does this principle extend? Can there be situations where a person might have a reasonable expectation of privacy even when exposed in public? Recall the public disclosure tort cases in Chapter 2, which indicate that sometimes a person does have a privacy interest even in the event of public exposure or being in a public place.

2. *Surveillance Cameras.* The use of surveillance cameras is increasing. Since 1994, in response to terrorist bombings, Britain has been watching city streets through a system of surveillance cameras monitored by closed circuit television (CCTV).[34] In 2002, the National Park Service announced plans to set up a surveillance system at all major monuments on the National Mall in Washington, D.C. Given the frequent use of surveillance cameras, do we still have an expectation of privacy not to be filmed in our day-to-day activities? Consider Marc Blitz:

> People also need privacy and anonymity in many aspects of public life — for example, when they explore controversial films, books, or ideas, have conversations in public places, or seek aid or counsel of a sort they can only find by venturing into the public sphere. Although walls and windows do not shield these public activities from everyone's view, other features of physical and social architecture, distinctive to public space, do shield them. Crowds and the diversity and separateness of the social circles that people move in allow people to find anonymity; the existence of isolated and unmonitored islands of public space allow them to find seclusion. . . . These privacy-enhancing features of public space cannot easily survive in a world of ubiquitous cameras, and the task of preserving them requires courts to do in a sense the opposite of what *Katz* recommends: They must abandon the task of identifying difficult-to-identify expectations of privacy . . . and instead return to the task of preserving the environment that makes privacy possible.[35]

What precisely are the harms of surveillance cameras? Consider Christopher Slobogin:

> Virtually all of us, no matter how innocent, feel somewhat unnerved when a police car pulls up behind us. Imagine now being watched by an officer, at a discreet distance and without any other intrusion, every time you walk through certain streets. Say you want to run (to catch a bus, for a brief bit of exercise or just for the hell of it). Will you? Or assume you want to obscure your face (because of the wind or a desire to avoid being seen by an officious acquaintance)? How about hanging out on the street corner (waiting for friends or because you have nothing else to do)?

---

[34] For more background about CCTV, see Clive Norris & Gary Armstrong, *The Maximum Surveillance Society: The Rise of CCTV* (1999); Jeffrey Rosen, *A Cautionary Tale for a New Age of Surveillance*, N.Y. Times Mag. (Oct. 7, 2001).

[35] Marc Jonathan Blitz, *Video Surveillance and the Constitution of Public Space: Fitting the Fourth Amendment to a World that Tracks Image and Identity*, 82 Tex. L. Rev. 1349, 1481 (2004).

In all of these scenarios, you will probably feel and perhaps act differently than when the officer is not there. Perhaps your hesitancy comes from uncertainty as to the officer's likely reaction or simply from a desire to appear completely law-abiding; the important point is that it exists. Government-run cameras are a less tangible presence than the ubiquitous cop, but better at recording your actions. A police officer in Liverpool, England may have said it best: A camera is like having a cop "on duty 24 hours a day, constantly taking notes."[36]

Are there any other harms you can think of? What are the benefits of surveillance cameras? Should they not be permissible as a low-cost way to extend the reach of police? Do the benefits outweigh the harms? Regarding the benefits of surveillance cameras, consider Jeff Rosen:

> In 2000, Britain's violent-crime rates actually increased by 4.3 percent, even though the cameras continued to proliferate. But CCTV cameras have a mysterious knack for justifying themselves regardless of what happens to crime. When crime goes up, the cameras get the credit for detecting it, and when crime goes down, they get the credit for preventing it.[37]

Would it be possible to design an empirical study that would test the effectiveness of surveillance cameras in preventing crime?

3. *Face Recognition Systems.* In Tampa, a computer software program called "FaceIt" linked to 36 cameras attempts to scan the faces of individuals on public streets to match them against mug shots of wanted fugitives. A similar system was used to scan faces at Super Bowl XXXV in January 2001. The Tampa Police Department argues that "FaceIt" is analogous to a police officer standing on a street holding a mug shot. Philip Agre contends that face recognition systems are different:

> A human being who spots me in the park has the accountability that someone can spot them as well. Cameras are much more anonymous and easy to hide. More important is the question of scale. Most people understand the moral difference between a single chance observation in a park and an investigator who follows you everywhere you go.[38]

Further, contends Agre, the information used and collected by face recognition systems could fall into the wrong hands and be potentially abused by the government to exercise social control. Additionally, such systems can have errors, resulting in the tracking and potential arrest of innocent persons. As a policy matter, do the costs of facial recognition systems outweigh the benefits? Given the information privacy law you have learned so far, assess the legality and constitutionality of facial recognition systems.

The Tampa face recognition system was ultimately scrapped because of high errors and general ineffectiveness.

---

[36] Christopher Slobogin, *Public Privacy: Camera Surveillance of Public Places and the Right to Anonymity*, 72 Miss. L.J. 213, 247 (2002).

[37] Jeffrey Rosen, *The Naked Crowd: Reclaiming Security and Freedom in an Anxious Age* 49 (2004).

[38] Philip E. Agre, *Your Face Is Not a Bar Code: Arguments Against Automatic Face Recognition in Public Places* (Sept. 9, 2001), http://dlis.gseis.ucla.edu/people/pagre/bar-code.html.

4. *Who Decides What Constitutes a Reasonable Expectation of Privacy?*
Currently, judges decide whether a defendant has a reasonable expectation of
privacy in a particular activity. Is this question appropriate for judges to
decide? Or should juries decide it? In all of the cases so far, observe the
sources that the Court cites to for support that there is no reasonable
expectation of privacy. How is a reasonable expectation of privacy to be
measured? Is it an empirical question about what most people in society
would generally consider to be private? If so, why aren't polls taken? If
you're an attorney arguing that there is a reasonable expectation of privacy in
something, what do you cite to? How should courts measure what society as a
whole thinks is private?

   Christopher Slobogin and Joseph Schumacher conducted a survey of
individuals, asking them to rate on a scale of 0 to 100 the intrusiveness of
certain types of searches or seizures, with 0 being nonintrusive and 100 being
extremely intrusive. Several searches that the Court has concluded do not
trigger a reasonable expectation of privacy rated in the middle of the scale.
The flyover in *Florida v. Riley* rated at 40.32 on this scale; the dog sniff in
United States v. Place rated at 58.33; the search of garbage in *California v.
Greenwood* rated at 44.95; and the use of a beeper to track a car in *United
States v. Knotts* rated at 54.46. Certain searches that the Court held do not
involve a reasonable expectation of privacy rated highly on the scale, such as
examining bank records in *United States v. Miller,* rated at 71.60. In other
highly ranked searches, the Court has concluded that the Fourth Amendment
applies, such as monitoring a phone for 30 days, rating at 87.67 and a body
cavity search at the border, rating at 90.14. The body cavity search was the
highest rated search, and a search of foliage in a public park was the lowest
rated at 6.48. Slobogin and Schumacher conclude that "the Supreme Court's
conclusions about the scope of the Fourth Amendment are often not in tune
with commonly held attitudes about police investigative techniques."[39]

   To what extent should empirical evidence such as this study be used by
courts in determining whether or not there is a reasonable expectation of
privacy? If such evidence should be used, at what point in the scale should the
line be drawn to establish the existence of a reasonable expectation of
privacy?

5. *Should the Reasonable Expectation of Privacy Test Be Empirical or
Normative?* There is an interesting paradox at the heart of the reasonable
expectation of privacy test: Legal protection is triggered by people's
expectations of privacy, but those expectations are, to a notable extent, shaped
by the extent of the legal protection of privacy. Consider the following
argument by Daniel Solove regarding the privacy of the postal letters:

> [I]n America, the privacy of letters was formed in significant part by a legal
> architecture that protected the confidentiality of letters from other people and
> government officials. In colonial America, mail was often insecure; it was

---

[39] Christopher Slobogin & Joseph E. Schumacher, *Reasonable Expectations of Privacy and
Autonomy in Fourth Amendment Cases: An Empirical Look at "Understandings Recognized and
Permitted by Society,"* 42 Duke L.J. 727 (1993).

difficult to seal letters; and the wax often used to keep letters sealed was not very effective. There was widespread suspicion of postal clerks reading letters; and a number of prominent individuals, such as Thomas Jefferson, Alexander Hamilton, and George Washington, decried the lack of privacy in their letters and would sometimes even write in code. . . . Despite these realities, and people's expectation that letters would not be confidential, the law evolved to provide strong protection of the privacy of letters. Benjamin Franklin, who was in charge of the colonial mails, required his employees to swear an oath not to open mail. In the late eighteenth and early nineteenth centuries, Congress passed several laws prohibiting the improper opening of mail. And the Supreme Court held in 1877 that despite the fact that people turned letters over to the government for delivery in the postal system, sealed parcels were protected from inspection by the Fourth Amendment. This example illustrates that privacy is not just found but constructed. By erecting a legal structure to protect the privacy of letters, our society shaped the practices of letter writing and using the postal system. It occurred because of the desire to make privacy an integral part of these practices rather than to preserve the status quo.[40]

Solove argues that societies seek to protect privacy with the law when they do not expect privacy but desire to have it. If Solove is right, then what should courts look to when applying the reasonable expectation of privacy test?

6. ***Critiques of the Reasonable Expectation of Privacy Test.*** Thomas Crocker argues that the Fourth Amendment protects more than privacy — it protects "political liberty." According to Crocker, "the Fourth Amendment fits into a broader political liberty framework, as it has increasingly focused on protecting a narrow conception of privacy and regulating everyday police practice." Instead, it should broadly "enable freedom of movement and social interaction in private and in public, secure from arbitrary search and seizure."[41] Crocker's argument suggests that the Fourth Amendment should protect assembly in public and other activities out in the open. Some might contend that his view of the Fourth Amendment is too broad and vague. Is it? What are the benefits and problems with Crocker's approach?

Daniel Solove argues that the reasonable expectation of privacy test should be abandoned because "current Fourth Amendment coverage often bears little relation to the problems caused by government investigative activities. It also bears little relation to whether it is best to have judicial oversight of law enforcement activity, what that oversight should consist of, how much limitation we want to impose on various government information gathering activities, and how we should guard against abuses of power." He recommends that "the Fourth Amendment should provide protection whenever a problem of reasonable significance can be identified with a

---

[40] Daniel J. Solove, *Conceptualizing Privacy*, 90 Cal. L. Rev. 1087, 1142-43 (2002); *see also* Shaun Spencer, *Reasonable Expectations and the Erosion of Privacy*, 39 San Diego L. Rev. 843 (2002).

[41] Thomas P. Crocker, *The Political Fourth Amendment*, 88 Wash. U. L. Rev. 303, 310-11 (2010).

particular form of government information gathering."[42] Is this approach workable? What are the benefits and problems with such an approach?

Susan Freiwald makes a similar argument in the context of communications:

> Courts should focus on the normative inquiry into whether users should be entitled to view their communications as private, but in doing so they should shift the inquiry away from users' apparent knowledge about whether their communications were vulnerable to interception. Instead, courts should discharge their responsibility to mediate the tension between law enforcement's interest in obtaining as much information as possible and users' interest in avoiding excessive government intrusion into their lives.[43]

Is looking at people's expectations the wrong inquiry? Freiwald suggests that courts look to four factors to determine whether Fourth Amendment regulation is appropriate — whether the surveillance is hidden, intrusive, indiscriminate, and continuous. Are these factors, as opposed to people's expectations of privacy, a more coherent and workable approach to determining whether the Fourth Amendment should regulate government surveillance activities?

(b) Sensory Enhancement Technology

DOW CHEMICAL CO. V. UNITED STATES

476 U.S. 227 (1986)

BURGER, C.J. . . . Petitioner Dow Chemical Co. operates a 2,000-acre facility manufacturing chemicals at Midland, Michigan. The facility consists of numerous covered buildings, with manufacturing equipment and piping conduits located between the various buildings exposed to visual observation from the air. At all times, Dow has maintained elaborate security around the perimeter of the complex barring ground-level public views of these areas. It also investigates any low-level flights by aircraft over the facility. Dow has not undertaken, however, to conceal all manufacturing equipment within the complex from aerial views. Dow maintains that the cost of covering its exposed equipment would be prohibitive.

In early 1978, enforcement officials of EPA, with Dow's consent, made an on-site inspection of two power plants in this complex. A subsequent EPA request for a second inspection, however, was denied, and EPA did not thereafter seek an administrative search warrant. Instead, EPA employed a commercial aerial photographer, using a standard floor-mounted, precision aerial mapping camera, to take photographs of the facility from altitudes of 12,000, 3,000, and 1,200 feet. At all times the aircraft was lawfully within navigable airspace.

---

[42] Daniel J. Solove, *Fourth Amendment Pragmatism,* 51 B.C. L. Rev. 1511, 1513-14 (2010). For more about these issues, see Daniel J. Solove, *Nothing to Hide: The False Tradeoff Between Privacy and Security* (2011).

[43] Susan Freiwald, *First Principles of Communications Privacy*, 2007 Stan. Tech. L. Rev. 3, 9.

EPA did not inform Dow of this aerial photography, but when Dow became aware of it, Dow brought suit in the District Court alleging that EPA's action violated the Fourth Amendment and was beyond EPA's statutory investigative authority. The District Court granted Dow's motion for summary judgment on the ground that EPA had no authority to take aerial photographs and that doing so was a search violating the Fourth Amendment. EPA was permanently enjoined from taking aerial photographs of Dow's premises and from disseminating, releasing, or copying the photographs already taken. . . .

The photographs at issue in this case are essentially like those commonly used in mapmaking. Any person with an airplane and an aerial camera could readily duplicate them. In common with much else, the technology of photography has changed in this century. These developments have enhanced industrial processes, and indeed all areas of life; they have also enhanced law enforcement techniques. . . .

. . . Dow claims EPA's use of aerial photography was a "search" of an area that, notwithstanding the large size of the plant, was within an "industrial curtilage" rather than an "open field," and that it had a reasonable expectation of privacy from such photography protected by the Fourth Amendment. . . .

. . . Dow concedes that a simple flyover with naked-eye observation, or the taking of a photograph from a nearby hillside overlooking such a facility, would give rise to no Fourth Amendment problem.

In *California v. Ciraolo*, 476 U.S. 207 (1986), decided today, we hold that naked-eye aerial observation from an altitude of 1,000 feet of a backyard within the curtilage of a home does not constitute a search under the Fourth Amendment.

In the instant case, two additional Fourth Amendment claims are presented: whether the common-law "curtilage" doctrine encompasses a large industrial complex such as Dow's, and whether photography employing an aerial mapping camera is permissible in this context. Dow argues that an industrial plant, even one occupying 2,000 acres, does not fall within the "open fields" doctrine of *Oliver v. United States* but rather is an "industrial curtilage" having constitutional protection equivalent to that of the curtilage of a private home. Dow further contends that any aerial photography of this "industrial curtilage" intrudes upon its reasonable expectations of privacy. Plainly a business establishment or an industrial or commercial facility enjoys certain protections under the Fourth Amendment. . . .

. . . The curtilage area immediately surrounding a private house has long been given protection as a place where the occupants have a reasonable and legitimate expectation of privacy that society is prepared to accept. . . .

Dow plainly has a reasonable, legitimate, and objective expectation of privacy within the interior of its covered buildings, and it is equally clear that expectation is one society is prepared to observe. Moreover, it could hardly be expected that Dow would erect a huge cover over a 2,000-acre tract. In contending that its entire enclosed plant complex is an "industrial curtilage," Dow argues that its exposed manufacturing facilities are analogous to the curtilage surrounding a home because it has taken every possible step to bar access from ground level. . . .

. . . The intimate activities associated with family privacy and the home and its curtilage simply do not reach the outdoor areas or spaces between structures and buildings of a manufacturing plant. . . .

It may well be, as the Government concedes, that surveillance of private property by using highly sophisticated surveillance equipment not generally available to the public, such as satellite technology, might be constitutionally proscribed absent a warrant. But the photographs here are not so revealing of intimate details as to raise constitutional concerns. Although they undoubtedly give EPA more detailed information than naked-eye views, they remain limited to an outline of the facility's buildings and equipment. The mere fact that human vision is enhanced somewhat, at least to the degree here, does not give rise to constitutional problems. An electronic device to penetrate walls or windows so as to hear and record confidential discussions of chemical formulae or other trade secrets would raise very different and far more serious questions; other protections such as trade secret laws are available to protect commercial activities from private surveillance by competitors. . . .

We hold that the taking of aerial photographs of an industrial plant complex from navigable airspace is not a search prohibited by the Fourth Amendment. . . .

POWELL, J. joined by BRENNAN, MARSHALL, and BLACKMUN, JJ. concurring in part and dissenting in part. The Fourth Amendment protects private citizens from arbitrary surveillance by their Government. For nearly 20 years, this Court has adhered to a standard that ensured that Fourth Amendment rights would retain their vitality as technology expanded the Government's capacity to commit unsuspected intrusions into private areas and activities. Today, in the context of administrative aerial photography of commercial premises, the Court retreats from that standard. It holds that the photography was not a Fourth Amendment "search" because it was not accompanied by a physical trespass and because the equipment used was not the most highly sophisticated form of technology available to the Government. Under this holding, the existence of an asserted privacy interest apparently will be decided solely by reference to the manner of surveillance used to intrude on that interest. Such an inquiry will not protect Fourth Amendment rights, but rather will permit their gradual decay as technology advances. . . .

NOTES & QUESTIONS

1. *New Surveillance Technologies.* One of the rationales of *Dow Chemical* is that the device could have been acquired by a member of the general public. Does the case turn on this point? Suppose the police used a special camera that was developed exclusively for law enforcement purposes.

The *Dow Chemical* Court stated: "It may well be, as the Government concedes, that surveillance of private property by using highly sophisticated surveillance equipment not generally available to the public, such as satellite technology, might be constitutionally proscribed absent a warrant." But does this sentence reflect contemporary technological reality? Mark Monmonier describes the rapid increase in the availability of commercial satellite capacities once the Cold War ended and the U.S. government lifted its restrictions in this area. The public now has cheaper and more detailed satellite images available to it than ever before.[44] As an example, look at maps.google.com, where free high-quality satellite imagery is available for most street maps.

Recall that in *The Right to Privacy*, Warren and Brandeis complained in 1890 of the then new ability to take candid photographs of individuals. Before the invention of the snap camera, people did not expect to be photographed without their consent. Clearly today the ability to take pictures in public is greatly enhanced. There are video cameras, night-vision cameras, powerful zoom lenses, and satellite images available for sale. Google Street View has mapped most of the United States at street level. Are these new technologies eroding our reasonable expectation of privacy?[45] How should the law respond?

2. *Flashlights.* The use of a flashlight "to illuminate a darkened area simply does not constitute a search, and thus triggers no Fourth Amendment protection." *Texas v. Brown*, 460 U.S. 730 (1983). If this conclusion seems evident, how is a flashlight different from other devices that enhance human senses? Is any device that enhances the human senses merely an extension of ordinary senses? What factors should be considered in determining which sense enhancement devices trigger a search under the Fourth Amendment and which do not?

3. *Beepers and Tracking Devices.* In *United States v. Knotts*, 460 U.S. 276 (1983), the police placed a beeper in a five-gallon drum of chloroform purchased by the defendants and placed in their car. The beeper transmitted signals that enabled the police to track the location of the defendants' vehicle. The Court held that the Fourth Amendment did not apply to the use of this device because a "person traveling in an automobile on public thoroughfares has no reasonable expectation of privacy in his movements from one place to another." Therefore, "[t]he governmental surveillance conducted by means of the beeper in this case amounted principally to the following of an automobile on public streets and highways." In *United States v. Karo*, 468 U.S. 705 (1984), law enforcement officials planted a beeper in a can of ether that the defendant bought from an informant. The officials tracked the movements of the can of ether through a variety of places, including within a residence. While the movements in *Knotts* were in public, the movements within the residence were not, and this amounted to an impermissible search of the residence:

> The monitoring of an electronic device such as a beeper is, of course, less intrusive than a full-scale search, but it does reveal a critical fact about the interior of the premises that the Government is extremely interested in knowing and that it could not have otherwise obtained without a warrant. The

---

[44] Mark Monmonier, *Spying with Maps* (2002).

[45] For an argument that people do have reasonable expectations of privacy in public, see Helen Nissenbaum, *Protecting Privacy in an Information Age: The Problem of Privacy in Public*, 17 Law & Phil. 559 (1998).

case is thus not like *Knotts*, for there the beeper told the authorities nothing about the interior of Knotts' cabin. The information obtained in *Knotts* was "voluntarily conveyed to anyone who wanted to look. . . ."

4. *Global Positioning System (GPS).* GPS is a radio navigation system, developed by the U.S. Department of Defense; it provides continuous worldwide positioning and timing information. GPS functions through use of 24 satellites in earth-based orbit, which are monitored by ground-based control stations. GPS devices raise technological issues similar to those at stake in *United States v. Karo* and *United States v. Knotts*.

The circuits are split on the extent to which law enforcement use of GPS devices require a warrant pursuant to the Fourth Amendment. The Seventh, Eighth, and Ninth Circuits have held that the use of a GPS device did not constitute a search under the Fourth Amendment. *United States v. Garcia*, 474 F.3d 994 (7th Cir. 2007); *United States v. Marquez*, 605 F.3d 604 (8th Cir. 2010); *United States v. Pineda-Morena*, 591 F.3d 1212 (9th Cir. 2010). For example, the Seventh Circuit considered use of a GPS device as similar to the practice of tracking a car "by means of cameras mounted on lampposts or satellite imaging," which it considered not to be a search. The Eighth Circuit found that if "police have reasonable suspicion that a particular vehicle is transporting drugs, a warrant is not required when, while the vehicle is parked in a public place, they install a non-invasive GPS tracking device on it for a reasonable period of time."

In contrast, the D.C. Circuit held that the warrantless use of a GPS device on a person's vehicle for 28 days constituted a search and required a warrant. *United States v. Maynard*, 615 F.3d 544 (D.C. Cir. 2010). It noted that the Supreme Court in *Knotts* had avoided the question whether "twenty-four hour surveillance" was a search by limiting its holding to the facts of the case before it. In considering "the issue of prolonged surveillance" in *Maynard*, the D.C. Circuit stated that "the whole of one's movements over the course of a month is not *actually* exposed to the public because the likelihood anyone will observe all those movement is effectively nil." Moreover, there was no constructive exposure of the whole of one's movements even when each individual movement was exposed "because that whole reveals more — sometimes a great deal more — than the sum of its parts." The Supreme Court recently granted certiorari on this case.

State courts have also issued opinions regarding the permissibility of warrantless use of GPS devices under their state constitutions. In interpreting the Washington State Constitution, the Washington Supreme Court in *State v. Jackson*, 76 P.3d 217 (Wash. 2003), concluded that the police need a warrant in order to attach a GPS device to a vehicle to track its movement — even in public:

> It is true that an officer standing at a distance in a lawful place may use binoculars to bring into closer view what he sees, or an officer may use a flashlight at night to see what is plainly there to be seen by day. However, when a GPS device is attached to a vehicle, law enforcement officers do not in fact follow the vehicle. Thus, unlike binoculars or a flashlight, the GPS device does not merely augment the officers' senses, but rather provides a

technological substitute for traditional visual tracking. Further, the devices in this case were in place for approximately two and one-half weeks. It is unlikely that the sheriff's department could have successfully maintained uninterrupted 24-hour surveillance throughout this time by following Jackson. Even longer tracking periods might be undertaken, depending upon the circumstances of a case. We perceive a difference between the kind of uninterrupted, 24-hour a day surveillance possible through use of a GPS device, which does not depend upon whether an officer could in fact have maintained visual contact over the tracking period, and an officer's use of binoculars or a flashlight to augment his or her senses.

Moreover, the intrusion into private affairs made possible with a GPS device is quite extensive as the information obtained can disclose a great deal about an individual's life. For example, the device can provide a detailed record of travel to doctors' offices, banks, gambling casinos, tanning salons, places of worship, political party meetings, bars, grocery stores, exercise gyms, places where children are dropped off for school, play, or day care, the upper scale restaurant and the fast food restaurant, the strip club, the opera, the baseball game, the "wrong" side of town, the family planning clinic, the labor rally. In this age, vehicles are used to take people to a vast number of places that can reveal preferences, alignments, associations, personal ails and foibles. The GPS tracking devices record all of these travels, and thus can provide a detailed picture of one's life.

In a similar fashion, the Court of Appeals of New York, the highest court in New York State, found that police placement of a GPS device inside the bumper of a person's van and monitoring of the device for 65 days without a warrant constituted an illegal search under the New York Constitution. It stated, "GPS is not a mere enhancement of human sensory capacity, it facilitates a new technological perception of the world in which the situation of any object may be followed and exhaustively recorded over, in most cases, a practically unlimited period." Do the decisions of the Washington Supreme Court and the New York Court of Appeals track the U.S. Supreme Court's reading of the Fourth Amendment in cases like *Karo* and *Knotts*?

KYLLO V. UNITED STATES

533 U.S. 27 (2001)

SCALIA, J. In 1991 Agent William Elliott of the United States Department of the Interior came to suspect that marijuana was being grown in the home belonging to petitioner Danny Kyllo, part of a triplex on Rhododendron Drive in Florence, Oregon. Indoor marijuana growth typically requires high-intensity lamps. In order to determine whether an amount of heat was emanating from petitioner's home consistent with the use of such lamps, at 3:20 A.M. on January 16, 1992, Agent Elliott and Dan Haas used an Agema Thermovision 210 thermal imager to scan the triplex. Thermal imagers detect infrared radiation, which virtually all objects emit but which is not visible to the naked eye. The imager converts radiation into images based on relative warmth — black is cool, white is hot, shades of gray connote relative differences; in that respect, it operates somewhat like a video camera showing heat images. The scan of Kyllo's home took only a few minutes and was performed from the passenger seat of Agent Elliott's vehicle across the street from the front of the house and also from the street in back of the house. The scan showed that the roof over the garage and a side wall of petitioner's home were relatively hot compared to the rest of the home and substantially warmer than neighboring homes in the triplex. Agent Elliott concluded that petitioner was using halide lights to grow marijuana in his house, which indeed he was. Based on tips from informants, utility bills, and the thermal imaging, a Federal Magistrate Judge issued a warrant authorizing a search of petitioner's home, and the agents found an indoor growing operation involving more than 100 plants. Petitioner was indicted on one count of manufacturing marijuana, in violation of 21 U.S.C. § 841(a)(1). He unsuccessfully moved to suppress the evidence seized from his home and then entered a conditional guilty plea. . . .

. . . "At the very core" of the Fourth Amendment "stands the right of a man to retreat into his own home and there be free from unreasonable governmental intrusion." With few exceptions, the question whether a warrantless search of a home is reasonable and hence constitutional must be answered no.

On the other hand, the antecedent question of whether or not a Fourth Amendment "search" has occurred is not so simple under our precedent. The permissibility of ordinary visual surveillance of a home used to be clear because, well into the 20th century, our Fourth Amendment jurisprudence was tied to common-law trespass. Visual surveillance was unquestionably lawful because "the eye cannot by the laws of England be guilty of a trespass." We have since decoupled violation of a person's Fourth Amendment rights from trespassory violation of his property, but the lawfulness of warrantless visual surveillance of a home has still been preserved. As we observed in *California v. Ciraolo*, 476 U.S. 207, (1986), "[t]he Fourth Amendment protection of the home has never been extended to require law enforcement officers to shield their eyes when passing by a home on public thoroughfares." . . .

The present case involves officers on a public street engaged in more than naked-eye surveillance of a home. We have previously reserved judgment as to how much technological enhancement of ordinary perception from such a vantage point, if any, is too much. While we upheld enhanced aerial photography of an industrial complex in *Dow Chemical*, we noted that we found "it important that this is not an area immediately adjacent to a private home, where privacy expectations are most heightened."

It would be foolish to contend that the degree of privacy secured to citizens by the Fourth Amendment has been entirely unaffected by the advance of technology. For example, as the cases discussed above make clear, the technology enabling human flight has exposed to public view (and hence, we have said, to official observation) uncovered portions of the house and its curtilage that once were private. The question we confront today is what limits there are upon this power of technology to shrink the realm of guaranteed privacy. . . .

. . . [I]n the case of the search of the interior of homes — the prototypical and hence most commonly litigated area of protected privacy — there is a ready criterion, with roots deep in the common law, of the minimal expectation of privacy that exists, and that is acknowledged to be reasonable. To withdraw protection of this minimum expectation would be to permit police technology to erode the privacy guaranteed by the Fourth Amendment. We think that obtaining by sense-enhancing technology any information regarding the interior of the home that could not otherwise have been obtained without physical "intrusion into a constitutionally protected area," *Silverman*, 365 U.S., at 512, constitutes a search — at least where (as here) the technology in question is not in general public use. This assures preservation of that degree of privacy against government that existed when the Fourth Amendment was adopted. On the basis of this criterion, the information obtained by the thermal imager in this case was the product of a search.[46]

The Government maintains, however, that the thermal imaging must be upheld because it detected "only heat radiating from the external surface of the house." The dissent makes this its leading point, contending that there is a fundamental difference between what it calls "off-the-wall" observations and "through-the-wall surveillance." But just as a thermal imager captures only heat emanating from a house, so also a powerful directional microphone picks up only sound emanating from a house — and a satellite capable of scanning from many miles away would pick up only visible light emanating from a house. We rejected such a mechanical interpretation of the Fourth Amendment in *Katz*, where the eavesdropping device picked up only sound waves that reached the exterior of the phone booth. Reversing that approach would leave the homeowner at the mercy of advancing technology — including imaging technology that could discern all human activity in the home. While the technology used in the present case was relatively crude, the rule we adopt must take account of more sophisticated systems that are already in use or in development. The dissent's reliance on the distinction between "off-the-wall" and "through-the-wall" observation is entirely incompatible with the dissent's belief, which we discuss below, that thermal-imaging observations of the intimate details of a home are impermissible. The most sophisticated thermal imaging devices continue to measure heat "off-the-wall" rather than "through-the-wall"; the dissent's disapproval of those more sophisticated thermal-imaging devices, is an acknowledgement that there is no substance to this distinction. As for the dissent's extraordinary assertion that anything learned through "an inference" cannot be a search, that would validate even the "through-the-wall" technologies that the dissent purports to disapprove. Surely the dissent does not believe that the through-the-wall radar or ultrasound technology produces an 8-by-10 Kodak glossy that needs no analysis (i.e., the making of inferences). And, of course, the

---

[46] The dissent's repeated assertion that the thermal imaging did not obtain information regarding the interior of the home is simply inaccurate. A thermal imager reveals the relative heat of various rooms in the home. The dissent may not find that information particularly private or important, but there is no basis for saying it is not information regarding the interior of the home. The dissent's comparison of the thermal imaging to various circumstances in which outside observers might be able to perceive, without technology, the heat of the home — for example, by observing snowmelt on the roof — is quite irrelevant. The fact that equivalent information could sometimes be obtained by other means does not make lawful the use of means that violate the Fourth Amendment. The police might, for example, learn how many people are in a particular house by setting up year-round surveillance, but that does not make breaking and entering to find out the same information lawful. In any event, on the night of January 16, 1992, no outside observer could have discerned the relative heat of Kyllo's home without thermal imaging.

novel proposition that inference insulates a search is blatantly contrary to *United States v. Karo*, 468 U.S. 705 (1984), where the police "inferred" from the activation of a beeper that a certain can of ether was in the home. The police activity was held to be a search, and the search was held unlawful.

The Government also contends that the thermal imaging was constitutional because it did not "detect private activities occurring in private areas." . . . The Fourth Amendment's protection of the home has never been tied to measurement of the quality or quantity of information obtained. In *Silverman*, for example, we made clear that any physical invasion of the structure of the home, "by even a fraction of an inch," was too much, and there is certainly no exception to the warrant requirement for the officer who barely cracks open the front door and sees nothing but the nonintimate rug on the vestibule floor. . . .

Limiting the prohibition of thermal imaging to "intimate details" would not only be wrong in principle; it would be impractical in application. . . . To begin with, there is no necessary connection between the sophistication of the surveillance equipment and the "intimacy" of the details that it observes—which means that one cannot say (and the police cannot be assured) that use of the relatively crude equipment at issue here will always be lawful. The Agema Thermovision 210 might disclose, for example, at what hour each night the lady of the house takes her daily sauna and bath—a detail that many would consider "intimate"; and a much more sophisticated system might detect nothing more intimate than the fact that someone left a closet light on. We could not, in other words, develop a rule approving only that through-the-wall surveillance which identifies objects no smaller than 36 by 36 inches, but would have to develop a jurisprudence specifying which home activities are "intimate" and which are not. And even when (if ever) that jurisprudence were fully developed, no police office would be able to know *in advance* whether his through-the-wall surveillance picks up "intimate" details—and thus would be unable to know in advance whether it is constitutional. . . .

We have said that the Fourth Amendment draws "a firm line at the entrance to the house." That line, we think, must be not only firm but also bright — which requires clear specification of those methods of surveillance that require a warrant. While it is certainly possible to conclude from the videotape of the thermal imaging that occurred in this case that no "significant" compromise of the homeowner's privacy has occurred, we must take the long view, from the original meaning of the Fourth Amendment forward. . . .

Where, as here, the Government uses a device that is not in general public use, to explore details of the home that would previously have been unknowable without physical intrusion, the surveillance is a "search" and is presumptively unreasonable without a warrant. . . .

STEVENS, J. joined by REHNQUIST, C.J. and O'CONNOR and KENNEDY, JJ. dissenting. . . . [S]earches and seizures of property in plain view are presumptively reasonable. Whether that property is residential or commercial, the basic principle is the same: "What a person knowingly exposes to the public, even in his own home or office, is not a subject of Fourth Amendment protection." That is the principle implicated here.

While the Court "take[s] the long view" and decides this case based largely on the potential of yet-to-be-developed technology that might allow "through-the-wall surveillance," this case involves nothing more than off-the-wall surveillance by law enforcement officers to gather information exposed to the general public from the outside of petitioner's home. All that the infrared camera did in this case was passively measure heat emitted from the exterior surfaces of petitioner's home; all that those measurements showed were relative differences in emission levels, vaguely indicating that some areas of the roof and outside walls were warmer than others. As still images from the infrared scans show, no details regarding the interior of petitioner's home were revealed. . . .

. . . Heat waves, like aromas that are generated in a kitchen, or in a laboratory or opium den, enter the public domain if and when they leave a building. A subjective expectation that they would remain private is not only implausible but also surely not "one that society is prepared to recognize as 'reasonable.'" . . .

Despite the Court's attempt to draw a line that is "not only firm but also bright," the contours of its new rule are uncertain because its protection apparently dissipates as soon as the relevant technology is "in general public use." Yet how much use is general public use is not even hinted at by the Court's opinion, which makes the somewhat doubtful assumption that the thermal imager used in this case does not satisfy that criterion. In any event, putting aside its lack of clarity, this criterion is somewhat perverse because it seems likely that the threat to privacy will grow, rather than recede, as the use of intrusive equipment becomes more readily available. . . .

Because the new rule applies to information regarding the "interior" of the home, it is too narrow as well as too broad. Clearly, a rule that is designed to protect individuals from the overly intrusive use of sense-enhancing equipment should not be limited to a home. If such equipment did provide its user with the functional equivalent of access to a private place — such as, for example, the telephone booth involved in *Katz*, or an office building — then the rule should apply to such an area as well as to a home. . . .

NOTES & QUESTIONS

1. ***Thermal Imagers vs. Canine Sniffs.*** How does the Court distinguish the thermal imager in *Kyllo* from the camera in *Dow Chemical* and the dog sniff in *Place*? Does this distinction make sense?

2. ***Canine Sniffs Revisited.*** The Court decided *Illinois v. Caballes,* another dog sniff case, subsequent to *Kyllo*. In *Caballes*, the majority opinion and Justice Souter's dissent all revisited *Kyllo*. For the *Caballes* majority, the distinction between the two cases was that the thermal-imaging device in *Kyllo* was able to detect lawful activities, such as when an individual enjoyed a hot sauna or bath. The *Caballes* majority stated: "The legitimate expectation that information about perfectly lawful activity will remain private is categorically distinguishable from respondent's hopes or expectations concerning the nondetection of contraband in the trunk of his car." Justice Souter, dissenting, argued: "[G]iven the fallibility of the dog, the sniff is the first step in a process that may disclose 'intimate details' without revealing contraband, just

as a thermal-imaging device might do, as described in *Kyllo v. United States.*" Is the dog sniff like a thermal-imaging device? Or is it, as the *Caballes* majority argues, simply *sui generis*?

3. ***The Limits on Sense-Enhancing Technology.*** The *Kyllo* Court notes that there must be some limits on sense-enhancement technology. What is the limiting principle according to the Court? Do you think this is the appropriate limiting principle?[47]

4. ***Technology in General Public Use.*** The majority based its holding on the fact that a thermal sensor was *"a device not in general public use."* However, a search of eBay reveals different kinds of thermal-imaging devices for sale at a variety of prices. Hence, the thermal sensor device is one that is publicly available. Is this "eBay test" relevant? How should a court decide when a technology is "in general public use"?

5. ***The Home.*** Justice Stevens argues that "a rule that is designed to protect individuals from the overly intrusive use of sense-enhancing equipment should not be limited to a home." Do you agree? Given the reasoning of the majority, would the Court reach the same result if the thermal imager had been used outside a person's office rather than her home?

6. ***"The Lady of the House."*** In her analysis of *Kyllo*, Jeannie Suk focuses on Scalia's discussion of how a heat-sensing device might reveal intimate information, including "at what hour each night the lady of the house takes her daily sauna and bath."[48] Suk argues:

> This anachronistic language . . . calls to mind more than the privacy interests of a person bathing. It also evokes the privacy interest of the man entitled to see the lady of the house naked, and his interest in shielding her body from prying eyes. Privacy is figured as a woman, object of the male gaze.

Are there other situations in which Suk's concept of domestic privacy would bolster a party's legal claim?

7. ***The Courts vs. Congress.*** Orin Kerr contends that when new technologies are involved, Congress, not the courts, should be the primary rulemaker. In particular, Kerr critiques the generally held view that "the Fourth Amendment should be interpreted broadly in response to technological change." According to Kerr:

> [C]ourts should place a thumb on the scale in favor of judicial caution when technology is in flux, and should consider allowing legislatures to provide the primary rules governing law enforcement investigations involving new technologies. . . . When technology is in flux, Fourth Amendment protections should remain relatively modest until the technology stabilizes.

---

[47] For background into sensory enhancement technology, see Christopher Slobogin, *Technologically-Assisted Physician Surveillance: The American Bar Association's Tentative Draft Standards*, 10 Harv. J.L. & Tech. 383 (1997); ABA Standards for Criminal Justice, Electronic Surveillance § B (3d ed. 1999) (technologically assisted physical surveillance), available at http://abanet.org/crimjust/standards/taps_toc.html.

[48] Jeannie Suk, *At Home in the Law* (2009).

Kerr justifies his conclusion by making an argument about the attributes of judicial versus legislative rulemaking:

> The first difference is that legislatures typically create generally applicable rules ex ante, while courts tend to create rules ex post in a case-by-case fashion. That is, legislatures enact generalized rules for the future, whereas courts resolve disputes settling the rights of parties arising from a past event. The difference leads to Fourth Amendment rules that tend to lag behind parallel statutory rules and current technologies by at least a decade, resulting in unsettled and then outdated rules that often make little sense given current technological facts. . . .
>
> A second difference between judicial and legislative rulemaking concerns their operative constraints. . . . Legislatures are up to the task [of adapting to technological change]; courts generally are not. Legislatures can experiment with different rules and make frequent amendments; they can place restrictions on both public and private actors; and they can even "sunset" rules so that they apply only for a particular period of time. The courts cannot. As a result, Fourth Amendment rules will tend to lack the flexibility that a regulatory response to new technologies may require. . . .
>
> The third important difference between judicial rules and legislative rules relates to the information environment in which rules are generated. Legislative rules tend to be the product of a wide range of inputs, ranging from legislative hearings and poll results to interest group advocacy and backroom compromises. Judicial rules tend to follow from a more formal and predictable presentation of written briefs and oral arguments by two parties. Once again, the difference offers significant advantages to legislative rulemaking. The task of generating balanced and nuanced rules requires a comprehensive understanding of technological facts. Legislatures are well-equipped to develop such understandings; courts generally are not.[49]

Peter Swire responds that Congress's privacy legislation was shaped by judicial decisions concerning the Fourth Amendment:

> At least four mutually reinforcing reasons underscore the importance of judicial decisions to how these privacy protections were enacted. First, the Supreme Court decision made the issue more salient, focusing attention on a topic that otherwise would not climb to the top of the legislative agenda. Second, the importance of the decision to the political process was greater because of what social scientists have called the "endowment effect" or "status quo bias." . . . [T]he concept is that individuals experience a loss as more important than a gain of equal size. . . . [T]he perceived "loss" of Fourth Amendment protections . . . would be a spur to legislative action. Third, the opinions of the Supreme Court shaped the legislative debates. Vigorous dissents in each case articulated reasons why privacy protections should be considered important. . . . Fourth, once the issue had moved high enough on the agenda to warrant a vote, there were persuasive public-policy arguments that some privacy protections were appropriate.[50]

---

[49] Orin S. Kerr, *The Fourth Amendment and New Technologies: Constitutional Myths and the Case for Caution*, 102 Mich. L. Rev. 801, 803-05, 868, 871, 875 (2004).

[50] Peter P. Swire, Katz *Is Dead. Long Live* Katz, 102 Mich. L. Rev. 904, 917 (2004).

Daniel Solove also disagrees with Kerr's conclusions: "Where the courts have left open areas for legislative rules to fill in, Congress has created an uneven fabric of protections that is riddled with holes and that has weak protections in numerous places." Further, Solove contends, legislative ex ante rules are not necessarily preferable to judicial ex post rules:

> The problem with ex ante laws is that they cannot anticipate all of the new and changing factual situations that technology brings about. Ex post rules, in contrast, are often much better tailored to specific types of technology, because such rules arise as technology changes, rather than beforehand. . . .

Solove argues that the "historical record suggests that Congress is actually far worse than the courts in reacting to new technologies." In response to Kerr's argument that the legislature is better equipped to understand new technologies than the judiciary, Solove responds that "merely shifting to a statutory regime will not eliminate Kerr's concern with judges misunderstanding technology. In fact, many judicial misunderstandings stem from courts trying to fit new technologies into old statutory regimes built around old technologies."[51]

B. FEDERAL ELECTRONIC SURVEILLANCE LAW

1. SECTION 605 OF THE FEDERAL COMMUNICATIONS ACT

Recall that in 1928, the Court in *Olmstead* declared that wiretapping did not constitute a Fourth Amendment violation. By the time *Olmstead* was decided, more than 25 states had made wiretapping a crime.

Six years later, responding to significant criticism of the *Olmstead* decision, Congress enacted the Federal Communications Act (FCA) of 1934. Section 605 of the Act provided that "no person not being authorized by the sender shall intercept any communication and divulge or publish the existence, contents, substance, purport, effect, or meaning of such intercepted communications to any person." Although § 605 did not expressly provide for an exclusionary rule, the Court in *Nardone v. United States*, 302 U.S. 379 (1937), held that federal officers could not introduce evidence obtained by illegal wiretapping in federal court.

Section 605 had significant limitations. States could still use evidence in violation of § 605 in state prosecutions. Further, § 605 only applied to wire communications and wiretapping, not to eavesdropping on nonwire communications. Thus, bugging was not covered.

In the words of Attorney General Nicholas Katzenback, § 605 was the "worst of all possible solutions." It prevented law enforcement from using information gleaned from wiretaps in court — even if pursuant to a warrant supported by probable cause. And it did little to restrict government wiretapping since it was

---

[51] Daniel J. Solove, *Fourth Amendment Codification and Professor Kerr's Misguided Call for Judicial Deference*, 74 Fordham L. Rev. 747, 761-74 (2005).

interpreted not to prohibit such activity so long as the evidence was not used in court.

With the absence of Fourth Amendment protections and the limited protections of § 605, the federal government engaged in extensive wiretapping. During World War II, J. Edgar Hoover, the director of the FBI, successfully urged President Franklin Roosevelt to allow FBI wiretapping to investigate subversive activities and threats to national security. During the Truman Administration, the justification for electronic surveillance expanded to include domestic security as well. In the 1950s, the FBI then expanded its electronic surveillance due to national concern about Communism and communist infiltration of government. During the Cold War Era and beyond, Hoover ordered wiretapping of hundreds of people, including political enemies, dissidents, Supreme Court Justices, professors, celebrities, writers, and others. Among Hoover's files were dossiers on John Steinbeck, Ernest Hemingway, Charlie Chaplin, Marlon Brando, Muhammad Ali, Albert Einstein, John Lennon, and numerous presidents and members of Congress.[52]

The FBI also placed Martin Luther King Jr. under extensive surveillance. Hoover believed King was a Communist (which he was not), and disliked him personally. When the FBI's electronic surveillance of King revealed King's extramarital affairs, the FBI sent copies of the tapes to King along with a letter insinuating that he should commit suicide or else the tapes would be leaked to the public. The FBI also sent the tapes to King's wife and played them to President Lyndon Johnson.[53] In reflecting on the FBI's campaign against King, Frederick Schwarz and Aziz Huq note that an important role was played by Hoover's "personal animus against King, and his profound distaste for the social changes pressed by the civil rights movement." Schwarz and Huq also observe: "But without an institutional underpinning, Hoover's bias would not have taken the form of a massive, multiyear surveillance and harassment campaign. The war against King highlights what happens when checks and balances are abandoned."[54]

During this time, state police also conducted wiretapping. To the extent that this wiretapping was regulated, this regulation was purely that of the individual states. Section 605 only applied at the federal level. In an influential study, Samuel Dash, Richard Schwartz, and Robert Knowlton revealed that regulation of wiretapping by the states was often ineffective. There were numerous unauthorized wiretaps and few checks against abuses.[55]

---

[52] Daniel J. Solove, *Reconstructing Electronic Surveillance Law,* 72 Geo. Wash. L. Rev. 1264, 1273-74 (2004).

[53] David J. Garrow, *The FBI and Martin Luther King, Jr.* (1980).

[54] Frederick A.O. Schwarz, Jr. & Aziz Z. Huq, *Unchecked and Unbalanced: Presidential Power in a Time of Terror* 23 (2007).

[55] *See* Samuel Dash, Richard Schwartz & Robert Knowlton, *The Eavesdroppers* (1959).

2. TITLE III

In 1968, in response to *Katz v. United States* and *Berger v. New York*, Congress enacted Title III of the Omnibus Crime Control and Safe Streets Act of 1968, Pub. L. No. 90-351, codified at 18 U.S.C. §§ 2510–2520. This Act is commonly referred to as "Title III" or, subsequent to its amendment in 1986, as the "Wiretap Act."

Title III extended far beyond § 605; it applied to wiretaps by federal and state officials as well as by private parties. Title III required federal agents to apply for a warrant before wiretapping. The Act criminalized private wiretaps. However, if any party to the conversation consented to the tapping, then there was no violation of Title III.

Title III authorized the Attorney General to apply to a federal judge for an order authorizing the interception of a "wire or oral communication." A judge could not issue a court order unless there was probable cause. Many other procedural safeguards were established.

Title III excluded wiretaps for national security purposes from any restrictions at all. President Nixon frequently used the national security exception to place internal dissidents and radicals under surveillance. However, in *United States v. United States District Court* (the *Keith* case), 407 U.S. 297 (1972), the Court unanimously rejected Nixon's approach, stating that Title III's national security exception does not apply to internal threats but only to foreign threats.

3. THE ELECTRONIC COMMUNICATIONS PRIVACY ACT

(a) Statutory Structure

In 1986, Congress modernized federal wiretap law by passing the Electronic Communications Privacy Act (ECPA).[56] The ECPA amended Title III (the Wiretap Act), and it also included two new acts in response to developments in computer technology and communication networks. Hence, federal electronic surveillance law on the domestic side contains three parts: (1) the Wiretap Act (the updated version of Title III, which ECPA shifted to its first Title); (2) the Stored Communications Act (SCA); and (3) the Pen Register Act.

Many of the provisions of federal electronic surveillance law apply not only to government officials, but to private individuals and entities as well. In particular, cases involving the violation of federal electronic surveillance law by private parties often occur in the employment context when employers desire to use forms of electronic surveillance on their employees.

---

[56] For more background on electronic surveillance law, see Patricia L. Bellia, *Surveillance Law Through Cyberlaw's Lens,* 72 Geo. Wash. L. Rev. 1375 (2004); Deirdre K. Mulligan, *Reasonable Expectations in Electronic Communications: A Critical Perspective on the Electronic Communications Privacy Act,* 72 Geo. Wash. L. Rev. 1557 (2004); Paul K. Ohm, *Parallel-Effect Statutes and E-mail "Warrants": Reframing the Internet Surveillance Debate,* 72 Geo. Wash. L. Rev. 1599 (2004); Susan Freiwald, *Online Surveillance: Remembering the Lessons of the Wiretap Act,* 56 Ala. L. Rev. 9 (2004). *See generally* Symposium, *The Future of Internet Surveillance Law,* 72 Geo. Wash. L. Rev. 1139-1617 (2004).

TYPES OF COMMUNICATIONS

In order to comprehend how each of the three acts comprising ECPA works, it is important to know that ECPA classifies all communications into three types: (1) "wire communications"; (2) "oral communications"; and (3) "electronic communications." Each type of communication is protected differently. As a general matter, wire communications receive the most protection and electronic communications receive the least.

Wire Communications. A "wire communication," defined in § 2510(1), involves all "aural transfers" that travel through a wire or a similar medium:

> (1) "wire communication" means any aural transfer made in whole or in part through the use of facilities for the transmission of communications by the aid of wire, cable, or other like connection between the point of origin and the point of reception (including the use of such connection in a switching station) furnished or operated by any person engaged in providing or operating such facilities for the transmission of interstate or foreign communications or communications affecting interstate or foreign commerce.

[most Protection]

An "aural transfer" is a communication containing the human voice at any point. § 2510(18). The human voice need only be a minor part of the communication. Further, the human voice need not always be present throughout the journey of the communication. Therefore, a communication that once consisted of the human voice that has been translated into code or tones still qualifies as an "aural transfer."

The aural transfer must travel through wire (i.e., telephone wires or cable wires) or a similar medium. The entire journey from origin to destination need not take place through wire, as many communications travel through a host of different mediums — wire, radio, satellite, and so on. Only part of the communication's journey must be through a wire.

Oral Communications. The second type of communication under federal wiretap law are "oral communications." Pursuant to § 2510(2), an "oral communication" is a communication "uttered by a person exhibiting an expectation that such communication is not subject to interception under circumstances justifying such expectation." Oral communications are typically intercepted through bugs and other recording or transmitting devices.

Electronic Communications. The final type of communication is an "electronic communication." Under § 2510(12), an electronic communication consists of all non-wire and non-oral communications:

> (12) "electronic communication" means any transfer of signs, signals, writing, images, sounds, data, or intelligence of any nature transmitted in whole or in part by a wire, radio, electromagnetic, photoelectronic or photooptical system that affects interstate or foreign commerce, but does not include —
>
> (A) any wire or oral communication. . . .

[least protection]

In other words, an electronic communication consists of all communications that do not constitute wire or oral communications. An example of an electronic communication is an e-mail — at least as long as it does not contain the human voice.

Although electronic communications are protected under the Stored Communications Act as well as the Wiretap Act, they are treated differently than wire and oral communications. The most notable difference is that the exclusionary rule in the Wiretap Act does not apply to electronic communications. Therefore, wire or oral communications that fall within the Wiretap Act are protected by the exclusionary rule, but not when they fall within the Stored Communications Act (which has no exclusionary rule). Electronic communications are not protected by the exclusionary rule in the Wiretap Act or the Stored Communications Act.

THE WIRETAP ACT

Interceptions. The Wiretap Act, which is codified at Title I of ECPA, 18 U.S.C. §§ 2510–2522, governs the interception of communications. In particular, § 2511 provides that:

(1) Except as otherwise specifically provided in this chapter any person who —

(a) intentionally intercepts, endeavors to intercept, or procures any other person to intercept or endeavor to intercept, any wire, oral, or electronic communication;

(b) intentionally uses, endeavors to use, or procures any other person to use or endeavor to use any electronic, mechanical, or other device to intercept any oral communication when —

(i) such device is affixed to, or otherwise transmits a signal through, a wire, cable, or other like connection used in wire communication; or

(ii) such device transmits communications by radio, or interferes with the transmission of such communication; or

(iii) such person knows, or has reason to know, that such device or any component thereof has been sent through the mail or transported in interstate or foreign commerce. . . .

(c) intentionally discloses, or endeavors to disclose, to any other person the contents of any wire, oral, or electronic communication, knowing or having reason to know that the information was obtained through the interception of a wire, oral, or electronic communication in violation of this subsection;

(d) intentionally uses, or endeavors to use, the contents of any wire, oral, or electronic communication, knowing or having reason to know that the information was obtained through the interception of a wire, oral, or electronic communication in violation of this subsection. . . .

As this provision indicates, the Wiretap Act applies to the intentional interception of a communication. To "intercept" a communication means to acquire its contents through the use of any "electronic, mechanical, or other device." § 2510(4). The classic example of an activity covered by the Act is the wiretapping of a phone conversation — a device is being used to listen to a conversation as it is occurring, as the words are moving through the wires. The

Wiretap Act applies when communications are intercepted contemporaneously with their transmission. Once the communication is completed and stored, then the Wiretap Act no longer applies.

In *Bartnicki v. Vopper*, 532 U.S. 514 (2001) (Chapter 2), the Court held that § 2511(1)(c) violated the First Amendment by restricting disclosures involving matters of public concern.

Exclusionary Rule. Under the Wiretap Act, "any aggrieved person . . . may move to suppress the contents of any wire or oral communication intercepted pursuant to this chapter, or evidence derived therefrom." § 2518 (10)(a).

Penalties. Violations of the Wiretap Act can result in fines of a minimum of $10,000 per violation as well as up to five years' imprisonment. *See* §§ 2511(4)(a); 2520(c)(2)(B).

Court Orders. Pursuant to § 2518, an application for a court wiretapping or electronic surveillance order must be made under oath and contain a variety of information, including details to justify the agent's belief that a crime has been, is being, or will be committed; specific description of place where communications will be intercepted; description of the type of communication; and period of time of interception. The judge may require the applicant to furnish additional testimony or documentary evidence in support of the application. The judge must find probable cause and that the particular communications concerning that offense will be obtained through the interception. Further, the court must find that alternatives to wiretapping were attempted and failed, or reasonably appear to be unlikely to succeed or to be too dangerous. The order can last for up to 30 days and can be renewed.

Under the Wiretap Act, only certain government officials are able to apply to a court for a wiretapping order — for federal law enforcement agencies, the relevant party is the attorney general, or a deputy or assistant attorney general; for state officials, the relevant party is the principal prosecuting attorney of a state or a local government, or any government attorney. In other words, the police themselves cannot obtain a wiretap order alone. The Wiretap Act also provides an exclusive list of crimes for which a wiretap order can be issued. The list is broad and includes most felonies. A wiretap order cannot be obtained, however, to investigate a misdemeanor.

Minimization. The Wiretap Act requires that interception must be minimized to avoid sweeping in communications beyond the purpose for which the order was sought. Pursuant to § 2518(6): "Every order and extension thereof shall contain a provision that the authorization to intercept shall be executed as soon as practicable, shall be conducted in such a way as to minimize the interception of communications not otherwise subject to interception under this chapter, and must terminate upon attainment of the authorized objective." For example, if law enforcement officials are wiretapping the home phone line of a person suspected of running an illegal gambling operation and the person's daughter is talking on the line to a friend about going to the movies, the officials should stop listening to the conversation.

Notice. After the surveillance is over, copies of the recorded conversations must be turned over to the court issuing the order. The court must notify the party that surveillance was undertaken within 90 days after the denial of a surveillance order or after the completion of the surveillance authorized by a granted surveillance order. § 2518(8)(d).

Exceptions. There are two notable exceptions under the Wiretap Act. First, the Act does not apply if one of the parties to the communication consents. § 2511(2)(c). For example, a person can secretly tap and record a communication to which that person is a party. Thus, secretly recording one's own phone conversations is not illegal under federal wiretap law. If they participate in the conversation, government agents and informants can record others without their knowledge. An exception to the consent exception is when an interception is carried out for the purpose of committing any criminal or tortious act. In that case, even when a party has consented, interception is illegal. § 2511(2)(d).

Second, a communications service provider is permitted "to intercept, disclose, or use that communication in the normal course of his employment while engaged in any activity which is a necessary incident to the rendition of his service or to the protection of the rights or property of the provider of that service." § 2511(2)(a). Also, a service provider may intentionally disclose intercepted communications to the proper authorities when criminal activity is afoot; with the consent of the originator, addressee, or intended recipient; or to any intermediary provider. § 2511(3).

THE STORED COMMUNICATIONS ACT

Stored Communications. Whereas communications in transmission are covered by the Wiretap Act, communications in storage are protected by the Stored Communications Act (SCA), codified at 18 U.S.C. §§ 2701–2711.[57] With many forms of modern communication, such as Internet service, communications and subscriber records are often maintained in storage by the electronic communications service provider. Section 2701 states:

> (a) Offense. — Except as provided in subsection (c) of this section whoever —
>
>> (1) intentionally accesses without authorization a facility through which an electronic communication service is provided; or
>> (2) intentionally exceeds an authorization to access that facility; and thereby obtains, alters, or prevents authorized access to a wire or electronic communication while it is in electronic storage in such system shall be punished as provided in subsection (b) of this section.

The definition of "electronic storage" in the Wiretap Act also applies to the term as used in the SCA. "Electronic storage" means:

> (A) any temporary, intermediate storage of a wire or electronic communication incidental to the electronic transmission thereof; and

---

[57] For more background about the SCA, see Orin S. Kerr, *A User's Guide to the Stored Communications Act, and a Legislator's Guide to Amending It,* 72 Geo. Wash. L. Rev. 1208 (2004).

(B) any storage of such communication by an electronic communications service for purposes of backup protection of such communication. § 2510(17).

Section 2701(a) does not apply to "the person or entity providing a wire or electronic communications service" (such as Internet Service Providers) or to "a user of that service with respect to a communication of or intended for that user." § 2701(c).

The SCA also forbids the disclosure of the contents of stored communications by communications service providers. *See* § 2702(a). There are a number of exceptions, including disclosures to the intended recipient of the communication, disclosures with the consent of the creator or recipient of the communication, disclosures that are "necessarily incident to the rendition of the service or to the protection of the rights or property of the provider of that service," and disclosures to a law enforcement agency under certain circumstances. *See* § 2702(b).

Penalties. The SCA has less severe criminal penalties and civil liability than Title I. Under § 2701(b), violations can result in fines of a minimum of $1,000 per violation and up to six months imprisonment. If the wiretap is done for commercial advantage or gain, then a violation can result in up to one year of imprisonment.

Exclusionary Rule. The SCA does not provide for an exclusionary rule.

Judicial Authority for Obtaining Stored Communications. Under the SCA, the judicial process required for obtaining permission to access stored communications held by electronic communications service providers is much less rigorous than under the Wiretap Act. If the government seeks access to the contents of a communication that has been in storage for 180 days or less, then it must first obtain a warrant supported by probable cause. § 2703(a). If the government wants to access a communication that has been in storage for more than 180 days, the government must provide prior notice to the subscriber and obtain an administrative subpoena, a grand jury subpoena, a trial subpoena, or a court order. § 2703(b). The court order does not require probable cause, only "specific and articulable facts showing that there are reasonable grounds" to believe communications are relevant to the criminal investigation. 18 U.S.C. § 2703(d). However, if the government seeks to access a communication that has been in storage for more than 180 days and does not want to provide prior notice to the subscriber, it must obtain a warrant. § 2703(b). Notice to the subscriber that the government obtained her communications can be delayed for up to 90 days. § 2705.

Court Orders to Obtain Subscriber Records. According to § 2703(c)(1)(B), communication service providers must disclose subscriber information (i.e., identifying information, address, phone number, etc.) to the government under certain circumstances:

(B) A provider of electronic communication service or remote computing service shall disclose a record or other information pertaining to a subscriber to or customer of such service (not including the contents of communications covered by subsection (a) or (b) of this section) to a governmental entity only when the governmental entity —

> (i) obtains a warrant issued under the Federal Rules of Criminal Procedure or equivalent State warrant;
> (ii) obtains a court order for such disclosure under subsection (d) of this section;
> (iii) has the consent of the subscriber or customer to such disclosure

Communications service providers who disclose stored communications in accordance with any of the above orders or subpoenas cannot be held liable for that disclosure. *See* § 2703(e).

Exceptions. Similar to the Wiretap Act, the SCA also has a consent exception, see § 2702(b), and a service provider exception, see § 2701(c)(1). Unlike the service provider exception for the Wiretap Act, which allows interceptions on a limited basis (those necessary to provide the communications service), the SCA's exception is broader, entirely exempting "the person or entity providing a wire or electronic communications service." § 2701(c)(1).

THE PEN REGISTER ACT

The Pen Register Act, codified at 18 U.S.C. §§ 3121–3127, governs pen registers and trap and trace devices — and their modern analogues. Recall *Smith v. Maryland,* earlier in this chapter, where the Court held that the Fourth Amendment did not extend to pen register information. The Pen Register Act provides some limited protection for such information. Subject to certain exceptions, "no person may install or use a pen register or a trap and trace device without first obtaining a court order." § 3121(a). Traditionally, a pen register was a device that records the telephone numbers dialled from a particular telephone line (phone numbers of outgoing calls). A trap and trace device is the reverse of a pen register — it records the telephone numbers where incoming calls originate.

Definition of "Pen Register." The Pen Register Act defines pen registers more broadly than phone number information:

> [T]he term "pen register" means a device or process which records or decodes dialing, routing, addressing, or signaling information transmitted by an instrument or facility from which a wire or electronic communication is transmitted, provided, however, that such information shall not include the contents of any communication . . . 18 U.S.C. § 3127(3)

Court Orders. If the government certifies that "the information likely to be obtained by such installation and use is relevant to an ongoing investigation," § 3123(a), then courts "shall authorize the installation and use of a pen register or a trap and trace device for a period not to exceed sixty days." § 3123(c). This standard is a low threshold. As Susan Freiwald contends: "[T]he language of the [pen register] court order requirement raises doubt as to its efficacy as a guard against fishing expeditions. . . . The relevance standard in the transaction records provision allows law enforcement to obtain records of people who may be tangentially involved in a crime, even as innocent victims."[58]

Enforcement. There is no exclusionary rule for violations of the Pen Register Act. Rather than a suppression remedy, the Pen Register Act provides: "Whoever knowingly violates subsection (a) shall be fined under this title or imprisoned not more than one year, or both." § 3121(d).

VIDEO SURVEILLANCE

Prior to the enactment of the ECPA, video surveillance was not encompassed within the language of Title III. When it amended federal electronic surveillance law in 1986 by enacting the ECPA, Congress again failed to address video surveillance. Of course, if the government intercepts a *communication* consisting of video images (such as a transmission of a webcam image or an e-mail containing a video clip), then the Wiretap Act applies. If the government accesses an individual's stored video clip, then the SCA applies. However, being watched by video *surveillance* (such as a surveillance camera) does not involve an interception or an accessing of stored images. The video surveillance must be silent video surveillance, or else it could be an "oral" communication subject to the Wiretap Act. In sum, silent video surveillance is not covered under federal electronic surveillance law. *See, e.g., United States v. Biasuci,* 786 F.2d 504 (2d Cir. 1986); *United States v. Koyomejian,* 970 F.2d 536 (9th Cir. 1992); *United States v. Falls,* 34 F.3d 674 (8th Cir. 1994).

In *United States v. Mesa-Rincon,* 911 F.2d 1433 (10th Cir. 1990), the court observed that although federal electronic surveillance law did not apply to video surveillance, the Fourth Amendment did:

> Unfortunately, Congress has not yet specifically defined the constitutional requirements for video surveillance. Nevertheless, the general fourth amendment requirements are still applicable to video surveillance; and suppression is required when the government fails to follow these requirements.
>
> Title III establishes elaborate warrant requirements for wiretapping and bugging. Unfortunately, Title III does not discuss television surveillance in any way. Thus, its requirements are not binding on this court in the context of video surveillance. However, the fact that Title III does not discuss television surveillance is no authority for the proposition that Congress meant to outlaw the practice.

ELECTRONIC SURVEILLANCE LAW AND THE FOURTH AMENDMENT

Electronic surveillance law operates independently of the Fourth Amendment. Even if a search is reasonable under the Fourth Amendment, electronic surveillance law may bar the evidence. Even if a search is authorized by a judge under federal electronic surveillance law, the Fourth Amendment could still prohibit the wiretap.

---

[58] Susan Freiwald, *Uncertain Privacy: Communications Attributes After the Digital Telephony Act,* 69 S. Cal. L. Rev. 949, 1005-06 (1996).

Moreover, procedures for obtaining a court order under the Wiretap Act are more stringent than those for obtaining a search warrant under the Fourth Amendment. As an example of how the Wiretap Act is stricter, under the Fourth Amendment, any law enforcement official can apply for a warrant. Under the Wiretap Act, in contrast, only certain officials (prosecuting attorneys) can apply.

In at least one significant way, federal electronic surveillance law is broader than the Fourth Amendment. Under the Fourth Amendment, search warrants generally authorize a single entry and prompt search. Warrants must be narrowly circumscribed. They are not a license for unlimited and continued investigation. Under the Wiretap Act, however, courts can authorize continuing surveillance — 24 hours a day for a 30-day period. This period can also be extended.

The Supreme Court has held that, pursuant to a warrant or an order under electronic surveillance law, the government can secretly enter one's residence or private property to install electronic surveillance devices, such as bugs. *See Dahlia v. United States*, 441 U.S. 238 (1979). The *Dahlia* Court further concluded that the Fourth Amendment does not require that an electronic surveillance order include a specific authorization to enter covertly the premises described in the order. In other words, the police need not request permission to make a covert entry when applying for an electronic surveillance order, and the order authorizing the use of electronic surveillance need not make any reference to a covert entry.

ELECTRONIC SURVEILLANCE ORDERS

The number of electronic surveillance orders issued under federal wiretap law has greatly expanded. In 1968, there were a total of 174 orders were approved. In 1980, 564 were approved; in 1990, 872 orders were approved; and in 1999, the number of approved orders was 1,350. In 2004, federal and state courts authorized 1,710 intercepts. In 2006, there was an increase to 1,839. In 2010, there were 3,194 intercepts authorized. This figure represents an increase of 34 percent in the number reported in 2009. The vast majority of requests for electronic surveillance orders have been granted. For example, from 1968 to 1996, about 20,000 requests for electronic surveillance orders were made, and only 28 have been denied.[59] In 2010, with a total of 3,194 orders granted, only one application for a wiretap was denied.[60]

Wiretap orders in the 1990s increasingly became a phenomenon of state rather than federal courts. In 1997, there were 569 federal orders and 617 state orders. In 2001, the breakdown was 486 federal and 1,005 state orders. In the twenty-first century, there are still more state than federal wiretap orders each year. Yet, the most important development has been the rapid increase in federal orders. In 2006, there were 461 federal orders and 1,378 state orders. In 2010, there were 1,207 federal orders and 1,987 state orders.

---

[59] *See* Title III Electronic Surveillance 1968-1999, http://www.epic.org/privacy/wiretap/stats/wiretap_stats.html.

[60] Administrative Office of the U.S. Courts, 2010 Wiretap Act Report, at http://www.uscourts.gov/uscourts/Statistics/WiretapReports/2010/2010WireTapReport.pdf

States vary greatly based on the extent to which they wiretap. Indeed, wiretaps are primarily a phenomenon of a handful of jurisdictions. At the state level in 2010, three states, California (657 orders), New York (480), and New Jersey (215) accounted for 68 percent of all wiretap orders. This pattern of use is likely independent of crime patterns in the United States. Rather, it probably reflects local norms of law enforcement practice, including prosecutorial familiarity with the complex set of legal requirements for obtaining wiretap orders.

In a comparative examination of statistics regarding electronic surveillance orders, Paul Schwartz examined trends in the United States and Germany. Schwartz found that in both countries, "law enforcement agencies in certain geographic areas generate a disproportionate amount of surveillance orders."[61] One German scholar, Johann Bizer, has observed that the differences between different German states cannot be explained by varying population structures or political orientation of state governments. Thus, in both Germany and the United States, requests for telecommunications surveillance appear to be driven by local enforcement norms as well as the law. What factors are likely to shape local enforcement norms and encourage or discourage the use of telecommunications surveillance?

Returning to the U.S. wiretap statistics, 96 percent of all wiretaps in 2010 involved mobile devices, such as cell phones and pagers. In 2010, there was an average of 3,199 intercepts and 188 persons involved per order. The average percentage of incriminating intercepts per wiretap order in 2010 was 26 percent, and this last statistic gives one pause. To be as clear as possible, this statistic is not inconsistent with each wiretap order leading to the collection of some incriminating intercepts. It means that on average 74 percent of the communications intercepted per order did not contain anything incriminating.

Is the glass 20 percent full or 80 percent empty? The Wiretap Act requires strict minimization of the collection of extraneous information once surveillance occurs. Are these statistics an indication that too much innocent communication is being monitored? Rarely will everything said by a particular person or on a particular phone line be incriminating. Is it practical to expect a much higher incriminating percentage than 20 percent?

As a final matter concerning these official statistics, the Wiretap Act Report details the results of wiretaps in terms of arrests as well as the number of motions made and granted to suppress with respect to interceptions. Wiretaps terminated in 2006 led to the arrest of 4,376 persons and the conviction of 711 persons. Wiretaps terminated in 2010 led to the arrest of 4,711 persons and the conviction of 800 persons.

In the analysis of Paul Schwartz, the entire system for statistical analysis of surveillance activity is deeply flawed. He argues that "rational inquiry about

---

[61] Paul M. Schwartz, *German and U.S. Telecommunications Privacy Law: Legal Regulation of Domestic Law Enforcement Surveillance*, 54 Hastings L.J. 751, 759-60 (2003); *see also* Paul M. Schwartz, *Evaluating Telecommunications Surveillance in Germany*, 72 Geo. Wash. L. Rev. 1244 (2004).

telecommunications surveillance is . . . largely precluded by the haphazard and incomplete information that the government collects about it."[62] Schwartz notes:

> [T]here has been a significant movement in surveillance activity away from the capturing of content pursuant to the Wiretap Act, which is the most carefully regulated and reported-on area of telecommunications surveillance. Of more importance today is the collection of telecommunications attributes under the Pen Register Act and the Stored Communications Act. Yet, we lack access to any statistical data about activities under the latter, and have less than full and up-to-date information regarding the former.

To counter this state of affairs, Schwartz proposes, among other measures, an annual index that would include information about law enforcement activity under the Stored Communications Act. The annual index also would harmonize information collected in order "to give a clear picture of how activities in different areas relate to another." As an example, FISA should be amended to separate statistics for physical and electronic searches so activity under FISA can be compared more clearly with that under the Wiretap Act and other statutory authorities.

STATE ELECTRONIC SURVEILLANCE LAW

A number of states have enacted their own versions of electronic surveillance law, some of which are more protective than federal electronic surveillance law. For example, several states require the consent of all parties to a conversation. Unless all parties consent, these states require a warrant for a wiretap. In contrast, federal wiretap law allows law enforcement to listen in to a conversation if any party to it consents to the surveillance.

One prominent example of a more protective state law was the indictment on July 30, 1999, of Linda Tripp on two counts of violating Maryland's wiretapping law. At the request of the Office of the Independent Counsel, Linda Tripp had secretly taped a phone conversation she had with Monica Lewinsky about Lewinsky's affair with President Clinton. Tripp then disclosed the contents of that conversation to a news magazine. Possible penalties under Maryland law included up to ten years' imprisonment and a $20,000 fine. Maryland's wiretapping law, in contrast to federal wiretap law, requires the consent of the other party to a communication. Tripp was indicted by a Maryland grand jury. Although Tripp was protected by a federal grant of immunity from prosecution, Maryland was not part of the immunity agreement and could prosecute Tripp. After a judicial ruling suppressing certain evidence, the case against Tripp was dropped.

Massachusetts also has an all-party-consent electronic surveillance law. Consider *Commonwealth v. Hyde,* 750 N.E.2d 963 (Mass. 2001). The defendant Michael Hyde was stopped by the police for a routine auto stop. The police searched the defendant, his passenger, and his car. No traffic citation was issued. Hyde filed a complaint at the police station about the stop, and he provided a hidden audio recording he had made of the encounter. The police subsequently

---

[62] Paul M. Schwartz, *Reviving Telecommunications Surveillance Law,* 75 U. Chi. L. Rev. 287 (2008).

charged Hyde with illegal electronic surveillance in violation of state law, G.L. c. 272, § 99, which provides that "any person who willfully commits an interception, attempts to commit an interception, or procures any other person to commit an interception or to attempt to commit an interception of any wire or oral communication shall be fined not more than ten thousand dollars, or imprisoned in the state prison for not more than five years, or imprisoned in a jail or house of correction for not more than two and one half years, or both so fined and given one such imprisonment." Hyde was convicted and sentenced to six months probation and a $500 fine.

The *Hyde* court concluded:

> We conclude that the Legislature intended G.L. c. 272, § 99, strictly to prohibit all secret recordings by members of the public, including recordings of police officers or other public officials interacting with members of the public, when made without their permission or knowledge. . . .
>
> We reject the defendant's argument that the statute is not applicable because the police officers were performing their public duties, and, therefore, had no reasonable expectation of privacy in their words. The statute's preamble expresses the Legislature's general concern that "the uncontrolled development and unrestricted use of modern electronic surveillance devices pose[d] grave dangers to the privacy of all citizens of the commonwealth" and this concern was relied on to justify the ban on the public's clandestine use of such devices. While we recognize that G.L. c. 272, § 99, was designed to prohibit the use of electronic surveillance devices by private individuals because of the serious threat they pose to the "privacy of all citizens," the plain language of the statute, which is the best indication of the Legislature's ultimate intent, contains nothing that would protect, on the basis of privacy rights, the recording that occurred here. In *Commonwealth v. Jackson, supra* at 506, 349 N.E.2d 337, this court rejected the argument that, because a kidnapper has no legitimate privacy interest in telephone calls made for ransom purposes, the secret electronic recording of that conversation by the victim's brother would not be prohibited under G.L. c. 272, § 99: "[W]e would render meaningless the Legislature's careful choice of words if we were to interpret 'secretly' as encompassing only those situations where an individual has a reasonable expectation of privacy." . . .
>
> Further, if the tape recording here is deemed proper on the ground that public officials are involved, then the door is opened even wider to electronic "bugging" or secret audio tape recording (both are prohibited by the statute and both are indistinguishable in the injury they inflict) of virtually every encounter or meeting between a person and a public official, whether the meeting or encounter is one that is stressful (like the one in this case or, perhaps, a session with a tax auditor) or nonstressful (like a routine meeting between a parent and a teacher in a public school to discuss a good student's progress). The door once opened would be hard to close, and the result would contravene the statute's broad purpose and the Legislature's clear prohibition of *all* secret interceptions and recordings by private citizens.

In dissent, Chief Justice Marshall wrote:

> The purpose of G.L. c. 272, § 99, is not to shield public officials from exposure of their wrongdoings. I have too great a respect for the Legislature to read any such meaning into a statute whose purpose is plain, and points in another direction entirely. Where the legislative intent is explicit, it violates a

fundamental rule of statutory construction to reach a result that is plainly contrary to that objective. To hold that the Legislature intended to allow police officers to conceal possible misconduct behind a cloak of privacy requires a more affirmative showing than this statute allows.

In our Republic the actions of public officials taken in their public capacities are not protected from exposure. Citizens have a particularly important role to play when the official conduct at issue is that of the police. Their role cannot be performed if citizens must fear criminal reprisals when they seek to hold government officials responsible by recording — secretly recording on occasion — an interaction between a citizen and a police officer. . . .

The court's ruling today also threatens the ability of the press — print and electronic — to perform its constitutional role of watchdog. As the court construes the Massachusetts wiretapping statute, there is no principled distinction to explain why members of the media would not be held to the same standard as all other citizens.

A few years later, Hyde was convicted again of secretly recording a police officer who had pulled him over in a traffic stop. Are all-party electronic surveillance laws too broad? What kinds of exceptions, if any, should be made?

Note as well that these all-party-consent statutes will also regulate surveillance by private sector entities. In *Kearney v. Salomon Smith Barney*, 137 P.2d 914 (Cal. 2006), two California clients sued a financial institution because their telephone calls to brokers in the institution's Georgia office were recorded without their consent. A California statute prohibited recording a telephone conversation without consent of all parties to it. In contrast, a Georgia statute permitted recording a telephone conversation if consent of one party had been granted. The California Supreme Court concluded that "comparative impairment analysis supports the application of California law in this context." It reached this conclusion by assessing the relative harm suffered to each state due to this conflict of law:

[I]n light of the substantial number of businesses operating in California that maintain out-of-state offices or telephone operators, a resolution of this conflict permitting all such businesses to regularly and routinely record telephone conversations made to or from California clients or consumers without the clients' or consumers' knowledge or consent would significantly impair the privacy policy guaranteed by California law, and potentially would place local California businesses (that would continue to be subject to California's protective privacy law) at an unfair competitive disadvantage vis-à-vis their out-of-state counterparts. At the same time, application of California law will not have a significant detrimental effect on Georgia's interests as embodied in the applicable Georgia law, because applying California law (1) will not adversely affect any privacy interest protected by Georgia law, (2) will affect only those business telephone calls in Georgia that are made to or are received from California clients, and (3) with respect to such calls, will not prevent a business located in Georgia from implementing or maintaining a practice of recording *all* such calls, but will require only that the business *inform* its clients or customers, at the outset of the call, of the company's policy of recording such calls. (. . . if a business informs a client or customer at the outset of a telephone call that the call is being recorded, the recording would not violate the applicable California statute.)

When state government officials are engaging in electronic surveillance, they are often subject to much less public scrutiny than their federal counterparts. Charles Kennedy and Peter Swire have concluded that there are likely to be significant differences between federal and state electronic surveillance because of differences in the respective "[i]nstitutions, procedures and training" of law enforcement personnel:

> Because state procedures are watched less systematically by the press and civil liberties organizations, abuses at the state level, whether deliberate or the result of inexperience, may not be detected. The under-reporting of state wiretaps . . . is both a symptom of and a contributing factor to this relative lack of oversight. The simple fact is that half of the states have wiretap powers, yet reported no wiretaps in 2001. The utter failure to file the annual wiretap report would be unthinkable at the federal level. In addition, the under-reporting of state wiretaps keeps the use and possible misuse of state wiretaps less visible.[63]

As noted above, moreover, wiretap orders over the last decade have increasingly become a phenomenon of state rather than federal courts. Yet, as Kennedy and Swire observe, we know far less about how state law enforcement agencies make use of their wiretap powers than federal ones. As for the lack of state wiretap reports from many states, the obligation to file a report with the Administrative Office of the U.S. Courts extends only to instances when the states actually make use of these powers. In other words, the Administrative Office does not require reports to be filed if no interception activity took place in the state during a given year.[64] As a simple, initial step at ending the ambiguity about the possible under-reporting of state wiretap orders, should states be required to file a report even if no surveillance activity takes place in it during a particular year?

4. THE COMMUNICATIONS ASSISTANCE FOR LAW ENFORCEMENT ACT

In *United States v. New York Telephone*, 434 U.S. 159 (1977), the Supreme Court held that 18 U.S.C. § 2518(4) required telecommunications providers to furnish "any assistance necessary to accomplish an electronic interception." However, the issue of whether a provider had to create and design its technology to facilitate authorized electronic surveillance remained an open question.

In the 1980s, new communications technology was developed to enable more wireless communications — cellular telephones, microwave, and satellite communications. As a result of fears that these new technologies would be harder to monitor, the law enforcement community successfully convinced Congress to

---

[63] Charles H. Kennedy & Peter P. Swire, *State Wiretaps and Electronic Surveillance After September 11,* 54 Hastings L.J. 971 (2003).

[64] Paul Schwartz, *German and U.S. Telecommunications Privacy Law*, 54 Hastings L.J. 751, 760 (2003).

force telecommunications providers to ensure that the government could continue to monitor electronic communications.[65]

The Communications Assistance for Law Enforcement Act (CALEA) of 1994, Pub. L. No. 103-414, (also known as the "Digital Telephony Act") requires telecommunication providers to help facilitate the government in executing legally authorized surveillance. The Act was passed against strong opposition from some civil liberties organizations. Congress appropriated federal funding of $500 million to telephone companies to make the proposed changes.

Requirements. CALEA requires all telecommunications providers to be able to isolate and intercept electronic communications and be able to deliver them to law enforcement personnel. If carriers provide an encryption service to users, then they must decrypt the communications. CALEA permits the telecommunications industry to develop the technology. Under a "safe harbor" provision, carriers that comply with accepted industry standards are in compliance with CALEA. 47 U.S.C. § 1006(a)(2).

Limits. CALEA contains some important limits. Carriers must "facilitat[e] authorized communications interceptions and access to call-identifying information . . . in a manner that protects . . . the privacy and security of communications and call-identifying information not authorized to be intercepted." § 1002(a)(4)(A). Further, CALEA is designed to provide "law enforcement no more and no less access to information than it had in the past." H.R. Rep. No. 103-827, pt. 1, at 22. Additionally, CALEA does not apply to "information services," such as e-mail and Internet access. §§ 1001(8)(C)(i), 1002(b)(2)(A).

The J-Standard. In *United States Telecom Ass'n v. FCC*, 227 F.3d 450 (D.C. Cir. 2000), the D.C. Circuit attempted to place certain limits on the FCC's interpretation of CALEA. This statute had set up a process by which the telecommunications industry "in consultation with law enforcement agencies, regulators, and consumers, [was] to develop its own technical standards for meeting the required surveillance capabilities." In 1995, the telecommunications industry started to develop this safe harbor standard, which was adopted by the industry in December 1997.

The standard is known as the Interim Standard/Trial Use Standard J-STD-025 (the "J-Standard"). The J-Standard sets forth the standards by which carriers can make communications and call-identifying information available to law enforcement officials. A group of industry associations as well as privacy organizations challenged the J-Standard and petitioned the Federal Communications Commission (FCC) to remove provisions that they argued extended beyond CALEA's authorization. In contrast, the Justice Department and FBI petitioned the FCC to add nine additional surveillance capabilities on its "punch list" to the J-Standard. The FCC refused the requests of the industry associations and privacy advocacy groups, but did add four of the nine items sought by the Justice Department and FBI to the J-Standard. The D.C. Circuit rejected the four chal-

---

[65] For a detailed analysis of CALEA, see Susan Freiwald, *Uncertain Privacy: Communication Attributes After the Digital Telephony Act*, 69 S. Cal. L. Rev. 949 (1996).

lenged items added to the J-Standard and remanded to the FCC to demonstrate compliance with CALEA, including the statutory requirement of the use of "cost-effective means."

An item on the original J-Standard was a requirement that carriers inform law enforcement officials of the nearest antenna tower to a mobile telephone user, giving officials the ability to track the location of mobile telephones. The D.C. court held that the requirement was valid under CALEA:

> Not only did the Commission elucidate the textual basis for interpreting "call-identifying information" to include location information, but it also explained how that result comports with CALEA's goal of preserving the same surveillance capabilities that law enforcement agencies had in POTS (plain old telephone service). "[I]n the wireline environment," the Commission explained, law enforcement agencies "have generally been able to obtain location information routinely from the telephone number because the telephone number usually corresponds with location." In the wireless environment, "the equivalent location information" is "the location of the cell sites to which the mobile terminal or handset is connected at the beginning and at the termination of the call." Accordingly, the Commission concluded, "[p]rovision of this particular location information does not appear to expand or diminish law enforcement's surveillance authority under prior law applicable to the wireline environment."

On remand, the FCC returned the four items that it had earlier approved from the law enforcement "punch list" once again to the J-Standard. *In the Matter of Communications Assistance for Law Enforcement Act*, FCC 02-108 (Apr. 5, 2002). One of these items concerned "post-cut-through dialed digit extraction," which is a list of any digits that a person dials after a call has been connected. The FCC required that a telecommunications carrier "have the ability to turn on and off the dialed digit extraction capability." It therefore mandated a "toggle feature" that would allow a carrier to turn off the capability if it "had reservations about the legal basis for providing all post-cut through digits" while it was, at the same time, providing "other punch list capabilities included in the same software."

Voice over Internet Protocol (VoIP). A new way to make telephone calls is to use a broadband Internet connection to transmit the call. This technique, VoIP, converts a voice signal into a digital signal that travels over the Internet and connects to a phone number. On August 4, 2004, the FCC unanimously adopted a Notice of Proposed Rulemaking and Declaratory Ruling regarding VoIP and CALEA. *In the Matter of Communications Assistance for Law Enforcement Act and Broadband Access and Services*, FCC 04-187 (Aug. 4, 2004). It tentatively declared that CALEA applies to any facilities-based providers of any type of broadband Internet access service — including wireline, cable modem, satellite, wireless, and powerline — and to managed or mediated VoIP services. This conclusion was based on an FCC judgment that these services fall under CALEA statutory language as "a replacement for a substantial portion of the local telephone service." 47 U.S.C. § 1001(8)B)(ii).

The FCC continued its work in this area by issuing an Order in 2005 that built on its previous Notice of Proposed Rulemaking. This rulemaking, upheld by the D.C. Circuit in June 2006, established that broadband and VoIP are "hybrid telecommunications-information services" that fall under CALEA to the extent that they qualify as "telecommunications carriers." Communications Assistance for Law Enforcement and Broadband Access and Services, 20 F.C.C.R. 14989, at ¶ 18 (2005); *American Council on Education v. FCC*, 451 F.3d 266 (D.C. Cir. 2006).

In May 2006, the FCC issued an additional order to address remaining issues to achieve CALEA compliance. Second Report and Order and Memorandum Opinion and Order (Order), FCC 06-56 (May 12, 2006). The FCC's overarching policy perspective concerned giving law enforcement agencies all the resources that CALEA authorizes to combat crime and support homeland security. As FCC Chairman Kevin J. Martin observed in a statement issued as part of the Order, "Enabling law enforcement to ensure our safety and security is of paramount importance." The Order set a May 14, 2007, compliance date for both facilities-based broadband Internet access and interconnected VoIP providers. It also permitted entities covered by CALEA to have the option of using Trusted Third Parties (TTPs) to help meet their CALEA obligations. The role of the TTPs would include processing requests for intercepts, conducting electronic surveillance, and delivering relevant information to law enforcement agencies.

Susan Landau and Whitfield Diffie argue that extension of CALEA requirements to the Internet will ironically make it less secure and create a potential for cyber-terrorism. The problem is that CALEA has now been interpreted to require that modifications be made to Internet protocols, which present the risk of introducing vulnerabilities into the system. In their view, inserting wiretap requirements into Internet protocols will make the Internet less secure. A system that permits "legally authorized security breaches" (such as a wiretap by law enforcement officers) is also more open to unauthorized security breaches (such as hacking and other kinds of unlawful intrusions). They argue:

> On balance we are better off with a secure computer infrastructure than with one that builds surveillance into the network fabric. At times this may press law enforcement to exercise more initiative and imagination in its investigations. On the other hand, in a society completely dependent on computer-to-computer communications, the alternative presents a hazard whose dimensions are as yet impossible to comprehend.[66]

5. THE USA PATRIOT ACT

On the morning of September 11, 2001, terrorists hijacked four planes and crashed three of them into the World Trade Center and the Pentagon, killing thousands of people. The nation was awakened into a world filled with new frightening dangers. Shortly after the September 11 attacks, a still unknown person or persons sent letters laced with the deadly bacteria anthrax through the mail to several prominent individuals in the news media and in politics. Acting with great haste, Congress passed a sweeping new law expanding the government's electronic surveillance powers in many significant ways.[67] Called

---

[66] Susan Landau & Whitfield Diffie, *Privacy on the Line* 331, 328 (2d ed. 2007).

[67] For background about the passage of the USA PATRIOT Act, see Beryl A. Howell, *Seven Weeks: The Making of the USA Patriot Act,* 72 Geo. Wash. L. Rev. 1145 (2004).

the "Uniting and Strengthening America By Providing Appropriate Tools Required To Intercept and Obstruct Terrorism Act" (USA PATRIOT Act), the Act made a number of substantial changes to several statutes, including the federal electronic surveillance statutes.

Definition of Terrorism. Section 802 of the USA PATRIOT Act added to 18 U.S.C. § 2331 a new definition of "domestic terrorism." According to the Act, domestic terrorism involves "acts dangerous to human life that are a violation of the criminal laws of the United States or of any State" that "appear to be intended: (i) to intimidate or coerce a civilian population; (ii) to influence the policy of a government by intimidation or coercion; or (iii) to affect the conduct of a government by mass destruction, assassination, or kidnapping; and . . . occur primarily within the territorial jurisdiction of the United States." According to many proponents of civil liberties, this definition is very broad and could potentially encompass many forms of civil disobedience, which, although consisting of criminal conduct (minor violence, threats, property damage), includes conduct that has historically been present in many political protests and has never been considered to be terrorism.

🗡 *Delayed Notice of Search Warrants.* Under the Fourth Amendment, the government must obtain a warrant and provide notice to a person before conducting a search or seizure. Case law provided for certain limited exceptions. Section 213 of the USA PATRIOT Act adds a provision to 18 U.S.C. § 3103a, enabling the government to delay notice if the court concludes that there is "reasonable cause" that immediate notice will create an "adverse result" such as physical danger, the destruction of evidence, delayed trial, flight from prosecution, and other circumstances. § 3103a(b). Warrants enabling a covert search with delayed notice are often referred to as "sneak and peek" warrants. Civil libertarians consider "sneak and peek" warrants dangerous because they authorize covert searches, thus preventing individuals from safeguarding their rights during the search. Moreover, there is little supervision of the government's carrying out of the search. Law enforcement officials argue that covert searches are necessary to avoid tipping off suspects that there is an investigation under way.

New Definition of Pen Registers and Trap and Trace Devices. Under the Pen Register Act of the ECPA, §§ 3121 *et seq.*, the definitions of pen registers and trap and trace devices focused primarily on telephone numbers. A pen register was defined under 18 U.S.C. § 3127(3) as

> a device which records or decodes electronic or other impulses which identify the numbers dialed or otherwise transmitted on the telephone line to which such device is attached. . . .

Section 216 of the USA PATRIOT Act changed the definition to read:

> a device *or process* which records or decodes *dialing, routing, addressing, or signaling information transmitted by an instrument or facility from which a wire or electronic communication is transmitted, provided, however, that such*

information shall not include the contents of any communication is attached . . . (changes emphasized).

These changes altered the definition of a pen register from applying not only to telephone numbers but also to Internet addresses, e-mail addressing information (the "to" and "from" lines on e-mail), and the routing information of a wide spectrum of communications. The inclusion of "or process" after "device" enlarges the means by which such routing information can be intercepted beyond the use of a physical device. The definition of a trap and trace device was changed in a similar way. Recall that under the Pen Register Act, a court order to obtain such information does not require probable cause, but merely certification that "the information likely to be obtained by such installation and use is relevant to an ongoing criminal investigation." 18 U.S.C. § 3123. The person whose communications are subject to this order need not even be a criminal suspect; all that the government needs to certify is relevance to an investigation.

Recall *Smith v. Maryland* earlier in this chapter, where the Court held that pen registers were not protected under the Fourth Amendment. Does the new definition of pen register and trap and trace device under the USA PATRIOT Act go beyond *Smith v. Maryland*? Are Internet addresses and e-mail addressing information analogous to pen registers?

Private Right of Action for Government Disclosures. The USA PATRIOT Act adds a provision to the Stored Communications Act that provides for civil actions against the United States for any "willful" violations. 18 U.S.C. § 2712. The court may assess actual damages or $10,000 (whichever is greater) and litigation costs. Such an action must first be presented before the "appropriate department or agency under the procedures of the Federal Tort Claims Act."

Reauthorization. When the USA PATRIOT Act was passed, several provisions had sunset provisions and would expire on a particular date. On March 9, 2006, President George W. Bush signed the USA PATRIOT Reauthorization Act, which made permanent 14 of 16 expiring USA PATRIOT Act sections. It created a new sunset of December 31, 2009 for USA PATRIOT Act sections 205 and 215 (which concern "roving" FISA wiretaps and FISA orders for business records), and for FISA's "lone wolf" amendments. This law also expanded the list of predicate offenses for which law enforcement could obtain wiretap orders.

C. DIGITAL SEARCHES AND SEIZURES

1. SEARCHING THE CONTENTS OF COMPUTERS

The Scope of Warrants to Search Computers. In *United States v. Lacy*, 119 F.3d 742 (9th Cir. 1997), the defendant challenged a search warrant authorizing the seizure of his computer hard drive and disks. The defendant contended that the warrant was too general because it applied to his entire computer system. The court upheld the warrant because "this type of generic classification is acceptable when a more precise description is not possible." Several other courts have followed a similar approach as in *Lacy*, upholding generic warrants. In *United States v. Upham*, 168 F.3d 532 (1st Cir. 1999), the court reasoned: "A sufficient chance of finding some needles in the computer haystack was established by the probable-cause showing in the warrant application; and a search of a computer and co-located disks is not inherently more intrusive than the physical search of an entire house for a weapon or drugs." *See also United States v. Hay*, 231 F.3d 630 (9th Cir. 2000) (following *Lacy* and upholding a "generic" warrant application).[68]

However, there are limits to the scope of a search of a computer. In *United States v. Carey*, 172 F.3d 1268 (10th Cir. 1999), an officer obtained a warrant to search a computer for records about illegal drug distribution. When the officer stumbled upon a pornographic file, he began to search for similar files. The court concluded that these actions amounted to an expansion of the scope of the search and would require the obtaining of a second warrant.

In *United States v. Campos*, 221 F.3d 1143 (10th Cir. 2000), the defendant e-mailed two images of child pornography to a person he talked to in a chat room. The person informed the FBI, and the FBI obtained a warrant to search the defendant's home and computer. The agents seized the defendant's computer, and a search revealed the two images of child pornography as well as six other images of child pornography. The defendant challenged the search as beyond the scope of the warrant because the agents "had grounds to search only for the two images that had been sent." However, the court rejected the defendant's contention, quoting from the FBI's explanation why it is not feasible to search only for particular computer files in one's home:

> . . . Computer storage devices . . . can store the equivalent of thousands of pages of information. Especially when the user wants to conceal criminal evidence, he often stores it in random order with deceptive file names. This requires searching authorities to examine all the stored data to determine whether it is included in the warrant. This sorting process can take weeks or months, depending on the volume of data stored, and it would be impractical to attempt this kind of data search on site. . . .
>
> Searching computer systems for criminal evidence is a highly technical process requiring expert skill and a properly controlled environment. The wide variety of computer hardware and software available requires even computer experts to specialize in some systems and applications, so it is difficult to know before a search which expert should analyze the system and its data. . . . Since computer evidence is extremely vulnerable to tampering or destruction (both from external sources or from destructive code embedded into the system as "booby trap"), the controlled environment of a laboratory is essential to its complete analysis. . . .

Computer Searches and Seizures. Searches and seizures for digital information in computers present some unique conceptual puzzles for existing Fourth Amendment doctrine. Thomas Clancy contends:

---

[68] For more about computer searches, see Raphael Winnick, *Searches and Seizures of Computers and Computer Data*, 88 Harv. J.L. & Tech. 75 (1994).

[C]omputers are containers. . . . They . . . contain electronic evidence, that is, a series of digitally stored 0s and 1s that, when combined with a computer program, yield such items as images, words, and spreadsheets. Accordingly, the traditional standards of the Fourth Amendment regulate obtaining the evidence in containers that happen to be computers.[69]

But is a computer a single container or is each computer file its own container? Orin Kerr argues:

A single physical storage device can store the private files of thousands of different users. It would be quite odd if looking at one file on a server meant that the entire server had been searched, and that the police could then analyze everything on the server, perhaps belonging to thousands of different people, without any restriction.[70]

Is copying a computer file or other digital information a seizure under the Fourth Amendment? In *United States v. Gorshkov*, 2001 WL 1024026 (W.D. Wash. 2001), the FBI remotely copied the contents of the defendant's computer in Russia. The court held: "The agents' act of copying the data on the Russian computers was not a seizure under the Fourth Amendment because it did not interfere with Defendant's or anyone else's possessory interest in the data." However, as Susan Brenner and Barbara Frederiksen contend:

[T]he information contained in computer files clearly belongs to the owner of the files. The ownership of information is similar to the contents of a private conversation in which the information belongs to the parties to the conversation. Copying computer data is analogous to recording a conversation. . . . Therefore, copying computer files should be treated as a seizure.[71]

Password-Protected Files. In *Trulock v. Freeh*, 275 F.3d 391 (4th Cir. 2001), Notra Trulock and Linda Conrad shared a computer but maintained separate files protected by passwords. They did not know each other's password and could not access each other's files. When FBI officials, without a warrant, asked to search and seize the computer, Conrad consented. The court held that the FBI could not search Trulock's files since Trulock had not consented:

Consent to search in the absence of a warrant may, in some circumstances, be given by a person other than the target of the search. Two criteria must be met in order for third party consent to be effective. First, the third party must have authority to consent to the search. Second, the third party's consent must be voluntary. . . .

We conclude that, based on the facts in the complaint, Conrad lacked authority to consent to the search of Trulock's files. Conrad and Trulock both used a computer located in Conrad's bedroom and each had joint access to the hard drive. Conrad and Trulock, however, protected their personal files with passwords; Conrad did not have access to Trulock's passwords. Although

---

[69] Thomas K. Clancy, *The Fourth Amendment Aspects of Computer Searches and Seizures: A Perspective and a Primer*, 75 Miss. L.J. 193, 196 (2005).

[70] Orin S. Kerr, *Searches and Seizures in a Digital World*, 119 Harv. L. Rev. 531, 556 (2005).

[71] Susan W. Brenner & Barbara A. Frederiksen, *Computer Searches and Seizures: Some Unresolved Issues*, 8 Mich. Telecomm. & Tech. L. Rev. 39, 111-12 (2002).

Conrad had authority to consent to a general search of the computer, her authority did not extend to Trulock's password-protected files.

UNITED STATES V. ANDRUS

483 F.3d 711 (10th Cir. 2007)

[Federal authorities believed that Ray Andrus was downloading child pornography to his home computer. Ray Andrus resided at his parents' house. Federal officials obtained the consent of Dr. Andrus (Andrus's father) to search the home. He also consented to their searching any computers in the home. The officials went into Ray Andrus's bedroom and a forensic expert examined the contents of the computer's hard drive with forensic software. The software enabled direct access to the computer, bypassing any password protection the user put on it. The officials discovered child pornography on the computer. Later on, the officials learned that Ray Andrus had protected his computer with a password and that his father did not know the password. Is the father's consent to search the computer valid since he did not know the password?]

MURPHY, J. . . . Subject to limited exceptions, the Fourth Amendment prohibits warrantless searches of an individual's home or possessions. Voluntary consent to a police search, given by the individual under investigation or by a third party with authority over the subject property, is a well-established exception to the warrant requirement. Valid third party consent can arise either through the third party's actual authority or the third party's apparent authority. A third party has actual authority to consent to a search "if that third party has either (1) mutual use of the property by virtue of joint access, or (2) control for most purposes." Even where actual authority is lacking, however, a third party has apparent authority to consent to a search when an officer reasonably, even if erroneously, believes the third party possesses authority to consent. *See Georgia v. Randolph,* 547 U.S. 103 (2006).

Whether apparent authority exists is an objective, totality-of-the-circumstances inquiry into whether the facts available to the officers at the time they commenced the search would lead a reasonable officer to believe the third party had authority to consent to the search. When the property to be searched is an object or container, the relevant inquiry must address the third party's relationship to the object. In *Randolph,* the Court explained, "The constant element in assessing Fourth Amendment reasonableness in consent cases . . . is the great significance given to widely shared social expectations." For example, the Court said, "[W]hen it comes to searching through bureau drawers, there will be instances in which even a person clearly belonging on the premises as an occupant may lack any perceived authority to consent." . . .

It may be unreasonable for law enforcement to believe a third party has authority to consent to the search of an object typically associated with a high expectation of privacy, especially when the officers know or should know the owner has indicated the intent to exclude the third party from using or exerting control over the object.

Courts considering the issue have attempted to analogize computers to other items more commonly seen in Fourth Amendment jurisprudence. Individuals' expectations of privacy in computers have been likened to their expectations of privacy in "a suitcase or briefcase." Password-protected files have been compared to a "locked footlocker inside the bedroom." *Trulock v. Freeh,* 275 F.3d 391, 403 (4th Cir. 2001).

Given the pervasiveness of computers in American homes, this court must reach some, at least tentative, conclusion about the category into which personal computers fall. A personal computer is often a repository for private information the computer's owner does not intend to share with others. . . .

The inquiry into whether the owner of a highly personal object has indicated a subjective expectation of privacy traditionally focuses on whether the subject suitcase, footlocker, or other container is physically locked. Determining whether a computer is "locked," or whether a reasonable officer should know a computer may be locked, presents a challenge distinct from that associated with other types of closed containers. Unlike footlockers or suitcases, where the presence of a locking device is generally apparent by looking at the item, a "lock" on the data within a computer is not apparent from a visual inspection of the outside of the computer, especially when the computer is in the "off" position prior to the search. Data on an entire computer may be protected by a password, with the password functioning as a lock, or there may be multiple users of a computer, each of whom has an individual and personalized password-protected "user profile." . . .

Courts addressing the issue of third party consent in the context of computers, therefore, have examined officers' knowledge about password protection as an indication of whether a computer is "locked" in the way a footlocker would be. For example, in *Trulock,* the Fourth Circuit held a live-in girlfriend lacked actual authority to consent to a search of her boyfriend's computer files where the girlfriend told police she and her boyfriend shared the household computer but had separate password-protected files that were inaccessible to the other. The court in that case explained, "Although Conrad had authority to consent to a general search of the computer, her authority did not extend to Trulock's password-protected files." . . .

In addition to password protection, courts also consider the location of the computer within the house and other indicia of household members' access to the computer in assessing third party authority. Third party apparent authority to consent to a search has generally been upheld when the computer is located in a common area of the home that is accessible to other family members under circumstances indicating the other family members were not excluded from using the computer. In contrast, where the third party has affirmatively disclaimed access to or control over the computer or a portion of the computer's files, even when the computer is located in a common area of the house, courts have been unwilling to find third party authority.

Andrus' case presents facts that differ somewhat from those in other cases. Andrus' computer was located in a bedroom occupied by the homeowner's fifty-one year old son rather than in a true common area. Dr. Andrus, however, had unlimited access to the room. Law enforcement officers did not ask specific questions about Dr. Andrus' use of the computer, but Dr. Andrus said nothing indicating the need for such questions. *Cf. Trulock,* 275 F.3d at 398 (when law enforcement questioned third party girlfriend about computer, she indicated she and boyfriend had separate password-protected files). The resolution of this appeal turns on whether the officers' belief in Dr. Andrus' authority was reasonable, despite the lack of any affirmative assertion by Dr. Andrus that he used the computer and despite the existence of a user profile indicating Ray Andrus' intent to exclude other household members from using the computer. For the reasons articulated below, this court concludes the officers' belief in Dr. Andrus' authority was reasonable. . . .

First, the officers knew Dr. Andrus owned the house and lived there with family members. Second, the officers knew Dr. Andrus' house had internet access and that Dr. Andrus paid the Time Warner internet and cable bill. Third, the officers knew the email address bandrus@kc.rr.com had been activated and used to register on a website that provided access to child pornography. Fourth, although the officers knew Ray Andrus lived in the center bedroom, they also knew that Dr. Andrus had access to the room at will. Fifth, the officers saw the computer in plain view on the desk in Andrus' room and it appeared available for use by other household members. Furthermore, the record indicates Dr. Andrus did not say or do anything to indicate his lack of ownership or control over the computer when Cheatham asked for his consent to conduct a computer search. It is uncontested that Dr. Andrus led the officers to the bedroom in which the computer was located, and, even after he saw Kanatzar begin to work on the computer, Dr. Andrus remained silent about any lack of authority he had over the computer. Even if Ray Andrus' computer was protected with a user name and password, there is no indication in the record that the officers knew or had reason to believe such protections were in place.

Andrus argues his computer's password protection indicated his computer was "locked" to third parties, a fact the officers would have known had they asked questions of Dr. Andrus prior to searching the computer. Under our case law, however, officers are not obligated to ask questions unless the circumstances are ambiguous. In essence, by suggesting the onus was on the officers to ask about password protection prior to searching the computer, despite the absence of any indication that Dr. Andrus' access to the computer was limited by a password, Andrus necessarily submits there is inherent ambiguity whenever police want to search a household computer and a third party has not affirmatively provided information about his own use of the computer or about password protection. Andrus' argument presupposes, however, that password protection of home computers is so common that a reasonable officer ought to know password protection is likely. Andrus has neither made this argument directly nor proffered any evidence to demonstrate a high incidence of password protection among home computer users. . . .

Viewed under the requisite totality-of-the-circumstances analysis, the facts known to the officers at the time the computer search commenced created an objectively reasonable perception that Dr. Andrus was, at least, *one* user of the computer. That objectively reasonable belief would have been enough to give Dr. Andrus apparent authority to consent to a search. Even if Dr. Andrus had no actual ability to use the computer and the computer was password protected, these mistakes of fact do not negate a determination of Dr. Andrus' apparent authority. In this case, the district court found Agent Cheatham properly halted the search when further conversation with Dr. Andrus revealed he did not use the computer and that Andrus' computer was the only computer in the house. These later revelations, however, have no bearing on the reasonableness of the officers' belief in Dr. Andrus' authority at the outset of the computer search.

McKAY, J., dissenting. This case concerns the reasonable expectation of privacy associated with password-protected computers. In examining the contours of a third party's apparent authority to consent to the search of a home computer, the majority correctly indicates that the extent to which law enforcement knows or should reasonably suspect that password protection is enabled is critical. . . . I take issue with the majority's implicit holding that law enforcement may use software deliberately designed to automatically bypass computer password protection based on third-party consent without the need to make a reasonable inquiry regarding the presence of password protection and the third party's access to that password.

The presence of security on Defendant's computer is undisputed. Yet, the majority curiously argues that Defendant's use of password protection is inconsequential because Defendant failed to argue that computer password protection is "commonplace." Of course, the decision provides no guidance on what would constitute sufficient proof of the prevalence of password protection, nor does it explain why the court could not take judicial notice that password protection is a standard feature of operating systems. Despite recognizing the "pervasiveness of computers in American homes," and the fact that the "personal computer is often a repository for private information the computer's owner does not intend to share with others," the majority requires the invocation of magical language in order to give effect to Defendant's subjective intent to exclude others from accessing the computer. . . .

The unconstrained ability of law enforcement to use forensic software such as the EnCase program to bypass password protection without first determining whether such passwords have been enabled does not "exacerbate[]" this difficulty; rather, it avoids it altogether, simultaneously and dangerously sidestepping the Fourth Amendment in the process. Indeed, the majority concedes that if such protection were "shown to be commonplace, law enforcement's use of forensic software like EnCase . . . may well be subject to question." But the fact that a computer password "lock" may not be *immediately* visible does not render it unlocked. I appreciate that unlike the locked file cabinet, computers have no handle to pull. But, like the padlocked footlocker, computers do exhibit outward signs of password protection: they display boot password screens, username/password log-in screens, and/or screen-saver reactivation passwords.

The fact remains that EnCase's ability to bypass security measures is well known to law enforcement. Here, ICE's forensic computer specialist found Defendant's computer turned off. Without turning it on, he hooked his laptop directly to the hard drive of Defendant's computer and ran the EnCase program. The agents made no effort to ascertain whether such security was enabled prior to initiating the search. . . .

The majority points out that law enforcement "did not ask specific questions" about Dr. Andrus' use of the computer or knowledge of Ray Andrus' use of password protection, but twice criticizes Dr. Andrus' failure to affirmatively disclaim ownership of, control over, or knowledge regarding the computer. Of course, the computer was located in Ray Andrus' very tiny bedroom, but the majority makes no effort to explain how this does not create an ambiguous situation as to ownership.

The burden on law enforcement to identify ownership of the computer was minimal. A simple question or two would have sufficed. Prior to the computer search, the agents questioned Dr. Andrus about Ray Andrus' status as a renter and Dr. Andrus' ability to enter his 51-year-old son's bedroom in order to determine Dr. Andrus' ability to consent to a search of the room, but the agents did not inquire whether Dr. Andrus used the computer, and if so, whether he had access to his son's password. At the suppression hearing, the agents testified that they were not immediately aware that Defendant's computer was the only one in the house, and they began to doubt Dr. Andrus' authority to consent when they learned this fact. The record reveals that, upon questioning, Dr. Andrus indicated that there was a computer in the house and led the agents to Defendant's room. The forensic specialist was then summoned. It took him approximately fifteen to twenty minutes to set up his equipment, yet, bizarrely, at no point during this period did the agents inquire about the presence of any other computers. . . .

Accordingly, in my view, given the case law indicating the importance of computer password protection, the common knowledge about the prevalence of password usage, and the design of EnCase or similar password bypass mechanisms, the Fourth Amendment and the reasonable inquiry rule, mandate that in consent-based, warrantless computer searches, law enforcement personnel inquire or otherwise check for the presence of password protection and, if a password is present, inquire about the consenter's knowledge of that password and joint access to the computer. . . .

NOTES & QUESTIONS

1. *A Question of Perspective?* Orin Kerr contends:

> From a virtual user's perspective, the child pornography was hidden to the father; it was behind a password-protected gate. Under these facts, the father couldn't consent to a search because he would lack common authority over it. From a physical perspective, however, the file was present on the hard drive just like all the other information. Under these facts, the father could consent to the search because he had access rights to the machine generally. . . .
>
> Viewed from the physical perspective, the investigators reasonably did not know about the user profile and reasonably believed that the father had rights to consent to that part of the hard drive.[72]

2. *Checking for Password Protection.* Was the investigators' belief about the father's authority over the computer reasonable? Should the investigators

---

[72] Orin Kerr, *Virtual Analogies, Physical Searches, and the Fourth Amendment,* Volokh Conspiracy, Apr. 26, 2007, http://www.volokh.com/posts/1177562355.shtml.

have asked the father more questions about his use of the computer first? Should they have turned on the machine to see if it was password-protected before hooking up the forensic software? What kinds of incentives does this decision engender for officers doing an investigation?

3. *The Right to Delete.* Paul Ohm contends that the Fourth Amendment should be read to encompass a right to delete: "The text of the Fourth Amendment seems broad enough to protect this 'right to destroy' or, in the computer context, 'right to delete' by its terms through its prohibition on unreasonable seizure."[73] If the government has engaged in an unreasonable search of a computer under the Fourth Amendment, the typical remedy is that the data is excluded from trial. Does it follow that people should also have the right to demand that the data seized by the government be deleted?

4. *Computer Searches at the Border—and Beyond.* Under the border search doctrine, the government need not obtain a warrant or even demonstrate reasonable suspicion to justify a search of persons or property at the international border. According to the Supreme Court, "It is axiomatic that the United States, as sovereign, has the inherent authority to protect, and a paramount interest in protecting, its territorial integrity." *United States v. Flores-Montano*, 541 U.S. 149 (2004). The Court has recognized only a few limits on the government's power to engage in searches at the border without any particularized suspicion, such as "invasive searches of the person." *Id.*

In *United States v. Arnold*, 533 F.3d 1003 (9th Cir. 2008), the Ninth Circuit considered whether this doctrine applied to computers and electronic devices at the border. The defendant argued that computers should be treated differently from regular property:

> Arnold argues that "laptop computers are fundamentally different from traditional closed containers," and analogizes them to "homes" and the "human mind." Arnold's analogy of a laptop to a home is based on his conclusion that a laptop's capacity allows for the storage of personal documents in an amount equivalent to that stored in one's home. He argues that a laptop is like the "human mind" because of its ability to record ideas, e-mail, internet chats and web-surfing habits.

The court rejected this argument:

> With respect to these searches, the Supreme Court has refused to draw distinctions between containers of information and contraband with respect to their quality or nature for purposes of determining the appropriate level of Fourth Amendment protection. Arnold's analogy to a search of a home based on a laptop's storage capacity is without merit. The Supreme Court has expressly rejected applying the Fourth Amendment protections afforded to homes to property which is "*capable of functioning as a home*" simply due to its size, or, distinguishing between "'worthy' and 'unworthy' containers."

---

[73] Paul Ohm, *The Fourth Amendment Right to Delete,* 119 Harv. L. Rev. F. 10 (2005). For an extensive normative argument for the right to delete, see Viktor Mayer-Schönberger, *Delete: The Virtues of Forgetting in the Digital Age* (2009).

In *United States v. Cotterman*, 637 F.3d 1068 (9th Cir. 2011), the Ninth Circuit upheld a search of a laptop computer that began at the nation's border and ended two days later in a governmental forensic computer laboratory that was 170 miles away from the border. The court stated, "So long as property has not been officially cleared for entry into the United States and remains in the control of the Government, any further search is simply a continuation of the original border search—the entirety of which is justified by the Government's border search power." According to the court, the defendant never regained his normal expectation of privacy in his computer, the 40-hour detention was reasonably related in scope to the circumstances justifying the initial detention at the border, and requiring forensic computer laboratories at all ports of entry throughout the United States would place an unreasonable burden on the government.

In dissent, Judge Betty Fletcher worried that "the scope of the search will be determined by the Government's desire to be thorough, and the length of seizure by the Government's convenience."

2. ENCRYPTION

Encryption includes the ability to keep communications secure by concealing the contents of a message. With encryption, even if a communication is intercepted, it still remains secure. Encryption works by translating a message into a code of letters or numbers called "cypher text." The parties to the communication hold a *key*, which consists of the information necessary to translate the code back to the original message, or "plain text." Since ancient times, code-makers have devised cryptographic systems to encode messages. But along with the code-makers arose code-breakers, who were able to figure out the keys to cryptographic systems by, for example, examining the patterns in the encoded messages and comparing them to patterns in a particular language and the frequency of use of certain letters in that language. Today, computers have vastly increased the complexity of encryption.

Encryption presents a difficult trade-off between privacy and surveillance. It is an essential technique to protect the privacy of electronic communications in an age when such communications can so easily be intercepted and monitored. On the other hand, it enables individuals to disguise their communications from detection by law enforcement officials.[74] As Whitfield Diffie and Susan Landau observe:

> The explosion in cryptography and the US government's attempts to control it have given rise to a debate between those who hail the new technology's contribution to privacy, business, and security and those who fear both its

---

[74] For more background on encryption, see Simon Singh, *The Code: The Evolution of Secrecy from Mary, Queen of Scots to Quantum Cryptography* (1999); Steven Levy, *Crypto: How the Code Rebels Beat the Government — Saving Privacy in the Digital Age* (2002); A. Michael Froomkin, *The Metaphor Is the Key: Cryptography, the Clipper Chip, and the Constitution*, 143 U. Pa. L. Rev. 709 (1995); Robert C. Post, *Encryption Source Code and the First Amendment*, 15 Berkeley Tech. L.J. 713 (2000); A. Michael Froomkin, *The Constitution and Encryption Regulation: Do We Need a "New Privacy"?*, 3 N.Y.U. J. Legis. & Pub. Pol'y 25 (1999).

interference with the work of police and its adverse effect on the collection of intelligence. Positions have often been extreme. The advocates for unfettered cryptography maintain that a free society depends on privacy to protect freedom of association, artistic creativity, and political discussion. The advocates of control hold that there will be no freedom at all unless we can protect ourselves from criminals, terrorists, and foreign threats. Many have tried to present themselves as seeking to maintain or restore the status quo. For the police, the status quo is the continued ability to wiretap. For civil libertarians, it is the ready availability of conversational privacy that prevailed at the time of the country's founding.[75]

The Clipper Chip. The U.S. government has become increasingly concerned that the growing sophistication of encryption would make it virtually impossible for the government to decrypt. In 1994, the government proposed implementing the "Clipper Chip," a federal encryption standard in which the government would retain a copy of the key in a system called "key escrow." By holding a "spare key," the government could readily decrypt encrypted communications if it desired. The Clipper Chip was strongly criticized, and the government's encryption standard has not been widely used.

Encryption and the First Amendment. In *Junger v. Daley*, 209 F.3d 481 (6th Cir. 2000), the Sixth Circuit concluded that encryption was protected speech under the First Amendment:

> Much like a mathematical or scientific formula, one can describe the function and design of encryption software by a prose explanation; however, for individuals fluent in a computer programming language, source code is the most efficient and precise means by which to communicate ideas about cryptography.

Junger relied on the reasoning of *Bernstein v. United States Dep't of Justice,* 176 F.3d 1132 (9th Cir. 1999) (opinion withdrawn), where the Ninth Circuit struck down a licensing scheme on encryption source code as a violation of the First Amendment:

> Bernstein has submitted numerous declarations from cryptographers and computer programmers explaining that cryptographic ideas and algorithms are conveniently expressed in source code. . . . [T]he chief task for cryptographers is the development of secure methods of encryption. While the articulation of such a system in layman's English or in general mathematical terms may be useful, the devil is, at least for cryptographers, often in the algorithmic details. By utilizing source code, a cryptographer can express algorithmic ideas with precision and methodological rigor that is otherwise difficult to achieve. . . .
>
> Thus, cryptographers use source code to express their scientific ideas in much the same way that mathematicians use equations or economists use graphs. . . .
>
> In light of these considerations, we conclude that encryption software, in its source code form and as employed by those in the field of cryptography, must be viewed as expressive for First Amendment purposes. . . .

---

[75] Whitfield Diffie & Susan Landau, *Privacy on the Line: The Politics of Wiretapping and Encryption* (1998).

Orin Kerr takes issue with *Junger*'s holding: "the court viewed source code using the close-up paradigm of what the code looked like, rather than the deeper functional perspective of what the code was actually supposed to do. . . . Just as viewing a Seurat painting from inches away reveals only dots, the *Junger* court's myopic view of source code revealed only communications that looked like speech in form, but lacked the deeper significance required to establish constitutional expression."[76]

In the view of Robert Post, the question of First Amendment coverage turns on a "constitutional sociology."[77] The relevant discussion for Post is "between encryption source code that is itself part of public dialogue and encryption source code that is meant merely to be used." He adds, moreover, that "even if encryption source code in not itself a subject of public discussion, its regulation might nevertheless affect public discussion in ways that ought to trigger First Amendment coverage." As an example, a licensing scheme for encryption code that engaged in viewpoint discrimination would be flawed. Even beyond viewpoint discrimination, a viewpoint neutral scheme of regulating encryption software would be flawed if it had a sufficient constitutional impact on "the various First Amendment media that employ" such software.

Consider *Karn v. United States Dep't of State*, 925 F. Supp. 1 (D.D.C. 1996), where the court came to the contrary conclusion from *Junger*:

> . . . The government regulation at issue here is clearly content-neutral. . . . The defendants are not regulating the export of the diskette because of the expressive content of the comments and or source code, but instead are regulating because of the belief that the combination of encryption source code on machine readable media will make it easier for foreign intelligence sources to encode their communications. . . .
>
> . . . [A] content-neutral regulation is justified . . . if it is within the constitutional power of the government, it "furthers an important or substantial governmental interest," and "the incidental restriction on alleged First Amendment freedoms is no greater than is essential to the furtherance of that interest." . . .
>
> . . . By placing cryptographic products on the ITAR, the President has determined that the proliferation of cryptographic products will harm the United States. . . .
>
> . . . [T]he plaintiff has not advanced any argument that the regulation is "substantially broader than necessary" to prevent the proliferation of cryptographic products. Nor has the plaintiff articulated any present barrier to the spreading of information on cryptography "by any other means" other than those containing encryption source code on machine-readable media. Therefore, the Court holds that the regulation of the plaintiff's diskette is narrowly tailored to the goal of limiting the proliferation of cryptographic products and that the regulation is justified. . . .

---

[76] Orin S. Kerr, *Are We Overprotecting Code? Thoughts on First-Generation Internet Law*, 57 Wash. & Lee L. Rev. 1287, 1292-93 (2000).

[77] Robert Post, *Encryption Source Code and the First Amendment*, 15 Berk. Tech. L.J. 713 (2000).

Encryption and the Fourth Amendment. Suppose law enforcement officials legally obtain an encrypted communication. Does the Fourth Amendment require a warrant before the government can decrypt an encrypted communication? Consider the following argument by Orin Kerr:

> Encryption is often explained as a lock-and-key system, in which a "key" is used to "lock" plaintext by turning it into ciphertext, and then a "key" is used to "unlock" the ciphertext by turning it into plaintext. We know that locking a container is a common way to create a reasonable expectation of privacy in its contents: the government ordinarily cannot break the lock and search a closed container without a warrant. . . .
>
> When we use a "lock" and "unlock" in the metaphorical sense to denote understanding, however, a lock cannot trigger the rights-based Fourth Amendment. If I tell you a riddle, I do not have a right to stop you from figuring it out. Although figuring out the secret of an inscrutable communication may "unlock" its meaning, the Fourth Amendment cannot regulate such a cognitive discovery. . . .[78]

Encryption and the Fifth Amendment. Can the government compel the production of a private key if it is stored on a personal computer? What if the key is known only to the individual and not stored or recorded?

3. E-MAIL

STEVE JACKSON GAMES, INC. V. UNITED STATES SECRET SERVICE
36 F.3d 457 (5th Cir. 1994)

BARKSDALE, J. Appellant Steve Jackson Games, Incorporated (SJG), publishes books, magazines, role-playing games, and related products. Starting in the mid-1980s, SJG operated an electronic bulletin board system, called "Illuminati" (BBS), from one of its computers. SJG used the BBS to post public information about its business, games, publications, and the role-playing hobby; to facilitate play-testing of games being developed; and to communicate with its customers and free-lance writers by electronic mail (E-mail).

Central to the issue before us, the BBS also offered customers the ability to send and receive private E-mail. Private E-mail was stored on the BBS computer's hard disk drive temporarily, until the addressees "called" the BBS (using their computers and modems) and read their mail. After reading their E-mail, the recipients could choose to either store it on the BBS computer's hard drive or delete it. In February 1990, there were 365 BBS users. Among other uses, appellants Steve Jackson, Elizabeth McCoy, William Milliken, and Steffan O'Sullivan used the BBS for communication by private E-mail. . . . [In addition, Lloyd Blankenship, an employee of Steve Jackson Games, operated a computer bulletin board system (BBS).] Blankenship had the ability to review, and perhaps delete any data on the BBS.

---

[78] Orin S. Kerr, *The Fourth Amendment in Cyberspace: Can Encryption Create a "Reasonable Expectation of Privacy?,"* 33 Conn. L. Rev. 503, 520-21, 522 (2001).

On February 28, 1990, [Secret Service] Agent Foley applied for a warrant to search SJG's premises and Blankenship's residence for evidence of violations of 18 U.S.C. §§ 1030 (proscribes interstate transportation of computer access information) and 2314 (proscribes interstate transportation of stolen property). A search warrant for SJG was issued that same day, authorizing the seizure of [computer hardware, software, and computer data.]

The next day, March 1, the warrant was executed by the Secret Service, including Agents Foley and Golden. Among the items seized was the computer which operated the BBS. At the time of the seizure, 162 items of unread, private E-mail were stored on the BBS, including items addressed to the individual appellants. . . .

Appellants filed suit in May 1991 against, among others, the Secret Service and the United States, claiming [among other things, a violation of] the Federal Wiretap Act, as amended by Title I of the Electronic Communications Privacy Act (ECPA), 18 U.S.C. §§ 2510-2521; and Title II of the ECPA, 18 U.S.C. §§ 2701-2711. . . .

As stated, the sole issue is a very narrow one: whether the seizure of a computer on which is stored private E-mail that has been sent to an electronic bulletin board, but not yet read (retrieved) by the recipients, constitutes an "intercept" proscribed by 18 U.S.C. § 2511(1)(a).

Section 2511 was enacted in 1968 as part of Title III of the Omnibus Crime Control and Safe Streets Act of 1968, often referred to as the Federal Wiretap Act. Prior to the 1986 amendment by Title I of the ECPA, it covered only wire and oral communications. Title I of the ECPA extended that coverage to electronic communications. In relevant part, § 2511(1)(a) proscribes "intentionally intercept[ing] . . . any wire, oral, or electronic communication," unless the intercept is authorized by court order or by other exceptions not relevant here. Section 2520 authorizes, *inter alia*, persons whose electronic communications are intercepted in violation of § 2511 to bring a civil action against the interceptor for actual damages, or for statutory damages of $10,000 per violation or $100 per day of the violation, whichever is greater. 18 U.S.C. § 2520.

The Act defines "intercept" as "the aural or other acquisition of the contents of any wire, electronic, or oral communication through the use of any electronic, mechanical, or other device." 18 U.S.C. § 2510(4). . . .

Webster's Third New International Dictionary (1986) defines "aural" as "of or relating to the ear" or "of or relating to the sense of hearing." And, the Act defines "aural transfer" as "a transfer containing the human voice at any point between and including the point of origin and the point of reception." 18 U.S.C. § 2510(18). This definition is extremely important for purposes of understanding the definition of a "wire communication," which is defined by the Act as

> any aural transfer made in whole or in part through the use of facilities for the transmission of communications by the aid of wire, cable, or other like connection between the point of origin and the point of reception (including the use of such connection in a switching station) . . . *and such term includes any electronic storage of such communication.*

18 U.S.C. § 2510(1) (emphasis added). In contrast, as noted, an "electronic communication" is defined as "any *transfer* of signs, signals, writing, images,

sounds, data, or intelligence of any nature transmitted in whole or in part by a wire, radio, electromagnetic, photoelectronic or photooptical system . . . but does not include . . . any wire or oral communication. . . ." 18 U.S.C. § 2510(12) (emphasis added).

Critical to the issue before us is the fact that, unlike the definition of "wire communication," *the definition of "electronic communication" does not include electronic storage of such communications. See* 18 U.S.C. § 2510(12). "Electronic storage" is defined as

> (A) any *temporary*, intermediate *storage* of a wire or *electronic communication incidental to the electronic transmission thereof;* and
> (B) any storage of such communication by an electronic communication service for purposes of backup protection of such communication. . . .

18 U.S.C. § 2510(17) (emphasis added). The E-mail in issue was in "electronic storage." Congress' use of the word "transfer" in the definition of "electronic communication," and its omission in that definition of the phrase "any electronic storage of such communication" (part of the definition of "wire communication") reflects that Congress did not intend for "intercept" to apply to "electronic communications" when those communications are in "electronic storage." . . .

Title II generally proscribes unauthorized access to stored wire or electronic communications. Section 2701(a) provides:

> Except as provided in subsection (c) of this section whoever —
>
> > (1) intentionally accesses without authorization a facility through which an electronic communication service is provided; or
> > (2) intentionally exceeds an authorization to access that facility; and thereby obtains, alters, or prevents authorized access to a wire or electronic communication *while it is in electronic storage in such system* shall be punished. . . .

18 U.S.C. § 2701(a) (emphasis added).

As stated, the district court found that the Secret Service violated § 2701 when it

> intentionally accesse[d] without authorization a facility [the computer] through which an electronic communication service [the BBS] is provided . . . and thereby obtain[ed] [and] prevent[ed] authorized access [by appellants] to a[n] . . . . electronic communication while it is in electronic storage in such system.

18 U.S.C. § 2701(a). The Secret Service does not challenge this ruling. We find no indication in either the Act or its legislative history that Congress intended for conduct that is clearly prohibited by Title II to furnish the basis for a civil remedy under Title I as well. . . .

NOTES & QUESTIONS

1. *Interception vs. Electronic Storage.* Is unread e-mail in storage because it is sitting on a hard drive at the ISP? Or is it in transmission because the recipient hasn't read it yet? Is the court applying an overly formalistic and strict reading of "interception"?

2. *The Fourth Amendment and E-mail: A Question of Perspective?* Suppose the police sought to obtain a person's unread e-mail messages that were stored with her ISP waiting to be downloaded. *Steve Jackson Games* demonstrates how ECPA would apply — the weaker provisions of the Stored Communications Act rather than the stronger protections of the Wiretap Act apply to e-mail temporarily stored with a person's ISP. *Steve Jackson Games* is a civil case. In the criminal law context, the Stored Communications Act requires a warrant to obtain e-mails stored at the ISP for 180 days or less. If the e-mails have been stored over 180 days, then the government can obtain them with a mere subpoena.

Would the Fourth Amendment apply? Orin Kerr argues that the answer depends upon the perspective by which one views the Internet. In the "internal perspective," the Internet is viewed as a virtual world, analogous to real space. From the "external perspective," we view the Internet as a network and do not analogize to real space. Kerr provides the following example:

> Does the Fourth Amendment require [the police] to obtain a search warrant [to obtain an e-mail]? . . . The answer depends largely upon whether they apply an internal or external perspective of the Internet.
>
> Imagine that the first officer applies an internal perspective of the Internet. To him, e-mail is the cyberspace equivalent of old-fashioned postal mail. His computer announces, "You've got mail!" when an e-mail message arrives and shows him a closed envelope. When he clicks on the envelope, it opens, revealing the message. From his internal perspective, the officer is likely to conclude that the Fourth Amendment places the same restriction on government access to e-mail that it places on government access to ordinary postal mail. He will then look in a Fourth Amendment treatise for the black letter rule on accessing postal mail. That treatise will tell him that accessing a suspect's mail ordinarily violates the suspect's "reasonable expectation of privacy," and that therefore the officer must first obtain a warrant. Because e-mail is the equivalent of postal mail, the officer will conclude that the Fourth Amendment requires him to obtain a warrant before he can access the e-mail.
>
> Imagine that the second police office approaches the same problem from an external perspective. To him, the facts look quite different. Looking at how the Internet actually works, the second police officer sees that when A sent the e-mail to B, A was instructing his computer to send a message to his Internet Service Provider (ISP) directing the ISP to forward a text message to B's ISP. To simplify matters, let's say that A's ISP is EarthLink, and B's ISP is America Online (AOL). . . .
>
> What process does the Fourth Amendment require? The second officer will reason that A sent a copy of the e-mail communication to a third party (the EarthLink computer), disclosing the communication to the third party and instructing it to send the communication to yet another third party (AOL). The officer will ask, what process does the Fourth Amendment require to obtain information that has been disclosed to a third party and is in the third party's possession? The officer will look in a Fourth Amendment treatise and locate to the black letter rule that the Fourth Amendment permits the government to obtain information disclosed to a third party using a mere subpoena. The officer can simply subpoena the system administrator to compel him to produce the e-mails. No search warrant is required.

Who is right? The first officer or the second? The answer depends on whether you approach the Internet from an internal or external perspective. From an internal perspective, the officers need a search warrant; from the external perspective, they do not.[79]

3. *Previously Read E-mail Stored at an ISP.* The e-mail stored on the ISP server in *Steve Jackson Games* had not yet been downloaded and read by the recipients. Many people continue to store their e-mail messages with their ISP even after having read them. Does the Stored Communications Act protect them in the same way? The answer to this question is currently in dispute. Daniel Solove observes:

> Because these messages are now stored indefinitely, according to the DOJ's interpretation . . . the e-mail is no longer in temporary storage and is "simply a remotely stored file." Therefore, under this view, it falls outside of much of the Act's protections. Since many people store their e-mail messages after reading them and the e-mail they send out, this enables the government to access their communications with very minimal limitations.[80]

In *Theofel v. Farey-Jones,* 359 F.3d 1066 (9th Cir. 2004), the court concluded that

> [t]he [Stored Communications] Act defines "electronic storage" as "(A) any temporary, intermediate storage of a wire or electronic communication incidental to the electronic transmission thereof; and (B) any storage of such communication by an electronic communication service for purposes of backup protection of such communication." Id. § 2510(17), incorporated by id. § 2711(1). Several courts have held that subsection (A) covers e-mail messages stored on an ISP's server pending delivery to the recipient. Because subsection (A) applies only to messages in "temporary, intermediate storage," however, these courts have limited that subsection's coverage to messages not yet delivered to their intended recipient.
>
> Defendants point to these cases and argue that messages remaining on an ISP's server after delivery no longer fall within the Act's coverage. But, even if such messages are not within the purview of subsection (A), they do fit comfortably within subsection (B). . . .
>
> An obvious purpose for storing a message on an ISP's server after delivery is to provide a second copy of the message in the event that the user needs to download it again — if, for example, the message is accidentally erased from the user's own computer. The ISP copy of the message functions as a "backup" for the user. Notably, nothing in the Act requires that the backup protection be for the benefit of the ISP rather than the user. Storage under these circumstances thus literally falls within the statutory definition.

See also Fraser v. Nationwide Mutual Insurance Co., 352 F.3d 108 (3d Cir. 2003) (suggesting that such e-mail messages were in backup storage under the definition of electronic storage).

---

[79] Orin S. Kerr, *The Problem of Perspective in Internet Law,* 91 Geo. L.J. 357, 361-62, 365-67 (2003).

[80] Daniel J. Solove, *Reconstructing Electronic Surveillance Law,* 72 Geo. Wash. L. Rev. 1264 (2004).

4. ***What Constitutes an Interception?*** In *United States v. Councilman,* 373 F.3d 197 (1st Cir. 2004), an Internet bookseller, Interloc, Inc., provided e-mail service for its customers, who were book dealers. Councilman, the vice president of Interloc, directed Interloc employees to draft a computer program to intercept all incoming communications from Amazon.com to the book dealers and make copies of them. Councilman and other Interloc then read the e-mails in order to gain a commercial advantage. Councilman was charged with criminal violations of the Wiretap Act. Councilman argued that he did not violate the Wiretap Act because the e-mails were in electronic storage, albeit very briefly, when they were copied. The court followed *Steve Jackson Games* and concluded that the e-mail was in temporary storage and therefore subject to the Stored Communications Act, not the Wiretap Act. However, unlike *Steve Jackson Games,* Interloc accessed the e-mails "as they were being transmitted and in real time."

The *Councilman* case received significant criticism by academic commentators and experts in electronic surveillance law for misunderstanding the fundamental distinction between the interception of a communication and the accessing of a stored communication. An interception occurs contemporaneously — as the communication is being transmitted. Accessing a stored communication occurs later, as the communication sits on a computer. This distinction has practical consequences, since interceptions are protected by the much more protective Wiretap Act rather than the Stored Communications Act. Does such a distinction still make sense? Is the contemporaneous interception of communications more troublesome than the accessing of the communications in *Steve Jackson Games*?

The case was reheard en banc, and the en banc court reversed the panel. *See United States v. Councilman,* 418 F.3d 67 (1st Cir. 2005) (en banc). The court concluded that "the term 'electronic communication' includes transient electronic storage that is intrinsic to the communication process, and hence that interception of an e-mail message in such storage is an offense under the Wiretap Act." The court declined to further elaborate on what constitutes and "interception."

5. ***Carnivore.*** Beginning in 1998, the FBI began using a hardware and software mechanism called "Carnivore" to intercept people's e-mail and instant messaging information from their Internet Service Providers (ISPs). After obtaining judicial authorization, the FBI would install Carnivore by connecting a computer directly to the ISP's server and initiating the program. Carnivore was designed to locate the e-mails of a suspect at the ISP when the ISP did not have the capacity to do so.

Carnivore was capable of analyzing the entire e-mail traffic of an ISP, although the FBI maintained it was only used to search for the e-mails of a suspect. The program filtered out the e-mail messages of ISP subscribers who are not the subject of the investigation; but to do so, it had to scan the e-mail headers that identify the senders and recipients. The FBI likened e-mail headers to the information captured by a pen register, a device that registers the phone numbers a person dials.

However, Carnivore could be programmed to search through the entire text of all e-mails, to capture e-mails with certain key words. In this way, Carnivore resembles a wiretap. Recall that under federal wiretap law, judicial approval for obtaining pen register information only requires a certification that "the information likely to be obtained by such installation and use is relevant to an ongoing investigation." 18 U.S.C. § 3123. In contrast, judicial approval of a wiretap requires a full panoply of requirements under Title I, including a showing of probable cause.

To eliminate the negative associations with the term "Carnivore," the device was renamed "DCS1000." Many members of Congress viewed Carnivore with great suspicion. Congress held hearings over the summer of 2000 pertaining to Carnivore, and several bills were proposed to halt or limit the use of Carnivore.

The anti-Carnivore sentiment abruptly ended after the September 11, 2001, World Trade Center and Pentagon terrorist attacks. Section 216 of the USA PATRIOT Act of 2001, in anticipation of the use of Carnivore, required reports on the use of Carnivore to be filed with a court. These reports, filed under seal, require (1) the names of the officers using the device; (2) when the device was installed, used, and removed; (3) the configuration of the device; and (4) the information collected by the device. 18 U.S.C. § 3133(a)(3).

The FBI discontinued use of Carnivore because ISPs can readily produce the information the FBI desires without the assistance of the Carnivore device and because commercially available software has similar functionality.

UNITED STATES V. WARSHAK

631 F.3d 266 (6th Cir. 2010)

[Steven Warshak ran several small businesses that sold products and advertisements, including a popular herbal supplement called "Enzyte," which was touted as increasing a man's erection. This supplement was made by Warshak's company, Berkeley Premium Nutraceuticals, Inc., which had 1,500 employees and sales of $250 million per year. A key component of Berkeley's business was the ability to process credit card payments. To do so, it had banks provide a line of credit. In 2002, one of the banks — the Bank of Kentucky — terminated its relationship with Berkeley because of too many "chargebacks" — when customers dispute a charge. In future applications to banks for similar lines of credit, Warshak filed false applications, including lying that he never had an account terminated. To prevent future problems with excessive chargebacks, Berkeley found ways to falsify the figures.

Warshak (along with his mother, Harriet Warshak, who was involved in the scheme) was eventually indicted for various crimes, including mail, wire, and bank fraud, making false statements to banks, and money laundering. He sought to exclude from evidence about 27,000 of his private e-mails seized from his ISP (NuVox). The trial court denied his motion, and he was convicted, sentenced to 25 years in prison, and ordered to forfeit nearly $500 million worth of proceeds.]

BOGGS, J. Warshak argues that the government's warrantless, *ex parte* seizure of approximately 27,000 of his private emails constituted a violation of the Fourth Amendment's prohibition on unreasonable searches and seizures. The government counters that, even if government agents violated the Fourth Amendment in obtaining the emails, they relied in good faith on the Stored Communications Act ("SCA"), 18 U.S.C. §§ 2701 *et seq.*, a statute that allows the government to obtain certain electronic communications without procuring a warrant. The government also argues that any hypothetical Fourth Amendment violation was harmless. We find that the government *did* violate Warshak's Fourth Amendment rights by compelling his Internet Service Provider ("ISP") to turn over the contents of his emails. However, we agree that agents relied on the SCA in good faith, and therefore hold that reversal is unwarranted. . . .

The Stored Communications Act ("SCA"), 18 U.S.C. §§ 2701 *et seq.*, "permits a 'governmental entity' to compel a service provider to disclose the contents of [electronic] communications in certain circumstances." *Warshak II,* 532 F.3d at 523. As this court explained in *Warshak II:*

> . . . The compelled-disclosure provisions give different levels of privacy protection based on whether the e-mail is held with an electronic communication service or a remote computing service and based on how long the e-mail has been in electronic storage. The government may obtain the contents of e-mails that are "in electronic storage" with an electronic communication service for 180 days or less "only pursuant to a warrant." 18 U.S.C. § 2703(a). The government has three options for obtaining communications stored with a remote computing service and communications that have been in electronic storage with an electronic service provider for more than 180 days: (1) obtain a warrant; (2) use an administrative subpoena; or (3) obtain a court order under § 2703(d). *Id.* § 2703(a), (b). . . .

The Fourth Amendment provides that "[t]he right of the people to be secure in their persons, houses, papers, and effects, against unreasonable searches and seizures, shall not be violated, and no Warrants shall issue, but upon probable cause. . . ." U.S. Const. amend. IV. . . .

A "search" occurs when the government infringes upon "an expectation of privacy that society is prepared to consider reasonable." This standard breaks down into two discrete inquiries: "first, has the [target of the investigation] manifested a subjective expectation of privacy in the object of the challenged search? Second, is society willing to recognize that expectation as reasonable?"

Turning first to the subjective component of the test, we find that Warshak plainly manifested an expectation that his emails would be shielded from outside scrutiny. As he notes in his brief, his "entire business and personal life was contained within the . . . emails seized." Given the often sensitive and sometimes damning substance of his emails, we think it highly unlikely that Warshak expected them to be made public, for people seldom unfurl their dirty laundry in plain view. Therefore, we conclude that Warshak had a subjective expectation of privacy in the contents of his emails.

The next question is whether society is prepared to recognize that expectation as reasonable. This question is one of grave import and enduring consequence, given the prominent role that email has assumed in modern communication.

Since the advent of email, the telephone call and the letter have waned in importance, and an explosion of Internet-based communication has taken place. People are now able to send sensitive and intimate information, instantaneously, to friends, family, and colleagues half a world away. Lovers exchange sweet nothings, and businessmen swap ambitious plans, all with the click of a mouse button. Commerce has also taken hold in email. Online purchases are often documented in email accounts, and email is frequently used to remind patients and clients of imminent appointments. In short, "account" is an apt word for the conglomeration of stored messages that comprises an email account, as it provides an account of its owner's life. By obtaining access to someone's email, government agents gain the ability to peer deeply into his activities. Much hinges, therefore, on whether the government is permitted to request that a commercial ISP turn over the contents of a subscriber's emails without triggering the machinery of the Fourth Amendment.

In confronting this question, we take note of two bedrock principles. First, the very fact that information is being passed through a communications network is a paramount Fourth Amendment consideration. Second, the Fourth Amendment must keep pace with the inexorable march of technological progress, or its guarantees will wither and perish.

With those principles in mind, we begin our analysis by considering the manner in which the Fourth Amendment protects traditional forms of communication. In *Katz,* the Supreme Court was asked to determine how the Fourth Amendment applied in the context of the telephone. There, government agents had affixed an electronic listening device to the exterior of a public phone booth, and had used the device to intercept and record several phone conversations. The Supreme Court held that this constituted a search under the Fourth Amendment, notwithstanding the fact that the telephone company had the capacity to monitor and record the calls. . . .

Letters receive similar protection. While a letter is in the mail, the police may not intercept it and examine its contents unless they first obtain a warrant based on probable cause. This is true despite the fact that sealed letters are handed over to perhaps dozens of mail carriers, any one of whom could tear open the thin paper envelopes that separate the private words from the world outside. Put another way, trusting a letter to an intermediary does not necessarily defeat a reasonable expectation that the letter will remain private.

Given the fundamental similarities between email and traditional forms of communication, it would defy common sense to afford emails lesser Fourth Amendment protection. It follows that email requires strong protection under the Fourth Amendment; otherwise, the Fourth Amendment would prove an ineffective guardian of private communication, an essential purpose it has long been recognized to serve.

If we accept that an email is analogous to a letter or a phone call, it is manifest that agents of the government cannot compel a commercial ISP to turn over the contents of an email without triggering the Fourth Amendment. An ISP is the intermediary that makes email communication possible. Emails must pass through an ISP's servers to reach their intended recipient. Thus, the ISP is the functional equivalent of a post office or a telephone company. As we have discussed above, the police may not storm the post office and intercept a letter, and they are likewise forbidden from using the phone system to make a clandestine recording of a telephone call—unless they get a warrant, that is. It only stands to reason that, if government agents compel an ISP to surrender the contents of a subscriber's emails, those agents have thereby conducted a Fourth Amendment search, which necessitates compliance with the warrant requirement absent some exception. . . .

[Earlier on in the litigation of this case,] the government argued that this conclusion was improper, pointing to the fact that NuVox contractually reserved the right to access Warshak's emails for certain purposes. While we acknowledge that a subscriber agreement might, in some cases, be sweeping enough to defeat a reasonable expectation of privacy in the contents of an email account, we doubt that will be the case in most situations, and it is certainly not the case here.

As an initial matter, it must be observed that the mere *ability* of a third-party intermediary to access the contents of a communication cannot be sufficient to extinguish a reasonable expectation of privacy. In *Katz,* the Supreme Court found it reasonable to expect privacy during a telephone call despite the ability of an operator to listen in. Similarly, the ability of a rogue mail handler to rip open a letter does not make it unreasonable to assume that sealed mail will remain private on its journey across the country. Therefore, the threat or possibility of access is not decisive when it comes to the reasonableness of an expectation of privacy. . . .

Our conclusion finds additional support in the application of Fourth Amendment doctrine to rented space. Hotel guests, for example, have a reasonable expectation of privacy in their rooms. *See United States v. Allen,* 106 F.3d 695, 699 (6th Cir. 1997). This is so even though maids routinely enter hotel rooms to replace the towels and tidy the furniture. Similarly, tenants have a legitimate expectation of privacy in their apartments. *See United States v. Washington,* 573 F.3d 279, 284 (6th Cir. 2009). That expectation persists, regardless of the incursions of handymen to fix leaky faucets. Consequently, we are convinced that some degree of routine access is hardly dispositive with respect to the privacy question.

Again, however, we are unwilling to hold that a subscriber agreement will *never* be broad enough to snuff out a reasonable expectation of privacy. As the panel noted in *Warshak I* [an earlier case in this litigation], if the ISP expresses an intention to "audit, inspect, and monitor" its subscriber's emails, that might be enough to render an expectation of privacy unreasonable. But where, as here, there is no such statement, the ISP's "control over the [emails] and ability to access them under certain limited circumstances will not be enough to overcome an expectation of privacy."

We recognize that our conclusion may be attacked in light of the Supreme Court's decision in *United States v. Miller,* 425 U.S. 435 (1976). In *Miller,* the Supreme Court held that a bank depositor does not have a reasonable expectation of privacy in the contents of bank records, checks, and deposit slips. The Court's holding in *Miller* was based on the fact that bank documents, "including financial statements and deposit slips, contain only information voluntarily conveyed to the banks and exposed to their employees in the ordinary course of business."

But *Miller* is distinguishable. First, *Miller* involved simple business records, as opposed to the potentially unlimited variety of "confidential communications" at issue here. Second, the bank depositor in *Miller* conveyed information to the bank so that the bank could put the information to use "in the ordinary course of business." By contrast, Warshak received his emails through NuVox. NuVox was an *intermediary,* not the intended recipient of the emails. Thus, *Miller* is not controlling.

Accordingly, we hold that a subscriber enjoys a reasonable expectation of privacy in the contents of emails "that are stored with, or sent or received through, a commercial ISP." The government may not compel a commercial ISP to turn over the contents of a subscriber's emails without first obtaining a warrant based on probable cause. Therefore, because they did not obtain a warrant, the government agents violated the Fourth Amendment when they obtained the contents of Warshak's emails. Moreover, to the extent that the SCA purports to permit the government to obtain such emails warrantlessly, the SCA is unconstitutional. . . .

Even though the government's search of Warshak's emails violated the Fourth Amendment, the emails are not subject to the exclusionary remedy if the officers relied in good faith on the SCA to obtain them. In [*Illinois v. Krull*, 480 U.S. 340 (1987),] the Supreme Court noted that the exclusionary rule's purpose of deterring law enforcement officers from engaging in unconstitutional conduct would not be furthered by holding officers accountable for mistakes of the legislature. Thus, even if a statute is later found to be unconstitutional, an officer "cannot be expected to question the judgment of the legislature." However, an officer cannot "be said to have acted in good-faith reliance upon a statute if its provisions are such that a reasonable officer should have known that the statute was unconstitutional."

Naturally, Warshak argues that the provisions of the SCA at issue in this case were plainly unconstitutional. He argues that any reasonable law enforcement officer would have understood that a warrant based on probable cause would be required to compel the production of private emails. . . .

However, we disagree that the SCA is so conspicuously unconstitutional as to preclude good-faith reliance. As we noted in *Warshak II,* "[t]he Stored Communications Act has been in existence since 1986 and to our knowledge has not been the subject of any successful Fourth Amendment challenges, in any context, whether to § 2703(d) or to any other provision." Furthermore, given the complicated thicket of issues that we were required to navigate when passing on the constitutionality of the SCA, it was not plain or obvious that the SCA was unconstitutional, and it was therefore reasonable for the government to rely upon the SCA in seeking to obtain the contents of Warshak's emails.

But the good-faith reliance inquiry does not end with the facial validity of the statute at issue. In *Krull,* the Supreme Court hinted that the good-faith exception does not apply if the government acted "outside the scope of the statute" on which it purported to rely. . . . Once the officer steps outside the scope of an unconstitutional statute, the mistake is no longer the legislature's, but the officer's. . . .

Warshak argues that the government violated several provisions of the SCA and should therefore be precluded from arguing good-faith reliance. First, Warshak argues that the government violated the SCA's notice provisions. Under § 2703(b)(1)(B), the government must provide notice to an account holder if it seeks to compel the disclosure of his emails through either a § 2703(b) subpoena or a § 2703(d) order. However, § 2705 permits the government to delay notification in certain situations. The initial period of delay is 90 days, but the government may seek to extend that period in 90-day increments. In this case, the government issued both a § 2703(b) subpoena and a § 2703(d) order to NuVox, seeking disclosure of Warshak's emails. At the time, the government made the requisite showing that notice should be delayed. However, the government did not seek to renew the period of delay. In all, the government failed to inform Warshak of either the subpoena or the order for over a year.

Conceding that it violated the notice provisions, the government argues that such violations are irrelevant to the issue of whether it reasonably relied on the SCA in *obtaining* the contents of Warshak's emails. We agree. As the government notes, the violations occurred *after* the emails had been obtained. Thus, the mistakes at issue had no bearing on the constitutional violations. Because the exclusionary rule was designed to deter constitutional violations, we decline to invoke it in this situation.

But Warshak does not hang his hat exclusively on the government's violations of the SCA's notice provisions. He also argues that the government exceeded its authority under another SCA provision — § 2703(f) — by requesting NuVox to engage in *prospective* preservation of his future emails. Under § 2703(f), "[a] provider of wire or electronic communication services or a remote computing service, upon the request of a governmental entity, shall take all necessary steps to *preserve* records and other evidence *in its possession* pending the issuance of a court order or other process." 18 U.S.C. § 2703(f) (emphasis added). Warshak argues that this statute permits only *retrospective* preservation—in other words, preservation of emails already in existence. . . .

Ultimately, however, this statutory violation, whether it occurred or not, is irrelevant to the issue of good-faith reliance. The question here is whether the government relied in good faith on § 2703(b) and § 2703(d) to *obtain* copies of Warshak's emails. True, the government might not have been able to gain access to the emails without the prospective preservation request, as it was NuVox's practice to delete all emails once they were downloaded to the account holder's computer. Thus, in a sense, the government's use of § 2703(f) was a but-for cause of the constitutional violation. But the actual violation at issue was obtaining the emails, and the government did not rely on § 2703(f) specifically to do that. Instead, the government relied on § 2703(b) and § 2703(d). The proper inquiry, therefore, is whether the government violated either of *those* provisions, and the preservation request is of no consequence to that inquiry. . . .

NOTES & QUESTIONS

1. ***E-mail and the Third Party Doctrine.*** Does the court convincingly distinguish e-mail maintained by an ISP from the third party doctrine cases (*Smith v. Maryland* and *United States v. Miller*)?

2. ***The SCA and E-mail.*** Do the SCA's different levels of protection of e-mail make sense? Consider Patricia Bellia and Susan Freiwald:

[W]arrant-level protection for stored e-mail should persist whether or not an e-mail has been opened, accessed, or downloaded. It is hard to imagine why the act of reading or preparing to read an e-mail, which is the entire point of communicating by e-mail, should somehow deprive a user of his reasonable expectation of privacy in the electronic communication. As discussed, the government's distinctions on this basis derive from a strained reading of out-of-date statutory provisions, and neither reflect nor should impact the Fourth Amendment status of stored e-mail.[81]

4. ISP RECORDS

UNITED STATES V. HAMBRICK

55 F. Supp. 2d 504 (W.D. Va. 1999)

MICHAEL, J. Defendant Scott M. Hambrick seeks the suppression of all evidence obtained from his Internet Service Provider ("ISP"), MindSpring, and seeks the suppression of all evidence seized from his home pursuant to a warrant issued by this court. For the reasons discussed below, the court denies the defendant's motion.

On March 14, 1998, J. L. McLaughlin, a police officer with the Keene, New Hampshire Police Department, connected to the Internet and entered a chat room called "Gay dads 4 sex." McLaughlin's screen name was "Rory14." In this chat room, Detective McLaughlin encountered someone using the screen name "Blowuinva." Based on a series of online conversations between "Rory14" (Det. McLaughlin) and "Blowuinva," McLaughlin concluded that "Blowuinva" sought to entice a fourteen-year-old boy to leave New Hampshire and live with "Blowuinva." Because of the anonymity of the Internet, Detective McLaughlin did not know the true identity of the person with whom he was communicating nor did he know where "Blowuinva" lived. "Blowuinva" had only identified himself as "Brad."

To determine Blowuinva's identity and location, McLaughlin obtained a New Hampshire state subpoena that he served on Blowuinva's Internet Service Provider, MindSpring, located in Atlanta, Georgia. The New Hampshire state subpoena requested that MindSpring produce "any records pertaining to the billing and/or user records documenting the subject using your services on March 14th, 1998 at 1210HRS (EST) using Internet Protocol Number 207.69.169.92." MindSpring complied with the subpoena. On March 20, 1998, MindSpring supplied McLaughlin with defendant's name, address, credit card number, e-mail address, home and work telephone numbers, fax number, and the fact that the Defendant's account was connected to the Internet at the Internet Protocol (IP) address.

A justice of the peace, Richard R. Richards, signed the New Hampshire state subpoena. Mr. Richards is not only a New Hampshire justice of the peace, but he is also a detective in the Keene Police Department, Investigation Division. Mr.

[81] Patricia L. Bellia & Susan Freiwald, *Fourth Amendment Protection for Stored E-Mail,* 2008 U. Chi. Legal F. 121, 135 (2008).

Richards did not issue the subpoena pursuant to a matter pending before himself, any other judicial officer, or a grand jury. At the hearing on the defendant's motion, the government conceded the invalidity of the warrant. The question before this court, therefore, is whether the court must suppress the information obtained from MindSpring, and all that flowed from it, because the government failed to obtain a proper subpoena. . . .

. . . [Under *Katz v. United States*,] the Fourth Amendment applies only where: (1) the citizen has manifested a subjective expectation of privacy, and (2) the expectation is one that society accepts as "objectively reasonable." . . . Applying the first part of the *Katz* analysis, Mr. Hambrick asserts that he had a subjective expectation of privacy in the information that MindSpring gave to the government. However, resolution of this matter hinges on whether Mr. Hambrick's expectation is one that society accepts as "objectively reasonable."

The objective reasonableness prong of the privacy test is ultimately a value judgment and a determination of how much privacy we should have as a society. In making this constitutional determination, this court must employ a sort of risk analysis, asking whether the individual affected should have expected the material at issue to remain private. The defendant asserts that the Electronic Communications Privacy Act ("ECPA") "legislatively resolves" this question. . . .

The information obtained through the use of the government's invalid subpoena consisted of the defendant's name, address, social security number, credit card number, and certification that the defendant was connected to the Internet on March 14, 1998. Thus, this information falls within the provisions of Title II of the ECPA.

The government may require that an ISP provide stored communications and transactional records only if (1) it obtains a warrant issued under the Federal Rules of Criminal Procedure or state equivalent, or (2) it gives prior notice to the online subscriber and then issues a subpoena or receives a court order authorizing disclosure of the information in question. *See* 18 U.S.C. § 2703(a)-(c)(1)(B). When an ISP discloses stored communications or transactional records to a government entity without the requisite authority, the aggrieved customer's sole remedy is damages.

Although Congress is willing to recognize that individuals have some degree of privacy in the stored data and transactional records that their ISPs retain, the ECPA is hardly a legislative determination that this expectation of privacy is one that rises to the level of "reasonably objective" for Fourth Amendment purposes. Despite its concern for privacy, Congress did not provide for suppression where a party obtains stored data or transactional records in violation of the Act. Additionally, the ECPA's concern for privacy extends only to government invasions of privacy. ISPs are free to turn stored data and transactional records over to nongovernmental entities. *See* 18 U.S.C. § 2703(c)(1)(A) ("[A] provider of electronic communication service or remote computing service may disclose a record or other information pertaining to a subscriber to or customer of such service . . . to any person other than a governmental entity."). For Fourth Amendment purposes, this court does not find that the ECPA has legislatively determined that an individual has a reasonable expectation of privacy in his name, address, social security number, credit card number, and proof of Internet connection. The fact that the ECPA does not proscribe turning over such information to private entities buttresses the conclusion that the ECPA does not create a reasonable expectation of privacy in that information. This, however, does not end the court's inquiry. This court must determine, within the constitutional framework that the Supreme Court has established, whether Mr. Hambrick's subjective expectation of privacy is one that society is willing to recognize.

To have any interest in privacy, there must be some exclusion of others. To have a reasonable expectation of privacy under the Supreme Court's risk-analysis approach to the Fourth Amendment, two conditions must be met: (1) the data must not be knowingly exposed to others, and (2) the Internet service provider's ability to access the data must not constitute a disclosure. In *Katz*, the Supreme Court expressly held that "what a person knowingly exposes to the public, even in his home or office, is not a subject of Fourth Amendment protection." Further, the Court "consistently has held that a person has no legitimate expectation of privacy in information he voluntarily turns over to third parties." *Smith v. Maryland*, 442 U.S. 735, 743-44 (1979). . . .

When Scott Hambrick surfed the Internet using the screen name "Blowuinva," he was not a completely anonymous actor. It is true that an average member of the public could not easily determine the true identity of "Blowuinva." Nevertheless, when Mr. Hambrick entered into an agreement to obtain Internet access from MindSpring, he knowingly revealed his name, address, credit card number, and telephone number to MindSpring and its employees. Mr. Hambrick also selected the screen name "Blowuinva." When the defendant selected his screen name it became tied to his true identity in all MindSpring records. MindSpring employees had ready access to these records in the normal course of MindSpring's business, for example, in the keeping of its records for billing purposes, and nothing prevented MindSpring from revealing this information to nongovernmental actors.[82] Also, there is nothing in the record to suggest that there was a restrictive agreement between the defendant and MindSpring that would limit the right of MindSpring to reveal the defendant's personal information to nongovernmental entities. Where such dissemination of information to nongovernment entities is not prohibited, there can be no reasonable expectation of privacy in that information.

Although not dispositive to the outcome of this motion, it is important to note that the court's decision does not leave members of cybersociety without privacy protection. Under the ECPA, Internet Service Providers are civilly liable when they reveal subscriber information or the contents of stored communications to the government without first requiring a warrant, court order, or subpoena. Here, nothing suggests that MindSpring had any knowledge that the facially valid subpoena submitted to it was in fact an invalid subpoena. Had MindSpring revealed the information at issue in this case to the government without first requiring a subpoena, apparently valid on its face, Mr. Hambrick could have sued MindSpring. This is a powerful deterrent protecting privacy in the online world and should not be taken lightly. . . .

---

[82] It is apparently common for ISPs to provide certain information that Mr. Hambrick alleges to be private to marketing firms and other organizations interested in soliciting business from Internet users.

NOTES & QUESTIONS

1. *Is There a Reasonable Expectation of Privacy in ISP Records?* The court in *Hambrick* concludes that there is no reasonable expectation of privacy in ISP records based on the third party doctrine in *Smith v. Maryland.* In *United States v. Kennedy,* 81 F. Supp. 2d 1103 (D. Kan. 2000), the court reached a similar conclusion:

   > Defendant has not demonstrated an objectively reasonable legitimate expectation of privacy in his subscriber information. . . . "[A] person has no legitimate expectation of privacy in information he voluntarily turns over to third parties." *Smith v. Maryland,* 442 U.S. 735 (1979). When defendant entered into an agreement with [his ISP], he knowingly revealed all information connected to [his IP address]. He cannot now claim to have a Fourth Amendment privacy interest in his subscriber information.

   Is *Smith v. Maryland* controlling on this issue? Is there a way to distinguish *Smith*?

2. *Statutes as a Basis for a Reasonable Expectation of Privacy?* Hambrick was not seeking relief directly under the Stored Communications Act of ECPA. Why not? Instead, Hambrick asserted he had Fourth Amendment protection in his subscriber records. He argued that under the *Katz* reasonable expectation of privacy test, the ECPA "legislatively resolves" that there is a reasonable expectation of privacy in information that Mindspring gave to the government. Should statutes that protect privacy serve as an indication of a societal recognition of a reasonable expectation of privacy? What are the consequences of using statutes such as ECPA to conclude that the Fourth Amendment applies?

3. *Is There a Remedy?* Mindspring couldn't release information to the government without a warrant or subpoena or else it would face civil liability. However, in this case, the government presented Mindspring with a subpoena that Mindspring had no knowledge was invalid. Therefore, it is unlikely that Mindspring would be liable. If the court is correct in its conclusion that 18 U.S.C. § 2703(a)–(c)(1)(B) of the ECPA only applies to the conduct of Internet Service Providers, then is there any remedy against Officer Richards's blatantly false subpoena? Could a police officer obtain a person's Internet subscriber information by falsifying a subpoena and escape without any civil liability or exclusionary rule?

MCVEIGH V. COHEN

983 F. Supp. 215 (D.D.C. 1998)

SPORKIN, J. . . . Plaintiff Timothy R. McVeigh, who bears no relation to the Oklahoma City bombing defendant, seeks to enjoin the United States Navy from discharging him under the statutory policy colloquially known as "Don't Ask, Don't Tell, Don't Pursue." See 10 U.S.C. § 654 ("new policy"). In the course of investigating his sexual orientation, the Plaintiff contends that the Defendants violated his rights under the Electronic Communications Privacy Act ("ECPA"), 18 U.S.C. § 2701 et seq., the Administrative Procedure Act ("APA") 5 U.S.C. § 706, the Department's own policy, and the Fourth and Fifth Amendments of the U.S. Constitution. Absent an injunction, the Plaintiff avers that he will suffer irreparable injury from the discharge, even if he were ultimately to prevail on the merits of his claims.

The Plaintiff, Senior Chief Timothy R. McVeigh, is a highly decorated seventeen-year veteran of the United States Navy who has served honorably and continuously since he was nineteen years old. At the time of the Navy's decision to discharge him, he was the senior-most enlisted man aboard the United States nuclear submarine U.S.S. Chicago.

On September 2, 1997, Ms. Helen Hajne, a civilian Navy volunteer, received an electronic mail ("email") message through the America Online Service ("AOL") regarding the toy-drive that she was coordinating for the Chicago crew members' children. The message box stated that it came from the alias "boysrch," but the text of the email was signed by a "Tim." Through an option available to AOL subscribers, the volunteer searched through the "member profile directory" to find the member profile for this sender. The directory specified that "boysrch" was an AOL subscriber named Tim who lived in Honolulu, Hawaii, worked in the military, and identified his marital status as "gay." Although the profile included some telling interests such as "collecting pics of other young studs" and "boy watching," it did not include any further identifying information such as full name, address, or phone number. . . .

Ms. Hajne proceeded to forward the email and directory profile to her husband, who, like Plaintiff, was also a noncommissioned officer aboard the U.S.S. Chicago. The material eventually found its way to Commander John Mickey, the captain of the ship and Plaintiff's commanding officer. In turn, Lieutenant Karin S. Morean, the ship's principal legal adviser and a member of the Judge Advocate General's ("JAG") Corps was called in to investigate the matter. By this point, the Navy suspected the "Tim" who authored the email might be Senior Chief Timothy McVeigh. Before she spoke to the Plaintiff and without a warrant or court order, Lieutenant Morean requested a Navy paralegal on her staff, Legalman First Class Joseph M. Kaiser, to contact AOL and obtain information from the service that could "connect" the screen name "boysrch" and accompanying user profile to McVeigh. Legalman Kaiser called AOL's toll-free customer service number and talked to a representative at technical services. Legalman Kaiser did not identify himself as a Naval serviceman. According to his testimony at the administrative hearing, he stated that he was "a third party in receipt of a fax sheet and wanted to confirm the profile sheet, [and] who it belonged to." The AOL representative affirmatively identified Timothy R. McVeigh as the customer in question.

Upon verification from AOL, Lieutenant Morean notified Senior Chief McVeigh that the Navy had obtained "some indication[] that he made a statement of homosexuality" in violation of § 654(b)(2) of "Don't Ask, Don't Tell." In light of the Uniform Code of Military Justice prohibition of sodomy and indecent acts, she then advised him of his right to remain silent. Shortly thereafter, in a memorandum dated September 22, 1997, the Navy advised Plaintiff that it was commencing an administrative discharge proceeding (termed by the Navy as an "administrative separation") against him. The reason stated was for "homosexual conduct, as evidenced by your statement that you are a homosexual."

On November 7, 1997, the Navy conducted an administrative discharge hearing before a three-member board. . . . At the conclusion of the administrative hearing, the board held that the government had sufficiently shown by a preponderance of the evidence that Senior Chief McVeigh had engaged in "homosexual conduct," a dischargeable offense. . . .

. . . Plaintiff is now scheduled to be discharged barring relief from this Court. . . .

. . . At its core, the Plaintiff's complaint is with the Navy's compliance, or lack thereof, with its new regulations under the "Don't Ask, Don't Tell, Don't Pursue" policy. Plaintiff contends that he did not "tell," as prescribed by the statute, but that nonetheless, the Navy impermissibly "asked" and zealously "pursued."

In short, this case raises the central issue of whether there is really a place for gay officers in the military under the new policy, "Don't Ask, Don't Tell, Don't Pursue." [This policy was adopted in 1993, and it prohibits the military from investigating sexual orientation unless there is "credible information" that a gay serviceman or servicewoman has the "propensity or intent to engage in homosexual acts."] . . .

The facts as stated above clearly demonstrate that the Plaintiff did not openly express his homosexuality in a way that compromised this "Don't Ask, Don't Tell" policy. Suggestions of sexual orientation in a private, anonymous email account did not give the Navy a sufficient reason to investigate to determine whether to commence discharge proceedings. In its actions, the Navy violated its own regulations. An investigation into sexual orientation may be initiated "only when [a commander] has received credible information that there is a basis for discharge," such as when an officer "has said that he or she is a homosexual or bisexual, or made some other statement that indicates a propensity or intent to engage in homosexual acts." Yet in this case, there was no such credible information that Senior Chief McVeigh had made such a statement. Under the Guidelines, "credible information" requires more than "just a belief or suspicion" that a Service member has engaged in homosexual conduct. In the examples provided, the Guidelines state that "credible information" would exist in this case only if "a reliable person" stated that he or she directly observed or heard a Service member make an oral or written statement that "a reasonable person would believe was intended to convey the fact that he or she engages in or has a propensity or intent to engage in homosexual acts."

Clearly, the facts as stated above in this case demonstrate that there was no such "credible information." All that the Navy had was an email message and user profile that it suspected was authored by Plaintiff. Under the military regulation, that information alone should not have triggered any sort of investigation. When the Navy affirmatively took steps to confirm the identity of the email respondent, it violated the very essence of "Don't Ask, Don't Pursue" by launching a search and destroy mission. Even if the Navy had a factual basis to believe that the email message and profile were written by Plaintiff, it was unreasonable to infer that they were necessarily intended to convey a propensity or intent to engage in homosexual conduct. Particularly in the context of cyberspace, a medium of "virtual reality" that invites fantasy and affords anonymity, the comments attributed to McVeigh do not by definition amount to a declaration of homosexuality. At most, they express "an abstract preference or desire to engage in homosexual acts." Yet the regulations specify that a statement professing homosexuality so as to warrant investigation must declare "more than an abstract preference or desire"; they must indicate a likelihood actually to carry out homosexual acts.

The subsequent steps taken by the Navy in its "pursuit" of the Plaintiff were not only unauthorized under its policy, but likely illegal under the Electronic Communications Privacy Act of 1986 ("ECPA"). The ECPA, enacted by Congress to address privacy concerns on the Internet, allows the government to obtain information from an online service provider — as the Navy did in this instance from AOL — but only if a) it obtains a warrant issued under the Federal Rules of Criminal Procedure or state equivalent; or b) it gives prior notice to the online subscriber and then issues a subpoena or receives a court order authorizing disclosure of the information in question. See 18 U.S.C. § 2703(b)(1)(A)-(B), (c)(1)(B).

In soliciting and obtaining over the phone personal information about the Plaintiff from AOL, his private on-line service provider, the government in this case invoked neither of these provisions and thus failed to comply with the ECPA. From the record, it is undisputed that the Navy directly solicited by phone information from AOL. Lieutenant Karin S. Morean, the ship's principal legal counsel and a member of the JAG corps, personally requested Legalman Kaiser to contact AOL and obtain the identity of the subscriber. Without this information, Plaintiff credibly contends that the Navy could not have made the necessary connection between him and the user profile which was the sole basis on which to commence discharge proceedings.

The government, in its defense, contends that the Plaintiff cannot succeed on his ECPA claim. It argues that the substantive provision of the statute that Plaintiff cites, 18 U.S.C. § 2703(c)(1)(B), puts the obligation on the online service provider to withhold information from the government, and not vice versa. In support of its position, Defendants cite to the Fourth Circuit opinion in *Tucker v. Waddell*, 83 F.3d 688 (4th Cir. 1996), which held that § 2703(c)(1)(B) only prohibits the actions of online providers, not the government. Accordingly, Defendants allege that Plaintiff has no cause of action against the government on the basis of the ECPA. . . .

. . . [However,] Section 2703(c)(1)(B) must be read in the context of the statute as a whole. In comparison, § 2703(a) and (b) imposes on the government a reciprocal obligation to obtain a warrant or the like before requiring disclosure. It appears from the face of the statute that all of the subsections of § 2703 were intended to work in tandem to protect consumer privacy. Even if, however, the government ultimately proves to be right in its assessment of § 2703(c)(1)(B), the Plaintiff has plead § 2703(a) and (b) as alternative grounds for relief. In his claim that the government, at the least, solicited a violation of the ECPA by AOL, the Court finds that there is likely success on the merits with regard to this issue. The government knew, or should have known, that by turning over the information without a warrant, AOL was breaking the law. Yet the Navy, in this case, directly solicited the information anyway. What is most telling is that the Naval investigator did not identify himself when he made his request. While the government makes much of the fact that § 2703(c)(1)(B) does not provide a cause of action against the government, it is elementary that information obtained improperly can be suppressed where an individual's rights have been violated. In these days of "big brother," where through technology and otherwise the privacy interests of individuals from all walks of life are being ignored or marginalized, it is imperative that statutes explicitly protecting these rights be strictly observed. . . .

. . . With literally the entire world on the world-wide web, enforcement of the ECPA is of great concern to those who bare the most personal information about their lives in private accounts through the Internet. . . .

. . . Although Officer McVeigh did not publicly announce his sexual orientation, the Navy nonetheless impermissibly embarked on a search and "outing" mission.

NOTES & QUESTIONS

1. *A Suppression Remedy?* Recall the following statement in *McVeigh*: "The government knew, or should have known, that by turning over the information without a warrant, AOL was breaking the law. . . . While the government makes much of the fact that § 2703(c)(1)(B) does not provide a cause of action against the government, it is elementary that information obtained improperly can be suppressed where an individual's rights have been violated." Is this last statement correct? The Stored Communications Act does not have a suppression remedy; the court is creating an exclusionary rule for the Stored Communications Act. Is this appropriate? Without a suppression remedy for the conduct of the government in this case, what would deter the government from violating the Stored Communications Act?

2. *Postscript.* Subsequent to *McVeigh v. Cohen,* Congress amended §§ 2703(a)-(c) to make it clear that these provisions applied not just to ISPs but also to government conduct. In *Freedman v. America Online, Inc.*, 303 F. Supp. 2d 121 (D. Conn. 2004), two police detectives signed a warrant themselves (rather than bring it before a judge) and served it to AOL. AOL responded by faxing plaintiff's name, address, phone numbers, account status, membership information, and his other AOL screen names. The district court concluded that the government had violated ECPA: "To conclude that the government may circumvent the legal processes set forth in the ECPA by merely requesting subscriber information from an ISP contradicts Congress's intent to protect personal privacy."

3. *Cell Site Location Information.* Recall the discussion of GPS tracking earlier in this chapter. Federal circuit courts are split as to whether a person has a reasonable expectation of privacy when the government uses a GPS device to track her movement and location in public. There is another way to obtain data about a person's movements or location — via records maintained by telecommunications service providers. Providers of cell phone or smart phone service have data about the location of that phone, which most often is the location of the user too. In *In re Application of the United States for an*

Order Authorizing the Release of Historical Cell-Site Info., 736 F. Supp. 2d 578 (E.D.N.Y. 2010), the federal government sought an order pursuant to 18 U.S.C. § 2703(c)-(d) of the SCA demanding from Sprint Nextel all the location information for a mobile phone over a 58-day period. Under the SCA, the government need only establish "specific and articulable facts showing that there are reasonable grounds to believe that the information sought is relevant and material to an ongoing criminal investigation." But the magistrate judge denied the government's order, holding that the Fourth Amendment required a warrant supported by probable cause. The magistrate reasoned that cell-site location information (CSLI) was analogous to GPS tracking that some federal circuit courts had held required a warrant under the Fourth Amendment. The district court, however, reversed the magistrate and granted the government's order without issuing an opinion.

In *In re Application of the United States for an Order Directing a Provider of Electronic Communications Services to Disclose Records to the Government*, 620 F.3d 304 (3d Cir. 2010), the court held that under the SCA, judges and magistrates retained discretion to issue orders under the more demanding warrant standard than the "specific and articulable facts" standard. The court did not engage in a Fourth Amendment analysis except to note that the third party doctrine under *Smith v. Maryland*, 442 U.S. 735 (1979) (telephone pen register information) and *United States v. Miller*, 425 U.S. 435 (1976) (bank records), was not applicable to CSLI:

> The Government argues that no CSLI can implicate constitutional protections because the subscriber has shared its information with a third party, i.e., the communications provider. . . .
>
> A cell phone customer has not "voluntarily" shared his location information with a cellular provider in any meaningful way. . . . [It] is unlikely that cell phone customers are aware that their cell phone providers *collect* and store historical location information. Therefore, "[w]hen a cell phone user makes a call, the only information that is voluntarily and knowingly conveyed to the phone company is the number that is dialed and there is no indication to the user that making that call will also locate the caller; when a cell phone user receives a call, he hasn't voluntarily exposed anything at all." (quoting brief of the Electronic Frontier Foundation).

Susan Freiwald concludes that CLSI should require a warrant and probable cause under the Fourth Amendment:

> Because government compulsion of disclosure of location data constitutes a search under the Fourth Amendment, the judicial oversight inherent in the probable cause warrant requirement is required. The power and intrusiveness of the method, and its susceptibility to abuse, mean that anything less would violate Fourth Amendment rights. While the probable cause standard will not necessarily be that much more demanding than the showing needed for a ["specific and articulable" facts] order [under the SCA], the need to provide notice to the target, after the fact judicial review, and meaningful remedies should make a significant difference. A warrant must be required for location data acquisition as a matter of law, and no Supreme Court precedents

pertaining to bumper-beepers, bank records, or telephone numbers counsel a different result.[83]

Based on the Supreme Court's Fourth Amendment cases — the third party doctrine, the beeper cases, and the cases finding no reasonable expectation of privacy in public — how does the Fourth Amendment apply to CSLI?

4. ***Historical vs. Real-Time Location Data.*** Is there a difference between historical versus real-time location data? Some courts have concluded that real-time location data requires a warrant whereas historical data does not. One rationale for the distinction is that historical data is stored in records and falls under the third party doctrine. According to Susan Freiwald, the distinction is spurious:

> [H]istorical location data may be at least as informative to law enforcement agents as prospective location data. Historical data may indicate with whom, where, and for how long targets have met. It may put a target at the scene of a crime at the time the crime was committed and thereby refute the target's alibi. Magistrate Judge Lenihan appropriately found that "the privacy and associational interests implicated [by acquisition of location data] are not meaningfully diminished by a delay in disclosure." Other courts have also recognized that law enforcement acquisition of records of historical location data, by virtue of creating a target's complete digital profile, should receive the same Fourth Amendment protection as acquisition of location data in real-time or prospectively.[84]

5. IP ADDRESSES AND URLS

UNITED STATES v. FORRESTER

512 F.3d 500 (9th Cir. 2008)

FISHER, J. . . . Defendants-appellants Mark Stephen Forrester and Dennis Louis Alba were charged with various offenses relating to the operation of a large Ecstasy-manufacturing laboratory, and were convicted on all counts following a jury trial. They now appeal their convictions and sentences. . . .

During its investigation of Forrester and Alba's Ecstasy-manufacturing operation, the government employed various computer surveillance techniques to monitor Alba's e-mail and Internet activity. The surveillance began in May 2001 after the government applied for and received court permission to install a pen register analogue known as a "mirror port" on Alba's account with PacBell Internet. The mirror port was installed at PacBell's connection facility in San Diego, and enabled the government to learn the to/from addresses of Alba's e-mail messages, the IP addresses of the websites that Alba visited and the total volume of information sent to or from his account. Later, the government obtained a warrant authorizing it to employ imaging and keystroke monitoring

---

[83] Susan Freiwald, Cell Phone Location Data and the Fourth Amendment: A Question of Law, Not Fact, 70 Md. L. Rev. 677, 742-43 (2011).

[84] *Id.* at 734.

techniques, but Alba does not challenge on appeal those techniques' legality or the government's application to use them.

Forrester and Alba were tried by jury. At trial, the government introduced extensive evidence showing that they and their associates built and operated a major Ecstasy laboratory. . . .

Alba contends that the government's surveillance of his e-mail and Internet activity violated the Fourth Amendment and fell outside the scope of the then-applicable federal pen register statute. We hold that the surveillance did not constitute a Fourth Amendment search and thus was not unconstitutional. We also hold that whether or not the computer surveillance was covered by the then-applicable pen register statute — an issue that we do not decide — Alba is not entitled to the suppression of any evidence (let alone the reversal of his convictions) as a consequence.

The Supreme Court held in *Smith v. Maryland* that the use of a pen register (a device that records numbers dialed from a phone line) does not constitute a search for Fourth Amendment purposes. According to the Court, people do not have a subjective expectation of privacy in numbers that they dial because they "realize that they must 'convey' phone numbers to the telephone company, since it is through telephone company switching equipment that their calls are completed." Even if there were such a subjective expectation, it would not be one that society is prepared to recognize as reasonable because "a person has no legitimate expectation of privacy in information he voluntarily turns over to third parties." Therefore the use of a pen register is not a Fourth Amendment search. Importantly, the Court distinguished pen registers from more intrusive surveillance techniques on the ground that "pen registers do not acquire the *contents* of communications" but rather obtain only the addressing information associated with phone calls.

Neither this nor any other circuit has spoken to the constitutionality of computer surveillance techniques that reveal the to/from addresses of e-mail messages, the IP addresses of websites visited and the total amount of data transmitted to or from an account. We conclude that the surveillance techniques the government employed here are constitutionally indistinguishable from the use of a pen register that the Court approved in *Smith.* First, e-mail and Internet users, like the telephone users in *Smith,* rely on third-party equipment in order to engage in communication. *Smith* based its holding that telephone users have no expectation of privacy in the numbers they dial on the users' imputed knowledge that their calls are completed through telephone company switching equipment. Analogously, e-mail and Internet users have no expectation of privacy in the to/from addresses of their messages or the IP addresses of the websites they visit because they should know that this information is provided to and used by Internet service providers for the specific purpose of directing the routing of information. Like telephone numbers, which provide instructions to the "switching equipment that processed those numbers," e-mail to/from addresses and IP addresses are not merely passively conveyed through third party equipment, but rather are voluntarily turned over in order to direct the third party's servers.

Second, e-mail to/from addresses and IP addresses constitute addressing information and do not necessarily reveal any more about the underlying contents of communication than do phone numbers. When the government obtains the to/from addresses of a person's e-mails or the IP addresses of websites visited, it does not find out the contents of the messages or know the particular pages on the websites the person viewed. At best, the government may make educated guesses about what was said in the messages or viewed on the websites based on its knowledge of the e-mail to/from addresses and IP addresses — but this is no different from speculation about the contents of a phone conversation on the basis of the identity of the person or entity that was dialed. Like IP addresses, certain phone numbers may strongly indicate the underlying contents of the communication; for example, the government would know that a person who dialed the phone number of a chemicals company or a gun shop was likely seeking information about chemicals or firearms. Further, when an individual dials a pre-recorded information or subject-specific line, such as sports scores, lottery results or phone sex lines, the phone number may even show that the caller had access to specific content information. Nonetheless, the Court in *Smith* and *Katz* drew a clear line between unprotected addressing information and protected content information that the government did not cross here.[85]

The government's surveillance of e-mail addresses also may be technologically sophisticated, but it is conceptually indistinguishable from government surveillance of physical mail. In a line of cases dating back to the nineteenth century, the Supreme Court has held that the government cannot engage in a warrantless search of the contents of sealed mail, but can observe whatever information people put on the outside of mail, because that information is voluntarily transmitted to third parties. E-mail, like physical mail, has an outside address "visible" to the third-party carriers that transmit it to its intended location, and also a package of content that the sender presumes will be read only by the intended recipient. The privacy interests in these two forms of communication are identical. The contents may deserve Fourth Amendment protection, but the address and size of the package do not. . . .

We therefore hold that the computer surveillance techniques that Alba challenges are not Fourth Amendment searches. However, our holding extends only to these particular techniques and does not imply that more intrusive techniques or techniques that reveal more content information are also constitutionally identical to the use of a pen register. . . .

Alba claims that the government's computer surveillance was not only unconstitutional but also beyond the scope of the then-applicable pen register statute, 18 U.S.C. § 3121-27 (amended October 2001). Under both the old and new versions of 18 U.S.C. § 3122, the government must apply for and obtain a court order before it can install and use a pen register. When the surveillance at issue here took place in May-July 2001, the applicable statute defined a pen register as a "device which records or decodes electronic or other impulses which

---

[85] Surveillance techniques that enable the government to determine not only the IP addresses that a person accesses but also the uniform resource locators ("URL") of the pages visited might be more constitutionally problematic. A URL, unlike an IP address, identifies the particular document within a website that a person views and thus reveals much more information about the person's Internet activity. For instance, a surveillance technique that captures IP addresses would show only that a person visited the New York Times' website at http://www.nytimes.com, whereas a technique that captures URLs would also divulge the particular articles the person viewed.

identify the numbers dialed or otherwise transmitted on the telephone line to which such device is attached." 18 U.S.C. § 3127(3). Notwithstanding the government's invocation of this provision and application for and receipt of a court order, Alba maintains that the computer surveillance at issue here did not come within the statutory definition of a "pen register."

Even assuming that Alba is correct in this contention, he would not be entitled to the suppression of the evidence obtained through the computer surveillance. As both the Supreme Court and this court have emphasized, suppression is a disfavored remedy, imposed only where its deterrence benefits outweigh its substantial social costs or (outside the constitutional context) where it is clearly contemplated by the relevant statute. . . . Alba does not point to any statutory language requiring suppression when computer surveillance that is similar but not technically equivalent to a pen register is carried out. Indeed, he does not even identify what law or regulation the government may have violated if its surveillance did not come within the scope of the then-applicable pen register statute. The suppression of evidence under these circumstances is plainly inappropriate.

Our conclusion is bolstered by the fact that suppression still would not be appropriate even if the computer surveillance was covered by the pen register statute. Assuming the surveillance violated the statute, there is no mention of suppression of evidence in the statutory text. Instead, the only penalty specified is that "[w]hoever knowingly violates subsection (a)" by installing or using a pen register without first obtaining a court order "shall be fined under this title or imprisoned not more than one year, or both." 18 U.S.C. § 3121(d).

NOTES & QUESTIONS

1. *IP Addresses vs. URLs.* The *Forrester* court concludes that e-mail headers and IP addresses are akin to pen registers and that the controlling case is *Smith v. Maryland.* Does *Smith* control because IP address and e-mail header information are not revealing of the contents of the communications or because this information is conveyed to a third party? Recall that in a footnote, the court observes that URLs "might be more constitutionally problematic" because a "URL, unlike an IP address, identifies the particular document within a website that a person views and thus reveals much more information about the person's Internet activity." However, although IP addresses do not reveal specific parts of a websites that a person visits, they do reveal the various websites that a person visits. Why isn't this revealing enough to trigger constitutional protections?

2. *Content vs. Envelope Information.* A key distinction under ECPA, as well as Fourth Amendment law, is between "content" and "envelope" information. Orin Kerr explains the distinction:

   . . . [E]very communications network features two types of information: the contents of communications, and the addressing and routing information that the networks use to deliver the contents of communications. The former is "content information," and the latter is "envelope information."

The essential distinction between content and envelope information remains constant across different technologies, from postal mail to email. With postal mail, the content information is the letter itself, stored safely inside its envelope. The envelope information is the information derived from the outside of the envelope, including the mailing and return addresses, the stamp and postmark, and the size and weight of the envelope when sealed.

Similar distinctions exist for telephone conversations. The content information for a telephone call is the actual conversation between participants that can be captured by an audio recording of the call. The envelope information includes the number the caller dials, the number from which the caller dials, the time of the call, and its duration.[86]

Under ECPA, content information is generally given strong protection (e.g., the Wiretap Act), whereas envelope information is not (e.g., the Pen Register Act). But is such a distinction viable?

Daniel Solove contends that the distinction breaks down:

When applied to IP addresses and URLs, the envelope/content distinction becomes even more fuzzy. An IP address is a unique number that is assigned to each computer connected to the Internet. Each website, therefore, has an IP address. On the surface, a list of IP addresses is simply a list of numbers; but it is actually much more. With a complete listing of IP addresses, the government can learn quite a lot about a person because it can trace how that person surfs the Internet. The government can learn the names of stores at which a person shops, the political organizations a person finds interesting, a person's sexual fetishes and fantasies, her health concerns, and so on.

Perhaps even more revealing are URLs. A URL is a pointer — it points to the location of particular information on the Internet. In other words, it indicates where something is located. When we cite to something on the Web, we are citing to its URL. . . . URLs can reveal the specific information that people are viewing on the Web. URLs can also contain search terms. . . .

[Therefore,] the content/envelope distinction is not always clear. In many circumstances, to adapt Marshall McLuhan, the "envelope" *is* the "content." Envelope information can reveal a lot about a person's private activities, sometimes as much (and even more) than can content information.[87]

Orin Kerr disagrees:

Professor Solove appears to doubt the wisdom of offering lower privacy protection for non-content information. He suggests that the acquisition of non-content information should require a full search warrant based on probable cause. . . .

Despite this, Solove's suggestion that the law should not offer lesser privacy protection for non-content information is unpersuasive. The main reason is that it is quite rare for non-content information to yield the equivalent of content information. It happens in very particular circumstances, but it remains quite rare, and usually in circumstances that are difficult to predict ex ante. In the Internet context, for example, non-content surveillance typically consists of collecting Internet packets; the packets disclose that a packet was sent from one

---

[86] Orin S. Kerr, Internet *Surveillance Law After the USA PATRIOT Act: The Big Brother That Isn't,* 97 Nw. U. L. Rev. 607, 611 (2003).

[87] Solove, *Surveillance Law, supra,* at 1287-88.

IP address to another IP address at a particular time. This isn't very private information, at least in most cases. Indeed, it is usually impossible to know who asked for the packet, or what the packet was about, or what the person who asked for the packet wanted to do, or even if it was a person (as opposed to the computer) who sent for the packet in the first place. Solove focuses on the compelling example of Internet search terms as an example of non-content information that can be the privacy equivalent of content information. This is a misleading example, however, as Internet search terms very well may be contents. . . . Thus, despite the fact that non-content information can yield private information, in the great majority of cases contents of communications implicate privacy concerns on a higher order of magnitude than non-content information, and it makes sense to give greater privacy protections for the former and lesser to the latter.[88]

Solove replies:

Kerr assumes that a compilation of envelope information is generally less revealing than content information. However, a person may care more about protecting the identities of people with whom she communicates than the content of those communications. Indeed, the identities of the people one communicates with implicates freedom of association under the First Amendment. The difficulty is that the distinction between content and envelope information does not correlate well to the distinction between sensitive and innocuous information. Envelope information can be quite sensitive; content information can be quite innocuous. Admittedly, in many cases, people do not care very much about maintaining privacy over the identities of their friends and associates. But it is also true that in many cases, the contents of communications are not very revealing as well. Many e-mails are short messages which do not reveal any deep secrets, and even Kerr would agree that this should not lessen their protection under the law. This is because content information has the potential to be quite sensitive — but this is also the case with envelope information.[89]

3. **The Scope of the Pen Register Act.** The version of the Pen Register Act in effect when the search took place in *Forrester* was the pre-USA PATRIOT Act version, which defined pen registers more narrowly as "numbers dialed." The USA PATRIOT Act expanded the definition of pen register to include "dialing, routing, addressing, or signaling information . . . provided, however, that such information shall not include the contents of any communication." Prior to the USA PATRIOT Act changes, it was an open question as to whether the Pen Register Act applied to e-mail headers, IP addresses, and URLs. The USA PATRIOT Act changes aimed to clarify that the Pen Register Act did apply beyond telephone numbers. E-mail headers seem to fit readily into the new Pen Register Act definition. But what about IP addresses and URLs? They involve "routing" and "addressing" information, but they

---

[88] Orin S. Kerr, *A User's Guide to the Stored Communications Act — and a Legislator's Guide to Amending It,* 72 Geo. Wash. L. Rev. 1208, 1229 n.142 (2004).

[89] Solove, *Surveillance Law, supra,* at 1288. Susan Freiwald contends that "the current categories of the ECPA do not cover web traffic data. At least one other category of protection is needed. Search terms entered, web-pages visited, and items viewed are neither message contents nor their to/from information." Freiwald, *Online Surveillance, supra,* at 71.

may also include "the contents" of communications. Do they involve "contents" or are they merely "envelope" information?

4. ***ECPA and the Exclusionary Rule.*** The *Forrester* court concludes that even if the acquisition of information violated the Pen Register Act, the exclusionary rule is not a remedy under the Act. As discussed earlier in this chapter, many provisions of electronic surveillance law lack an exclusionary rule. In the Wiretap Act, wire and oral communications are protected with an exclusionary rule, but electronic communications are not. Solove argues that "[s]ince e-mail has become a central mode of communication, this discrepancy is baseless."[90] Is it? Can you think of a reason why e-mail should receive lesser protection than a phone conversation, which would be protected by the exclusionary rule under the Wiretap Act? Additionally, the Stored Communications Act and Pen Register Act have no exclusionary remedies for any type of communication.

Orin Kerr argues the absence of an exclusionary rule in many of ECPA's provisions leads to inadequate judicial attention to ECPA. Without an exclusionary rule, Kerr contends, "criminal defendants have little incentive to raise challenges to the government's Internet surveillance practices." Therefore, many challenges to Internet surveillance practices "tend to be in civil cases between private parties that raise issues far removed from those that animated Congress to pass the statutes." Adding an exclusionary remedy, Kerr argues, would "benefit both civil libertarian and law enforcement interests alike." He writes:

> On the civil libertarian side, a suppression remedy would considerably increase judicial scrutiny of the government's Internet surveillance practices in criminal cases. The resulting judicial opinions would clarify the rules that the government must follow, serving the public interest of greater transparency. Less obviously, the change could also benefit law enforcement by altering the type and nature of the disputes over the Internet surveillance laws that courts encounter. Prosecutors would have greater control over the types of cases the courts decided, enjoy more sympathetic facts, and have a better opportunity to explain and defend law enforcement interests before the courts. The statutory law of Internet surveillance would become more like the Fourth Amendment law: a source of vital and enforceable rights that every criminal defendant can invoke, governed by relatively clear standards that by and large respect law enforcement needs and attempt to strike a balance between those needs and privacy interests.[91]

5. ***The Internet vs. the Telephone.*** Susan Freiwald contends that while the 1968 Wiretap Act (Title III) provided powerful and effective protection for telephone communications, ECPA in 1986 did not do the same for online communications:

> . . . [O]nline surveillance is even more susceptible to law enforcement abuse and even more threatening to privacy. Therefore, one might expect regulation

---

[90] Solove, *Surveillance Law, supra,* at 1282.

[91] Orin S. Kerr, *Lifting the "Fog" of Internet Surveillance: How a Suppression Remedy Would Change Computer Crime Law,* 54 Hastings L.J. 805, 824, 807-08 (2003).

of online surveillance to be more privacy-protective than traditional wiretapping law. That could not be further from the truth. The law provides dramatically less privacy protection for online activities than for traditional telephone calls and videotapings. Additionally, what makes the Wiretap Act complex makes online surveillance law chaotic. Almost all of the techniques designed to rein in law enforcement have been abandoned in the online context. And, while Congress resolved much of its ambivalence towards wiretapping in 1968, current law suggests the outright hostility of all branches of government to online privacy.[92]

In what ways does federal electronic surveillance law protect Internet communication differently from telephone communication? Should the privacy protections differ in these areas?

6. KEY LOGGING DEVICES

UNITED STATES V. SCARFO

180 F. Supp. 2d 572 (D.N.J. 2001)

POLITAN, J. . . . Acting pursuant to federal search warrants, the F.B.I. on January 15, 1999, entered Scarfo and Paolercio's business office, Merchant Services of Essex County, to search for evidence of an illegal gambling and loansharking operation. During their search of Merchant Services, the F.B.I. came across a personal computer and attempted to access its various files. They were unable to gain entry to an encrypted file named "Factors."

Suspecting the "Factors" file contained evidence of an illegal gambling and loansharking operation, the F.B.I. returned to the location and, pursuant to two search warrants, installed what is known as a "Key Logger System" ("KLS") on the computer and/or computer keyboard in order to decipher the passphrase to the encrypted file, thereby gaining entry to the file. The KLS records the keystrokes an individual enters on a personal computer's keyboard. The government utilized the KLS in order to "catch" Scarfo's passphrases to the encrypted file while he was entering them onto his keyboard. Scarfo's personal computer features a modem for communication over telephone lines and he possesses an America Online account. The F.B.I. obtained the passphrase to the "Factors" file and retrieved what is alleged to be incriminating evidence.

On June 21, 2000, a federal grand jury returned a three count indictment against the Defendants charging them with gambling and loansharking. The Defendant Scarfo then filed his motion for discovery and to suppress the evidence recovered from his computer. After oral argument was heard on July 30, 2001, the Court ordered additional briefing by the parties. In an August 7, 2001, Letter Opinion and Order, this Court expressed serious concerns over whether the government violated the wiretap statute in utilizing the KLS on Scarfo's computer. Specifically, the Court expressed concern over whether the

---

[92] Susan Freiwald, *Online Surveillance: Remembering the Lessons of the Wiretap Act*, 56 Ala. L. Rev. 9, 14 (2004).

KLS may have operated during periods when Scarfo (or any other user of his personal computer) was communicating via modem over telephone lines, thereby unlawfully intercepting wire communications without having applied for a wiretap pursuant to Title III, 18 U.S.C. § 2510.

As a result of these concerns, on August 7, 2001, this Court ordered the United States to file with the Court a report explaining fully how the KLS device functions and describing the KLS technology and how it works vis-à-vis the computer modem, Internet communications, e-mail and all other uses of a computer. In light of the government's grave concern over the national security implications such a revelation might raise, the Court permitted the United States to submit any additional evidence which would provide particular and specific reasons how and why disclosure of the KLS would jeopardize both ongoing and future domestic criminal investigations and national security interests.

The United States responded by filing a request for modification of this Court's August 7, 2001, Letter Opinion and Order so as to comply with the procedures set forth in the Classified Information Procedures Act, Title 18, United States Code, Appendix III, § 1 *et seq.* ("CIPA"). [The FBI contended that a detailed disclosure of how the KLS worked would negatively affect national security and that this information was classified. After an in camera, ex parte hearing with several officials from the Attorney General's office and the FBI, the court granted the government's request not to release the details of how KLS functioned. Instead, the government would provide Scarfo and his attorneys with an unclassified summary about how KLS worked. Based on that summary, Scarfo contended that the KLS violated the Fourth Amendment because the KLS had the capability of collecting data on all of his keystrokes, not merely those of his passphrase.]

Where a search warrant is obtained, the Fourth Amendment requires a certain modicum of particularity in the language of the warrant with respect to the area and items to be searched and/or seized. The particularity requirement exists so that law enforcement officers are constrained from undertaking a boundless and exploratory rummaging through one's personal property. . . . Because the encrypted file could not be accessed via traditional investigative means, Judge Haneke's Order permitted law enforcement officers to "install and leave behind software, firmware, and/or hardware equipment which will monitor the inputted data entered on Nicodemo S. Scarfo's computer in the TARGET LOCATION so that the F.B.I. can capture the password necessary to decrypt computer files by recording the key related information as they are entered." The Order also allowed the F.B.I. to

> search for and seize business records in whatever form they are kept (e.g., written, mechanically or computer maintained and any necessary computer hardware, including computers, computer hard drives, floppy disks or other storage disks or tapes as necessary to access such information, as well as, seizing the mirror hard drive to preserve configuration files, public keys, private keys, and other information that may be of assistance in interpreting the password) — including address and telephone books and electronic storage devices; ledgers and other accounting-type records; banking records and statements; travel records; correspondence; memoranda; notes; calendars; and diaries — that contain information about the identities and whereabouts of

conspirators, betting customers and victim debtors, and/or that otherwise reveal the origin, receipt, concealment or distribution of criminal proceeds relating to illegal gambling, loansharking and other racketeering offenses.

On its face, the Order is very comprehensive and lists the items, including the evidence in the encrypted file, to be seized with more than sufficient specificity. *See Andresen v. Maryland,* 427 U.S. 463, 480-81 (1976) (defendant's general warrant claim rejected where search warrant contained, among other things, a lengthy list of specified and particular items to be seized). One would be hard pressed to draft a more specified or detailed search warrant than the May 8, 1999 Order. Indeed, it could not be written with more particularity. It specifically identifies each piece of evidence the F.B.I. sought which would be linked to the particular crimes the F.B.I. had probable cause to believe were committed. Most importantly, Judge Haneke's Order clearly specifies the key piece of the puzzle the F.B.I. sought — Scarfo's passphrase to the encrypted file.

That the KLS certainly recorded keystrokes typed into Scarfo's keyboard *other* than the searched-for passphrase is of no consequence. This does not, as Scarfo argues, convert the limited search for the passphrase into a general exploratory search. During many lawful searches, police officers may not know the exact nature of the incriminating evidence sought until they stumble upon it. Just like searches for incriminating documents in a closet or filing cabinet, it is true that during a search for a passphrase "some innocuous [items] will be at least cursorily perused in order to determine whether they are among those [items] to be seized."

Hence, "no tenet of the Fourth Amendment prohibits a search merely because it cannot be performed with surgical precision." Where proof of wrongdoing depends upon documents or computer passphrases whose precise nature cannot be known in advance, law enforcement officers must be afforded the leeway to wade through a potential morass of information in the target location to find the particular evidence which is properly specified in the warrant. . . . Accordingly, Scarfo's claim that the warrants were written and executed as general warrants is rejected. . . .

The principal mystery surrounding this case was whether the KLS intercepted a wire communication in violation of the wiretap statute by recording keystrokes of e-mail or other communications made over a telephone or cable line while the modem operated. These are the only conceivable wire communications which might emanate from Scarfo's computer and potentially fall under the wiretap statute. . . .

The KLS, which is the exclusive property of the F.B.I., was devised by F.B.I. engineers using previously developed techniques in order to obtain a target's key and key-related information. As part of the investigation into Scarfo's computer, the F.B.I. "did not install and operate any component which would search for and record data entering or exiting the computer from the transmission pathway through the modem attached to the computer." Neither did the F.B.I. "install or operate any KLS component which would search for or record any fixed data stored within the computer."

Recognizing that Scarfo's computer had a modem and thus was capable of transmitting electronic communications via the modem, the F.B.I. configured the

KLS to avoid intercepting electronic communications typed on the keyboard and simultaneously transmitted in real time via the communication ports. . . . Hence, when the modem was operating, the KLS did not record keystrokes. It was designed to prohibit the capture of keyboard keystrokes whenever the modem operated. Since Scarfo's computer possessed no other means of communicating with another computer save for the modem, the KLS did not intercept any wire communications. Accordingly, the Defendants' motion to suppress evidence for violation of Title III is denied. . . .

NOTES & QUESTIONS

1. *Did the Court Need to Reach the Main Issue?* Judge Politan discusses the government's actions in *Scarfo* as if a suppression remedy were available for Scarfo. He finds that a search warrant was not required under the Wiretap Act because of the way in which the FBI's keylogging device worked; the KLS did not function when the modem was operating. But there was a simpler way to deny Scarfo's motion: the Wiretap Act does not provide a suppression remedy for electronic communications. Did Judge Politan assume that a remedy existed according to some theory similar to the *McVeigh* case? Was he simply eager to rule on the KLS issue?

2. *Recording Thoughts and Ideas.* Consider the following argument by Raymond Ku:

   . . . By monitoring what an individual enters into her computer as she enters it, the government has the ability to monitor thought itself. Keystroke-recording devices allow the government to record formless thoughts and ideas an individual never intended to share with anyone, never intended to save on the hard drive and never intended to preserve for future reference in any form. The devices also allow the government to record thoughts and ideas the individual may have rejected the moment they were typed. . . .

   . . . [T]he techniques used in the Scarfo case bring us closer to a world in which the only privacy we are guaranteed is the privacy found in the confines of our own minds. [93]

3. *Old Technologies in New Bottles?* A common defense of new technological surveillance devices is that they are analogous to existing technologies. Carnivore can be likened to pen registers; the keystroke monitor in the Scarfo case can be analogized to a bug. To what extent are these analogies apt? Are new surveillance technologies, simply old forms of surveillance in new bottles? Or is there something different involved? If so, what is new with these technologies, and how ought they be regulated?

4. *Magic Lantern.* The FBI has developed technology through which a keystroke logging device can be installed into a person's computer through a computer virus that is e-mailed to the suspect's computer. The virus keeps track of keystrokes and secretly transmits the information to the government. Thus, the government can install a keystroke logging device without ever

---

[93] Raymond Ku, *Think Twice Before You Type*, 163 N.J. L.J. 747 (Feb. 19, 2001).

having to physically enter one's office or home. Recall your Fourth Amendment analysis of Carnivore. How does Magic Lantern differ with respect to its Fourth Amendment implications? How does your Fourth Amendment analysis of Magic Lantern differ from that of the keystroke logging device in *Scarfo*?

D. NATIONAL SECURITY AND FOREIGN INTELLIGENCE

1. IS NATIONAL SECURITY DIFFERENT?

Should the law treat investigations involving national security differently than other criminal investigations? In Fourth Amendment law, this question has long remained unresolved. In a footnote to *Katz v. United States,* 389 U.S. 347 (1967), the Court stated that perhaps a warrant might not be required in situations involving national security:

> Whether safeguards other than prior authorization by a magistrate would satisfy the Fourth Amendment in a situation involving the national security is a question not presented by this case.

Justice White, in a concurring opinion, declared:

> In joining the Court's opinion, I note the Court's acknowledgment that there are circumstance in which it is reasonable to search without a warrant. In this connection . . . the Court points out that today's decision does not reach national security cases. Wiretapping to protect the security of the Nation has been authorized by successive Presidents. The present Administration would apparently save national security cases from restrictions against wiretapping. We should not require the warrant procedure and the magistrate's judgment if the President of the United States or his chief legal officer, the Attorney General, has considered the requirements of national security and authorized electronic surveillance as reasonable.

Justices Douglas and Brennan, in another concurring opinion, took issue with Justice White:

> . . . Neither the President nor the Attorney General is a magistrate. In matters where they believe national security may be involved they are not detached, disinterested, and neutral as a court or magistrate must be. . . .
>
> There is, so far as I understand constitutional history, no distinction under the Fourth Amendment between types of crimes. Article III, § 3, gives "treason" a very narrow definition and puts restrictions on its proof. But the Fourth Amendment draws no lines between various substantive offenses. The arrests on cases of "hot pursuit" and the arrests on visible or other evidence of probable cause cut across the board and are not peculiar to any kind of crime.
>
> I would respect the present lines of distinction and not improvise because a particular crime seems particularly heinous. When the Framers took that step, as they did with treason, the worst crime of all, they made their purpose manifest.

UNITED STATES V. UNITED STATES DISTRICT COURT
(THE *KEITH* CASE)
407 U.S. 297 (1972)

POWELL, J. . . . The issue before us is an important one for the people of our country and their Government. It involves the delicate question of the President's power, acting through the Attorney General, to authorize electronic surveillance in internal security matters without prior judicial approval. Successive Presidents for more than one-quarter of a century have authorized such surveillance in varying degrees, without guidance from the Congress or a definitive decision of this Court. This case brings the issue here for the first time. Its resolution is a matter of national concern, requiring sensitivity both to the Government's right to protect itself from unlawful subversion and attack and to the citizen's right to be secure in his privacy against unreasonable Government intrusion.

This case arises from a criminal proceeding in the United States District Court for the Eastern District of Michigan, in which the United States charged three defendants with conspiracy to destroy Government property. . . . One of the defendants, Plamondon, was charged with the dynamite bombing of an office of the Central Intelligence Agency in Ann Arbor, Michigan.

Title III of the Omnibus Crime Control and Safe Streets Act, 18 U.S.C. §§ 2510-2520, authorizes the use of electronic surveillance for classes of crimes carefully specified in 18 U.S.C. § 2516. Such surveillance is subject to prior court order. Section 2518 sets forth the detailed and particularized application necessary to obtain such an order as well as carefully circumscribed conditions for its use. The Act represents a comprehensive attempt by Congress to promote more effective control of crime while protecting the privacy of individual thought and expression. Much of Title III was drawn to meet the constitutional requirements for electronic surveillance enunciated by this Court in *Berger v. New York,* and *Katz v. United States*.

The Government relies on § 2511(3). It argues that "in excepting national security surveillances from the Act's warrant requirement Congress recognized the President's authority to conduct such surveillances without prior judicial approval." The section thus is viewed as a recognition or affirmance of a constitutional authority in the President to conduct warrantless domestic security surveillance such as that involved in this case.

We think the language of § 2511(3), as well as the legislative history of the statute, refutes this interpretation. The relevant language is that: "Nothing contained in this chapter . . . shall limit the constitutional power of the President to take such measures as he deems necessary to protect . . ." against the dangers specified. At most, this is an implicit recognition that the President does have certain powers in the specified areas. Few would doubt this, as the section refers — among other things — to protection "against actual or potential attack or other hostile acts of a foreign power." But so far as the use of the President's electronic surveillance power is concerned, the language is essentially neutral.

Section 2511(3) certainly confers no power, as the language is wholly inappropriate for such a purpose. It merely provides that the Act shall not be interpreted to limit or disturb such power as the President may have under the

Constitution. In short, Congress simply left presidential powers where it found them.

Our present inquiry, though important, is . . . a narrow one. It addresses a question left open by *Katz*:

> Whether safeguards other than prior authorization by a magistrate would satisfy the Fourth Amendment in a situation involving the national security. . . .

We begin the inquiry by noting that the President of the United States has the fundamental duty, under Art. II, § 1, of the Constitution, to "preserve, protect and defend the Constitution of the United States." Implicit in that duty is the power to protect our Government against those who would subvert or overthrow it by unlawful means. In the discharge of this duty, the President — through the Attorney General — may find it necessary to employ electronic surveillance to obtain intelligence information on the plans of those who plot unlawful acts against the Government. The use of such surveillance in internal security cases has been sanctioned more or less continuously by various Presidents and Attorneys General since July 1946.

Though the Government and respondents debate their seriousness and magnitude, threats and acts of sabotage against the Government exist in sufficient number to justify investigative powers with respect to them.[94] The covertness and complexity of potential unlawful conduct against the Government and the necessary dependency of many conspirators upon the telephone make electronic surveillance an effective investigatory instrument in certain circumstances. The marked acceleration in technological developments and sophistication in their use have resulted in new techniques for the planning, commission, and concealment of criminal activities. It would be contrary to the public interest for Government to deny to itself the prudent and lawful employment of those very techniques which are employed against the Government and its lawabiding citizens. . . .

But a recognition of these elementary truths does not make the employment by Government of electronic surveillance a welcome development — even when employed with restraint and under judicial supervision. There is, understandably, a deep-seated uneasiness and apprehension that this capability will be used to intrude upon cherished privacy of law-abiding citizens. We look to the Bill of Rights to safeguard this privacy. Though physical entry of the home is the chief evil against which the wording of the Fourth Amendment is directed, its broader spirit now shields private speech from unreasonable surveillance. Our decision in *Katz* refused to lock the Fourth Amendment into instances of actual physical trespass.

. . . [N]ational security cases, moreover, often reflect a convergence of First and Fourth Amendment values not present in cases of "ordinary" crime. Though the investigative duty of the executive may be stronger in such cases, so also is there greater jeopardy to constitutionally protected speech. . . . The danger to

---

[94] The Government asserts that there were 1,562 bombing incidents in the United States from January 1, 1971, to July 1, 1971, most of which involved Government related facilities. Respondents dispute these statistics as incorporating many frivolous incidents as well as bombings against nongovernmental facilities. The precise level of this activity, however, is not relevant to the disposition of this case.

political dissent is acute where the Government attempts to act under so vague a concept as the power to protect "domestic security." Given the difficulty of defining the domestic security interest, the danger of abuse in acting to protect that interest becomes apparent.

The price of lawful public dissent must not be a dread of subjection to an unchecked surveillance power. Nor must the fear of unauthorized official eavesdropping deter vigorous citizen dissent and discussion of Government action in private conversation. For private dissent, no less than open public discourse, is essential to our free society.

As the Fourth Amendment is not absolute in its terms, our task is to examine and balance the basic values at stake in this case: the duty of Government to protect the domestic security, and the potential danger posed by unreasonable surveillance to individual privacy and free expression. If the legitimate need of Government to safeguard domestic security requires the use of electronic surveillance, the question is whether the needs of citizens for privacy and the free expression may not be better protected by requiring a warrant before such surveillance is undertaken. We must also ask whether a warrant requirement would unduly frustrate the efforts of Government to protect itself from acts of subversion and overthrow directed against it. . . .

[C]ontentions in behalf of a complete exemption from the warrant requirement, when urged on behalf of the President and the national security in its domestic implications, merit the most careful consideration. We certainly do not reject them lightly, especially at a time of worldwide ferment and when civil disorders in this country are more prevalent than in the less turbulent periods of our history. There is, no doubt, pragmatic force to the Government's position.

[W]e do not think a case has been made for the requested departure from Fourth Amendment standards. The circumstances described do not justify complete exemption of domestic security surveillance from prior judicial scrutiny. Official surveillance, whether its purpose be criminal investigation or ongoing intelligence gathering, risks infringement of constitutionally protected privacy of speech. Security surveillances are especially sensitive because of the inherent vagueness of the domestic security concept, the necessarily broad and continuing nature of intelligence gathering, and the temptation to utilize such surveillances to oversee political dissent. We recognize, as we have before, the constitutional basis of the President's domestic security role, but we think it must be exercised in a manner compatible with the Fourth Amendment. In this case we hold that this requires an appropriate prior warrant procedure.

We cannot accept the Government's argument that internal security matters are too subtle and complex for judicial evaluation. Courts regularly deal with the most difficult issues of our society. There is no reason to believe that federal judges will be insensitive to or uncomprehending of the issues involved in domestic security cases. . . . If the threat is too subtle or complex for our senior law enforcement officers to convey its significance to a court, one may question whether there is probable cause for surveillance.

Nor do we believe prior judicial approval will fracture the secrecy essential to official intelligence gathering. The investigation of criminal activity has long involved imparting sensitive information to judicial officers who have respected the confidentialities involved. Judges may be counted upon to be especially conscious of security requirements in national security cases. Title III of the Omnibus Crime Control and Safe Streets Act already has imposed this responsibility on the judiciary in connection with such crimes as espionage, sabotage, and treason, §§ 2516(1)(a) and (c), each of which may involve domestic as well as foreign security threats. Moreover, a warrant application involves no public or adversary proceedings: it is an ex parte request before a magistrate or judge. Whatever security dangers clerical and secretarial personnel may pose can be minimized by proper administrative measures, possibly to the point of allowing the Government itself to provide the necessary clerical assistance. . . .

We emphasize, before concluding this opinion, the scope of our decision. As stated at the outset, this case involves only the domestic aspects of national security. We have not addressed and express no opinion as to, the issues which may be involved with respect to activities of foreign powers or their agents. . . .

Moreover, we do not hold that the same type of standards and procedures prescribed by Title III are necessarily applicable to this case. We recognize that domestic security surveillance may involve different policy and practical considerations from the surveillance of "ordinary crime." The gathering of security intelligence is often long range and involves the interrelation of various sources and types of information. The exact targets of such surveillance may be more difficult to identify than in surveillance operations against many types of crime specified in Title III. Often, too, the emphasis of domestic intelligence gathering is on the prevention of unlawful activity or the enhancement of the Government's preparedness for some possible future crisis or emergency. Thus, the focus of domestic surveillance may be less precise than that directed against more conventional types of crime.

Given those potential distinctions between Title III criminal surveillances and those involving the domestic security, Congress may wish to consider protective standards for the latter which differ from those already prescribed for specified crimes in Title III. Different standards may be compatible with the Fourth Amendment if they are reasonable both in relation to the legitimate need of Government for intelligence information and the protected rights of our citizens. For the warrant application may vary according to the governmental interest to be enforced and the nature of citizen rights deserving protection. . . .

DOUGLAS, J. concurring. While I join in the opinion of the Court, I add these words in support of it. . . .

If the Warrant Clause were held inapplicable here, then the federal intelligence machine would literally enjoy unchecked discretion. Here, federal agents wish to rummage for months on end through every conversation, no matter how intimate or personal, carried over selected telephone lines, simply to seize those few utterances which may add to their sense of the pulse of a domestic underground. . . .

That "domestic security" is said to be involved here does not draw this case outside the mainstream of Fourth Amendment law. Rather, the recurring desire of reigning officials to employ dragnet techniques to intimidate their critics lies at the core of that prohibition. For it was such excesses as the use of general warrants and the writs of assistance that led to the ratification of the Fourth Amendment. . . .

[W]e are currently in the throes of another national seizure of paranoia, resembling the hysteria which surrounded the Alien and Sedition Acts, the Palmer Raids, and the McCarthy era. Those who register dissent or who petition their governments for redress are subjected to scrutiny by grand juries, by the FBI, or even by the military. Their associates are interrogated. Their homes are bugged and their telephones are wiretapped. They are befriended by secret government informers. Their patriotism and loyalty are questioned. . . .

We have as much or more to fear from the erosion of our sense of privacy and independence by the omnipresent electronic ear of the Government as we do from the likelihood that fomenters of domestic upheaval will modify our form of governing.

NOTES & QUESTIONS

1. *Domestic Security vs. Foreign Threats.* The *Keith* Court draws a distinction between electronic surveillance in (1) criminal investigations, regulated under Title III (now ECPA); (2) domestic security investigations; and (3) investigations involving "activities of foreign powers and their agents."

    Regarding the first category, the *Keith* Court stated that there was no debate regarding "the necessity of obtaining a warrant in the surveillance of crimes unrelated to the national security interest." Regarding the second category, the focus of the *Keith* Court's opinion, its holding was that the Fourth Amendment required the issuing of a warrant in domestic security investigations. It also held that the precise requirements for issuing a requirement to investigate domestic security need not be the same as for Title III criminal surveillance. Finally, it stated that it did not address issues involving foreign powers and their agents. Does this tripartite distinction seem useful as a policy matter?

    How does one distinguish between security surveillance (category two) and surveillance for ordinary crime (category one)? Daniel Solove argues that such a distinction ought not to be made: "'National security' has often been abused as a justification not only for surveillance but also for maintaining the secrecy of government records as well as violating the civil liberties of citizens." He further contends that "the line between national security and regular criminal activities is very blurry, especially in an age of terrorism."[95] On the other hand, Richard Posner contends that the word "unreasonable" in the Fourth Amendment "invites a wide-ranging comparison between the benefits and costs of a search or seizure." He proposes a "sliding scale" standard where "the level of suspicion require to justify the search or seizure should fall . . . as the magnitude of the crime under investigation rises."[96] Paul Rosenzweig argues: "In this time of terror, some adjustment of the balance

---

[95] Solove, *Surveillance Law*, 72 Geo. Wash. L. Rev. 1264, 1301-02 (2004).

[96] Richard Posner, *Law, Pragmatism, and Democracy* 303 (2003); *see also* Akhil Reed Amar, *The Constitution and Criminal Procedure* 31 (1997) ("The core of the Fourth Amendment . . . is neither a warrant nor probable cause but reasonableness.").

between liberty and security is both necessary and appropriate. . . . [T]he very text of the Fourth Amendment — with its prohibition only of 'unreasonable' searches and seizures — explicitly recognizes the need to balance the harm averted against the extent of governmental intrusion."[97]

2. ***The Church Committee Report.*** In 1976, a congressional committee led by Senator Frank Church (called the "Church Committee") engaged in an extensive investigation of government national security surveillance. It found extensive abuses, which it chronicled in its famous report known as the Church Committee Report:

> Too many people have been spied upon by too many Government agencies and too much information has been collected. The Government has often undertaken the secret surveillance of citizens on the basis of their political beliefs, even when those beliefs posed no threat of violence or illegal acts on behalf of a hostile foreign power. The Government, operating primarily through secret informants, but also using other intrusive techniques such as wiretaps, microphone "bugs," surreptitious mail opening, and break-ins, has swept in vast amounts of information about the personal lives, views, and associations of American citizens. . . . Groups and individuals have been harassed and disrupted because of their political views and their lifestyles. Investigations have been based upon vague standards whose breadth made excessive collection inevitable. . . .
>
> The FBI's COINTELPRO — counterintelligence program — was designed to "disrupt" groups and "neutralize" individuals deemed to be threats to domestic security. The FBI resorted to counterintelligence tactics in part because its chief officials believed that existing law could not control the activities of certain dissident groups, and that court decisions had tied the hands of the intelligence community. Whatever opinion one holds about the policies of the targeted groups, many of the tactics employed by the FBI were indisputably degrading to a free society. . . .
>
> Since the early 1930's, intelligence agencies have frequently wiretapped and bugged American citizens without the benefit of judicial warrant. . . .
>
> There has been, in short, a clear and sustained failure by those responsible to control the intelligence community and to ensure its accountability.[98]

The Church Committee Report was influential in the creation of FISA as well as the Attorney General Guidelines.

3. ***National Security vs. Civil Liberties.*** Eric Posner and Adrian Vermeule argue that the legislature and judiciary should defer to the executive in times of emergency and that it is justified to curtail civil liberties when national security is threatened:

> The essential feature of the emergency is that national security is threatened; because the executive is the only organ of government with the resources, power, and flexibility to respond to threats to national security, it is natural,

---

[97] Paul Rosenzweig, *Civil Liberty and the Response to Terrorism,* 42 Duq. L. Rev. 663 (2004).
[98] *Intelligence Activities and the Rights of Americans* (Vol. 2), Final Report of the Select Committee to Study Government Operations with Respect to Intelligence Activities 5, 10, 15 (Apr. 26, 1976).

inevitable, and desirable for power to flow to this branch of government. Congress rationally acquiesces; courts rationally defer. . . .

During emergencies, when new threats appear, the balance shifts; government should and will reduce civil liberties in order to enhance security in those domains where the two must be traded off. . . .

In emergencies . . . judges are at sea, even more so than are executive officials. The novelty of the threats and of the necessary responses makes judicial routines and evolved legal rules seem inapposite, even obstructive. There is a premium on the executive's capacities for swift, vigorous, and secretive action.[99]

4. ***The Fourth Amendment and Foreign Intelligence Surveillance.*** *Keith* did not address how the Fourth Amendment would govern foreign intelligence surveillance (category three). Circuit courts examining the issue have concluded that at a minimum, no warrant is required by the Fourth Amendment for foreign intelligence surveillance. In *United States v. Butenko*, 494 F.2d 593 (3d Cir. 1974) (en banc), the court justified this conclusion by reasoning that "foreign intelligence gathering is a clandestine and highly unstructured activity, and the need for electronic surveillance often cannot be anticipated in advance." Reaching a similar conclusion in *United States v. Truong Dinh Hung*, 629 F.2d 908 (4th Cir. 1980), the court reasoned: "[T]he needs of the executive are so compelling in the area of foreign intelligence, unlike the area of domestic security, that a uniform warrant requirement would, following *Keith,* 'unduly frustrate' the President in carrying out his foreign affairs responsibilities."

2. THE FOREIGN INTELLIGENCE SURVEILLANCE ACT

In the *Keith* case, the Court explicitly refused to address whether the Fourth Amendment would require a warrant for surveillance of agents of foreign powers.

The Foreign Intelligence Surveillance Act (FISA) of 1978, Pub. L. No. 95-511, codified at 50 U.S.C. §§ 1801–1811, establishes standards and procedures for use of electronic surveillance to collect "foreign intelligence" within the United States. § 1804(a)(7)(B). FISA creates a different regime than ECPA, the legal regime that governs electronic surveillance for law enforcement purposes. The regime created by FISA is designed primarily for intelligence gathering agencies to regulate how they gain general intelligence about foreign powers and agents of foreign powers within the borders of the United States. In contrast, the regime of ECPA is designed for domestic law enforcement to govern the gathering of information for criminal investigations involving people in United States.

---

[99] Eric A. Posner & Adrian Vermeule, *Terror in the Balance: Security, Liberty, and the Courts* 4, 5, 18 (2006). For another defense of the curtailment of civil liberties for national security, see Richard A. Posner, *Not a Suicide Pact: The Constitution in a Time of National Emergency* (2006).

Applicability of FISA. When does FISA govern rather than ECPA? FISA generally applies when foreign intelligence gathering is "a significant purpose" of the investigation. 50 U.S.C. § 1804(a)(7)(B) and § 1823(a)(7)(B). The language of "a significant purpose" comes from the USA PATRIOT Act of 2001. Prior to the USA PATRIOT Act, FISA as interpreted by the courts required that the collection of foreign intelligence be the primary purpose for surveillance. After the USA PATRIOT Act, foreign intelligence gathering need no longer be the primary purpose. A further expansion of the FISA occurred in 2008 with amendments to that law, which we discuss below.

The Foreign Intelligence Surveillance Court (FISC). Requests for FISA orders are reviewed by a special court of federal district court judges. The USA PATRIOT Act increased the number of judges on the FISC from 7 to 11. 50 U.S.C. § 1803(a). The proceedings are ex parte, with the Department of Justice (DOJ) making the applications to the court on behalf of the CIA and other agencies. The Court meets in secret, and its proceedings are generally not revealed to the public or to the targets of the surveillance.

In 2007, the FISC declined an ACLU request to access its documents relating to alleged unauthorized surveillance. *In re Motion for Release of Court Records*, 526 F. Supp. 2d (2007). This case was an exception to the usual procedure of *ex parte* only hearings before the FISC. The court found that it had jurisdiction to entertain motions for release of its documents, and then denied the request. It stated:

> The FISC is a unique court. Its entire docket relates to the collection of foreign intelligence by the federal government. The applications submitted to it by the government are classified, as are the overwhelming majority of the FISC's orders. Court sessions are held behind closed doors in a secure facility, and every proceeding in its history prior to this one has been ex parte, with the government the only party. . . . Other courts operate primarily in public with secrecy the exception; the FISC operates primarily in secret, with public access the exception.

Perhaps most importantly, the court noted that "the proper functioning of the FISA process would be adversely affected if submitting sensitive information to the FISC could subject the Executive Branch's classification to a heightened form of judicial review."

Court Orders. The legal test for surveillance under FISA is not whether probable cause exists that the party to be monitored is involved in criminal activity. Rather, the court must find probable cause that the party to be monitored is a "foreign power" or "an agent of a foreign power." § 1801. Therefore, unlike ECPA or the Fourth Amendment, FISA surveillance is not tied to any required showing of a connection to criminal activity. However, if the monitored party is a "United States person" (a citizen or permanent resident alien), the government must establish probable cause that the party's activities "may" or "are about to" involve a criminal violation. § 1801(b)(2)(A).

The number of FISA electronic surveillance orders expanded from 199 orders (1979) to 886 (1999).[100] In 2001, the FISA court approved 934 applications for electronic surveillance orders. None were denied.[101] The USA PATRIOT Act of 2001 eased the standard for obtaining a FISA order. There were 1,228 orders in 2002, 1,727 orders in 2003 (4 were denied), and 1,758 applications in 2004. This represents an increase of 88 percent from 2001.

Surveillance Without Court Orders. In certain circumstances, FISA authorizes surveillance without having to first obtain a court order. § 1802. In particular, the surveillance must be "solely directed at" obtaining intelligence exclusively from "foreign powers." § 1802(a). There must be "no substantial likelihood that the surveillance will acquire the contents of any communications to which a United States person is a party." § 1802(a)(1)(B). Electronic surveillance without a court order requires the authorization of the President, through the Attorney General, in writing under oath. § 1802(a)(1).

Video Surveillance. Unlike ECPA, FISA explicitly regulates video surveillance. In order to have court approval for video surveillance, the FISA requires the government to submit, among other things, "a detailed description of the nature of the information sought and the type of communications or activities to be subjected to the surveillance," § 1804(a)(6); "a certification . . . that such information cannot reasonably be obtained by normal investigative techniques," § 1804(a)(7); and "a statement of the period of time for which the electronic surveillance is required to be maintained," § 1804(a)(10). Video surveillance orders can last for 90 days.

The FISA Amendments Act. In 2008, Congress enacted significant amendments to FISA. The FISA Amendments Act (FAA) was passed in response to the revelation in 2005 that since 9/11 the National Security Agency (NSA) was engaging in an extensive program of warrantless wiretapping of international phone calls. Subsequently, several lawsuits were brought against the telecommunications companies that participated in the surveillance for violating FISA and ECPA. One of the most controversial aspects of the FAA was a grant of retroactive immunity to these companies. The NSA surveillance program and the ensuing litigation will be discussed later on in this chapter.

In its other aspects, the FAA both expanded the government's surveillance abilities and added new privacy protections. The FAA explicitly permits collection of information from U.S. telecommunications facilities where it is not possible in advance to know whether a communication is purely international (that is, all parties to it are located outside of the United States) or whether the communication involves a foreign power or its agents. David Kris explains, "With the advent of web-based communication and other developments, the government cannot always determine — consistently, reliably, and in real time

---

[100] Foreign Intelligence Surveillance Act Orders 1979-1999, http://www/epic.org/privacy/wiretap/stats/fisa_stats.html.

[101] Office of Attorney General, *2001 Annual FISA Report to Congress,* available at www.usdoj.gov/o4foia/readingrooms/2001annualfisareporttocongress.htm.

— the location of parties to an e-mail message."[102] It is also possible to collect information and then examine it (through data mining) to look for links with a foreign power or its agents. The perceived need, Kris states, was for a kind of "vacuum-cleaner" capacity that would enable the government to sift through large amounts of information without meeting FISA's traditional warrant requirements.

FAA amends FISA to permit "targeting of persons reasonably believed to be located outside the United States to acquire foreign intelligence information." § 702(a). The person targeted must be a non-USA person, or certain more restrictive measures apply. §§ 703–04. The critical substantive requirements are that the "target" of the surveillance be someone overseas and that a "significant purpose" of the surveillance be to acquire "foreign intelligence information," which is broadly defined.

The collection of this information must be carried out in accordance with certain "targeting procedures" to ensure that the collection is directed at persons located outside the United States. § 702(c)(1)(A). The acquisition must also involve new minimization procedures, which the Attorney General is to adopt. § 702(e). The Justice Department and the Director of National Intelligence must certify in advance of the surveillance activity that targeting and minimization procedures meet the statutory standards and that "a significant purpose" of the surveillance is to acquire foreign intelligence information. § 702(g)(2). The FAA also states that the government may not engage in a kind of "reverse-targeting" — the government cannot target "a person reasonably believed to be outside the United States if the purpose of such acquisition is to target a particular, known person reasonably believed to be in the United States." § 702(b)(2).

The FISC is to review certifications and the targeting and minimization procedures adopted. If a certification does not "contain all the required elements" or the procedures "are not consistent with the requirements" of the FAA or the Fourth Amendment to the U.S. Constitution, the FISC is to issue an order directing the government to correct any deficiencies. § 702(i)(3).

As for its expansion of privacy protections, the FAA requires that the FISC approve surveillance of a U.S. citizen abroad based on a showing that includes a finding that the person is "an agent of a foreign power, or an officer or employee of a foreign power." Previously, FISA did not regulate surveillance of targets, whether U.S. citizens or not, when located outside the United States. The FAA also contains new mechanisms for congressional oversight and crafts new audit functions for the Inspector Generals of the Department Justice.

---

[102] David Kris, *A Guide to the New FISA Bill, Part I*, Balkanization (June 21, 2008), at http://balkin.blogspot.com/2008/06/guide-to-new-fisa-bill-part-i.html. Kris is co-author of the leading treatise, J. Douglas Wilson & David Kris, *National Security Investigations and Prosecutions* (2007).

GLOBAL RELIEF FOUNDATION, INC. V. O'NEIL

207 F. Supp. 779 (N.D. Ill. 2002)

. . . [A]gents of the FBI arrived at the corporate headquarters of Global Relief [a U.S.-based Islamic humanitarian relief organization] and the home of its executive director on December 14, 2001 and seized a considerable amount of material they felt was relevant to their investigation of Global Relief's activities. As the defendants have conceded in their briefs, no warrant had been obtained before the FBI arrived either at Global Relief's headquarters or the executive director's residence. Nevertheless, FISA includes a provision which states that, when the Attorney General declares that "an emergency situation exists with respect to the execution of a search to obtain foreign intelligence information" prior to the Foreign Intelligence Surveillance Court acting on the application, a warrantless search is authorized. 50 U.S.C. § 1824(e)(1)(B)(i). When such an emergency situation arises, the government must submit a warrant application to the Foreign Intelligence Surveillance Court within 72 hours of the warrantless search for approval. *See* 50 U.S.C. § 1824(e). In this case, the failure of the FBI agents to present a FISA warrant on December 14 was caused by the Assistant Attorney General's declaration that an emergency situation existed with respect to the targeted documents and material. The defendants did submit a warrant application to the Foreign Intelligence Surveillance Court on December 15, as required by 50 U.S.C. § 1824(e). We have reviewed the warrant that issued and the submissions to the Foreign Intelligence Surveillance Court in support of that warrant.

We conclude that the FISA application established probable cause to believe that Global Relief and the executive director were agents of a foreign power, as that term is defined for FISA purposes, at the time the search was conducted and the application was granted. . . . Given the sensitive nature of the information upon which we have relied in making this determination and the Attorney General's sworn assertion that disclosure of the underlying information would harm national security, it would be improper for us to elaborate further on this subject.

This Court has concluded that disclosure of the information we have reviewed could substantially undermine ongoing investigations required to apprehend the conspirators behind the September 11 murders and undermine the ability of law enforcement agencies to reduce the possibility of terrorist crimes in the future. Furthermore, this Court is persuaded that the search and seizure made by the FBI on December 14 were authorized by FISA. Accordingly, we decline plaintiff's request that we declare the search invalid and order the immediate return of all items seized.

NOTES & QUESTIONS

1. *Probable Cause.* Searches under the Wiretap Act require a "super warrant," including a showing of probable cause that an individual has committed or is about to commit an enumerated offense. 18 U.S.C. § 2518(3). What is the

required showing of probable cause for a FISA search? FISA requires a judicial finding, as the *O'Neill* case indicates, that probable cause exists to believe that the target is an agent of a foreign power. It also states that no U.S. person can be considered an agent of a foreign power based solely on First Amendment activities.

2. *Defendants' Rights?* In *Global Relief Foundation*, the court finds that disclosure of the information that it reviewed in deciding on the validity of the search was not to be revealed to the defendant because it "could substantially undermine ongoing investigations required to apprehend the conspirators behind the September 11 murders and undermine the ability of law enforcement agencies to reduce the possibility of terrorist crimes in the future." However, FISA requires that defendants receive notice about "any information obtained or derived from an electronic surveillance of that aggrieved person" pursuant to FISA when the government seeks to use information at trial or other official proceedings. 50 U.S.C. § 1806(c).

3. *The Three* **Keith** *Categories.* Recall the *Keith* Court's distinction between electronic surveillance in (1) criminal investigations; (2) domestic security investigations; and (3) investigations involving "activities of foreign powers and their agents." Today, ECPA regulates electronic surveillance in criminal investigations (category one above). The Foreign Intelligence Surveillance Act (FISA), as enacted in 1978, regulates electronic and other kinds of surveillance in cases involving foreign powers and their agents (category three).

What then of the *Keith* category of "domestic security investigations" (category two)? Recall that the defendants in the underlying criminal proceeding were charged with a conspiracy to destroy government property. One of the defendants, for example, was charged with "the dynamite bombing" of a CIA office in Michigan. *Keith* makes it clear that it would be consistent with the Fourth Amendment for Congress to create different statutory requirements for issuing warrants for surveillance in cases involving domestic security. But Congress has not enacted such rules, and, as a consequence, law enforcement is required to carry out surveillance of criminal activities similar to those in *Keith* under the requirements of Title III and other parts of ECPA.

4. *The Lone Wolf Amendment.* The *Keith* categories and related rules remain unaltered by the "lone wolf" amendment to FISA in 2004. That year, Congress amended FISA to include any non-U.S. person who "engages in international terrorism or activities in preparation therefor" in the definition of "agent of a foreign power." The change means that the "lone wolf" terrorist need not be tied to a foreign power, but must be a non-U.S. person engaged in or plotting "international terrorism." FISA defines "international terrorism" as involving, among other things, activities that "[o]ccur totally outside the U.S., or transcend national boundaries in terms of the means by which they accomplished, the persons they appear intended to coerce or intimidate, or the locale in which their perpetrators operate or seek asylum." 50 U.S.C. § 1801(c). As an illustration of the coverage of the "Lone Wolf" amendment, it

would not cover Timothy McVeigh, the Oklahoma City bomber.

5. *A New Agency for Domestic Intelligence?* Francesca Bignami notes that in European countries, one governmental agency typically gathers intelligence on threats abroad posed by foreign governments, and another agency "is charged with gathering intelligence at home, on activities sponsored by foreign powers (counter-intelligence) as well as on home-grown security threats."[103] Both of these agencies are generally overseen not by judiciary, but by legislative and executive branches. Both intelligence agencies generally carry out surveillance under a more permissive set of legal rules than the domestic police. In contrast, in the United States, the FBI is charged with both domestic intelligence investigations and criminal investigations of violations of federal law.

Judge Richard Posner has emerged as the leading critic of the assignment of this double function to the FBI. He contends that the combination of criminal investigation and domestic intelligence at the FBI has not been successful: "If the incompatibility between the law enforcement and intelligence cultures is conceded, then it follows that an agency 100 percent dedicated to domestic intelligence would be likely to do a better job than the FBI, which is at most 20 percent intelligence and thus at least 80 percent criminal investigation and in consequence dominated by the criminal investigations."[104] Posner calls for creation of a "pure" domestic intelligence agency, one without any law enforcement responsibilities and located outside of the FBI. For Posner, the new U.S. Security Intelligence Surveillance can be modeled on the United Kingdom's MI5 or the Canadian Security Intelligence Service. What should the rules be for such a domestic intelligence agency concerning telecommunications surveillance? Should the FISA rules be applied to it?

UNITED STATES V. ISA

923 F.2d 1300 (8th Cir. 1991)

[The FBI obtained an order pursuant to FISA to bug the home of Zein Hassan Isa and his wife, Maria Matias. The FBI suspected Isa, a naturalized U.S. citizen, of being an agent of the Palestine Liberation Organization (PLO). One evening, the FBI's recording tapes of the bugged home captured Zein and Maria's murder of their 16-year-old daughter, Tina. Zein and Maria became angry at Tina's general rebelliousness and her defiance of their order not to date a particular young man. On the tape, Zein said to Tina: "Here, listen, my dear daughter, do you know that this is the last day? Tonight, you're going to die!" Tina responded in disbelief: "Huh?" Maria held Tina down while Zein stabbed her six times in the chest. While Tina screamed, Zein said: "Quiet, little one! Die my daughter, die!" The FBI turned the tapes over to the State of Missouri, where the Isas resided, where

---

[103] Francesca Bignami, *European versus American Liberty*, 48 B.C. L. Rev. 609, 621 (2007).
[104] Richard A. Posner, *Uncertain Shield* 101-02 (2006).

they were used to convict the Isas of murder. The Isas were sentenced to death.[105] Zein Isa argued that the recording should be suppressed because it captured events that had no relevance to the FBI's foreign intelligence gathering.]

GIBSON, J. . . . [A]ppellant argues that his fourth amendment rights were violated because the government failed to comply with the minimization procedures defined in 50 U.S.C. § 1801(h). Specifically, he contends that the tapes turned over to the State of Missouri record a "private domestic matter," which is not relevant material under the Foreign Intelligence Surveillance Act and must therefore be destroyed. In support of this argument, he cites isolated sentences regarding required minimization procedures from the legislative history of the Foreign Intelligence Surveillance Act:

> Minimization procedures might also include restrictions on the use of surveillance to times when foreign intelligence information is likely to be obtained, ... [Furthermore, a target's] communications which are clearly not relevant to his clandestine intelligence activities should be destroyed. S. Rep. No. 95-701, 95th Cong., 2d Sess. 4.

Notwithstanding the minimization procedures required by [FISA], the Act specifically authorizes the retention of information that is "evidence of a crime," 50 U.S.C. § 1801(h)(3), and provides procedures for the retention and dissemination of such information. 50 U.S.C. § 1806(b)-(f). There is no requirement that the "crime" be related to foreign intelligence. . . .

Thus, we conclude that the tapes are "evidence of crime" and that the district court correctly denied appellant's motion to suppress. 50 U.S.C. § 1801(h)(3).

NOTES & QUESTIONS

1. *Use of Information Obtained Through FISA Orders.* As the *Isa* court notes, information obtained via FISA can be used in criminal trials. However, the standard to obtain a FISA order does not require probable cause. Is it appropriate to allow the use of evidence that would ordinarily required a warrant with probable cause to obtain? On the other hand, the FISA order in *Isa* was properly obtained, and the agents unexpectedly obtained evidence of a murder. If the order is obtained properly in good faith, and evidence of a crime is unexpectedly gathered, why should it be excluded from use in a criminal prosecution?

2. *Minimization Procedures and Information Screening "Walls."* As illustrated by *Isa,* FISA allows the use of information properly obtained under FISA to be used in a criminal prosecution. What prevents the government from using the often more lax standards of FISA to gather evidence in a criminal investigation? The standards of FISA are often much less stringent than those of ECPA. Government officials would merely need to say that they are conducting "intelligence gathering" and obtain a FISA order rather than an

---

[105] The Eighth Circuit opinion contains a very meager account of the facts on this case. The facts contained in this book are taken from *Terror and Death at Home Are Caught in F.B.I. Tape,* N.Y. Times, Oct. 28, 1991, at A14.

order under ECPA — and then, if they uncover evidence of a crime, they could use it to prosecute. FISA has some built-in protections against this. For example, it requires that "the purpose" of the surveillance be foreign intelligence gathering. This language was interpreted by courts as the "primary" purpose.

FISA requires that procedures be implemented to minimize the collection, retention, and dissemination of information about United States persons. § 1801(h)(1). Minimization procedures are designed to prevent the broad power of "foreign intelligence gathering" from being used for routine criminal investigations. In a number of instances, however, there are overlaps between foreign intelligence gathering and criminal investigations.

One common minimization procedure is what is known as an "information screening wall." With the "wall," an official not involved in the criminal investigation must review the raw materials gathered by FISA surveillance and only pass on information that might be relevant evidence. The wall is designed to prevent criminal justice personnel from initiating or directing the FISA surveillance. The wall does not prevent the sharing of information; rather, it prevents criminal prosecutors from becoming involved in the front end of the investigation rather than on the back end.

How should terrorism investigations, which involve both intelligence gathering and the collection of evidence for criminal prosecution, fit into this scheme?

THE 9/11 COMMISSION REPORT

Excerpt from pp. 254-75 (2004)

"The System Was Blinking Red"

As 2001 began, counterterrorism officials were receiving frequent but fragmentary reports about threats. Indeed, there appeared to be possible threats almost everywhere the United States had interests — including at home. . . .

Threat reports surged in June and July, reaching an even higher peak of urgency. The summer threats seemed to be focused on Saudi Arabia, Israel, Bahrain, Kuwait, Yemen, and possibly Rome, but the danger could be anywhere — including a possible attack on the G-8 summit in Genoa. . . .

A terrorist threat advisory distributed in late June indicated a high probability of near-term "spectacular" terrorist attacks resulting in numerous casualties. Other reports' titles warned, "Bin Ladin Attacks May Be Imminent" and "Bin Ladin and Associates Making Near-Term Threats." . . .

Most of the intelligence community recognized in the summer of 2001 that the number and severity of threat reports were unprecedented. Many officials told us that they knew something terrible was planned, and they were desperate to stop it. Despite their large number, the threats received contained few specifics regarding time, place, method, or target. . . .

["Jane," an FBI analyst assigned to the FBI's investigation of the terrorist attack on the USS *Cole*] began drafting what is known as a lead for the FBI's New York Field Office. A lead relays information from one part of the FBI to another and requests that a particular action be taken. . . . [H]er draft lead was not sent until August 28. Her email told the New York agent that she wanted him to get started as soon as possible, but she labeled the lead as "Routine" — a designation that informs the receiving office that it has 30 days to respond.

The agent who received the lead forwarded it to his squad supervisor. That same day, the supervisor forwarded the lead to an intelligence agent to open an intelligence case — an agent who thus was behind "the wall" keeping FBI intelligence information from being shared with criminal prosecutors. He also sent it to the *Cole* case agents and an agent who had spent significant time in Malaysia searching for another Khalid: Khalid Sheikh Mohammad.

The suggested goal of the investigation was to locate Mihdhar, [a member of al Qaeda and a 9/11 hijacker] determine his contacts and reasons for being in the United States, and possibly conduct an interview. Before sending the lead, "Jane" had discussed it with "John," the CIA official on detail to the FBI. . . . The discussion seems to have been limited to whether the search should be classified as an intelligence investigation or as a criminal one. It appears that no one informed higher levels of management in either the FBI or CIA about the case. . . .

One of the *Cole* case agents read the lead with interest, and contacted "Jane" to obtain more information. "Jane" argued, however, that because the agent was designated a "criminal" FBI agent, not an intelligence FBI agent, the wall kept him from participating in any search for Mihdhar. In fact, she felt he had to destroy his copy of the lead because it contained NSA information from reports that included caveats ordering that the information not be shared without OIPR's permission. The agent asked "Jane" to get an opinion from the FBI's National Security Law Unit (NSLU) on whether he could open a criminal case on Mihdhar.

"Jane" sent an email to the *Cole* case agent explaining that according to the NSLU, the case could be opened only as an intelligence matter, and that if Mihdhar was found, only designated intelligence agents could conduct or even be present at any interview. She appears to have misunderstood the complex rules that could apply to this situation.

The FBI agent angrily responded:

> Whatever has happened to this — someday someone will die — and the wall or not — the public will not understand why we were not more effective at throwing every resource we had at certain "problems." . . .

"Jane" replied that she was not making up the rules; she claimed that they were in the relevant manual and "ordered by the [FISA] Court and every office of the FBI is required to follow them including FBI NY."

It is now clear that everyone involved was confused about the rules governing the sharing and use of information gathered in intelligence channels. Because Mihdhar was being sought for his possible connection to or knowledge of the *Cole* bombing, he could be investigated or tracked under the existing *Cole* criminal case. No new criminal case was need for the criminal agent to begin searching for Mihdhar. And as NSA had approved the passage of its information to the criminal agent, he could have conducted a search using all available information. As a result of this confusion, the criminal agents who were knowledgeable about al Qaeda and experienced with criminal investigative techniques, including finding suspects and possible criminal charges, were thus excluded from the search. . . .

We believe that if more resources had been applied and a significantly different approach taken, Mihdhar and Hazmi might have been found. They had used their true names in the United States. Still, the investigators would have needed luck as well as skill to find them prior to September 11 even if such searches had begun as early as August 23, when the lead was first drafted.

Many FBI witnesses have suggested that even if Mihdhar had been found, there was nothing the agents could have done except follow him onto the planes. We believe this is incorrect. Both Hazmi and Mihdhar could have been held for immigration violations or as material witnesses in the *Cole* bombing case. Investigation or interrogation of them, and investigation of their travel and financial activities, could have yielded evidence of connections to other participants in the 9/11 plot. The simple fact of their detention could have derailed the plan. In any case, the opportunity did not arise. . . .

On August 15, 2001, the Minneapolis FBI Field Office initiated an intelligence investigation on Zacarias Moussaoui. . . . [H]e had entered the United States in February 2001, and had begun flight lessons at Airman Flight School in Norman, Oklahoma. He resumed his training at the Pan Am International Flight Academy in Eagan, Minnesota, starting on August 13. He had none of the usual qualifications for light training on Pan Am's Boeing 747 flight simulators. He said he did not intend to become a commercial pilot but wanted the training as an "ego boosting thing." Moussaoui stood out because with little knowledge of flying, he wanted to learn to "take off and land" a Boeing 747.

The agent in Minneapolis quickly learned that Moussaoui possessed jihadist beliefs. Moreover, Moussaoui had $32,000 in a bank account but did not provide a plausible explanation for this sum of money. He traveled to Pakistan but became agitated when asked if he had traveled to nearby countries while in Pakistan. He planned to receive martial arts training, and intended to purchase a global positioning receiver. The agent also noted that Moussaoui became extremely agitated whenever he was questioned regarding his religious beliefs. The agent concluded that Moussaoui was "an Islamic extremist preparing for some future act in furtherance of radical fundamentalist goals." He also believed Moussaoui's plan was related to his flight training.

Moussaoui can be seen as an al Qaeda mistake and a missed opportunity. An apparently unreliable operative, he had fallen into the hands of the FBI. . . . If Moussaoui had been connected to al Qaeda, questions should instantly have arisen about a possible al Qaeda plot that involved piloting airliners, a possibility that had never been seriously analyzed by the intelligence community. . . .

As a French national who had overstayed his visa, Moussaoui could be detained immediately. The INS arrested Moussaoui on the immigration violation. A deportation order was signed on August 17, 2001.

The agents in Minnesota were concerned that the U.S. Attorney's office in Minneapolis would find insufficient probable cause of a crime to obtain a criminal warrant to search Moussaoui's laptop computer. Agents at FBI headquarters believed there was insufficient probable cause. Minneapolis therefore sought a special warrant under the Foreign Intelligence Surveillance Act. . . .

To do so, however, the FBI needed to demonstrate probable cause that Moussaoui was an agent of a foreign power, a demonstration that was not required to obtain a criminal warrant but was a statutory requirement for a FISA warrant. The agent did not have sufficient information to connect Moussaoui to a "foreign power," so he reached out for help, in the United States and overseas. . .

[Based on information supplied by the French government, Moussaoui was linked to a rebel leader in Chechnya.] This set off a spirited debate between the Minneapolis Field Office, FBI headquarters, and the CIA as to whether Chechen rebels . . . were sufficiently associated with a terrorist organization to constitute a "foreign power" for purposes of the FISA statute. FBI headquarters did not believe this was good enough, and its National Security Law Unit declined to submit a FISA application. . . .

Although the Minneapolis agents wanted to tell the FAA from the beginning about Moussaoui, FBI headquarters instructed Minneapolis that it could not share the more complete report the case agent had prepared for the FAA. . . .

NOTES & QUESTIONS

1. *Confusion About the Law Before 9/11.* The 9/11 Commission Report excerpted above indicated that many law enforcement officials were confused about what FISA required and how information could be shared. The 9/11 Commission Report stated that the FBI headquarters concluded that Moussaoui's association with Chechen rebels was not adequate to justify a FISA order because Chechen rebels were not "sufficiently associated with a terrorist organization to constitute a 'foreign power' for purposes of the FISA statute." Does FISA require that a foreign power involve a terrorist organization? Consider the following excerpt from a Senate Report discussing the problems with the Moussaoui investigation:

> *First,* key FBI personnel responsible for protecting our country against terrorism did not understand the law. The SSA at FBI Headquarters responsible for assembling the facts in support of the Moussaoui FISA application testified before the Committee in a closed hearing that he did not know that "probable cause" was the applicable legal standard for obtaining a FISA warrant. In addition, he did not have a clear understanding of what the probable cause standard meant. . . . In addition to not understanding the probable cause standard, the SSA's supervisor (the Unit Chief) responsible for reviewing FISA applications did not have a proper understanding of the legal definition of the "agent of a foreign power" requirement.[106]

A footnote in the report explained that the FBI agent "was under the incorrect impression that the statute required a link to an already identified or 'recognized' terrorist organization, an interpretation that the FBI and the supervisor himself admitted was incorrect."

---

[106] Senate Report No. 108-040.

According to Senator Arlen Specter (R-PA), the consequences of this misunderstanding of law were grave:

> The failure to obtain a warrant under the Foreign Intelligence Surveillance Act for Zacarias Moussaoui was a matter of enormous importance, and it is my view that if we had gotten into Zacarias Moussaoui's computer, a treasure trove of connections to Al-Qeada, in combination with the FBI report from Phoenix where the young man with Osama bin Laden's picture seeking flight training, added to [the fact that] the CIA knew about two men who turned out to be terrorist pilots on 9/11 . . . there was a veritable blueprint and 9/11 might well have been prevented. . . .
>
> [I]n a way which was really incredulous, the FBI agents didn't know the standard. They didn't know it when they were dealing with the Moussaoui case, and they didn't know it almost a year later when we had the closed-door hearing.[107]

Does this indication regarding law enforcement confusion point to a need for changes in the law, changes in FBI training, or some other action?

2. *What Did the FISA "Wall" Require?* Since information validly obtained pursuant to a FISA court order can be used for criminal prosecution, the FISA "wall" prevented criminal enforcement officials from directing the implementation of FISA orders. Consider the following remarks by Jamie Gorelick, who was part of the 9/11 Commission:

> At last week's hearing, Attorney General John Ashcroft, facing criticism, asserted that "the single greatest structural cause for September 11 was the wall that segregated criminal investigations and intelligence agents" and that I built that wall through a March 1995 memo. This simply is not true.
>
> First, I did not invent the "wall," which is not a wall but a set of procedures implementing a 1978 statute (the Foreign Intelligence Surveillance Act, or FISA) and federal court decisions interpreting it. In a nutshell, that law, as the courts read it, said intelligence investigators could conduct electronic surveillance in the United States against foreign targets under a more lenient standard than is required in ordinary criminal cases, but only if the "primary purpose" of the surveillance were foreign intelligence rather than a criminal prosecution.
>
> Second, according to the FISA Court of Review, it was the justice departments under Presidents Ronald Reagan and George H.W. Bush in the 1980s that began to read the statute as limiting the department's ability to obtain FISA orders if it intended to bring a criminal prosecution. . . .
>
> [N]othing in the 1995 guidelines prevented the sharing of information between criminal and intelligence investigators. Indeed, the guidelines require that FBI foreign intelligence agents share information with criminal investigators and prosecutors whenever they uncover facts suggesting that a crime has been or may be committed. . . .[108]

According to Gorelick, why was the "wall" in place? What function did it serve? What precisely did it require?

---

[107] *The USA Patriot Act in Practice: Shedding Light on the FISA Process,* S. Hearing 107-947 (Sept. 10, 2002).

[108] Jamie S. Gorelick, *The Truth About "the Wall,"* Wash. Post, Apr. 18, 2004, at B7.

3. *FISA and the USA PATRIOT Act.* Prior to the USA PATRIOT Act, FISA applied when foreign intelligence gathering was "the purpose" of the investigation. Courts interpreted "the purpose" to mean that the primary purpose of the investigation had to be foreign intelligence gathering. Criminal enforcement could be a secondary purpose, but not the primary one. The USA PATRIOT Act, § 204, changed this language to make FISA applicable when foreign intelligence gathering is "a significant purpose" of the investigation. 50 U.S.C. §§ 1804(a)(7)(B) and 1823(a)(7)(B). Why do you think that this change was made in the USA PATRIOT Act?

IN RE SEALED CASE

310 F.3d 717 (FIS Ct. Rev. 2002)

[In 2002, Attorney General John Ashcroft submitted to the FISA court new procedures for minimization, which significantly curtailed the screening walls. The procedures were reviewed by the FISA court in *In re All Matters Submitted to the Foreign Intelligence Surveillance Court* (May 17, 2002). The court expressed concern over the new procedures in light of the fact that in September 2000, the government had confessed error in about 75 FISA applications, including false statements that the targets of FISA surveillance were not under criminal investigations, that intelligence and criminal investigations were separate, and that information was not shared with FBI criminal investigators and assistant U.S. attorneys. The FISA court rejected the proposed procedures because they would allow criminal prosecutors to advise on FISA information gathering activities. The government appealed to the Foreign Intelligence Surveillance (FIS) Court of Review, which is composed of three judges on the D.C. Circuit. In 2002, the FIS Court of Review published its first and, thus far, only opinion.]

PER CURIAM. This is the first appeal from the Foreign Intelligence Surveillance Court to the Court of Review since the passage of the Foreign Intelligence Surveillance Act (FISA) in 1978. The appeal is brought by the United States from a FISA court surveillance order which imposed certain restrictions on the government. . . .

The court's decision from which the government appeals imposed certain requirements and limitations accompanying an order authorizing electronic surveillance of an "agent of a foreign power" as defined in FISA. There is no disagreement between the government and the FISA court as to the propriety of the electronic surveillance; the court found that the government had shown probable cause to believe that the target is an agent of a foreign power and otherwise met the basic requirements of FISA. . . . The FISA court authorized the surveillance, but imposed certain restrictions, which the government contends are neither mandated nor authorized by FISA. Particularly, the court ordered that law enforcement officials shall not make recommendations to intelligence officials concerning the initiation, operation, continuation or expansion of FISA searches or surveillances. Additionally, the FBI and the Criminal Division [of the

Department of Justice] shall ensure that law enforcement officials do not direct or control the use of the FISA procedures to enhance criminal prosecution, and that advice intended to preserve the option of a criminal prosecution does not inadvertently result in the Criminal Division's directing or controlling the investigation using FISA searches and surveillances toward law enforcement objectives.

To ensure the Justice Department followed these strictures the court also fashioned what the government refers to as a "chaperone requirement"; that a unit of the Justice Department, the Office of Intelligence Policy and Review (OIPR) (composed of 31 lawyers and 25 support staff), "be invited" to all meetings between the FBI and the Criminal Division involving consultations for the purpose of coordinating efforts "to investigate or protect against foreign attack or other grave hostile acts, sabotage, international terrorism, or clandestine intelligence activities by foreign powers or their agents." . . .

[The FISA court opinion below] appears to proceed from the assumption that FISA constructed a barrier between counterintelligence/intelligence officials and law enforcement officers in the Executive Branch — indeed, it uses the word "wall" popularized by certain commentators (and journalists) to describe that supposed barrier.

The "wall" emerges from the court's implicit interpretation of FISA. The court apparently believes it can approve applications for electronic surveillance only if the government's objective is *not* primarily directed toward criminal prosecution of the foreign agents for their foreign intelligence activity. But the court neither refers to any FISA language supporting that view, nor does it reference the Patriot Act amendments, which the government contends specifically altered FISA to make clear that an application could be obtained even if criminal prosecution is the primary counter mechanism.

Instead the court relied for its imposition of the disputed restrictions on its statutory authority to approve "minimization procedures" designed to prevent the acquisition, retention, and dissemination within the government of material gathered in an electronic surveillance that is unnecessary to the government's need for foreign intelligence information. 50 U.S.C. § 1801(h). . . .

. . . [I]t is quite puzzling that the Justice Department, at some point during the 1980s, began to read the statute as limiting the Department's ability to obtain FISA orders if it intended to prosecute the targeted agents — even for foreign intelligence crimes. To be sure, section 1804, which sets forth the elements of an application for an order, required a national security official in the Executive Branch — typically the Director of the FBI — to certify that "the purpose" of the surveillance is to obtain foreign intelligence information (amended by the Patriot Act to read "a significant purpose"). But as the government now argues, the definition of foreign intelligence information includes evidence of crimes such as espionage, sabotage or terrorism. Indeed, it is virtually impossible to read the 1978 FISA to exclude from its purpose the prosecution of foreign intelligence crimes, most importantly because, as we have noted, the definition of an agent of a foreign power — if he or she is a U.S. person — is grounded on criminal conduct. . . .

. . . In October 2001, Congress amended FISA to change "the purpose" language in § 1804(a)(7)(B) to "a significant purpose." It also added a provision allowing "Federal officers who conduct electronic surveillance to acquire foreign intelligence information" to "consult with Federal law enforcement officers to coordinate efforts to investigate or protect against" attack or other grave hostile acts, sabotage or international terrorism, or clandestine intelligence activities, by foreign powers or their agents. 50 U.S.C. § 1806(k)(1). . . . Although the Patriot Act amendments to FISA expressly sanctioned consultation and coordination between intelligence and law enforcement officials, in response to the first applications filed by OIPR under those amendments, in November 2001, the FISA court for the first time adopted the 1995 Procedures, as augmented by the January 2000 and August 2001 Procedures, as "minimization procedures" to apply in all cases before the court.

The Attorney General interpreted the Patriot Act quite differently. On March 6, 2002, the Attorney General approved new "Intelligence Sharing Procedures" to implement the Act's amendments to FISA. The 2002 Procedures supersede prior procedures and were designed to permit the complete exchange of information and advice between intelligence and law enforcement officials. They eliminated the "direction and control" test and allowed the exchange of advice between the FBI, OIPR, and the Criminal Division regarding "the initiation, operation, continuation, or expansion of FISA searches or surveillance." . . .

Unpersuaded by the Attorney General's interpretation of the Patriot Act, the court ordered that the 2002 Procedures be adopted, *with modifications,* as minimization procedures to apply in all cases. . . .

. . . [W]hen Congress explicitly authorizes consultation and coordination between different offices in the government, without even suggesting a limitation on who is to direct and control, it necessarily implies that either could be taking the lead. . . .

That leaves us with something of an analytic conundrum. On the one hand, Congress did not amend the definition of foreign intelligence information which, we have explained, includes evidence of foreign intelligence crimes. On the other hand, Congress accepted the dichotomy between foreign intelligence and law enforcement by adopting the significant purpose test. Nevertheless, it is our task to do our best to read the statute to honor congressional intent. The better reading, it seems to us, excludes from the purpose of gaining foreign intelligence information a sole objective of criminal prosecution. We therefore reject the government's argument to the contrary. Yet this may not make much practical difference. Because, as the government points out, when it commences an electronic surveillance of a foreign agent, typically it will not have decided whether to prosecute the agent (whatever may be the subjective intent of the investigators or lawyers who initiate an investigation). So long as the government entertains a realistic option of dealing with the agent other than through criminal prosecution, it satisfies the significant purpose test.

The important point is — and here we agree with the government — the Patriot Act amendment, by using the word "significant," eliminated any justification for the FISA court to balance the relative weight the government places on criminal prosecution as compared to other counterintelligence responses. If the certification of the application's purpose articulates a broader objective than criminal prosecution — such as stopping an ongoing conspiracy — and includes other potential non-prosecutorial responses, the government meets the statutory test. Of course, if the court concluded that the government's sole objective was merely to gain evidence of past criminal conduct — even foreign intelligence crimes — to punish the agent rather than halt ongoing espionage or terrorist activity, the application should be denied. . . .

It can be argued, however, that by providing that an application is to be granted if the government has only a "significant purpose" of gaining foreign intelligence information, the Patriot Act allows the government to have a primary objective of prosecuting an agent for a non-foreign intelligence crime. Yet we think that would be an anomalous reading of the amendment. . . . That is not to deny that ordinary crimes might be inextricably intertwined with foreign intelligence crimes. For example, if a group of international terrorists were to engage in bank robberies in order to finance the manufacture of a bomb, evidence of the bank robbery should be treated just as evidence of the terrorist act itself. But the FISA process cannot be used as a device to investigate wholly unrelated ordinary crimes.

Having determined that FISA, as amended, does not oblige the government to demonstrate to the FISA court that its primary purpose in conducting electronic surveillance is *not* criminal prosecution, we are obliged to consider whether the statute as amended is consistent with the Fourth Amendment. . . . [I]n asking whether FISA procedures can be regarded as reasonable under the Fourth Amendment, we think it is instructive to compare those procedures and requirements with their Title III counterparts. Obviously, the closer those FISA procedures are to Title III procedures, the lesser are our constitutional concerns. . . .

With limited exceptions not at issue here, both Title III and FISA require prior judicial scrutiny of an application for an order authorizing electronic surveillance. 50 U.S.C. § 1805; 18 U.S.C. § 2518. And there is no dispute that a FISA judge satisfies the Fourth Amendment's requirement of a "neutral and detached magistrate."

The statutes differ to some extent in their probable cause showings. Title III allows a court to enter an *ex parte* order authorizing electronic surveillance if it determines on the basis of the facts submitted in the government's application that "there is probable cause for belief that an individual is committing, has committed, or is about to commit" a specified predicate offense. 18 U.S.C. § 2518(3)(a). FISA by contrast requires a showing of probable cause that the target is a foreign power or an agent of a foreign power. 50 U.S.C. § 1805(a)(3). We have noted, however, that where a U.S. person is involved, an "agent of a foreign power" is defined in terms of criminal activity. . . . FISA surveillance would not be authorized against a target engaged in purely domestic terrorism because the government would not be able to show that the target is acting for or on behalf of a foreign power. . . .

FISA's general programmatic purpose, to protect the nation against terrorists and espionage threats directed by foreign powers, has from its outset been distinguishable from "ordinary crime control." After the events of September 11, 2001, though, it is hard to imagine greater emergencies facing Americans than those experienced on that date.

We acknowledge, however, that the constitutional question presented by this case — whether Congress' disapproval of the primary purpose test is consistent with the Fourth Amendment — has no definitive jurisprudential answer.

. . . Our case may well involve the most serious threat our country faces. Even without taking into account the President's inherent constitutional authority to conduct warrantless foreign intelligence surveillance, we think the procedures and government showings required under FISA, if they do not meet the minimum Fourth Amendment warrant standards, certainly come close.

NOTES & QUESTIONS

1. *Assessing the Benefits and Problems of the "Wall."* Paul Rosenzweig argues: "Prior to the Patriot Act, a very real wall existed. . . . While information could be 'thrown over the wall' from intelligence officials to prosecutors, the decision to do so always rested with national security personnel — even though law-enforcement agents are in a better position to determine what evidence is pertinent to their case."[109]

Consider Peter Swire:

> The principal argument [in favor of the wall] is that criminal prosecutions should be based on the normal rules of criminal procedure, not on evidence gathered in a secret court system. The norm should be the usual constitutional protections rather than the exceptional circumstances that arise in foreign intelligence investigations. . . .
>
> "[T]he wall" serves essential purposes. . . . [R]emoval of "the wall" may violate the Constitution for investigations that are primarily not for foreign intelligence purposes. At some point an investigation is so thoroughly domestic and criminal that the usual Fourth Amendment and other protections apply. . . . Second, "the wall" may be important in preventing the spread of the secret FISA system over time. As of 2002, seventy-one percent of the federal electronic surveillance orders were FISA orders rather than Title III orders. The Patriot Act reduction of safeguards in the FISA system means that this figure may climb in the future. . . .
>
> . . . [E]arly in an investigation, it may be difficult or impossible for investigators to know whether the evidence will eventually be used for intelligence purposes or in an actual prosecution. For instance, imagine that a FISA wiretap is sought for a group of foreign agents who are planning a bomb attack. On these facts, there would be a strong foreign intelligence purpose, to frustrate the foreign attack. In addition, there would be a strong law enforcement basis for surveillance, to create evidence that would prove conspiracy beyond a reasonable doubt. On these facts, it would be difficult for officials to certify honestly that "the primary purpose" of the surveillance was for foreign intelligence rather than law enforcement. The honest official might say that the surveillance has a dual use — both to create actionable foreign intelligence information and to create evidence for later prosecution.
>
> Faced with this possibility of dual use, the Patriot Act amendment was to require only that "a significant purpose" of the surveillance be for foreign

---

[109] Paul Rosenzweig, *Civil Liberty and the Response to Terrorism,* 42 Duq. L. Rev. 663 (2004).

intelligence. Under the new standard, an official could honestly affirm both a significant purpose for foreign intelligence and a likely use for law enforcement.

Swire is troubled by the USA PATRIOT Act's changing FISA's requirement that "the purpose" of the investigation be foreign intelligence gathering to a looser requirement that "a significant purpose" of the investigation constituting foreign intelligence gathering:

> The problem with the "significant purpose" standard, however, is that it allows too much use of secret FISA surveillance for ordinary crimes. The FISCR interpreted the new statute in a broad way: "So long as the government entertains a realistic option of dealing with the agent other than through criminal prosecution, it satisfies the significant purpose test." The range of "realistic options" would seem to be so broad, however, that FISA orders could issue for an enormous range of investigations that ordinarily would be handled in the criminal system. . . . The Patriot Act amendment, as interpreted by the FISCR, thus allows the slippery slope to occur. A potentially immense range of law enforcement surveillance could shift into the secret FISA system.[110]

In lieu of the standard that "a significant purpose" of the investigation consist of foreign intelligence gathering, Swire recommends that FISA orders should be granted only if the surveillance is "sufficiently important for foreign intelligence purposes." Will Swire's proposed standard ("sufficiently important for foreign intelligence purposes") make a material difference from that of "a significant purpose"?

2. *The Constitutionality of FISA and the Protect America Act.* At the end of *In re Sealed Case,* the court concludes: "[W]e think the procedures and government showings required under FISA, if they do not meet the minimum Fourth Amendment warrant standards, certainly come close." Is coming close to meeting minimum warrant standards adequate enough to be constitutional?

Prior to the USA PATRIOT Act amendments, a few courts considered the constitutionality of FISA, with all concluding that the statute passed constitutional muster. For example, in *United States v. Duggan,* 743 F.2d 59 (2d Cir. 1984), the Second Circuit concluded that FISA did not violate the Fourth Amendment because

> [p]rior to the enactment of FISA, virtually every court that had addressed the issue had concluded that the President had the inherent power to conduct warrantless electronic surveillance to collect foreign intelligence information, and that such surveillances constituted an exception to the warrant requirement of the Fourth Amendment. The Supreme Court specifically declined to address this issue in *United States v. United States District Court,* but it had made clear that the requirements of the Fourth Amendment may change when differing governmental interests are at stake, and it observed . . . that the governmental interests presented in national security investigations

---

[110] Peter Swire, *The System of Foreign Intelligence Surveillance Law,* 72 Geo. Wash. L. Rev. 1306, 1342, 1360-65 (2004).

differ substantially from those presented in traditional criminal investigations.
. . .

Against this background, Congress passed FISA to settle what it believed to be the unresolved question of the applicability of the Fourth Amendment warrant requirement to electronic surveillance for foreign intelligence purposes, and to "remove any doubt as to the lawfulness of such surveillance."
. . .

We regard the procedures fashioned in FISA as a constitutionally adequate balancing of the individual's Fourth Amendment rights against the nation's need to obtain foreign intelligence information. . . .

In 2008, the Foreign Intelligence Surveillance Court of Review (FISCR) upheld the constitutionality of the Protect America Act (PAA) of 2007, a stopgap law enacted before the FISA Amendment Act of 2008. *In re Directives [redacted text]*, 551 F.3d 1004 (FISCR 2008). The FISCR found that the PAA, applied through the relevant directives, satisfied the Fourth Amendment's reasonableness requirements. It observed, "The more important the government's interest, the greater the intrusion that may be constitutionally tolerated under the Fourth Amendment." Moreover, the PAA and accompanying directives provide safeguards, including "targeting procedures, minimization procedures, [and] a procedure to ensure that a significant purpose of a surveillance is to obtain foreign intelligence information." It concluded that "our decision recognizes that where the government has instituted several layers of serviceable safeguards to protect individuals against unwarranted harms and to minimize incidental intrusions, its effort to protect national security should not be frustrated by the courts."

Why should different Fourth Amendment requirements exist for foreign intelligence purposes as opposed to regular domestic law enforcement? Is the distinction between foreign intelligence and domestic law enforcement tenable in light of international terrorism, where investigations often have both a foreign intelligence and domestic law enforcement purpose? Do the USA PATRIOT Act amendments affect FISA's constitutionality?

3. *After-the-Fact Reasonableness Review?* In a critique of the FISA warrant-procedure as amended by the PATRIOT Act, a Note in the *Yale Law Journal* proposes that FISA be repealed and that the United States return to use of warrantless foreign intelligence surveillance in which "targets could challenge the reasonableness of the surveillance in an adversary proceeding in an Article III court after the surveillance was complete."[111]

Do you think that the foreign intelligence context is well-suited to the proposed warrantless regime? For the Note, "the possibility of after-the-fact reasonableness review of the merits of their decisions in Article III courts (in camera or note) would help guarantee careful and calm DOJ decisionmaking." Is reasonableness a sufficiently strict standard of review? Furthermore, one of the hallmarks of the Fourth Amendment's warrant procedure is before-the-fact review; law enforcement officials must seek judicial authorization *before* they conduct their search. Would after-the-fact review result in hindsight

---

[111] Nola K. Breglio, Note, *Leaving FISA Behind: The Need to Return to Warrantless Foreign Intelligence Surveillance*, 113 Yale L.J. 179, 203-04, 209, 212 (2003).

bias? Another consideration is the extent to which warrantless surveillance would allow the government to "bootstrap" an investigation — the government could undertake broad, unregulated surveillance knowing that it could lead to evidence that may be admissible in court.

3. THE ATTORNEY GENERAL'S FBI GUIDELINES

Unlike many government agencies, the FBI was not created by Congress through a statute. In 1907, Attorney General Charles Bonaparte requested that Congress authorize him to create a national detective force in the Department of Justice (DOJ). The DOJ had been using investigators from the Secret Service, but Bonaparte wanted a permanent force. Congress rejected his request due to concerns over this small group developing into a secret police system. Nevertheless, Bonaparte went ahead with his plans and formed a new subdivision of the DOJ, called the "Bureau of Investigation." President Theodore Roosevelt later authorized the subdivision through an executive order in 1908. J. Edgar Hoover began running the Bureau, which was renamed the Federal Bureau of Investigation in 1935.[112]

The FBI grew at a great pace. In 1933, the FBI had 353 agents and 422 support staff; in 1945, it had 4,380 agents and 7,422 support staff.[113] Today, the FBI has 11,000 agents and 16,000 support staff, as well as 56 field offices, 400 satellite offices, and 40 foreign liaison posts.[114]

FBI surveillance activities are regulated through the U.S. Constitution and electronic surveillance laws, as well as by guidelines promulgated by the Attorney General. In 1976, responding to Hoover's abuses of power, Attorney General Edward Levi established guidelines to control FBI surveillance activities.[115] As William Banks and M.E. Bowman observe:

> The most pertinent Levi Guidelines focused on freedom of speech and freedom of the press. First, investigations based solely on unpopular speech, where there is no threat of violence, were prohibited. Second, techniques designed to disrupt organizations engaged in protected First Amendment activity, or to discredit individuals would not be used in any circumstance.
>
> At the same time, Attorney General Levi emphasized that the Guidelines were intended to permit domestic security investigations where the activities under investigation "involve or will involve the use of force or violence and the violation of criminal law." . . .
>
> On March 7, 1983, Attorney General William French Smith revised the Guidelines regarding domestic security investigations. . . .
>
> The Smith Guidelines were intended to increase the investigative avenues available to the FBI in domestic terrorism cases. Where the Levi/Civiletti Guidelines had established a predicate investigative standard of "specific and articulable facts," the Smith version lowered the threshold to require only a "reasonable indication" as the legal standard for opening a "full"

---

[112] Curt Gentry, *J. Edgar Hoover: The Man and the* Secrets 111-13 (1991).

[113] Ronald Kessler, *The Bureau: The Secret History of the FBI* 57 (2002).

[114] Federal Bureau of Investigation, Frequently Asked Questions, http://www.fbi.gov/aboutus/faqs/faqsone.html (Dec. 4, 2003).

[115] *See* United States Attorney General Guidelines on Domestic Security Investigation (1976).

investigation. . . . The "reasonable indication" standard is significantly lower than the Fourth Amendment standard of probable cause required in law enforcement. To balance the lowered threshold for opening an investigation, Attorney General Smith emphasized that investigations would be regulated and would "not be based solely on activities protected by the First Amendment or the lawful exercise of other rights secured by the Constitution."

Nonetheless, the Smith Guidelines authorized FBI Headquarters to approve the use of informants to infiltrate a group "in a manner that may influence the exercise of rights protected by the First Amendment." The Smith Guidelines also stated: "In the absence of any information indicating planned violence by a group or enterprise, mere speculation that force or violence might occur during the course of an otherwise peaceable demonstration is not sufficient grounds for initiation of an investigation." . . .

According to the criminal guidelines, a full investigation may be opened where there is "reasonable indication" that two or more persons are engaged in an enterprise for the purpose of furthering political or social goals wholly or in part through activities that involve force or violence and are a violation of the criminal laws of the United States. . . .

In order to determine whether an investigation should be opened, the FBI must also take into consideration the magnitude of the threat, the likelihood that the threat will come to fruition, and the immediacy of the jeopardy. In addition to physical danger, the FBI must consider the danger to privacy and free expression posed by an investigation. For example, unless there is a reasonable indication that force or violence might occur during the course of a demonstration, initiation of an investigation is not appropriate. . . .[116]

In 2002, Attorney General John Ashcroft issued revised FBI guidelines. Whereas under the preexisting guidelines, the FBI could engage in surveillance of public political activity and search the Internet when "facts or circumstances reasonably indicate that a federal crime has been, is being, or will be committed,"[117] Ashcroft's guidelines eliminate this requirement. The FBI is permitted to gather "publicly available information, whether obtained directly or through services or resources (whether nonprofit or commercial) that compile or analyze such information; and information voluntarily provided by private entities." The FBI can also "carry out general topical research, including conducting online searches and accessing online sites and forums."[118]

Daniel Solove argues that Congress should pass a legislative charter to regulate the FBI:

. . . [E]xecutive orders and guidelines can all be changed by executive fiat, as demonstrated by Ashcroft's substantial revision to the guidelines in 2002. Moreover, the Attorney General Guidelines are not judicially enforceable. The problem with the current system is that it relies extensively on self-regulation by the executive branch. Much of this regulation has been effective, but it can too readily be changed in times of crisis without debate or discussion. Codifying the

---

[116] William C. Banks & M.E. Bowman, *Executive Authority for National Security Surveillance,* 50 Am. U. L. Rev. 1, 69-74 (2000).

[117] The Attorney General's Guidelines on General Crimes, Racketeering Enterprise and Domestic Security/Terrorism Investigations § II.C.1 (Mar. 21, 1989).

[118] The Attorney General's Guidelines on General Crimes, Racketeering Enterprise and Terrorism Enterprise Investigations § VI (May 30, 2002).

internal executive regulations of the FBI would also allow for public input into the process. The FBI is a very powerful arm of the executive branch, and if we believe in separation of powers, then it is imperative that the legislative branch, not the executive alone, become involved in the regulation of the FBI. The guidelines should be judicially enforceable to ensure that they are strictly followed.[119]

Should other government security agencies have more oversight? Does Solove overlook the FBI's internal administrative processes that serve to limit its power?

4. THE HOMELAND SECURITY ACT

In 2002, Congress passed the Homeland Security Act, 6 U.S.C. § 222, which consolidated 22 federal agencies into the Department of Homeland Security (DHS). Agencies and other major components at the DHS include the Transportation Security Administration, Customs and Border Protection, Federal Emergency Management Agency, U.S. Citizenship and Immigration Services, U.S. Coast Guard, and U.S. Secret Service. The Office of the Secretary of DHS includes the Office of the Chief Privacy Officer, the Office of Civil Rights and Civil Liberties, the Office of Counter Narcotics, and the Office of State and Local Government Coordination.

Among other things, the Act creates a Privacy Office. 6 U.S.C. § 222. The Secretary must "appoint a senior official to assume primary responsibility for privacy policy." The privacy official's responsibilities include ensuring compliance with the Privacy Act of 1974; evaluating "legislative and regulatory proposals involving the collection, use, and disclosure of personal information by the Federal Government"; and preparing an annual report to Congress.

5. THE INTELLIGENCE REFORM AND TERRORISM PREVENTION ACT

Information Sharing and Institutional Culture. The 9/11 Commission found that in addition to the legal restrictions on sharing of foreign intelligence information, limitations in the FBI's institutional culture as well as technology had also prevented the circulation of data. In its final report, the 9/11 Commission stated: "The importance of integrated, all-source analysis cannot be overstated. Without it, it is not possible to 'connect the dots.'"[120] The 9/11 Commission called for a restructuring of the United States Intelligence Community (USIC) through creation of a National Intelligence Director to oversee this process.

In an Executive Order of August 27, 2004, President Bush required executive branch agencies to establish an environment to facilitate sharing of terrorism information.[121] Responding to the 9/11 Commission Report, Congress passed the Intelligence Reform and Terrorism Prevention Act of 2004 (IRPTA), codifying

---

[119] Daniel J. Solove, *Reconstructing Electronic Surveillance Law,* 72 Geo. Wash. L. Rev. 1264, 1304 (2004).

[120] The 9/11 Commission Report 408 (2004).

[121] Exec. Order No. 13356, 69 Fed. Reg. 53,599, 53,600-01 (Sept. 1, 2004).

the requirements in Bush's Executive Order. The Act mandates that intelligence be "provided in its most shareable form" that the heads of intelligence agencies and federal departments "promote a culture of information sharing."

The Privacy and Civil Liberties Oversight Board. The IRTPA seeks to establish protection of privacy and civil liberties by setting up a five-member Privacy and Civil Liberties Oversight Board. The Board gives advice to the President and agencies of the executive branch and provides an annual report of activities to Congress. Among its oversight activities, the Board is to review whether "the information sharing practices of the departments, agencies, and elements of the executive branch . . . appropriately protect privacy and civil liberties." The Board is also to "ensure that privacy and civil liberties are appropriately considered in the development and implementation of . . . regulations and executive branch policies." Regarding FISA surveillance, IRTPA mandates that the Attorney General provide more detailed reporting to Congress on governmental surveillance practices and the government's legal interpretations of FISA.

The Privacy and Civil Liberties Board has been the subject of controversy. A year after its creation, in February 2006, the Board still had not met a single time. When the Board issued its first annual report in May 2007, it led to the resignation of Lanny Davis, the Board's only Democratic member. The Bush Administration made more than 200 revisions to the report. The White House defending the actions as "standard operating procedure," and stated that it was appropriate because the board was legally under the President's supervision. In his resignation letter, Davis contested "the extensive redlining of the board's report to Congress by administration officials and the majority of the Board's willingness to accept most [of the edits.]"

Later that year, Congress enacted legislation to strengthen the independence and authority of the Board. It is now an "independent agency" located within the executive branch. No more than three members of the same political party can be appointed to the Board, and the Senate is to confirm all appointments to it. As before, however, the Board cannot issue subpoenas itself. Rather, a majority of Board members have the power to ask the Attorney General to issue a subpoena.[122]

6. THE NSA SURVEILLANCE PROGRAM

In December 2005, a front page article in the *New York Times* first revealed that the National Security Agency (NSA) was intercepting communications where one party was located outside the United States and another party inside the United States.[123] The Bush Administration named this surveillance program the "Terrorist Surveillance Program" (TSP).

Created in 1952, the NSA collects and analyzes foreign communications. As Frederick Schwarz and Aziz Huq explain, "The NSA collects signals intelligence

---

[122] Ronald D. Lee & Paul M. Schwartz, *Beyond the "War on Terrorism": Towards the New Intelligence Network*, 103 Mich. L. Rev. 1446 (2005).

[123] James Risen & Eric Lichtblau, *Bush Lets U.S. Spy on Callers Without Courts*, N.Y. Times, Dec. 16. 2005, at A1.

from telegrams, telephones, faxes, e-mails, and other electronic communications, and then disseminates this information among other agencies of the executive branch."[124] Schwarz and Huq also point out that the Church Committee investigation in 1975-76 found that "the NSA had not exercised its vast power with restraint or due regard for the Constitution." In the past, the NSA had engaged in activities such as collecting every international telegram sent from the United States and maintaining watch lists of U.S. citizens involved in political protests.

After 9/11, the NSA again began secret surveillance activities within the United States. Although the Bush Administration has discussed aspects of the NSA surveillance of telecommunications, the complete dimensions of the NSA activities remain unknown. And while the Department of Justice has issued a white paper justifying these activities,[125] the legal opinions said to declare the program lawful are secret.

Several lawsuits ensued, challenging the legality of the NSA surveillance. Some of these cases were brought against telecommunications companies that cooperated with the NSA in conducting the surveillance. Plaintiffs alleged that these companies violated FISA and ECPA.

Early in 2007, a secret FISC decision denied permission for certain NSA surveillance activities. The FISC judgment was said to concern a NSA request for a so-called "basket warrant," under which warrants are issued not on a case-by-case basis for specific suspects, but more generally for surveillance activity involving multiple targets. One anonymous official was quoted as saying that the FISC ruling concerned cases "where one end is foreign and you don't know where the other is."[126] The Administration leaked information about this ruling and argued that it impeded the government's ability to investigate threats of imminent terrorist attacks.

In the summer of 2007, Congress enacted the Protect America Act to authorize the NSA surveillance program.[127] This statute was subject to sunset in 120 days, and it expired without Congress enacting a new law or renewing it.[128] At that point, without the Protect America Act's amendments, the original FISA once again took effect, until Congress enacted FAA in July 2008.

A major roadblock to amending FISA had been the subject of immunity for the telecommunications companies that participated or participate in TSP or similar programs. President Bush stated that telecommunications immunity was needed to provide "meaningful liability protection to those who are alleged to have assisted our nation following the attacks of September 11, 2001." FISA

---

[124] Frederick A.O. Schwarz Jr. & Aziz Z. Huq, *Unchecked and Unbalanced: Presidential Power in a Time of Terror* 127 (2007).

[125] United States Department of Justice, *Legal Authorities Supporting the Activities of the National Security Agency Described by the President* (Jan. 19, 2006).

[126] Greg Miller, *Court Puts Limits on Surveillance Abroad*, L.A. Times, Aug. 2, 2007.

[127] The Protect America Act created an exception to FISA's requirements. The exception was found in the statute's § 105A. This part of the law exempted all communications "directed at" people outside of the United States from FISA's definition of "electronic surveillance." Once a communication fell within § 105A, the government could carry it out subject to § 105B and its requirements — rather than FISA and its obligation to seek a warrant from the FISC.

[128] As discussed above, the Foreign Intelligence Surveillance Court of Review upheld the constitutionality of the PAA. *In re Directives [redacted text]*, 551 F.3d 1004 (FISCR 2008).

already did contain immunity provisions, and this language was in effect at the time that the TSP began. *See* 18 U.S.C. § 2511(2)(a)(ii). The cooperation of the telecommunication companies with the NSA must have been outside the existing safe harbor language.

The FAA of 2008, discussed earlier in this chapter, establishes new rules for at least some of this NSA behavior. Title II of the FAA raises a new challenge to the litigation against the NSA behavior prior to its enactments — it provides statutory defenses for the telecommunications companies that assisted the NSA. Specifically, the FAA prohibits "a civil action" against anyone "for providing assistance to an element of the intelligence community" in connection "with an intelligence activity involving communications" following a specific kind of certification by the Attorney General. § 802. The certification in question requires a determination that the assistance was (1) authorized by the President during the period beginning on September 11, 2001 and ending on January 17, 2007; (2) designed to detect or prevent a terrorist attack; and (3) the subject of a written request from the Attorney General or the head of the intelligence community. A court presented with such a certificate is to review it for the support of "substantial evidence."

Before enactment of FAA, several courts heard challenges to the NSA warrantless wiretapping program. One of the most important issues in this litigation was the state secrets privilege, which is a common law evidentiary rule. The state secrets privilege protects information from discovery when disclosure of it would harm national security. Subsequently, courts interpreted the effect of the FAA on these cases as well as the relationship between the state secrets privilege. In the following pages, we examine the path of two important cases: *Al-Haramain Islamic Foundation v. Bush* and *Hepting v. AT&T*.

AL-HARAMAIN ISLAMIC FOUNDATION V. BUSH

507 F.3d 1190 (9th Cir. 2007)

McKEOWN, J. Following the terrorist attacks on September 11, 2001, President George W. Bush authorized the National Security Agency ("NSA") to conduct a warrantless communications surveillance program. The program intercepted international communications into and out of the United States of persons alleged to have ties to Al Qaeda and other terrorist networks. Though its operating parameters remain murky, and certain details may forever remain so, much of what is known about the Terrorist Surveillance Program ("TSP") was spoon-fed to the public by the President and his administration.

After *The New York Times* first revealed the program's existence in late 2005, government officials moved at lightning-speed to quell public concern and doled out a series of detailed disclosures about the program. Only one day after *The New York Times'* story broke, President Bush informed the country in a public radio address that he had authorized the interception of international communications of individuals with known links to Al Qaeda and related terrorist organizations. Two days after President Bush's announcement, then-Attorney General Alberto Gonzales disclosed that the program targeted communications where the government had concluded that one party to the communication was a member of, or affiliated with, Al Qaeda. The Department of Justice followed these and other official disclosures with a lengthy white paper in which it both confirmed the existence of the surveillance program and also offered legal justification of the intercepts.

The government's plethora of voluntary disclosures did not go unnoticed. Al-Haramain Islamic Foundation, a designated terrorist organization, and two of its attorneys (collectively, "Al-Haramain") brought suit against President Bush and other executive branch agencies and officials. They claimed that they were subject to warrantless electronic surveillance in 2004 in violation of the Foreign Intelligence Surveillance Act ("FISA"), various provisions of the United States Constitution, and international law. The government countered that the suit is foreclosed by the state secrets privilege, an evidentiary privilege that protects national security and military information in appropriate circumstances.

Essential to substantiating Al-Haramain's allegations against the government is a classified "Top Secret" document (the "Sealed Document") that the government inadvertently gave to Al-Haramain in 2004 during a proceeding to freeze the organization's assets. Faced with the government's motions to dismiss and to bar Al-Haramain from access to the Sealed Document, the district court concluded that the state secrets privilege did not bar the lawsuit altogether. The court held that the Sealed Document was protected by the state secrets privilege and that its inadvertent disclosure did not alter its privileged nature, but decided that Al-Haramain would be permitted to file *in camera* affidavits attesting to the contents of the document based on the memories of lawyers who had received copies. . . .

Al-Haramain is a Muslim charity which is active in more than 50 countries. Its activities include building mosques and maintaining various development and education programs. The United Nations Security Council has identified Al-Haramain as an entity belonging to or associated with Al Qaeda. In February 2004, the Office of Foreign Assets Control of the Department of Treasury temporarily froze Al-Haramain's assets pending a proceeding to determine whether to declare it a "Specially Designated Global Terrorist" due to the organization's alleged ties to Al Qaeda. Ultimately, Al-Haramain and one of its directors, Soliman Al-Buthi, were declared "Specially Designated Global Terrorists."

In August 2004, during Al-Haramain's civil designation proceeding, the Department of the Treasury produced a number of unclassified materials that were given to Al-Haramain's counsel and two of its directors. Inadvertently included in these materials was the Sealed Document, which was labeled "TOP SECRET." Al-Haramain's counsel copied and disseminated the materials, including the Sealed Document, to Al-Haramain's directors and co-counsel, including Wendell Belew and Asim Ghafoor. In August or September of 2004, a reporter from *The Washington Post* reviewed these documents while researching an article. In late August, the FBI was notified of the Sealed Document's inadvertent disclosure. In October of 2004, the FBI retrieved all copies of the Sealed Document from Al-Haramain's counsel, though it did not seek out Al-Haramain's directors to obtain their copies. The Sealed Document is located in a Department of Justice Sensitive Compartmented Information Facility.

Al-Haramain alleges that after *The New York Times* story broke in December 2005, it realized that the Sealed Document was proof that it had been subjected to warrantless surveillance in March and April of 2004. Though the government has acknowledged the existence of the TSP, it has not disclosed the identities of the specific persons or entities surveilled under the program, and disputes whether Al-Haramain's inferences are correct. . . .

Although we have not previously addressed directly the standard of review for a claim of the state secrets privilege, we have intimated that our review is de novo. De novo review as to the legal application of the privilege and clear error review as to factual findings make sense, as the determination of privilege is essentially a legal matter based on the underlying facts. . . .

The state secrets privilege is a common law evidentiary privilege that permits the government to bar the disclosure of information if "there is a reasonable danger" that disclosure will "expose military matters which, in the interest of national security, should not be divulged." *United States v. Reynolds,* 345 U.S. 1, 10 (1953). The privilege is not to be lightly invoked. . . .

We agree with the district court's conclusion that the very subject matter of the litigation — the government's alleged warrantless surveillance program under the TSP — is not protected by the state secrets privilege. Two discrete sets of unclassified facts support this determination. First, President Bush and others in the administration publicly acknowledged that in the months following the September 11, 2001, terrorist attacks, the President authorized a communications surveillance program that intercepted the communications of persons with suspected links to Al Qaeda and related terrorist organizations. Second, in 2004, Al-Haramain was officially declared by the government to be a "Specially Designated Global Terrorist" due to its purported ties to Al Qaeda. The subject matter of the litigation — the TSP and the government's warrantless surveillance of persons or entities who, like Al-Haramain, were suspected by the NSA to have connections to terrorists — is simply not a state secret. At this early stage in the litigation, enough is known about the TSP, and Al-Haramain's classification as a "Specially Designated Global Terrorist," that the subject matter of Al-Haramain's lawsuit can be discussed, as it has been extensively in publicly-filed pleadings, televised arguments in open court in this appeal,[129] and in the media and the blogosphere, without disturbing the dark waters of privileged information.

Because cases in this area are scarce, no court has put a fine point on how broadly or narrowly "subject matter" is defined in the context of state secrets. Application of this principle must be viewed in the face of the specific facts alleged and the scope of the lawsuit. In this case, the analysis is not difficult because Al-Haramain challenges warrantless surveillance authorized under the TSP. Significantly, until disclosure of the program in 2005, the program and its details were a highly prized government secret.

The first disclosure may have come from *The New York Times,* but President Bush quickly confirmed the existence of the TSP just one day later, on December 17, 2005, in a radio address to the nation. The President's announcement that he

---

[129] Pursuant to a camera request filed before argument, we permitted C-SPAN to record the proceeding for later broadcast.

had authorized the NSA to intercept the international communications of individuals with known links to Al Qaeda cast the first official glimmer of light on the TSP. Since then, government officials have made voluntary disclosure after voluntary disclosure about the TSP, selectively coloring in the contours of the surveillance program and even hanging some of it in broad daylight.

Two days after President Bush's announcement, Attorney General Gonzales disclosed that the TSP intercepted communications where one party was outside the United States, and the government had "a reasonable basis to conclude that one party to the communication is a member of al Qaeda, affiliated with al Qaeda, or a member of an organization affiliated with al Qaeda, or working in support of al Qaeda." Attorney General Gonzales confirmed that surveillance occurred without FISA warrants . . . and that American citizens could be surveilled only if they communicated with a suspected or known terrorist . . . .

In an address to the National Press Club on January 23, 2006, General Hayden volunteered further details about the TSP . . . General Hayden's statements provided to the American public a wealth of information about the TSP. The public now knows the following additional facts about the program, beyond the general contours outlined by other officials: (1) at least one participant for each surveilled call was located outside the United States; (2) the surveillance was conducted without FISA warrants; (3) inadvertent calls involving purely domestic callers were destroyed and not reported; (4) the inadvertent collection was recorded and reported; and (5) U.S. identities are expunged from NSA records of surveilled calls if deemed non-essential to an understanding of the intelligence value of a particular report. These facts alone, disclosed by General Hayden in a public address, provide a fairly complete picture of the scope of the TSP.

. . . [T]he government's many attempts to assuage citizens' fears that *they* have not been surveilled now doom the government's assertion that the very subject matter of this litigation, the existence of a warrantless surveillance program, is barred by the state secrets privilege. . . .

Al-Haramain's case does involve privileged information, but that fact alone does not render the very subject matter of the action a state secret. Accordingly, we affirm the district court's denial of dismissal on that basis.

Although the very subject matter of this lawsuit does not result in automatic dismissal, we must still address the government's invocation of the state secrets privilege as to the Sealed Document and its assertion that Al-Haramain cannot establish either standing or a prima facie case without the use of state secrets. . . .

Having reviewed it *in camera,* we conclude that the Sealed Document is protected by the state secrets privilege, along with the information as to whether the government surveilled Al-Haramain. We take very seriously our obligation to review the documents with a very careful, indeed a skeptical, eye, and not to accept at face value the government's claim or justification of privilege. Simply saying "military secret," "national security" or "terrorist threat" or invoking an ethereal fear that disclosure will threaten our nation is insufficient to support the privilege. Sufficient detail must be-and has been-provided for us to make a meaningful examination. . . . That said, we acknowledge the need to defer to the Executive on matters of foreign policy and national security and surely cannot legitimately find ourselves second guessing the Executive in this arena. . . . [O]ur judicial intuition about this proposition is no substitute for documented risks and threats posed by the potential disclosure of national security information. . . .

It is no secret that the Sealed Document has something to do with intelligence activities. Beyond that, we go no further in disclosure. The filings involving classified information, including the Sealed Document, declarations and portions of briefs, are referred to in the pleadings as *In Camera or Ex Parte* documents. Each member of the panel has had unlimited access to these documents.

We have spent considerable time examining the government's declarations (both publicly filed and those filed under seal). We are satisfied that the basis for the privilege is exceptionally well documented. Detailed statements underscore that disclosure of information concerning the Sealed Document and the means, sources and methods of intelligence gathering in the context of this case would undermine the government's intelligence capabilities and compromise national security. Thus, we reach the same conclusion as the district court: the government has sustained its burden as to the state secrets privilege.

We must next resolve how the litigation should proceed in light of the government's successful privilege claim. . . .

After correctly determining that the Sealed Document was protected by the state secrets privilege, the district court then erred in forging an unusual path forward in this litigation. Though it granted the government's motion to deny Al-Haramain access to the Sealed Document based on the state secrets privilege, the court permitted the Al-Haramain plaintiffs to file *in camera* affidavits attesting to the contents of the document from their memories.

The district court's approach—a commendable effort to thread the needle—is contrary to established Supreme Court precedent. If information is found to be a privileged state secret, there are only two ways that litigation can proceed: (1) if the plaintiffs can prove "the essential facts" of their claims "without resort to material touching upon military secrets," *Reynolds,* 345 U.S. at 11, or (2) in accord with the procedure outlined in FISA. By allowing *in camera* review of affidavits attesting to individuals' memories of the Sealed Document, the district court sanctioned "material touching" upon privileged information, contrary to *Reynolds.*

Moreover, the district court's solution is flawed: if the Sealed Document is privileged because it contains very sensitive information regarding national security, permitting the same information to be revealed through reconstructed memories circumvents the document's absolute privilege. *See Reynolds,* 345 U.S. at 10 (A court "should not jeopardize the security which the privilege is meant to protect by insisting upon an examination of the evidence, even by the judge alone, in chambers."). That approach also suffers from a worst of both worlds deficiency: either the memory is wholly accurate, in which case the approach is tantamount to release of the document itself, or the memory is inaccurate, in which case the court is not well-served and the disclosure may be even more problematic from a security standpoint. The state secrets privilege, because of its unique national security considerations, does not lend itself to a compromise solution in this case. The Sealed Document, its contents, and any individuals' memories of its contents, even well-reasoned speculation as to its contents, are completely barred from further disclosure in this litigation by the common law state secrets privilege.

The requirements for standing are well known to us from the Supreme Court's decision in *Lujan v. Defenders of Wildlife,* 504 U.S. 555 (1992). Standing requires that (1) the plaintiff suffered an injury in fact, *i.e.,* one that is sufficiently "concrete and particularized" and "actual or imminent, not conjectural or hypothetical," (2) the injury is "fairly traceable" to the challenged conduct, and (3) the injury is "likely" to be "redressed by a favorable decision."

Al-Haramain cannot establish that it suffered injury in fact, a "concrete and particularized" injury, because the Sealed Document, which Al-Haramain alleges proves that its members were unlawfully surveilled, is protected by the state secrets privilege. At oral argument, counsel for Al-Haramain essentially conceded that Al-Haramain cannot establish standing without reference to the Sealed Document. . . . It is not sufficient for Al-Haramain to speculate that it might be subject to surveillance under the TSP simply because it has been designated a "Specially Designated Global Terrorist." . . .

Because we affirm the district court's conclusion that the Sealed Document, along with data concerning surveillance, are privileged, and conclude that no testimony attesting to individuals' memories of the document may be admitted to establish the contents of the document, Al-Haramain cannot establish that it has standing, and its claims must be dismissed, unless FISA preempts the state secrets privilege.

Under FISA, 50 U.S.C. §§ 1801 *et seq.,* if an "aggrieved person" requests discovery of materials relating to electronic surveillance, and the Attorney General files an affidavit stating that the disclosure of such information would harm the national security of the United States, a district court may review *in camera* and ex parte the materials "as may be necessary to determine whether the surveillance of the aggrieved person was lawfully authorized and conducted." 50 U.S.C. § 1806(f). The statute further provides that the court may disclose to the aggrieved person, using protective orders, portions of the materials "where such disclosure is necessary to make an accurate determination of the legality of the surveillance." *Id.* The statute, unlike the common law state secrets privilege, provides a detailed regime to determine whether surveillance "was lawfully authorized and conducted." *Id.*

As an alternative argument, Al-Haramain posits that FISA preempts the state secrets privilege. The district court chose not to rule on this issue. Now, however, the FISA issue remains central to Al-Haramain's ability to proceed with this lawsuit. Rather than consider the issue for the first time on appeal, we remand to the district court to consider whether FISA preempts the state secrets privilege and for any proceedings collateral to that determination.

IN RE NATIONAL SECURITY AGENCY TELECOMMUNICATIONS RECORDS LITIGATION [I]

564 F. Supp. 2d 1109 (N.D. Cal. 2008)

WALKER, C.J. The court of appeals has remanded the above case [*Al-Haramain Islamic Foundation v. Bush*] for this court "to consider whether FISA preempts the state secrets privilege and for any proceedings collateral to that determination". . . . For the reasons stated herein, the court has determined that: (1) FISA preempts the state secrets privilege in connection with electronic surveillance for intelligence purposes and would appear to displace the state secrets privilege for purposes of plaintiffs' claims. . . .

"Preemption" usually refers to Congress asserting its authority under the Supremacy Clause to override state law that interferes with federal interests. In the present context, "preemption" refers to Congress overriding or replacing the interstitial lawmaking that judges create through federal common law. In *Milwaukee v. Illinois*, 451 U.S. 304 (1981) the Supreme Court explained the latter type of preemption: "Federal common law is a 'necessary expedient' and when Congress addresses a question previously governed by a decision rested on federal common law the need for such an unusual exercise of lawmaking by federal courts disappears."

The court is charged with determining whether FISA preempts or displaces not a common-law set of rules for conducting foreign intelligence surveillance, but rather a privilege asserted by the government to avoid public and judicial scrutiny of its activities related to national security. In this case, those activities include foreign intelligence surveillance, the subject matter that Congress through FISA sought comprehensively to regulate. This imperfect overlap between the preempting statute and the common-law rule being preempted does not, however, create serious problems with finding the state secrets privilege preempted or displaced by FISA in the context of matters within FISA's purview. FISA does not preempt the state secrets privilege as to matters that are not within FISA's purview; for such matters, the lack of comprehensive federal legislation leaves an appropriate role for this judge-made federal common law privilege. . . .

"The state secrets privilege is a common law evidentiary privilege that protects information from discovery when disclosure would be inimical to the national security. [It] has its modern roots in *United States v. Reynolds*." *In re United States*, 872 F.2d 472 (D.C. Cir. 1989). . . . *Reynolds* largely demarcated the state secrets privilege as it is understood today, that is: it belongs to the government; it must be properly invoked by means of a "formal claim of privilege, lodged by the head of the department which has control over the matter" after "actual consideration"; the court must then "determine whether the circumstances are appropriate for the claim of privilege, and yet do so without forcing a disclosure of the very thing the privilege is designed to protect"; the precise nature, extent and manner of this inquiry depends in part on the extent of a party's need for the information sought tested against the strength of the government's claim of privilege; and in camera review might be appropriate in some cases, but not all.

Plaintiffs argue that the in camera procedure described in FISA's section 1806(f) applies to preempt the protocol described in *Reynolds* in this case. The court agrees. Section 1806(f) . . . provides that in cases in federal courts in which "aggrieved persons" seek to discover materials relating to, or information derived from, electronic surveillance, the United States attorney general may file "an affidavit under oath that disclosure or an adversary hearing would harm the national security of the United States." In that event, the court "shall" conduct an in camera, ex parte review of such materials relating to the surveillance "as may be necessary to determine whether the surveillance . . . was lawfully authorized and conducted." The procedure described in section 1806(f), while not identical to the procedure described in *Reynolds,* has important characteristics in common with it — enough, certainly, to establish that it preempts the state secrets privilege as to matters to which it relates. Section 1806(f) is Congress's specific and detailed prescription for how courts should handle claims by the government that the disclosure of material relating to or derived from electronic surveillance would harm national security; it leaves no room in a case to which section 1806(f) applies for a *Reynolds*-type process. Moreover, its similarities are striking enough to suggest that section 1806(f), which addresses a range of circumstances in which information derived from electronic surveillance might become relevant to judicial proceedings, is in effect a codification of the state secrets privilege for purposes of relevant cases under FISA, as modified to reflect Congress's precise directive to the federal courts for the handling of materials and information with purported national security implications.

IN RE NATIONAL SECURITY AGENCY TELECOMMUNICATIONS RECORDS LITIGATION [II]
700 F. Supp. 2d 1182 (N.D. Cal. 2010)

WALKER, C.J. Contending that United States government officials acting without warrants intercepted and eavesdropped on their international telephone conversations, plaintiffs Al-Haramain Islamic Foundation, Inc., an Oregon nonprofit corporation ("Al-Haramain"), and Wendell Belew and Asim Ghafoor, individuals who allege they are United States citizens and attorneys for Al-Haramain, seek summary judgment of liability on their FISA claim. Defendants, certain high-ranking government officials and associated government agencies, oppose plaintiffs' motion and bring their fourth motion for dismissal and/or summary judgment. In compliance with the court's orders of June 3 and June 5, 2009, the parties have presented only non-classified evidence to the court in support of these motions. Upon consideration of that evidence and the arguments presented by the parties, the court now GRANTS plaintiffs' motion and DENIES defendants' motions. . . .

[The court found that the plaintiffs submitted sufficient information under § 1806(f) to make a prima facie case of electronic surveillance. The burden then shifted to the government to affirm or deny those charges with an affidavit. The court then described FISA procedures available to the government.]

50 USC § 1806(f) provides a procedure by which the government may do this in camera, thus avoiding the disclosure of sensitive national security

information. Defendants declined to avail themselves of section 1806(f)'s in camera review procedures and have otherwise declined to submit anything to the court squarely addressing plaintiffs' prima facie case of electronic surveillance. . . .

In summary, because FISA displaces the [State Secrets Privilege, or "SSP"] in cases within its purview, the existence of a FISA warrant is a fact that cannot be concealed through the device of the SSP in FISA litigation for the reasons stated in the court's July 8, 2008 order. Plaintiffs have made out a prima facie case and defendants have foregone multiple opportunities to show that a warrant existed, including specifically rejecting the method created by Congress for this very purpose. Defendants' possession of the exclusive knowledge whether or not a FISA warrant was obtained, moreover, creates such grave equitable concerns that defendants must be deemed estopped from arguing that a warrant might have existed or, conversely, must be deemed to have admitted that no warrant existed. The court now determines, in light of all the aforementioned points and the procedural history of this case, that there is no genuine issue of material fact whether a warrant was obtained for the electronic surveillance of plaintiffs. For purposes of this litigation, there was no such warrant for the electronic surveillance of any of plaintiffs.

NOTES & QUESTIONS

1. ***The Holding in* Al-Haramain.** The path of this case was complicated, and we first wish to summarize the litigation. In *Al-Haramain Islamic Foundation*, the Ninth Circuit decided that the Bush Administration had revealed too much about the TSP to claim that the very subject matter of the litigation was a state secret. Yet, it did agree that the Sealed Document, which the Treasury Department had inadvertently provided to the Al-Haramain Islamic Foundation, was protected by the state secrets doctrine. The Ninth Circuit also found that the state secrets privilege prevented the plaintiffs, the Al-Haramain Foundation, from reconstructing "the essence of the document through memory." Without reference to the Sealed Document, Al-Haramain could not establish that it suffered injury-in-fact. Hence, it lacked standing.

   As a final matter, the Ninth Circuit remanded the case back to the lower court on the issue of whether FISA preempts the state secrets privilege. It was this statutory framework that was found to displace the evidentiary privilege. The district court then found in *In re NSA Telecommunications Records Litigation [I]* that FISA did, in fact, preempt the state secrets privilege. After the government refused to supply information to the court pursuant to FISA procedures under § 1806(f), the district found for the plaintiffs in *In re NSA Telecommunications Records Litigation [II]*.

2. ***The* Reynolds *Precedent*.** The birth of the modern state secrets privilege is *Reynolds v. United States*, 345 U.S. 1 (1953). In this Cold War era case, the Supreme Court drew on English precedents regarding crown privilege. The *Reynolds* Court found that the "occasion for the privilege is appropriate when a court finds 'from all the circumstances of the case, that there is a reasonable

danger that compulsion of the evidence will expose military matters, which, in the interests of national security, should not be divulged.'"

In *Reynolds*, a B-29 military aircraft had crashed and killed members of its crew as well as three civilian observers on board the flight. Their widows sued the government under the Federal Tort Claims Act and sought discovery of the official accident investigation of the Air Force. The Supreme Court found both a "reasonable danger that the accident investigation report would contain" state secrets and a "dubious showing of necessity" by the plaintiffs. It reversed the Third Circuit's decision and sustained the government's claim of privilege.

In 2000, the Air Force declassified the accident report at stake in *Reynolds*. As William Weaver and Robert M. Pallitto summarize, "The material originally requested by the plaintiffs in *Reynolds* has recently been made public through Freedom of Information Act requests, and it contained no classified or national security information."[130] In 2005, the Third Circuit heard a claim from a surviving widow and five heirs of the other, now deceased widows, in the original action. In this case, *Herring v. United States*, 424 F.3d 383 (3d Cir. 2005), the plaintiffs' claim was that the officials "fraudulently misrepresented the nature of the [accident] report in a way that caused the widows to settle their case for less than its full value."

The Third Circuit rejected this claim. The plaintiffs failed to show a fraud upon the court related to the Air Force's assertions of military secrets privilege for the contested accident report in the *Reynolds*. It found that the statements of the government officials at the time of the *Reynolds* litigation were "susceptible of a truthful interpretation." For the *Herring* court, the question was not whether the accident report actually contained sensitive information about the mission and the electronic equipment involvement. Rather, it would be enough if these reports could reasonably be read "to assert privilege over technical information about the B-29." The statements could be read in that fashion; "the claim of privilege referred to the B-29 itself rather than solely the secret mission and equipment."

Note as well that the *Reynolds* Court had not examined the documents itself, or sought to release the information to plaintiffs in redacted form. Courts continue to be reluctant to examine information about which the government has claimed the state secrets privilege. As Weaver and Pallitto state, "In less than one-third of reported cases in which the privilege has been invoked have the courts required in camera inspection of documents, and they have only required such inspection five times out of the twenty-three reported cases since the presidency of George H.W. Bush."[131]

3. **State Secrets in Civil Cases.** In an extensive empirical study of the state secrets doctrine, Laura Donohue demonstrates that "the shadow of state secrets casts longer and broader than previously acknowledged: more than 400 state secret cases emerged in the aftermath of *Reynolds*. In hundreds of

[130] William G. Weaver & Robert M. Pallitto, *State Secrets and Executive Power*, 120 Pol. Sci. Q. 85, 99 (2005).
[131] *Id.* at 101.

additional cases, moreover, state secrets doctrine played a significant role."[132] Donohue's research finds, moreover, that government contractors now leverage the doctrine in a kind of "greymail." As part of a civil suit, companies claim that state secrets are involved, and seek to have the government intervene to invoke the privilege and help that party block the emergence of certain information. Donohue writes, "Should the government initially refuse to support the corporation's state secrets claim, companies deeply embedded in the state may threaten to air legally or politically damaging information."

Is the state secrets doctrine in need of reform? If so, how should it be altered?

4. *The* **Al-Haramain** *Damages.* In a final case, the district court assessed the extent of damages to be awarded after finding for the plaintiffs in *In re NSA Telecommunications Records Litigation [II]*. The court denied any damages to plaintiff Al-Haramain. *In re: National Security Agency Telecommunications Records Litigation*, 2010 U.S. Dist. LEXIS 136156 (N.D. Cal. 2010). It stated, "The distribution of any funds to plaintiff Al-Haramain is impossible because Al-Haramain's assets are blocked as a result of its designation as a [Specially Designated Global Terrorist, or SDGT] organization." Pursuant to the International Emergency Economic Powers Act and Executive Order No. 13,224, the U.S. Treasury has authority to designated SDGT organizations and block all their assets. As for plaintiffs Ghafoor and Belew, the attorneys for Al-Haramain, the court awarded each $20,400 in liquidated damages. These were calculated according to FISA § 1801(a) at a rate of $100 per day for violations of a period of 204 days.

The court denied the request for $183,600 per plaintiff in punitive damages. In its view, the government did not demonstrate "reckless or callous indifference" to federal rights. Moreover, "it is essential to remember that the precise limits of the President's power to act in defense of the nation are not specifically delineated, and due to the nature of our constitution will never be spelled out in every detail." Finally, the court awarded reasonable attorney fees and expenses to Ghafoor and Belew of $2.5 million.

Does FISA provide adequate remedies to encourage plaintiffs to defend their interests under it? In *NSA [II]*, in a part of the opinion not excerpted above, the court had noted, "The parties have cited no other case in which a plaintiff has actually brought suit under section 1810, let alone secured a civil judgment under it." It concluded, "section 1810 is not user-friendly."

5. *Background on* **Al-Haramain:** *The Sealed Document.* How did the Sealed Document in *Al-Haramain* wind up sealed? Where did it come from? Patrick Radden Keefe has interviewed Al-Haramain's attorneys, including Lynne Bernabei, to whom the Treasury Department had accidently sent the top secret material.[133] Based on these interviews, he explains:

---

[132] Laura K. Donohue, *The Shadow of State Secrets*, 159 U. Pa. L. Rev. 77 (2010).
[133] Patrick Radden Keefe, *Annals of Surveillance: State Secrets*, New Yorker, Apr. 28, 2008.

The document that the Treasury Department turned over to Bernabei appears to have been a summary of intercepted telephone conversations between two of Al Haramain's American lawyers, in Washington, and one of the charity's officers, in Saudia Arabia. The government had evidently passed along proof of surveillance to the targets of that surveillance, and supplied the Oregon branch of Al Haramian — a suspected terrorist organization — with ammunition to challenge the constitutionality of the warrantless-wiretapping program.

Keefe explains that the FBI itself retrieved almost all copies of this document from Bernabei, her fellow attorneys, and her clients. It did not, however, seek to retrieve the copies of these documents that went to two of her clients then living in the Middle East. At some point in the litigation, these copies were sent back to Al-Haramain's attorneys, who turned them over to the district court, which then segregated them from the other evidence.

HEPTING V. AT&T CORP.

439 F. Supp. 974 (N.D. Cal. 2006)

WALKER, J. Plaintiffs allege that AT&T Corporation (AT&T) and its holding company, AT&T Inc, are collaborating with the National Security Agency (NSA) in a massive warrantless surveillance program that illegally tracks the domestic and foreign communications and communication records of millions of Americans. . . .

In determining whether a factual statement is a secret for purposes of the state secrets privilege, the court should look only at publicly reported information that possesses substantial indicia of reliability and whose verification or substantiation possesses the potential to endanger national security. That entails assessing the value of the information to an individual or group bent on threatening the security of the country, as well as the secrecy of the information. . . .

Accordingly, in determining whether a factual statement is a secret, the court considers only public admissions or denials by the government, AT&T and other telecommunications companies, which are the parties indisputably situated to disclose whether and to what extent the alleged programs exist. In determining what is a secret, the court at present refrains from relying on the declaration of Mark Klein. Although AT&T does not dispute that Klein was a former AT&T technician and he has publicly declared under oath that he observed AT&T assisting the NSA in some capacity and his assertions would appear admissible in connection with the present motions, the inferences Klein draws have been disputed. To accept the Klein declaration at this juncture in connection with the state secrets issue would invite attempts to undermine the privilege by mere assertions of knowledge by an interested party. Needless to say, this does not reflect that the court discounts Klein's credibility, but simply that what is or is not secret depends on what the government and its alleged operative AT&T and other telecommunications providers have either admitted or denied or is beyond reasonable dispute.

Likewise, the court does not rely on media reports about the alleged NSA programs because their reliability is unclear. To illustrate, after Verizon and BellSouth denied involvement in the program described in *USA Today* in which communication records are monitored, *USA Today* published a subsequent story somewhat backing down from its earlier statements and at least in some measure substantiating these companies' denials.

Finally, the court notes in determining whether the privilege applies, the court is not limited to considering strictly admissible evidence. . . . [T]he court may rely upon reliable public evidence that might otherwise be inadmissible at trial because it does not comply with the technical requirements of the rules of evidence.

With these considerations in mind, the court at last determines whether the state secrets privilege applies here. . . .

In sum, the government has disclosed the general contours of the "terrorist surveillance program," which requires the assistance of a telecommunications provider, and AT&T claims that it lawfully and dutifully assists the government in classified matters when asked. . . .

[I]t is important to note that even the state secrets privilege has its limits. While the court recognizes and respects the executive's constitutional duty to protect the nation from threats, the court also takes seriously its constitutional duty to adjudicate the disputes that come before it. See *Hamdi v. Rumsfeld,* 542 U.S. 507, 536 (2004) (plurality opinion) ("Whatever power the United States Constitution envisions for the Executive in its exchanges with other nations or with enemy organizations in times of conflict, it most assuredly envisions a role for all three branches when individual liberties are at stake."). To defer to a blanket assertion of secrecy here would be to abdicate that duty, particularly because the very subject matter of this litigation has been so publicly aired. The compromise between liberty and security remains a difficult one. But dismissing this case at the outset would sacrifice liberty for no apparent enhancement of security. . . .

The government also contends the issue whether AT&T received a certification authorizing its assistance to the government is a state secret.

The procedural requirements and impact of a certification under Title III are addressed in 18 U.S.C. § 2511(2)(a)(ii):

> Notwithstanding any other law, providers of wire or electronic communication service, their officers, employees, and agents, . . . are authorized to provide information, facilities, or technical assistance to persons authorized by law to intercept wire, oral, or electronic communications or to conduct electronic surveillance, as defined in section 101 of [FISA] . . . . if such provider, its officers, employees, or agents, . . . has been provided with — . . . .
>
> (B) a certification in writing by a person specified in section 2518(7) of this title [18 U.S.C.S. § 2518(7)] or the Attorney General of the United States that no warrant or court order is required by law, that all statutory requirements have been met, and that the specified assistance is required. . . .

Although it is doubtful whether plaintiffs' *constitutional* claim would be barred by a valid certification under section 2511(2)(a)(ii), this provision on its face makes clear that a valid certification would preclude the *statutory* claims asserted here. See 18 U.S.C. § 2511(2)(a)(ii) ("No cause of action shall lie in any court against any provider of wire or electronic communication service . . . for providing information, facilities, or assistance in accordance with the terms of a . . . certification under this chapter.").

As noted above, it is not a secret for purposes of the state secrets privilege that AT&T and the government have some kind of intelligence relationship. Nonetheless, the court recognizes that uncovering whether and to what extent a certification exists might reveal information about AT&T's assistance to the government that has not been publicly disclosed. Accordingly, in applying the state secrets privilege to the certification question, the court must look deeper at what information has been publicly revealed about the alleged electronic surveillance programs. The following chart summarizes what the government has disclosed about the scope of these programs in terms of (1) the individuals whose communications are being monitored, (2) the locations of those individuals and (3) the types of information being monitored:

	Purely Domestic	Domestic-Foreign	
	Communication Content	Communication Content	Communication Records
General Public	Government DENIES	Government DENIES	Government NEITHER CONFIRMS NOR DENIES
Al Qaeda or affiliate member/agent	Government DENIES	Government CONFIRMS	

As the chart relates, the government's public disclosures regarding monitoring of "communication content" (i.e., wiretapping or listening in on a communication) differ significantly from its disclosures regarding "communication records" (i.e., collecting ancillary data pertaining to a communication, such as the telephone numbers dialed by an individual). . . .

Beginning with the warrantless monitoring of "communication content," the government has confirmed that it monitors "contents of communications where . . . one party to the communication is outside the United States" and the government has "a reasonable basis to conclude that one party to the communication is a member of al Qaeda, affiliated with al Qaeda, or a member of an organization affiliated with al Qaeda, or working in support of al Qaeda." The government denies listening in without a warrant on any purely domestic communications or communications in which neither party has a connection to al Qaeda or a related terrorist organization. In sum, regarding the government's monitoring of "communication content," the government has disclosed the universe of possibilities in terms of *whose* communications it monitors and *where* those communicating parties are located.

Based on these public disclosures, the court cannot conclude that the existence of a certification regarding the "communication content" program is a state secret. If the government's public disclosures have been truthful, revealing whether AT&T has received a certification to assist in monitoring communication content should not reveal any new information that would assist a terrorist and adversely affect national security. And if the government has not been truthful, the state secrets privilege should not serve as a shield for its false public statements. In short, the government has opened the door for judicial inquiry by publicly confirming and denying material information about its monitoring of communication content.

Accordingly, the court concludes that the state secrets privilege will not prevent AT&T from asserting a certification-based defense, as appropriate, regarding allegations that it assisted the government in monitoring communication content. The court envisions that AT&T could confirm or deny the existence of a certification authorizing monitoring of communication content through a combination of responses to interrogatories and *in camera* review by the court. Under this approach, AT&T could reveal information at the level of generality at which the government has publicly confirmed or denied its monitoring of communication content. This approach would also enable AT&T to disclose the non-privileged information described here while withholding any incidental privileged information that a certification might contain.

Turning to the alleged monitoring of communication records, the court notes that despite many public reports on the matter, the government has neither confirmed nor denied whether it monitors communication records and has never publicly disclosed whether the NSA program reported by *USA Today* on May 11, 2006, actually exists. Although BellSouth, Verizon and Qwest have denied participating in this program, AT&T has neither confirmed nor denied its involvement. Hence, unlike the program monitoring communication content, the general contours and even the existence of the alleged communication records program remain unclear. . . .

[T]he court recognizes that it is not in a position to estimate a terrorist's risk preferences, which might depend on facts not before the court. For example, it may be that a terrorist is unable to avoid AT&T by choosing another provider or, for reasons outside his control, his communications might necessarily be routed through an AT&T facility. Revealing that a communication records program exists might encourage that terrorist to switch to less efficient but less detectable forms of communication. And revealing that such a program does not exist might encourage a terrorist to use AT&T services when he would not have done so otherwise. Accordingly, for present purposes, the court does not require AT&T to disclose what relationship, if any, it has with this alleged program.

The court stresses that it does not presently conclude that the state secrets privilege will necessarily preclude AT&T from revealing later in this litigation information about the alleged communication records program. While this case has been pending, the government and telecommunications companies have made substantial public disclosures on the alleged NSA programs. It is conceivable that these entities might disclose, either deliberately or accidentally, other pertinent information about the communication records program as this litigation proceeds. The court recognizes such disclosures might make this program's existence or non-existence no longer a secret. Accordingly, while the court presently declines to permit any discovery regarding the alleged communication records program, if appropriate, plaintiffs can request that the court revisit this issue in the future.. . . .

[F]or purposes of the present motion to dismiss, plaintiffs have stated sufficient facts to allege injury-in-fact for all their claims. "At the pleading stage, general factual allegations of injury resulting from the defendant's conduct may suffice, for on a motion to dismiss we 'presume that general allegations embrace those specific facts that are necessary to support the claim.'" *Lujan,* 504 U.S. at 561 (quoting *Lujan v. National Wildlife Federation,* 497 U.S. 871 (1990)). Throughout the complaint, plaintiffs generally describe the injuries they have allegedly suffered because of AT&T's illegal conduct and its collaboration with the government. . . . Here, the alleged injury is concrete even though it is widely shared. Despite AT&T's alleged creation of a dragnet to intercept all or substantially all of its customers' communications, this dragnet necessarily inflicts a concrete injury that affects each customer in a distinct way, depending on the content of that customer's communications and the time that customer spends using AT&T services. Indeed, the present situation resembles a scenario in which "large numbers of individuals suffer the same common-law injury (say, a widespread mass tort)."

IN RE NATIONAL SECURITY AGENCY TELECOMMUNICATIONS RECORDS LITIGATION [III]
633 F. Supp. 2d 949 (N.D. Cal. 2008)

WALKER, C.J. The United States has moved to dismiss "all claims against the electronic communication service providers" in the cases in this multidistrict litigation (MDL) matter brought by individuals against telecommunications companies. The single ground for dismissal in the government's motion is section 802 of FISA, part of the FISA Amendments Act of 2008 (FISAAA), enacted July 10, 2008 and codified at 50 U.S.C. § 1885a. In response to the government's motion to dismiss, plaintiffs, alleged to be customers of the various telecommunications companies named as defendants in these actions, have advanced a variety of constitutional challenges to the provisions of FISAAA upon which the government relies in seeking dismissal. For the reasons presented herein, these challenges must be rejected and the government's motion to dismiss GRANTED.

In December 2005, news agencies began reporting that President George W Bush had ordered the National Security Agency (NSA) to conduct eavesdropping of some portion of telecommunications in the United States without warrants and that the NSA had obtained the cooperation of telecommunications companies to tap into a significant portion of the companies' telephone and e-mail traffic, both domestic and international. See, e.g., James Risen and Eric Lichtblau, *Bush Lets U.S. Spy on Callers Without Courts,* N.Y. Times (Dec. 16, 2005). In January 2006, the first of dozens of lawsuits by customers of telecommunications companies were filed alleging various causes of action related to such cooperation with the NSA in warrantless wiretapping of customers' communications. See, e.g., *Hepting v. AT & T Corp.*, C 06-0672 VRW, 2006 WL 324036 (N.D. Cal. 2006). . . .

On August 9, 2006, the Judicial Panel on Multidistrict Litigation ordered all cases arising from the alleged warrantless wiretapping program by the NSA transferred to the Northern District of California and consolidated before the undersigned judge.

On July 7, 2008, after months of election-year legislative exertion that received considerable press coverage, Congress enacted FISAAA. The new law included an immunity provision for the benefit of telecommunications companies that would be triggered if and when the Attorney General of the United States certified certain facts to the relevant United States district court. On September 19, 2008, the United States filed its motion to dismiss all claims against telecommunications company defendants in these cases, including the pending master consolidated complaints.

FISAAA contains four titles. The government's motion rests on a provision of Title II, which bears the heading "Protections for Electronic Communication Service Providers" and contains section 802, concerning "procedures for implementing statutory defenses under [FISA]."

Section 802(a) contains the new immunity provision upon which the United States relies in seeking dismissal:

(a) REQUIREMENT FOR CERTIFICATION. — Notwithstanding any other provision of law, a civil action may not lie or be maintained in a Federal or State court against any person for providing assistance to an element of the intelligence community, and shall be promptly dismissed, if the Attorney General certifies to the district court of the United States in which such action is pending that —

(1) any assistance by that person was provided pursuant to an order of the court established under section 103(a) directing such assistance;

(2) any assistance by that person was provided pursuant to a certification in writing under section 2511(2)(a)(ii)(B) or 2709(b) of title 18, United States Code;

(3) any assistance by that person was provided pursuant to a directive under section 102(a)(4), 105B(e), as added by section 2 of the Protect America Act of 2007 (Public Law 110-55), or 702(h) directing such assistance;

(4) in the case of a covered civil action, the assistance alleged to have been provided by the electronic communication service provider was —

(A) in connection with an intelligence activity involving communications that was —

(i) authorized by the President during the period beginning on September 11, 2001, and ending on January 17, 2007; and

(ii) designed to detect or prevent a terrorist attack, or activities in preparation for a terrorist attack, against the United States; and

(B) the subject of a written request or directive, or a series of written requests or directives, from the Attorney General or the head of an element of the intelligence community (or the deputy of such person) to the electronic communication service provider indicating that the activity was —

(i) authorized by the President; and

(ii) determined to be lawful; or
(5) the person did not provide the alleged assistance.

The government has submitted a public certification by former Attorney General Michael Mukasey which includes the following statement: "I hereby certify that the claims asserted in the civil actions pending in these consolidated proceedings brought against electronic communication service providers fall within at least one provision contained in Section 802(a)." In addition, the government has submitted classified certifications in support of its motion.

Section 802(b)(1) sets out the standard for judicial review of a certification: "A certification under subsection (a) shall be given effect unless the court finds that such certification is not supported by substantial evidence provided to the court pursuant to this section." The statute does not define "substantial evidence," so courts presumably are to employ definitions of that standard articulated in other contexts. The United States, for example, cites a social security case, *McCarthy v. Apfel,* 221 F.3d 1119 (9th Cir. 2000), which defines the substantial evidence standard as "such relevant evidence as a reasonable mind might, upon consideration of the entire record, accept as adequate to support a conclusion." . . .

Section 802(c) specifies the manner in which the court is to deal with classified information. If the Attorney General files an unsworn statement under penalty of perjury that disclosure of the certification and related materials would harm the national security, the court is obligated under section 802(c) to do two things: (1) review the certification and any supplemental materials in camera and ex parte; and (2) limit public disclosure concerning such certification and the supplemental materials, including any public order following such in camera and ex parte review, to a statement whether the case is dismissed and a description of the legal standards that govern the order, without disclosing the specific subparagraph within subsection (a) that is the basis for the certification. . . .

FISAAA's section 802 appears to be *sui generis* among immunity laws: it creates a retroactive immunity for past, completed acts committed by private parties acting in concert with governmental entities that allegedly violated constitutional rights. The immunity can only be activated by the executive branch of government and may not be invoked by its beneficiaries. Section 802 also contains an unusual temporal limitation confining its immunity protections to suits arising from actions authorized by the president between September 11, 2001 and January 7, 2007. The government contends that section 802 is valid and enforceable and fully applicable to all the cases in the MDL brought by individuals against telecommunications companies. The government now invokes section 802's procedures in seeking dismissal of these actions. . . .

[The court upheld the FISAAA against constitutional claims, such as violating separation of powers doctrine, due process, and the First Amendment. It also found that the statute did not violate requirements of the Administrative Procedure Act.]

. . . Congress has manifested its unequivocal intention to create an immunity that will shield the telecommunications company defendants from liability in these actions. The Attorney General, in submitting the certifications, is acting pursuant to and in accordance with that congressional grant of authority, in effect, to administer the newly-created immunity provision. . . .

While plaintiffs have made a valiant effort to challenge the sufficiency of certifications they are barred by statute from reviewing, their contentions under section 802 are not sufficiently substantial to persuade the court that the intent of Congress in enacting the statute should be frustrated in this proceeding in which the court is required to apply the statute. The court has examined the Attorney General's submissions and has determined that he has met his burden under section 802(a). The court is prohibited by section 802(c)(2) from opining further. The United States' motion to dismiss must therefore be, and hereby is, GRANTED.

NOTES & QUESTIONS

1. *The Holding in* **Hepting.** In *Hepting*, the plaintiffs alleged that AT&T was collaborating with the NSA in a massive warrantless surveillance program, namely, the TSP. As customers of AT&T, the plaintiffs alleged that they suffered injury from this surveillance. But what about the state secrets privilege? Recall that in *Al-Haramain*, the plaintiffs' ability to demonstrate an injury turned on access to the Sealed Document or their memories of it. Without access to the document, the Ninth Circuit found that the Al-Haramain Foundation and other plaintiffs could not show standing.

   In contrast, the *Hepting* plaintiffs alleged injury due to *non-targeted* surveillance under the TSP. The *Hepting* court found that the existence of the TSP was itself not a state secret. It found that (1) the Bush Administration had disclosed "the general contours" of the TSP, which (2) "requires the assistance of a telecommunications provider," and (3) AT&T helps the government in classified matters when asked. This litigation ended, however, due to *In re NSA Telecommunications Records Litigation [III]*. In that case, the district court found that the FISA Amendments Act had provided retroactive immunity for the defendants and dismissed the action.

2. *The FISA Amendment Act and* **Hepting.** The FISA Amendment Act effectively foreclosed litigation against telecommunication providers who participated in the TSP.[134] The court in *In re: NSA [III]* found that Congress in enacting the statute "manifested an unequivocal intention to create an immunity that will shield the telecommunications company defendants from liability in these actions." At the time of the debates around this law, Congress also considered laws that would have capped the possible liability exposure of the telecommunications companies at fairly modest amounts, but allow the litigation against them to proceed. Do you think that this approach would have been superior to the FISA Amendment Act's outright grant of immunity?

---

[134] As for the constitutionality of the FISA Amendment Act, the Second Circuit has found that a group of plaintiffs have sufficient standing to permit their claim. *Amnesty International USA v. Clapper*, 683 F.3d 118 (2d Cir. 2011).

3. ***The End of FISA?*** William Banks argues: "At a minimum, the unraveling of FISA and emergence of the TSP call into question the virtual disappearance of effective oversight of our national security surveillance. The Congress and federal courts have become observers of the system, not even participants, much less overseers."[135] He proposes: "If FISA is to have any meaningful role for the next thirty years, its central terms will have to be restored, one way or another."

In contrast, John Yoo argues that such surveillance should be permitted where there is a reasonable chance that terrorists will appear, or communicate, even if we do not know their specific identities. A law professor, Yoo was in government service at the time of the TSP and wrote the government memorandums at the Department of Justice's Office of Legal Counsel that approved the program.[136] Subsequently, he has proposed that in cases where there is a likelihood, perhaps "a 50 percent chance" that terrorists would use a certain kind of avenue for reaching each other, "[a] FISA-based approach would prevent computers from searching through that channel for keywords or names that might suggest terrorist communications."[137]

A third approach is proposed by Orin Kerr, who would update FISA beyond its current approach, which depends "on the identity and location of who is being monitored.[138] In contrast to this "person-focused" approach, Kerr would add "a complementary set of data-focused authorities" to the statute. Under this second approach, "Surveillance practices should be authorized when the government establishes a likelihood that surveillance would yield what I call 'terrorist intelligence information' — information relevant to terrorism investigations. . . ." Kerr is unwilling to state, however, whether the data-focused approach ("used when identities and/or location are unknown") should or should not require any kind of warrant.

---

[135] William C. Banks, *The Death of FISA*, 91 Minn. L. Rev. 1209, 1297 (2007).

[136] For a discussion of Yoo's role, see *In re: National Security Telecommunications Records Litigation*, 2010 U.S. Dist. LEXIS 136156, *38-*40 (N.D. Cal. 2010)

[137] John Yoo, *War By Other Means: An Insider's Accounts of the War on Terror* 112 (2006).

[138] Orin Kerr, *Updating the Foreign Intelligence Surveillance Act*, 75 U. Chi. L. Rev. 238 (2008).

CHAPTER 3

PRIVACY AND GOVERNMENT RECORDS AND DATABASES

In the United States, government began to use records widely about citizens after the rise of the administrative state in the early part of the twentieth century. The administrative state's extensive and complex systems of regulation, licensing, and entitlements demanded the collection of a significant amount of personal information. For example, the Social Security system, created in 1935, required that records be kept about every employed individual's earnings. To ensure that each record was correctly identified, the Social Security Administration assigned each individual a unique nine-digit number known as a Social Security number (SSN).

Technology has also been developed that helps government create detailed databases of personal information. Indeed, one of the greatest catalysts for the creation of government records has been technology — namely, the computer. The invention of the mainframe computer in 1946 sparked a revolution in recordkeeping. By the 1960s, computers provided a fast, efficient, and inexpensive way to store, analyze, and transfer information. Federal and state agencies began to computerize their records, often using SSNs as identifiers for these records.[1]

Today, federal agencies maintain thousands of databases. States also keep a panoply of public records, pertaining to births, marriages, divorces, property ownership, licensing, voter registration, and the identity and location of sex offenders. State public records will be covered later in this chapter.

The vast stores of personal information spread throughout government databases have given rise to significant fears that one day this information might be combined to create a file on each citizen. In his influential book on privacy from 1971, Arthur Miller warned of the "possibility of constructing a

---

[1] See Alan F. Westin & Michael A. Baker, *Databanks in a Free Society: Computers, Record-Keeping and Privacy* 229 (1972); Priscilla Regan, *Legislating Privacy* 69 (1995); Daniel J. Solove, *Privacy and Power: Computer Databases and Metaphors for Information Privacy*, 53 Stan. L. Rev. 1393, 1400-03 (2001).

sophisticated data center capable of generating a comprehensive womb-to-tomb dossier on every individual and transmitting it to a wide range of data users over a national network."[2] Several times, the federal government has seriously considered the idea of creating a national database of personal information. In the 1960s, for example, the Johnson Administration proposed a National Data Center that would combine data held by various federal agencies into one large computer database. However, the plan was abandoned after a public outcry. Following the terrorist attacks on September 11, 2001, there was a new effort to build a national database based on records contained in state motor vehicle agencies. Unlike the earlier proposal that envisioned a centralized system of records management, the new system would be based on standardized record formats and data linkages to enable information sharing among federal and state agencies.

A. PUBLIC ACCESS TO GOVERNMENT RECORDS

1. PUBLIC RECORDS AND COURT RECORDS

As noted above, states maintain a panoply of records about individuals, many available to the public. These records contain varying kinds of information. Birth records often disclose one's name, date of birth, place of birth, the names and ages of one's parents, and one's mother's maiden name. States also maintain driver's license records, as well as accident reports. Voting records, which can disclose one's political party affiliation, date of birth, e-mail address, home address, and telephone number, are publicly available in many states. Several types of professions require state licensing, such as doctors, attorneys, engineers, nurses, police, and teachers. Property ownership records contain a physical description of one's property, including the number and size of rooms as well as the value of the property. Police records, such as records of arrests, are also frequently made publicly available.

Court records are public in all states, though settlements in civil actions are sometimes sealed. A significant amount of personal data can find its way into court records. In a civil case, for example, medical and financial information often is entered into evidence. The names, addresses, and occupations of jurors become part of the court record, as well as the jurors' answers to voir dire questions. In some states, family court proceedings are public.

For information in court records, privacy is protected by way of protective orders, which are issued at the discretion of trial court judges. Courts also have the discretion to seal certain court proceedings or portions of court proceedings from the public, as well as to permit parties to proceed anonymously under special circumstances.

Privacy in records maintained by state agencies is protected under each state's freedom of information law. Most states have some form of exemption for privacy, often patterned after the federal Freedom of Information Act's (FOIA)

---

[2] Arthur Miller, *Assault on Privacy* 39 (1971).

privacy exemptions. Not all states interpret their privacy exemptions as broadly as the Supreme Court has interpreted FOIA's. Further, certain state FOIAs do not have privacy exemptions.

Until recently, public and court records were difficult to access. These documents were only available in local offices. The Internet revolution has now made it possible to access records from anywhere. Furthermore, private sector entities have consolidated these records into gigantic new databases.

DOE V. SHAKUR

164 F.R.D. 359 (S.D.N.Y. 1996)

CHIN, J. This diversity action raises the difficult question of whether the victim of a sexual assault may prosecute a civil suit for damages under a pseudonym. Plaintiff has brought this action charging that defendants Tupac A. Shakur and Charles L. Fuller sexually assaulted her on November 18, 1993. On December 1, 1994, a jury trial in Supreme Court, New York County, found Shakur and Fuller guilty of sexual abuse and not guilty of sodomy, attempted sodomy and weapons violations. They were sentenced on February 7, 1995 and an appeal is pending.

This civil suit was filed approximately two weeks after Shakur and Fuller were sentenced. The complaint seeks $10 million in compensatory damages and $50 million in punitive damages. Before filing her complaint, plaintiff obtained an order *ex parte* from Judge Sprizzo, sitting as Part I judge, sealing the complaint and permitting plaintiff to file a substitute complaint using a pseudonym in place of her real name. Neither defendant filed a timely answer and thus the Clerk of the Court entered a default.

Shakur has moved to vacate the entry of default. In his motion papers, which have not yet been filed with the Clerk of the Court but which have been served on plaintiff, Shakur identifies plaintiff by her real name. Shakur justifies his use of plaintiff's name by noting that Judge Sprizzo's order allowing plaintiff to file her complaint using a pseudonym was signed after an *ex parte* appearance and merely sealed the complaint. That order did not provide that this entire proceeding was to be conducted under seal. In response, plaintiff claims that Judge Sprizzo's order requires all papers filed with the Court to use plaintiff's pseudonym. In the alternative, plaintiff requests that I issue such an order now.

As a threshold matter, it is plain from the face of Judge Sprizzo's order that he did not decide the issue now before me. Judge Sprizzo's order merely allowed plaintiff to file the *complaint* under seal. Judge Sprizzo did not order that all documents filed in this case be sealed. Nor did Judge Sprizzo hold that plaintiff could prosecute the entire lawsuit under a pseudonym. Nor do I believe that Judge Sprizzo, sitting as Part I judge on the basis of an *ex parte* application, intended to foreclose defendants from being heard on the issue.

Rule 10(a) of the Federal Rules of Civil Procedure provides that a complaint shall state the names of all the parties. The intention of this rule is to apprise parties of who their opponents are and to protect the public's legitimate interest in knowing the facts at issue in court proceedings. Nevertheless, in some circumstances a party may commence a suit using a fictitious name.

It is within a court's discretion to allow a plaintiff to proceed anonymously. *Doe v. Bell Atlantic Business Sys. Servs., Inc.,* 162 F.R.D. 418, 420 (D. Mass. 1995). In exercising its discretion, a court should consider certain factors in determining whether plaintiffs may proceed anonymously. These factors include (1) whether the plaintiff is challenging governmental activity; (2) whether the plaintiff would be required to disclose information of the utmost intimacy; (3) whether the plaintiff would be compelled to admit his or her intention to engage in illegal conduct, thereby risking criminal prosecution; (4) whether the plaintiff would risk suffering injury if identified; and (5) whether the party defending against a suit brought under a pseudonym would be prejudiced.

In considering these and other factors, a court must engage in a balancing process. As the Eleventh Circuit has held,

> The ultimate test for permitting a plaintiff to proceed anonymously is whether the plaintiff has a substantial privacy right which outweighs the "customary and constitutionally-embedded presumption of openness in judicial proceedings." It is the exceptional case in which a plaintiff may proceed under a fictitious name.

Frank, 951 F.2d at 323 (*citing Doe v. Stegall,* 653 F.2d 180, 186 (5th Cir. 1981)).

The present case is a difficult one. If the allegations of the complaint are true, plaintiff was the victim of a brutal sexual assault. Quite understandably, she does not want to be publicly identified and she has very legitimate privacy concerns. On balance, however, these concerns are outweighed by the following considerations.

First, plaintiff has chosen to bring this lawsuit. She has made serious charges and has put her credibility in issue. Fairness requires that she be prepared to stand behind her charges publicly.

Second, this is a civil suit for damages, where plaintiff is seeking to vindicate primarily her own interests. This is not a criminal case where rape shield laws might provide some anonymity to encourage victims to testify to vindicate the public's interest in enforcement of our laws. *See id.* (rape shield laws "apply to situations where the government chooses to prosecute a case, and offer[ ] anonymity to a victim who does not have a choice in or control over the prosecution"). Indeed, the public's interest in bringing defendants to justice for breaking the law — assuming that they did — is being vindicated in the criminal proceedings.

Third, Shakur has been publicly accused. If plaintiff were permitted to prosecute this case anonymously, Shakur would be placed at a serious disadvantage, for he would be required to defend himself publicly while plaintiff could make her accusations from behind a cloak of anonymity.

Finally, the public has a right of access to the courts. Indeed, "lawsuits are public events and the public has a legitimate interest in knowing the facts involved in them. Among those facts is the identity of the parties." . . .

Plaintiff argues that Shakur's notoriety will likely cause this case to attract significant media attention, and she contends that disclosure of her name will cause her to be "publicly humiliated and embarrassed." Such claims of public humiliation and embarrassment, however, are not sufficient grounds for allowing a plaintiff in a civil suit to proceed anonymously, as the cases cited above demonstrate. Moreover, plaintiff has conceded that the press has known her name for some time. Indeed, plaintiff makes it clear that the press has been aware of both her residence and her place of employment. Hence, her identity is not unknown.

Plaintiff's allegation that she has been subjected to death threats would provide a legitimate basis for allowing her to proceed anonymously. Plaintiff has not, however, provided any details, nor has she explained how or why the use of her real name in court papers would lead to harm, since those who presumably would have any animosity toward her already know her true identity. Thus, plaintiff simply has not shown that she is entitled to proceed under a pseudonym in this action.

It may be, as plaintiff suggests, that victims of sexual assault will be deterred from seeking relief through civil suits if they are not permitted to proceed under a pseudonym. That would be an unfortunate result. For the reasons discussed above, however, plaintiff and others like her must seek vindication of their rights publicly.

NOTES & QUESTIONS

1. ***Pseudonymous Litigation.*** *Doe v. Shakur* involved a party's request to proceed under a pseudonym. The court refused this request. The standard for allowing a party to proceed with a fictitious name gives significant room for judicial discretion. Consider *Doe v. Blue Cross & Blue Shield United of Wisconsin*, 112 F.3d 869 (7th Cir. 1997):

> The plaintiff is proceeding under a fictitious name because of fear that the litigation might result in the disclosure of his psychiatric records. The motion to proceed in this way was not opposed, and the district judge granted it without comment. The judge's action was entirely understandable given the absence of objection and the sensitivity of psychiatric records, but we would be remiss if we failed to point out that the privilege of suing or defending under a fictitious name should not be granted automatically even if the opposing party does not object. The use of fictitious names is disfavored, and the judge has an independent duty to determine whether exceptional circumstances justify such a departure from the normal method of proceeding in federal courts. *See United States v. Microsoft Corp.,* 56 F.3d 1448, 1463-64 (D.C. Cir. 1995) (per curiam), and cases cited there, and our recent dictum in *K.F.P. v. Dane County,* 110 F.3d 516, 518-19 (7th Cir. 1997). Rule 10(a) of the Federal Rules of Civil Procedure, in providing that the complaint shall give the names of all the parties to the suit (and our plaintiff's name is *not* "John Doe"), instantiates the principle that judicial proceedings, civil as well as criminal, are to be conducted in public. Identifying the parties to the proceeding is an important dimension of publicness. The people have a right to know who is using their courts.
>
> There are exceptions. Records or parts of records are sometimes sealed for good reasons, including the protection of state secrets, trade secrets, and informers; and fictitious names are allowed when necessary to protect the privacy of children, rape victims, and other particularly vulnerable parties or witnesses. But the fact that a case involves a medical issue is not a sufficient reason for allowing the use of a fictitious name, even though many people are

understandably secretive about their medical problems. "John Doe" suffers, or at least from 1989 to 1991 suffered, from a psychiatric disorder — obsessive-compulsive syndrome. This is a common enough disorder — some would say that most lawyers and judges suffer from it to a degree — and not such a badge of infamy or humiliation in the modern world that its presence should be an automatic ground for concealing the identity of a party to a federal suit. To make it such would be to propagate the view that mental illness is shameful. Should "John Doe"'s psychiatric records contain material that would be highly embarrassing to the average person yet somehow pertinent to this suit and so an appropriate part of the judicial record, the judge could require that this material be placed under seal.

Also consider *Doe No. 2 v. Kolko*, 242 F.R.D. 193 (2006). An adult plaintiff alleged that he was sexually abused as a child by a rabbi at a private Jewish school. The court allowed the plaintiff to proceed anonymously by looking to several factors, including: the public's strong interest in protecting sexual abuse victims; the opinion of the plaintiff's psychologist that the alleged abuse had caused the plaintiff severe psychological and emotional injuries; plaintiff's assertion that he feared retaliation and ostracism if his name was disclosed; a lack of showing that knowledge of plaintiff's identity was widespread; any additional prejudice to defendant's reputation due to pursuit of legal action under pseudonym was minimal due to two similar lawsuits against the rabbi by named plaintiffs; and, finally, a lack of showing that defendants' ability to conduct discovery or impeach plaintiff's credibility would be impaired by allowing plaintiff to proceed anonymously. On the final point, the court noted that defendants would need to make redactions and take measures not to disclose plaintiff's identity, but would otherwise not be hampered by plaintiff's mere anonymity in court papers. These restrictions could also be reconsidered before the case went to trial.

When is it appropriate for a judge to allow a party to proceed under a pseudonym? Does the test give too much discretion to judges to make this determination? If so, how would you draft a rule that limits judicial discretion in approaching this issue?

Lior Strahilevitz proposes that pseudonymity be used as a tool to have parties raise their grievances in the appropriate forums — either formally through litigation or informally via other dispute resolution mechanisms. Strahilevitz argues that pseudonymity should be granted in cases where we want parties to use litigation to resolve their disputes. The issue of whether a party can litigate pseudonymously should be resolved at the conclusion of the litigation rather than at the beginning:

> There is no reason why the issue of pseudonymity needs to be resolved at the outset of the litigation. A court is free to keep the identity of a party or both parties under seal until a final judgment is entered and all appeals are exhausted. It would be straightforward to unseal the parties' identities at that later date, via an amended opinion. At that point, a court can more reliably answer questions about whether the plaintiff raised novel legal issues, whether her injuries were serious enough to warrant judicial intervention, and whether

alternatives to litigation might have ameliorated the controversy more efficiently.[3]

As an alternative, Strahilevitz proposes that parties should be able to obtain pseudonymity if they prevail in the litigation. However, will the uncertainty associated with any determination of pseudonymity deter plaintiffs from pursuing their claims in court? Are there other benefits and costs of pseudonymous litigation for which Strahilevitz's theory does not account?

2. ***Protective Orders.*** Federal Rule of Civil Procedure 26(c) provides that judges may, "for good cause shown," issue protective orders where disclosure of information gleaned in discovery might cause a party "annoyance, embarrassment, oppression, or undue burden or expense." In other words, a protective order serves to place limits on the process of discovery. Most states have protective order provisions similar to the federal one. There is a presumption in favor of access to information through discovery, and the party seeking the protective order must overcome this presumption. Courts will issue a protective order when a party's interest in privacy outweighs the public interest in disclosure.[4] Although the standard for obtaining a protective order is easier to satisfy than the standard for proceeding under a pseudonym, the thumb on the scale is on the side of public access. Consider the "good cause shown" standard of Federal Rule of Civil Procedure 26(c). Does it grant too much discretion to a court in granting protective orders?

3. ***Personal Information in Court Records.*** Under some court practices, certain information is categorically excluded from court records. As Natalie Gomez-Velez notes:

> The list of data elements categorically excluded from case records varies from state to state, depending to some extent on the degree to which case records are being made available and the extent to which a particular state precludes public access to certain categories of cases and information. . . .
>
> To a great extent, the federal courts, New York, Indiana, and courts in other states that exclude whole classes of sensitive cases like matrimonial, adoption, juvenile, and family law cases from public access, have fewer problems to solve than courts that permit public access to these kinds of cases.[5]

2. THE FREEDOM OF INFORMATION ACT

Until the second half of the twentieth century, only a few states had created a statutory right of public access to government records. The federal government had no such statute until the passage in 1966 of the Freedom of Information Act (FOIA). President Lyndon Johnson, in signing FOIA into law, stated:

---

[3] Lior Jacob Strahilevitz, *Pseudonymous Litigation*, 77 U. Chi. L. Rev. 1239 (2010).

[4] For more information about court records, see Gregory M. Silverman, *Rise of the Machines: Justice Information Systems and the Question of Public Access to Court Records Over the Internet*, 79 Wash. L. Rev. 175 (2004).

[5] Natalie Gomez-Velez, *Internet Access to Court Records — Balancing Public Access and Privacy*, 51 Loy. L. Rev. 365, 434-35 (2005).

This legislation springs from one of our most essential principles: A democracy works best when the people have all the information that the security of the Nation permits. No one should be able to pull curtains of secrecy around decisions which can be revealed without injury to the public interest.[6]

Significant amendments to FOIA in 1974 strengthened the Act. *See* Pub. L. No. 93-502. Key provisions established administrative deadlines, reduced fees, imposed sanctions for arbitrary and capricious withholding of agency records, and provided for attorneys' fees and costs.

Right to Access. FOIA grants all persons the right to inspect and copy records and documents maintained by any federal agency, federal corporation, or federal department. Certain documents must be disclosed automatically — without anybody explicitly requesting them. FOIA requires disclosure in the Federal Register of descriptions of agency functions, procedures, rules, and policies. 5 U.S.C. § 552(a)(1). FOIA also requires that opinions, orders, administrative staff manuals, and other materials be automatically released into the public domain. § 552(a)(2).

To obtain a document under FOIA, a requester must invoke FOIA in the request and follow the "published rules stating the time, place, fees (if any), and procedures to be followed." § 552(a)(3)(A). The agency must make "reasonable efforts" to answer any request that "reasonably describe[s]" the information sought. §§ 552(a)(3)(A)-(C). A requester can submit a request by mail or through an online form. The agency receiving the request is required to respond to the request within 20 business days unless the agency requests extra time based on "unusual circumstances." § 552(a)(6)(A). A requester may ask for expedited processing upon a showing of "compelling need." § 552(a)(6)(E)(i)(I).

There is an administrative appeals process to challenge any agency denial of a request that an agency must detail in its denial letter. § 552(a)(6)(A). The requester has 20 business days to invoke the process. After exhausting any administrative appeals or if any agency fails to adhere to statutory time limits, a requester may also file a complaint against the agency in federal court. § 552(a)(4)(B).

Exemptions. FOIA contains nine enumerated exemptions to disclosure. Pursuant to § 552(b):

(b) This section does not apply to matters that are —

(1)(A) specifically authorized under criteria established by an Executive order to be kept secret in the interest of national defense or foreign policy and (B) are in fact properly classified pursuant to such Executive order;

(2) related solely to the internal personnel rules and practices of an agency;

(3) specifically exempted from disclosure by statute (other than section 552b of this title), provided that such statute (A) requires that the

---

[6] 2 *Public Papers of the Presidents of the United States: Lyndon B. Johnson* 699 (1967), quoted in H.R. Rep. 104-795 (104th Cong. 2d Sess.), at 8 (1996).

matters be withheld from the public in such a manner as to leave no discretion on the issue, or (B) establishes particular criteria for withholding or refers to particular types of matters to be withheld;

(4) trade secrets and commercial or financial information obtained from a person and privileged or confidential;

(5) inter-agency or intra-agency memorandums or letters which would not be available by law to a party other than an agency in litigation with the agency;

(6) personnel and medical files and similar files the disclosure of which would constitute a clearly unwarranted invasion of personal privacy;

(7) records or information compiled for law enforcement purposes, but only to the extent that the production of such law enforcement records or information (A) could reasonably be expected to interfere with enforcement proceedings, (B) would deprive a person of a right to a fair trial or an impartial adjudication, (C) could reasonably be expected to constitute an unwarranted invasion of personal privacy, (D) could reasonably be expected to disclose the identity of a confidential source, including a State, local, or foreign agency or authority or any private institution which furnished information on a confidential basis, and, in the case of a record or information compiled by a criminal law enforcement authority in the course of a criminal investigation or by an agency conducting a lawful national security intelligence investigation, information furnished by a confidential source, (E) would disclose techniques and procedures for law enforcement investigations or prosecutions, or would disclose guidelines for law enforcement investigations or prosecutions if such disclosure could reasonably be expected to risk circumvention of the law, or (F) could reasonably be expected to endanger the life or physical safety of any individual;

(8) contained in or related to examination, operating, or condition reports prepared by, on behalf of, or for the use of an agency responsible for the regulation or supervision of financial institutions; or

(9) geological and geophysical information and data, including maps, concerning wells.

Redaction. If a portion of a document that falls under an exemption can be redacted (blacked out), then the remainder of the document must be provided to the requester:

Any reasonably segregable portion of a record shall be provided to any person requesting such record after deletion of the portions which are exempt under this subsection. § 552(b).

The Privacy Exemptions. Two of the exemptions involve privacy concerns. Exemption (6) exempts from disclosure "personnel and medical files and similar files the disclosure of which would constitute a clearly unwarranted invasion of personal privacy." § 552(b)(6). Exemption (7)(C) exempts from disclosure "records or information compiled for law enforcement purposes . . . which could reasonably be expected to constitute an unwarranted invasion of personal privacy." § 552(b)(7)(C). Further, FOIA provides that "[t]o the extent required to prevent a clearly unwarranted invasion of personal privacy, an agency may delete identifying details when it makes available or publishes an opinion, statement of policy, interpretation, or staff manual or instruction." § 552(a)(2). Consider the textual differences between Exemptions (6) and 7(c). Which exemption is more protective of privacy interests?

The exemptions are permissive; that is, agencies are not required to apply the exemptions. Only the government agency can raise Exemptions 6 and 7(C). The individual to whom the information pertains has no right to litigate the issue if the agency does not choose to; nor does the individual have a right to be given notice that her personal information falls within a FOIA request.[7]

The Law Enforcement Exemption. Exemption § 552(b)(7) depends upon the agency demonstrating "that the files were generated during legitimate law enforcement activity." *Freeman v. United States Dep't of Justice,* 723 F. Supp. 1115 (D. Md. 1988). "Exemption 7(E) may not be used to withhold information regarding investigative techniques that are illegal or of questionable legality." *Wilkinson v. FBI,* 633 F. Supp. 336, 349-50 (C.D. Cal. 1986). However, even if people become "an object of investigation because their names were obtained from an unlawful search," FOIA does not "require that documents generated in the investigation . . . be turned over." *Becker v. Internal Revenue Service,* 34 F.2d 398 (7th Cir. 1994).

State FOIAs. Since the passage of FOIA in 1966, a number of states have enacted their own open records statutes. Today, every state has an open records law, most of which are patterned after the federal FOIA. These statutes are often referred to as "freedom of information," "open access," "right to know," or "sunshine" laws.

UNITED STATES DEPARTMENT OF JUSTICE V. REPORTERS COMMITTEE FOR FREEDOM OF THE PRESS
489 U.S. 749 (1989)

STEVENS, J. The Federal Bureau of Investigation (FBI) has accumulated and maintains criminal identification records, sometimes referred to as "rap sheets," on over 24 million persons. The question presented by this case is whether the disclosure of the contents of such a file to a third party "could reasonably be expected to constitute an unwarranted invasion of personal privacy" within the meaning of the Freedom of Information Act (FOIA), 5 U.S.C. § 552(b)(7)(C). . . .

In 1924 Congress appropriated funds to enable the Department of Justice (Department) to establish a program to collect and preserve fingerprints and other criminal identification records. That statute authorized the Department to exchange such information with "officials of States, cities and other institutions." Six years later Congress created the FBI's identification division, and gave it

---

[7] For more background about FOIA's privacy exemptions, see James T. O'Reilly, *Expanding the Purpose of Federal Records Access: New Private Entitlement or New Threat to Privacy?*, 50 Admin. L. Rev. 371 (1998); Patricia M. Wald, *The Freedom of Information Act: A Short Case Study in the Perils and Paybacks of Legislating Democratic Values,* 33 Emory L.J. 649 (1984); Anthony T. Kronman, *The Privacy Exemption to the Freedom of Information Act,* 9 J. Legal Stud. 727 (1980).

responsibility for "acquiring, collecting, classifying, and preserving criminal identification and other crime records and the exchanging of said criminal identification records with the duly authorized officials of governmental agencies, of States, cities, and penal institutions." Rap sheets compiled pursuant to such authority contain certain descriptive information, such as date of birth and physical characteristics, as well as a history of arrests, charges, convictions, and incarcerations of the subject. Normally a rap sheet is preserved until its subject attains age 80. . . .

. . . As a matter of executive policy, the Department has generally treated rap sheets as confidential and, with certain exceptions, has restricted their use to governmental purposes. . . .

Although much rapsheet information is a matter of public record, the availability and dissemination of the actual rap sheet to the public is limited. Arrests, indictments, convictions, and sentences are public events that are usually documented in court records. In addition, if a person's entire criminal history transpired in a single jurisdiction, all of the contents of his or her rap sheet may be available upon request in that jurisdiction. That possibility, however, is present in only three States. All of the other 47 States place substantial restrictions on the availability of criminal-history summaries even though individual events in those summaries are matters of public record. Moreover, even in Florida, Wisconsin, and Oklahoma, the publicly available summaries may not include information about out-of-state arrests or convictions. . . .

The statute known as FOIA is actually a part of the Administrative Procedure Act (APA). Section 3 of the APA as enacted in 1946 gave agencies broad discretion concerning the publication of governmental records. In 1966 Congress amended that section to implement "'a general philosophy of full agency disclosure.'" . . . The amendment . . . requires every agency "upon any request for records which . . . reasonably describes such records" to make such records "promptly available to any person." If an agency improperly withholds any documents, the district court has jurisdiction to order their production. Unlike the review of other agency action that must be upheld if supported by substantial evidence and not arbitrary or capricious, FOIA expressly places the burden "on the agency to sustain its action" and directs the district courts to "determine the matter de novo."

Congress exempted nine categories of documents from FOIA's broad disclosure requirements. Three of those exemptions are arguably relevant to this case. Exemption 3 applies to documents that are specifically exempted from disclosure by another statute. § 552(b)(3). Exemption 6 protects "personnel and medical files and similar files the disclosure of which would constitute a clearly unwarranted invasion of personal privacy." § 552(b)(6). Exemption 7(C) excludes records or information compiled for law enforcement purposes, "but only to the extent that the production of such [materials] . . . could reasonably be expected to constitute an unwarranted invasion of personal privacy." § 552(b)(7)(C). . . .

This case arises out of requests made by a CBS news correspondent and the Reporters Committee for Freedom of the Press (respondents) for information concerning the criminal records of four members of the Medico family. The Pennsylvania Crime Commission had identified the family's company, Medico

Industries, as a legitimate business dominated by organized crime figures. Moreover, the company allegedly had obtained a number of defense contracts as a result of an improper arrangement with a corrupt Congressman.

FOIA requests sought disclosure of any arrests, indictments, acquittals, convictions, and sentences of any of the four Medicos. Although the FBI originally denied the requests, it provided the requested data concerning three of the Medicos after their deaths. In their complaint in the District Court, respondents sought the rap sheet for the fourth, Charles Medico (Medico), insofar as it contained "matters of public record." . . .

Exemption 7(C) requires us to balance the privacy interest in maintaining, as the Government puts it, the "practical obscurity" of the rap sheets against the public interest in their release.

The preliminary question is whether Medico's interest in the nondisclosure of any rap sheet the FBI might have on him is the sort of "personal privacy" interest that Congress intended Exemption 7(C) to protect.[8] . . . Because events summarized in a rap sheet have been previously disclosed to the public, respondents contend that Medico's privacy interest in avoiding disclosure of a federal compilation of these events approaches zero. We reject respondents' cramped notion of personal privacy.

To begin with, both the common law and the literal understandings of privacy encompass the individual's control of information concerning his or her person. In an organized society, there are few facts that are not at one time or another divulged to another. Thus the extent of the protection accorded a privacy right at common law rested in part on the degree of dissemination of the allegedly private fact and the extent to which the passage of time rendered it private. According to Webster's initial definition, information may be classified as "private" if it is "intended for or restricted to the use of a particular person or group or class of persons: not freely available to the public." Recognition of this attribute of a privacy interest supports the distinction, in terms of personal privacy, between scattered disclosure of the bits of information contained in a rap sheet and revelation of the rap sheet as a whole. The very fact that federal funds have been spent to prepare, index, and maintain these criminal-history files demonstrates that the individual items of information in the summaries would not otherwise be "freely available" either to the officials who have access to the underlying files or to the general public. Indeed, if the summaries were "freely available," there would be no reason to invoke the FOIA to obtain access to the information they contain. Granted, in many contexts the fact that information is not freely available is no reason to exempt that information from a statute generally requiring its dissemination. But the issue here is whether the compilation of otherwise hard-to-obtain information alters the privacy interest implicated by disclosure of that information. Plainly there is a vast difference between the public records that might be found after a diligent search of courthouse files, county

---

[8] The question of the statutory meaning of privacy under the FOIA is, of course, not the same as the question whether a tort action might lie for invasion of privacy or the question whether an individual's interest in privacy is protected by the Constitution. *See, e.g., Cox Broadcasting Corp. v. Cohn*, 420 U.S. 469 (1975) (Constitution prohibits State from penalizing publication of name of deceased rape victim obtained from public records). . . .

archives, and local police stations throughout the country and a computerized summary located in a single clearinghouse of information. . . .

We have also recognized the privacy interest in keeping personal facts away from the public eye. In *Whalen v. Roe*, 429 U.S. 589 (1977), we held that "the State of New York may record, in a centralized computer file, the names and addresses of all persons who have obtained, pursuant to a doctor's prescription, certain drugs for which there is both a lawful and an unlawful market." In holding only that the Federal Constitution does not prohibit such a compilation, we recognized that such a centralized computer file posed a "threat to privacy":

> We are not unaware of the threat to privacy implicit in the accumulation of vast amounts of personal information in computerized data banks or other massive government files. The collection of taxes, the distribution of welfare and social security benefits, the supervision of public health, the direction of our Armed Forces, and the enforcement of the criminal laws all require the orderly preservation of great quantities of information, much of which is personal in character and potentially embarrassing or harmful if disclosed. The right to collect and use such data for public purposes is typically accompanied by a concomitant statutory or regulatory duty to avoid unwarranted disclosures. Recognizing that in some circumstances that duty arguably has its roots in the Constitution, nevertheless New York's statutory scheme, and its implementing administrative procedures, evidence a proper concern with, and protection of, the individual's interest in privacy.

In sum, the fact that "an event is not wholly 'private' does not mean that an individual has no interest in limiting disclosure or dissemination of the information." The privacy interest in a rap sheet is substantial. The substantial character of that interest is affected by the fact that in today's society the computer can accumulate and store information that would otherwise have surely been forgotten long before a person attains age 80, when the FBI's rap sheets are discarded. . . .

Exemption 7(C), by its terms, permits an agency to withhold a document only when revelation "could reasonably be expected to constitute an unwarranted invasion of personal privacy." We must next address what factors might warrant an invasion of the interest described [above].

Our previous decisions establish that whether an invasion of privacy is warranted cannot turn on the purposes for which the request for information is made. Except for cases in which the objection to disclosure is based on a claim of privilege and the person requesting disclosure is the party protected by the privilege, the identity of the requesting party has no bearing on the merits of his or her FOIA request. . . . As we have repeatedly stated, Congress "clearly intended" the FOIA "to give any member of the public as much right to disclosure as one with a special interest [in a particular document]."

Thus whether disclosure of a private document under Exemption 7(C) is warranted must turn on the nature of the requested document and its relationship to "the basic purpose of the Freedom of Information Act 'to open agency action to the light of public scrutiny,'" rather than on the particular purpose for which the document is being requested. In our leading case on FOIA, we declared that the Act was designed to create a broad right of access to "official information." *EPA v. Mink,* 410 U.S. 73, 80, (1973). In his dissent in that case, Justice Douglas characterized the philosophy of the statute by quoting this comment by Henry Steele Commager:

> "'The generation that made the nation thought secrecy in government one of the instruments of Old World tyranny and committed itself to the principle that a democracy cannot function unless the people are permitted to know *what their government is up to.*'" (quoting from *The New York Review of Books*, Oct. 5, 1972, p. 7) (emphasis added).

. . . This basic policy of "'full agency disclosure unless information is exempted under clearly delineated statutory language,'" indeed focuses on the citizens' right to be informed about "what their government is up to." Official information that sheds light on an agency's performance of its statutory duties falls squarely within that statutory purpose. That purpose, however, is not fostered by disclosure of information about private citizens that is accumulated in various governmental files but that reveals little or nothing about an agency's own conduct. In this case — and presumably in the typical case in which one private citizen is seeking information about another — the requester does not intend to discover anything about the conduct of the agency that has possession of the requested records. Indeed, response to this request would not shed any light on the conduct of any Government agency or official. . . .

Respondents argue that there is a two-fold public interest in learning about Medico's past arrests or convictions: He allegedly had improper dealings with a corrupt Congressman, and he is an officer of a corporation with defense contracts. But if Medico has, in fact, been arrested or convicted of certain crimes, that information would neither aggravate nor mitigate his allegedly improper relationship with the Congressman; more specifically, it would tell us nothing directly about the character of the Congressman's behavior. Nor would it tell us anything about the conduct of the Department of Defense (DOD) in awarding one or more contracts to the Medico Company. . . . Conceivably Medico's rap sheet would provide details to include in a news story, but, in itself, this is not the kind of public interest for which Congress enacted the FOIA. In other words, although there is undoubtedly some public interest in anyone's criminal history, especially if the history is in some way related to the subject's dealing with a public official or agency, the FOIA's central purpose is to ensure that the Government's activities be opened to the sharp eye of public scrutiny, not that information about private citizens that happens to be in the warehouse of the Government be so disclosed. . . .

. . . The privacy interest in maintaining the practical obscurity of rap-sheet information will always be high. When the subject of such a rap sheet is a private citizen and when the information is in the Government's control as a compilation, rather than as a record of "what the Government is up to," the privacy interest protected by Exemption 7(C) is in fact at its apex while the FOIA-based public interest in disclosure is at its nadir. Such a disparity on the scales of justice holds for a class of cases without regard to individual circumstances; the standard virtues of bright-line rules are thus present, and the difficulties attendant to ad hoc adjudication may be avoided. Accordingly, we hold as a categorical matter that a third party's request for law enforcement records or information about a private citizen can reasonably be expected to invade that citizen's privacy, and that when the request seeks no "official information" about a Government agency, but merely records that the Government happens to be storing, the invasion of privacy is "unwarranted." . . .

BLACKMUN J., joined by BRENNAN, J. concurring in the judgment: I concur in the result the Court reaches in this case, but I cannot follow the route the Court takes to reach that result. In other words, the Court's use of "categorical balancing" under Exemption 7(C), I think, is not basically sound. Such a bright-line rule obviously has its appeal, but I wonder whether it would not run aground on occasion, such as in a situation where a rap sheet discloses a congressional candidate's conviction of tax fraud five years before. Surely, the FBI's disclosure of that information could not "reasonably be expected" to constitute an invasion of personal privacy, much less an unwarranted invasion, inasmuch as the candidate relinquished any interest in preventing the dissemination of this information when he chose to run for Congress. In short, I do not believe that Exemption 7(C)'s language and its legislative history, or the case law, support interpreting that provision as exempting all rap-sheet information from the FOIA's disclosure requirements.

NOTES & QUESTIONS

1. *The Privacy Interest and "Practical Obscurity."* Many courts, including the Supreme Court in other contexts, have held that once information is exposed to the public, it can no longer be considered private. In *Reporters Committee,* however, the Court recognizes a privacy interest in the rap sheets despite the fact that they are compiled from information in public records. The Court concludes that "there is a vast difference between the public records that might be found after a diligent search of courthouse files, county archives, and local police stations throughout the country and a computerized summary located in a single clearinghouse of information." Is the Court stretching privacy too far by claiming it can be violated by altering "practical obscurity"?

   Daniel Solove argues in support of the Court's conception of privacy: "Privacy involves an expectation of a certain degree of accessibility of information. . . . Privacy can be violated by altering levels of accessibility, by taking obscure facts and making them widely accessible."[9] Is such a conception of privacy feasible?

2. *The Interest in Public Access.* The Court also denies access to the rap sheets because "this [FOIA] request would not shed any light on the conduct of any Government agency or official." What kind of use of government records is being sought in *Reporters Committee*? Does this use contribute to the public interest? Does the use comport with the purpose of FOIA?

3. *The Court's Rationale Beyond the FOIA Context.* In a footnote, the Court stated that the reasoning of this case is confined to the FOIA context. As a

---

[9] Daniel J. Solove, *Access and Aggregation: Public Records, Privacy, and the Constitution,* 86 Minn. L. Rev. 1137, 1176-78 (2002).

hypothetical case, imagine that there were no privacy exemptions to FOIA, and the FBI disclosed the rap sheets. The Medicos sue, claiming a violation of their constitutional right to information privacy. What would the result likely be? Can the Court coherently claim that people have a privacy interest in their rap sheet information under FOIA but not in the context of the constitutional right to information privacy?

4. ***Exemption 6.*** The *Reporters Committee* case concerned Exemption 7(C). Exemption 6 provides that FOIA's disclosure provisions do not apply to *"personnel and medical files and similar files* the disclosure of which would constitute a clearly unwarranted invasion of personal privacy." § 552(b)(6) (emphasis added). Does Exemption 6 only apply to "personnel and medical files"? What does "similar files" mean?

The Supreme Court answered these questions in *United States Dep't of State v. Washington Post Co.*, 456 U.S. 595 (1982). There, the *Washington Post* requested documents indicating whether two Iranian nationals were holding valid United States passports. According to the Department of State, the two individuals were prominent figures in Iran's Revolutionary Government; several Iranian revolutionary leaders had been strongly criticized in Iran for ties to the United States; and the two could be subject to violence if United States ties, such as passports, were disclosed. The *Washington Post* contended that the language of Exemption 6 simply did not cover these types of documents. The Court disagreed:

> The language of Exemption 6 sheds little light on what Congress meant by "similar files." Fortunately, the legislative history is somewhat more illuminating. The House and Senate Reports, although not defining the phrase "similar files," suggest that Congress' primary purpose in enacting Exemption 6 was to protect individuals from the injury and embarrassment that can result from the unnecessary disclosure of personal information. . . .
>
> . . . Congress' statements that it was creating a "general exemption" for information contained in "great quantities of files," suggest that the phrase "similar files" was to have a broad, rather than a narrow, meaning. This impression is confirmed by the frequent characterization of the "clearly unwarranted invasion of personal privacy" language as a "limitation" which holds Exemption 6 "within bounds." Had the words "similar files" been intended to be only a narrow addition to "personnel and medical files," there would seem to be no reason for concern about the exemption's being "held within bounds," and there surely would be clear suggestions in the legislative history that such a narrow meaning was intended. We have found none.
>
> A proper analysis of the exemption must also take into account the fact that "personnel and medical files," the two benchmarks for measuring the term "similar files," are likely to contain much information about a particular individual that is not intimate. Information such as place of birth, date of birth, date of marriage, employment history, and comparable data is not normally regarded as highly personal, and yet respondent does not disagree that such information, if contained in a "personnel" or "medical" file, would be exempt from any disclosure that would constitute a clearly unwarranted invasion of personal privacy. . . .
>
> . . . "[T]he protection of an individual's right of privacy" which Congress sought to achieve by preventing "the disclosure of [information] which might

harm the individual," surely was not intended to turn upon the label of the file which contains the damaging information. . . .

In sum, we do not think that Congress meant to limit Exemption 6 to a narrow class of files containing only a discrete kind of personal information. Rather, "[t]he exemption [was] intended to cover detailed Government records on an individual which can be identified as applying to that individual." When disclosure of information which applies to a particular individual is sought from Government records, courts must determine whether release of the information would constitute a clearly unwarranted invasion of that person's privacy. . . .

5. **Definition of Agency.** FOIA requires only that "agencies" respond to requesters. Congress is not a federal agency and is therefore not subject to the Act. Nor is the President or his advisors, whose "sole function" is to "advise and assist" the President. For similar reasons, the National Security Council is not an agency. *Armstrong v. Executive Office of the President*, 90 F.3d 556 (D.C. Cir. 1996).

NATIONAL ARCHIVES AND RECORDS ADMINISTRATION V. FAVISH

541 U.S. 157 (2004)

KENNEDY, J. This is case requires us to interpret the Freedom of Information Act (FOIA), 5 U.S.C. § 552. FOIA does not apply if the requested data fall within one or more exemptions. Exemption 7(C) excuses from disclosure "records or information compiled for law enforcement purposes" if their production "could reasonably be expected to constitute an unwarranted invasion of personal privacy." § 552(b)(7)(C).

In *Department of Justice v. Reporters Comm. for Freedom of Press,* 489 U.S. 749 (1989), we considered the scope of Exemption 7(C) and held that release of the document at issue would be a prohibited invasion of the personal privacy of the person to whom the document referred. The principal document involved was the criminal record, or rap sheet, of the person who himself objected to the disclosure. Here, the information pertains to an official investigation into the circumstances surrounding an apparent suicide. The initial question is whether the exemption extends to the decedent's family when the family objects to the release of photographs showing the condition of the body at the scene of death. If we find the decedent's family does have a personal privacy interest recognized by the statute, we must then consider whether that privacy claim is outweighed by the public interest in disclosure.

Vincent Foster, Jr., deputy counsel to President Clinton, was found dead in Fort Marcy Park, located just outside Washington, D.C. The United States Park Police conducted the initial investigation and took color photographs of the death scene, including 10 pictures of Foster's body. The investigation concluded that Foster committed suicide by shooting himself with a revolver. Subsequent investigations by the Federal Bureau of Investigation, committees of the Senate and the House of Representatives, and independent counsels Robert Fiske and Kenneth Starr reached the same conclusion. Despite the unanimous finding of these five investigations, a citizen interested in the matter, Allan Favish, remained skeptical. Favish is now a respondent in this proceeding. . . .

It is common ground among the parties that the death-scene photographs in [the Office of Independent Counsel's, or] OIC's possession are "records or information compiled for law enforcement purposes" as that phrase is used in Exemption 7(C). This leads to the question whether disclosure of the four photographs "could reasonably be expected to constitute an unwarranted invasion of personal privacy." Favish contends the family has no personal privacy interest covered by Exemption 7(C). . . .

We disagree. The right to personal privacy is not confined, as Favish argues, to the "right to control information about oneself.". . . To say that the concept of personal privacy must "encompass" the individual's control of information about himself does not mean it cannot encompass other personal privacy interests as well. *Reporters Committee* had no occasion to consider whether individuals whose personal data are not contained in the requested materials also have a recognized privacy interest under Exemption 7(C). *Reporters Committee* explained, however, that the concept of personal privacy under Exemption 7(C) is not some limited or "cramped notion" of that idea. 489 U.S. at 763. Records or information are not to be released under the Act if disclosure "could reasonably be expected to constitute an unwarranted invasion of personal privacy." 5 U.S.C. § 552(b)(7). This provision is in marked contrast to the language in Exemption 6, pertaining to "personnel and medical files," where withholding is required only if disclosure "would constitute a clearly unwarranted invasion of personal privacy." § 552(b)(6). The adverb "clearly," found in Exemption 6, is not used in Exemption 7(C). In addition, "whereas Exemption 6 refers to disclosures that 'would constitute' an invasion of privacy, Exemption 7(C) encompasses any disclosure that 'could reasonably be expected to constitute' such an invasion." *Reporters Committee*, 489 U.S., at 756. . . .

Law enforcement documents obtained by Government investigators often contain information about persons interviewed as witnesses or initial suspects but whose link to the official inquiry may be the result of mere happenstance. There is special reason, therefore, to give protection to this intimate personal data, to which the public does not have a general right of access in the ordinary course. In this class of cases where the subject of the documents "is a private citizen," "the privacy interest . . . is at its apex."

. . . Foster's relatives . . . invoke their own right and interest to personal privacy. They seek to be shielded by the exemption to secure their own refuge from a sensation-seeking culture for their own peace of mind and tranquility, not for the sake of the deceased. . . .

. . . We have little difficulty . . . in finding in our case law and traditions the right of family members to direct and control disposition of the body of the deceased and to limit attempts to exploit pictures of the deceased family member's remains for public purposes.

Burial rites or their counterparts have been respected in almost all civilizations from time immemorial. See generally 26 *Encyclopaedia Britannica* 851 (15th ed. 1985) (noting that "[t]he ritual burial of the dead" has been practiced "from the very dawn of human culture and . . . in most parts of the world"); 5 *Encyclopedia of Religion* 450 (1987) ("[F]uneral rites . . . are the conscious cultural forms of one of our most ancient, universal, and unconscious impulses"). They are a sign of the respect a society shows for the deceased and for the surviving family members. The power of Sophocles' story in Antigone maintains its hold to this day because of the universal acceptance of the heroine's right to insist on respect for the body of her brother. *See* Antigone of Sophocles, 8 *Harvard Classics: Nine Greek Dramas* 255 (C. Eliot ed. 1909). The outrage at seeing the bodies of American soldiers mutilated and dragged through the streets is but a modern instance of the same understanding of the interests decent people have for those whom they have lost. Family members have a personal stake in honoring and mourning their dead and objecting to unwarranted public exploitation that, by intruding upon their own grief, tends to degrade the rites and respect they seek to accord to the deceased person who was once their own.

In addition this well-established cultural tradition acknowledging a family's control over the body and death images of the deceased has long been recognized at common law. Indeed, this right to privacy has much deeper roots in the common law than the rap sheets held to be protected from disclosure in *Reporters Committee.* An early decision by the New York Court of Appeals is typical:

> It is the right of privacy of the living which it is sought to enforce here. That right may in some cases be itself violated by improperly interfering with the character or memory of a deceased relative, but it is the right of the living, and not that of the dead, which is recognized. A privilege may be given the surviving relatives of a deceased person to protect his memory, but the privilege exists for the benefit of the living, to protect their feelings, and to prevent a violation of their own rights in the character and memory of the deceased. *Schuyler v. Curtis,* 147 N.Y. 434 (1895). . . .

We can assume Congress legislated against this background of law, scholarship, and history when it enacted FOIA and when it amended Exemption 7(C) to extend its terms. . . .

We have observed that the statutory privacy right protected by Exemption 7(C) goes beyond the common law and the Constitution. See *Reporters Committee,* 489 U.S., at 762, n.13 (contrasting the scope of the privacy protection under FOIA with the analogous protection under the common law and the Constitution). . . . It would be anomalous to hold in the instant case that the statute provides even less protection than does the common law.

The statutory scheme must be understood, moreover, in light of the consequences that would follow were we to adopt Favish's position. As a general rule, withholding information under FOIA cannot be predicated on the identity of the requester. See *Reporters Committee, supra,* at 771. We are advised by the Government that child molesters, rapists, murderers, and other violent criminals often make FOIA requests for autopsies, photographs, and records of their deceased victims. Our holding ensures that the privacy interests of surviving family members would allow the Government to deny these gruesome requests in appropriate cases. We find it inconceivable that Congress could have intended a definition of "personal privacy" so narrow that it would allow convicted felons to obtain these materials without limitations at the expense of surviving family members' personal privacy.

. . . [W]e hold that FOIA recognizes surviving family members' right to personal privacy with respect to their close relative's death-scene images. Our holding is consistent with the unanimous view of the Courts of Appeals and other lower courts that have addressed the question. . . .

Our ruling that the personal privacy protected by Exemption 7(C) extends to family members who object to the disclosure of graphic details surrounding their relative's death does not end the case. Although this privacy interest is within the terms of the exemption, the statute directs nondisclosure only where the information "could reasonably be expected to constitute an unwarranted invasion" of the family's personal privacy. The term "unwarranted" requires us to balance the family's privacy interest against the public interest in disclosure. . . .

FOIA is often explained as a means for citizens to know "what the Government is up to." This phrase should not be dismissed as a convenient formalism. It defines a structural necessity in a real democracy. The statement confirms that, as a general rule, when documents are within FOIA's disclosure provisions, citizens should not be required to explain why they seek the information. A person requesting the information needs no preconceived idea of the uses the data might serve. The information belongs to citizens to do with as they choose. Furthermore, as we have noted, the disclosure does not depend on the identity of the requester. As a general rule, if the information is subject to disclosure, it belongs to all.

When disclosure touches upon certain areas defined in the exemptions, however, the statute recognizes limitations that compete with the general interest in disclosure, and that, in appropriate cases, can overcome it. In the case of Exemption 7(C), the statute requires us to protect, in the proper degree, the personal privacy of citizens against the uncontrolled release of information compiled through the power of the state. The statutory direction that the information not be released if the invasion of personal privacy could reasonably be expected to be unwarranted requires the courts to balance the competing interests in privacy and disclosure. To effect this balance and to give practical meaning to the exemption, the usual rule that the citizen need not offer a reason for requesting the information must be inapplicable.

Where the privacy concerns addressed by Exemption 7(C) are present, the exemption requires the person requesting the information to establish a sufficient reason for the disclosure. First, the citizen must show that the public interest sought to be advanced is a significant one, an interest more specific than having the information for its own sake. Second, the citizen must show the information is likely to advance that interest. Otherwise, the invasion of privacy is unwarranted.

. . . In the case of photographic images and other data pertaining to an individual who died under mysterious circumstances, the justification most likely to satisfy Exemption 7(C)'s public interest requirement is that the information is necessary to show the investigative agency or other responsible officials acted negligently or otherwise improperly in the performance of their duties. . . .

We hold that, where there is a privacy interest protected by Exemption 7(C) and the public interest being asserted is to show that responsible officials acted negligently or otherwise improperly in the performance of their duties, the requester must establish more than a bare suspicion in order to obtain disclosure.

Rather, the requester must produce evidence that would warrant a belief by a reasonable person that the alleged Government impropriety might have occurred. In *Department of State v. Ray,* 502 U.S. 164 (1991), we held there is a presumption of legitimacy accorded to the Government's official conduct. The presumption perhaps is less a rule of evidence than a general working principle. However the rule is characterized, where the presumption is applicable, clear evidence is usually required to displace it. . . . Given FOIA's prodisclosure purpose, however, the less stringent standard we adopt today is more faithful to the statutory scheme. Only when the FOIA requester has produced evidence sufficient to satisfy this standard will there exist a counterweight on the FOIA scale for the court to balance against the cognizable privacy interests in the requested records. . . . It would be quite extraordinary to say we must ignore the fact that five different inquiries into the Foster matter reached the same conclusion. . . . Favish has not produced any evidence that would warrant a belief by a reasonable person that the alleged Government impropriety might have occurred to put the balance into play. . . .

NOTES & QUESTIONS

1. ***Characterizing the Public Interest in Disclosure.*** Consider Lior Strahilevitz:

> [T]he *Favish* Court's conclusion that the autopsy photographs were made less newsworthy as a result of the previous investigations is unsatisfying. Favish requested the photographs because he believed that there was a conspiracy to cover up Foster's murder, and the Court noted that multiple separate investigations had debunked that murder theory. But suppose Favish had sought the release of the photographs to suggest different wrongdoing by the government—not its murder of a high government official, but its wasteful expenditure of resources on multiple investigations of what was obviously an open-and-shut case of suicide. Under the reasoning of the *Favish* opinion, a person seeking the disclosure of the autopsy photographs under such a theory ought to be able to prevail under the Court's balancing approach. If we take the reasoning of the opinion seriously, you or I should be able to obtain the Foster autopsy photos if we just recharacterize the government's misconduct.[10]

Had the Court characterized the public interest in disclosure as Strahilevitz suggests, should that tip the balance to disclosure? Conspiracy theorists might question the validity of any government investigation, no matter how thorough or convincing. Should the Court make qualitative judgments about when curiosity about a matter is legitimate as opposed to unjustified or paranoid?

2. ***The Implications of Post-Mortem Privacy.*** Apart from the narrow context of FOIA, how will post-mortem privacy interests function in other areas of law? Are there other privacy interests that should or should not exist after one's death?

3. ***Corporations and Exemption 7(c).*** In *Federal Communications Commission v. AT&T,* 131 S. Ct. 1177 (2011), the Supreme Court, in a unanimous opinion,

---

[10] Lior Jacob Strahilevitz, *Reunifying Privacy Law,* 98 Cal. L. Rev. 2007, 2024 (2010).

found that corporations did not have "personal privacy" for the purposes of FOIA's Exemption 7(c). As a result, corporations cannot claim that this exemption shields corporate documents from release. Part of the Court's argument was linguistic; part turned on the specific context of FOIA. Regarding FOIA's language, the Court declared, "in ordinary usage, a noun and its adjective form may have meanings as disparate as any two unrelated words." Thus, while FOIA defined "person" to include corporations, this definition was not dispositive for the word "personal" in Exemption 7(c). The Court noted that, "we often use the word 'personal' to mean precisely the *opposite* of business-related: We speak of personal expenses and business expenses, personal life and work life, personal opinion and a company's view."

As far as FOIA was concerned, the Court noted that Exemption 7(c) used language that traced Exemption 6, which concerns "personnel and medical files" as well any "similar" file and not the language in Exemption 4, which pertains to "trade secrets and commercial or financial information." Exemption 4 clearly pertains to corporations, and Congress did not follow the language that "plainly covered" corporations.[11]

4. *National Security and Critical Infrastructure Information.* Post 9/11, the federal government has taken a new restrictive approach to FOIA. First, as part of the Homeland Security Act, the Bush Administration oversaw enactment of a new exemption to FOIA in the Critical Infrastructure Information Act of 2002 (CIIA). The CIIA exempts from FOIA disclosure any information that a private party voluntarily provides to the Department of Homeland Security (DHS) if the information relates to the security of vital infrastructure.

"Critical infrastructure information" is "information not customarily in the public domain and related to the security of critical infrastructure or protected [computer] systems." 6 U.S.C. § 131. In a report prepared for Rep. Henry A. Waxman (Waxman Report), the Minority Staff, Special Investigation Division, Committee on Government Reform, stated:

> Communications from the private sector to government agencies are routinely released under FOIA (apart from confidential business information). This is an important check against capture of governmental agencies by special interests. But under the critical infrastructure information exemption even routine communications can be withheld from disclosure.[12]

In an op-ed in the *Washington Post*, Mark Tapscott of the Heritage Foundation asked for clarification of "what constitutes vulnerabilities" of infrastructure in order to prevent the CIIA from being "manipulated by clever

---

[11] In closing his opinion for the Court in *Federal Communications v. AT&T*, Chief Justice Roberts concludes with a great closing quip: "The protection in FOIA against disclosure of law enforcement information on the ground that it would constitute an unwarranted invasion of personal privacy does not extend to corporation. We trust that AT&T will not take it personally."

[12] U.S. House of Representatives, *Committee on Government Reform, Minority Staff, Special Investigations Division, Secrecy in the Bush Administration* 9 (Sept. 14, 2004).

corporate and government operators to hide endless varieties of potentially embarrassing and/or criminal information from public view."

The Waxman Report also noted that CIIA exempts from FOIA all information that is marked critical infrastructure information. As a consequence, the CIIA may not permit the redaction that is otherwise normally carried out under FOIA. As the Report states, "None of the information in a submission marked as critical infrastructure information is likely to be disclosed, even when portions of the information do not themselves constitute critical infrastructure information."[13]

Second, beyond the enactment of CIIA, a further move toward a restrictive approach to FOIA was made through the Executive Branch's introduction of the concept of "sensitive but unclassified information." On March 19, 2002, Andrew Card, White House Chief of Staff, issued an important memorandum that instructs federal agencies to deny disclosure of "sensitive but unclassified information."[14] The Card Memorandum urged agencies to safeguard records regarding weapons of mass destruction and "other information that could be misused to harm the security of our Nation and the safety of our people." The Card Memorandum urged agencies to apply FOIA's Exemption 2 or Exemption 4 in withholding such records. Please reread these exemptions reprinted earlier in this section. How do you think they are being extended to apply to "sensitive but unclassified information"?

Consider the following argument by Mary-Rose Papandrea:

> FOIA is riddled with large, undefined exceptions. When information arguably involves national security, courts are too timid to force the executive branch to provide a thorough explanation for continued secrecy. . . .
>
> The "right to know" has encountered additional and more disturbing problems since the terrorist attacks of September 11. Not only has the courts' tendency to defer to the Executive's national security risk assessment become exaggerated, but courts now appear overtly hostile to the very existence of a right of access during a time of crisis. Instead, they suggest that an enforceable right to know is unnecessary because the political process is adequate to force government disclosure.[15]

David Vladek has offered a similar negative view of FOIA.[16] He faults the slow process of "drafting and submitting FOIA requests and waiting for the agency's response." Vladek also argues that it has been "subject to political manipulation by administrations that are intent on limiting public access to government held information" and undercut by judicial interpretation of its provisions.

---

[13] *Id.* at 10.

[14] Andrew H. Card, Jr., Assistant to the President and Chief of Staff, *Memorandum for the Heads of Executive Departments and Agencies; Subject: Action to Safeguard Information Regarding Weapons of Mass Destruction and Other Sensitive Documents Relating to Homeland Security* (Mar. 19, 2002), at http://www.usdoj.gov/oip/foiapost/2002foiapost10.htm.

[15] Mary-Rose Papandrea, *Under Attack: The Public's Right to Know and the War on Terror*, 25 B.C. Third World L.J. 35, 79-80 (2005).

[16] David C. Vladek, *Information Access: Surveying the Current Legal Landscape of Federal Right-to-Know Laws*, 86 Tex. L. Rev. 1787 (2008).

Finally, Seth Kreimer provides a positive analysis of the impact of FOIA.[17] In his judgment, it "must be understood as functioning within a broader ecology of transparency." Moreover, "[a]s part of that system, it has done underappreciated service in the past half-decade and partakes of virtues of resiliency and efficacy that should be acknowledged and preserved." Kreimer identifies a number of successful FOIA actions that have taken place in the context of the "Global War on Terror." He finds, "It has been predominately the availability of well-financed NGOs, combined with the possibility of assistance from the private bar, that has made FOIA a force to be reckoned with in this arena."

How should open government be reconciled with national security concerns?

5. ***Desired and Undesired Privacy.*** In *Associated Press v. Department of Defense*, 554 F.3d 274 (2d Cir. 2009), the Associated Press requested from the Department of Defense (DOD) identifying information about detainees alleging abuse at the Guantanamo Bay detention facility as well as identifying information about the detainee's family members. The DOD asserted that disclosure would violate the detainees' privacy interests and that the FOIA privacy Exemptions 6 and 7(C) applied. Regarding the detainees, the court held that Exemption 7(C) barred disclosure of their identities. The court first concluded that the detainees had a right to privacy:

> We first consider the detainees who allegedly have been abused by military personnel or other detainees. Certainly they have an interest in both keeping the personal facts of their abuse from the public eye and in avoiding disclosure of their identities in order to prevent embarrassment. As victims of abuse, they are entitled to some protection of personal information that would be revealed if their names were associated with the incidents of abuse. The disclosure of their names could certainly subject them to embarrassment and humiliation. . .
>   .

Turning to the public interest in the disclosure of the detainee identities, the court held:

> AP's first argument appears to suggest that the alleged government impropriety in handling these allegations of various abuses may be tied to the nationalities or religions of the detainees involved. In essence, AP implies that DOD may have responded differently to allegations of abuse depending on the nationalities or religions of the abused detainees. Without that underlying assumption, knowing the detainees' nationalities or religions would not serve the public interest because it would shed no light on what the government is up to. AP's argument in this regard is squarely foreclosed by *Favish,* in which the Supreme Court held:

---

[17] Seth F. Kreimer, *The Freedom of Information Act and the Ecology of Transparency*, 10 U. Pa. J. Const. L. 101 (2008).

[W]here there is a privacy interest protected by Exemption 7(C) and the public interest being asserted is to show that responsible officials acted negligently or otherwise improperly in the performance of their duties, the requester must establish more than a bare suspicion in order to obtain disclosure. Rather, the requester must produce evidence that would warrant a belief by a reasonable person that the alleged Government impropriety might have occurred.

. . . AP has produced no evidence that DOD responded differently to allegations of abuse depending on the nationalities or religions of the detainees involved. Because there is no evidence of government impropriety in that regard, we cannot find that the public interest would be furthered based on a rationale grounded in disclosure of an individual's religion or nationality.

AP's second argument, that the names and identifying information would allow the public to track these detainees' treatment in other aspects of DOD actions, including transfer and release decisions, deserves more attention. . . . [I]f the identities of the detainees involved in the abuse allegations were known, it might be possible to see whether those allegations affected the government's decision to transfer, release, or continue to detain them. Although under this rationale the public interest might be further served, the speculative nature of the result is insufficient to outweigh the detainees' privacy interest in nondisclosure.

AP's third argument, that the information will allow the public to seek out the detainees' side of the story, calls upon a "derivative use" theory. That theory posits that the public interest can be read more broadly to include the ability to use redacted information to obtain additional as yet undiscovered information outside the government files. . . . [T]he Supreme Court [has] reasoned that "[m]ere speculation about hypothetical public benefits cannot outweigh a demonstrably significant invasion of privacy."

Lior Strahilevitz argues that some of the detainees would have welcomed the disclosure of their identities. In a footnote to the opinion, the court reasoned that it was not analyzing the privacy interests of the prisoners categorically or individually, but Strahilevitz counters that the logical implication of the court's ruling was to choose the categorical approach. As Strahilevitz explains:

A categorical approach necessarily would result in complete disclosure or non-disclosure, whereas an individuated approach — constructive partition of the list of detainees — necessarily would result in partial disclosure. By ruling in favor of complete non-disclosure, the court had to embrace a categorical basis for deciding the issue, its protests to the contrary notwithstanding.

As the court saw it, the fact that some detainees wanted their identities disclosed was irrelevant. Moreover, under the court's holding, and its categorical-though-ostensibly-not-categorical approach, the objections of one privacy seeking detainee would trump the desires of scores of other publicity-seeking detainees.[18]

Should the court have examined the desires of the detainees individually? Was the government using "privacy" as a tool to make it harder for the press to investigate the alleged abuse?

---

[18] Lior Jacob Strahilevitz, *Information and Exclusion* (2011).

3. CONSTITUTIONAL REQUIREMENTS OF PUBLIC ACCESS

The Common Law Right to Access Public Records. As the Supreme Court held in *Nixon v. Warner Communications, Inc.,* 435 U.S. 589 (1978): "It is clear that the courts of this country recognize a general right to inspect and copy public records and documents, including judicial records and documents." The right to access public records is justified by "the citizen's desire to keep a watchful eye on the workings of public agencies, and in a newspaper publisher's intention to publish information concerning the operation of government." Thus, under the common law, the Court concluded, there is a general right to access public records and court records. The Court noted that the right to access is not absolute.

Court Records. Courts have a long tradition of allowing open access to court records. In *Nixon v. Warner Communications, Inc.,* 435 U.S. 589 (1978), the Supreme Court stated: "Every court has supervisory power over its own records and files, and access has been denied where court files might have become a vehicle for improper purposes." Access to court records is "best left to the sound discretion of the trial court, a discretion to be exercised in light of the relevant facts and circumstances of the particular case." In *Seattle Times Co. v. Rhinehart,* 467 U.S. 20, 33 (1984), the Court held that "pretrial depositions and interrogatories are not public components of a civil trial. Such proceedings were not open to the public at common law, and, in general, they are conducted in private as a matter of modern practice."

The First Amendment Right to Access. The First Amendment requires that certain judicial proceedings be open to the public. In *Globe Newspaper v. Superior Court,* 457 U.S. 596 (1982), the Supreme Court articulated a test to determine whether the First Amendment requires public access to a proceeding: (1) whether the proceeding "historically has been open to the press and general public" and (2) whether access "plays a particularly significant role in the functioning of the judicial process and the government as a whole." The court in *Globe* concluded that the First Amendment requires public access to criminal trials, and the government can deny access only if "the denial is necessitated by a compelling governmental interest and is narrowly tailored to serve that interest." According to the Court, the First Amendment right to access extends to voir dire in a capital murder trial. *Press-Enterprise Co. v. Superior Court* ("*Press-Enterprise I*"), 464 U.S. 501 (1984). It also extends to pre-trial proceedings. *Press-Enterprise Co. v. Superior Court* ("*Press-Enterprise II*"), 478 U.S. 1 (1986).

Privacy of Litigants and Jurors. A court can permit plaintiffs to proceed under a pseudonym, although "it is the exceptional case in which a plaintiff may proceed under a fictitious name." *Doe v. Frank,* 951 F.2d 320, 323 (11th Cir. 1992). Courts can also provide for jurors to remain anonymous. Is such anonymity appropriate?

Consider the case of Juror Number Four. In a well-publicized criminal trial against Tyco International executive L. Dennis Kozlowski, during the jury's 12 days of deliberating, newspapers identified Juror Number Four by name because she appeared to gesture an "O.K." sign to the defense table. The articles stated that she lived on the Upper East Side of Manhattan and that the apartment building staff found her to be cold and stingy. The newspapers reported that friends described her as opinionated and stubborn. Extensive coverage of the juror continued. As a result of the coverage, the juror received a threatening note, and the judge declared a mistrial. On the one hand, the media was reporting on possible juror misconduct. On the other hand, the media coverage interfered with the trial. Suppose on retrial, the judge were to order that the identities of all the jurors shall not be disclosed. Would such an order be constitutional?

Consider *United States v. Blagojevich*, 612 F.3d 558 (7th Cir. 2010), where the court held that jurors' names in the highly publicized case of former Illinois Governor Rod Blagojevich must be released to the public. The court based its decision on the common law right to access public records. Dissenting from a denial to rehear the case en banc, Judge Posner wrote:

> Whatever the situation in England, there is no *general* federal common-law right of public access to information relating to federal litigation. Such a right would create a presumption of access to jury deliberations, appellate judicial deliberations, depositions whether or not used at trial, terms of settlement, grand jury proceedings, judges' discussions with their law clerks, and so on. No one thinks that the media can demand access to any of these phases of the litigation process, or that if they do the judge must hold a hearing to consider their demand; why should the media have a presumptive right to the names of the jurors before a trial ends?
>
> The panel cites *Nixon v. Warner Communications, Inc.*, 435 U.S. 589 (1978), which created a "presumption . . . in favor of public access to judicial records" to enable the public to "monitor the functioning of our courts, thereby insuring quality, honesty and respect for our legal system." But jurors' *names*—as distinct from evidence, materials attached to dispositive motions, and judicial rulings—are not judicial records. "The courts have not extended [the common law right of access] beyond materials on which a court relies in determining the litigants' substantive rights." *Anderson v. Cryovac, Inc.*, 805 F.2d 1, 13 (1st Cir. 1986).

In some jurisdictions, the court records of divorce cases are made public. Is such a policy advisable? This issue is best illustrated by what happened in June 2004, when at the request of the *Chicago Tribune* and a TV station, a judge ordered the unsealing of the divorce records of Illinois Republican Senate candidate Jack Ryan and his wife, actress Jeri Ryan. Both Jack and Jeri had vigorously objected to the unsealing of the records, which they contended would cause harm to them as well as their nine-year-old child. The records revealed Jeri's accusations that Jack had taken her to sex clubs and asked her to perform sex acts that made her uncomfortable. A few days after the release of the records, Jack abandoned his quest for the Senate. Was the release of the records appropriate in this case? Jack was a political candidate, and Jeri was a well-known actress. Does their public figure status affect the analysis? Should it? To what extent should the effect of the release of the information on a couple's children be a factor in the analysis?

LOS ANGELES POLICE DEPARTMENT V. UNITED REPORTING PUBLISHING CORP.

528 U.S. 32 (1999)

REHNQUIST, C.J. California Government Code § 6254(f)(3) places two conditions on public access to arrestees' addresses — that the person requesting an address declare that the request is being made for one of five prescribed purposes, and that the requestor also declare that the address will not be used directly or indirectly to sell a product or service.

The District Court permanently enjoined enforcement of the statute, and the Court of Appeals affirmed, holding that the statute was facially invalid because it unduly burdens commercial speech. We hold that the statutory section in question was not subject to a "facial" challenge.

Petitioner, the Los Angeles Police Department, maintains records relating to arrestees. Respondent, United Reporting Publishing Corporation, is a private publishing service that provides the names and addresses of recently arrested individuals to its customers, who include attorneys, insurance companies, drug and alcohol counselors, and driving schools.

Before July 1, 1996, respondent received arrestees' names and addresses under the old version of § 6254, which generally required state and local law enforcement agencies to make public the name, address, and occupation of every individual arrested by the agency. Cal. Govt. Code § 6254(f). Effective July 1, 1996, the state legislature amended § 6254(f) to limit the public's access to arrestees' and victims' current addresses. The amended statute provides that state and local law enforcement agencies shall make public:

> [T]he current address of every individual arrested by the agency and the current address of the victim of a crime, where the requester declares under penalty of perjury that the request is made for a scholarly, journalistic, political, or governmental purpose, or that the request is made for investigation purposes by a licensed private investigator . . . except that the address of the victim of [certain crimes] shall remain confidential. Address information obtained pursuant to this paragraph shall not be used directly or indirectly to sell a product or service to any individual or group of individuals, and the requester shall execute a declaration to that effect under penalty of perjury. Cal. Govt. Code § 6254(f)(3).

Sections 6254(f)(1) and (2) require that state and local law enforcement agencies make public, inter alia, the name, occupation, and physical description, including date of birth, of every individual arrested by the agency, as well as the circumstances of the arrest. Thus, amended § 6254(f) limits access only to the arrestees' addresses.

Before the effective date of the amendment, respondent sought declaratory and injunctive relief pursuant to 42 U.S.C. § 1983 to hold the amendment unconstitutional under the First and Fourteenth Amendments to the United States Constitution. On the effective date of the statute, petitioner and other law enforcement agencies denied respondent access to the address information because, according to respondent, "[respondent's] employees could not sign section 6254(f)(3) declarations." Respondent did not allege, and nothing in the record before this Court indicates, that it ever "declar[ed] under penalty of perjury" that it was requesting information for one of the prescribed purposes and that it would not use the address information to "directly or indirectly . . . sell a product or service," as would have been required by the statute. *See* § 6254(f)(3).

Respondent then amended its complaint and sought a temporary restraining order. The District Court issued a temporary restraining order, and, a few days later, issued a preliminary injunction. Respondent then filed a motion for summary judgment, which was granted. In granting the motion, the District Court construed respondent's claim as presenting a facial challenge to amended § 6254(f). The court held that the statute was facially invalid under the First Amendment.

The Court of Appeals affirmed the District Court's facial invalidation. The court concluded that the statute restricted commercial speech, and, as such, was entitled to "'a limited measure of protection, commensurate with its subordinate position in the scale of First Amendment values.'" The court applied the test set out in *Central Hudson Gas & Elec. Corp. v. Public Serv. Comm'n of N.Y.*, 447 U.S. 557 (1980), and found that the asserted governmental interest in protecting arrestees' privacy was substantial. But, the court held that "the numerous exceptions to § 6254(f)(3) for journalistic, scholarly, political, governmental, and investigative purposes render the statute unconstitutional under the First Amendment." The court noted that "[h]aving one's name, crime, and address printed in the local paper is a far greater affront to privacy than receiving a letter from an attorney, substance abuse counselor, or driving school eager to help one overcome his present difficulties (for a fee, naturally)," and thus that the exceptions "undermine and counteract" the asserted governmental interest in preserving arrestees' privacy. Thus, the Court of Appeals affirmed the District Court's grant of summary judgment in favor of respondent and upheld the injunction against enforcement of § 6254(f)(3). We granted certiorari.

We hold that respondent was not, under our cases, entitled to prevail on a "facial attack" on § 6254(f)(3).

Respondent's primary argument in the District Court and the Court of Appeals was that § 6254(f)(3) was invalid on its face, and respondent maintains that position here. But we believe that our cases hold otherwise.

The traditional rule is that "a person to whom a statute may constitutionally be applied may not challenge that statute on the ground that it may conceivably be applied unconstitutionally to others in situations not before the Court."

Prototypical exceptions to this traditional rule are First Amendment challenges to statutes based on First Amendment overbreadth. "At least when statutes regulate or proscribe speech . . . the transcendent value to all society of constitutionally protected expression is deemed to justify allowing 'attacks on overly broad statutes with no requirement that the person making the attack demonstrate that his own conduct could not be regulated by a statute drawn with the requisite narrow specificity.'" "This is deemed necessary because persons whose expression is constitutionally protected may well refrain from exercising their right for fear of criminal sanctions provided by a statute susceptible of application to protected expression." . . .

Even though the challenge be based on the First Amendment, the overbreadth doctrine is not casually employed. "Because of the wide-reaching effects of striking down a statute on its face at the request of one whose own conduct may be punished despite the First Amendment, we have recognized that the overbreadth doctrine is 'strong medicine' and have employed it with hesitation, and then 'only as a last resort.'" . . .

The Court of Appeals held that § 6254(f)(3) was facially invalid under the First Amendment. Petitioner contends that the section in question is not an abridgment of anyone's right to engage in speech, be it commercial or otherwise, but simply a law regulating access to information in the hands of the police department.

We believe that, at least for purposes of facial invalidation, petitioner's view is correct. This is not a case in which the government is prohibiting a speaker from conveying information that the speaker already possesses. The California statute in question merely requires that if respondent wishes to obtain the addresses of arrestees it must qualify under the statute to do so. Respondent did not attempt to qualify and was therefore denied access to the addresses. For purposes of assessing the propriety of a facial invalidation, what we have before us is nothing more than a governmental denial of access to information in its possession. California could decide not to give out arrestee information at all without violating the First Amendment.

To the extent that respondent's "facial challenge" seeks to rely on the effect of the statute on parties not before the Court — its potential customers, for example — its claim does not fit within the case law allowing courts to entertain facial challenges. No threat of prosecution, for example, or cutoff of funds hangs over their heads. They may seek access under the statute on their own just as respondent did, without incurring any burden other than the prospect that their request will be denied. Resort to a facial challenge here is not warranted because there is "no possibility that protected speech will be muted." . . .

GINSBURG, J. joined by O'CONNOR, SOUTER, and BREYER, JJ. concurring. I join the Court's opinion, which recognizes that California Government Code § 6254(f)(3) is properly analyzed as a restriction on access to government information, not as a restriction on protected speech. That is sufficient reason to reverse the Ninth Circuit's judgment.

As the Court observes, the statute at issue does not restrict speakers from conveying information they already possess. Anyone who comes upon arrestee address information in the public domain is free to use that information as she sees fit. It is true, as Justice Scalia suggests, that the information could be provided to and published by journalists, and § 6254(f)(3) would indeed be a speech restriction if it then prohibited people from using that published information to speak to or about arrestees. But the statute contains no such prohibition. Once address information is in the public domain, the statute does not restrict its use in any way.

California could, as the Court notes, constitutionally decide not to give out arrestee address information at all. It does not appear that the selective disclosure of address information that California has chosen instead impermissibly burdens speech. To be sure, the provision of address information is a kind of subsidy to people who wish to speak to or about arrestees, and once a State decides to make such a benefit available to the public, there are no doubt limits to its freedom to decide how that benefit will be distributed. California could not, for example, release address information only to those whose political views were in line with the party in power. But if the award of the subsidy is not based on an illegitimate criterion such as viewpoint, California is free to support some speech without supporting other speech.

Throughout its argument, respondent assumes that § 6254(f)(3)'s regime of selective disclosure burdens speech in the sense of reducing the total flow of information. Whether that is correct is far from clear and depends on the point of comparison. If California were to publish the names and addresses of arrestees for everyone to use freely, it would indeed be easier to speak to and about arrestees than it is under the present system. But if States were required to choose between keeping proprietary information to themselves and making it available without limits, States might well choose the former option. In that event, disallowing selective disclosure would lead not to more speech overall but to more secrecy and less speech. As noted above, this consideration could not justify limited disclosures that discriminated on the basis of viewpoint or some other proscribed criterion. But it does suggest that society's interest in the free flow of information might argue for upholding laws like the one at issue in this case rather than imposing an all-or-nothing regime under which "nothing" could be a State's easiest response.

STEVENS, J. joined by KENNEDY, J. dissenting. . . . To determine whether the Amendment is valid as applied to respondent, it is similarly not necessary to invoke the overbreadth doctrine. That doctrine is only relevant if the challenger needs to rely on the possibility of invalid applications to third parties. In this case, it is the application of the Amendment to respondent itself that is at issue. Nor, in my opinion, is it necessary to do the four-step *Central Hudson* dance, because I agree with the majority that the Amendment is really a restriction on access to government information rather than a direct restriction on protected speech. For this reason, the majority is surely correct in observing that "California could decide not to give out arrestee information at all without violating the First Amendment." Moreover, I think it equally clear that California could release the information on a selective basis to a limited group of users who have a special, and legitimate, need for the information.

A different, and more difficult, question is presented when the State makes information generally available, but denies access to a small disfavored class. In this case, the State is making the information available to scholars, news media, politicians, and others, while denying access to a narrow category of persons solely because they intend to use the information for a constitutionally protected purpose. As Justice Ginsburg points out, if the State identified the disfavored persons based on their viewpoint, or political affiliation, for example, the discrimination would clearly be invalid.

What the State did here, in my opinion, is comparable to that obviously unconstitutional discrimination. In this case, the denial of access is based on the fact that respondent plans to publish the information to others who, in turn, intend to use it for a commercial speech purpose that the State finds objectionable. Respondent's proposed publication of the information is indisputably lawful — petitioner concedes that if respondent independently acquires the data, the First Amendment protects its right to communicate it to others. Similarly, the First Amendment supports the third parties' use of it for commercial speech purposes. Thus, because the State's discrimination is based on its desire to prevent the information from being used for constitutionally protected purposes, I think it must assume the burden of justifying its conduct.

The only justification advanced by the State is an asserted interest in protecting the privacy of victims and arrestees. Although that interest would explain a total ban on access, or a statute narrowly limiting access, it is insufficient when the data can be published in the news media and obtained by private investigators or others who meet the Amendment's vague criteria. . . . By allowing such widespread access to the information, the State has eviscerated any rational basis for believing that the Amendment will truly protect the privacy of these persons.

That the State might simply withhold the information from all persons does not insulate its actions from constitutional scrutiny. For even though government may withhold a particular benefit entirely, it "may not deny a benefit to a person on a basis that infringes his constitutionally protected interests — especially his interest in freedom of speech." A contrary view would impermissibly allow the government to "'produce a result which [it] could not command directly.'" It is perfectly clear that California could not directly censor the use of this information or the resulting speech. It follows, I believe, that the State's discriminatory ban on access to information — in an attempt to prohibit persons from exercising their constitutional rights to publish it in a truthful and accurate manner — is equally invalid.

Accordingly, I respectfully dissent.

NOTES & QUESTIONS

1. *Reconciling Privacy and Transparency.* Consider the following argument by Daniel Solove:

> How can the tension between transparency and privacy be reconciled? Must access to public records be sacrificed at the altar of privacy? Or must privacy be compromised as the price for a government disinfected by sunlight?
>
> It is my thesis that both transparency and privacy can be balanced through limitations on the access and use of personal information in public records. . . . We can make information accessible for certain purposes only. When government discloses information, it can limit how it discloses that information by preventing it from being amassed by companies for commercial purposes, to be sold to others, or to be combined with other information and sold back to the government. . . .
>
> . . . [B]y making access conditional on accepting certain responsibilities when using data — such as using it for specific purposes, not disclosing it to

others, and so on, certain functions of transparency can be preserved at the same time privacy is protected.[19]

However, does this approach, as Justice Stevens contends in his dissent, impermissibly single out certain types of speakers? What if the California statute limited disclosure of the information to anybody who would use a form of mass communication or widespread publicity to disclose that information? In other words, what if it excluded journalists and the media from access?

2. **Florida Star v. B.J.F.** In *Florida Star v. B.J.F.,* 491 U.S. 524 (1989), the Supreme Court struck down a Florida law that prohibited the press from publishing a rape victim's name that inadvertently appeared in a public record. The Court held: "[W]here a newspaper publishes truthful information which it has lawfully obtained, punishment may lawfully be imposed, if at all, only when narrowly tailored to a state interest of the highest order." Daniel Solove notes:

> Governments can make a public record available *on the condition that* certain information is not disclosed or used in a certain manner. However, governments cannot establish post-access restrictions on the disclosure or use of information that is publicly available. Once the information is made available to the public, the *Florida Star* cases prohibit a state from restricting use.[20]

Is *United Reporting* consistent with *Florida Star*? Suppose Florida passed a law that in order for the press to access its police reports about sexual assaults, journalists would have to agree to not disclose rape victims' names from the reports. Would this law be constitutional?

3. *Disclosure of Social Security Numbers in Public Records.* In *Ostergren v. Cuccinelli,,* 615 F.3d 263 (4th Cir. 2010), privacy activist Betty Ostergren obtained real estate records for politicians and disclosed them online with unredacted Social Security numbers (SSNs) to demonstrate the problems of the availability of SSNs in public records. Ostergren challenged a law criminalizing the intentional communication of another person's SSN to the general public. The court held:

> Virginia argues that the unredacted SSNs on Ostergren's website should not be protected under the First Amendment because they facilitate identity theft and are no essential part of any exposition of ideas. Although these observations might be true under certain circumstances, we cannot agree with Virginia's argument here. The unredacted SSNs on Virginia land records that Ostergren has posted online are integral to her message. Indeed, they *are* her message. Displaying them proves Virginia's failure to safeguard private information and powerfully demonstrates why Virginia citizens should be concerned. . . . Thus, although we do not foreclose the possibility that communicating SSNs might be found unprotected in other situations, we conclude, on these facts,

---

[19] Daniel J. Solove, *Access and Aggregation: Public Records, Privacy, and the Constitution,* 86 Minn. L. Rev. 1137 (2002).

[20] *Id.*

that the First Amendment does reach Ostergren's publication of Virginia land records containing unredacted SSNs.

After concluding that Ostergren's posting of the records was protected by the First Amendment, the Fourth Circuit proceeded to analyze whether the state law survived strict scrutiny. The court concluded that protecting people's SSNs from disclosure was an interest of the highest order. The law, however, was not narrowly tailored to achieve this goal:

> We cannot conclude that prohibiting Ostergren from posting public records online would be narrowly tailored to protecting individual privacy when Virginia currently makes those same records available through secure remote access without having redacted SSNs. The record reflects that 15 clerks of court have not finished redacting SSNs from their land records, which are nonetheless available online. Under *Cox Broadcasting* and its progeny, the First Amendment does not allow Virginia to punish Ostergren for posting its land records online without redacting SSNs when numerous clerks are doing precisely that. *Cf. Florida Star,* 491 U.S. at 535 ("[W]here the government has made certain information publicly available, it is highly anomalous to sanction persons other than the source of its release."). Virginia could curtail SSNs' public disclosure much more narrowly by directing clerks not to make land records available through secure remote access until after SSNs have been redacted.

4. CONSTITUTIONAL LIMITATIONS ON PUBLIC ACCESS

(a) Public Records

Like the federal FOIA, many states have privacy exemptions in their freedom of information laws. But not all states balance privacy and transparency equally. Are there limitations on what information governments can release to the public? Consider the cases below:

KALLSTROM V. CITY OF COLUMBUS [*KALLSTROM I*]
136 F.3d 1055 (6th Cir. 1998)

MOORE, J. . . . The three plaintiffs, Melissa Kallstrom, Thomas Coelho, and Gary Householder, are undercover officers employed by the Columbus Police Department. All three were actively involved in the drug conspiracy investigation of the Short North Posse, a violent gang in the Short North area of Columbus, Ohio. In *United States v. Derrick Russell, et al.,* No. CR-2 95-044, (S.D. Ohio), forty-one members of the Short North Posse were prosecuted on drug conspiracy charges. Plaintiffs testified at the trial of eight of the *Russell* defendants.

During the *Russell* criminal trial, defense counsel requested and obtained from the City Kallstrom's personnel and pre-employment file, which defense counsel appears to have passed on to several of the *Russell* defendants. Officers Coelho and Householder also suspect that copies of their personnel and pre-employment files were obtained by the same defense attorney. The City additionally released Officer Coelho's file to the Police Officers for Equal Rights organization following its request for the file in the fall of 1995 in order to investigate possible discriminatory hiring and promotion practices by the City. The officers' personnel files include the officers' addresses and phone numbers; the names, addresses, and phone numbers of immediate family members; the names and addresses of personal references; the officers' banking institutions and corresponding account information, including account balances; their social security numbers; responses to questions regarding their personal life asked during the course of polygraph examinations; and copies of their drivers' licenses, including pictures and home addresses. The district court found that in light of the Short North Posse's propensity for violence and intimidation, the release of these personnel files created a serious risk to the personal safety of the plaintiffs and those relatives named in the files.

Prior to accepting employment with the City, the plaintiffs were assured by the City that personal information contained in their files would be held in strict confidence. Despite its earlier promise of confidentiality, however, the City believed Ohio's Public Records Act, Ohio Rev. Code Ann. § 149.43, required it to release the officers' files upon request from any member of the public.

The officers brought suit under 42 U.S.C. §§ 1983 and 1988 against the City, claiming that the dissemination of personal information contained in their personnel files violates their right to privacy as guaranteed by the Due Process Clause of the Fourteenth Amendment. . . . In addition to seeking compensatory damages, the officers request an injunction restraining the City from releasing personal information regarding them. . . .

Section 1983 imposes civil liability on a person acting under color of state law who deprives another of the "rights, privileges, or immunities secured by the Constitution and laws." 42 U.S.C. § 1983. The threshold question, therefore, is whether the City deprived the officers of a right "secured by the Constitution and laws." . . .

In *Whalen v. Roe,* the Supreme Court declared that the constitutional right to privacy grounded in the Fourteenth Amendment respects not only individual autonomy in intimate matters, but also the individual's interest in avoiding divulgence of highly personal information. The court echoed these sentiments in *Nixon v. Administrator of Gen. Servs.,* 433 U.S. 425 (1977), acknowledging that "[o]ne element of privacy has been characterized as 'the individual interest in avoiding disclosure of personal matters.'" Although *Whalen* and *Nixon* appear to recognize constitutional protection for an individual's interest in safeguarding personal matters from public view, in both cases the Court found that public interests outweighed the individuals' privacy interests.

This circuit has read *Whalen* and *Nixon* narrowly, and will only balance an individual's interest in nondisclosure of informational privacy against the public's interest in and need for the invasion of privacy where the individual privacy interest is of constitutional dimension. . . . We hold that the officers' privacy interests do indeed implicate a fundamental liberty interest, specifically their interest in preserving their lives and the lives of their family members, as well as preserving their personal security and bodily integrity. . . .

In light of the Short North Posse's propensity for violence and intimidation, the district court found that the City's release of the plaintiffs-appellants' addresses, phone numbers, and driver's licenses to defense counsel in the *Russell* case, as well as their family members' names, addresses, and phone numbers, created a serious risk to the personal safety of the plaintiffs and those relatives named in the files. We see no reason to doubt that where disclosure of this personal information may fall into the hands of persons likely to seek revenge upon the officers for their involvement in the *Russell* case, the City created a very real threat to the officers' and their family members' personal security and bodily integrity, and possibly their lives. Accordingly, we hold that the City's disclosure of this private information about the officers to defense counsel in the *Russell* case rises to constitutional dimensions, thereby requiring us . . . to balance the officers' interests against those of the City.

The district court found that although there was no indication that the Police Officers for Equal Rights organization posed any threat to the officers and their family members, disclosure even to that group of the officers' phone numbers, addresses, and driver's licenses, and their family members' names, addresses and phone numbers "increases the risk that the information will fall into the wrong hands." . . . Since the district court did not indicate its view of the severity of risks inherent in disclosure of information to the Police Officers for Equal Rights organization, we remand to the district court for reconsideration in light of this opinion of issues regarding disclosure of personal information to that organization.

In finding that the City's release of private information concerning the officers to defense counsel in the *Russell* case rises to constitutional dimensions by threatening the personal security and bodily integrity of the officers and their family members, we do not mean to imply that every governmental act which intrudes upon or threatens to intrude upon an individual's body invokes the Fourteenth Amendment. But where the release of private information places an individual at substantial risk of serious bodily harm, possibly even death, from a perceived likely threat, the "magnitude of the liberty deprivation . . . strips the very essence of personhood." . . .

Where state action infringes upon a fundamental right, such action will be upheld under the substantive due process component of the Fourteenth Amendment only where the governmental action furthers a compelling state interest, and is narrowly drawn to further that state interest. Having found that the officers have a fundamental constitutional interest in preventing the release of personal information contained in their personnel files where such disclosure creates a substantial risk of serious bodily harm, we must now turn to whether the City's actions narrowly serve a compelling public purpose.

The City believed Ohio's Public Records Act, Ohio Rev. Code Ann. § 149.43, required it to disclose the personal information contained in the officers' records. Ohio's Public Records Act requires the state to make available all public records to any person, unless the record falls within one of the statute's enumerated exceptions. The State mandates release of state agency records in order to shed light on the state government's performance, thereby enabling Ohio citizens to understand better the operations of their government. In the judicial setting, courts have long recognized the importance of permitting public access to judicial records so that citizens may understand and exercise oversight over the judicial system. We see no reason why public access to government agency records should be considered any less important. For purposes of this case, we assume that the interests served by allowing public access to agency records rises to the level of a compelling state interest. Nevertheless, the City's release to the criminal defense counsel of the officers' and their family members' home addresses and phone numbers, as well as the family members' names and the officers' driver's licenses, does not narrowly serve these interests.

While there may be situations in which the release of the this type of personal information might further the public's understanding of the workings of its law enforcement agencies, the facts as presented here do not support such a conclusion. The City released the information at issue to defense counsel in a large drug conspiracy case, who is asserted to have passed the information onto his clients. We simply fail to see how placing this personal information into the hands of the *Russell* defendants in any way increases public understanding of the City's law enforcement agency where the *Russell* defendants and their attorney make no claim that they sought this personal information about the officers in order to shed light on the internal workings of the Columbus Police Department. We therefore cannot conclude that the disclosure narrowly serves the state's interest in ensuring accountable governance. Accordingly, we hold that the City's actions in automatically disclosing this information to any member of the public requesting it are not narrowly tailored to serve this important public interest. . . .

Injunctive relief involving matters subject to state regulation may be no broader than necessary to remedy the constitutional violation. . . . [T]he constitutional violation arises when the release of private information about the officers places their personal security, and that of their families, at substantial risk without narrowly serving a compelling state interest. Thus, the officers are entitled to notice and an opportunity to be heard prior to the release of private information contained in their personnel files only where the disclosure of the requested information could potentially threaten the officers' and their families' personal security. As discussed above, release of the officers' addresses, phone numbers, and driver's licenses, as well as their family members' names, addresses, and phone numbers, is likely to result in a substantial risk to their personal security. On remand, the district court should consider whether release of other private information contained in the officers' personnel files also poses the same risk. . . . [B]ecause the City's decision to continue releasing this information potentially places the officers and their families at risk of irreparable harm that cannot be adequately remedied at law, the officers are entitled to injunctive relief prohibiting the City from again disclosing this information without first providing the officers meaningful notice.

KALLSTROM V. CITY OF COLUMBUS [*KALLSTROM II*]

165 F. Supp. 2d 686 (S.D. Ohio 2001)

SMITH, J. In this case, the Court is being asked to limit the freedom of the press by preventing the news media from obtaining public information contained in the city's personnel files. City police officers fear its publication may endanger themselves and their families.

To deny members of the press access to public information solely because they have the ability to disseminate it would silence the most important critics of governmental activity. This not only violates the Constitution, but eliminates the very protections the Founders envisioned a free press would provide.

Plaintiffs, who are three Columbus police officers ("Officers"), filed suit against defendant City of Columbus ("City") seeking compensatory damages under 42 U.S.C. §§ 1983 and 1988 and an injunction to prevent further dissemination of their personal information. Specifically, plaintiffs claim defendant violated their rights to privacy as guaranteed by the Due Process Clause of the Fourteenth Amendment by making their personnel records available to a criminal defense attorney pursuant to the Ohio Public Records Act, Ohio Rev. Code § 149.43. In October 1998, intervenors, a group of ten Ohio news organizations, joined the lawsuit without opposition after the City, citing the Sixth Circuit decision in this case, denied their request to see plaintiffs' personnel files. . . .

Using the Sixth Circuit's framework, the Court finds the Fourteenth Amendment does not prevent the City from allowing intervenors to inspect or copy the requested information from plaintiffs' personnel files. . . .

Intervenors have requested the home addresses of each plaintiff; summaries of investigations of plaintiffs' backgrounds; memos and reports of any assaults in which the plaintiffs were either perpetrators or victims; memos and reports related to any motor vehicle accidents in which City vehicles operated by plaintiffs were damaged or caused property damage or personal injury to others; memos and notices related to any disciplinary charges; and, answers to personal history questions. The request specifically excludes information identifying the Officers' banking institutions and financial account numbers; personal credit card numbers; social security numbers; information about any psychological conditions the Officers may have; responses to polygraph examinations; and, "medical records" or any other recorded information exempt from mandatory disclosure under Ohio Revised Code § 149.43. Further, intervenors do not object to the City redacting the names of any minor dependents of plaintiffs unless the dependent is employed by the City, any information made confidential by the Americans with Disabilities Act, 42 U.S.C. § 12101 et seq., or records which the Ohio Public Records Act would not require the City to disclose.

The Court finds plaintiffs do not have a constitutional privacy interest in the information requested by intervenors. Under the Sixth Circuit standard, plaintiffs must show that the release of information they wish to keep private would place them "at substantial risk of serious bodily harm, possibly even death, from a perceived likely threat." *Kallstrom,* 136 F.3d at 1064. The Court could fathom information contained in plaintiffs' personnel files that satisfies this stringent constitutional standard. Yet, that is not the Court's responsibility. The Sixth Circuit requires this Court to look at a "clear development of the factual circumstances" surrounding any future release of personal information from the Officers' personnel files. Plaintiffs have failed to provide any potentially admissible evidence to suggest that the release of any information contained in the three personnel files may place any of the plaintiffs at any risk of serious bodily harm. Nor have they identified a current "perceived likely threat."[21] This

---

[21] The Court sympathizes with plaintiffs' initial fears of retaliation from the Short North Posse. . . . [H]owever, plaintiffs have not developed clear and factual circumstances, outside of

is fatal to their claims. By not identifying any real potential danger that could arise from the release of information in their personnel files, plaintiffs have failed to make a showing sufficient to establish the existence of an element essential to their case for which they carry the burden.

Further, the majority of intervenors' request focuses on each plaintiff's disciplinary records, incident complaints from citizens, and other documents detailing how each officer is performing his or her job. Although plaintiffs may wish maintain the confidentiality of their employment histories, the Constitution does not provide a shield against disclosure of potentially embarrassing or even improper activities by public servants.

Finally, plaintiffs' interests in their home addresses also fail to meet the stringent constitutional standard set by the Sixth Circuit. Addresses are part of the public domain. Anyone with an individual's name and either Internet access or the initiative to visit a local government office can scan county property records, court records, or voter registration records for such information as an individual's address, the exact location of his or her residence, and even a floor plan of the home. The Supreme Court has found that "[t]he interests in privacy fade when the information involved already appears on the public record." *Cox Broad. Corp. v. Cohn,* 420 U.S. 469 (1975). In this case, plaintiffs have voluntarily revealed their own identities. For instance, plaintiffs initiated this lawsuit in their own names and describe their profession in the pleadings as "undercover narcotics officers." Plaintiffs also chose to testify without a pseudonym in the Posse trial. As plaintiffs have revealed their identities, their addresses are easily accessible in the public domain.

Even assuming plaintiffs have a constitutional interest in the information contained in their personnel files, the balancing test described by the Sixth Circuit still weighs in favor of disclosure. Where a state action infringes upon a fundamental right, the action will be upheld only where it furthers a compelling state interest and is narrowly drawn to further that state interest. In *Kallstrom,* the Sixth Circuit assumed that the state interests served by allowing public access to agency records were compelling, but held that the City's release of plaintiffs' personnel files to counsel for a criminal defendant did not narrowly achieve these interests.

Ohio's Public Records Act requires the state to make available all public records to any person unless the record falls within one of the statute's exceptions. Ohio Rev. Code § 149.43(B). The state has an interest in releasing its governmental agency records to "ensure accountability of government to those being governed." *See State ex rel. Strothers v. Wertheim,* 80 Ohio St. 3d 155 (1997). In *Kallstrom,* the Sixth Circuit acknowledged "there may be situations in which the release of this type of personal information might further the public's understanding of the workings of its law enforcement agencies." *Kallstrom,* 136 F.3d at 1065. This is one of those situations. The information intervenors request details the functioning of the City's police force. The personnel files reveal, among other things, the character and background of the City's police officers, whether the officers are using City property responsibly, and whether the City is

---

mere speculation, that this threat still exists. The only evidence in the record suggests, fortunately, the threat never developed.

enforcing the residency requirement for City employees as required by the City's charter. The state has a compelling interest in releasing this type of information to enlighten the public about the performance of its law enforcement agencies and ensure government accountability. The importance of public access to these files as a restraint on government activity is evident from cases such as the U.S. Justice Department's civil rights action against the City concerning police practices, which is currently pending in this courthouse.

Further, the City's disclosure of public records, including police officer personnel files, is narrowly tailored to achieve this compelling state interest. In *Kallstrom,* the Sixth Circuit failed "to see how placing [the Officers'] personal information into the hands of the *Russell* defendants in any way increases public understanding of the City's law enforcement agency." The press, however, is a different entity. . . .

The full disclosure of these personnel files is necessary to enable the press to do its job. As nothing less than full disclosure will ensure transparency in government, the Court finds full disclosure is narrowly tailored to meet the state's compelling interest. . . .

The intervenors seek a second declaration that the City is violating the First Amendment by denying the news organizations a state law right because they might publish accurate reports of the contents of public records. The Court agrees and grants summary judgment for intervenors on their second ground for declaratory judgment. . . .

Neither the First Amendment nor the Fourteenth Amendment mandates a right of access to government information or sources of information within the government's control. . . . In this case, the doors have been opened by the Ohio Public Records Act. Thus, the issue becomes whether the City can deny intervenors their state law right to these public records because, as members of the news media, they have the ability to disseminate the information contained in plaintiffs' personnel files.

The Supreme Court has held that the government may not single out the press to bear special burdens without violating the First Amendment. *Minneapolis Star & Tribune Co. v. Minnesota Comm'r of Revenue,* 460 U.S. 575 (1983). In *Minneapolis Star,* the Supreme Court found that Minnesota's use tax on paper and ink violated the First Amendment for "singling out the press for taxation" that did not apply to other enterprises. Courts, however, have not been hesitant to extend this rationale beyond taxation. *See, e.g., Legi-Tech, Inc. v. Keiper,* 766 F.2d 728 (2d Cir. 1985) (suggesting denial of press access to a public legislative database would face "hostile scrutiny" as singling out the press for a special burden). . . .

Due to these important considerations, a state-imposed burden on the press is always "subject to at least some degree of heightened First Amendment scrutiny." When the government specially burdens the press, "the appropriate method of analysis thus is to balance the burden implicit in singling out the press against the interest asserted by the State." The burden "can survive only if the governmental interest outweighs the burden and cannot be achieved by means that do not infringe First Amendment rights as significantly."

In its pleadings, the City states its interest as preventing members of the press from accessing plaintiffs' personnel records because news organizations have the ability to disseminate the information to "wide and diverse audiences, including the Short North Posse." Since the second part of the *Minneapolis Star* test is dispositive, the Court finds it unnecessary to balance the City's interest with the burden implicit in singling out the press. The Court concludes the City's decision to single out the press for disparate treatment does not satisfactorily accomplish its stated purpose.

Treating the press differently will not prevent the harm the City is seeking to avoid. The City's denial of the intervenors' public records request because of their ability to disseminate information suggests that the same records would have been provided to anyone who did not have this capability. Any member of the public would have access to these records — including Short North Posse members, their friends, and their families. Silencing the press makes no difference as to whether these people have access to plaintiffs' personal information.

Further, this distinction does not prevent the press from gaining access to the materials. The news organizations could have a surrogate request the records and provide copies to the press. Even a reporter for one of the intervenors could request the records as a citizen, without revealing his or her professional affiliation, and use plaintiffs' personal information in the same manner as if the news organization had requested the records as an entity. Allowing the City to impose these arbitrary burdens threatens to eviscerate the ability of the press to serve as a restraint on government activity, poses inherent dangers to free expression, and presents great potential for censorship or manipulation. . . .

In choosing to deny intervenors' request based on their ability to disseminate the information, however, the City placed a burden on the press that would not have attached to any other request for those public records. The City's arbitrary treatment of the press is not only thoroughly ineffective at achieving its objective, but also highly offensive to the First Amendment. . . .

NOTES & QUESTIONS

1. ***How Broad Is the* Kallstrom II *Decision?*** In his reading of *Kallstrom I*, Paul Schwartz argues that the case showed that "[o]nly the threat of life-threatening harm to officers and their families and the City of Columbus' plan for automatic disclosure of this information" allowed an interest in nondisclosure to triumph.[22] Schwartz also notes that the Sixth Circuit granted merely a limited injunction to the undercover officers that allowed them a chance to object when someone requested their personal data. In this fashion, the *Kallstrom II* court left the door open for release of this information under other circumstances. What is left of the Sixth Circuit's opinion after *Kallstrom II*? Under what basis did the district court in *Kallstrom II* decide that the information should be released to the press?

In *Barber v. Overton*, 496 F.3d 449 (6th Cir. 2007), the Sixth Circuit revisited the *Kallstrom I* and found that this decision was not implicated by a (mistaken) release of Social Security numbers and birth dates of prison

---

[22] Paul M. Schwartz, *Internet Privacy and the State*, 32 Conn. L. Rev. 815, 828-29 (2000).

officers to prisoners: "*Kallstrom* created a narrowly tailored right, limited to circumstances where the information was particularly sensitive and the persons to whom it was disclosed were particularly dangerous *vis-à-vis the plaintiffs*" (emphasis in original). In sum, the *Barber* court stated that the release of the information "was not sensitive enough nor the threat of retaliation apparent enough to warrant constitution protection here."

2. ***Statutory vs. Constitutional Privacy Exemptions.*** Contrast the operation of statutory privacy exemptions to FOIA and exceptions based on the constitutional right to information privacy, as in *Kallstrom I*. How does the presence of the Ohio Public Records Act affect the analysis in *Kallstrom II*?

3. ***The Scope of Privacy Exemptions.*** In *Moak v. Philadelphia Newspapers, Inc.*, 336 A.2d 920 (Pa. 1975), the court held that the employee records of a police department, which contained the name, gender, date of birth, salary, and other personal information about the employees, did not fall within the privacy exemption to Pennsylvania's Right to Know Law because the records would not "operate to the prejudice or impairment of a person's reputation or personal security." Should the privacy of personal information turn on whether it will harm a person's reputation or security?

4. ***Public Records in a Digital World.*** Public records are increasingly being stored in electronic format. The paper records of the past were difficult to access. Now, they can be collected in databases and searched en masse. To what extent should the increased accessibility of records created by the digital age affect open record laws?

In 2001, the Judicial Conference Committee on Court Administration and Case Management issued a report with policies regarding public access to electronic case files. As Peter Winn describes it:

> Before the Judicial Conference Committee on Court Administration and Case Management (Committee) issued the Report, a study of the problem was prepared by the staff of the Administrative Office of the United States Courts. The staff white paper described two general approaches to the problem. One approach was to treat electronic judicial records as governed by exactly the same rules as paper records — what the white paper calls the "public is public" approach. The second approach advocated treating electronic and paper files differently in order to respect the practical obscurity of paper case files, urging that the rules regulating electronic court records reflect the fact that unrestricted online access to court records would undoubtedly, as a practical matter, compromise privacy, as well as increase the risk of personal harm to litigants and third parties whose private information appeared in case files. The white paper suggested that different levels of privileges could be created to govern electronic access to court records. Under this approach, judges and court staff would generally have broad, although not unlimited, remote access to all electronic case files, as would other key participants in the judicial process, such as the U.S. Attorney, the U.S. Trustee, and bankruptcy case trustees. Litigants and their attorneys would have unrestricted access to the files relevant to their own cases. The general public would have remote access to a subset of the full case file, including, in most cases, pleadings, briefs, orders, and opinions. Under this approach, the entire electronic case file

could still be viewed at the clerk's office, just as the paper file is available now for inspection, but would not generally be made available on the Internet.

Unfortunately, at least with respect to civil cases and bankruptcy cases, few, if any, of the suggestions contained in the staff white paper were ultimately adopted in the Report. Instead, the Committee adopted the "public is public" approach to the problem, rejecting the view that courts have a responsibility to adopt rules governing the use of their computer systems to try to recreate in cyberspace the practical balance that existed in the world of paper judicial records. In supporting this decision, the Committee took the position that attempting to recreate the "practical obscurity" of the brick and mortar world was simply too complicated an exercise for the courts to undertake. The Report does appear to recognize a limited responsibility on the part of the courts to adopt rules in order to limit the foreseeable harms of identity theft and online stalking. The Report recommends that certain "personal data identifiers," such as Social Security numbers, dates of birth, financial account numbers, and names of minor children, be partially redacted by the litigants. . . .

The Report recommends that criminal court records not be placed online, for the present, finding that any benefits of remote electronic access to criminal files would be outweighed by the safety and law enforcement risks such access would create. The Report expressed the concern that allowing defendants and others easy access to information regarding the cooperation and other activities of co-defendants would increase the risk that the information would be used to intimidate, harass, and possibly harm victims, defendants, and their families. In addition, the Report noted that merely sealing such documents would not adequately address the problems of online access, since the fact that a document is sealed signals probable defendant cooperation and covert law enforcement initiatives.[23]

In March 2004, the Judicial Conference issued a report recommending that, with certain exceptions, all criminal records be placed online accessible to the public.[24]

5. *911 Calls.* In many states, the recordings of 911 calls are disclosed to the public. Is such a practice a violation of the constitutional right to information privacy? When these calls involve celebrities, gossip sites on the Internet, such as TMZ or Radaronline, will post the audio of the call on their sites. One example is the 911 call made from Michael Jackson's house on June 25, 2009, as he was dying. As this example shows, many 911 calls involve matters about people's physical health and times of extreme stress. Matters of mental health can also be discussed in 911 calls.

Doctors and nurses are under a duty of confidentiality, so why not 911 call centers, especially when people are revealing medical information? On the other hand, proponents of making 911 calls available to the public might contend that publicly disclosing the calls is necessary for the public to vet how well the 911 operators respond to calls, and to provide background on

---

[23] Peter A. Winn, *Online Court Records: Balancing Judicial Accountability and Privacy in an Age of Electronic Information*, 79 Wash. L. Rev. 307, 322-25 (2004).

[24] http://www.privacy.uscourts.gov/crimimpl.htm.

subsequent police or medical action. What interests should be predominate in the balance?

(b) Police Records

PAUL V. DAVIS
424 U.S. 693 (1976)

REHNQUIST, J. . . . Petitioner Paul is the Chief of Police of the Louisville, Ky., Division of Police, while petitioner McDaniel occupies the same position in the Jefferson County, Ky., Division of Police. In late 1972 they agreed to combine their efforts for the purpose of alerting local area merchants to possible shoplifters who might be operating during the Christmas season. In early December petitioners distributed to approximately 800 merchants in the Louisville metropolitan area a "flyer," which began as follows:

TO: BUSINESS MEN IN THE METROPOLITAN AREA

The Chiefs of The Jefferson County and City of Louisville Police Departments, in an effort to keep their officers advised on shoplifting activity, have approved the attached alphabetically arranged flyer of subjects known to be active in this criminal field.

This flyer is being distributed to you, the business man, so that you may inform your security personnel to watch for these subjects. These persons have been arrested during 1971 and 1972 or have been active in various criminal fields in high density shopping areas.

Only the photograph and name of the subject is shown on this flyer, if additional information is desired, please forward a request in writing. . . .

The flyer consisted of five pages of "mug shot" photos, arranged alphabetically. [Each page had the heading: "ACTIVE SHOPLIFTERS."]

In approximately the center of page 2 there appeared photos and the name of the respondent, Edward Charles Davis III.

Respondent appeared on the flyer because on June 14, 1971, he had been arrested in Louisville on a charge of shoplifting. He had been arraigned on this charge in September 1971, and, upon his plea of not guilty, the charge had been "filed away with leave (to reinstate)," a disposition which left the charge outstanding. Thus, at the time petitioners caused the flyer to be prepared and circulated respondent had been charged with shoplifting but his guilt or innocence of that offense had never been resolved. Shortly after circulation of the flyer the charge against respondent was finally dismissed by a judge of the Louisville Police Court.

At the time the flyer was circulated respondent was employed as a photographer by the Louisville Courier-Journal and Times. The flyer, and respondent's inclusion therein, soon came to the attention of respondent's supervisor, the executive director of photography for the two newspapers. This individual called respondent in to hear his version of the events leading to his appearing in the flyer. Following this discussion, the supervisor informed respondent that although he would not be fired, he "had best not find himself in a similar situation" in the future.

Respondent thereupon brought this § 1983 action in the District Court for the Western District of Kentucky, seeking redress for the alleged violation of rights guaranteed to him by the Constitution of the United States. . . .

Respondent's due process claim is grounded upon his assertion that the flyer, and in particular the phrase "Active Shoplifters" appearing at the head of the page upon which his name and photograph appear, impermissibly deprived him of some "liberty" protected by the Fourteenth Amendment. His complaint asserted that the "active shoplifter" designation would inhibit him from entering business establishments for fear of being suspected of shoplifting and possibly apprehended, and would seriously impair his future employment opportunities. Accepting that such consequences may flow from the flyer in question, respondent's complaint would appear to state a classical claim for defamation actionable in the courts of virtually every State. Imputing criminal behavior to an individual is generally considered defamatory per se, and actionable without proof of special damages.

Respondent brought his action, however, not in the state courts of Kentucky, but in a United States District Court for that State. He asserted not a claim for defamation under the laws of Kentucky, but a claim that he had been deprived of rights secured to him by the Fourteenth Amendment of the United States Constitution. Concededly if the same allegations had been made about respondent by a private individual, he would have nothing more than a claim for defamation under state law. But, he contends, since petitioners are respectively an official of city and of county government, his action is thereby transmuted into one for deprivation by the State of rights secured under the Fourteenth Amendment. . . .

If respondent's view is to prevail, a person arrested by law enforcement officers who announce that they believe such person to be responsible for a particular crime in order to calm the fears of an aroused populace, presumably obtains a claim against such officers under § 1983. And since it is surely far more clear from the language of the Fourteenth Amendment that "life" is protected against state deprivation than it is that reputation is protected against state injury, it would be difficult to see why the survivors of an innocent bystander mistakenly shot by a policeman or negligently killed by a sheriff driving a government vehicle, would not have claims equally cognizable under § 1983.

It is hard to perceive any logical stopping place to such a line of reasoning. Respondent's construction would seem almost necessarily to result in every legally cognizable injury which may have been inflicted by a state official acting under "color of law" establishing a violation of the Fourteenth Amendment. We think it would come as a great surprise to those who drafted and shepherded the adoption of that Amendment to learn that it worked such a result, and a study of our decisions convinces us they do not support the construction urged by respondent. . . .

The second premise upon which the result reached by the Court of Appeals could be rested that the infliction by state officials of a "stigma" to one's reputation is somehow different in kind from infliction by a state official of harm to other interests protected by state law is equally untenable. The words "liberty" and "property" as used in the Fourteenth Amendment do not in terms single out reputation as a candidate for special protection over and above other interests that may be protected by state law. While we have in a number of our prior cases pointed out the frequently drastic effect of the "stigma" which may result from defamation by the government in a variety of contexts, this line of cases does not establish the proposition that reputation alone, apart from some more tangible interests such as employment, is either "liberty" or "property" by itself sufficient to invoke the procedural protection of the Due Process Clause. . . .

Respondent's complaint also alleged a violation of a "right to privacy guaranteed by the First, Fourth, Fifth, Ninth, and Fourteenth Amendments." . . .

While there is no "right of privacy" found in any specific guarantee of the Constitution, the Court has recognized that "zones of privacy" may be created by more specific constitutional guarantees and thereby impose limits upon government power. *See Roe v. Wade*, 410 U.S. 113 (1973). Respondent's case, however, comes within none of these areas. He does not seek to suppress evidence seized in the course of an unreasonable search. *See Katz v. United States*, 389 U.S. 347 (1967). And our other "right of privacy" cases, while defying categorical description, deal generally with substantive aspects of the Fourteenth Amendment. In *Roe* the Court pointed out that the personal rights found in this guarantee of personal privacy must be limited to those which are "fundamental" or "implicit in the concept of ordered liberty" as described in *Palko v. Connecticut*, 302 U.S. 319 (1937). The activities detailed as being within this definition were ones very different from that for which respondent claims constitutional protection matters relating to marriage, procreation, contraception, family relationships, and child rearing and education. In these areas it has been held that there are limitations on the States' power to substantively regulate conduct.

Respondent's claim is far afield from this line of decisions. He claims constitutional protection against the disclosure of the fact of his arrest on a shoplifting charge. His claim is based, not upon any challenge to the State's ability to restrict his freedom of action in a sphere contended to be "private," but instead on a claim that the State may not publicize a record of an official act such as an arrest. None of our substantive privacy decisions hold this or anything like this, and we decline to enlarge them in this manner. . .

NOTES & QUESTIONS

1. **Wisconsin v. Constantineau.** Five years prior to *Paul*, the Court was more receptive to constitutional protection for reputational harms in *Wisconsin v. Constantineau*, 400 U.S. 433 (1971). There, the Court struck down a law authorizing the posting of names of people who had been designated excessive drinkers in retail liquor outlets. Alcohol was not to be sold to these individuals. The Court reasoned:

   > Where a person's good name, reputation, honor, or integrity is at stake because of what the government is doing to him, notice and an opportunity to be heard are essential. "Posting" under the Wisconsin Act may to some be merely the mark of illness, to others it is a stigma, an official branding of a person. The label is a degrading one. Under the Wisconsin Act, a resident of Hartford is given no process at all. This appellee was not afforded a chance to defend herself. She may have been the victim of an official's caprice. Only

when the whole proceedings leading to the pinning of an unsavory label on a person are aired can oppressive results be prevented.

Is *Paul* consistent with this case?

2. **Paul v. Davis** *vs.* **Whalen v. Roe.** *Paul v. Davis* was decided one year prior to *Whalen v. Roe,* 429 U.S. 589 (1977), where the Supreme Court recognized that the constitutional right to privacy involves "the individual interest in avoiding disclosure of personal matters." How does *Paul* square with *Whalen*? Does *Whalen* implicitly overrule *Paul* by recognizing a constitutional right to avoid disclosure of certain information? How can these cases be reconciled?

CLINE V. ROGERS
87 F.3d 176 (6th Cir. 1996)

BATCHELDER, J. . . . The plaintiff-appellant, Jackie Ray Cline ("Cline"), alleges that in 1992, a private citizen contacted the Sheriff's Department of McMinn County, Tennessee ("the County"), and asked Sheriff George Rogers to check Cline's arrest record. According to Cline, Rogers searched state and local records and requested a computer search of National Crime Information Center ("NCIC") records of the Federal Bureau of Investigation ("FBI"). Cline alleges that Rogers disclosed to the private citizen the information Rogers obtained regarding Cline's criminal history, in violation of both Tennessee and federal law.

Cline filed this lawsuit against Rogers, individually and in his official capacity as sheriff. Cline also named the County as a defendant, alleging that improper searches of criminal records is "a routine and customary practice in McMinn County," that the County "lacks adequate controls to ensure that access to criminal records is for authorized purposes only," that the County did not have in place an adequate system to detect misuse of criminal records, that the County had provided inadequate training to prevent such abuse, and that the County had "been indifferent to the civil rights of private citizens by allowing such abuses to continue."

Cline's complaint sought damages under 42 U.S.C. § 1983 for violation of his federal civil rights. . . . [The district court dismissed Cline's complaint, and Cline appealed.]

There is no violation of the United States Constitution in this case because there is no constitutional right to privacy in one's criminal record. Nondisclosure of one's criminal record is not one of those personal rights that is "fundamental" or "implicit in the concept of ordered liberty." *See Whalen v. Roe.* In *Whalen*, the Supreme Court distinguished fundamental privacy interests in "matters relating to marriage, procreation, contraception, family relationships, and child rearing and education" and "individual interest in avoiding disclosure of personal matters."

Moreover, one's criminal history is arguably not a private "personal matter" at all, since arrest and conviction information are matters of public record. *See Paul v. Davis* (rejecting a similar claim based on facts more egregious than those alleged here). Although there may be a dispute among the circuit courts regarding the existence and extent of an individual privacy right to nondisclosure of "personal matters," see *Slayton v. Willingham*, 726 F.2d 631 (10th Cir. 1984); *Fadjo v. Coon*, 633 F.2d 1172, 1176 (5th Cir. Unit B 1981) (both opining that *Paul* has been at least partially overruled by the Supreme Court's decisions in *Whalen* and *Nixon*), this circuit does not recognize a constitutional privacy interest in avoiding disclosure of, e.g., one's criminal record. See *DeSanti*, 653 F.2d at 1090 (regarding disclosure of juvenile delinquents' "social histories"); see also *Doe v. Wigginton*, 21 F.3d 733 (6th Cir. 1994) (disclosure of inmate's HIV infection did not violate constitutional right of privacy).

Because there is no privacy interest in one's criminal record that is protected by the United States Constitution, Cline could prove no set of facts that would entitle him to relief; therefore, the district court correctly dismissed this claim. . .

SCHEETZ V. THE MORNING CALL, INC.

946 F.2d 202 (3d Cir. 1991)

NYGAARD, J. . . . Kenneth Scheetz is a police officer in the City of Allentown. Rosann Scheetz is his wife. In the course of an argument between them in their home in January of 1988, Kenneth struck Rosann. Rosann left the house, but returned approximately a half an hour later. The argument resumed, and Kenneth again struck Rosann.

Rosann called the Allentown police. Two officers responded and prepared a standard "offense/incident" report, consisting of a face sheet and supplemental reports. The "face sheet" of this report[25] stated that Rosann Scheetz had reported a domestic disturbance, that two police cars had responded, and that Rosann had left the home.

In the meantime, Rosann had driven to the Allentown police station, apparently with the intention of filing a Pennsylvania Protection From Abuse Petition. The officers who interviewed Rosann prepared two "supplemental reports" and made them part of the file. They reveal that Rosann stated that her husband had beaten her before and had refused counseling. The police gave Rosann three options: file criminal charges, request a protection from abuse order, or initiate department disciplinary action against Kenneth. These supplements also note that Rosann had visible physical injuries, that Rosann did not want to return home and that she was permitted to spend the night in the shift commander's office.

Chief Wayne Stephens filed a third supplement to the report. He had spoken to Kenneth about the incident, and the third supplement memorialized this fact, as well as Kenneth's statement to the Chief that he and his wife were scheduled to speak with a marriage counselor. None of the supplements indicated that the Chief took any disciplinary action against Kenneth.

Shortly after the incident, Kenneth Scheetz was named "Officer of the Year" by Chief Stephens. Several months later, as part of "Respect for Law Week,"

---

[25] The "face sheet" is a public document similar to a police blotter. The parties agree that this document is a public record. The parties dispute whether the "supplemental reports" are public records available under Pennsylvania's Right to Know Law. There is some evidence that these reports were generally available, subject to the approval of a police supervisor.

press releases and photos of Kenneth were released. A dinner and official ceremony were held in Kenneth's honor. The Morning Call ("The Call"), a local newspaper, published a story and photo on this honor.

Terry Mutchler, a reporter for The Call, became interested in investigating the prior incident involving Kenneth and Rosann. Another reporter from the paper had tried to get the police report from the police, who refused to release it. Mutchler's request for a copy of the report from the department was also formally refused. Mutchler nonetheless managed to get a copy of the report.

Mutchler then interviewed Chief Stephens about the incident. Chief Stephens initially denied the incident, but when confronted with Mutchler's information, he claimed that the report was stolen and refused further comment. Chief Stephens did, however, offer his insights into the subject of spousal abuse, stating "people fake it" and "women . . . tear their dresses and rip up their bras and say they were raped." Mutchler also interviewed Deputy Chief Monaghan, who offered assorted rationalizations for why no follow-up had been done on the Scheetz incident. The Scheetzes refused comment on the incident.

The Call published an article by Mutchler titled "Police didn't investigate assault complaint against officer." Eight paragraphs of the article were comprised of quotes from the police report of the beating incident which detailed the injuries Rosann received. The bulk of the article, however, focused on the lack of investigation and follow-up by the police department. Chief Stephens was quoted as saying that the incident had not been investigated. The article also quoted the comments Chief Stephens had made to Mutchler about domestic abuse, as well as Deputy Chief Monaghan's explanations for why no charges were pressed. The last two columns of the article consisted of quotes from Kenneth's superiors praising his work. . . .

. . . Kenneth and Rosann then sued Mutchler, The Call, and "John or Jane Doe." The complaint alleged that Mutchler and The Call had conspired with an unknown state actor (the Doe defendant) to deprive the Scheetzes of their constitutional right to privacy in violation of 42 U.S.C. § 1983. The complaint also raised several pendent state law claims. . . .

The district court granted the defendants' motion for summary judgment in part, denied it in part, granted judgment to the defendants on the § 1983 claim, dismissed the pendent state claims, dismissed the Doe defendant and dismissed all remaining motions as moot. The Scheetzes appeal. . . .

. . . Because we conclude that the Scheetzes have not alleged a violation of a constitutionally protected privacy interest, we will affirm.

The defendants rely on dicta in *Paul v. Davis* to support their argument that "garden variety" invasion of privacy claims are not actionable under section 1983. . . . The Supreme Court rejected the proposition that reputation alone was a liberty or property interest within the meaning of the due process clause. In dicta, the Court went on to consider the alternative argument that the police chiefs' action constituted a violation of the plaintiff's right to privacy. After first noting that privacy decisions had been limited in the past to family and procreative matters, the Court concluded that publication by the state of an official act such as an arrest could not constitute invasion of the constitutional right to privacy.

The very next year, however, the Court held in *Whalen v. Roe*, that the right to privacy extends to both "the individual interest in avoiding disclosure of personal matters, and . . . the interest in independence in making certain kinds of important decisions." *Whalen* recognized that the information contained in medical records is constitutionally protected under the confidentiality branch of the privacy right.

Thus, some confidential information is protected under the confidentiality branch of the right to privacy, the dicta in *Paul* notwithstanding.[26] Accordingly, the Scheetzes in this case contend that the information contained in the police incident report is similarly protected by the federal right.

Although cases exploring the autonomy branch of the right of privacy are legion, the contours of the confidentiality branch are murky. We have recognized that some confidential information, such as medical records, is constitutionally protected under the confidentiality branch of the federal privacy right. Other courts have similarly recognized that § 1983 may be used to redress violations of a constitutional confidentiality right.

Concluding that violations of the confidentiality right of privacy may be actionable under § 1983 does not, however, end our inquiry. Although defendants are wrong in arguing that *Paul* prohibits any privacy § 1983 action, we conclude that they correctly argue that the Scheetzes did not have a constitutionally protected privacy interest in the information they divulged in a police report. . . .

Although the outlines of the confidentiality right are not definite, the information that has been protected in other cases was information that the disclosing person reasonably expected to remain private. In reporting this potential crime to the police, Rosann Scheetz could not reasonably expect the information to remain secret. The police could have brought charges without her concurrence, at which point all the information would have wound up on the public record, where it would have been non-confidential. *See Cox Broadcasting Corp. v. Cohn*, 420 U.S. 469 (1975) (privacy interest fades when information is in the public record). This information is not like medical or financial records (which have been accorded some constitutional protection by this court) where there is a reasonable expectation that privacy will be preserved. When police are called, a private disturbance loses much of its private character. We conclude that the information Rosann Scheetz disclosed in the police reports is not constitutionally protected. . . .

MANSMANN, J. dissenting. . . . I agree that some of the information contained in the police report, specifically that information contained in the "Offense/Incident Report," is not protected under a constitutional privacy interest. Because the "Offense/Incident Report" is classified as a public document under the police department's policy, that information was not treated as confidential. . . .

Some of the information reported by The Call, however, was contained only in confidential portions of the police report entitled "Investigative Supplements" and was not discernable from the public portion of the report. That information detailed the private facts of the Scheetzes' marital counseling and precise details of their marital disturbance, including a description of Rosann's injuries and her

---

[26] *Paul* can be reconciled with *Whalen* since the information at issue in *Paul* (the fact of plaintiff's arrest for shoplifting) is not the kind of information entitled to constitutional protection.

statements. Since this information is clearly confidential, I would then examine the nature of the Scheetzes' privacy interest in keeping it confidential. . . .

. . . The majority suggests that because the information could have been publicly disclosed, the Scheetzes had no privacy interest. While it is true that criminal charges could have been brought without Rosann's concurrence, it does not necessarily follow that in spite of the fact that she declined to press charges or take alternative legal action, and no legal action ensued, Rosann Scheetz could have reasonably expected public disclosure of the confidential information that had remained quietly dormant in confidential police department reports.

This is especially true where the public disclosure occurred 16 months after the incident. *See, e.g., Briscoe v. Reader's Digest Ass'n,* 483 P.2d 34 (Cal. 1971) (common law right to privacy infringed by publication of truck hijacking conviction of 11 years ago); *Melvin v. Reid,* 297 P. 91 (Cal. 1931) (liability for common law invasion of privacy imposed upon producers of movie that revealed prior life of prostitution and crime of woman who had long since taken a new name and established a respectable life). . . .

. . . Because this confidential information had lain undisclosed in the confidential police department files for over a year and Rosann Scheetz had not pursued any legal action, the Scheetzes could reasonably have expected that the confidential information would never be publicly disclosed. In light of this delay, I cannot agree with the majority's otherwise appropriate assertion that "[w]hen police are called, a private disturbance loses much of its private character." Information that has remained confidential over a period of time, absent any legal action, can reasonably be expected to recede from public notice. . . .

NOTES & QUESTIONS

1. ***Privacy as a Way to Conceal a Scandal.*** The information about the police department's treatment of Ken Scheetz's abuse of his wife is highly newsworthy. The information reveals a police department that praised rather than disciplined Ken Scheetz and virtually ignored his wife's complaints of abuse. Is privacy being used to cover up the scandalous way the police department reacted to Rosann Scheetz's complaint?

2. ***Deterring Reporting of Spousal Abuse.*** Would routine disclosure of complaints of spousal abuse inhibit victims such as Rosann Scheetz from coming forward? Keep in mind that it is Rosann Scheetz, in addition to her husband, who is suing for a violation of her privacy.

3. ***Limits on Police Reports.*** The court concluded that Rosann Scheetz lacked an expectation of privacy in the information because it was included in a police report: "In reporting this potential crime to the police, Rosann Scheetz could not reasonably expect the information to remain secret. The police could have brought charges without her concurrence, at which point all the information would have wound up on the public record, where it would have been non-confidential." Are there limits to what information the police should include in a police report?

4. ***Police Threats to Disclose.*** Consider *Sterling v. Borough of Minersville*, 232 F.3d 190 (3d Cir. 2000). Marcus Wayman, 18 years old, was in a parked car along with a 17-year-old male friend. The car was parked in a lot adjacent to a beer distributor. F. Scott Wilinsky, a police officer, observed the vehicle and became suspicious that the youths might be attempting to burglarize the beer distributor. Wilinsky called for backup. After investigating, the officers determined that a break-in had not occurred at the beer distributor, but that the youths had been drinking. Wilinsky searched the vehicle and discovered two condoms and asked about the boys' sexual orientation. The boys said that they were gay, and that they were in the lot to engage in consensual sex. The boys were arrested for underage drinking and taken to the police station, where Wilinsky lectured them that homosexual activity was contrary to the dictates of the Bible. Wilinsky then told Wayman that he must inform his grandfather about his homosexuality or else Wilinsky himself would inform Wayman's grandfather. When he was released from custody, Wayman committed suicide. Wayman's mother filed a § 1983 suit against the Borough of Minersville, Wilinksy, and other officers and officials alleging, among other things, a violation of the constitutional right to information privacy. The court reasoned:

> We first ask whether Wayman had a protected privacy right concerning Wilinsky's threat to disclose his suspected sexual orientation. . . .
> It is difficult to imagine a more private matter than one's sexuality and a less likely probability that the government would have a legitimate interest in disclosure of sexual identity.
> We can, therefore, readily conclude that Wayman's sexual orientation was an intimate aspect of his personality entitled to privacy protection under *Whalen*. . . .
> Before we can definitely conclude that a constitutional tort has occurred, however, we must further ask whether Wilinsky's threat of disclosure, rather than actual disclosure, constituted a violation of Wayman's right to privacy. . . .
> The threat to breach some confidential aspect of one's life . . . is tantamount to a violation of the privacy right because the security of one's privacy has been compromised by the threat of disclosure. Thus, Wilinsky's threat to disclose Wayman's suspected homosexuality suffices as a violation of Wayman's constitutionally protected privacy interest. . . .

(c) Megan's Laws

In 1994, in New Jersey, a seven-year-old girl, Megan Kanka, was brutally raped and murdered by her neighbor, Jesse Timmendequas, who had two earlier sexual assault convictions. Nobody in Megan's family knew about Timmendequas's prior criminal record. Seventeen days after Megan's death, New Jersey Assembly Speaker Chuck Haytaian declared a legislative emergency. A law was proposed, called "Megan's Law," to establish a system for people to learn of the whereabouts of sexual offenders who were released from prison. The statute passed without committee hearings and without supportive research. Within three months of Megan's death, the law was signed by Governor Christie Whitman and became law. Similar laws appeared in other states. These laws, commonly called "Megan's Laws," set up databases of personal information about sexual offenders so that people can learn their identities and where they live.

In 1996, Congress passed a federal Megan's Law restricting states from receiving federal anti-crime funds unless they agreed to "release relevant information that is necessary to protect the public" from released sex offenders. *See* Pub. L. No. 104-145, codified at 42 U.S.C. § 14071(d)(2). Today, all 50 states have passed a version of Megan's Law. Sex offender registries under Megan's Law often contain information such as the sex offender's Social Security number, photograph, address, prior convictions, and places of employment.

States differ in how they disseminate sexual offender information. In California, booths are set up at county fairs so that individuals can browse through the registry. Some states have 1-800 or 1-900 numbers where people can call in and ask if particular people are sex offenders. At least 16 states have made their registries available on the Internet.

PAUL P. V. VERNIERO

170 F.3d 396 (3d Cir. 1999)

SLOVITER, J. Plaintiff Paul P. sues on his behalf and on behalf of a class of persons who, having been convicted of specified sex crimes, are required to comply with N.J. Stat. Ann. § 2c:7-1 et seq., known as "Megan's Law," which provides for a system of registration and community notification. . . .

In a related action, *E.B. v. Verniero*, 119 F.3d 1077 (3d Cir. 1997), this court rejected the claims of comparably situated persons that the community notification requirements violate the Double Jeopardy Clause or the Ex Post Facto Clause of the United States Constitution. That holding of *E.B.* was predicated on the conclusion that the notification required by Megan's Law does not constitute punishment. . . .

In this case, plaintiffs raise a challenge to Megan's Law that they claim is different from that considered in *E.B.* They argue that the statutory requirement that the class members provide extensive information to local law enforcement personnel, including each registrant's current biographical data, physical description, home address, place of employment, schooling, and a description and license plate number of the registrant's vehicle, and the subsequent community notification is a violation of their constitutionally protected right to privacy.

The statutory scheme is described in detail in *E.B.*, and we refer only briefly to the salient details. We explained the registration requirements as follows:

The registrant must provide the following information to the chief law enforcement officer of the municipality in which he resides: name, social security number, age, race, sex, date of birth, height, weight, hair and eye color, address of legal residence, address of any current temporary legal residence, and date and place of employment. N.J.S.A. 2C:7-4b(1). He must confirm his address every ninety days, notify the municipal law enforcement agency if he moves, and re-

register with the law enforcement agency of any new municipality. N.J.S.A. 2C:7-2d to e.

The information provided by the registrant is put into a central registry, open to other law enforcement personnel but not to public inspection. Law enforcement officials then use the data provided to apply a "Risk Assessment Scale," a numerical scoring system, to determine the registrant's "risk of offense" and the tier in which the registrant should be classified. In the case of Tier 1 registrants, notification is given only to law enforcement agents "likely to encounter" the registrant. Tier 2, or "moderate risk," notification is given to law enforcement agents, schools, and community organizations "likely to encounter" the registrant. Tier 3, or "high risk," notification goes to all members of the public "likely to encounter" the registrant. Notifications generally contain a warning that the information is confidential and should not be disseminated to others, as well as an admonition that actions taken against the registrant, such as assaults, are illegal.

The prosecutor must provide the registrant with notice of the proposed notification. A pre-notification judicial review process is available for any registrant who wishes to challenge his or her classification.

The plaintiffs are Tier 2 and Tier 3 registrants who have been certified as a class and whose offenses were committed after the enactment of Megan's Law. . . .

The legal foundation for plaintiffs' claim is the Supreme Court's recognition that there is "a right of personal privacy, or a guarantee of certain areas or zones of privacy," protected by the United States Constitution. *Roe v. Wade*, 410 U.S. 113, 152 (1973). This "guarantee of personal privacy" covers "only personal rights that can be deemed 'fundamental' or 'implicit in the concept of ordered liberty.'" This privacy right "has some extension to activities relating to marriage, procreation, contraception, family relationships, and child rearing and education."

Plaintiffs argue that Megan's Law infringes upon their constitutionally protected privacy interests in two ways. One is by the dissemination of information about them, most particularly by disseminating both their home addresses and a "compilation of information which would otherwise remain 'scattered' or 'wholly forgotten.'" Their other claim is that the community notification infringes upon their "privacy interests in their most intimate relationships — those with their spouses, children, parents, and other family members."

Plaintiffs thus seek to invoke the two categories of privacy interests identified by the Supreme Court in *Whalen v. Roe*. . . .

The parties dispute the extent to which our decision in *E.B.* is dispositive of the privacy issue before us in this case. Plaintiffs contend that no privacy issue was raised, briefed, or argued in *E.B.* and that the discussion in *E.B.* relating to cases on which they rely is dictum. The State defendants, on the other hand, regard "[t]he portions of the *E.B.* decision holding that community notification does not implicate a fundamental privacy interest and the finding of a compelling state interest in protecting the public from recidivist sex offenders," as "control[ling] the decision in this case." We thus turn to examine the *E.B.* decision.

The privacy issue arose in *E.B.* during our analysis of whether community notification mandated by Megan's Law constitutes punishment for purposes of the Ex Post Facto and Double Jeopardy Clauses. In that context, we stated that the "primary sting from Megan's law notification comes by way of injury to what is denoted . . . as reputational interests. This includes . . . the myriad of . . . ways in which one is treated differently by virtue of being known as a potentially dangerous sex offender." *E.B.*, 119 F.3d at 1102. We then referred to the Supreme Court's holding in *Paul v. Davis*, stating:

> Just as Davis sought constitutional protection from the consequences of state disclosure of the fact of his shoplifting arrest and law enforcement's assessment that he was a continuing risk, so registrants seek protection from what may follow disclosure of facts related to their sex offense convictions and the resulting judgment of the state that they are a continuing risk. It follows that, just as the officers' publication of the official act of Davis' arrest did not violate any fundamental privacy right of Davis', neither does New Jersey's publication (through notification) of registrants' convictions and findings of dangerousness implicate any interest of fundamental constitutional magnitude.

We rejected the contention that dissemination of information about criminal activity beyond law enforcement personnel is analogous to historical punishments, such as the stocks, cages, and scarlet letters. We found instead that the dissemination is more like the dissemination of "rap sheet" information to regulatory agencies, bar associations, prospective employers, and interested members of the public that public indictment, public trial, and public imposition of sentence necessarily entail. We noted that although the Supreme Court later recognized in *United States Department of Justice v. Reporters Committee for Freedom of the Press*, 489 U.S. 749 (1989), that the dissemination of "rap sheets" implicates a privacy interest, the Court there was determining whether a "rap sheet" fell under the "privacy interest" protected by an exemption to the Freedom of Information Act ("FOIA"), not that protected by the Constitution. We pointed out that the Supreme Court itself made the distinction between the two types of privacy interest, and we quoted its statement in *Reporters Committee*, that "[t]he question of the statutory meaning of privacy under the FOIA is, of course, not the same as the question . . . whether an individual's interest in privacy is protected by the Constitution." . . .

. . . Finally, we concluded in *E.B.* that even if a "fundamental right" were implicated, "the state's interest here would suffice to justify the deprivation." . . .

The District Court here concluded that there was no privacy interest in the plaintiffs' home addresses, stating that "[b]ecause such information is public, plaintiffs' privacy interests are not implicated." As to the argument based on the "compilation" of various information, the court held that "[i]t is of little consequence whether this public information is disclosed piecemeal or whether it is disclosed in compilation."

To the extent that plaintiffs' alleged injury stems from the disclosure of their sex offender status, alone or in conjunction with other information, the District Court's opinion is in line with other cases in this court and elsewhere holding specifically that arrest records and related information are not protected by a right to privacy. See *Fraternal Order of Police*, 812 F.2d at 117 (holding that "arrest records are not entitled to privacy protection" because they are public); *Cline v. Rogers*, 87 F.3d 176, 179 (6th Cir.) (holding that "there is no constitutional right to privacy in one's criminal record" because "arrest and conviction information are matters of public record"). . . .

We are not insensitive to the argument that notification implicates plaintiffs' privacy interest by disclosing their home addresses. The compilation of home addresses in widely available telephone directories might suggest a consensus that these addresses are not considered private were it not for the fact that a significant number of persons, ranging from public officials and performers to just ordinary folk, choose to list their telephones privately, because they regard their home addresses to be private information. Indeed, their view is supported by decisions holding that home addresses are entitled to privacy under FOIA, which exempts from disclosure personal files "the disclosure of which would constitute a clearly unwarranted invasion of personal privacy." 5 U.S.C. § 552(b)(6). . . .

Although these cases are not dispositive, they reflect the general understanding that home addresses are entitled to some privacy protection, whether or not so required by a statute. We are therefore unwilling to hold that absent a statute, a person's home address is never entitled to privacy protection. . . .

Accepting therefore the claim by the plaintiffs that there is some nontrivial interest in one's home address by persons who do not wish it disclosed, we must engage in the balancing inquiry repeatedly held appropriate in privacy cases. . . .

The nature and significance of the state interest served by Megan's Law was considered in *E.B.* There, we stated that the state interest, which we characterized as compelling, "would suffice to justify the deprivation even if a fundamental right of the registrant's were implicated." We find no reason to disagree. The public interest in knowing where prior sex offenders live so that susceptible individuals can be appropriately cautioned does not differ whether the issue is the registrant's claim under the Double Jeopardy or Ex Post Facto Clauses, or is the registrant's claim to privacy. . . .

The other argument raised by plaintiffs as part of their privacy claim is that community notification infringes upon their fundamental interest in family relationships. . . . In *E.B.*, we recognized that Megan's Law "impose[s] no restrictions on a registrant's ability to live and work in a community," but that plaintiffs complain of the law's "indirect effects: Actions that members of the community may take as a result of learning of the registrant's past, his potential danger, and his presence in the community." Even if we concede, as the District Court did, that "being subject to Megan's Law community notification places a constitutionally cognizable strain upon familial relationships," these indirect effects which follow from plaintiffs' commission of a crime are too substantially different from the government actions at issue in the prior cases to fall within the penumbra of constitutional privacy protection. Megan's Law does not restrict plaintiffs' freedom of action with respect to their families and therefore does not intrude upon the aspect of the right to privacy that protects an individual's independence in making certain types of important decisions. . . .

During the pendency of this appeal, appellants filed a series of motions under seal, six in all, seeking to supplement the record with evidence of recent incidents which have caused serious adverse consequences to them and their families. . . .

. . . [T]his court has previously held that "[t]he fact that protected information must be disclosed to a party who has a particular need for it . . . does not strip the information of its protection against disclosure to those who have no similar need," and we have required the government to implement adequate safeguards against unnecessary disclosure. Because these motions were filed in this court in the first instance, the District Court has not had the opportunity to consider the information contained therein and to determine whether any action is appropriate in light of our precedent.

[We] will remand this matter so that the District Court can consider whether plaintiffs' interest in assuring that information is disclosed only to those who have a particular need for it has been accorded adequate protection in light of the information set forth in the motions. . . .

NOTES & QUESTIONS

1. **The Privacy Interest.** In *Russell v. Gregoire*, 124 F.3d 1079 (9th Cir. 1997), the court considered a similar challenge under the constitutional right to information privacy to Washington's version of Megan's Law, which involved public dissemination of the offender's photo, name, age, birth date, other identifying information, and a summary of his or her crime. It includes the general vicinity of his or her residence, but not the exact address. Wash. Rev. Code § 9A.44.130(1). The court held that the statute did not run afoul of the constitutional right to information privacy:

> In this case, the collection and dissemination of information is carefully designed and narrowly limited. Even if *Whalen* and *Nixon* had established a broad right to privacy in data compilations, the Act does not unduly disseminate private information about Russell and Stearns.
>
> Moreover, any such right to privacy, to the extent it exists at all, would protect only personal information. The information collected and disseminated by the Washington statute is already fully available to the public and is not constitutionally protected, with the exception of the general vicinity of the offender's residence (which is published) and the offender's employer (which is collected but not released to the public). Neither of these two items are generally considered "private."

Recall that in *Paul P. v. Verniero,* the court held that the reasoning of *United States Department of Justice v. Reporters Committee for Freedom of the Press*, 489 U.S. 749 (1989), was inapplicable to the constitutional right to information privacy. In *Reporters Committee*, the Court concluded that the disclosure of FBI "rap sheets" (compilations of a person's arrests, charges, and convictions) under the Freedom of Information Act (FOIA) implicated a privacy interest:

> In an organized society, there are few facts that are not at one time or another divulged to another. Thus, the extent of the protection accorded a privacy right at common law rested in part on the degree of dissemination of the allegedly private fact and the extent to which the passage of time rendered it private. . . . Recognition of this attribute of a privacy interest supports the distinction, in

terms of personal privacy, between scattered disclosure of the bits of information contained in a rap sheet and revelation of the rap sheet as a whole.

The reasoning of this case suggests that sexual offenders have a privacy interest in their prior convictions. Should the reasoning of *Reporters Committee* apply to the constitutional right to information privacy?

Prior to *Paul P.*, the New Jersey Supreme Court had upheld New Jersey's Megan's Law in *Doe v. Poritz*, 662 A.2d 367 (N.J. 1995). There, the court, relying on *Reporters Committee*, recognized a privacy interest in some of the information divulged by New Jersey's Megan's Law:

> . . . We find . . . that considering the totality of the information disclosed to the public, the Notification Law implicates a privacy interest. That the information disseminated under the Notification Law may be available to the public, in some form or other, does not mean that plaintiff has no interest in limiting its dissemination. As the Court recognized in *United States Department of Justice v. Reporters Committee for Freedom of the Press*, 489 U.S. 749 (1989), privacy "encompass[es] the individual's control of information concerning his or her person." . . .
>
> . . . [T]he Court recognized a "distinction . . . between scattered disclosure of the bits of information contained in a rap sheet and revelation of the rap sheet as a whole." . . . The Court noted, furthermore, that there was a "privacy interest inherent in the nondisclosure of certain information even when the information may have been at one time public." . . .
>
> In exposing those various bits of information to the public, the Notification Law links various bits of information — name, appearance, address, and crime — that otherwise might remain unconnected. However public any of those individual pieces of information may be, were it not for the Notification Law, those connections might never be made. We believe a privacy interest is implicated when the government assembles those diverse pieces of information into a single package and disseminates that package to the public, thereby ensuring that a person cannot assume anonymity — in this case, preventing a person's criminal history from fading into obscurity and being wholly forgotten. Those convicted of crime may have no cognizable privacy interest in the fact of their conviction, but the Notification Law, given the compilation and dissemination of information, nonetheless implicates a privacy interest. The interests in privacy may fade when the information is a matter of public record, but they are not non-existent. . . .

The court, however, concluded that the state interest outweighed the sexual offender's privacy interest:

> There is an express public policy militating toward disclosure: the danger of recidivism posed by sex offenders. The state interest in protecting the safety of members of the public from sex offenders is clear and compelling. The Legislature has determined that there is a substantial danger of recidivism by sex offenders, and public notification clearly advances the purpose of protecting the public from that danger. . . .

Compare the treatment of *Reporters Committee* in *Paul P.* and *Poritz*. How do the cases differ in the way they deal with the import of *Reporters Committee*?[27]

2. ***Postscript to* Paul P.** Following the Third Circuit's decision in *Paul P.*, the district court on remand held that the Megan's Law regulations in New Jersey did not sufficiently protect against unauthorized disclosures. The plaintiffs had cited to 45 instances where information had been released to unauthorized persons, with one disclosure resulting in the offender's name and address being printed in an article on the front page of a newspaper. Although noting that zero leakage is unattainable, the court stated that the government must avoid "unreasonably impinging on the 'nontrivial' privacy interests" of the plaintiffs and that the current Megan's Law regulations failed to meet this standard. *Paul P. v. Farmer*, 80 F. Supp. 2d 320 (D.N.J. 2000). The state attorney general promulgated new guidelines that were approved by the district court and affirmed on appeal. *See Paul P. v. Farmer*, 227 F.3d 98 (3d Cir. 2000). The new guidelines permit two forms of notice. An "unredacted notice" contains all information. A "redacted notice" omits the specific home address of the offender as well as the name and address of the employer. To receive an unredacted notice, the recipient must sign a form agreeing to be bound by court order and submitting to the jurisdiction of the court. The recipient must agree to share information only with her household and those caring for her children. If the person refuses to sign the receipt, then she can only receive the redacted notice.

In 2000, New Jersey amended its constitution by a referendum that provided that nothing in the New Jersey Constitution shall prohibit the disclosure of Megan's Law information over the Internet. New Jersey subsequently posted its sexual offender data on a website, excluding the offenders' current home addresses.

In *A.A. v. New Jersey*, 341 F.3d 206 (3d Cir. 2003), the Third Circuit upheld New Jersey's Megan's Law against a privacy claim against a public Internet registry posting personal information against convicted sex offenders. The court found that the Internet registry, which contains information about certain high-risk and moderate-risk sex offenders, was permissible due to the state's compelling interest to prevent sex offenses. Although the convicted sex offenders have a "nontrivial" privacy interest in their home addresses, the court concluded that a need exists to access information in a mobile society. The court stated: "Consider parents with young children who want to purchase a new home in New Jersey. Without the Registry, they would not be notified of the presence of convicted sex offenders, even those with a high risk of re-offense, until they had already purchased their new home which may be in the proximity of a Registrant's home. . . . So too a family planning a vacation at the New Jersey shore."

---

[27] *See also Cutshall v. Sundquist*, 193 F.3d 466 (6th Cir. 1999) (rejecting reliance on *Reporters Committee* and concluding that constitutional right to information privacy is not implicated by Megan's Law).

Like New Jersey, many states are placing their Megan's Law information on the Internet. Is such a practice going too far? Or is it necessary to make accessing the information more convenient? Consider Daniel Solove's critique of posting Megan's Law disclosures on the Internet:

> Megan's Law disclosures may be relevant for certain types of relationships, such as child care. Still, what most Megan's Laws lose sight of the use of the information in question. Megan's Law data is beneficial when disclosed for certain purposes, but not necessarily for all purposes. When placed on the Internet for any curious individual around the world to see, Megan's Law information becomes disconnected from its goals.[28]

3. *The Breadth of Megan's Laws.* Megan's Law does not merely involve offenses against children. It encompasses a wide range of sex offenses, which can range from sodomy, prostitution, consensual homosexual acts, masturbation in public places, flashing, and statutory rape. In some states, the disclosure does not indicate what particular sexual offense the offender committed. Is such a general listing appropriate? Is Megan's Law justified under the constitutional right to information privacy for every offense that a state classifies as a sexual offense? Or does the balance weigh in favor of Megan's Law only for specific offenses? If so, how should such offenses be distinguished from ones in which the balance does not weigh in favor of Megan's Law?[29]

4. *Recidivism Rates.* One of the justifications for Megan's Law is that sexual offenders have a high recidivism rate and, hence, pose a threat to the community. But sexual offenders have a lower recidivism rate than those who commit other forms of violent crime, such as robbers. In one study of offenders re-arrested within three years for any crime, previously convicted murderers had approximately a 42 percent re-arrest rate; rapists had a 51.5 percent re-arrest rate; other sexual offenders had a 48 percent re-arrest rate; and robbers had a 66 percent re-arrest rate. However, re-arrest rates, without more information, are misleading. Of the 51.5 percent of rapists who were re-arrested within three years after being released, only 7.7 percent were re-arrested for a sex crime. Further, different types of sexual offenders have different recidivism rates.[30]

5. *Family Stigma.* The majority of sexual offenses against children are committed by family members or close friends of the family (estimated at

---

[28] Daniel J. Solove, *The Virtues of Knowing Less: Justifying Privacy Protections Against Disclosure*, 53 Duke L.J. 967, 1061 (2003).

[29] For more on the privacy implications of Megan's Laws, see Caroline Louise Lewis, *The Jacob Wetterling Crimes Against Children and Sexually Violent Offender Registration Act: An Unconstitutional Deprivation of the Right to Privacy and Substantive Due Process*, 31 Harv. C.R.-C.L. L. Rev. 89 (1996); Symposium, *Critical Perspectives on Megan's Law: Protection vs. Privacy*, 13 N.Y.L. Sch. J. Hum. Rts. 1 (1996).

[30] *See* Jane A. Small, *Who Are the People in Your Neighborhood? Due Process, Public Protection, and Sex Offender Notification Laws*, 74 N.Y.U. L. Rev. 1451 (1999). For a contrary view regarding recidivism rates for sex offenders, see Daniel L. Feldman, *The "Scarlet Letter Laws" of the 1990s: A Response to Critics*, 60 Alb. L. Rev. 1081 (1997).

about 92 percent).[31] When a child's parent is released and is listed in the sex offender registry, the child's privacy can also be compromised because the entire family is under the stigma of harboring a sexual offender.

In *Doe v. Quiring,* 686 N.W.2d 918 (S.D. 2004), a young woman, who was the victim of incest by her father, brought suit to have her father's name removed from the sex offender public registry. Among the information that the registry contains is the type of crime that the offender committed. The victim argued that "public access to incest offenders and their crimes through the Registry 'necessarily' involves the 'release of . . . identifying information regarding the victim of the crime.'" Pursuant to South Dakota's Megan's Law: "Nothing in this section allows the release of the name or any identifying information regarding the victim of the crime to any person other than law enforcement agencies, and such victim identifying information is confidential." SDCL 22-22-40. The victim contended that "because the crime of incest involves familial relationships, the very definition of the crime of incest 'so narrows the group of possible victims that identification of the victim is necessarily implicated by the name of the offense.'" The court, however, disagreed:

> [B]ecause the Registry does not reveal the victim's familial relationship, age, physical description, address, or gender, a victim could be any one of a number of less than 21-year-old relatives of the offender. Under these circumstances, we believe that the mere listing of the offender and type of offense is not the disclosure of the "identifying information" that the Legislature intended to prohibit. . . .

In dissent, Justices Meierhenry and Sabers argued:

> Initially, the legislative purpose "of alerting the public in the interest of community safety" is satisfied by identifying the crime as "rape" or "sexual contact." To note the crime specifically as incest only serves to narrow the class of victims to a small number capable of being identified. The size of the class of incest victims is limited to family members. The number of family members under the age of twenty-one is even smaller and, in some cases, may include only a couple of children. Publicly identifying the crime as "incest" significantly increases the risk of providing "identifying information of the victim" and may bring opprobrium on family members who were not victims. It may also have the effect of making victims or family members reluctant to report the crimes knowing the registry will list the crime as incest. Often incest crimes go unreported because of the fear of public exposure and embarrassment created for the family, victim, and perpetrator. Michele L. Earl-Hubbard, *The Child Sex Offender Registration Laws: The Punishment, Liberty Deprivation, and Unintended Results Associated with the Scarlet Letter Laws of the 1990s,* 90 N.W. U. L. Rev. 788, 856 (1996). As one author noted, "Ironically, Megan's Laws may stigmatize the very victims of sex offenses whom they are designed to protect, many of whom are children living in the same house as the sex offender." Daniel J. Solove, *The Virtues of*

---

[31] Michele L. Earl-Hubbard, Comment, *The Child Sex Offender Registration Laws: The Punishment, Liberty Deprivation, and Unintended Results Associated with the Scarlet Letter Laws of the 1990s,* 90 Nw. U. L. Rev. 788, 851-52 (1996).

Knowing Less: Justifying Privacy Protections Against Disclosure, 53 Duke L.J. 967, 1060 (2003).

6. ***Shaming Punishments.*** In colonial America, marking criminals with branding, mutilation, or letter-wearing (such as the scarlet letter) was common. Marks would be burned into the convict's hand or forehead. This was often done because there was no way of imprisoning people. Nathaniel Hawthorne's *The Scarlet Letter* involves a famous example of a shaming punishment where Hester Prynne was made to stitch a red letter "A" to her clothing to punish her for adultery. Does Megan's Law amount to a shaming punishment? Is this form of punishment appropriate?

   Amitai Etzioni has praised shaming in the context of Megan's Law. He argues: "[S]haming is particularly communitarian in that it does not occur unless the community approves of the values at stake."[32] In his view, moreover, due to recidivism among sex offenders, a likely alternative to publicizing the presence of the sex offender in the community plus shaming will be "to keep the offender longer in jail" to protect the community. Will antisocial behavior expand in the absence of shaming?

7. ***Shaming in Other Contexts.*** Today, shaming punishments are making a comeback. In a move broader than Megan's Law, some localities are publicizing the names of certain arrestees. For example, in 1997, Kansas City created "John TV," broadcasting on television the names, photographs, addresses, and ages of people who had been arrested for soliciting prostitutes. Similar programs have been started in other cities. Is this activity more or less problematic to you than Megan's Law?

8. ***Is Megan's Law a Punishment?*** In *Smith v. Doe,* 538 U.S. 84 (2003), the Supreme Court examined whether Alaska's Megan's Law violated the constitutional prohibitions on ex post facto laws. An ex post facto law is a law that applies after the fact. In other words, the federal government and the states cannot pass a law that criminalizes past actions. Pursuant to U.S. Constitution art. I, § 9, "No . . . ex post facto Law shall be passed" by the federal government. U.S. Constitution art. I, § 10 provides that "No state shall . . . pass any . . . ex post facto Law."

   Alaska's Megan's Law makes public the following information: "name, aliases, address, photograph, physical description, description [,] license [and] identification numbers of motor vehicles, place of employment, date of birth, crime for which convicted, date of conviction, place and court of conviction, length and conditions of sentence, and a statement as to whether the offender or kidnapper is in compliance with [the update] requirements . . . or cannot be located." Alaska Stat. § 18.65.087(b). The Supreme Court noted that if the sex offender registration and notification law is designed to "impose punishment," then it "constitutes retroactive punishment" and is an impermissible ex post facto law. The Court concluded that "the intent of the Alaska Legislature was to create a civil, nonpunitive regime." Further, the Court concluded that the

---

[32] Amitai Etzioni, The *Limits of Privacy* 60-61 (1999).

effect of the law did not "negate Alaska's intention to establish a civil regulatory scheme." In reaching this latter conclusion, the Court dismissed an argument that Megan's Law resembles the "shaming punishments of the colonial period."

> Any initial resemblance to early punishments is, however, misleading. Punishments such as whipping, pillory, and branding inflicted physical pain and staged a direct confrontation between the offender and the public. Even punishments that lacked the corporal component, such as public shaming, humiliation, and banishment, involved more than the dissemination of information. They either held the person up before his fellow citizens for face-to-face shaming or expelled him from the community. By contrast, the stigma of Alaska's Megan's Law results not from public display for ridicule and shaming but from the dissemination of accurate information about a criminal record, most of which is already public. Our system does not treat dissemination of truthful information in furtherance of a legitimate governmental objective as punishment. On the contrary, our criminal law tradition insists on public indictment, public trial, and public imposition of sentence. Transparency is essential to maintaining public respect for the criminal justice system, ensuring its integrity, and protecting the rights of the accused. The publicity may cause adverse consequences for the convicted defendant, running from mild personal embarrassment to social ostracism. In contrast to the colonial shaming punishments, however, the State does not make the publicity and the resulting stigma an integral part of the objective of the regulatory scheme.

The Court reasoned that although the "reach of the Internet is greater than anything which could have been designed in colonial times," the goal of the notification is "to inform the public for its own safety, not to humiliate the offender. . . . The Internet makes the document search more efficient, cost effective, and convenient for Alaska's citizenry."

Justices Stevens, Ginsburg, and Breyer dissented. In Justices Ginsburg and Breyer's dissent, they observed:

> And meriting heaviest weight in my judgment, the Act makes no provision whatever for the possibility of rehabilitation: Offenders cannot shorten their registration or notification period, even on the clearest demonstration of rehabilitation or conclusive proof of physical incapacitation. However plain it may be that a former sex offender currently poses no threat of recidivism, he will remain subject to long-term monitoring and inescapable humiliation.
>
> John Doe I, for example, pleaded *nolo contendere* to a charge of sexual abuse of a minor nine years before the Alaska Act was enacted. He successfully completed a treatment program, and gained early release on supervised probation in part because of his compliance with the program's requirements and his apparent low risk of re-offense. He subsequently remarried, established a business, and was reunited with his family. He was also granted custody of a minor daughter, based on a court's determination that he had been successfully rehabilitated. The court's determination rested in part on psychiatric evaluations concluding that Doe had "a very low risk of re-offending" and is "not a pedophile." Notwithstanding this strong evidence of rehabilitation, the Alaska Act requires Doe to report personal information to

the State four times per year, and permits the State publicly to label him a "Registered Sex Offender" for the rest of his life.

9. ***Megan's Law Disclosures for All Crimes?*** A growing number of states are furnishing online databases of all of their current inmates and parolees. Do these databases serve the statutory purpose of protecting the community? Should registries of felons stop at sexual offenders? Why not all people convicted of a crime?

10. ***How Far Can Disclosure Go?*** In May 2001, Judge J. Manuel Banales of Texas ordered 21 convicted sex offenders to post signs in their front yards stating: "Danger! Registered Sex Offender Lives Here." Additionally, the offenders must place bumper stickers on their cars stating: "Danger! Registered Sex Offender in Vehicle." Other offenders were ordered to send letters to all the people who lived within three blocks of their homes. Compliance is monitored by the probation department. "The whole idea is that everybody is looking at you," Judge Banales said to the offenders. "You have no one else to blame but yourself." Under the reasoning of either *Russell* or *Paul P.*, is this court order a violation of the constitutional right to information privacy?

11. ***A Prison-Privacy Trade-off?*** Suppose that instead of enacting Megan's Laws, society just decided to extend the sentences for sexual offenses and lock up sexual offenders for life. Perhaps if states could not enact a Megan's Law, they would resort to more life sentences for sexual offenders. Most likely, many offenders would choose a regime where they would be released from prison and subject to Megan's Law to a regime where they would spend the rest of their lives in prison. What do you think about this potential trade-off?

B. GOVERNMENT RECORDS OF PERSONAL INFORMATION

1. FAIR INFORMATION PRACTICES

In the 1960s, the increasing use of computers gave rise to a significant public debate about privacy. In particular, commentators expressed opposition to the increasing amount of personal information collected by government agencies and stored in computer databases.

In 1973, the Department of Housing, Education, and Welfare (HEW) issued a highly influential report about government records maintained in computer databases. The HEW Report characterized the growing concern over privacy:

> It is no wonder that people have come to distrust computer-based record-keeping operations. Even in non-governmental settings, an individual's control over the personal information that he gives to an organization or that an organization obtains about him, is lessening as the relationship between the giver and receiver of personal data grows more attenuated, impersonal, and

diffused. There was a time when information about an individual tended to be elicited in face-to-face contacts involving personal trust and a certain symmetry, or balance, between giver and receiver. Nowadays, an individual must increasingly give information about himself to large and relatively faceless institutions, for handling and use by strangers — unknown, unseen, and, all too frequently, unresponsive. Sometimes the individual does not even know that an organization maintains a record about him. Often he may not see it, much less contest its accuracy, control its dissemination, or challenge its use by others. . . .

The poet, the novelist, and the social scientist tell us, each in his own way, that the life of a small-town man, woman, or family is an open book compared to the more anonymous existence of urban dwellers. Yet the individual in a small town can retain his confidence because he can be more sure of retaining control. He lives in a face-to-face world, in a social system where irresponsible behavior can be identified and called to account. By contrast, the impersonal data system, and faceless users of the information it contains, tend to be accountable only in the formal sense of the word. In practice they are for the most part immune to whatever sanctions the individual can invoke.

To remedy these growing concerns over the accumulation and use of personal information by the government, the HEW Report recommended that a Code of Fair Information Practices be established:

- There must be no personal-data record-keeping systems whose very existence is secret.

- There must be a way for an individual to find out what information about him is in a record and how it is used.

- There must be a way for an individual to prevent information about him obtained for one purpose from being used or made available for other purposes without his consent.

- There must be a way for an individual to correct or amend a record of identifiable information about him.

- Any organization creating, maintaining, using, or disseminating records of identifiable personal data must assure the reliability of the data for their intended use and must take reasonable precautions to prevent misuse of the data.[33]

Fair Information Practices can be understood most simply as the rights and responsibilities that are associated with the transfer and use of personal information. Since the intent is to correct information asymmetries that result from the transfer of personal data from an individual to an organization, Fair Information Practices typically assign rights to individuals and responsibilities to organizations.

---

[33] U.S. Dep't of Health, Educ. & Welfare, Records, *Computers, and the Rights of Citizens: Report of the Secretary's Advisory Comm. on Automated Personal Data Systems* 29-30, 41-42 (1973) ("HEW Report").

MARC ROTENBERG, *FAIR INFORMATION PRACTICES AND*
THE ARCHITECTURE OF PRIVACY (WHAT LARRY DOESN'T GET)

2001 Stan. Tech. L. Rev. 1

. . . Not only have Fair Information Practices played a significant role in framing privacy laws in the United States, these basic principles have also contributed to the development of privacy laws around the world and even to the development of important international guidelines for privacy protection. The most well known of these international guidelines are the Organization for Economic Cooperation and Development's Recommendations Concerning and Guidelines Governing the Protection of Privacy and Transborder Flows of Personal Data ("OECD Guidelines"). The OECD Guidelines set out eight principles for data protection that are still the benchmark for assessing privacy policy and legislation: Collection Limitation; Data Quality; Purpose Specification; Use Limitation; Security Safeguards; Openness; Individual Participation; and Accountability. The principles articulate in only a couple of pages a set of rules that have guided the development of national law and increasingly the design of information systems.

It is generally understood that the challenge of privacy protection in the information age is the application and enforcement of Fair Information Practices and the OECD Guidelines. While some recommendations for improvement have been made, the level of consensus, at least outside of the United States, about the viability of Fair Information Practices as a general solution to the problem of privacy protection is remarkable. As recently as 1998 the OECD reaffirmed support for the 1980 guidelines, and countries that are adopting privacy legislation have generally done so in the tradition of Fair Information Practices.

While some commentators have made recommendations for updating or expanding the principles, there is general agreement that the concept of Fair Information Practices and the specific standards set out in the OECD Guidelines continue to provide a useful and effective framework for privacy protection in information systems.

Commentators have also noted a remarkable convergence of privacy policies. Countries around the world, with very distinct cultural backgrounds and systems of governance, nonetheless have adopted roughly similar approaches to privacy protection. Perhaps this is not so surprising. The original OECD Guidelines were drafted by representatives from North America, Europe, and Asia. The OECD Guidelines reflect a broad consensus about how to safeguard the control and use of personal information in a world where data can flow freely across national borders. Just as it does today on the Internet. . . .

Viewed against this background, the problem of privacy protection in the United States in the early 1990s was fairly well understood. The coverage of U.S. law was uneven: Fair Information Practices were in force in some sectors and not others. There was inadequate enforcement and oversight. Technology continued to outpace the law. And the failure to adopt a comprehensive legal framework to safeguard privacy rights could jeopardize transborder data flows with Europe and other regions. These factors should all have played a significant role in coding a solution to the privacy problem. . . .

2. THE PRIVACY ACT

Influenced by the HEW Report's Fair Information Practices and inspired by the Watergate scandal, Congress enacted the Privacy Act of 1974 four months after President Nixon resigned from office. In passing the Privacy Act, Congress found that "the privacy of an individual is directly affected by the collection, maintenance, use, and dissemination of personal information by Federal agencies" and that "the increasing use of computers and sophisticated information technology, while essential to the efficient operations of the Government, has greatly magnified the harm to individual privacy that can occur from any collection, maintenance, use, or dissemination of personal information."

Purposes of the Privacy Act. The Privacy Act's stated purposes are, among other things, to: (1) "permit an individual to determine what records pertaining to him are collected, maintained, used, or disseminated by [federal] agencies"; (2) "permit an individual to prevent records pertaining to him obtained by such agencies for a particular purpose from being used or made available for another purpose without his consent"; (3) allow an individual to access and correct his personal data maintained by federal agencies; and (4) ensure that information is "current and accurate for its intended use, and that adequate safeguards are provided to prevent misuse of such information."

Applicability and Scope. The Privacy Act applies to federal agencies. It does not apply to businesses or private sector organizations. Moreover, it does not apply to state and local agencies—only federal ones.

In order to establish a violation of the Privacy Act, a plaintiff must prove several things:

First, the plaintiff must prove that the agency violated its obligations under the Act (most often, that the agency improperly disclosed information).

Second, the information disclosed must be a "record" contained within a "system of records." A "record" must be identifiable to an individual (contain her name or other identifying information) and must contain information about the individual. § 552a(a)(4). The record must be kept as part of a "system of records," which is "a group of any records under the control of any agency from which information is retrieved by the name of the individual or by some identifying number, symbol, or other identifying particular assigned to the individual." § 552a(a)(5).

Third, to collect damages, the plaintiff must show that an adverse impact resulted from the Privacy Act violation and that the violation was "willful or intentional."

Limits on Disclosure. Pursuant to the Privacy Act:

No agency shall disclose any record which is contained in a system of records by any means of communication to any person, or to another agency, except pursuant to a written request by, or with prior written consent of, the individual to whom the record pertains. 5 U.S.C. § 552a(b).

Responsibilities for Recordkeeping. The Privacy Act establishes restrictions and responsibilities for agencies maintaining records about individuals. Agencies shall maintain "only such information about an individual as is relevant and necessary to accomplish a purpose of the agency required to be accomplished by statute or by executive order of the President." § 552a(e)(1). Additionally, agencies shall "collect information to the greatest extent practicable directly from the subject individual when the information may result in adverse determinations about an individual's rights, benefits, and privileges under Federal programs." § 552a(e)(2). Agencies shall inform individuals who make a request about how their personal information will be used. § 552a(e)(3). Agencies must publish in the Federal Register notices about the systems of records they maintain. § 552a(e)(4). Agencies must also "establish appropriate administrative, technical, and physical safeguards to insure the security and confidentiality of records." § 552a(e)(10).

Right to Access and Correct Records. Pursuant to the federal Privacy Act, upon request, individuals can review their records and can ask that the agency correct any inaccuracies in their records. § 552a(d).

Enforcement. If an agency fails to comply with any provision of the Privacy Act, or refuses to comply with an individual's request to obtain access to her records or correct her records, individuals can bring a civil action in federal court. § 552a(g)(1). The court can enjoin the agency from withholding access of records. § 552a(g)(3). In limited circumstances, monetary damages may be awarded:

> (4) In any suit brought under the provisions of subsection (g)(1)(C) or (D) of this section in which the court determines that the agency acted in a manner which was intentional or willful, the United States shall be liable to the individual in an amount equal to the sum of —
>
>> (A) actual damages sustained by the individual as a result of the refusal or failure, but in no case shall a person entitled to recovery receive less than the sum of $1,000; and
>> (B) the costs of the action together with reasonable attorney fees as determined by the court. § 552a(g)(4).

Law Enforcement Exceptions. Pursuant to § 552a(j), the "head of any agency may promulgate rules . . . to exempt any system of records within the agency from any part of [the Privacy Act] if the system of records" is (1) maintained by the CIA or (2) maintained by a law enforcement agency and consists of (A) identifying and criminal history information compiled to identify criminal offenders or (B) "information compiled for the purpose of criminal investigation, including reports of informants and investigators, and associated with an identifiable individual"; or (C) "reports identifiable to an individual compiled at any stage of the process of enforcement of the criminal laws from arrest or indictment through release from supervision." This exception does not apply to § 552a(b), §§ 552a(c)(1) and (2), and certain portions of § 552(e).

Additionally, § 552(k)(2) allows the head of any agency to promulgate rules to exempt "investigatory material compiled for law enforcement purposes" from the Act's accounting and access provisions. However, "if any individual is denied any right, privilege, or benefit that we would otherwise be entitled by Federal law . . . as a result of the maintenance of such material, such material shall be provided to the individual, except to the extent that the disclosure of such material would reveal the identity of a [government informant]."

FOIA Exception. When FOIA requires that information be released, the Privacy Act does not apply. § 552a(b)(3).

Routine Use Exception. The broadest exception under the Privacy Act is that information may be disclosed for any "routine use" if disclosure is "compatible" with the purpose for which the agency collected the information. § 552a(b)(3).

Information Sharing Among Agencies. The Privacy Act permits one agency to disclose information "to another agency or to an instrumentality of any governmental jurisdiction within or under the control of the United States for a civil or criminal law enforcement activity" if the agency or instrumentality's head makes "a written request to the agency which maintains the record." § 552a(b)(7).

Other Exceptions. In all, there are about a dozen exceptions to the Privacy Act. Other exceptions allow disclosure to the Census Bureau, "to a person pursuant to a showing of compelling circumstances affecting the health or safety of an individual"; to Congress; to the Comptroller General, pursuant to a court order, or to a credit reporting agency. § 552a(b).

State Privacy Acts. Although every state has a statute comparable to the federal FOIA, requiring public access to government records, most states do not have a statute comparable to the federal Privacy Act. Only about a third of states have adopted such a statute.

QUINN V. STONE
978 F.2d 126 (3d Cir. 1992)

HIGGINBOTHAM, J. Appellants Randall Quinn (Quinn) and Marianne Merritt (Merritt) are married to each other and work at the Letterkenny Army Depot (LEAD) in Chambersburg, Pennsylvania as civilian employees. Appellee Michael P.W. Stone is the Secretary of the Army and the second appellee is the Department of the Army. At LEAD, Quinn is a natural resource manager and Merritt is an environmentalist. Quinn is responsible for controlling the deer population on LEAD property by setting the length of the hunting season and determining the types of deer to be killed. . . .

In addition to their professional interest in LEAD's wildlife, Quinn and Merritt are both deer hunters and hunt deer on LEAD property with other hunters. Quinn and Merritt are registered with the Pennsylvania Game Commission and possess valid Pennsylvania hunting licenses. Quinn and Merritt also have "bonus tags" which allow the holder to kill one additional deer during the hunting season. Both also possess valid LEAD hunting permits.

On January 6, 1990, Quinn and Merritt went hunting on LEAD property. At check-in Post 2, both Quinn and Merritt complied with the LEAD procedures whereby all hunters are required to produce their Pennsylvania hunting licenses and LEAD hunting permits. As part of this check-in procedure, the LEAD Security employees annotate a computer-generated hunting roster, which lists all hunters with LEAD hunting permits. Each entry on this roster corresponds to a single hunter and consists of:

    a. the LEAD permit number
    b. the Pennsylvania hunting license number
    c. the name of the hunter
    d. the address of the hunter
    e. the phone number of the hunter.

The hunting roster is computer-generated at the beginning of the hunting day, with the check-in time, check-out time, and kill information added by hand as the day progresses.

The computer-generated LEAD hunting roster for January 6, 1990 incorrectly gave separate addresses and phone numbers for Quinn and Merritt. The roster indicated that Quinn lived at an address in St. Thomas, Pennsylvania and Merritt in Chambersburg, Pennsylvania. Both parties agree that Merritt's listed address was incorrect and out-of-date. Apparently, her prior address was never changed in the LEAD files, even though Merritt had written her new address on her LEAD hunting permit application, her LEAD hunting license, her application for a Pennsylvania hunting license, and her Pennsylvania hunting license for the 1988-89 and 1989-90 hunting seasons.

Two of Security personnel conducting the check-in at Post 2 during the day were Lark Myers (Myers) and Statler. Statler personally observed Quinn and Merritt checking in to hunt. Shortly after Quinn and Merritt checked in, Myers mentioned to Statler that Quinn had previously brought a deer to Myers' fiance's butcher shop to be butchered. Statler questioned how Quinn could still be hunting this season if he had already killed one deer. Statler reviewed the roster and found Quinn's name. Statler then looked for Quinn's wife's name but did not recognize Merritt's name. He then asked Myers what Quinn's wife's name was and Myers told him that she thought Merritt continued to go by the name of Merritt after her marriage to Quinn. Statler again reviewed the hunting roster and found Merritt's entry. Statler noted that the home address listed for Merritt was different from that listed for Quinn and remarked on this to Myers.

Later that morning, Statler reported to David Miller (Miller), an investigator in LEAD Security, the information that Quinn and Merritt were hunting and that they had taken a deer to be butchered earlier during the hunting season. Miller then informed Jody Eyer (Eyer), a part-time Deputy Wildlife Conservation Officer with the Pennsylvania Game Commission, of Quinn's and Merritt's hunting even though Quinn had previously killed a deer that season. Eyer believed that there were grounds to suspect that a hunting violation had occurred since a hunter is generally allowed to kill only one deer a season. Eyer contacted Statler and spoke with him directly. He also reviewed the hunting roster. Eyer turned the case over to Frank Clark (Clark), a full-time PGC Wildlife Conservation Officer, for investigation, although Eyer continued to aid in the investigation.

On January 9, 1990, LEAD's Miller met with PGC's Clark. In this meeting, Clark reviewed the hunting roster generated at Post 2 and noted the discrepancies between Quinn's and Merritt's listed addresses. To Clark, the two addresses raised the possibility that Quinn and Merritt "had used two addresses to illegally obtain two sets of hunting licenses." At this meeting, Clark requested that LEAD review available files to determine the correct addresses. LEAD investigator Fox (Fox) did so but was unable to determine the correct addresses. . . .

[After an extensive investigation, Clark concluded that there "was no evidence to charge Quinn and Merritt with hunting violations."]

The appellants allege that both suffered occupational and health damage as a result of the disclosures. Quinn alleges that he suffered damage to his professional image, reputation, integrity and working relationship with LEAD and PGC personnel. Merritt alleges that her reputation for "law-abidingness and integrity" was damaged. Quinn also alleges suffering from stress, headaches, hypertension, chest pains, sinusitis, nervousness, and inability to sleep. Merritt alleges she suffered stress, nervousness, and inability to sleep. Both allege they suffered emotional anguish.

Quinn and Merritt filed separate actions alleging violations of the Privacy Act, 5 U.S.C. § 552a, and seeking an order directing the Army to purge its files of records relating to the plaintiffs and damages for violations of the Act. The district court granted the defendants' motion to consolidate the actions and on September 18, 1991 granted the defendants' motion for summary judgment. Plaintiffs filed a timely appeal. . . .

This appeal presents several different issues relating to three of the four necessary elements for a damages suit under the Privacy Act. As we explain in this opinion, in order to maintain a suit for damages under the catch-all provision of 5 U.S.C. § 552a(g)(1)(D) for a violation of the Act's central prohibition against disclosure, § 552a(b), a plaintiff must advance evidence to support a jury's finding of four necessary elements: (1) the information is covered by the Act as a "record" contained in a "system of records"; (2) the agency "disclose[d]" the information; (3) the disclosure had an "adverse effect" on the plaintiff (an element which separates itself into two components: (a) an adverse effect standing requirement and (b) a causal nexus between the disclosure and the adverse effect); and (4) the disclosure was "willful or intentional."

The appellees first argue that the district court properly granted summary judgment because the information relating to Merritt on the LEAD hunting roster and on her time card is not information covered by the Act. We disagree.

The Act defines a "record" to mean:

> any item, collection, or grouping of information about an individual that is maintained by an agency, including, but not limited to, his education, financial transactions, medical history, and criminal or employment history and that contains his name, or the identifying particular assigned to the individual, such as a finger or voice print or a photograph.

5 U.S.C. § 552a(a)(4). Further, the Act's prohibition on disclosure relates to "any record which is contained in a system of records." § 552a(b). Fitting the statutory definitions of a protected record, the information allegedly disclosed from both the hunting roster and the time card contained an identifying particular (the plaintiff's name) and was maintained within a system of records.

Appellees propose two separate arguments that the information contained in the hunting roster is not a "record" within the meaning of the Act. First, they argue that stale or incorrect information, such as Merritt's out-of-date address and telephone number, is not covered by the Act because this information is not meaningful. We cannot accept this argument in this case. The Third Circuit has recently re-affirmed that, at the very least, there is a "meaningful" privacy interest in home addresses. *Federal Labor Relations Authority v. U.S. Department of the Navy,* 966 F.2d 747 (3d Cir. 1992) (en banc). As we noted there, the disclosure of home addresses "can identify specific and sometimes personal characteristics about residents." In the light of the other information disclosed in this case, the disclosure of the existence of an out-of-date address, different from the one at which Merritt was currently living, revealed the meaningful information that Merritt had maintained an address apart from Quinn's, an address that might be used to manipulate Pennsylvania's hunting laws. As this case demonstrates, the meaningful privacy interest in a particular piece of information may be lessened by the passage of time, but such an interest is unlikely to be extinguished. We conclude that this out-of-date home address was meaningful information and was protected by the Privacy Act.

Second, the appellees argue that the Act protects only information which discloses a characteristic or quality of an individual. The appellees contend that Merritt's information on the hunting roster did not constitute a "record" because "none of the information disclosed a characteristic or quality about her." Applying this argument also to the time card, appellees argue that "[t]he fact that an individual was working or not on a weekday is not information which discloses a characteristic [or] quality about the person."

At first blush, this argument seems close to the requirement that the information must be meaningful, but appellees here propose a different gloss on the statute than that of meaningfulness. They would read the Act to protect only that category of information which is intimate or personal, information which directly reflects a specific or personal characteristic about a person (as opposed to information which might reveal such specific and personal characteristics but only in conjunction with other pieces of information). . . .

[W]e think that such information does reveal a "quality or characteristic" about that person. Time card information regarding taking time off from work as compensation for overtime, as sick leave, or for vacation can easily be considered descriptive of an individual.

More significantly, we reject appellees' underlying argument that the information covered by the Act as a "record" is limited to the information that directly reflects a characteristic or quality of the individual. . . . [W]e find such an interpretation contrary to the language of the statute. On its face, § 552a(a)(4)'s statutory definition of a record as "any item, collection, or grouping of information about an individual" appears to us to have a broad meaning encompassing *any* information about an individual that is linked to that individual through an identifying particular and is not to be restricted to information that reflects a characteristic or quality of an individual. Moreover, our interpretation is consistent with the thrust of the statutory definition. A "record" may be "any item, collection, or grouping of information about an individual." 5 U.S.C. § 552a(a)(4). While a record can therefore consist of a single piece of information, it may also be a collection or grouping of pieces of information. Thus, even if a piece of information could not meet a "characteristic or quality" test standing alone, it could still be included within a "record" as statutorily defined and protected by the Act if that piece of information were linked with an identifying particular (or was itself an identifying particular) and maintained within a system of records.

We thus . . . conclude in this case that both the information on the hunting roster and time card was information that was covered by the Act.

Even if the information on the hunting roster and on the time card were covered by the Act, appellees make two arguments that this information was not "disclosed" within the meaning of 552a(b). The appellees contend that, while Quinn's home address and telephone number were records, they were not disclosed within the meaning of 5 U.S.C. § 552a(b) because the information had been previously disclosed by Quinn to the Pennsylvania Game Commission. Appellees argue that disclosure contemplates release of information not otherwise known to the recipient.

We agree the Act is not violated where the agency makes available information which is already known by the recipient.

There is no basis, however, in this record to make such an argument. Clearly, there was no prior knowledge of the information on the time card. Likewise, there is no evidence on this record that Eyer and Clark, the investigators in the field, already had any actual knowledge of the home address information. There is, by contrast, evidence that Eyer and Clark received the partially out-of-date information about Quinn's and Merritt's addresses by means of a disclosure of the hunting roster. Without evidence that Eyer and Clark otherwise knew the information disclosed, the appellees' argument fails.

The appellees next contend that no disclosure of information occurs when the information, even if not actually known by the recipient, is otherwise public. Appellees may be making either of two arguments here. To say that information is public can mean either that such information is readily accessible to the members of the public or that each individual member of the public should be presumed to know this information. We reject both arguments.

Appellees have cited to this court no case that stands for the proposition that there is no violation of the Act if the information is merely readily accessible to the members of the public (such as in the local telephone book) and our research has discovered none. We doubt if any court would so hold. To do so would eviscerate the Act's central prohibition, the prohibition against disclosure. For instance, such an argument would short-circuit the delicate balancing courts now engage in between the FOIA and the Privacy Act under 5 U.S.C. § 552a(b)(2). See *FLRA v. U.S. Department of the Navy,* 966 F.2d 747 (3d Cir. 1992) (en banc). To define disclosure so narrowly as to exclude information that is readily accessible to the public would render superfluous the detailed statutory scheme of twelve exceptions to the prohibition on disclosure. We conclude that making available information which is readily accessible to the members of the public is a disclosure under 552a(b), subject, of course, to the Act's exceptions. . . .

We thus conclude that not only was the information contained in the hunting roster and the time card covered by the Act, but it was also disclosed within the Act's terms.

What remains is to examine the Act's "adverse effect" requirement. The Privacy Act's civil remedies section, in relevant part, provides as follows:

> (g)(1) Civil remedies. — Whenever any agency . . .
> (D) fails to comply with any other provision of this section, or any rule promulgated thereunder, in such a way as to have an adverse effect on an individual,
> the individual may bring a civil action against the agency, and the district courts of the United States shall have jurisdiction in the matters under the provisions of this subsection.

This section thus gives an individual adversely affected by any agency violation of the Act a judicial remedy whereby the individual may seek damages. Thus, there are two limitations placed on the right to sue. First, the adverse effect requirement of (g)(1)(D) is, in effect, a standing requirement. Allegations of mental distress, emotional trauma, or embarrassment have been held sufficient to confer standing. *Albright v. United States,* 732 F.2d 181 (D.C. Cir. 1984). Second, to state a claim under the Act, the plaintiff must also allege a causal connection between the agency violation and the adverse effect. . . .

Appellees argue that neither of these two requirements were met in this case. First, they argue that Merritt makes no assertion that the release of time card information had an adverse effect on her sufficient to confer standing. Upon any fair reading of the record, however, appellees' argument cannot be sustained. As we have recounted above, both appellants allege that they have undergone stress and emotional anguish. Both also allege that they have suffered occupational losses due to the PGC investigation allegedly caused by the disclosures. We think these allegations sufficient to satisfy the Act's adverse effect standing requirement.

With greater vigor, appellees argue there is no causal connection between the disclosures and the adverse effects. They assert that the PGC's investigation was begun prior to and independent of the disclosure of the hunting roster. Appellees claim that the only information passed along to the PGC was Statler's personal observation that plaintiffs were hunting on Jan. 6, 1990 and Myers' observation that they had previously taken a deer to the butcher's. Defendants also claim that the time card disclosure had no causal connection to the adverse effects suffered by the plaintiffs.

We believe, however, that the record amply shows a causal connection between the disclosures and the alleged adverse effects on Quinn and Merritt by means of the PGC investigation. First, there is sufficient evidence for a jury to find that the PGC investigation was initially caused in significant part by the disclosure of the discrepant addresses. There is evidence that the varying addresses were passed along by LEAD Security employee Statler to Eyer of the PGC from the beginning of the investigation. . . .

A trier of fact could infer that the address discrepancy was part of the impetus for Eyer to turn the investigation over to Clark, the full-time investigator.

We thus cannot agree with the district court that the difference in addresses which initially raised the suspicion of the PGC investigator was "only a small part of his investigation." This piece of information was present from the very beginning of the investigation and may have played a significant role in the crucial decisions to initiate and pursue the investigation.

Second, there is sufficient evidence for a jury to conclude that the disclosure of Merritt's time card information served to fuel and to keep the investigation going even after the discrepancy in the addresses had been resolved. . . .

The issue of the "routine use" exception to the Act's prohibition on disclosure has been argued before this court by both parties. However, the issue was not argued before the district court in support of the defendants' motion for summary judgment and the district court did not consider the issue. We thus consider this issue waived for purposes of this appeal. . . .

We recognize that some persons might feel that a lengthy opinion such as this that explores whether or not it was permissible to reveal matters so mundane as information on a hunting record and a time card is a trivialization of the federal litigation process. However, Congress has made the choice that there are some areas of privacy which must be recognized by the federal government in its management of information and, as we read the present record, the appellants should not be precluded from proving their allegations. The district court's grant of summary judgment in favor of the appellees will be reversed in part and affirmed in part and the case remanded for further proceedings consistent with this opinion.

NYGAARD, J. dissenting. While I agree with most of the conclusions reached by the majority, because I believe that the disclosure of the contents of these records was pursuant to a "routine use," I respectfully dissent.

The Privacy Act states that records are not protected from disclosure if the disclosure is pursuant to a "routine use." 5 U.S.C. § 552a(b)(3). A routine use is defined as "the use of such record for a purpose which is compatible with the purpose for which it was collected." 5 U.S.C. § 552a(a)(7). In addition, the Privacy Act states that the agencies must publish a notice each year in the Federal Register indicating the routine uses for which protected records may be used. 5 U.S.C. § 552a(e)(4). This information must include "the categories of users and the purpose of such use." 5 U.S.C. § 552a(e)(4)(D).

In compliance with the Privacy Act, the DOD published in the Federal Register, "blanket routine uses" which are applicable to every record system maintained by its various branches, including the army.

One of these provisions entitled "Routine Use-Law Enforcement," states:

> In the event that a system of records maintained by this component to carry out its functions indicates a violation or potential violation of law . . . the relevant records in the system of records may be referred, as a routine use, to the appropriate agency, whether federal, state, local, or foreign, charged with the responsibility of *investigating or prosecuting such violation* [.] Fed. Reg., May 29, 1985. (emphasis added.) . . . .

These routine uses fairly cover the facts of this case. The disclosure of the hunting roster information was for use by the Pennsylvania Game Commission's wildlife conservation officers to investigate possible violations of state hunting laws. This was precisely the type of "state law enforcement" the regulations covered.

Here, one of the main purposes for the collection of the information on the hunting roster was to monitor hunting in order to prevent unlawful overkilling of deer. The disclosure was made to help PGC find out if appellants were trying to hunt deer lawfully. . . .

The disclosure of Merritt's time card information to PGC investigator Clark creates a tougher question. . . .

In general, the main reason time cards are collected is to determine employees' work hours in order to compute payroll. It is not to collect information about an employee which can be used against him in a criminal investigation.

Nonetheless, the *main* purpose for which time cards are collected certainly is not the *only* purpose. One of the reasons time card information is collected is to find out if an employee was at work on a given day-the precise reason for which it was used in this case. LEAD disclosed information on Merritt's time card precisely for this purpose. . . .

For this reason, I would affirm the district court's grant of summary judgment as to both Merritt's time card and the hunting roster.

NOTES & QUESTIONS

1. *Information in the Public Domain.* The court in *Quinn* holds that even publicly accessible information is protected against disclosure by the Privacy Act because holding otherwise "would eviscerate the Act's central prohibition, the prohibition against disclosure." The court noted that it could find no court to conclude that information already in the public domain would not be protected. Subsequently, some courts have so concluded. For example,

in *Barry v. U.S. Department of Justice*, 63 F. Supp. 2d 25 (D.D.C. 1999), the court concluded that a record widely accessible to the public was not protected by the Privacy Act. It distinguished *Quinn* along with other "decisions involving information that may have been 'public,' but that could be found only in isolated public records." The court concluded that because the record in question was publicly available in a way not "isolated or obscure," it was not protected by the Privacy Act. Did *Quinn* turn on the fact that the addresses were "obscure or isolated"? Should information already available to the public be protected against disclosure by the Privacy Act?

2. ***The "Routine Use" Exemption: "The Biggest Loophole."*** Consider Robert Gellman:

> The act limits use of personal data to those officers and employees of the agency maintaining the data who have a need for the data in the performance their duties. This vague standard is not a significant barrier to the sharing of personal information within agencies. . . . No administrative process exists to control or limit internal agency uses. Suits have been brought by individuals who objected to specific uses, but most uses have been upheld. . . .
>
> The legislation left most decisions about external uses to the agencies, and this created the biggest loophole in the law.
>
> An agency can establish a "routine use" if it determines that a disclosure is compatible with the purpose for which the record was collected. This vague formula has not created much of a substantive barrier to external disclosure of personal information. . . . Later legislation, political pressures, and bureaucratic convenience tended to overwhelm the law's weak limitations. Without any effective restriction on disclosure, the Privacy Act lost much of its vitality and became more procedural and more symbolic.[34]

Other observers have noted the problematic nature of the Privacy Act's "routine use" exemption. According to the Privacy Act's language, a routine use must be "a purpose which is compatible with the purpose for which it was collected." 5 U.S.C. § 552a(7). Paul Schwartz observes:

> Not only is the "routine use" exemption applied in a fashion that ignores relevant statutory language, such agency practice continues despite prolonged and well-placed criticism of it. As early as 1977, the Privacy Protection Study Commission, a blue-ribbon commission created by Congress at the time of the Privacy Act's enactment, noted its disapproval of overbroad applications of the routine use exemption. In 1983, the House Committee on Government Operations issued a condemnation of such agency practice. Three years later, the Congressional Office of Technology Assessment complained that the routine use exemption had become "a catchall exemption." . . . David Flaherty, in a pathbreaking comparative study of data protection law, *Protecting Privacy in Surveillance Societies*, called the American routine use exemption "a huge loophole." Despite these comments, agencies continue to justify almost any use of information as a "routine use" of the data.[35]

---

[34] Robert Gellman, *Does Privacy Law Work? in Technology and Privacy: The New Landscape* (Philip E. Agre & Marc Rotenberg eds. 1997).

[35] Paul M. Schwartz, *Privacy and Participation*, 80 Iowa L. Rev. 553, 586 (1995).

Only a few courts have placed substantive limits on an agency's proposed "routine use" of personal information. Justin Franklin and Robert Bouchard conclude: "In practice, many of the cases where a 'routine use' defense is raised are resolved in favor of the government."[36]

3. ***What Is an "Agency"?*** The Privacy Act only applies to federal agencies. In *Tripp v. Executive Office of the President,* 200 F.R.D. 140 (D.D.C. 2001), Linda Tripp sued the Executive Office of the President (EOP), the Department of Defense (DOD), and the FBI. Tripp, the friend of Monica Lewinsky who secretly recorded their conversations to assist Kenneth Starr in his investigation of President Clinton, contended that the EOP, DOD, and FBI leaked confidential information about her to the media in retaliation for her role in the Clinton investigation. The EOP moved to dismiss claiming that it was not an "agency" within the meaning of the Privacy Act. The Privacy Act adopts FOIA's definition of "agency," which "includes any executive department . . . . or other establishment in the executive branch of the Government (including the Executive Office of the President), or any independent regulatory agency." 5 U.S.C. § 552(f). However, the court concluded:

> The plain language of the Privacy Act directs one to look to the FOIA for the definition of "agency." 5 U.S.C. § 552a(1). While on its face, the FOIA states that the definition of "agency" includes the Executive Office of the President, the U.S. Supreme Court, the D.C. Circuit, and Congress, through the FOIA's legislative history, have all made it abundantly clear this does not include the Office of the President.

Unlike the EOP, the FBI and DOD are agencies under the Privacy Act. In 2003, Tripp settled her Privacy Act suit against the Defense Department for $590,000.

4. ***What Constitutes a "Record" in a "System of Records"?*** The Privacy Act does not apply to all information or records that an agency maintains. Rather, it applies to records contained in a "system of records." A "system of records" is a group of records where data is retrieved by an individual's name or other identifying information. 5 U.S.C. § 552a(a)(4). A "record" is "any item, collection, or grouping of information about an individual . . . that contains his name [or other identifying information]." In *Albright v. United States,* 631 F.2d 915 (D.C. Cir. 1980), the court analyzed whether a videotape of a meeting constituted a "record" under the Privacy Act. The court concluded that it was: "As long as the tape contains a means of identifying an individual by picture or voice, it falls within the definition of 'record' under the Privacy Act."

---

[36] Justin D. Franklin & Robert E. Bouchard, *Guidebook to the Freedom of Information and Privacy Acts* §2:18 (2007).

DOE V. CHAO

540 U.S. 614 (2004)

SOUTER, J. The United States is subject to a cause of action for the benefit of at least some individuals adversely affected by a federal agency's violation of the Privacy Act of 1974. The question before us is whether plaintiffs must prove some actual damages to qualify for a minimum statutory award of $1,000. We hold that they must.

Petitioner Buck Doe filed for benefits under the Black Lung Benefits Act, 83 Stat. 792, 30 U.S.C. § 901 *et seq.,* with the Office of Workers' Compensation Programs, the division of the Department of Labor responsible for adjudicating it. The application form called for a Social Security number, which the agency then used to identify the applicant's claim, as on documents like "multicaptioned" notices of hearing dates, sent to groups of claimants, their employers, and the lawyers involved in their cases. The Government concedes that following this practice led to disclosing Doe's Social Security number beyond the limits set by the Privacy Act. See 5 U.S.C. § 552a(b).

Doe joined with six other black lung claimants to sue the Department of Labor, alleging repeated violations of the Act and seeking certification of a class of "'all claimants for Black Lung Benefits since the passage of the Privacy Act.'" Pet. for Cert. 6a. Early on, the United States stipulated to an order prohibiting future publication of applicants' Social Security numbers on multicaptioned hearing notices, and the parties then filed cross-motions for summary judgment. The District Court denied class certification and entered judgment against all individual plaintiffs except Doe, finding that their submissions had raised no issues of cognizable harm. As to Doe, the court accepted his uncontroverted evidence of distress on learning of the improper disclosure, granted summary judgment, and awarded $1,000 in statutory damages under 5 U.S.C. § 552a(g)(4).

A divided panel of the Fourth Circuit affirmed in part but reversed on Doe's claim, holding the United States entitled to summary judgment across the board. 306 F.3d 170 (2002). The Circuit treated the $1,000 statutory minimum as available only to plaintiffs who suffered actual damages because of the agency's violation, and then found that Doe had not raised a triable issue of fact about actual damages, having submitted no corroboration for his claim of emotional distress, such as evidence of physical symptoms, medical treatment, loss of income, or impact on his behavior. In fact, the only indication of emotional affliction was Doe's conclusory allegations that he was " 'torn . . . all to pieces' " and " 'greatly concerned and worried' " because of the disclosure of his Social Security number and its potentially " 'devastating' " consequences.

Doe petitioned for review of the holding that some actual damages must be proven before a plaintiff may receive the minimum statutory award. . . .

"[I]n order to protect the privacy of individuals identified in information systems maintained by Federal agencies, it is necessary . . . to regulate the collection, maintenance, use, and dissemination of information by such agencies." Privacy Act of 1974. The Act gives agencies detailed instructions for managing their records and provides for various sorts of civil relief to individuals aggrieved by failures on the Government's part to comply with the requirements.

Subsection (g)(1) recognizes a civil action for agency misconduct fitting within any of four categories (the fourth, in issue here, being a catchall), 5 U.S.C. §§ 552a(g)(1)(A)–(D), and then makes separate provision for the redress of each. The first two categories cover deficient management of records: subsection (g)(1)(A) provides for the correction of any inaccurate or otherwise improper material in a record, and subsection (g)(1)(B) provides a right of access against any agency refusing to allow an individual to inspect a record kept on him. . . .

Like the inspection and correction infractions, breaches of the statute with adverse consequences are addressed by specific terms governing relief:

> In any suit brought under the provisions of subsection (g)(1)(C) or (D) of this section in which the court determines that the agency acted in a manner which was intentional or willful, the United States shall be liable to the individual in an amount equal to the sum of —
>
>> (A) actual damages sustained by the individual as a result of the refusal or failure, but in no case shall a person entitled to recovery receive less than the sum of $1,000; and
>> (B) the costs of the action together with reasonable attorney fees as determined by the court. § 552a(g)(4).

Doe argues that subsection (g)(4)(A) entitles any plaintiff adversely affected by an intentional or willful violation to the $1,000 minimum on proof of nothing more than a statutory violation: anyone suffering an adverse consequence of intentional or willful disclosure is entitled to recovery. The Government claims the minimum guarantee goes only to victims who prove some actual damages. We think the Government has the better side of the argument.

To begin with, the Government's position is supported by a straightforward textual analysis. When the statute gets to the point of guaranteeing the $1,000 minimum, it not only has confined any eligibility to victims of adverse effects caused by intentional or willful actions, but has provided expressly for liability to such victims for "actual damages sustained." It has made specific provision, in other words, for what a victim within the limited class may recover. When the very next clause of the sentence containing the explicit provision guarantees $1,000 to a "person entitled to recovery," the simplest reading of that phrase looks back to the immediately preceding provision for recovering actual damages, which is also the Act's sole provision for recovering anything (as distinct from equitable relief). With such an obvious referent for "person entitled to recovery" in the plaintiff who sustains "actual damages," Doe's theory is immediately questionable in ignoring the "actual damages" language so directly at hand and instead looking for "a person entitled to recovery" in a separate part of the statute devoid of any mention either of recovery or of what might be recovered.

Nor is it too strong to say that Doe does ignore statutory language. When Doe reads the statute to mean that the United States shall be liable to any adversely affected subject of an intentional or willful violation, without more, he treats willful action as the last fact necessary to make the Government "liable," and he is thus able to describe anyone to whom it is liable as entitled to the $1,000 guarantee. But this way of reading the statute simply pays no attention to the fact that the statute does not speak of liability (and consequent entitlement to recovery) in a freestanding, unqualified way, but in a limited way, by reference to enumerated damages.

Doe's manner of reading "entitle[ment] to recovery" as satisfied by adverse effect caused by intentional or willful violation is in tension with more than the text, however. It is at odds with the traditional understanding that tort recovery requires not only wrongful act plus causation reaching to the plaintiff, but proof of some harm for which damages can reasonably be assessed. Doe, instead, identifies a person as entitled to recover without any reference to proof of damages, actual or otherwise. Doe might respond that it makes sense to speak of a privacy tort victim as entitled to recover without reference to damages because analogous common law would not require him to show particular items of injury in order to receive a dollar recovery. Traditionally, the common law has provided such victims with a claim for "general" damages, which for privacy and defamation torts are presumed damages: a monetary award calculated without reference to specific harm. . . .

This [conclusion] . . . is underscored by drafting history showing that Congress cut out the very language in the bill that would have authorized any presumed damages. The Senate bill would have authorized an award of "actual and general damages sustained by any person," with that language followed by the guarantee that "in no case shall a person entitled to recovery receive less than the sum of $1,000." S. 3418, 93d Cong., 2d Sess., § 303(c)(1) (1974). Although the provision for general damages would have covered presumed damages, this language was trimmed from the final statute, subject to any later revision that might be recommended by the Commission. The deletion of "general damages" from the bill is fairly seen, then, as a deliberate elimination of any possibility of imputing harm and awarding presumed damages. The deletion thus precludes any hope of a sound interpretation of entitlement to recovery without reference to actual damages.

Finally, Doe's reading is open to the objection that no purpose is served by conditioning the guarantee on a person's being entitled to recovery. As Doe treats the text, Congress could have accomplished its object simply by providing that the Government would be liable to the individual for actual damages "but in no case . . . less than the sum of $1,000" plus fees and costs. Doe's reading leaves the reference to entitlement to recovery with no job to do, and it accordingly accomplishes nothing. . . .

Next, Doe also suggests there is something peculiar in offering some guaranteed damages, as a form of presumed damages not requiring proof of amount, only to those plaintiffs who can demonstrate actual damages. But this approach parallels another remedial scheme that the drafters of the Privacy Act would probably have known about. At common law, certain defamation torts were redressed by general damages but only when a plaintiff first proved some "special harm," i.e., "harm of a material and generally of a pecuniary nature." 3 Restatement of Torts § 575, Comments a and b (1938) (discussing defamation torts that are "not actionable per se"). Plaintiffs claiming such torts could recover presumed damages only if they could demonstrate some actual, quantifiable pecuniary loss. Because the recovery of presumed damages in these cases was supplemental to compensation for specific harm, it was hardly unprecedented for

Congress to make a guaranteed minimum contingent upon some showing of actual damages, thereby avoiding giveaways to plaintiffs with nothing more than "abstract injuries." . . .

The "entitle[ment] to recovery" necessary to qualify for the $1,000 minimum is not shown merely by an intentional or willful violation of the Act producing some adverse effect. The statute guarantees $1,000 only to plaintiffs who have suffered some actual damages.

GINSBURG, STEVENS, and BREYER, JJ. dissenting. "It is 'a cardinal principle of statutory construction' that 'a statute ought, upon the whole, to be so construed that, if it can be prevented, no clause, sentence, or word shall be superfluous, void, or insignificant.'" The Court's reading of § 552a(g)(4) is hardly in full harmony with that principle. Under the Court's construction, the words "a person entitled to recovery" have no office, and the liability-determining element "adverse effect" becomes superfluous, swallowed up by the "actual damages" requirement. Further, the Court's interpretation renders the word "recovery" nothing more than a synonym for "actual damages," and it turns the phrase "shall be liable" into "may be liable." . . .

The purpose and legislative history of the Privacy Act, as well as similarly designed statutes, are in harmony with the reading of § 552a(g)(4) most federal judges have found sound. Congress sought to afford recovery for "*any* damages" resulting from the "willful or intentional" violation of "any individual's rights under th[e] Act." § 2(b)(6), 88 Stat. 1896 (emphasis added). Privacy Act violations commonly cause fear, anxiety, or other emotional distress — in the Act's parlance, "adverse effects." Harm of this character must, of course, be proved genuine. In cases like Doe's, emotional distress is generally the only harm the claimant suffers, *e.g.,* the identity theft apprehended never materializes. . . .

The Government, although recognizing that "actual damages" may be slender and easy to generate, fears depletion of the federal fisc were the Court to adopt Doe's reading of § 552a(g)(4). Experience does not support those fears. As the Government candidly acknowledged at oral argument: "[W]e have not had a problem with enormous recoveries against the Government up to this point." No doubt mindful that Congress did not endorse massive recoveries, the District Court in this very case denied class-action certification, and other courts have similarly refused to certify suits seeking damages under § 552a(g)(4) as class actions. Furthermore, courts have disallowed the runaway liability that might ensue were they to count every single wrongful disclosure as a discrete basis for a $1,000 award.

The text of § 552a(g)(4), it is undisputed, accommodates two concerns. Congress sought to give the Privacy Act teeth by deterring violations and providing remedies when violations occur. At the same time, Congress did not want to saddle the Government with disproportionate liability. . . .

Congress has used language similar to § 552a(g)(4) in other privacy statutes. See 18 U.S.C. § 2707(c); 26 U.S.C. § 6110(j)(2); 26 U.S.C. § 7217(c) (1976 ed., Supp. V). These other statutes have been understood to permit recovery of the $1,000 statutory minimum despite the absence of proven actual damages. . . .

Doe has standing to sue, the Court agrees, based on "allegations that he was 'torn . . . all to pieces' and 'greatly concerned and worried' because of the disclosure of his Social Security number and its potentially 'devastating' consequences." Standing to sue, but not to succeed, the Court holds, unless Doe also incurred an easily arranged out-of-pocket expense. In my view, Congress gave Privacy Act suitors like Doe not only standing to sue, but the right to a recovery if the fact trier credits their claims of emotional distress brought on by an agency's intentional or willful violation of the Act. For the reasons stated in this dissenting opinion, which track the reasons expressed by Circuit Judge Michael dissenting in part in the Fourth Circuit, I would reverse the judgment of the Court of Appeals.

NOTES & QUESTIONS

1. *Postscript.* In subsequent litigation, the district court concluded that Buck Doe was still entitled to attorneys' fees and costs under the Privacy Act because he established that the government had willfully violated the Act. The court awarded $57,520.97 for attorneys' fees and costs. On appeal, in *Doe v. Chao*, 435 F.3d 492 (4th Cir. 2006), the Fourth Circuit held that attorneys' fees and costs could still be recovered despite failing to show actual damages. However, the court concluded that the district court erred in assessing the amount of the award because it failed to "give primary consideration to the amount of damages awarded as compared to the amount sought." On remand, the district court awarded $15,887.50 in attorneys' fees and costs to Doe's counsel.

2. *Damages Under the Privacy Act.* One of the difficulties in privacy cases that involve the leakage of personal information is establishing damages. In most cases, people might be made more vulnerable to harms like identity theft, but they might not yet be victimized. Damages for the violation of many Privacy Act violations will involve emotional distress rather than overt physical or psychological harm. By requiring "actual damages" in order to receive statutory damages, does the Court's holding in *Doe v. Chao* make it nearly impossible to recover for a Privacy Act violation? On the other hand, should any violation of the Privacy Act result in automatic damages for thousands of dollars?

   What constitutes "actual damages" under the Privacy Act? The *Chao* Court did not reach an opinion on the issue, noting in a footnote:

   > The Courts of Appeals are divided on the precise definition of actual damages. Compare *Fitzpatrick v. IRS*, 665 F.2d 327, 331 (11th Cir. 1982) (actual damages are restricted to pecuniary loss), with *Johnson v. Department of Treasury, IRS*, 700 F.2d 971, 972-974 (5th Cir. 1983) (actual damages can cover adequately demonstrated mental anxiety even without any out-of-pocket loss). That issue is not before us. . . . We assume without deciding that the Fourth Circuit was correct to hold that Doe's complaints in this case did not rise to the level of alleging actual damages. We do not suggest that out-of-pocket expenses are necessary for recovery of the $1,000 minimum; only that they suffice to qualify under any view of actual damages.

Recently, the Ninth Circuit weighed in on the issue and concluded that actual damages encompasses both pecuniary and nonpecuniary injuries. In *Cooper v. Federal Aviation Administration,* 596 F.3d 538 (9th Cir. 2010), the court reasoned:

> Congress's intent that the Act offer relief in the form of "any damages" resulting from a violation of one's right of privacy begs the question of what types of injuries typically result from the violation of such a right. The Supreme Court has observed that "[i]n the 'right of privacy' cases the primary damage is the mental distress from having been exposed to public view." *Time, Inc. v. Hill,* 385 U.S. 374 (1967). The related common-law tort of defamation also provides monetary relief for nonpecuniary harms. . . . Given the nature of the injuries that most frequently flow from privacy violations, it is difficult to see how Congress's stated goal of subjecting federal agencies to civil suit for any damages resulting from a willful or intentional violation of the Act could be fully realized unless the Act encompasses both pecuniary and nonpecuniary injuries.

The Supreme Court has granted certiorari in this case, and will decide it during the 2011-2012 Term.

3. ***The Linda Tripp Case.*** Recall the Linda Tripp case above in the notes to *Quinn v. Stone.* The Department of Defense (DOD) settled the case for $590,000. In light of *Doe v. Chao,* should the DOD have settled?

4. ***Willful vs. Negligent Violations of the Privacy Act.*** In *Andrews v. Veterans Administration,* 838 F.2d 418 (10th Cir. 1988), an employee of the Veterans Administration (VA) was responding to a FOIA request for proficiency reports of various nurses. The VA employee attempted to redact the identities of nurses from the reports, but failed to do so properly. As a result, several nurses could be identified on their reports. At trial, the district court concluded that the nurses "suffered some degree of anguish, embarrassment, or other mental trauma" from the disclosure and that the VA employee "acted conscientiously, in good faith, though inadvertently negligently, in releasing the proficiency reports in an inadequately sanitized condition." Furthermore, the district court concluded that the VA was grossly negligent in failing to adequately train the employee about the release of personal information. On appeal, the Tenth Circuit concluded that the disclosure of the information was improper. The identities of the nurses were protected under Exemption 6 of FOIA. However, the VA, despite acting with gross negligence, could not be held liable to the nurses:

> . . . [E]ven if the Privacy Act is violated, no punishment may be imposed unless the agency acted in a manner which was intentional or willful. In this case the district court equated "intentional or willful" with gross negligence. . . .
>
> . . . [T]he term "willful or intentional" clearly requires conduct amounting to more than gross negligence. We are persuaded by the District of Columbia Circuit's definitions of willful or intentional that contemplate action "so 'patently egregious and unlawful' that anyone undertaking the conduct should have known it 'unlawful,'" or conduct committed "without grounds for believing it to be lawful" or action "flagrantly disregarding others' rights under the Act," and we adopt those definitions, and add the view . . . that the

conduct must amount to, at the very least, reckless behavior. Those, and similar definitions, describe conduct more extreme than gross negligence.

Applying that standard to this case, our review of the record convinces us that the VA's conduct falls far short of a "willful or intentional" violation of the Privacy Act. Indeed, we find that it falls short of even the gross negligence standard applied by the district court to that conduct. . . .

According to Paul Schwartz, "individuals who seek to enforce their rights under the Privacy Act face numerous statutory hurdles, limited damages, and scant chance to affect an agency's overall behavior."[37] The most common form of improper disclosure of records is due to carelessness rather than willful behavior. Does the requirement that disclosure be done "willfully and intentionally" make damages under the Privacy Act virtually impossible to collect? What if the standard for collecting damages were negligence? Would agencies that must handle millions of records and respond to thousands of FOIA requests be exposed to too great a risk of liability? Consider Robert Gellman:

> The Privacy Act contains civil and criminal penalties for violations, but it is far from clear that the enforcement methods are useful. . . . In more than 20 years, federal prosecutors have brought no more than a handful of criminal cases, and perhaps only one, under the Privacy Act.
>
> The basic method for enforcing the Privacy Act is the individual lawsuit. Aggrieved individuals can sue the government for violations. . . . The former General Counsel to the Privacy Protection Study Commission testified that the act was "to a large extent, unenforceable by individuals." The main reasons are that it is difficult to recover damages and that limited injunctive relief is available under the law. Individual enforcement does not offer any significant incentive for agencies to comply more carefully with the Privacy Act's provisions.[38]

5. ***The Interaction Between the Privacy Act and FOIA.*** The Privacy Act does not apply to information that must be disclosed pursuant to FOIA. § 552a(k)(1). However, if one of FOIA's privacy exceptions applies, then the Privacy Act would require that the government refrain from disclosing certain information.

United States Dep't of Defense v. Federal Labor Relations Authority, 510 U.S. 487 (1994), clearly illustrates the interaction between these two statutes. There, two local unions requested the names and home addresses of employees in federal agencies. The agencies disclosed the employees' names and work stations to the unions but refused to release their home addresses. The unions filed unfair labor practice charges with the Federal Labor Relations Authority (FLRA), arguing that federal labor law required the agencies to disclose the addresses. Pursuant to the Federal Service Labor-Management Relations Statute, 5 U.S.C. §§ 7101–7135, agencies must, "to the extent not prohibited by law," furnish unions with data necessary for

---

[37] Paul M. Schwartz, *Privacy and Participation*, 80 Iowa L. Rev. 553, 596 (1995).

[38] Robert Gellman, *Does Privacy Law Work?* in *Technology and Privacy: The New Landscape* (Philip E. Agre & Marc Rotenberg eds. 1997).

collective-bargaining purposes. § 7114(b)(4). The agencies argued that disclosure of the home addresses was prohibited by the Privacy Act. The Court agreed with the agencies:

> The employee addresses sought by the unions are "records" covered by the broad terms of the Privacy Act. Therefore, unless FOIA would require release of the addresses, their disclosure is "prohibited by law," and the agencies may not reveal them to the unions.
>
> We turn, then, to FOIA. . . . The exemption potentially applicable to employee addresses is Exemption 6, which provides that FOIA's disclosure requirements do not apply to "personnel and medical files and similar files the disclosure of which would constitute a clearly unwarranted invasion of personal privacy." 5 U.S.C. § 552(b)(6).
>
> Thus, although this case requires us to follow a somewhat convoluted path of statutory cross-references, its proper resolution depends upon a discrete inquiry: whether disclosure of the home addresses "would constitute a clearly unwarranted invasion of [the] personal privacy" of bargaining unit employees within the meaning of FOIA. . . .
>
> We must weigh the privacy interest of bargaining unit employees in nondisclosure of their addresses against the only relevant public interest in the FOIA balancing analysis — the extent to which disclosure of the information sought would "she[d] light on an agency's performance of its statutory duties" or otherwise let citizens know "what their government is up to."
>
> The relevant public interest supporting disclosure in this case is negligible, at best. Disclosure of the addresses might allow the unions to communicate more effectively with employees, but it would not appreciably further "the citizens' right to be informed about what their government is up to." Indeed, such disclosure would reveal little or nothing about the employing agencies or their activities. . . .
>
> Against the virtually nonexistent FOIA-related public interest in disclosure, we weigh the interest of bargaining unit employees in nondisclosure of their home addresses. . . .
>
> It is true that home addresses often are publicly available through sources such as telephone directories and voter registration lists, but "[i]n an organized society, there are few facts that are not at one time or another divulged to another." *Reporters Comm.* The privacy interest protected by Exemption 6 "encompass[es] the individual's control of information concerning his or her person." An individual's interest in controlling the dissemination of information regarding personal matters does not dissolve simply because that information may be available to the public in some form. Here, for the most part, the unions seek to obtain the addresses of nonunion employees who have decided not to reveal their addresses to their exclusive representative. . . . Whatever the reason that these employees have chosen not to become members of the union or to provide the union with their addresses, however, it is clear that they have *some* nontrivial privacy interest in nondisclosure, and in avoiding the influx of union-related mail, and, perhaps, union-related telephone calls or visits, that would follow disclosure.
>
> Many people simply do not want to be disturbed at home by work-related matters. . . . Moreover, when we consider that other parties, such as commercial advertisers and solicitors, must have the same access under FOIA as the unions to the employee address lists sought in this case, it is clear that

the individual privacy interest that would be protected by nondisclosure is far from insignificant.

Because the privacy interest of bargaining unit employees in nondisclosure of their home addresses substantially outweighs the negligible FOIA-related public interest in disclosure, we conclude that disclosure would constitute a "clearly unwarranted invasion of personal privacy." 5 U.S.C. § 552(b)(6). FOIA, thus, does not require the agencies to divulge the addresses, and the Privacy Act, therefore, prohibits their release to the unions. . . .

Suppose the agencies opted not to litigate and disclosed the addresses of their employees. Would an employee have a cause of action under the Privacy Act for the disclosure of her address? Would that employee likely prevail in such an action? What type of remedy could the employee obtain?

6. ***The Complementary Values of the Privacy Act and FOIA.*** Although the Privacy Act restricts disclosures and the FOIA promotes disclosures, Marc Rotenberg contends that these statutes promote "complementary values." He observes:

> In enacting both the Privacy Act of 1974 and adopting the amendments that same year which significantly strengthened the Freedom of Information Act, Congress sought to ensure that personal information collected and maintained by federal agencies would be properly protected while also seeking to ensure that public information in the possession of federal agencies would be widely available to the public. The complementary goals of safeguarding individual liberty and ensuring government accountability were enabled by legislation that protected privacy on the one hand and promoted government oversight on the other.[39]

7. ***The Accuracy of the National Crime Information Center Database.*** In 2003, the Justice Department stated that the FBI would no longer be required to ensure the accuracy of its National Crime Information Center (NCIC) database, which consists of nearly 40 million criminal records. The NCIC provides access to fingerprints, mug shots, people with outstanding arrest warrants, missing persons, suspected terrorists, and gang members. The NCIC database is used by law enforcement officials around the country. Under the Privacy Act, can the FBI be exempted from maintaining the accuracy of NCIC?

8. ***Government Access to Private Sector Databases.*** The Privacy Act also applies to private companies that contract with the government to administer systems of records. 5 U.S.C. § 552a(m). However, as Christopher Hoofnagle observes, "a database of information that originates at a [commercial data broker] would not trigger the requirements of the Privacy Act." Hoofnagle goes on to observe:

> This limitation to the Privacy Act is critical — it allows [commercial data brokers] to amass huge databases that the government is legally prohibited

---

[39] Marc Rotenberg, *Privacy and Secrecy After September 11*, 86 Minn. L. Rev. 1115, 1129 (2002).

from creating. Then, when the government needs the information, it can request it from the [commercial data broker].[40]

9. ***Law Enforcement Access to Privacy Act Records.*** After 9/11, there were extensive complaints about restrictions on the ability of agencies to share personal information. To what extent does the Privacy Act permit such information sharing? Examine § 552a(b)(7).

10. ***The First Amendment Restriction.*** Pursuant to the Privacy Act, 5 U.S.C. § 552a(e)(7), agencies shall

> maintain no record describing how any individual exercises rights guaranteed by the First Amendment unless expressly authorized by statute or by the individual about whom the record is maintained or unless pertinent to and within the scope of an authorized law enforcement activity.

In *Becker v. Internal Revenue Service,* 34 F.2d 398 (7th Cir. 1994), three brothers, Thomas, Jeffrey, and Steven Becker, sought to have IRS records about them expunged pursuant to the Privacy Act. The files pertained to a criminal investigation of their failure to pay taxes and their activities as "tax protestors." Some of the records in the IRS's files pertained to the brothers' First Amendment rights, such as "a flyer advertising a book and a collection of newspaper articles regarding various IRS actions against certain individuals and groups who are alleged tax protesters or cheats."

The district court concluded that maintaining these materials in the Beckers' records "unquestionably implies that they are associated with the tax protesters and cheats described in the newspaper articles" and thus describes "how the plaintiffs exercise their First Amendment rights of speech and association." However, the district court concluded that the documents are "pertinent to and within the scope of an authorized law enforcement activity." Accordingly, the district court concluded, "the IRS may lawfully maintain these records and may withhold this information from plaintiffs under the Privacy Act pursuant to 5 U.S.C. § 552a(k)(2)." Section 552a(k)(2) allows agencies to exempt certain systems of records from individual access. The IRS claimed that it exempted the records because "to grant access to an investigative file could interfere with investigative and enforcement proceedings . . . and disclose investigative techniques and procedures."

The Seventh Circuit, however, concluded that § 551a(k)(2) does not allow agencies to be exempt from the First Amendment activities exclusion. The court noted that these documents were contained in files closed several years ago, and that the Beckers' ultimate objective was to have the records removed from their files, not just to gain access. The court reasoned:

> We conclude that the IRS has not sufficiently justified the maintenance of the documents in the Beckers' files. The IRS asserts that it may maintain these articles for possible future uses. Under some circumstances, this may be a legitimate justification for maintaining documents in a file for an extended period of time. We have examined the material, and any thought that it could

---

[40] Christopher Jay Hoofnagle, *Big Brother's Little Helpers: How ChoicePoint and Other Commercial Data Brokers Collect and Package Your Data for Law Enforcement,* 29 N.C. J. Int'l L. & Com. Reg. 595, 623 (2004).

be helpful in future enforcement activity concerning the Beckers is untenable. The material consists of newspaper articles dating from the middle to late 1980s, with no reference to the Beckers; any potential advantage to having these documents in the Beckers' files, at some uncertain date, is minuscule (and the IRS does not elaborate on how this material would be helpful). This indefinite use must be viewed in light of the fact that Judge Alesia found the Beckers' First Amendment rights are implicated. As the Senate Report on the Privacy Act pointed out,

> This section's [5 U.S.C. § 552a(e)(7)] restraint is aimed particularly at preventing collection of protected information not immediately needed, about law-abiding Americans, on the off-chance that Government or the particular agency might possibly have to deal with them in the future. S. Rep. No. 1183, 93d Cong., 2d Sess., *reprinted in* 1974 U.S.C.C.A.N. 6916, 6971.

There is a remote possibility that a part of the newspaper articles (describing practices of tax protesters) would be helpful in investigation of persons in general. We are not, however, presented with a situation where documents are maintained in a general file rather than in a specific individual's file.

Because we conclude that the IRS has not carried its burden in establishing that the materials are exempt from Privacy Act requirements, the documents should be expunged. . . .

Consider the following case, which came to a different conclusion regarding the First Amendment restriction:

J. RODERICK MACARTHUR FOUNDATION V. FEDERAL BUREAU OF INVESTIGATION

102 F.3d 600 (D.C. Cir. 1996)

GINSBURG, J. . . . The J. Roderick MacArthur Foundation and its former president Lance E. Lindblom seek to compel the Federal Bureau of Investigation to expunge its records relating to their associational activities and to refrain from maintaining such records in the future. Lindblom invokes both the Privacy Act, 5 U.S.C. § 552a, and the First Amendment to the Constitution of the United States; the Foundation relies solely upon the first amendment. . . .

As president of the Foundation, which provides grants to organizations involved with various political, social, and economic issues, Lindblom occasionally met with foreign leaders and political dissidents. At some point Lindblom's associations caught the attention of the FBI. When Lindblom and the Foundation later got wind of the FBI's interest they asked the Bureau, pursuant to the Freedom of Information Act, 5 U.S.C. § 552(a), for copies of all documents it had relating to them. The FBI informed them that it had a file on Lindblom consisting of 23 pages of materials and that, although the FBI did not have a file on the Foundation, it had located in other files five pages on which the Foundation's name appears. . . . The FBI released redacted copies of several of the documents relating to Lindblom and the Foundation but refused to release others. . . . At least some of the documents that the FBI released from the Lindblom file refer to Lindblom's associational activities. . . .

Section (e)(7) of the [Privacy] Act provides in relevant part that a government agency "shall . . . maintain no record describing how any individual exercises rights guaranteed by the First Amendment unless . . . pertinent to and within the scope of an authorized law enforcement activity." 5 U.S.C. § 552a(e)(7). . . .

Lindblom does not challenge the FBI's having collected information about him, and we assume that the information was pertinent to an authorized law enforcement activity when it was collected. Lindblom's claim is that an agency may not maintain (that is, retain) such lawfully collected information unless there is a current law enforcement necessity to do so. More specifically, he claims that "information which may have been properly collected as part of a legitimate law enforcement investigation may not be permanently kept under the name of the individual, especially when that individual is not the target of the investigation." . . .

Lindblom's primary assertion, that the Act forbids maintenance of information about first amendment activities unless that information serves a "current law enforcement necessity," requires more extended analysis. . . .

Looking at the terms of § (e)(7), we find no support for Lindblom's argument that the Act authorizes an agency to maintain a record describing first amendment activities only if and so long as there is a "current law enforcement necessity" to do so. The noun "record" in § (e)(7) is modified in only two ways: the record must be "[1] pertinent to and [2] within the scope of an authorized law enforcement activity." We do not understand this to mean, as Lindblom would in essence require, that the record must be pertinent to an active investigation; "an authorized law enforcement activity" such as foreign counter-intelligence, is a concept far broader than either an active investigation or a "current law enforcement necessity." . . .

Information that was pertinent to an authorized law enforcement activity when collected does not later lose its pertinence to that activity simply because the information is not of current interest (let alone "necessity") to the agency — a point seemingly lost upon our dissenting colleague. . . .

. . . Lindblom's interpretation of the Act would place new and daunting burdens, both substantive and administrative, upon the FBI and other government agencies, with little or no gain to individual privacy. If a law enforcement agency were required to purge its files of information regarding an individual so requesting whenever it had closed a particular investigation, then its ability to accomplish its mission would inevitably suffer. As we have said before, intelligence gathering is "akin to the construction of a mosaic"; to appreciate the full import of a single piece may require the agency to take a broad view of the whole work. Suppose, for example, that a citizen is contacted by a foreign agent but the FBI, after investigation, determines that the contact is innocent. If the same individual is later contacted by another foreign agent and perhaps thereafter by a third, then what had earlier appeared to be innocent when viewed in isolation may, when later viewed as part of a larger whole, acquire a more sinister air. Simply put, information that was once collected as part of a now-closed investigation may yet play a role in a new or reopened investigation. If the earlier record had been purged, however, then the agency's later investigation could not be informed by the earlier event(s).

Furthermore, if federal law enforcement agencies were required upon request to purge all such records, then they would surely be inundated with requests to do so. Responding to each such request could be difficult and time-consuming. . . . [W]e are reluctant to think that the Congress required so formidable an undertaking, with so little potential benefit, absent a clear statement to that effect. . . .

Accordingly, we hold that the Privacy Act does not prohibit an agency from maintaining records about an individual's first amendment activities if the information was pertinent to an authorized law enforcement activity when the agency collected the information. The Act does not require an agency to expunge records when they are no longer pertinent to a current law enforcement activity. . . .

The Foundation and Lindblom both claim that the FBI violated the first amendment by creating files on them based upon their associational activity. The FBI responds that it has no file on the Foundation and that its maintenance of lawfully gathered information about Lindblom does not violate his rights under the first amendment. We need not, however, decide whether the FBI violated the Constitution because the appellants lack standing so to claim.

"In order to establish standing under Article III, a complainant must allege (1) a personal injury-in-fact that is (2) 'fairly traceable' to the defendant's conduct and (3) redressable by the relief requested." *Branton v. FCC,* 993 F.2d 906 (D.C. Cir. 1992). The injury-in-fact requirement has two elements: The plaintiff must show that it has suffered "an invasion of a legally protected interest which is (a) concrete and particularized and (b) actual or imminent, not conjectural or hypothetical." *Lujan v. Defenders of Wildlife,* 504 U.S. 555, 560 (1992).

Consider first the case of the Foundation. It claims to have been injured because the FBI's maintenance of records on the Foundation inhibited its pursuit of activities protected by the first amendment. More specifically, the Foundation claims that the FBI's maintenance of records regarding the Foundation (1) may deter potential grantees from seeking money from the Foundation and (2) may make it more difficult for current Foundation employees to find jobs elsewhere in the future. . . .

The affiants declare, among other things, that "in the close-knit philanthropic community, an FBI file potentially limits the future employability of foundation personnel" and that "it is likely that some grantees' behavior will be affected by the maintenance of FBI files on foundations."

These affidavits speak broadly of stigma and harm to the Foundation's reputation. A "potential" limitation upon employees' future "employability" lacks concreteness. The Foundation points to not a single Foundation employee whose job prospects have been dimmed because of the FBI records. Nor does either affidavit indicate even generally how "some grantees' behavior will be affected" by the FBI records on the Foundation. The Foundation does not point to a single grantee or even type of grantee that would be any less likely to seek money from the Foundation because the FBI maintains records on it. This is not enough to establish an injury to the Foundation.

The Foundation's claim of injury also lacks immediacy. Because the Foundation does not allege that it has yet suffered any injury in the form of diminished job prospects for its employees or decreased interest from potential grantees, its only hope for standing rests upon showing that a threatened harm is "*certainly* impending." It is not enough for the Foundation to assert that it might suffer an injury in the future, or even that it is likely to suffer an injury at some unknown future time. Such "someday" injuries are insufficient. . . .

Lindblom also raises a first amendment claim, but he offers no separate arguments or affidavits in support of his standing. . . . Lindblom does not claim that the FBI's interest in him has limited or may limit his prospects for employment. . . . Lindblom has failed to show that he has suffered any injury in his individual capacity, we hold that Lindblom lacks standing to press a constitutional claim against the FBI. . . .

TATEL, J. concurring in part and dissenting in part. . . . The statute defines "maintain" as including both "maintain" and "collect." 5 U.S.C. § 552a(a)(3) (1994). To collect means "to gather together." To maintain means "to keep in existence or continuance; preserve." *Random House Unabridged Dictionary* 403, 1160 (2d ed.1993).In order to give each of these verbs its meaning, I would interpret section (e)(7), as a whole, to require that records be pertinent to "an authorized law enforcement activity" — words undefined in the statute — not only at the time of gathering, i.e., collecting, but also at the time of keeping, i.e., maintaining. In other words, if there is no *current* law enforcement activity to which a record has pertinence, the agency may not maintain it. Not only does this approach avoid effectively reading the word "maintain" out of that term's statutory definition, but it furthers the Act's purpose to protect citizens from the unnecessary collection *and* retention of personal information by the government. . . .

Because Congress chose to use the word "maintain" in section (e)(7), and to define that term as both "maintain" and "collect," we know that Congress must have meant something more than just "collect." . . .

Congress passed the Privacy Act to give individuals some defenses against governmental tendencies towards secrecy and "Big Brother" surveillance. *See* S. Rep. No. 93-1183, at 1 (Privacy Act "is designed to prevent the kind of illegal, unwise, overbroad, investigation and record surveillance of law-abiding citizens produced in recent years from actions of some over-zealous investigators, and the curiosity of some government administrators, or the wrongful disclosure and use, in some cases, of personal files held by Federal agencies."). The fewer unnecessary files describing First Amendment activities the government keeps on law-abiding citizens, the lesser the chance of any future abuse of those files.

NOTES & QUESTIONS

1. *The Scope of the First Amendment Restriction.* Which court, *Becker* or *MacArthur Foundation,* comes to a more convincing interpretation of the First Amendment restriction? Based on the *MacArthur Foundation* court's interpretation, to what would the First Amendment restriction apply?

2. *The Fourth Amendment and Information Collection and Recordkeeping.* Does the Fourth Amendment have any applicability in this context? Or does the Fourth Amendment only focus on information gathering activities?

3. *What Constitutes "Law Enforcement Activity" Under § 552a(e)(7)?* In *Bassiouni v. FBI,* 436 F.3d 712 (7th Cir. 2006), a law professor sought to have his records amended or expunged pursuant to the Privacy Act. Mahmoud Cherif Bassiouni, a DePaul University law professor, obtained access to FBI records about himself. The records listed groups labeled as "terrorist" groups, including the Popular Front for the Liberation of Palestine, a group currently designated by the Department of State as a terrorist group. The records did not conclude that Bassiouni was a member of any of these groups. The FBI stated "that it does not suspect him of ties to terrorist groups." Contending that he was not a member of these groups, Bassiouni demanded that the FBI amend or expunge his records because they were outdated and inaccurate. Among other things, Bassiouni contended that the maintenance of the records was a violation of § 552a(e)(7). The court, however, disagreed because § 552a(e)(7) does not apply to information "pertinent to and within the scope of an authorized law enforcement activity." According to the court:

> In this case, the Bureau, through Special Agent Krupkowski's declaration, identifies the ways in which Mr. Bassiouni's file is related to its law enforcement activities. First, the FBI notes its ongoing investigations into the threats posed by terrorist groups, specifically those originating in the Middle East. According to the declaration, "the FBI has amended its investigative priorities, naming as its number one priority to 'protect the United States from terrorist attack.'" Because of the nature of these investigative activities, and because of the breadth of Mr. Bassiouni's contacts with the Middle East, the FBI anticipates that it will continue to receive information about Mr. Bassiouni. The Bureau's file on Mr. Bassiouni will provide context for evaluating that new information.
>
> Perhaps more importantly, the public Krupkowski Declaration states that the records are important for evaluating the continued reliability of its intelligence sources. The Declaration explains that the process of verifying source information, and therefore determining whether a source is reliable, takes place over "years, even decades." . . .
>
> We believe that the purposes identified by the Bureau fall within "authorized law enforcement activity" conducted by the FBI. We note at the outset that the realm of national security belongs to the executive branch, and we owe considerable deference to that branch's assessment in matters of national security. Furthermore, although the Privacy Act certainly does not authorize collection and maintenance of information of private citizens on the "off-hand" chance that such information may someday be useful, it does not require law enforcement agencies to purge, on a continuous basis, properly collected information with respect to individuals that the agency has good reason to believe may be relevant on a continuing basis in the fulfillment of the agency's statutory responsibilities. The Privacy Act does not give any indication that Congress intended law enforcement agencies to begin from scratch with every investigation. Nor do we believe that Congress meant to deprive such agencies of the benefit of historical analysis.
>
> Mr. Bassiouni, however, urges us to reject the proffered law enforcement justifications as inadequate. He maintains, first, that, in order to fall within the law enforcement exception of (e)(7) the FBI must be "*currently* involved in a law enforcement investigation of Plaintiff." However, as we have noted

already, no court that has considered the meaning of law enforcement activity in (e)(7) has interpreted the term so narrowly.

3. THE USE OF GOVERNMENT DATABASES

(a) The Computer Matching and Privacy Protection Act

In 1977, the federal government initiated Project Match, a program where it compared computer employee records to records of people receiving benefits through Aid to Families with Dependent Children to detect fraud. This was considered by the government to be exempted from the Privacy Act under the "routine use" exception. According to Priscilla Regan:

> . . . The scope of computer matches . . . raises Fourth Amendment questions. Computer matches are generalized electronic searches of millions of records. Under the Fourth Amendment, the Supreme Court has determined that searches must not be overly inclusive; no "fishing expeditions" or "dragnet investigations" are allowed. Yet in computer matches, many people who have not engaged in fraud or are not actually suspected of criminal activity are subject to the computer search. This raises questions about the presumption of innocence, as reflected in Fourth and Fifth Amendment case law. If matches are considered a Fourth Amendment search, then some limitations on the breadth of the match and/or justifications for a match are necessary. For example, a government agency could be required to show that a less intrusive means of carrying out the search was not available and that procedural safeguards limiting the dangers of abuse and agency discretion were applied. Additionally, procedural safeguards are required under due process protections. A final constitutional issue is whether matching conflicts with the equal protection clause because categories of people, not individual suspects, are subject to computer matches. Two groups — federal employees and welfare recipients — are most often the subjects of computer matching.
>
> Despite these arguments about the constitutionality of computer matches, the courts have generally not upheld individual privacy claims in cases challenging computer-matching programs. Moreover, there has been little litigation in this area for two reasons. First, the damage requirements of the Privacy Act are so difficult to prove that they serve as a deterrent to its use. . . . Secondly, in large-scale computer matching, single individuals are rarely sufficiently harmed to litigate claims and most individuals are not even aware of the match. . . . [41]

In 1988, Congress passed the Computer Matching and Privacy Protection Act (CMPPA), Pub. L. No. 100-503, to regulate the practice of computer matching. The CMPPA amends the Privacy Act and provides that in order for agencies to disclose records to engage in computer matching programs, they must establish "a written agreement between the source agency and the recipient agency or non-Federal agency stating" the purpose and legal authority for the program, a justification for the program, a description of the records to be matched, procedures for the accuracy of the information, and prohibitions on redisclosure of the records. § 552a(o)(1). These agreements must be available upon request to the public.

---

[41] Priscilla Regan, *Legislating Privacy* 89-90 (1995).

The CMPPA establishes Data Integrity Boards within each agency to oversee matching, requires agencies to perform a cost-benefit analysis of proposed matching endeavors, and requires agencies to notify individuals of the termination of benefits due to computer matching and permit them an opportunity to refute the termination. § 552a(p).

Is computer matching a violation of the Fourth Amendment? If you believe that matching contravenes the Fourth Amendment, are the due process rights provided by the CMPPA sufficient to cure the constitutional deficiencies?[42]

(b) Airline Passenger Screening

THE 9/11 COMMISSION REPORT

Excerpts from pp. 1-4, 392-95 (2004)

Boston: American 11 and United 175. [Mohamed] Atta and [Abdul Aziz al] Omari boarded a 6:00 A.M. flight from Portland [Maine] to Boston's Logan International Airport.

When he checked in for his flight to Boston, Atta was selected by a computerized prescreening system known as CAPPS (Computer Assisted Passenger Prescreening System), created to identify passengers who should be subject to special security measures. Under the security rules in place at the time, the only consequence of Atta's selection by CAPPS was that his checked bags were held off the plane until it was confirmed that he boarded the aircraft. This did not hinder Atta's plans. . . .

While Atta had been selected by CAPPS in Portland, three members of his hijacking team — Suqami, Wail al Shehri, and Waleed al Shehri — were selected in Boston. Their selection affected only the handling of their checked bags, not their screening at the checkpoint.

Washington Dulles: American 77. Hundreds of miles southwest of Boston, at Dulles International Airport . . . five more men were preparing to take their early morning flight. At 7:15, a pair of them, Khalid al Mihdhar and Majed Moqed, checked in at the American Airlines ticket counter for Flight 77, bound for Los Angeles. Within the next 20 minutes, they would be followed by Nani Hanjour and two brothers, Nawaf al Hazmi and Salem al Hazmi.

Hani Hanjour, Khalid al Mihdhar, and Majed Moqed were flagged by CAPPS. The Hazmi brothers were also selected for extra scrutiny by the airline's customer service representative at the check-in counter. He did so because one of the brothers did not have photo identification nor could he understand English, and because the agent found both of the passengers to be suspicious. The only consequence of their selection was that their checked bags were held off the plane until it was confirmed that they had boarded the aircraft. . . .

---

[42] For an interesting account of the psychological effects and other harms caused by endeavors such as computer matching on welfare recipients, see John Gilliom, *Overseers of the Poor: Surveillance, Resistance, and the Limits of Privacy* (2001).

[Overall, on] 9/11, the 19 hijackers were screened by a computer-assisted screening system called CAPPS. More than half were identified for further inspection, which applied only to their checked luggage.

Under current practices, air carriers enforce government orders to stop certain known and suspected terrorists from boarding commercial flights and to apply secondary screening procedures to others. The "no-fly" and "automatic selectee" lists include only those individuals who the U.S. government believes pose a direct threat of attacking aviation.

Because air carriers implement the program, concerns about sharing intelligence information with private firms and foreign countries keep the U.S. government from listing all terrorist and terrorist suspects who should be included. The TSA has planned to take over this function when it deploys a new screening system to take the place of CAPPS. The deployment of this system has been delayed because of claims it may violate civil liberties.

Recommendation: Improved use of "no-fly" and "automatic selectee" lists should not be delayed while the argument about a successor to CAPPS continues. This screening function should be performed by the TSA, and it should utilize the larger set of watchlists maintained by the federal government. Air carriers should be required to supply the information needed to test and implement this new system. . . .

NOTES & QUESTIONS

1. *False Positives.* The 9/11 Report mentioned the number of "hits" that the CAPPS system made, flagging more than half of the 19 terrorists. Each day, there are approximately 1.9 million airline passengers. Imagine a false positive rate of just 1 percent, which by current estimates of such rates would be quite a good rate. At a 1 percent error rate, 19,000 people would be flagged as false positives. Merely talking about the "hits" rather than the "misses" paints only a partial picture of the effectiveness of the system.

After 9/11, the airline screening system incorrectly singled out a number of high-profile individuals. For example, Senator Edward Kennedy (D-Mass.) and Rep. Donald E. Young (R-Alaska) were tapped for secondary screening. Cat Stevens, a singer who now goes by the name Yusuf Islam, was placed on the no-fly list. According to *Time* magazine, this incident rested in a spelling mistake: "According to aviation sources with access to the list, there is no Yusuf Islam on the no-fly registry, though there is a 'Youssouf Islam.'" The article goes on, however, to state that the U.S. Transportation Safety Administration "alleges that Islam has links to terrorist groups, which he has denied; British foreign minister Jack Straw said the TSA action 'should never have been taken.'"[43]

Supporters of computerized airline screening argue that even with a significant number of false positives, CAPPS is useful in singling out

---

[43] Sally B. Donnelly, *You Say Yusuf, I Say Youssouf* . . . , Time.com, Sept. 25, 2004, www.time.com/time/nation/article/0,8599,702062,00.html.

passengers for extra scrutiny, since the most extensive screening cannot be done on 1.9 million passengers each day.

Some argue that if the government were able to collect more data, the false positives would drop. Is the answer obtaining more data? Are screening systems like CAPPS effective security measures? Bruce Schneier, a noted security expert, discusses whether a system like CAPPS might in the end be worth the trade-offs:

> System like CAPPS will be likely to single out lone terrorists who meet the profile, or a terrorist group whose entire membership fits the profile, or copycat terrorist groups without the wisdom, time, and resources to probe [the system]. But terrorists are a surprisingly diverse group . . . CAPPS works best combined with random screening.

Schneier also notes two basic problems with CAPPS. First, it can be probed. In other words, "a terrorist organization can probe the system repeatedly and identify which of its people, or which ticket characteristics, are less likely to be searched." Second, a system "that is more likely to select a certain class of passenger is also less likely to select other classes of passengers."[44] As a consequence, terrorists who do not fit a profile may slip by unnoticed.

2. *The Evolution of Airline Passenger Screening.* Since September 11th, the government has been attempting to design an airline passenger screening program. In 2001, the FAA created two lists — a list of people who were barred from flying and a list of people selected for secondary screening. In 2002, the Transportation Security Administration (TSA) was created, and it took over the security functions from the FAA. The Terrorist Screening Center in the FBI maintains the no-fly list as well as the selectee list. The no-fly list, which had only 16 names on it in 2001, now has over 20,000 names. The precise number remains unknown. The names on these lists are kept secret.

In 2003, the federal government announced the creation of CAPPS II, which was to be the successor to CAPPS. CAPPS II would have classified people according to their "threat level" when flying. Passengers would be classified as green, yellow, or red. Green passengers would be screened normally; yellow ones would be given extra scrutiny; and red passengers would not be allowed to fly.

Critics of CAPPS II criticized the lack of transparency in the system. They objected that the data used in the profiling along with the factors that go into the profiles would not be publicly disclosed. What are the costs and benefits of requiring public disclosure of the types of information and the logic used in the profiling?

In July 2004, the government announced that it was abandoning CAPPS II. Shortly thereafter, the Transportation Security Agency proposed a new screening system called "Secure Flight." This system became operational in 2009.

---

[44] Bruce Schneier, *Beyond Fear* 164-65 (2003).

Some argue that the benefit of a computerized airline passenger screening system is that without such a system, more individuals must be subjected to extensive searching. With the system, only those individuals profiled as a risk will be subject to extra scrutiny. Therefore, airline screening systems such as Secure Flight protect privacy by narrowing the number of people who must be intrusively searched. On the other hand, the system has costs in terms of both privacy and equality. Privacy is affected not just in a search, but in the gathering of data for profiling. Equality is implicated because some passengers, very possibly based on race and nationality, will be treated differently than other passengers. How do you weigh the costs and benefits? What about the people who are banned from flying? What kind of legal challenge should they have?

3. *PNR Data.* Airline passenger screening systems rely on passenger name record (PNR) data, which commercial airlines maintain for each passenger. This record includes financial information, such as credit card numbers, as well as itineraries for travel, phone numbers, and any special meal requests. After 9/11, the government requested that airlines turn over their PNR data. Although sharing the information with the government was not authorized in their privacy policies, many airlines willingly complied. Is it problematic for the government to have PNR data? What can be learned about an individual through PNR data?

In 2005, it was revealed that the FBI was keeping 257.5 million PNR records on people who flew between June and September 2001.[45] To what extent does the Privacy Act restrict the FBI from retaining this information?

(c) Government Data Mining

Data mining involves examining personal information in databases to look for patterns or unusual activity, or to identify links between a suspect and other individuals. Computer matching programs are an example of data mining — they seek to detect fraud by making comparisons in personal information residing in different databases.

Total Information Awareness. In 2002, the press reported that the Department of Defense was developing a project called "Total Information Awareness" (TIA), headed by Admiral John Poindexter. TIA would consist of a database of dossiers of people constructed with information about their finances, education, travel, health, and more. The information would be obtained from various private sector companies. The information would then be used to profile people to single out those engaged in terrorist activities. TIA generated a significant public outcry, and the Senate amended its spending bill early in 2003 to bar funding for TIA until the details of the program were explained to Congress.

In its report to Congress on May 20, 2003, the Department of Defense renamed the program "Terrorism Information Awareness" and stated that the

---

[45] Leslie Miller, *FBI Keeping Records on Pre-9/11 Travelers*, Associated Press, Jan. 14, 2005.

program would be protective of privacy. Later in 2003, the Senate voted to deny funding for TIA. According to some media reports, however, classified part of the federal budget still contain funding for certain aspects of TIA.[46] What laws or constitutional rights would be implicated by TIA or a similar program?

Consider K.A. Taipale:

> [I]t is my view that the recent defunding of DARPA's Information Awareness Office ("IAO") and its Terrorism Information Awareness program and related projects will turn out to be a pyrrhic "victory" for civil liberties as the program provided a focused opportunity around which to publicly debate the rules and procedures for the future use of these technologies and, importantly, to oversee the development of the appropriate technical features required to support any concurred upon implementation or oversight policies to protect privacy.[47]

Daniel Solove predicted in 2004 that TIA was far from dead:

> . . . TIA is only one part of the story of government access to personal information and its creation of dossiers on American citizens. In fact, for quite some time, the government has been increasingly contracting with businesses to acquire databases of personal information. Database firms are willing to supply the information and the government is willing to pay for it. Currently, government agencies such as the FBI and IRS are purchasing databases of personal information from private-sector companies. A private company called ChoicePoint, Inc. has amassed a database of 10 billion records and has contracts with at least 35 federal agencies to share the data with them. . . .
>
> Thus, we are increasingly seeing collusion, partly voluntary, partly coerced, between the private sector and the government. While public attention has focused on the Total Information Awareness project, the very same goals and techniques of the program continue to be carried out less systematically by various government agencies and law enforcement officials. We are already closer to Total Information Awareness than we might think.[48]

Pattern-Based vs. Subject-Based Data Mining. There are at least two general types of data mining. "Subject-based" data mining involves searching the data of a specific identified person. It might involve examining whom that person associates and does business with. "Pattern-based" data mining involves starting with a particular profile for terrorist activity and then analyzing databases to see which individuals' patterns of activity match that profile. Do these forms of data mining present different privacy concerns? If so, what are they? How should each type of data mining be regulated?

---

[46] Ira S. Rubinstein, Ronald D. Lee & Paul M. Schwartz, *Data Mining and Internet Profiling*, 75 U. Chi. L. Rev. 261, 265 (2008).

[47] K.A. Taipale, *Data Mining and Domestic Security: Connecting the Dots to Make Sense of Data*, 5 Colum. Sci. & Tech. L. Rev. 9-12 (2003).

[48] Daniel J. Solove, *The Digital Person: Technology and Privacy in the Information Age* 169, 175 (2004).

DATA MINING: FEDERAL EFFORTS COVER A WIDE RANGE OF USES

U.S. General Accountability Office, excerpt from pp. 2-3 (May 2004)

Federal agencies are using data mining for a variety of purposes, ranging from improving service or performance to analyzing and detecting terrorist patterns and activities. Our survey of 128 federal departments and agencies on their use of data mining shows that 52 agencies are using or are planning to use data mining. These departments and agencies reported 199 data mining efforts, of which 68 were planned and 131 were operational. . . .

The Department of Defense reported having the largest number of data mining efforts aimed at improving service or performance and at managing human resources. Defense was also the most frequent user of efforts aimed at analyzing intelligence and detecting terrorist activities, followed by the Departments of Homeland Security, Justice, and Education. . . .

Data mining efforts for detecting criminal activities or patterns, however, were spread relatively evenly among the reporting agencies.

In addition, out of all 199 data mining efforts identified, 122 used personal information. For these efforts, the primary purposes were detecting fraud, waste, and abuse; detecting criminal activities or patterns; analyzing intelligence and detecting terrorist activities; and increasing tax compliance.

Agencies also identified efforts to mine data from the private sector and data from other federal agencies, both of which could include personal information. Of 54 efforts to mine data from the private sector (such as credit reports or credit card transactions), 36 involve personal information. Of 77 efforts to mine data from other federal agencies, 46 involve personal information (including student loan application data, bank account numbers, credit card information, and taxpayer identification numbers).

Data mining enables corporations and government agencies to analyze massive volumes of data quickly and relatively inexpensively. The use of this type of information retrieval has been driven by the exponential growth in the volumes and availability of information collected by the public and private sectors, as well as by advances in computing and data storage capabilities. In response to these trends, generic data mining tools are increasingly available for — or built into — major commercial database applications. Today, mining can be performed on many types of data. . . .

MARY DeROSA, DATA MINING AND DATA ANALYSIS FOR COUNTERTERRORISM

Center for Strategic and International Studies (CSIS) 6-8 (2004)

A relatively simple and useful data-analysis tool for counterterrorism is subject-based "link analysis." This technique uses aggregated public records or other large collections of data to find links between a subject — a suspect, an address, or other piece of relevant information — and other people, places, or things. This can provide additional clues for analysts and investigators to follow. Link analysis is a tool that is available now and is used for, among other things, background checks of applicants for sensitive jobs and as an investigatory tool in national security and law enforcement investigations.

A hindsight analysis of the September 11 attacks provides an example of how simple, subject-based link analysis could be used effectively to assist investigations or analysis of terrorist plans. By using government watch list information, airline reservation records, and aggregated public record data, link analysis could have identified all 19 September 11 terrorists — for follow-up investigation — before September 11. The links can be summarized as follows:

Direct Links — Watch List Information

- Khalid Almihdhar and Nawaf Alhazmi, both hijackers of American Airlines (AA) Flight 77, which crashed into the Pentagon, appeared on a U.S. government terrorist watch list. Both used their real names to reserve their flights. . . .

Link Analysis — One Degree of Separation

- Two other hijackers used the same contact address for their flight reservations that Khalid Almihdhar listed on his reservation. These were Mohamed Atta, who hijacked AA Flight 11, which crashed into the World Trade Center North Tower, and Marwan Al Shehhi, who hijacked UA Flight 175.

- Salem Alhazmi, who hijacked AA Flight 77, used the same contact address on his reservation as Nawaf Alhazmi.

- The frequent flyer number that Khalid Almihdhar used to make his reservation was also used by hijacker Majed Moqed to make his reservation on AA Flight 77.

- Hamza Alghamdi, who hijacked UA Flight 175, used the same contact address on his reservation as Ahmed Alghamdi used on his.

- Hani Hanjour, who hijacked AA Flight 77, lived with both Nawaf Alhazmi and Khalid Almihdhar, a fact that searches of public records could have revealed. . . .

Thus, if the government had started with watch list data and pursued links, it is at least possible that all of the hijackers would have been identified as subjects for further investigation. Of course, this example does not show the false positives — names of people with no connection to the terror attacks that might also have been linked to the watch list subjects.

Pattern-based data analysis also has potential for counterterrorism in the longer term, if research on uses of those techniques continues. . . . [D]ata-mining research must find ways to identify useful patterns that can predict an extremely rare activity — terrorist planning and attacks. It must also identify how to separate the "signal" of pattern from the "noise" of innocent activity in the data. One possible advantage of pattern-based searches — if they can be perfected — would be that they could provide clues to "sleeper" activity by unknown terrorists who have never engaged in activity that would link them to known terrorists. Unlike subject-based queries, pattern-based searches do not require a link to a known suspicious subject.

Types of pattern-based searches that could prove useful include searches for particular combinations of lower-level activity that together are predictive of terrorist activity. For example, a pattern of a "sleeper" terrorist might be a person in the country on a student visa who purchases a bomb-making book and 50 medium-sized loads of fertilizer. Or, if the concern is that terrorists will use large trucks for attacks, automated data analysis might be conducted regularly to identify people who have rented large trucks, used hotels or drop boxes as addresses, and fall within certain age ranges or have other qualities that are part of a known terrorist pattern. Significant patterns in e-mail traffic might be discovered that could reveal terrorist activity and terrorist "ringleaders." Pattern-based searches might also be very useful in response and consequence management. For example, searches of hospital data for reports of certain combinations of symptoms, or of other databases for patterns of behavior, such as pharmaceutical purchases or work absenteeism might provide an early signal of a terrorist attack using a biological weapon. . . .

NOTES & QUESTIONS

1. *The TAPAC Committee Report.* The Technology and Privacy Advisory Committee (TAPAC) was appointed by Secretary of Defense Donald Rumsfeld to examine the privacy implications of data mining. In its report, it noted that TIA was "a flawed effort to achieve worthwhile ends. It was flawed by its perceived insensitivity to critical privacy issues, the manner in which it was presented to the public, and the lack of clarity and consistency with which it was described." The report recommended:

> If the data mining is limited to searches based on particularized suspicion about a specific individual, we believe existing law should govern. Because, by definition, there is enough evidence about such a person to warrant further investigation, and that investigation is clearly subject to the protections of the Fourth Amendment, supplemented by federal statutes, we rely on existing law. We understand this category of data mining to include searches seeking to identify or locate a specific individual (e.g., a suspected terrorist) from airline or cruise ship passenger manifests or other lists of names or other non-sensitive information about U.S. persons. . . .
>
> For all other government data mining that involves personally identifiable information about U.S. persons, we recommend below that the government be required to first establish a predicate demonstrating the need for the data mining to prevent or respond to terrorism, and second, unless exigent circumstances are present, obtain authorization from the Foreign Intelligence Surveillance Court for its data mining activities. As we stress, that authorization may be sought either for programs that include data mining known or likely to include information on U.S. persons, or for specific applications of data mining where the use of personally identifiable information concerning U.S. persons is clearly anticipated. Legislation will be

required for the Foreign Intelligence Surveillance Court to fulfill the role we recommend.[49]

The TAPAC Report's central recommendation is for a secret Foreign Intelligence Surveillance Act (FISA) court to approve various data mining projects. Is this a viable way to regulate data mining?

2. *The Markle Foundation Reports.* The Markle Foundation, a private sector philanthropic organization, established a Task Force on National Security in the Information Age that has issued two reports about government data mining. In these reports, the Markle Task Force is enthusiastic about the potential benefits of government data mining and recommends moving ahead with projects that will draw on this technique. The Markle Task Force recommends that government have ready access to private sector databases, but that the databases not be combined into a centralized database like the one envisioned for TIA:

> Attempting to centralize [databases of personal] information is not the answer because it would not link the information to the dispersed analytical capabilities of the network. Centralization could also lead to information becoming obsolete, since a centralized analytical entity would not have the ability to keep up-to-date much of the information collected from dispersed sources. . . .
>
> Our Task Force's fundamental objective, then, is to identify the technological tools and infrastructure, the policies, and the processes necessary to link these different communities so that important information can be shared among the people who need it, and as rapidly as possible. . . .
>
> Today, the private sector is on the frontline of the homeland security effort. Its members are holders of the data that may prove crucial to identifying and locating terrorists or thwarting terrorist attacks. . . . We therefore start from the premise that the government must have access to that information, which is needed to protect our country, and that through a combination of well-crafted guidelines, careful articulation of the types of information needed for identified purposes, and effective oversight using modern information technology, it will be possible to assure that government gets that information in a way that protects our essential liberties.[50]

Is decentralization sufficient to safeguard privacy? While mentioning privacy and civil liberty concerns, the Markle Foundation Task Force does not suggest much in the way of legal controls, but it mentions the possibility of technology to help protect privacy. The report does not, however, explain what concrete limitations should be established to protect privacy.

3. *The CMPPA and Government Data Mining.* To what extent does the Computer Matching and Privacy Protection Act (CMPPA) regulate government data mining? Consider the view of the Markle Foundation:

---

[49] Technology and Privacy Advisory Committee (TAPAC), *Safeguarding Privacy in the Fight Against Terrorism*, vii-x, 45-49 (2004).

[50] Markle Foundation Task Force, *Creating a Trusted Information Network for Homeland Security* 14-15 (2003).

Based upon past applications of the routine use exception [to the Privacy Act], it seems likely that future government initiatives promoting increased interagency information sharing to protect national security will meet with little resistance. A routine use need only meet [two requirements] to be valid: (1) compatible with the purpose of the information collection and (2) published in the Federal Register. . . .

In today's age of information, data mining has the potential to become one of the government's most powerful tools for analyzing information on terrorism. Congress, however, has restricted the kinds of data mining federal agencies can do. In 1977, the Department of Health, Education, and Welfare initiated Project Match to identify federal employees fraudulently receiving welfare payments. . . . Over the next decade, such computer matching became pervasive. In a 1986 study, the Office of Technology Assessment reported that in 1984, eleven cabinet level departments and four independent agencies conducted 110 separate computer matching programs, consisting of 700 total matches and involving seven billion records. . . .

The widespread disclosure of information across agencies promoted Congress to act in 1988. To address these problems, Congress amended the Privacy Act by passing the Computer Matching Act, which precluded government agencies from treating computer matching as a routine use in most cases. Congress, however, explicitly excluded "matches performed for foreign counterintelligence purposes or to produce background checks for security clearances of Federal personnel." . . . Thus, so long as an agency lists something like "analyzing information to improve national security or prevent terrorism" as a routine use for the agency's information, a counterterrorism intelligence agency should be able to data mine the agency's records.[51]

4. ***The Privacy Act and Government Data Mining.*** What, if any, limits would the Privacy Act place on the kinds of government data mining discussed earlier in this section? Do any other laws discussed thus far regulate the practice?

Consider the following observation by Stewart Baker in the Markle Foundation Report regarding the limitations of the Privacy Act:

[The Privacy Act] requirements are just restrictive enough to make it awkward for the government to take direct access of private databases for data-mining analysis. As a result, one of the emerging solutions being adopted by the government is to encourage or even require industry to keep the databases in private hands, run pattern recognition themselves, and report suspicious results to the government. . . . [T]his approach has been used in the anti-money-laundering context. The Administration has discussed adopting similar approaches with respect to other records that might be of interest in counter-terrorism investigations.[52]

---

[51] Markle Foundation Task Force, *Protecting America's Freedom in the Information Age* 131 (2002).

[52] Markle Foundation Task Force, *Protecting America's Freedom in the Information Age* 169 (2002).

UNITED STATES V. SOKOLOW

490 U.S. 1 (1989)

Respondent Andrew Sokolow was stopped by Drug Enforcement Administration (DEA) agents upon his arrival at Honolulu International Airport. The agents found 1,063 grams of cocaine in his carry-on luggage. When respondent was stopped, the agents knew, *inter alia,* that (1) he paid $2,100 for two airplane tickets from a roll of $20 bills; (2) he traveled under a name that did not match the name under which his telephone number was listed; (3) his original destination was Miami, a source city for illicit drugs; (4) he stayed in Miami for only 48 hours, even though a round-trip flight from Honolulu to Miami takes 20 hours; (5) he appeared nervous during his trip; and (6) he checked none of his luggage. A divided panel of the United States Court of Appeals for the Ninth Circuit held that the DEA agents did not have a reasonable suspicion to stop respondent, as required by the Fourth Amendment. 831 F.2d 1413 (CA9 1987). We take the contrary view.

This case involves a typical attempt to smuggle drugs through one of the Nation's airports. On a Sunday in July 1984, respondent went to the United Airlines ticket counter at Honolulu Airport, where he purchased two round-trip tickets for a flight to Miami leaving later that day. The tickets were purchased in the names of "Andrew Kray" and "Janet Norian" and had open return dates. Respondent paid $2,100 for the tickets from a large roll of $20 bills, which appeared to contain a total of $4,000. He also gave the ticket agent his home telephone number. The ticket agent noticed that respondent seemed nervous; he was about 25 years old; he was dressed in a black jumpsuit and wore gold jewelry; and he was accompanied by a woman, who turned out to be Janet Norian. Neither respondent nor his companion checked any of their four pieces of luggage.

After the couple left for their flight, the ticket agent informed Officer John McCarthy of the Honolulu Police Department of respondent's cash purchase of tickets to Miami. Officer McCarthy determined that the telephone number respondent gave to the ticket agent was subscribed to a "Karl Herman," who resided at 348-A Royal Hawaiian Avenue in Honolulu. Unbeknownst to McCarthy (and later to the DEA agents), respondent was Herman's roommate. The ticket agent identified respondent's voice on the answering machine at Herman's number. Officer McCarthy was unable to find any listing under the name "Andrew Kray" in Hawaii. McCarthy subsequently learned that return reservations from Miami to Honolulu had been made in the names of Kray and Norian, with their arrival scheduled for July 25, three days after respondent and his companion had left. He also learned that Kray and Norian were scheduled to make stopovers in Denver and Los Angeles.

On July 25, during the stopover in Los Angeles, DEA agents identified respondent. He "appeared to be very nervous and was looking all around the waiting area." Later that day, at 6:30 p.m., respondent and Norian arrived in Honolulu. As before, they had not checked their luggage. Respondent was still wearing a black jumpsuit and gold jewelry. The couple proceeded directly to the street and tried to hail a cab, where Agent Richard Kempshall and three other

DEA agents approached them. Kempshall displayed his credentials, grabbed respondent by the arm, and moved him back onto the sidewalk. Kempshall asked respondent for his airline ticket and identification; respondent said that he had neither. He told the agents that his name was "Sokolow," but that he was traveling under his mother's maiden name, "Kray."

Respondent and Norian were escorted to the DEA office at the airport. There, the couple's luggage was examined by "Donker," a narcotics detector dog, which alerted on respondent's brown shoulder bag. The agents arrested respondent. He was advised of his constitutional rights and declined to make any statements. The agents obtained a warrant to search the shoulder bag. They found no illicit drugs, but the bag did contain several suspicious documents indicating respondent's involvement in drug trafficking. The agents had Donker reexamine the remaining luggage, and this time the dog alerted on a medium-sized Louis Vuitton bag. By now, it was 9:30 p.m., too late for the agents to obtain a second warrant. They allowed respondent to leave for the night, but kept his luggage. The next morning, after a second dog confirmed Donker's alert, the agents obtained a warrant and found 1,063 grams of cocaine inside the bag.

Respondent was indicted for possession with the intent to distribute cocaine in violation of 21 U.S.C. § 841(a)(1). The United States District Court for Hawaii denied his motion to suppress the cocaine and other evidence seized from his luggage, finding that the DEA agents had a reasonable suspicion that he was involved in drug trafficking when they stopped him at the airport. . . .

The United States Court of Appeals for the Ninth Circuit reversed respondent's conviction by a divided vote, holding that the DEA agents did not have a reasonable suspicion to justify the stop. The majority divided the facts bearing on reasonable suspicion into two categories. In the first category, the majority placed facts describing "ongoing criminal activity," such as the use of an alias or evasive movement through an airport; the majority believed that at least one such factor was always needed to support a finding of reasonable suspicion. In the second category, it placed facts describing "personal characteristics" of drug couriers, such as the cash payment for tickets, a short trip to a major source city for drugs, nervousness, type of attire, and unchecked luggage. The majority believed that such characteristics, "shared by drug couriers and the public at large," were only relevant if there was evidence of ongoing criminal behavior and the Government offered "[e]mpirical documentation" that the combination of facts at issue did not describe the behavior of "significant numbers of innocent persons." Applying this two-part test to the facts of this case, the majority found that there was no evidence of ongoing criminal behavior, and thus that the agents' stop was impermissible. . . .

Our decision . . . turns on whether the agents had a reasonable suspicion that respondent was engaged in wrongdoing when they encountered him on the sidewalk. In *Terry v. Ohio,* 392 U.S. 1 (1968), we held that the police can stop and briefly detain a person for investigative purposes if the officer has a reasonable suspicion supported by articulable facts that criminal activity "may be afoot," even if the officer lacks probable cause.

The officer, of course, must be able to articulate something more than an "inchoate and unparticularized suspicion or 'hunch.'" The Fourth Amendment requires "some minimal level of objective justification" for making the stop. That level of suspicion is considerably less than proof of wrongdoing by a preponderance of the evidence. We have held that probable cause means "a fair probability that contraband or evidence of a crime will be found," *Illinois v. Gates,* 462 U.S. 213 (1983), and the level of suspicion required for a *Terry* stop is obviously less demanding than that for probable cause. . . .

In evaluating the validity of a stop such as this, we must consider "the totality of the circumstances — the whole picture." . . .

The rule enunciated by the Court of Appeals, in which evidence available to an officer is divided into evidence of "ongoing criminal behavior," on the one hand, and "probabilistic" evidence, on the other, is not in keeping with the quoted statements from our decisions. It also seems to us to draw a sharp line between types of evidence, the probative value of which varies only in degree. The Court of Appeals classified evidence of traveling under an alias, or evidence that the suspect took an evasive or erratic path through an airport, as meeting the test for showing "ongoing criminal activity." But certainly instances are conceivable in which traveling under an alias would not reflect ongoing criminal activity: for example, a person who wished to travel to a hospital or clinic for an operation and wished to concealed that fact. One taking an evasive path through an airport might be seeking to avoid a confrontation with an angry acquaintance or with a creditor. This is not to say that each of these types of evidence is not highly probative, but they do not have the sort of ironclad significance attributed to them by the Court of Appeals.

On the other hand, the factors in this case that the Court of Appeals treated as merely "probabilistic" also have probative significance. Paying $2,100 in cash for two airplane tickets is out of the ordinary, and it is even more out of the ordinary to pay that sum from a roll of $20 bills containing nearly twice that amount of cash. Most business travelers, we feel confident, purchase airline tickets by credit card or check so as to have a record for tax or business purposes, and few vacationers carry with them thousands of dollars in $20 bills. We also think the agents had a reasonable ground to believe that respondent was traveling under an alias; the evidence was by no means conclusive, but it was sufficient to warrant consideration. While a trip from Honolulu to Miami, standing alone, is not a cause for any sort of suspicion, here there was more: surely few residents of Honolulu travel from that city for 20 hours to spend 48 hours in Miami during the month of July.

Any one of these factors is not by itself proof of any illegal conduct and is quite consistent with innocent travel. But we think taken together they amount to reasonable suspicion. Indeed, *Terry* itself involved "a series of acts, each of them perhaps innocent" if viewed separately, "but which taken together warranted further investigation." . . .

We do not agree with respondent that our analysis is somehow changed by the agents' belief that his behavior was consistent with one of the DEA's "drug courier profiles." A court sitting to determine the existence of reasonable suspicion must require the agent to articulate the factors leading to that conclusion, but the fact that these factors may be set forth in a "profile" does not somehow detract from their evidentiary significance as seen by a trained agent. . . .

We hold that the agents had a reasonable basis to suspect that respondent was transporting illegal drugs on these facts. . . .

MARSHALL and BRENNAN, JJ. dissenting. Because the strongest advocates of Fourth Amendment rights are frequently criminals, it is easy to forget that our interpretations of such rights apply to the innocent and the guilty alike. In the present case, the chain of events set in motion when respondent Andrew Sokolow was stopped by Drug Enforcement Administration (DEA) agents at Honolulu International Airport led to the discovery of cocaine and, ultimately, to Sokolow's conviction for drug trafficking. But in sustaining this conviction on the ground that the agents reasonably suspected Sokolow of ongoing criminal activity, the Court diminishes the rights of *all* citizens "to be secure in their persons," U.S. Const., Amdt. 4, as they traverse the Nation's airports. Finding this result constitutionally impermissible, I dissent.

The Fourth Amendment cabins government's authority to intrude on personal privacy and security by requiring that searches and seizures usually be supported by a showing of probable cause. The reasonable-suspicion standard is a derivation of the probable-cause command, applicable only to those brief detentions which fall short of being full-scale searches and seizures and which are necessitated by law enforcement exigencies such as the need to stop ongoing crimes, to prevent imminent crimes, and to protect law enforcement officers in highly charged situations. By requiring reasonable suspicion as a prerequisite to such seizures, the Fourth Amendment protects innocent persons from being subjected to "overbearing or harassing" police conduct carried out solely on the basis of imprecise stereotypes of what criminals look like, or on the basis of irrelevant personal characteristics such as race.

To deter such egregious police behavior, we have held that a suspicion is not reasonable unless officers have based it on "specific and articulable facts." It is not enough to suspect that an individual has committed crimes in the past, harbors unconsummated criminal designs, or has the propensity to commit crimes. On the contrary, before detaining an individual, law enforcement officers must reasonably suspect that he is engaged in, or poised to commit, a criminal act *at that moment*. . . .

Evaluated against this standard, the facts about Andrew Sokolow known to the DEA agents at the time they stopped him fall short of reasonably indicating that he was engaged at the time in criminal activity. It is highly significant that the DEA agents stopped Sokolow because he matched one of the DEA's "profiles" of a paradigmatic drug courier. In my view, a law enforcement officer's mechanistic application of a formula of personal and behavioral traits in deciding whom to detain can only dull the officer's ability and determination to make sensitive and fact-specific inferences "in light of his experience," *Terry, supra*, particularly in ambiguous or borderline cases. Reflexive reliance on a profile of drug courier characteristics runs a far greater risk than does ordinary, case-by-case police work of subjecting innocent individuals to unwarranted police harassment and detention. This risk is enhanced by the profile's "chameleon-like way of adapting to any particular set of observations." *Compare, e.g., United States v. Moore,* 675 F.2d 802 (CA6 1982) (suspect was first to deplane), cert. denied, 460 U.S. 1068 (1983), *with United States v. Mendenhall,* 446 U.S. 544 (1980) (last to deplane), *with United States v. Buenaventura-Ariza,* 615 F.2d 29 (CA2 1980) (deplaned from middle); *United*

States v. Sullivan, 625 F.2d 9 (CA4 1980) (one-way tickets), *with United States v. Craemer,* 555 F.2d 594 (CA6 1977) (round-trip tickets), with *United States v. McCaleb,* 552 F.2d 717 (CA6 1977) (nonstop flight), with *United States v. Sokolow,* 808 F.2d 1366, (CA9) (changed planes); *Craemer, supra* (no luggage), *with United States v. Sanford,* 658 F.2d 342 (CA5 1981) (gym bag), with *Sullivan, supra,* at 12 (new suitcases); *United States v. Smith,* 574 F.2d 882 (CA6 1978) (traveling alone), *with United States v. Fry,* 622 F.2d 1218 (CA5 1980) (travelling with companion); *United States v. Andrews,* 600 F.2d 563 (CA6 1979) (acted nervously), *with United States v. Himmelwright,* 551 F.2d 991 (CA5) (acted too calmly). . . . In asserting that it is not "somehow" relevant that the agents who stopped Sokolow did so in reliance on a prefabricated profile of criminal characteristics, the majority thus ducks serious issues relating to a questionable law enforcement practice, to address the validity of which we granted certiorari in this case. . . .

[T]raveler Sokolow gave no indications of evasive activity. On the contrary, the sole behavioral detail about Sokolow noted by the DEA agents was that he was nervous. With news accounts proliferating of plane crashes, near collisions, and air terrorism, there are manifold and good reasons for being agitated while awaiting a flight, reasons that have nothing to do with one's involvement in a criminal endeavor.

The remaining circumstantial facts known about Sokolow, considered either singly or together, are scarcely indicative of criminal activity. . . . [T]he fact that Sokolow took a brief trip to a resort city for which he brought only carry-on luggage also "describe[s] a very large category of presumably innocent travelers." That Sokolow embarked from Miami, "a source city for illicit drugs," is no more suggestive of illegality; thousands of innocent persons travel from "source cities" every day and, judging from the DEA's testimony in past cases, nearly every major city in the country may be characterized as a source or distribution city. That Sokolow had his phone listed in another person's name also does not support the majority's assertion that the DEA agents reasonably believed Sokolow was using an alias; it is commonplace to have one's phone registered in the name of a roommate, which, it later turned out, was precisely what Sokolow had done. That Sokolow was dressed in a black jumpsuit and wore gold jewelry also provides no grounds for suspecting wrongdoing, the majority's repeated and unexplained allusions to Sokolow's style of dress notwithstanding. For law enforcement officers to base a search, even in part, on a "pop" guess that persons dressed in a particular fashion are likely to commit crimes not only stretches the concept of reasonable suspicion beyond recognition, but also is inimical to the self-expression which the choice of wardrobe may provide.

Finally, that Sokolow paid for his tickets in cash indicates no imminent or ongoing criminal activity. The majority "feel[s] confident" that "[m]ost business travelers . . . purchase airline tickets by credit card or check." Why the majority confines its focus only to "business travelers" I do not know, but I would not so lightly infer ongoing crime from the use of legal tender. Making major cash purchases, while surely less common today, may simply reflect the traveler's aversion to, or inability to obtain, plastic money. . . .

NOTES & QUESTIONS

1. ***Profiling.*** What sorts of criteria would be sufficient to find reasonable suspicion for a *Terry* stop for potential terrorist activity at an airport? Having a one-way ticket? Having only carry-on luggage? One of the difficulties in creating a profile of a terrorist, Anita Ramasastry notes, is that "[t]here is no well-defined and reinforced profile for terrorists. Further, attacks are relatively infrequent, making it harder to reinforce any profiles that do exist."[53]

Is the use of profiles to detain or search people problematic? Fred Schauer contends that making generalizations is not necessarily problematic, even when doing so leads to some mistakes:

> Here Justice Marshall [dissenting in *Sokolow*] went right to the heart of the matter. He recognized that the question of the profile is not about profiles as such, but is about *rules*. The issue is whether preexisting and general rules should be employed to determine which people to stop, as the majority was willing to permit, or whether that determination must, as Justice Marshall insisted, be made on a particularistic basis by individual officers using their own best judgment in each case, even if that best judgment can itself be seen as just another version of profiling. Once we understand that the issue is not about whether to use profiles or not but instead about whether to use (or to prefer) formal written profiles or informal unwritten ones, it becomes clear that this is not a question of profiles or not, but a question about discretion. Should individual customs officers have the discretion to create their own profiles, as Justice Marshall preferred, or is it at least permissible, even if not constitutionally mandatory, for formal written profiles to be used as a way of regularizing the process and limiting the discretion of individual officers?
>
> Once we understand the choice as being one between profiles that are constructed in advance and have the potential to be both under- and overinclusive, on the one hand, and profiles that are constructed on a case-by-case basis by law-enforcement officials making, in Justice Marshall's words, "sensitive and fact-specific inferences in light of [their] experience," on the other, we can see that the issue is not about profiling at all, for profiling is inevitable.[54]

Is the use of data mining laudable because it involves a computer searching for written pre-established patterns rather than the ad hoc discretion of airline screening officials at the security checkpoints? Pre-established profiles can eliminate the use of race or other problematic factors that might be used in an official's ad hoc discretion. Then again, even pre-established profiles can employ improper factors.

What factors should be considered to be improper? Should information about a person's associations and group memberships be included? Information about a person's political and expressive activity? Information about a person's religion or race?

---

[53] Anita Ramasastry, *Lost in Translation? Data Mining, National Security, and the "Adverse Inference" Problem*, 22 Santa Clara Computer & High Tech. L.J. 757, 773 (2006).

[54] Frederick Schauer, *Profiles, Probabilities, and Stereotypes* 173-74 (2003).

Fred Schauer examines the issue of whether race should be a factor in the profile:

> Those who commit acts of airplane terrorism, both before and after September 11, 2001, are disproportionately younger Muslim men of Middle Eastern background. . . .
>
> On the evidence we now have, it is more than plausible to suppose that Middle Eastern ethnicity is a significant contributory factor, such that including it in the algorithm will make the algorithm substantially more effective than excluding it.
>
> Because allowing the use of race and ethnicity imposes a cost on those members of the targeted groups who are in the area of overinclusion — Middle Easterners who have done nothing wrong — it might be preferable to distribute the cost more broadly, and in doing so raise the cost without lowering the degree of security. If excluding the relevant factor of Middle Eastern appearance from the algorithm made it necessary to increase the scrutiny of everyone — if excluding ethnicity while still including everything else increased waiting time at airports an average of thirty minutes per passenger — this might still be a price worth paying. . . . Put starkly, the question of racial or ethnic profiling in air travel is not the question of whether racial and ethnic sensitivity must be bought at the price of thousands of lives. Rather, it is most often the question of whether racial and ethnic sensitivity should be bought at the price of arriving thirty minutes earlier at the airport.[55]

Consider the following document obtained by the Electronic Privacy Information Center from NASA regarding airline passenger data:

> ISLE ran a simple anomaly detection algorithm that it developed as part of this project on a subset of the census database, and it found some interesting anomalies. Many of the anomalies were people from unusual countries. One anomaly was a 22-year-old African American man who was not a college graduate but had over $100,000 in capital gains.
>
> We ran Gritbot on a subset of the census database. It discovered many interesting anomalies, including a woman whose ancestry is Mexican but who speaks Chinese at home, a 16-year-old veteran, and some people who reported their race to be white and their ancestry to be African-American. . . .[56]

Profiles ultimately involve human judgment about what patterns should be singled out as suspicious. One difficulty with data mining is that if the profiles remain secret, how can there be oversight to prevent improper factors from being used? Who decides what factors are appropriate?

2. *An Assessment of Government Data Mining.* Consider the following account of the problems of government data mining by Daniel Solove:

> Usually, the government has some form of particularized suspicion, a factual basis to believe that a particular person may be engaged in illegal conduct. Particularized suspicion keeps the government's profound investigative powers in check, preventing widespread surveillance and snooping into the lives and affairs of all citizens. Computer matches . . . investigate everyone, and most people who are investigated are innocent.

---

[55] *Id.* at 181-90.
[56] NASA Documents, available at http://www.epic.org/privacy/airtravel/nasa/.

With the new information supplied by the private sector, there is an increased potential for more automated investigations, such as searches for all people who purchase books about particular topics or those who visit certain websites, or perhaps even people whose personal interests fit a profile for those likely to engage in certain forms of criminal activity. Profiles work similarly to the way that Amazon.com predicts which products customers will want to buy. They use particular characteristics and patterns of activity to predict how people will behave in the future. Of course, profiles can be mistaken, but they are often accurate enough to tempt people to rely on them. But there are even deeper problems with profiles beyond inaccuracies. Profiles can be based on stereotypes, race, or religion. A profile is only as good as its designer. Profiles are often kept secret, enabling prejudices and faulty assumptions to exist unchecked by the public.[57]

3. ***A Hypothetical Data Mining Problem.*** Suppose the FBI receives a tip from a credible source that two young males, both naturalized U.S. citizens, who are Muslim and who were originally born in Saudi Arabia, have rented a U-Haul truck and are planning to use it to detonate a bomb at a crowded building or place in Los Angeles, CA within the next week. The source says he met the two males at his mosque, which has over 1,000 worshippers. This is all the information the FBI agents have. The FBI would like to: (1) obtain the records of the people who attend the mosque; (2) obtain the records of U-Haul. The FBI would like to engage in data mining on the records to narrow their search for the two males. Notwithstanding existing law, should the FBI agents be permitted to obtain the records? If so, what privacy protections should be established?

ARIZONA V. EVANS

514 U.S. 1 (1995)

REHNQUIST, J. This case presents the question whether evidence seized in violation of the Fourth Amendment by an officer who acted in reliance on a police record indicating the existence of an outstanding arrest warrant — a record that is later determined to be erroneous — must be suppressed by virtue of the exclusionary rule regardless of the source of the error. . . .

In January 1991, Phoenix police officer Bryan Sargent observed respondent Isaac Evans driving the wrong way on a one-way street in front of the police station. The officer stopped respondent and asked to see his driver's license. After respondent told him that his license had been suspended, the officer entered respondent's name into a computer data terminal located in his patrol car. The computer inquiry confirmed that respondent's license had been suspended and also indicated that there was an outstanding misdemeanor warrant for his arrest. Based upon the outstanding warrant, Officer Sargent placed respondent under arrest. While being handcuffed, respondent dropped a hand-rolled cigarette that

---

[57] Daniel J. Solove, *The Digital Person: Technology and Privacy in the Information Age* 179-85 (2004).

the officers determined smelled of marijuana. Officers proceeded to search his car and discovered a bag of marijuana under the passenger's seat.

The State charged respondent with possession of marijuana. When the police notified the Justice Court that they had arrested him, the Justice Court discovered that the arrest warrant previously had been quashed and so advised the police. Respondent argued that because his arrest was based on a warrant that had been quashed 17 days prior to his arrest, the marijuana seized incident to the arrest should be suppressed as the fruit of an unlawful arrest. Respondent also argued that "[t]he 'good faith' exception to the exclusionary rule [was] inapplicable . . . because it was police error, not judicial error, which caused the invalid arrest.". . .

"The question whether the exclusionary rule's remedy is appropriate in a particular context has long been regarded as an issue separate from the question whether the Fourth Amendment rights of the party seeking to invoke the rule were violated by police conduct." The exclusionary rule operates as a judicially created remedy designed to safeguard against future violations of Fourth Amendment rights through the rule's general deterrent effect. As with any remedial device, the rule's application has been restricted to those instances where its remedial objectives are thought most efficaciously served. Where the exclusionary rule does not result in appreciable deterrence, then, clearly, its use . . . is unwarranted. . . .

If court employees were responsible for the erroneous computer record, the exclusion of evidence at trial would not sufficiently deter future errors so as to warrant such a severe sanction. First, as we noted in [*United States v. Leon,* 468 U.S. 897 (1984)], the exclusionary rule was historically designed as a means of deterring police misconduct, not mistakes by court employees. Second, respondent offers no evidence that court employees are inclined to ignore or subvert the Fourth Amendment or that lawlessness among these actors requires application of the extreme sanction of exclusion. To the contrary, the Chief Clerk of the Justice Court testified at the suppression hearing that this type of error occurred once every three or four years.

Finally, and most important, there is no basis for believing that application of the exclusionary rule in these circumstances will have a significant effect on court employees responsible for informing the police that a warrant has been quashed. Because court clerks are not adjuncts to the law enforcement team engaged in the often competitive enterprise of ferreting out crime, they have no stake in the outcome of particular criminal prosecutions. The threat of exclusion of evidence could not be expected to deter such individuals from failing to inform police officials that a warrant had been quashed. . . .

In fact, once the court clerks discovered the error, they immediately corrected it, and then proceeded to search their files to make sure that no similar mistakes had occurred. There is no indication that the arresting officer was not acting objectively reasonably when he relied upon the police computer record. Application of the *Leon* framework supports a categorical exception to the exclusionary rule for clerical errors of court employees. . . .

O'CONNOR, SOUTER, and BREYER, JJ. concurring. The evidence in this case strongly suggests that it was a court employee's departure from established recordkeeping procedures that caused the record of respondent's arrest warrant to remain in the computer system after the warrant had been quashed. Prudently, then, the Court limits itself to the question whether a court employee's departure from such established procedures is the kind of error to which the exclusionary rule should apply. . . .

In limiting itself to that single question, however, the Court does not hold that the court employee's mistake in this case was necessarily the *only* error that may have occurred and to which the exclusionary rule might apply. While the police were innocent of the court employee's mistake, they may or may not have acted reasonably in their reliance *on the recordkeeping system itself.* Surely it would *not* be reasonable for the police to rely, say, on a recordkeeping system, their own or some other agency's, that has no mechanism to ensure its accuracy over time and that routinely leads to false arrests, even years after the probable cause for any such arrest has ceased to exist (if it ever existed). . . .

In recent years, we have witnessed the advent of powerful, computer-based recordkeeping systems that facilitate arrests in ways that have never before been possible. The police, of course, are entitled to enjoy the substantial advantages this technology confers. They may not, however, rely on it blindly. With the benefits of more efficient law enforcement mechanisms comes the burden of corresponding constitutional responsibilities.

GINSBURG and STEVENS, JJ. dissenting. This case portrays the increasing use of computer technology in law enforcement; it illustrates an evolving problem this Court need not, and in my judgment should not, resolve too hastily. . . .

Widespread reliance on computers to store and convey information generates, along with manifold benefits, new possibilities of error, due to both computer malfunctions and operator mistakes. Most germane to this case, computerization greatly amplifies an error's effect, and correspondingly intensifies the need for prompt correction; for inaccurate data can infect not only one agency, but the many agencies that share access to the database. The computerized data bases of the Federal Bureau of Investigation's National Crime Information Center (NCIC), to take a conspicuous example, contain over 23 million records, identifying, among other things, persons and vehicles sought by law enforcement agencies nationwide. NCIC information is available to approximately 71,000 federal, state, and local agencies. Thus, any mistake entered into the NCIC spreads nationwide in an instant.

Isaac Evans' arrest exemplifies the risks associated with computerization of arrest warrants. Though his arrest was in fact warrantless — the warrant once issued having been quashed over two weeks before the episode in suit — the computer reported otherwise. Evans' case is not idiosyncratic. . . .

In the instant case, the Court features testimony of the Chief Clerk of the Justice Court in East Phoenix to the effect that errors of the kind Evans encountered are reported only "on[c]e every three or four years." But the same witness also recounted that, when the error concerning Evans came to light, an immediate check revealed that three other errors of the very same kind had occurred on "that same day." . . .

In the Court's view, exclusion of evidence, even if capable of deterring police officer errors, cannot deter the carelessness of other governmental actors. Whatever federal precedents may indicate — an issue on which I voice no opinion — the Court's conclusion is not the lesson inevitably to be drawn from logic or experience.

In this electronic age, particularly with respect to recordkeeping, court personnel and police officers are not neatly compartmentalized actors. Instead, they serve together to carry out the State's information-gathering objectives. Whether particular records are maintained by the police or the courts should not be dispositive where a single computer data base can answer all calls. Not only is it artificial to distinguish between court clerk and police clerk slips; in practice, it may be difficult to pinpoint whether one official, *e.g.,* a court employee, or another, *e.g.,* a police officer, caused the error to exist or to persist. Applying an exclusionary rule as the Arizona court did may well supply a powerful incentive to the State to promote the prompt updating of computer records. . . .

NOTES & QUESTIONS

1. *Accuracy.* Pattern-based data mining is often not a highly accurate way of identifying suspects. Daniel Steinbock explores the arguments relating to data mining's accuracy:

   > It must be noted at the outset that, in one sense, accuracy is not a particularly high priority in data matching and data mining. To the extent that their results are used for heightened scrutiny or for terrorist profiling, even the staunchest advocates would not pretend that these indicators are foolproof, but would simply respond that they do not need to be. This is especially true for predictive uses; the goal is simply to sort the higher from the lower risks and, perhaps, to see if a certain threshold of risk has been reached. On the other hand, even with predictive uses, errors in the data will produce a larger number of falsely positive results, thereby imposing unnecessary harms. This effectively externalizes the error costs of the computer-generated decision onto its subjects.[58]

   Anita Ramasastry notes that data can often be "lost in translation" when it is taken from other contexts and used for government data mining purposes:

   > First, data may not be accurate when provided initially by a consumer or may only reflect a partial truth. Second, data may get mistranslated due to human error (e.g. typing in a birth date incorrectly) when placed into a database. Third, when data is used in a new context, it may not be interpreted in the same way as previously used, because the new party using the data may not understand how the data was originally classified. For example, racial or ethnic classifications in one database may be different than in a new database. Fourth, when data from different sources is combined into a larger database, it may be incorrectly integrated. In other words, data from different people who share the same surname might be incorrectly merged, creating a new profile that is incorrect. Thus, there are multiple ways in which data may be

---

[58] Daniel J. Steinbock, *Data Matching, Data Mining, and Due Process*, 40 Ga. L. Rev. 1, 82-83 (2005).

erroneous. Where human agents are involved in compiling or aggregating different data, data sources can be mistranslated.[59]

2. *Due Process.* Consider Daniel Steinbock:

> The most striking aspect of virtually all antiterrorist and data mining decisions is the total absence of even the most rudimentary procedures for notice, hearing, or other opportunities for meaningful participation before, or even after, the deprivation is imposed.

Steinbock examines four ways to bring due process to data mining programs:

> One is summary hearings, along the lines of those required in brief school suspensions, prior to denial of access to flights or infringements of other liberty or property rights. A second involves correction opportunities after the initial data matching or data mining consequence, in a fuller process with disclosure and a right to respond. A third means of redress is after-the-fact compensatory damages for false positives in outcome. This solution allows for less process but makes wrongly identified persons whole, at least monetarily. Finally, given the frequent need for secrecy in data matching and data mining decision algorithms and the difficulty of addressing challenges to them in individual hearings, this Article proposes examination of their validity by independent oversight bodies. Evaluating whether a decisional system meets constitutional demands of due process requires attention to all stages of the process.[60]

3. *Transparency.* Consider Daniel Solove:

> The problem with many data mining programs is that they lack adequate transparency. The reason for the secrecy of the programs is that exposing the algorithms and patterns that trigger identification as a possible future terrorist will tip off terrorists about what behaviors to avoid. This is indeed a legitimate concern. Our society, however, is one of open government, public accountability, and oversight of government officials — not one of secret blacklists maintained in clandestine bureaucracies. Without public accountability, unelected bureaucrats can administer data mining programs in ways often insulated from any scrutiny at all. For example, the information gathered about people for use in data mining might be collected from sources that do not take sufficient steps to maintain its accuracy. Without oversight, it is unclear what level of accuracy the government requires for the information it gathers and uses. If profiles are based on race, speech, or other factors that society might not find desirable to include, how is this to be aired and discussed? If a person is routinely singled out based on a profile and wants to challenge the profile, there appears no way to do so unless the profile is revealed.
>
> The lack of transparency in data mining programs makes it nearly impossible to balance the liberty and security interests. Given the significant potential privacy issues and other constitutional concerns, combined with speculative and unproven security benefits as well as many other alternative

---

[59] Anita Ramasastry, *Lost in Translation? Data Mining, National Security, and the "Adverse Inference" Problem*, 22 Santa Clara Computer & High Tech. L.J. 757, 778 (2006).

[60] Steinbock, Data Mining, supra, at 57.

means of promoting security, should data mining still be on the table as a viable policy option?[61]

UNITED STATES V. ELLISON
462 F.3d 557 (6th Cir. 2006)

GIBBONS, J. . . . The central issue in this case is whether the Fourth Amendment is implicated when a police officer investigates an automobile license plate number using a law enforcement computer database. While on routine patrol, Officer Mark Keeley of the Farmington Hills (Michigan) Police Department pulled into a two-lane service drive adjacent to a shopping center. Keeley testified that a white van, with a male driver inside, was idling in the lane closest to the stores, in an area marked with "Fire Lane" and "No Parking" signs. Keeley did not issue the van a citation for being illegally parked, nor did he request that the driver move the van. Rather, he moved into a parking spot to observe the van and entered the vehicle's license plate number into his patrol car's Law Enforcement Information Network ("LEIN") computer. The LEIN search revealed that the vehicle was registered to Curtis Ellison, who had an outstanding felony warrant. Following standard procedure, Keeley radioed for back-up and continued observing the van. After two minutes, another male got into the van, and it drove away. Officer Keeley followed the van until his back-up was nearby, and then activated his lights and stopped the van.

Officer Keeley approached the driver's-side window as his back-up arrived. He advised the driver that he was being stopped for parking in a fire lane and asked for license, registration and proof of insurance. The driver, identified as Edward Coleman, stated that he had only stopped in front of the store to wait for the passenger. At this time the passenger stated that he was the registered owner of the vehicle. Keeley verified the passenger's identity as Curtis Ellison and moved to the passenger side of the van. Keeley notified Ellison that he was being arrested on the outstanding warrant. Ellison stepped out of the van, and during the routine safety pat-down, two firearms were found. Coleman was released with a warning about parking in a fire lane.

Ellison was indicted for being a felon in possession of a firearm in violation of 18 U.S.C. § 922(g). Prior to trial, he made a timely motion to suppress the firearm as the fruit of an illegal search. After holding a hearing, the district court made a factual finding that the van was not parked illegally, and thus, the officer did not have probable cause to run the LEIN check of Ellison's license plate. The court issued a Memorandum Opinion and Order granting the motion to suppress under the "fruit of the poisonous tree" doctrine. . . .

The government argues on appeal that Ellison had no reasonable expectation of privacy in the information contained on his license plate, and thus, no probable cause was required for Officer Keeley to run the LEIN check. . . .

Although the district court did not expressly state that Ellison had a reasonable expectation of privacy in the information contained on his license

---

[61] Daniel J. Solove, *Data Mining and the Security-Liberty Debate*, 74 U. Chi. L. Rev. 343 (2008).

plate, such a conclusion was necessarily implied by the court's ruling that a Fourth Amendment violation occurred. Thus, the district court could only find that the LEIN search violated the Fourth Amendment if it first concluded that Ellison had a "constitutionally protected reasonable expectation of privacy" in his license plate number. . . .

A tenet of constitutional jurisprudence is that the Fourth Amendment protects only what an individual seeks to keep private. *Katz,* 389 U.S. at 351-52. "What a person knowingly exposes to the public . . . is not a subject of Fourth Amendment protection." It is also settled that "objects falling in the plain view of an officer who has a right to be in the position to have that view are subject to seizure." . . .

No argument can be made that a motorist seeks to keep the information on his license plate private. The very purpose of a license plate number, like that of a Vehicle Identification Number, is to provide identifying information to law enforcement officials and others. . . .

The dissent implies that even if an individual has no expectation of privacy in a license plate number, a privacy interest is somehow created by the entry of this information into a law-enforcement computer database. This argument flies in the face of established Fourth Amendment doctrine. First, despite the dissent's concerns over the information available in a LEIN search, Ellison had no privacy interest in the information retrieved by Officer Keely. The obvious purpose of maintaining law enforcement databases is to make information, such as the existence of outstanding warrants, readily available to officers carrying out legitimate law enforcement duties. The dissent fails to state how using a license plate number-in which there is no expectation of privacy-to retrieve other non-private information somehow creates a "search" for the purposes of the Fourth Amendment. . . . This is not a case where the police used a technology not available to the public to discover evidence that could not otherwise be obtained without "intrusion into a constitutionally-protected area." *Kyllo v. United States,* 533 U.S. 27, 34-35 (2001) (holding that the use of thermal-imaging technology to detect heat inside a private home violates the Fourth Amendment). The technology used in this case does not allow officers to access any previously-unobtainable information; it simply allows them to access information more quickly. As the information was obtained without intruding upon a constitutionally-protected area, there was no "search" for Fourth Amendment purposes. . . .

MOORE, J. dissenting. . . . The majority rests its conclusion that the Fourth Amendment was not implicated by the LEIN search on the relatively uncontroversial fact that the operator of a vehicle has no privacy interest in the particular combination of letters and numerals that make up his license-plate number, but pays short shrift to the crucial issue of how the license-plate information is used. . . . This approach misses the crux of the issue before the court: even if there is no privacy interest in the license-plate number per se, can the police, without any measure of heightened suspicion or other constraint on their discretion, conduct a search using the license-plate number to access information about the vehicle and its operator that may not otherwise be public or accessible by the police without heightened suspicion? . . . .

The use of a computer database to acquire information about drivers through their license-plate numbers without any heightened suspicion is in tension with many of the Fourth Amendment concerns expressed in *Delaware v. Prouse,* 440 U.S. 648, 655-63 (1979). In *Prouse,* the Supreme Court held that an officer may not stop a vehicle to check the operator's license and registration without "at least articulable and reasonable suspicion that a motorist is unlicensed or that an automobile is not registered, or that either the vehicle or an occupant is otherwise subject to seizure for violation of law," despite the fact that the state requires drivers to be licensed and vehicles to be registered. The Court stated that the Fourth Amendment aims "to safeguard the privacy and security of individuals against arbitrary invasions. . . . Thus, the permissibility of a particular law enforcement practice is judged by balancing its intrusion on the individual's Fourth Amendment interests against its promotion of legitimate governmental interests." The Court then explained the constitutional concerns that flow from the unbridled discretion associated with permitting random searches of drivers' information:

> To insist neither upon an appropriate factual basis for suspicion directed at a particular automobile nor upon some other substantial and objective standard or rule to govern the exercise of discretion "would invite intrusions upon constitutionally guaranteed rights based on nothing more substantial than inarticulate hunches. . . ." *Terry v. Ohio,* 392 U.S. [1], at 22 [1968]. . . . When there is not probable cause to believe that a driver is violating any one of the multitude of applicable traffic and equipment regulations — or other articulable basis amounting to reasonable suspicion that the driver is unlicensed or his vehicle unregistered — we cannot conceive of any legitimate basis upon which a patrolman could decide that stopping a particular driver for a spot check would be more productive than stopping any other driver. This kind of standardless and unconstrained discretion is the evil the Court has discerned when in previous cases it has insisted that the discretion of the official in the field be circumscribed, at least to some extent. . . .

Although the license-plate search at issue here is arguably less invasive than a license-and-registration check, the constitutional concerns regarding abuse of discretion do not disappear simply because drivers are not stopped to conduct the license-plate search. First, a search can implicate the Fourth Amendment even when the individual does not know that she is being searched. Second, the balancing of Fourth Amendment interests also requires consideration of "psychological intrusion[s] visited upon" the individuals searched in assessing the extent of intrusion that a particular police practice imposes. *See Prouse,* 440 U.S. at 657. The psychological invasion that results from knowing that one's personal information is subject to search by the police, for no reason, at any time one is driving a car is undoubtedly grave.

Because the government incorrectly limits its Fourth Amendment analysis to the plain view of the license plate without exploring the constitutional implications of the subsequent LEIN search, it does not provide any explanation as to the governmental interests promoted by license-plate searches. . . .

In addition, the possibility and the reality of errors in the computer databases accessed by MDT systems lead to great concern regarding the potential for license-plate searches to result in unwarranted intrusions into privacy in the form of stops made purely on the basis of incorrect information. . . .

NOTES & QUESTIONS

1. *The Fourth Amendment and Government Data Mining.* Does the Fourth Amendment provide any limits on government data mining? Lee Tein argues that it does:

> The use of patterns discovered through data mining raises . . . particularity issues. Imagine a database of a million people and a hypothesis that those who meet certain criteria are highly likely to be terrorists. But you don't know whether any of these million people actually do meet these criteria; if you did, you wouldn't need to run the search. The basic problem is lack of particularized suspicion; data about these persons would be "searched" without any reason to believe either that the database contains evidence of terrorist activity or that any person "in" the database is a terrorist. . . .[62]

When the government engages in data mining, it often analyzes information that it already possesses. Is this a search? If the government has information about a person in its records and analyzes it, does this trigger the Fourth Amendment?

In contrast, Richard Posner argues in favor of data mining: "Computer searches do not invade privacy because search programs are not sentient beings. Only the human search should raise constitutional or other legal issues."[63] Consider the following argument in response to Posner: "[T]here is human intervention in data mining even before the first automated search is run; humans will write the software, shape the database parameters, and decide on the kinds of matches that count. And the task of data mining itself is guided by some degree of human interaction."[64] To the extent there is a human element in data mining, how ought it to be regulated? Do the problems of data mining stem solely from the human element?

4. THE DRIVER'S PRIVACY PROTECTION ACT

For decades, many states had been selling to private sector companies their motor vehicle records. Motor vehicle records contain information such as one's name, address, phone number, Social Security number, medical information, height, weight, gender, eye color, photograph, and date of birth. This information was highly desired by marketers, who paid states millions of dollars to obtain these records. In 1994, Congress passed the Driver's Privacy Protection Act (DPPA), 18 U.S.C. §§ 2721–2725, to halt this practice.

---

[62] Lee Tien, Privacy, *Technology and Data Mining*, 30 Ohio N.U. L. Rev. 389, 405 (2004).

[63] Richard Posner, *Privacy, Surveillance, and Law*, 75 U. Chi. L. Rev. 245 (2008).

[64] Ira Rubinstein, Ronald D. Lee & Paul M. Schwartz, *Data Mining and Internet Profiling*, 75 U. Chi. L. Rev. 261 (2008).

Restriction on Disclosure. Pursuant to DPPA:

> [A] State department of motor vehicles . . . shall not knowingly disclose or otherwise make available to any person or entity personal information about any individual obtained by the department in connection with a motor vehicle record. 18 U.S.C. § 2721(a).

"Personal information" is defined as data "that identifies an individual, including an individual's photograph, social security number, driver identification number, name, address (but not the 5-digit zip code), telephone number, and medical or disability information." § 2725(3). The definition of "personal information" specifically excludes "information on vehicular accidents, driving violations, and driver's status." § 2725(3).

DPPA applies to state DMVs and their officials and employees. Further, DPPA only applies to motor vehicle records.

Consent. State DMVs can disclose personal information in motor vehicle records if the individual consents. In order to disclose a driver's personal information for marketing or other restricted uses, the driver must affirmatively indicate her consent (opt in). § 2721(b) and (d).

Exceptions. The DPPA contains a number of exceptions. Personal information can be disclosed for purposes of law enforcement, recalls, legal proceedings, and insurance claims investigations. § 2721(b). Additionally, DPPA permits disclosure to licensed private investigative agencies. § 2721(b). Ironically, the event that motivated Congress to pass the DPPA was the murder of actress Rebecca Shaeffer. Her murderer ascertained her address from a private detective, who had received it from the DMV.[65]

Restrictions on Further Dissemination. If private entities obtain motor vehicle record information, they cannot resell or further disseminate that information. 18 U.S.C. § 2721(c). However, if the driver consents to the disclosure of her data, then information may be disseminated for any purpose.

Enforcement. The DPPA establishes criminal fines for any "person" who knowingly obtains or discloses motor vehicle record data in ways prohibited by the DPPA. §§ 2722, 2723(a), 2725(2).

The DPPA, § 2724, provides for a private right to action for violations:

> A person who knowingly obtains, discloses or uses personal information, from a motor vehicle record, for a purpose not permitted under this chapter shall be liable to the individual to whom the information pertains, who may bring a civil action in a United States district court.

Note that this section purportedly applies to any "person who knowingly obtains, discloses or uses personal information, from a motor vehicle record." In other words, it does not just apply to state DMVs but to anybody who uses data

---

[65] *See* Charles J. Sykes, *The End of Privacy: Personal Rights in the Surveillance Society* 30-31 (1999).

from a motor vehicle record. States and state agencies are generally excluded from the DPPA, but the U.S. Attorney General may impose a civil penalty of up to $5,000 per day for state agencies that maintain a "policy or practice of substantial noncompliance" with the DPPA. § 2723(b).

In *Margan v. Niles*, 250 F. Supp. 2d 63 (N.D.N.Y. 2003), the court found that the DPPA provided a cause of action beyond the motor operator whose motor vehicle record was disclosed. The court found that "any individual whose address was obtained from a motor vehicle record is a proper plaintiff." Hence, in *Niles*, the spouse and children of an individual whose address was obtained from a motor vehicle record could "maintain an action under the DPPA where the spouse and children share the same address as that individual." The court also found that a municipality whose agent violated the DPPA could be held vicariously liable under this statute. *See also Luparello v. The Incorporated Village of Garden City*, 290 F. Supp. 2d 341 (E.D.N.Y. 2003).

The Scope of Congressional Power. In *Reno v. Condon*, 528 U.S. 141 (2000), the Supreme Court upheld the DPPA against a constitutional challenge that DPPA violated the Tenth and Eleventh Amendments:

> The United States asserts that the DPPA is a proper exercise of Congress' authority to regulate interstate commerce under the Commerce Clause, U.S. Const., Art. I, § 8, cl. 3. The United States bases its Commerce Clause argument on the fact that the personal, identifying information that the DPPA regulates is a "thin[g] in interstate commerce," and that the sale or release of that information in interstate commerce is therefore a proper subject of congressional regulation. We agree with the United States' contention. The motor vehicle information which the States have historically sold is used by insurers, manufacturers, direct marketers, and others engaged in interstate commerce to contact drivers with customized solicitations. The information is also used in the stream of interstate commerce by various public and private entities for matters related to interstate motoring. Because drivers' information is, in this context, an article of commerce, its sale or release into the interstate stream of business is sufficient to support congressional regulation.

Based on *Reno v. Condon*, what is the extent of Congress's power to regulate information maintained by the states? Suppose Congress amended the Privacy Act to apply not just to federal agencies but to all state and local governments as well. Would such an extension of the Privacy Act be constitutional?

CHAPTER 4

PRIVACY OF FINANCIAL AND COMMERCIAL DATA

A. THE FINANCIAL SERVICES INDUSTRY AND PERSONAL DATA

1. THE FAIR CREDIT REPORTING ACT

Increasingly, companies in the United States make sales based on credit. Since 1980, almost all homes and most new cars are purchased on credit. Well over half of retail items are purchased on credit as well.[1]

As a result of the centrality of different forms of consumer borrowing, credit reporting agencies play an ever-greater role in economic transactions. Credit reporting agencies prepare credit reports about people's credit history for use by creditors seeking to loan people money. Credit reports contain financial information such as bankruptcy filings, judgments and liens, mortgage foreclosures, and checking account data. Some companies also prepare investigative consumer reports, which supplement the credit report with information about an individual's character and lifestyle. Creditors depend upon credit reports to determine whether or not to offer a person a loan as well as what interest rate to charge that person. Credit reports are also reviewed by some landlords before renting out an apartment.

Credit reports contain a "credit score" that is used to assess a person's credit risk. In many cases, a low score will not necessarily mean the denial of a loan, mortgage, or credit card; rather, it means that a higher rate of interest will be charged. As Evan Hendricks notes:

> According to the Fair Isaac Corporation, a leading developer of credit scoring models, one delinquent account can lower a credit score from 70 to 120 points. A consumer with excellent credit (credit score of 720-850) would pay about 7.85% interest rate for a home equity loan, while a consumer with marginal

---

[1] *See generally* Robert Ellis Smith, *Ben Franklin's Web Site: Privacy and Curiosity from Plymouth Rock to the Internet* 313-25 (2000); Steven L. Nock, *The Costs of Privacy: Surveillance and Reputation in America* (1993).

credit (640-659) would pay 9.2% and one with poor credit (500-559) would pay a 12.1% rate. The rate swings for a new car loan are even greater, with good credit risks paying a 5.2% rate, moderate risks paying 11.4% and poor risks paying 17.2%.[2]

Credit reports are not only used in connection with granting credit. Employers use credit reports to make hiring and promotion decisions. The issuance of professional licenses, such as admittance to the bar, also can require the examination of one's credit report.

There are three major national credit reporting agencies: Experian, Equifax, and Trans Union. Each of these three companies has information on virtually every adult American citizen, and they routinely prepare credit reports about individuals.

According to Peter Swire, our financial system has been shifting toward more traceable payment transactions: "The shift from cash to checks to credit and debit cards shows an evolution toward creating records, placing the records automatically in databases, and potentially linking the databases to reveal extremely detailed information about an individual's purchasing history."[3] This evolution is generating new problems for the protection of privacy.

In 1970, Congress passed the Fair Credit Reporting Act (FCRA), Pub. L. No. 90-321, to regulate credit reporting agencies. The Act was inspired by allegations of abuse and lack of responsiveness of credit agencies to consumer complaints. In its statement of purpose, the FCRA states: "There is a need to insure that consumer reporting agencies exercise their grave responsibilities with fairness, impartiality, and a respect for the consumer's right to privacy." 15 U.S.C. § 1681. The FCRA requires credit reporting companies to provide an individual access to her records, establishes procedures for correcting information, and sets limitations on disclosure.

Scope. FCRA applies to "any consumer reporting agency" that furnishes a "consumer report." 15 U.S.C. § 1681b. As a consequence, the scope of the FCRA turns on the definitions of "consumer report" and "consumer reporting agencies." Pursuant to § 1681b(d):

> The term "consumer report" means any written, oral, or other communication of any information by a consumer reporting agency bearing on a consumer's credit worthiness, credit standing, credit capacity, character, general reputation, personal characteristics, or mode of living which is used or expected to be used or collected in whole or in part for the purpose of serving as a factor in establishing the consumer's eligibility for
>
> > (A) credit or insurance to be used primarily for personal, family, or household purposes;
> > (B) employment purposes; or
> > (C) any other purpose authorized under [§ 1681b].

---

[2] Evan Hendricks, *Credit Scores and Credit Reports: How the System Really Works, What You Can Do* 3-4 (2004).

[3] Peter P. Swire, *Financial Privacy and the Theory of High-Tech Government Surveillance*, 77 Wash. U. L.Q. 461 (1999).

A "consumer reporting agency" is defined as

[a]ny person which, for monetary fees, dues, or on a cooperative nonprofit basis, regularly engages in whole or in part in the practice of assembling or evaluating consumer credit information or other information on consumers for the purpose of furnishing consumer reports to third parties, and which uses means or facility of interstate commerce for the purpose of preparing or furnishing consumer reports. § 1681b(f).

Courts have held that "even if a report is used or expected to be used for a non-consumer purpose, it may still fall within the definition of a consumer report if it contains information that was originally collected by a consumer reporting agency with the expectation that it would be used for a consumer purpose." *Ippolito v. WNS, Inc.*, 864 F.2d 440 (7th Cir. 1988); *Bakker v. McKinnon*, 152 F.3d 1007 (8th Cir. 1998).

Permissible Uses of Credit Reports. Pursuant to 15 U.S.C. § 1681(a), a consumer reporting agency can furnish a consumer report only under certain circumstances or for certain uses: (1) in response to a court order or grand jury subpoena; (2) to the person to whom the report pertains; (3) to a "person which [the agency] has reason to believe" intends to use the information in connection with (a) the extension of credit to a consumer; (b) employment purposes; (c) insurance underwriting; (d) licensing or the conferral of government benefits; (e) assessment of credit risks associated with an existing credit obligation; (f) "legitimate business need" when engaging in "a business transaction involving the consumer"; (4) to establish a person's capacity to pay child support.

Credit Reports for Employment Purposes. When an employer or potential employer seeks a credit report for employment purposes, she must first disclose in writing to the consumer that a credit report may be obtained, and the consumer must authorize in writing that the report can be obtained. The person seeking the report from a credit reporting agency must certify that she obtained the consent of the individual and that she will not use the information in violation of any equal employment opportunity law or regulation. § 1681b(b). If the person who obtained the report takes adverse action based in any way on the report, she must provide the consumer a copy of the report and a description of the consumer's rights under the FCRA. § 1681b(b).

Pursuant to § 1681b(g):

A consumer reporting agency shall not furnish for employment purposes, or in connection with a credit or insurance transaction or a direct marketing transaction, a consumer report that contains medical information about a consumer, unless the consumer consents to the furnishing of the report.

Law Enforcement Access. Pursuant to FCRA, "a consumer reporting agency may furnish identifying information respecting any customer, limited to his name, address, former addresses, places of employment, or former places of employment, to a governmental agency." § 1681f. The FBI can obtain "the names and addresses of all financial institutions . . . at which a consumer maintains or has maintained an account" by presenting a written request to a consumer reporting agency. § 1681u(a). Additionally, pursuant to a written request by the FBI, a consumer reporting agency must disclose "identifying information respecting a consumer, limited to name, address, former addresses, places of employment, or former places of employment." The FBI, however, must certify that the information is sought in an investigation to protect against "international terrorism or clandestine intelligence activities" and that the investigation "is not conducted solely upon the basis of activities protected by the first amendment to the Constitution of the United States." § 1681u(b). To obtain additional information from a credit report, the FBI must obtain a court order and meet the same standard as above. § 1681u(c).

Moreover, § 1681v provides a broad release exemption "to a government agency authorized to conduct investigations of, or intelligence or counterintelligence activities or analysis related to, international terrorism." These entities can obtain a consumer report on an individual when the government agency provides "a written certification" to a consumer reporting agency that the information is "necessary" for an agency investigation or other agency activity.

Unauthorized Disclosures of Credit Reports: Prescreening. A typical American receives a flood of credit cards offers each year. These offers follow due to the practice of "prescreening" consumers for such offers, which FCRA permits. A credit reporting agency can furnish a credit report, without the consumer's authorization, if

> (i) the transaction consists of a firm offer of credit or insurance;
> (ii) the consumer reporting agency has complied with subsection (e); and
> (iii) there is not in effect the election by the consumer, made in accordance with subsection (e), to have the consumer's name and address excluded from lists of names provided by the agency pursuant to this paragraph. § 1681b(c).

Subsection (e) of § 1681b provides the consumer with a right to opt out of such unauthorized disclosures. If the consumer notifies the credit reporting agency by phone, the opt out shall last for two years and then expire. If the consumer notifies the credit reporting agency by submitting a signed opt-out form, then the opt out remains effective until the consumer notifies the agency otherwise. § 1681b(e).

Limitations on Information Contained in Credit Reports. Credit reporting agencies are excluded from providing certain information in credit reports, such as bankruptcy proceedings more than ten years old; suits and judgments more than seven years old; paid tax liens more than seven years old; and records of arrest, indictment, or conviction of a crime more than seven years old. § 1681c(a). These limitations do not apply, however, when a company is preparing a credit report used in connection with a credit transaction more than $150,000; underwriting a life insurance policy more than $150,000; or employing an individual with an annual salary more than $75,000. § 1681c(b).

Investigative Consumer Reports. An "investigative consumer report" is "a consumer report or portion thereof in which information on a consumer's character, general reputation, personal characteristics, or mode of living is obtained through personal interviews, with neighbors, friends, or associates." § 1681a(f). The FCRA provides limitations on investigative consumer reports. These reports cannot be prepared unless "it is clearly and accurately disclosed to the consumer that an investigative consumer report including information as to his character, general reputation, personal characteristics and mode of living, whichever are applicable, may be made." § 1681d(a)(1). The consumer, if she requests, can require disclosure "of the nature and scope of the investigation requested." § 1681d(b). Further, if the report contains any adverse information about a person gleaned from interviews with neighbors, friends, or associates, the agency must take reasonable steps to corroborate that information "from an additional source that has independent and direct knowledge of the information" or ensure that "the person interviewed is the best possible source of the information." § 1681d(d).

Accuracy. "Whenever a consumer reporting agency prepares a consumer report it shall follow reasonable procedures to assure maximum possible accuracy of the information concerning the individual about whom the report relates." § 1681e(b).

Disclosures to the Consumer. The FCRA requires that credit reporting agencies, upon request of the consumer, disclose, among other things:

(1) All information in the consumer's file at the time of the request, except . . . any information concerning credit scores or any other risk scores or predictors relating to the consumer.
(2) The sources of the information. . . .
(3) Identification of each person . . . that procured a consumer report [within two years for employment purposes; within one year for all other purposes] . . . .
(4) The dates, original payees, and amounts of any checks upon which is based any adverse characterization of the consumer, included in the file at the time of disclosure. . . . § 1681g.

Responsiveness to Consumer Complaints. National credit reporting agencies must provide consumers who request disclosures under the FCRA with a toll-free telephone number at which personnel are accessible to respond to consumer inquiries during normal business hours. § 1681g(c).

Procedures in Case of Disputed Accuracy. Pursuant to § 1681i(a)(1):

If the completeness or accuracy of any item of information contained in a consumer's file at a consumer reporting agency is disputed by the consumer and the consumer notifies the agency directly of such dispute, the agency shall reinvestigate free of charge and record the current status of the disputed information or delete the item from the file. . . .

The consumer reporting agency must provide written notice to a consumer of the results of a reinvestigation within five business days after completing the investigation. § 1681i.

If the information is found to be inaccurate or incomplete or cannot be verified, the consumer reporting agency must promptly delete it from the file. § 1681i. At the request of the consumer, the credit reporting agency must furnish notification that the item has been deleted to "any person specifically designated by the consumer who has within two years prior thereto received a consumer report for employment purposes, or within six months prior thereto received a consumer report for any other purpose." § 1681i(d).

"If the reinvestigation does not resolve the dispute, the consumer may file a brief statement setting forth the nature of the dispute." § 1681i(b).

In any subsequent credit report, the agency must clearly note that the information in question is disputed by the consumer and provide the consumer's statement. § 1681i(c).

Public Record Information for Employment Purposes. If a credit reporting agency furnishes a credit report for employment purposes containing information obtained in public records that is likely to have an adverse effect on the consumer, it must either notify the consumer of the fact that public record information is being reported along with the name and address of the person to whom the information is being reported or "maintain strict procedures designed to insure that whenever public record information which is likely to have an adverse effect on a consumer's ability to obtain employment is reported it is complete and up to date." § 1681k.

Requirements on Users of Consumer Reports. If a user of a credit report takes any adverse action on a consumer based in any way on the report, the user shall provide notice of the adverse action to the consumer, information for the consumer to contact the credit reporting agency that prepared the report, and notice of the consumer's right to obtain a free copy of the report and to dispute the accuracy of the report. § 1681m(a). Whenever credit is denied based on information obtained through sources other than a credit report, upon the consumer's written request, the person or entity denying credit shall disclose the nature of that information. § 1681m(b).

Civil Liability. A person who "willfully fails to comply with any requirement" of the FCRA is liable to the consumer for actual damages or damages between $100 and $1,000, as well as punitive damages and attorneys' fees and costs. § 1681n. Negligent failure to comply with any requirement of the FCRA results in liability to the consumer for actual damages as well as attorneys' fees and costs. § 1681. The FTC also has the power to enforce the FCRA.

The FCRA states that an action to enforce liability under the Act must be brought within two years "from the date on which the liability arises." § 1681p. However, when the defendant has "willfully misrepresented any information required under [the FCRA] to be disclosed and the information . . . is material to [a claim under the FCRA], the actions may be brought at a time within two years after [the plaintiff's] discovery of the misrepresentation." § 1681p.

The Fair and Accurate Credit Transactions Act. In 2003, Congress passed the Fair and Accurate Credit Transactions Act (FACTA), which amended FCRA. Evan Hendricks explains the impetus for passing the FACTA:

> [K]ey provisions of the FCRA that preempted State law were set to expire on December 31, 2003. These provisions dealt with issues affecting billions of dollars in commerce: pre-approved credit card offers, duties on creditors (furnishers) to report accurately and to reinvestigate, and the sharing of personal data among corporate affiliates. Industry expressed fears that if legislation was not passed and the preemption expired, state legislatures would begin passing conflicting laws that would raise compliance costs, and worse, interfere with profits.
>
> To consumer and privacy groups, legislation was long overdue because the 1996 FCRA Amendments were not getting the job done. All of the long-standing problems related to privacy and fair information practices persisted: inaccuracy, faulty reinvestigations, reinsertion, non-responsiveness, and lax security. More dramatically, identity theft had been crowned the nation's "fastest growing crime," and the biggest harm from identity theft, everyone knew, was to the privacy of credit reports. . . .
>
> Both sides wanted legislation, but not the same legislation. Industry wanted a simple, straightforward bill that would do nothing more than make FCRA preemption permanent.
>
> Consumer privacy groups called for a detailed reform bill that would set a "floor" of new protections, but which would leave the states free to go further.[4]

One-Call Fraud Alerts. The FACTA amends FCRA to enable consumers to alert only one credit reporting agency of potential fraud rather than all of them. That agency must notify the other credit reporting agencies. 15 U.S.C. § 1681c-1.

Business Transaction Data. The FACTA gives victims of identity theft the right to require certain disclosures from the creditors used by the identity thief; these disclosures concern information about the fraudulent transactions carried out in the victim's name. 15 U.S.C. § 1681g(e)(1). To obtain this information from the creditors, however, the victim must provide one form of identification from a list (that the business gets to pick) as well as proof of the claim of identity theft (police report, affidavit). The victim's request must be in writing and must specify the date of the transaction and other transaction data. Business entities can decline this request if they believe in good faith that there is not "a high degree of confidence in knowing the true identity of the individual requesting the information." § 1681g(e)(2). Further, business entities cannot be sued if they make a disclosure in good faith under these provisions. § 1681g(e)(7). Business entities are not required to alter their record-keeping practices to provide the information required by these provisions. § 1681g(e)(8).

Block of Identity Theft Information. The FACTA amends the FCRA to provide:

---

[4] Hendricks, *Credit Scores, supra*, at 307-08.

(a) *Block*. Except as otherwise provided in this section, a consumer reporting agency shall block the reporting of any information in the file of a consumer that the consumer identifies as information that resulted from an alleged identity theft, not later than 4 business days after the date of receipt by such agency of —

(1) appropriate proof of the identity of the consumer;
(2) a copy of an identity theft report;
(3) the identification of such information by the consumer; and
(4) a statement by the consumer that the information is not information relating to any transaction by the consumer.

(b) *Notification*. A consumer reporting agency shall promptly notify the furnisher of information identified by the consumer under subsection (a) —

(1) that the information may be a result of identity theft;
(2) that an identity theft report has been filed;
(3) that a block has been requested under this section; and
(4) of the effective dates of the block. § 1681c-2.

SSN Truncation. If a consumer requests it, credit reporting agencies must not disclose the first five digits of the consumer's SSN. § 1681g(a)(1)(A).

Free Credit Reports. FACTA requires credit reporting agencies to provide a free credit report once a year at the request of a consumer. § 1681j.

Disclosure of Credit Scores. FACTA requires credit reporting agencies to disclose to a consumer her credit score. Many credit reporting agencies previously would not divulge a person's credit score. § 1681g.

Statute of Limitations. FCRA's statute of limitation extends to two years after the date when the plaintiff discovers the violation or five years after the date of the violation, whichever occurs earlier.

Preemption. The FACTA preempts state laws that address many business practices. State laws that deal with these topics — even if they provide more protection to consumers — are preempted. Before FACTA, FCRA contained a list of limited preemptions for certain specified "subject matters," and set these preemptions to expire in 2004. In FACTA, Congress made permanent all existing preemptions in FCRA, and added a list of new and permanent preemptions. In so doing, it also reversed some existing state safeguards. For example, FACTA reversed one aspect of California's S.B. 1, which required customers to be permitted to "opt out," or indicate their refusal to information sharing before an organization could share such personal information with its affiliates. § 1681a(d)(1). For caselaw finding that FACTA's preemption voids some but not all of S.B. 1's affiliate sharing provisions, see *American Bankers Ass'n v. Lockyer*, 541 F.3d 1214 (9th Cir. 2008).

FACTA also made an important innovation in the jurisprudence of preemption by limiting some of its preemptions only to a new and narrow category of "required conduct" rather than the broader category of "subject matter."[5] §§ 1681c-1, 1681t(b)(5). As an example of a "required conduct" preemption, FACTA requires consumer agencies to place fraud alerts on consumer credit files under certain circumstances. At the same time, it permits states to engage in further regulation regarding the larger subject area, which is identity theft.

SMITH V. BOB SMITH CHEVROLET, INC.

275 F. Supp. 2d 808 (W.D. Ky. 2003)

HEYBURN, J. Christopher Smith ("Plaintiff") alleges that Defendant Bob Smith Chevrolet, Inc. violated the Fair Credit Reporting Act, 15 U.S.C. § 1681 *et seq.,* and invaded his privacy in violation of Kentucky common law. . . . [B]oth parties have moved for summary judgment on the issue of whether Smith Chevrolet lacked a permissible purpose when it accessed Plaintiff's credit report; Smith Chevrolet moved to dismiss the Kentucky invasion of privacy claim. . . .

The underlying facts concern the disputed sale of a 2001 GMC Suburban. Having decided that he wanted to purchase a car, on December 13, 2000, Plaintiff completed a GMAC credit application to determine his eligibility for financing. On December 23, 2000, Plaintiff went to Smith Chevrolet with the intention of purchasing the Suburban to use on a family Christmas vacation.

After arriving at the dealership, Plaintiff met with a company employee to discuss the terms of the sale. Two factors complicated the sale. First, Plaintiff wanted to trade in his 1997 Mercury Villager. Second, as an employee of General Electric — a General Motors ("GM") supplier — he was entitled to a standard discount upon proof of employment. Although Plaintiff did have the 1997 Mercury Villager to trade-in on December 23, 2000, he did not have the proper documentation needed to secure the discount. Notwithstanding this fact, a Smith Chevrolet representative agreed to sell Plaintiff the Suburban at the GM discounted price provided he proved his entitlement to the full discount at a later date. After calculating the Villager's trade-in value and the GM discount, the two sides agreed on a price and set forth the terms of the sale in a handwritten purchase order. . . .

On January 10, 2001, Plaintiff faxed and mailed proof of his eligibility for the GM discount. Shortly thereafter, Plaintiff's bank issued Smith Chevrolet a check in the amount of the balance due.

About a week or ten days later, another dispute arose which gives rise to the current litigation. At that point Smith Chevrolet claims it realized the employee who generated the typewritten Purchase Agreement inadvertently doubled the amount of Plaintiff's discount. Smith Chevrolet contacted Plaintiff, explained the calculation error and told Plaintiff that he owed the dealership more money. Furthermore, Smith Chevrolet told Plaintiff that, until he paid the difference, it refused to transfer the Suburban's title and pay off the outstanding loan attached on the Villager trade-in. These were both actions Smith Chevrolet had promised Plaintiff it would take when Plaintiff left the lot on December 23, 2000.

---

[5] For a discussion, see Paul M. Schwartz, *Preemption and Privacy*, 118 Yale L.J. 902, 943-44 (2009).

Following from this dispute, on February 21, 2000, Smith Chevrolet accessed Plaintiff's consumer report. The decision to access Plaintiff's report was made by Drew Smith, Smith Chevrolet's chief executive officer and part-owner. Smith Chevrolet says it accessed Plaintiff's report to determine whether Plaintiff was (1) continuing to make payments on the Villager's loan and (2) maintaining insurance on the Villager. Plaintiff disputes Smith Chevrolet's motivations in this regard and claims that it simply wanted to invade Plaintiff's privacy.

When the parties could not agree on the amount due, Plaintiff sued Smith Chevrolet in Jefferson Circuit Court for breach of the sale contract. He demanded specific performance so that he could receive the Suburban's title and transfer the Villager loan obligations to Smith Chevrolet. About a year later, a state court jury found in Plaintiff's favor. One day earlier, on May 13, 2002, Plaintiff filed this suit in federal court. . . .

The heart of [Plaintiff's] case is the contention that Smith Chevrolet violated the FCRA when it accessed Plaintiff's credit report on February 21, 2001. Specifically, Plaintiff contends Smith Chevrolet is liable for negligently and willfully violating the responsibilities imposed by the FCRA. *See* 15 U.S.C. § 1681o (creating a private cause of action for negligent violations of the FCRA); 15 U.S.C. § 1681n (creating a private cause of action for willful violations). Both sides have filed motions for summary judgment addressing whether Smith Chevrolet had a "permissible purpose" for accessing Plaintiff's credit report. The facts central to this claim are not in dispute. Smith Chevrolet may access Plaintiff's credit report only if, as a matter of law, its actions are consistent with one of the permissible purposes set forth in 15 U.S.C. § 1681b(a)(3).

The FCRA identifies a limited set of "permissible purposes" for obtaining and using a consumer report. *See* 15 U.S.C. § 1681b(a)(3); *see also* 15 U.S.C. § 1681b(f). Those permissible purposes provide that a person may only access a consumer report if he:

> (A) intends to use the information in connection with a credit transaction involving the consumer on whom the information is to be furnished and involving the extension of credit to, or review or collection of an account of, the consumer; or
>
> (B) intends to use the information for employment purposes; or
>
> (C) intends to use the information in connection with the underwriting of insurance involving the consumer; or
>
> (D) intends to use the information in connection with a determination of the consumer's eligibility for a license or other benefit granted by a governmental instrumentality required by law to consider an applicant's financial responsibility or status; or
>
> (E) intends to use the information, as a potential investor or servicer, or current insurer, in connection with a valuation of, or an assessment of the credit or prepayment risks associated with, an existing credit obligation; or
>
> (F) otherwise has a legitimate business need for the information—
>
>> (i) in connection with a business transaction that is initiated by the consumer; or
>>
>> (ii) to review an account to determine whether the consumer continues to meet the terms of the account.

15 U.S.C. § 1681b(a)(3).

In its summary judgment motion, Smith Chevrolet contends it had three bases for accessing Plaintiff's credit report. The Court now addresses each of these arguments.

First and most persuasively, Smith Chevrolet contends its actions complied with § 1681b(a)(3)(f)(i). That section provides that one may obtain a consumer report if it "has a legitimate business need for the information . . . in connection with a business transaction that is initiated by the consumer. . ." Smith Chevrolet argues that because the transaction was in dispute, it needed to ascertain the value of its collateral. If it appeared that Plaintiff was not current on his payments for the Mercury Villager, then his indebtedness would have increased over and above the amount owed Smith Chevrolet.

As a starting point, the Court begins with the FCRA's text. The applicability of this permissible purpose boils down to whether Smith Chevrolet's use of the credit report was "in connection with a transaction initiated by the consumer," as the statute uses those terms. That restriction to the actual statutory usage is important here because, in the abstract, it is true Smith Chevrolet accessed Plaintiff's credit report in connection with a transaction Plaintiff at one point initiated. The Court concludes, however, that the statute uses the terms "in connection with a transaction initiated by the consumer" more restrictively.

Turning to the text at issue, when Congress defined the term "consumer report," it stated:

> The term "consumer report" means any written, oral, or other communication of any information by a consumer reporting agency bearing on a consumer's credit worthiness, credit standing, credit capacity, character, general reputation, personal characteristics, or mode of living which is used or expected to be used or collected in whole or in part for the purpose of serving as a factor in establishing the consumer's eligibility for—
>
> > (A) credit or insurance to be used primarily for personal, family, or household purposes;
> >
> > (B) employment purposes; or
> >
> > (C) any other purpose authorized under section 604 [15 U.S.C. § 1681b].

15 U.S.C. § 1681a(d).

This definition suggests that Congress primarily envisioned consumer reports being disseminated for the purposes of assessing "eligibility." Then, in § 1681b(a)(3), Congress listed additional specific permissible purposes pertaining to the extension of credit, collection of an account, employment purposes, the underwriting of insurance for a consumer, determining a consumer's eligibility for a governmental benefit, and the valuation of a consumer's credit risk. The rule of *ejusdem generis* provides that when general words follow an enumeration of specific terms, the general words are construed to embrace only objects similar in nature to those objects enumerated by the preceding specific words. The definition of "consumer report" therefore includes those reports needed to assess a consumer's eligibility for a benefit, as well as other predictable needs — such as collecting money owed under an agreement and assessing a particular consumer's credit or insurance risk — that arise in the midst of a typical business transaction. In fact, in every one of these situations, the consumer report is obtained either to provide a benefit to a consumer or to collect a pre-existing debt.

Tellingly, the two permissible purposes stated in § 1681b(a)(3)(F) can also be read to effectuate these same ends. That is, § 1681b(a)(3)(F)(i) suggests the retention of a credit report for the purpose of furthering a business transaction initiated by a consumer and § 1681b(a)(3)(F)(ii) permits the use of a credit report to determine whether a consumer continues to be eligible for a benefit. It is a basic principle of statutory construction that a statute should be read and construed as a whole. Like the definition of "consumer report" and consistent with the other five specific permissible purposes, these two permissible purposes also suggest that Congress intended to allow access to a consumer report either when that access would benefit a consumer or would facilitate the collection of pre-existing debt.

To be precise, Smith Chevrolet's stated reason for accessing the credit report was not in connection with a standard business transaction that Plaintiff initiated. Instead, and quite significantly in this Court's view, Smith Chevrolet accessed the credit report to determine how much additional money it could collect, apart from what the two parties agreed upon in a standard business transaction. Almost certainly, it did not access Plaintiff's credit report for a reason beneficial to the consumer. Nor did it access the credit report to collect on a pre-existing debt. Rather, it accessed the report for its own business purposes and as part of a new event: the recovery of the duplicative discount. Although this is a fine distinction, it may be an important one. Smith Chevrolet's interpretation of the phrase "in connection with" is limitless. Under its reading, so long as any company had a reason to question any part of a transaction, it could access a consumer's credit report "in connection with a business transaction" that at some point was "initiated by the consumer." That is, five weeks, five months, or five years down the line, Smith Chevrolet could access Plaintiff's credit report if some dispute ever arose about the contracted price. In the Court's view, such an interpretation would give commercial entities an unlimited blank check to access and *reaccess* a consumer credit report long after the typical issues of eligibility, price, and financing were determined. Neither the specific language nor the overall scope of the FCRA can be said to support such an interpretation. . . .

Moreover, nearly every federal court addressing this issue has similarly held that the "legitimate business need" permissible purpose should be narrowly construed in the context of the other five enumerated purposes. . . .

The Court concludes, therefore, that when Smith Chevrolet accessed Plaintiff's credit report it was not, as a practical matter, part of the transaction which Plaintiff initiated. That transaction, in so far as Plaintiff's eligibility and debt was concerned, ended when the parties created a contract for the car's price and Plaintiff paid that price in full. Under any conceivable interpretation of the facts in this case, Smith Chevrolet cannot be said to have a "legitimate business need" for Plaintiff's credit report "in connection with a transaction initiated by the consumer." § 604(a)(3)(F)(i).

Smith Chevrolet also argues that its actions were protected both by §§ 1681b(3)(A) and 1681b(a)(1)(F)(ii) which provide that:

> Any consumer reporting agency may furnish a consumer report under the following circumstances and no other: . . .
>
> (A) to a person which it has reason to believe intends to use the information in connection with a credit transaction involving the consumer on whom the information is to be furnished and involving the extension of credit to, or review or collection of an account of the consumer; or . . .
>
> (F) otherwise has a legitimate business need for the information . . . (ii) to review an account to determine whether the consumer continues to meet the terms of the account.

Smith Chevrolet claims that it had a permissible purpose under both of these provisions because, due to its own error, Plaintiff received twice the discount he was entitled to and so a debt remained. Therefore, Smith Chevrolet says that it was reviewing whether Plaintiff owed any additional debt. And, because reviewing the size of the debt Plaintiff owed is synonymous with "collection of an account" and with determining "whether [Chris Smith] continue[d] to meet the terms of the account," Smith Chevrolet contends it therefore clearly had a permissible purpose.

The problem with this argument is that there was no outstanding debt and, consequently, there was no "account" to collect on. To be sure, Smith Chevrolet thought there *should be* an outstanding debt. Thinking there *should be* a debt, Smith Chevrolet contacted Plaintiff and ordered him to pay. At that point, Plaintiff refused to pay. Only then did Smith Chevrolet access Plaintiff's credit report.

Whether a debt or existing account exists simply cannot be a function of whether Smith Chevrolet alleges the existence of a debt. To do so would allow Smith Chevrolet infinite opportunities to access Plaintiff's credit report, so long as he could come up with a reason for thinking the account should continue in existence. As this Court has explained elsewhere, the FCRA intended to strike a balance between protecting the needs of commerce and the consumer's privacy interest. The Court finds that Smith Chevrolet must have a reasonable belief that the debt existed. Here, Smith Chevrolet's decision to investigate Plaintiff's credit report was not based on a reasonable belief that debt was owed; it was based on a belief that the original transaction was mistaken. Plaintiff had no reason to suspect that any new debt would arise after the initial transaction was completed. For all practical purposes that transaction was closed when the vehicle was delivered and Plaintiff made his payment. To find these permissible purposes applicable in this instance would extend the FCRA's language well beyond its intended purpose. . . .

Both sides have also moved for summary judgment on Plaintiff's claim of willful non-compliance. Section 1681n provides for civil liability in cases where the defendant willfully fails to comply with FCRA. In such a case, punitive damages may be awarded. 15 U.S.C. § 1681n(a)(2). This Court has recently explained the standard for liability under § 1681n, stating that, "[t]o show willful noncompliance with the FCRA, [the Plaintiff] must show that [defendant] knowingly and intentionally committed an act in conscious disregard for the rights of others, but need not show malice or evil motive."

Questions involving a party's state of mind are generally appropriately resolved by a jury rather than on summary judgment. From what the Court can ascertain at this point, the following facts are undisputed. Carol Hodges, a former Finance and Insurance Manager for Smith Chevrolet, has testified that the company did not have "written polices" regarding the acquisition of credit reports. She said that salespeople could freely access consumer credit reports. Hodges also said that the company had some unwritten rules for accessing customer credit reports, but these rules were not strictly followed. In fact, Smith Chevrolet's practices were "haphazard" and "very sloppy." Hodges had no part in the February 21, 2001, events and has no idea if Smith Chevrolet acted responsibly the day it accessed Plaintiff's credit report.

Based on these disputed facts, the Court cannot enter summary judgment on the issue of Smith Chevrolet's state of mind and will therefore deny the parties cross motions for summary judgment as they pertain to § 1681n.

Last, Smith Chevrolet has moved for summary judgment on Plaintiff's invasion of privacy claim. The Supreme Court of Kentucky adopted the principles for invasion of privacy as enunciated in the Restatement (Second) of Torts (1976) in *McCall v. Courier-Journal and Louisville Times Co.,* 623 S.W.2d 882, 887 (Ky. 1981). . . .

NOTES & QUESTIONS

1. *Legitimate Business Need.* In *Smith Chevrolet,* a critical element in the court's decision is its finding that the auto dealership must have a "reasonable belief" that the debt existed to access the credit report. But the decision to investigate the credit report was based, in fact, on a belief that the Plaintiff should owe the car dealer more than he did (due to the mistaken double discount). How does the court interpret the FCRA's statutory provision that allows businesses access to consumer credit reports when there is "a legitimate business need for the information"?

2. *Permissible Uses of Consumer Reports.* The FCRA contains a provision for civil liability for "obtaining a consumer report under false pretenses or knowingly without a permissible purpose." 15 U.S.C. § 1681n(a)(1)(B). But what, exactly, is a "consumer report"? A consumer report is defined based on the purposes for which it is used. These purposes include credit, insurance, and employment background checks, among others. 15 U.S.C. § 1681b.

In *Phillips v. Grendahl,* 312 F.3d 357 (8th Cir. 2002), Mary Grendahl became suspicious of her daughter Sarah's fiancée, Lavon Phillips. She believed he was lying about being an attorney as well as his ex-wives and girlfriends. Grendahl contacted Kevin Fitzgerald, a friend who worked for a detective agency. By searching computer databases, Fitzgerald obtained Phillips's Social Security number and previous addresses. He then submitted the data to Econ Control to obtain a report called a "Finder's Report." A Finder's Report includes a person's "address, aliases, birthdate, employer addresses, and the identity of firms with which the consumer had credit accounts and firms that had made inquiries about the consumer."

When Phillips discovered the investigation, he sued Grendahl, the detective agency Fitzgerald worked for, and Econ Control. The court concluded that the Finder's Report was a "consumer report" under FCRA. It also concluded that the defendants did not have a valid purpose under FCRA for obtaining the report:

> The only purpose for obtaining the report was to obtain information on Mary Grendahl's prospective son-in-law. Investigating a person because he wants to marry one's daughter is not a statutory consumer purpose under section 1681b(a). Even if getting married can be characterized as a consumer transaction under section 1681b(a)(3), it was not Mary Grendahl, but her daughter, whom Phillips was engaged to marry. He had no business transaction pending with Mary Grendahl. There was no permissible purpose for obtaining or using a consumer report.

3. ***Liability Under FCRA.*** FCRA creates liability for willfully or negligently failing to comply with its requirements. People can recover actual damages or statutory damages between $100 and $1,000 for willful violations, plus punitive damages and attorneys' fees and costs. § 1681n. People can recover actual damages and attorneys' fees and costs for negligent violations. § 1681n. Willful means that one intentionally commits an act "in conscious disregard for the rights of others." In *Safeco Insurance Co. v. Burr*, 551 U.S. 47 (2007), the Supreme Court held that acting in "reckless disregard" of a consumer's rights under FCRA was sufficient to establish willfulness.

Jeff Sovern notes that the FCRA's fault standard for liability — negligence — is inadequate to allow many victims to pursue relief because victims "are not normally aware of the procedures a credit bureau uses when issuing an erroneous credit report or what constitutes reasonable procedures." Because each individual consumer's losses will not be very high, consumers may not bring valid cases because of high litigation costs. Therefore, Sovern argues, credit reports should "be made strictly liable for attributing the transactions of identity thieves to innocent customers." Sovern also recommends liquidated damages for identity theft cases in order to reduce litigation costs.[6]

4. ***Furnishing Information to a Consumer Reporting Agency.*** In *Lema v. Citibank*, 935 F. Supp. 695 (D. Md. 1996), Citibank issued the plaintiff a credit card. When the plaintiff's account became delinquent, Citibank reported the information to consumer reporting agencies. The plaintiff sued Citibank under FCRA, claiming that the information it supplied to the consumer reporting agencies was inaccurate. The court dismissed the claim:

> The FCRA imposes civil liability only on consumer reporting agencies and users of consumer information. Thus, plaintiff must show that defendants are either of those entities in order to withstand defendants' summary judgment motion. . . .
> Plaintiff alleges only that defendants reported to third parties information regarding transactions between defendants and plaintiff. Defendants did not

---

[6] Jeff Sovern, *The Jewel of Their Souls: Preventing Identity Theft Through Loss Allocation Rules,* 64 U. Pitt. L. Rev. 343, 393, 406-07 (2003).

therefore furnish a consumer report regarding plaintiff, nor did they act as a consumer reporting agency with respect to him.

The court noted that the FCRA, § 1681h, provides qualified immunity for those that furnish allegedly false information to consumer reporting agencies. Plaintiffs can "bring a state law claim of defamation, invasion of privacy or negligence, provided such plaintiff alleges that defendants acted with malice or willful intent to injure plaintiff."

SARVER V. EXPERIAN INFORMATION SOLUTIONS

390 F.3d 969 (7th Cir. 2004)

EVANS, J. Lloyd Sarver appeals from an order granting summary judgment to Experian Information Solutions, Inc., a credit reporting company, on his claim under the Fair Credit Reporting Act (FCRA), 15 U.S.C. §§ 1681 *et seq.*

Experian reported inaccurate information on Sarver's credit report, which on August 2, 2002, caused the Monogram Bank of Georgia to deny him credit. Monogram cited the Experian credit report and particularly a reference to a bankruptcy which appeared on the report. Both before and after Monogram denied him credit, Sarver asked for a copy of his credit report. He received copies both times and both reports showed that accounts with Cross Country Bank were listed as having been "involved in bankruptcy." No other accounts had that notation, although other accounts had significant problems. A Bank One installment account had a balance past due 180 days, and another company, Providian, had written off $3,099 on a revolving account.

On August 29, 2002, Sarver wrote Experian informing it that the bankruptcy notation was inaccurate and asking that it be removed from his report. Sarver provided his full name and address but no other identifying information. On September 11, Experian sent Sarver a letter requesting further information, including his Social Security number, before it could begin an investigation. Sarver did not provide the information, but instead filed the present lawsuit, which resulted in summary judgment for Experian. It was later confirmed that the notation on the Cross Country Bank account was inaccurate and, as it turned out, another Lloyd Sarver was the culprit on that account.

In this appeal from the judgment dismissing his case, Sarver claims summary judgment was improper because issues of fact exist as to whether Experian violated FCRA, §§ 1681i and 1681e(b). . . .

Section 1681i requires a credit reporting agency to reinvestigate items on a credit report when a consumer disputes the validity of those items. An agency can terminate a reinvestigation if it determines the complaint is frivolous, "including by reason of a failure by a consumer to provide sufficient information to investigate the disputed information." § 1681i(a)(3). We do not need to decide whether Sarver's failure to provide the information Experian requested rendered his complaint frivolous; his claim under § 1681i(a) fails for another reason, a lack of evidence of damages. In order to prevail on his claims, Sarver must show that he suffered damages as a result of the inaccurate information. As we have said in *Crabill v. Trans Union, L.L.C.,* 259 F.3d 662, 664 (7th Cir. 2001):

Without a causal relation between the violation of the statute and the loss of credit, or some other harm, a plaintiff cannot obtain an award of "actual damages."

On this point, the district court concluded that there were no damages. Our review of the record leads us to agree.

Sarver, however, disagrees and claims that he suffered damages when he was denied credit from Monogram Bank of Georgia on August 2, 2002. This letter cannot be a basis for his damage claim, however, because as of August 2, Experian had no notice of any inaccuracies in the report. Even though Sarver asked for a copy of his report on July 18, he did not notify Experian of a problem until a month and a half later. Experian must be notified of an error before it is required to reinvestigate. As we have made clear, the FCRA is not a strict liability statute. *Henson v. CSC Credit Servs.*, 29 F.3d 280 (7th Cir. 1994).

Sarver also does not show that he suffered pecuniary damages between August 29 (when he notified Experian of the error) and February 20, 2003 (when the Cross Country account was removed from his file). He does not claim that he applied for credit during that time period or that a third party looked at his report. In addition, his claim for emotional distress fails. We have maintained a strict standard for a finding of emotional damage "because they are so easy to manufacture." *Aiello v. Providian Fin. Corp.*, 239 F.3d 876, 880 (7th Cir. 2001). We have required that when "the injured party's own testimony is the only proof of emotional damages, he must explain the circumstances of his injury in reasonable detail; he cannot rely on mere conclusory statements." *Denius v. Dunlap*, 330 F.3d 919, 929 (7th Cir. 2003). Finally, to obtain statutory damages under FCRA § 1681n(a), Sarver must show that Experian willfully violated the Act. There is similarly no evidence of willfulness. Summary judgment was properly granted on this claim.

We turn to Sarver's claim under § 1681e(b), which requires that a credit reporting agency follow "reasonable procedures to assure maximum possible accuracy" when it prepares a credit report. The reasonableness of a reporting agency's procedures is normally a question for trial unless the reasonableness or unreasonableness of the procedures is beyond question. *Crabill*, 259 F.3d at 663. However, to state a claim under the statute,

> a consumer must sufficiently allege "that a credit reporting agency prepared a report containing 'inaccurate' information." However, the credit reporting agency is not automatically liable even if the consumer proves that it prepared an inaccurate credit report because the FCRA "does not make reporting agencies strictly liable for all inaccuracies." A credit reporting agency is not liable under the FCRA if it followed "reasonable procedures to assure maximum possible accuracy," but nonetheless reported inaccurate information in the consumer's credit report.

Henson, 29 F.3d at 284. The Commentary of the Federal Trade Commission to the FCRA, 16 C.F.R. pt. 600, app., section 607 at 3.A, states that the section does not hold a reporting agency responsible where an item of information, received from a source that it reasonably believes is reputable, turns out to be inaccurate unless the agency receives notice of systemic problems with its procedures.

Experian has provided an account of its procedures. The affidavit of David Browne, Experian's compliance manager, explains that the company gathers credit information originated by approximately 40,000 sources. The information is stored in a complex system of national databases, containing approximately 200 million names and addresses and some 2.6 billion trade lines, which include information about consumer accounts, judgments, etc. The company processes over 50 million updates to trade information each day. Lenders report millions of accounts to Experian daily; they provide identifying information, including address, social security number, and date of birth. The identifying information is used to link the credit items to the appropriate consumer. Mr. Browne also notes that Experian's computer system does not store complete credit reports, but rather stores the individual items of credit information linked to identifying information. The credit report is generated at the time an inquiry for it is received.

One can easily see how, even with safeguards in place, mistakes can happen. But given the complexity of the system and the volume of information involved, a mistake does not render the procedures unreasonable. In his attempt to show that Experian's procedures are unreasonable, Sarver argues that someone should have noticed that only the Cross Country accounts were shown to have been involved in bankruptcy. That anomaly should have alerted Experian, Sarver says, to the fact that the report was inaccurate. What Sarver is asking, then, is that each computer-generated report be examined for anomalous information and, if it is found, an investigation be launched. In the absence of notice of prevalent unreliable information from a reporting lender, which would put Experian on notice that problems exist, we cannot find that such a requirement to investigate would be reasonable given the enormous volume of information Experian processes daily.

We found in *Henson* that a consumer reporting agency was not liable, as a matter of law, for reporting information from a judgment docket unless there was prior notice from the consumer that the information might be inaccurate. We said that a

> contrary rule of law would require credit reporting agencies to go beyond the face of numerous court records to determine whether they correctly report the outcome of the underlying action. Such a rule would also require credit reporting agencies to engage in background research which would substantially increase the cost of their services. In turn, they would be forced to pass on the increased costs to their customers and ultimately to the individual consumer.

Henson, 29 F.3d at 285. The same could be said for records from financial institutions. As we said, in his affidavit Mr. Browne proclaims, and there is nothing in the record to make us doubt his statement, that lenders report many millions of accounts to Experian daily. Sarver's report, dated August 26, 2002, contains entries from six different lenders. The increased cost to Experian to examine each of these entries individually would be enormous. We find that as a matter of law there is nothing in this record to show that Experian's procedures are unreasonable.

NOTES & QUESTIONS

1. *A Critical Perspective on* **Sarver.** Consider Elizabeth De Armond:

> In justifying the agency's failure to resolve the anomalies within the records attributed to the plaintiff, the court emphasized the 200 million names and addresses, the 2.6 billion trade lines, and the complexity of the system. This reasoning overlooks that the very complexity of the system reveals the ability of the agency to control the high volume of individuals and records, and that ability should alert the agency to the high risk of misattributing information. The court ruled that the agency's failure to investigate the inconsistency was not unreasonable because the agency had no notice that the specific lender who had provided information about the impaired accounts was unreliable. However, the question, in order to protect individuals from reckless attribution, should not be whether any single provider is unreliable. The question should have been whether reporting it as the plaintiff's without checking it, given the obvious inconsistency, was reckless. Where the agency was aware of the risk of misattribution from fuzzy matching, and that matching produced a record that was unlike the others, a jury should decide whether the failure to take any steps to verify the anomalous data breached the FCRA's accuracy standard.
>
> The *Sarver* court also reasoned that to require an agency to further investigate the accuracy of a consumer's records when an anomaly appeared would impose "enormous" increased costs. However, the court did not refer to any estimate of the costs or explain why an already complex system capable of making many comparisons among different records could not inexpensively adjust to cross-checking data when reliability was at issue. Furthermore, when an anomaly appears that would work to the consumer's detriment, an agency could simply decline to attribute the negative data should it not want to take the extra effort of verifying it. The decision allows the agency all of the benefits of its database technology with none of the responsibilities.[7]

This criticism raises a baseline issue: who should bear the costs of relative degrees of inaccuracy and accuracy in the credit system? If credit agency's need investigate more kinds of inconsistencies in credit reports, will consumers as a group bear the additional costs?

2. *Is FCRA Too Deferential to Industry Interests?* Consider De Armond on the flaws of FCRA:

> [FCRA] inadequately protects individuals from the consequential and emotional damages caused by misattributed acts for several reasons. . . .
>
> The Act's most significant flaw is that it imposes meaningful accuracy requirements only after a false and negative item has been reported, has already been put into the data sea. However, given that digitized data is far more available, accessible, duplicable, and transmittable than old paper records, once a false record has been put into the data sea, it is very hard to ever completely cull it out. . . .
>
> The Act is designed to impose meaningful accuracy standards only after inaccurate information has already been provided by a data provider and reported by a data aggregator. The Act permits the original data provider,

---

[7] Elizabeth D. De Armond, *Frothy Chaos: Modern Data Warehousing and Old-Fashioned Defamation*, 41 Val. U. L. Rev. 1061, 1099-1102, 1108 (2007).

called a furnisher under the Act, to furnish nearly any item in a consumer's name without first verifying that it belongs to that consumer. But the Act only prohibits the furnisher from furnishing information that the furnisher either "knows or has reasonable cause to believe" to be inaccurate. A furnisher only has "'reasonable cause to believe that an item of information is inaccurate'" if the furnisher has "specific knowledge, other than solely allegations by the consumer, that would cause a reasonable person to have substantial doubts about the accuracy of the information." . . .

Thus, the agency acquires information that likely has not been subjected to any scrutiny, let alone verified. The agency acquires the information, either electronically or via magnetic tape from the provider, and stores it electronically, where it sits until needed for a report. Just as the Act imposes a relatively weak accuracy requirement on data providers at the point of initial provision, the Act places only loose limits on aggregators that then report the information. When a subscriber requests a report on a particular consumer, the aggregator, the consumer reporting agency, must only follow "reasonable procedures to assure maximum possible accuracy" of the information that it returns to the subscriber. The provision does not in fact require agencies to ensure the maximum possible accuracy of every item of information, or to do much if anything to match, verify, or cross-check the information. . . .

It is only after an individual has learned that an agency has falsely charged him or her with negative data that the individual can require an aggregator to examine the data. . . .

As *Sarver* also points out, the Experian computer system does not store computer credit reports, but only generates them when an inquiry is received. Individual items of credit information are stored linked to identifying information, which allows their retrieval and compilation into a credit report. Should individual items of information be reviewed for accuracy at the initial time that the credit agency collects them?

3. ***What Constitutes Negligence in Investigating Errors in Consumer Reports?*** In *Dennis v. BEH-1, LLC*, 504 F.3d 892 (9th Cir. 2007), Jason Dennis was sued by his landlord, but the parties agreed to drop the lawsuit after reaching a settlement. The parties filed a "Request for Dismissal" with the court clerk, and the court register properly registered the dismissal. Later on, Experian Information Solutions, Inc. stated on Dennis's credit report that a civil claim judgment had been entered against him for $1,959. Dennis contacted Experian to complain about the error. Experian had Hogan Information Services, a third party contractor, verify Dennis's claims. Hogan replied that Experian's information was correct and sent along a copy of the stipulation of settlement between Dennis and his landlord. Experian told Dennis that it would not correct his report. Dennis sued under FCRA, contending that Experian failed to maintain "reasonable procedures" under § 1681e(b) to ensure the accuracy of credit reports and that it failed to adequately reinvestigate the disputed information under § 1681i. The district court dismissed Dennis's case on summary judgment. The court of appeals, however, concluded:

> The district court erred insofar as it held that Dennis couldn't make the prima facie showing of inaccurate reporting required by sections 1681e and 1681i. Experian's credit report on Dennis *is* inaccurate. Because the case against

Dennis was dismissed, there could have been no "Civil claim judgment" against him: "A dismissal without prejudice . . . has the effect of a final judgment *in favor* of the defendant." Dennis has made the prima facie showing of inaccuracy required by sections 1681e and 1681i.

The district court also seems to have awarded summary judgment to Experian because Dennis didn't offer evidence of "actual damages" as required by section 1681*o*(a)(1). Here, too, the district court erred. Dennis testified that he hoped to start a business and that he diligently paid his bills on time for years so that he would have a clean credit history when he sought financing for the venture. The only blemish on his credit report in April 2003 was the erroneously reported judgment. According to Dennis, that was enough to cause several lenders to decline his applications for credit, dashing his hopes of starting a new business. Dennis also claims that Experian's error caused his next landlord to demand that Dennis pay a greater security deposit. In addition to those tangible harms, Dennis claims that Experian's inaccurate report caused him emotional distress, which we've held to be "actual damages."

The court of appeals reasoned that Hogan failed to understand the meaning of the Request for Dismissal document and that Experian could readily have detected this mistake:

Experian could have caught Hogan's error if it had consulted the Civil Register in Dennis's case, which can be viewed free of charge on the Los Angeles Superior Court's excellent website. As described above, the Register clearly indicates that the case against Dennis was dismissed. Experian apparently never looked at the Register.

Experian also could have detected Hogan's mistake by examining the document Hogan retrieved from Dennis's court file. Hogan mistakenly believed that this document proved that judgment had been entered against Dennis; in fact, the document confirms Dennis's account of what happened. The document is a written stipulation between Dennis and his landlord that no judgment would be entered against Dennis so long as Dennis complied with the payment schedule. The parties couldn't have been clearer on this point: "If paid, case dismissed. If not paid, judgment to enter upon [landlord's] declaration of non-payment. . . ."

The court of appeals further concluded that it had no need to remand the case for a jury trial regarding Experian's negligence:

Even accepting as true everything Experian has claimed, no rational jury could find that the company wasn't negligent. The stipulation Hogan retrieved from Dennis's court file may be unusual, but it's also unambiguous, and Experian was negligent in mis-interpreting it as an entry of judgment. Experian is also responsible for the negligence of Hogan, the investigation service it hired to review Dennis's court file. . . .

When conducting a reinvestigation pursuant to 15 U.S.C. § 1681i, a credit reporting agency must exercise reasonable diligence in examining the court file to determine whether an adverse judgment has, in fact, been entered against the consumer. A reinvestigation that overlooks documents in the court file expressly stating that *no* adverse judgment was entered falls far short of this standard. On our own motion, therefore, we grant summary judgment to Dennis on his claim that Experian negligently failed to conduct a reasonable reinvestigation in violation of section 1681i. Whether Experian's failure was also willful, in violation of section 1681n, is a question for the jury on remand.

This case illustrates how important it is for Experian, a company that traffics in the reputations of ordinary people, to train its employees to understand the legal significance of the documents they rely on. Because Experian negligently failed to conduct a reasonable reinvestigation, we grant summary judgment to Dennis on this claim. We remand only so that the district court may calculate damages and award attorney's fees. As to all other claims under the Fair Credit Reporting Act, we reverse summary judgment for Experian and remand for trial. Dennis is also entitled to attorney's fees for an entirely successful appeal. 15 U.S.C. § 1681*o*(a)(2). . . .

4. ***Defamation, Privacy, and FCRA's Qualified Immunity.*** Can the credit reporting agencies be sued under state tort law for defamation or for invasion of privacy? Regarding defamation, recall that the Supreme Court held in *Dun & Bradstreet, Inc. v. Greenmoss Builders, Inc.,* 472 U.S. 749 (1985), that a credit reporting agency reporting on an individual is engaging in "speech on matters of purely private concern" and, consequently, receives less First Amendment protection than other forms of speech. Therefore, for such cases of defamation, the First Amendment limits established by *New York Times v. Sullivan,* 376 U.S. 254 (1964), and *Gertz v. Robert Welch, Inc.,* 418 U.S. 323 (1974), do not apply. All forms of damages (compensatory, presumed, and punitive) are available without showing "actual malice."

However, FCRA provides qualified immunity to credit reporting agencies and to the furnishers of information to credit reporting agencies:

> Except as provided in sections 1681n and 1681o of this title, no consumer may bring any action or proceeding in the nature of defamation, invasion of privacy, or negligence with respect to the reporting of information against any consumer reporting agency, or any user of information, or any person who furnishes information to a consumer reporting agency, based on information disclosed pursuant to section 1681g, 1681h, or 1681m of this title, or based on information disclosed by a user of a consumer report to or for a consumer against whom the user has taken adverse action, based in whole or in part on the report except as to false information furnished with malice or wilful intent to injure such consumer. § 1681h(e).

Therefore, although the Constitution doesn't require actual malice to establish defamation for the false reporting of credit information, the FCRA does. Actual malice exists if one states false information with knowledge of its falsity or in reckless disregard for the truth.

Establishing malice can be difficult. Consider *Morris v. Equifax Information Services, L.L.C.,* 457 F.3d 460 (5th Cir. 2006):

> While Morris has presented evidence that Equifax knew that Morris claimed that there were false statements in the information that Equifax was publishing about Morris, this evidence does not show that Equifax knew these statements were false. Morris also argues that Equifax had a reckless disregard for whether the statements were false because "Equifax continued to publish the same false information about Morris without lifting a finger to determine whether the information was false or not." To show "reckless disregard,"

however, Morris must present "sufficient evidence to permit the conclusion that the defendant *in fact entertained serious doubts* as to the truth of his publication." *St. Amant v. Thompson*, 390 U.S. 727 (1968) (emphasis added). In this case, there is no such evidence.

How does a person establish that a credit reporting agency "entertained serious doubts" about the truth of its report? The difficulty is that the reporting is an automated process involving hundreds of millions of people. If a person calls to point out an error, should that be sufficient to show that the credit reporting agency had knowledge? Or does it make it too easy for any person to establish reckless disregard, as it would be established anytime a person merely made an allegation of falsity?

Elizabeth De Armond recommends that notwithstanding the requirement of proving actual malice, defamation and false light can serve as a good way to protect victims of credit reporting mistakes. She argues that credit reporting agencies offer special services to protect people from identity theft if people pay for it, but the existence of these services demonstrates that credit reporting agencies "have the analytical capacity to discern unusual activity in a particular consumer's name, at least if the consumer is willing to pay for it." De Armond contends that "data providers and data aggregators should be well aware that data may not belong to whom it appears. Failing to acknowledge that risk, by verifying identities of doers of the deeds they report, surpasses the standard of recklessness." Specifically, with regard to the *Sarver* case, she argues: "In *Sarver,* where the aggregator, a consumer reporting agency, attributed accounts that indicated the borrower's bankruptcy to the wrong individual, the agency acted recklessly . . . when it repeated the misattribution, even after the plaintiff had notified the agency of its error."[8]

2. THE USE AND DISCLOSURE OF FINANCIAL INFORMATION

(a) The Breach of Confidentiality Tort and Financial Institutions

Recall the breach of confidentiality tort from Chapter 4. Under the common law, a doctor can be liable to a patient if she discloses the patient's personal information. A number of jurisdictions extend the tort of breach of confidentiality to disclosures by banks and financial institutions of their customers' financial information. In *Peterson v. Idaho First Nat'l Bank*, 367 P.2d 284 (Idaho 1961), the court held that a bank could be sued for breach of confidentiality for disclosing customer information:

It is generally stated that the relation between a bank and its general depositor is that of debtor and creditor. . . . But it is also said that in discharging its obligation to a depositor a bank must do so subject to the rules of agency. . . .

All agree that a bank should protect its business records from the prying eyes of the public, moved by curiosity or malice. No one questions its right to protect

---

[8] De Armond, *supra,* at 1139, 1132, 1130.

its fiduciary relationship with its customers, which, in sound banking practice, as a matter of common knowledge, is done everywhere. . . .

To give such information to third persons or to the public at the instance of the customer or depositor is certainly not beyond the scope of banking powers. It is a different matter, however, when such information is sought from the bank without the consent of the depositor or customer of the bank. Indeed, it is an implied term of the contract between the banker and his customer that the banker will not divulge to third persons, without the consent of the customer, express or implied, either the state of the customer's account or any of his transactions with the bank, or any information relating to the customer acquired through the keeping of his account. . . .

It is inconceivable that a bank would at any time consider itself at liberty to disclose the intimate details of its depositors' accounts. Inviolate secrecy is one of the inherent and fundamental precepts of the relationship of the bank and its customers or depositors.

Several other jurisdictions have held likewise. *See, e.g., Barnett Bank of West Florida v. Hooper*, 498 So. 2d 923 (Fla. 1986); *Indiana Nat'l Bank v. Chapman*, 482 N.E.2d 474 (Ind. App. 1985); *Suburban Trust Co. v. Waller*, 408 A.2d 758 (Md. App. 1979); *Richfield Bank & Trust Co. v. Sjogren*, 244 N.W.2d 648 (Minn. 1976); *McGuire v. Shubert,* 722 A.2d 1087 (Pa. Super. 1998).

(b) The Gramm-Leach-Bliley Act

In 1999, Congress passed the Financial Services Modernization Act, more commonly known as the Gramm-Leach-Bliley (GLB) Act, Pub. L. No. 106-102, codified at 15 U.S.C. §§ 6801–6809. The GLB Act was designed to restructure financial services industries, which had long been regulated under the Glass-Steagall Act of 1933. The Glass-Steagall Act, passed in response to the Great Depression, prevented different types of financial institutions (e.g., banks, brokerage houses, insurers) from affiliating with each other. The GLB Act enables the creation of financial conglomerates that provide a host of different forms of financial services.

The law authorizes widespread sharing of personal information by financial institutions such as banks, insurers, and investment companies. The law permits sharing of personal information between companies that are joined together or affiliated with each other as well as sharing of information between unaffiliated companies. To protect privacy, the Act requires a variety of agencies (FTC, Comptroller of Currency, SEC, and a number of others) to establish "appropriate standards for the financial institutions subject to their jurisdiction" to "insure security and confidentiality of customer records and information" and "protect against unauthorized access" to the records. 15 U.S.C. § 6801.

Nonpublic Personal Information. The privacy provisions of the GLB Act only apply to "nonpublic personal information" that consists of "personally identifiable financial information." § 6809(4). Thus, the law only protects *financial* information that is *not public.*

Sharing of Information with Affiliated Companies. The GLB Act permits financial institutions that are joined together to share the "nonpublic personal information" that each affiliate possesses. For example, suppose an affiliate has access to a person's medical information. This information could be shared with an affiliate bank that could then turn down a person for a loan. Affiliates must tell customers that they are sharing such information. § 6802(a). The disclosure can be in the form of a general disclosure in a privacy policy. § 6803(a). There is no way for individuals to block this sharing of information.

Sharing of Information with Nonaffiliated Companies. Financial institutions can share personal information with nonaffiliated companies only if they first provide individuals with the ability to opt out of the disclosure. § 6802(b). However, people cannot opt out if the financial institution provides personal data to nonaffiliated third parties "to perform services for or functions on behalf of the financial institution, including marketing of the financial institution's own products and services, or financial products or services offered pursuant to joint agreements between two or more financial institutions." § 6802(b)(2). The financial institution must disclose the information sharing and must have a contract with the third party requiring the third party to maintain the confidentiality of the information. § 6802(b)(2). Third parties receiving personal data from a financial institution cannot reuse that information. § 6802(c). These provisions do not apply to disclosures to credit reporting agencies.

Limits on Disclosure. Financial institutions cannot disclose (other than to credit reporting agencies) account numbers or credit card numbers for use in direct marketing (telemarketing, e-mail, or mail). § 6802(d).

Privacy Notices. The GLB Act requires that financial institutions inform customers of their privacy policies. In particular, customers must be informed about policies concerning the disclosure of personal information to affiliates and other companies and categories of information that are disclosed and the security of personal data. § 6803(a).

Security. The GLB Act requires the FTC and other agencies to establish security standards for nonpublic personal information. *See* 15 U.S.C. §§ 6801(b), 6805(b)(2). The FTC issued its final regulations on May 23, 2002. According to the regulations, financial institutions "shall develop, implement, and maintain a comprehensive information security program" that is appropriate to the "size and complexity" of the institution, the "nature and scope" of the institution's activities, and the "sensitivity of any customer information at issue." 16 C.F.R. § 314.3(a). An "information security program" is defined as "the administrative, technical, or physical safeguards [an institution uses] to access, collect, distribute, process, store, use, transmit, dispose of, or otherwise handle customer information." § 314.2(b).

Preemption. The GLB Act does not preempt state laws that provide greater protection to privacy. § 6807(b). As will be discussed below, Vermont has made use of this provision and requires opt in, or affirmative consumer consent, before a financial institution can share nonpublic personal financial information pertaining to a consumer to a nonaffiliated third party.

Critics and Supporters. Consider the following critique by Ted Janger and Paul Schwartz:

> The GLB Act has managed to disappoint both industry leaders and privacy advocates alike. Why are so many observers frustrated with the GLB Act? We have already noted the complaint of financial services companies regarding the expense of privacy notices. These organizations also argue that there have been scant pay-off from the costly mailings — and strong evidence backs up this claim. For example, a survey from the American Banker's Association found that 22% of banking customers said that they received a privacy notice but did not read it, and 41% could not even recall receiving a notice. The survey also found only 0.5% of banking customers had exercised their opt-out rights. . . .
>
> Not only are privacy notices difficult to understand, but they are written in a fashion that makes it hard to exercise the opt-out rights that GLB Act mandates. For example, opt-out provisions are sometimes buried in privacy notices. As the Public Citizen Litigation Group has found, "Explanations of how to opt-out invariably appear at the end of the notices. Thus, before they learn how to opt-out, consumers must trudge through up to ten pages of fine print. . . ." Public Citizen also identified many passages regarding opt-out that "are obviously designed to discourage consumers from exercising their rights under the statute." For example, some financial institutions include an opt-out box only "in a thicket of misleading statements.". . . A final tactic of GLB Act privacy notices is to state that consumers who opt-out may fail to receive "valuable offers." . . .
>
> The GLB Act merely contains an opt-out requirement; as a result, information can be disclosed to non-affiliated entities unless individuals take affirmative action, namely, informing the financial entity that they refuse this sharing of their personal data. By setting its default as an opt-out, the GLB Act fails to create any penalty on the party with superior knowledge, the financial entity, should negotiations fail to occur. In other words, the GLB leaves the burden of bargaining on the less informed party, the individual consumer. These doubts about the efficacy of opt-out are supported, at least indirectly, by the evidence concerning sometimes confusing, sometimes misleading privacy notices. . . . An opt-out default creates incentives for privacy notices that lead to *inaction* by the consumer.[9]

Marcy Peek argues that the GLB Act has actually done more to facilitate information sharing than to protect privacy. Enabling greater information uses so long as customers have a right to opt out has resulted in much more information sharing since "the opt-out right is meaningless in practice; the right to opt out of the trafficking of one's personal information is explained in lengthy, legalistic privacy policies that most people throw away as just more junk mail." More

---

[9] Ted Janger & Paul M. Schwartz, *The Gramm-Leach-Bliley Act, Information Privacy, and the Limits of Default Rules*, 86 Minn. L. Rev. 1219, 1230-32, 1241 (2002).

broadly, Peek argues, several laws purporting to protect privacy often "represent a façade of protection for consumers, keeping them complacent in the purported knowledge that someone is protecting their privacy interests." In the end, Peek argues, "corporate power drives information privacy law."[10]

In contrast, Peter Swire argues that the GLB Act "works surprisingly well as privacy legislation":

> Recognizing the criticisms to date, and the limits of the available evidence, I would like to make the case for a decidedly more optimistic view of the effect of the GLB notices. Even in their current flawed form and even if not a single consumer exercised the opt-out right, I contend that a principal effect of the notices has been to require financial institutions to inspect their own practices. In this respect, the detail and complexity of the GLB notices is actually a virtue. In order to draft the notice, many financial institutions undertook an extensive process, often for the first time, to learn just how data is and is not shared between different parts of the organization and with third parties. Based on my extensive discussions with people in the industry, I believe that many institutions discovered practices that they decided, upon deliberation, to change. One public example of this was the decision of Bank of America no longer to share its customers' data with third parties, even subject to opt-out. The detailed and complex notice, in short, created a more detailed roadmap for privacy compliance.[11]

The critics of the GLB Act and Swire appear to be looking at the statute from two different perspectives. The critics are looking at it from a consumer-centric view; Swire sees the positive effect that the statute has on practices within institutions. Is there a way for a statute to have a positive impact in both areas?

(c) State Financial Regulation

The Vermont Opt-in Approach. In contrast to the GLB approach, Vermont permits sharing of personal data by financial institutions with nonaffiliated companies only if companies obtain an individual's consent. This requirement of a positive response before information can be shared is termed an "opt in." State of Vermont, Department, Insurance, Securities & Health Care Administration, Banking Division, Regulation B-2001-01, Privacy of Consumer Financial and Health Information Regulation. This regulation also carefully defines the acceptable form of and process for opt-in notice. For example, when consumers want to revoke their opting in to information sharing, financial institutions cannot force "the consumer to write his or her own letter." Financial institutions also cannot make consumers "use a check-off box that was provided with the initial notice but [that] is not included with subsequent notices."

---

[10] Marcy E. Peek, Information *Privacy and Corporate Power: Towards a Re-Imagination of Information Privacy Law*, 37 Seton Hall L. Rev. 127, 147-49, 137 (2006).

[11] Peter P. Swire, *The Surprising Virtues of the New Financial Privacy Law*, 86 Minn. L. Rev. 1263, 1315-16 (2002).

California's SB1. California's Financial Information Privacy Act, known as "SB1," Cal. Fin. Code §§ 4050–4060, was enacted "to afford persons greater privacy protections that those provided in . . . the federal Gramm-Leach-Bliley Act." § 4051. Specifically, the California legislature found that the Gramm-Leach-Bliley Act "increases the likelihood that the personal financial information of California residents will be widely shared among, between, and within companies" and that "the policies intended to protect financial privacy imposed by the Gramm-Leach-Bliley Act are inadequate to meet the privacy concerns of California residents." § 4051.5.

In contrast to the Gramm-Leach-Bliley Act, which provides people with an opt-out right, SB1, like the Vermont regulation, requires opt in:

> [A] financial institution shall not sell, share, transfer, or otherwise disclose nonpublic personal information to or with any nonaffiliated third parties without the explicit prior consent of the consumer to whom the nonpublic personal information relates. § 4052.5.

SB1 permits financial institutions to offer incentives or discounts for people to opt in. § 4053.

Financial institutions challenged SB1, arguing that it was preempted by the FCRA. In *American Bankers Association v. Gould*, 412 F.3d 1081 (9th Cir. 2005), the court concluded that "SB1 is preempted [by FCRA] to the extent that it applies to information shared between affiliates concerning consumers' 'credit worthiness, credit standing, credit capacity, character, general reputation, personal characteristics, or mode of living' that is used, expected to be used, or collected for the purpose of establishing eligibility for 'credit or insurance,' employment, or other authorized purpose." The court remanded for the district court to determine which portions of SB1 survived preemption.

On remand, *American Bankers Association v. Lockyer*, 2005 WL 2452798 (E.D. Cal. 2005) (not reported in F. Supp. 2d), the court held that "no portion of SB1's affiliate sharing provision survives" preemption. Among the difficulties for the court was that, as plaintiffs argued before it, "it would be virtually impossible to ascertain in advance whether or not information collected and shared by a financial institution would satisfy a FCRA authorized purpose." The district court explained:

> A financial institution may gather and share information with its affiliates believing in good faith that it is not required to comply with SB1 because the information will be used for an FCRA authorized purpose. If, in fact, the information is not so used, the financial institution would have acted in violation of SB1 exposing it to the penalties thereunder. This creates the untenable situation of forcing California financial institutions to either risk violation of SB1 or comply therewith whether or not the information is for an FCRA authorized purpose.

The North Dakota Opt-in Referendum and Other States. In June 2002, North Dakotans overwhelmingly rejected, by a 73 percent vote, a 2001 state law that had established an opt-out rather than opt-in standard for financial institutions in North Dakota. The Privacy Rights Clearinghouse noted: "The referendum in North Dakota was the first time this issue has been taken directly to voters."[12] New Mexico has also provided an opt-in requirement for financial institutions before sharing of personal consumer data is permitted with nonaffiliated companies.

3. IDENTITY THEFT

Identity theft is one of the most rapidly growing forms of crime. Identity theft occurs when a criminal obtains an individual's personal information and uses it to open new bank accounts, acquire credit cards, and obtain loans in that individual's name. Consider the following example from journalist Bob Sullivan:

> Starting in August 1998, Anthony Lemar Taylor spent a year successfully pretending to be the golf superstar [Tiger Woods]. Taylor's $50,000 spending spree included a big-screen television, stereo speakers, a living room set, even a U-Haul to move all the stolen goods. Taylor, who looks nothing like the golf legend, simply obtained a driver's license using Tiger's real name, Eldrick Woods; then, he used Wood's Social Security number to get credit in his name. . . .
>
> When Tiger himself testified during the case in 2001, Taylor, a 30-year-old career criminal, didn't stand a chance. Wood's star power helped the state throw the book at Taylor. . . . The firm, swift justice might have made other potential identity thieves think twice, but for this: Precious few identity thefts are even investigated, let alone prosecuted to the full extent of the law. The average victim has enough trouble getting the police to bother filling out an incident report. . . .
>
> The real world of identity theft . . . is . . . a haunting, paperwork nightmare, one often compared to financial rape, littered with small and large tragedies. . . . Couples can't buy homes because their credit is damaged. Identity theft victims are often denied access to the lowest interest rates and can pay as much as 50 percent more to borrow money. . . . And thousands of people face hundreds of hours of electronic trials against their erroneous credit reports and eventually end with fraudulent debts and endless nightly threatening calls from collection agencies.[13]

According to a 2007 report to the FTC, "approximately 8.3 million U.S. adults discovered that they were victims of some form of ID theft in 2005."[14] According to this report's estimates, the total losses from ID theft in that year were $15.6 billion. Moreover, "victims of all types of ID theft spent hours of their time resolving the various problems that result from ID theft. The median value for the number of hours spent resolving problems by all victims was four. However, 10 percent of all victims spent at least 55 hours resolving their problems."

In an important caveat, however, this report also notes that it may not capture all types of identity theft. In particular, it does not measure "synthetic ID theft." This activity involves a criminal creating a fictitious identity by combining information from one or more consumers. Affected consumers face considerable

---

[12] Privacy Rights Clearinghouse, *North Dakota Votes for "Opt-In" Financial Privacy*, June 21, 2002, at www.privacyrights.org/ar/nd_optin.htm.

[13] Bob Sullivan, *Your Evil Twin: Behind the Identity Theft Epidemic* 35-36 (2004).

[14] Synovate, Federal Trade Commission — 2006 Identity Theft Survey Report (Nov. 2007).

obstacles in detecting synthetic ID theft; therefore, any survey of identity theft, which depends on consumer self-reporting, is likely to underreport it.

Chris Hoofnagle proposes that policy responses to identity theft are hobbled by a lack of information about the dimensions of the problem.[15] He argues: "We are asking the wrong people about the crime. . . . Victims often do not know how their personal data were stolen or who stole the information." Hoofnagle's solution is to create a reporting requirement on financial institutions, including all lenders and organizations that control access to accounts (such as PayPal and Western Union). There would be three disclosure requirements for these entities: "(1) the number of identity theft incidents suffered or avoided; (2) the forms of identity theft attempted and the financial products targeted (e.g., mortgage loan or credit card); and (3) the amount of loss suffered or avoided."

Hoofnagle's larger hope is that if statistics were available by individual institution on identity theft, financial institutions would have a "new product differentiator, similar to low interest rates and fee-free access accounts." In other words, consumers would be able to choose to have a financial relationship with one organization rather than another based on its track record in providing safe financial products. Do you think that consumers would respond to such market information and actually switch accounts from one organization to another? Personal information might be stolen from nonfinancial institutions, such as a college, and then used by a criminal for fraud at a bank. How can incentives be provided for nonfinancial institutions to have adequate security?

(a) Identity Theft Statutes

The Identity Theft Assumption and Deterrence Act. Congress responded to the growth of identity theft by passing the Identity Theft and Assumption Deterrence Act in 1998. The Act makes it a federal crime to "knowingly transfer or use, without lawful authority, a means of identification of another person with the intent to commit, or to aid or abet, any unlawful activity that constitutes a violation of Federal law, or that constitutes a felony under any applicable State or local law." 18 U.S.C. § 1028.

The Fair Credit Reporting Act. The Fair Credit Reporting Act (FCRA), as amended by the Fair and Accurate Credit Transactions Act (FACTA), has provisions that address identity theft. We discuss these provisions below.

State Legislative Responses. The vast majority of states now have statutes concerning identity theft. Before 1998, only three states had enacted statutes dealing explicitly with identity theft.[16] Arizona was one of these states; it punishes identity thefts as low-grade felony, but its statute does not address victims' rights and remedies. Ariz. Rev. Stat. Ann. § 13-2008(D). The passage of

---

[15] Chris Jay Hoofnagle, *Identity Theft: Making the Known Unknowns Known*, 21 Harv. J. L. & Tech. 97 (2007).

[16] U.S. General Accountability Office, *Report to the Honorable Sam Johnson House of Representatives, Identity Theft: Greater Awareness and Use of Existing Data Are Needed* 7 (June 2002).

the federal Identity Theft Assumption and Deterrence Act in 1998 sparked most states to pass their own identity theft legislation — more than 40 states now have identity theft statutes on the books.[17]

Many identity theft statutes focus on defining criminal penalties for the crime. Penalties are tied to the amount of money the thief steals. For example, in Florida, identity theft is a second-degree felony if it results in an injury of $75,000 or more, Fla. Stat. Ann. § 817.568(2)(b), but is only a first-degree misdemeanor if the individual is harassed without having reached the $75,000 threshold. Fla. Stat. Ann. § 817.568(3). New Jersey likewise penalizes identity thefts resulting in injury over $75,000 as a second-degree crime; injuries between $500 and $75,000 constitute a third-degree crime; injuries between $200 and $500 constitute a fourth-degree crime; and injuries less than $200 constitute a disorderly persons offense. N.J.S.A. §§ 2C:21-17(c)(1)–(2). Pennsylvania punishes identity thefts in a similar manner. *See* Pa. Stat. Ann. tit. 18, § 4120(c)(1).

Should penalties be tied to the dollar value of the things the thief wrongfully took or to the mental distress and harm caused to the victims, which might not be correlated to such a dollar value?

California, in contrast to most other states, has some of the most comprehensive and powerful identity theft laws. For example, California permits victims to obtain the fraudulent applications that the identity thief made as well as a record of the thief's transactions in the victim's name. Cal. Penal Code § 530.8; Cal. Civil Code § 1748.95. California also assists victims in stopping debt collectors from continuing to try to collect debts that the thief created. Cal. Civ. Code § 1788.18. The central difference between California's approach and that of other states is that California grants powerful rights to victims to assist them in fixing the damage of an identity theft. California also requires companies to notify consumers of data security breaches where personal information about consumers is compromised. Cal. Civ. Code § 1798.82(a).

Assessing Identity Theft Statutes. Daniel Solove contends that many statutes addressing identity theft focus mainly on enhancing criminal penalties and ignore the real roots of the problem:

> [T]he prevailing approach toward dealing with identity theft — by relying on increasing criminal penalties and by depending upon individuals to take great lengths to try to protect themselves against their vulnerabilities to identity theft — has the wrong focus. . . . The underlying cause of identity theft is an architecture that makes us vulnerable to such crimes and unable to adequately repair the damage. . . .
>
> This architecture is not created by identity thieves; rather, it is exploited by them. It is an architecture of vulnerability, one where personal information is not protected with adequate security, where identity thieves have easy access to data and the ability to use it in detrimental ways. We are increasingly living with what I call "digital dossiers" about our lives, and these dossiers are not controlled by us but by various entities, such as private-sector companies and the government. These dossiers play a profound role in our lives in modern

---

[17] *Id.* at 6.

society. The identity thief taps into these dossiers and uses them, manipulates them, and pollutes them. The identity thief's ability to so easily access and use our personal data stems from an architecture that does not provide adequate security to our personal information and that does not afford us with a sufficient degree of participation in the collection, dissemination, and use of that information. Consequently, it is difficult for the victim to figure out what is going on and how she can remedy the situation. . . .

Private sector entities lack adequate ways of controlling access to records and accounts in a person's name, and numerous companies engage in the common practice of using SSNs, mother's maiden names, and addresses for access to account information. Additionally, creditors give out credit and establish new accounts if the applicant supplies a name, SSN, and address.[18]

Lynn LoPucki and Solove agree that the problem of identity theft is caused by the frequent use of SSNs as identifiers. According to LoPucki:

The problem is not that thieves have access to personal information, but that creditors and credit-reporting agencies often lack both the means and the incentives to correctly identify the persons who seek credit from them or on whom they report.[19]

LoPucki suggests that the problem is caused by the lack of a reliable means for identification. He proposes a system where the government maintains a database of identification information that people submit, such as biometric data, photographs, and other personal information. Solove argues that more sophisticated identification systems come with other problems, such as an increase in data gathering about people and an inability of people who are the victims of abusive spouses or stalkers to hide. However, both Solove and LoPucki agree that identity theft is, in large part, a problem caused by the system in which credit is granted in the United States.

(b) Tort Law

WOLFE V. MBNA AMERICA BANK
485 F. Supp. 2d 874 (W.D. Tenn. 2007)

DONALD, J. Before the Court is Defendant MBNA America Bank's ("Defendant") Motion to Dismiss Plaintiff's Fourth Amended Complaint made pursuant to Rule 12(b)(6) of the Federal Rules of Civil Procedure. Plaintiff Mark Wolfe ("Plaintiff") filed his Fourth Amended Complaint on September 15, 2006, alleging a claim under the Tennessee Consumer Protection Act of 1977 ("TCPA"), Tenn. Code Ann. § 47-18-104(a)-(b), as well as claims for negligence, gross negligence, and defamation.

---

[18] Daniel J. Solove, *Identity Theft, Privacy, and the Architecture of Vulnerability,* 54 Hastings L.J. 1227 (2003). For a response to Solove's proposals for solutions and a defense of his own proposed solution, see Lynn M. LoPucki, *Did Privacy Cause Identity Theft?*, 54 Hastings L.J. 1277 (2003).

[19] Lynn M. LoPucki, *Human Identification Theory and the Identity Theft Problem,* 80 Tex. L. Rev. 89, 94 (2001).

Plaintiff, now a twenty-seven year old male, is a resident of the State of Tennessee. In or about April 2000, Defendant received a credit account application in Plaintiff's name from a telemarketing company. The application listed Plaintiff's address as 3557 Frankie Carolyn Drive, Apartment 4, Memphis, Tennessee 38118. Plaintiff did not reside and had never resided at this address.

Upon receipt of the application, Defendant issued a credit card bearing Plaintiff's name to an unknown and unauthorized individual residing at the address listed on the application. Plaintiff alleges that Defendant, prior to issuing the card, did not attempt to verify whether the information contained in the credit account application was authentic and accurate. After receiving the card, the unknown and unauthorized individual charged $864.00 to the credit account, exceeding the account's $500.00 credit limit. When no payments were made on the account, Defendant, without investigating whether the account was obtained using a stolen identity, declared the account delinquent and transferred the account to NCO Financial Systems, Inc. ("NCO"), a debt collection agency. Defendant also notified various credit reporting agencies that the account was delinquent.

In order to collect the debt on the delinquent account, NCO hired an attorney, who discovered Plaintiff's actual address. The attorney, in a letter dated November 29, 2004, notified Plaintiff of the delinquent account and requested payment. Upon receipt of this letter, Plaintiff contacted the attorney to inquire about the account, but was told that he would receive information about the account in thirty (30) days. Plaintiff never received any further information.

In January 2005, Plaintiff applied for a job with a bank, but Plaintiff was not hired due to his poor credit score. Following this denial, Plaintiff contacted Defendant numerous times to dispute the delinquent account but was unable to obtain any "adequate or real explanation" from Defendant. At some point in time, Defendant mailed a notice of arbitration proceedings to the address listed on the credit account application, which subsequently resulted in an arbitration award against Plaintiff. Despite Plaintiff notifying Defendant that his identity was stolen, Defendant continues to list the credit account bearing Plaintiff's name as delinquent and has not corrected the information provided to credit reporting agencies regarding the account. . . .

A motion to dismiss for failure to state a claim only tests whether the plaintiff has pleaded a cognizable claim. . . .

Plaintiff alleges that Defendant had a *duty to verify* "the accuracy and authenticity of a credit application completed in Plaintiff's name before issuing a credit card." . . . Plaintiff alleges that Defendant failed to comply with [its duty to verify], and thus, is negligent and/or grossly negligent.

In Tennessee, negligence is established if a plaintiff demonstrates: "(1) a duty of care owed by the defendant to the plaintiff; (2) conduct falling below the applicable standard of care amounts to a breach of that duty; (3) an injury or loss; (4) causation in fact; and (5) proximate, or legal cause." To establish gross negligence, a plaintiff "must demonstrate ordinary negligence and must then prove that the defendant acted 'with utter unconcern for the safety of others, or . . . with such reckless disregard for the rights of others that a conscious indifference to consequences is implied in law'". . . .

Addressing the first context or duty, Defendant asserts that Plaintiff's negligence and gross negligence claims should be dismissed because Tennessee negligence law does not impose a duty on Defendant to verify the authenticity and accuracy of a credit account application prior to issuing a credit card. Defendant, characterizing Plaintiff's claim as one for the "negligent enablement of identity theft," argues that a duty to verify essentially constitutes a duty to prevent third-party criminal activity. Defendant argues that Tennessee courts have never held that commercial banks have a common law duty to prevent the theft of a non-customer's identity. Defendant further argues that it, like Plaintiff, is a victim of identity theft.

Under Tennessee negligence law, a duty is defined as "the legal obligation a defendant owes to a plaintiff to conform to the reasonable person standard of care in order to protect against unreasonable risks of harm." "Whether a defendant owes a duty to a plaintiff in any given situation is a question of law for the court." The "existence and scope of the duty of the defendant in a particular case rests on all the relevant circumstances, including the foreseeability of harm to the plaintiff and other similarly situated persons." A harm is foreseeable "if a reasonable person could foresee the probability of its occurrence or if the person was on notice that the likelihood of danger to the party to whom is owed a duty is probable."

Because Tennessee courts have not specifically addressed whether Tennessee negligence law imposes a duty to verify on commercial banks, Defendant cites in support of its argument the Supreme Court of South Carolina's decision in *Huggins v. Citibank, N.A.,* 585 S.E.2d 275 (S.C. 2003). In *Huggins,* the plaintiff alleged, among other things, that the defendant bank was negligent for issuing a credit card in the plaintiff's name to an unknown and unauthorized person "without any investigation, verification, or corroboration" of the authenticity and accuracy of the credit account application. The defendant argued that under South Carolina negligence law, it had no duty to verify the accuracy and authenticity of the credit account application because plaintiff was technically a non-customer. The South Carolina Supreme Court, despite finding that "it is foreseeable that injury may arise by the negligent issuance of a credit card," ultimately found that no duty to verify existed because "[t]he relationship, if any, between credit card issuers and potential victims of identity theft is far too attenuated to rise to the level of a duty between them." Noting the similarity between negligence law in Tennessee and South Carolina, Defendant argues that its relationship with Plaintiff, like the parties in *Huggins,* was and is too attenuated to warrant the imposition of a duty to verify.

Upon review, the Court finds the South Carolina Supreme Court's conclusion in *Huggins* to be flawed. In reaching its conclusion, the *Huggins* court relied heavily on the fact that there was no prior business relationship between the parties, that is, the plaintiff was not a customer of the defendant bank. The Court believes that the court's reliance on this fact is misplaced. While the existence of a prior business relationship might have some meaning in the context of a contractual dispute, a prior business relationship has little meaning in the context of negligence law. Instead, to determine whether a duty exists between parties, the Court must examine all relevant circumstances, with emphasis on the foreseeability of the alleged harm. As to the issue of foreseeability, the South

Carolina Supreme Court found that "it is foreseeable that injury may arise by the negligent issuance of a credit card" and that such injury "could be prevented if credit card issuers carefully scrutinized credit card applications." The Court agrees with and adopts these findings.

With the alarming increase in identity theft in recent years, commercial banks and credit card issuers have become the first, and often last, line of defense in preventing the devastating damage that identity theft inflicts. Because the injury resulting from the negligent issuance of a credit card is foreseeable and preventable, the Court finds that under Tennessee negligence law, Defendant has a duty to verify the authenticity and accuracy of a credit account application before issuing a credit card. The Court, however, emphasizes that this duty to verify does not impose upon Defendant a duty to prevent all identity theft. The Court recognizes that despite banks utilizing the most reasonable and vigilant verification methods, some criminals will still be able to obtain enough personal information to secure a credit card with a stolen identity. Rather, this duty to verify merely requires Defendant to implement reasonable and cost-effective verification methods that can prevent criminals, in some instances, from obtaining a credit card with a stolen identity. Whether Defendant complied with this duty before issuing a credit card in Plaintiff's name is an issue for the trier of fact. Accordingly, Defendant's motion to dismiss Plaintiff's negligence and gross negligence claims in the first factual context is DENIED.

NOTES & QUESTIONS

1. *Tort Law to the Rescue?* In *Wolfe*, the district court located a duty in tort law that required a bank to take steps to verify identity before issuing a credit card in the plaintiff's name to a person. The court operated under a negligence theory: the bank need not prevent all identity theft (strict liability), but merely to use reasonable verification methods. What kind of practical steps might a bank take to make sure that the person to whom it issues a credit card is, in fact, the intended person? In light of the Lo Pucki-Solove debate (excerpted above) about the flawed system for checking and otherwise verifying identity, how successful are any "reasonable" means likely to be?

(c) The Fair Credit Reporting Act

A significant amount of identity theft involves the credit reporting system. When an identity thief starts creating delinquent debts in a person's name, creditors report the delinquencies to the credit reporting agencies, and the delinquencies begin to appear on the person's credit report. This can severely affect the person's credit score and make it impossible for the person to secure credit. What are the responsibilities of credit reporting agencies in ensuring that the data it reports about individuals really pertains to them rather than to the identity thief who impersonated them?

SLOANE V. EQUIFAX INFORMATION SERVICES, LLC

510 F.3d 495 (4th Cir. 2007)

DIANA GRIBBON MOTZ, J. After Suzanne Sloane discovered that a thief had stolen her identity and ruined her credit, she notified the police and sought to have Equifax Information Services, LLC, a credit reporting service, correct the resulting errors in her credit report. The police promptly arrested and jailed the thief. But twenty-one months later, Equifax still had not corrected the errors in Suzanne's credit report. Accordingly, Suzanne brought this action against Equifax for violations of the Fair Credit Reporting Act (FCRA), 15 U.S.C.A. §§ 1681 *et seq.* A jury found that Equifax had violated the Act in numerous respects and awarded Suzanne $351,000 in actual damages ($106,000 for economic losses and $245,000 for mental anguish, humiliation, and emotional distress). The district court entered judgment in the amount of $351,000. In addition, without permitting Equifax to file a written opposition, the court also awarded Suzanne attorney's fees in the amount of $181,083. On appeal, Equifax challenges the award of damages and attorney's fees. We affirm in part and reverse and remand in part.

On June 25, 2003, Suzanne Sloane entered Prince William Hospital to deliver a baby. She left the hospital not only a new mother, but also the victim of identity theft. A recently hired hospital employee named Shovana Sloan noticed similarity in the women's names and birth dates and, in November and December 2003, began using Suzanne's social security number to obtain credit cards, loans, cash advances, and other goods and services totaling more than $30,000. At the end of January 2004, Suzanne discovered these fraudulent transactions when Citibank notified her that it had cancelled her credit card and told her to contact Equifax if she had any concerns.

Unable to reach Equifax by telephone on a Friday evening, Suzanne went instead to the Equifax website, where she was able to access her credit report and discovered Shovana Sloan's name and evidence of the financial crimes Shovana had committed. Suzanne promptly notified the police, and contacted Equifax, which assertedly placed a fraud alert on her credit file. Equifax told Suzanne to "roll up her sleeves" and start calling all of her "20-some" creditors to notify them of the identity theft. Suzanne took the next two days off from work to contact each of her creditors, and, at their direction, she submitted numerous notarized forms to correct her credit history.

Suzanne, however, continued to experience problems with Equifax. On March 31, 2004, almost two months after reporting the identity theft to Equifax and despite her efforts to work with individual creditors as Equifax had advised, Suzanne and her husband, Tracey, tried to secure a pre-qualification letter to buy a vacation home, but were turned down. The loan officer told them that Suzanne's credit score was "terrible" — in fact, the "worst" the loan officer had ever seen — and that no loan would be possible until the numerous problems in Suzanne's Equifax credit report had been corrected. The loan officer also told Suzanne not to apply for additional credit in the meantime, because each credit inquiry would appear on her credit report and further lower her score.

Chagrined that Equifax had not yet corrected these errors in her credit report, Suzanne refrained from applying for any type of consumer credit for seven months. But, in October 2004, after the repeated breakdown of their family car, Suzanne and Tracey attempted to rely on Suzanne's credit to purchase a used car at a local dealership. Following a credit check, the car salesman pulled Tracey aside and informed him that it would be impossible to approve the financing so long as Suzanne's name appeared on the loan. Similarly, when the Sloanes returned to the mortgage company to obtain a home loan in January 2005, eight months after their initial visit, they were offered only an adjustable rate loan instead of a less expensive 30-year fixed rate loan in part because of Equifax's still inaccurate credit report.

In frustration, on March 9, 2005, more than thirteen months after first reporting the identity theft to Equifax, Suzanne sent a formal letter to the credit reporting agency, disputing twenty-four specific items in her credit report and requesting their deletion. Equifax agreed to delete the majority of these items, but after assertedly verifying two accounts with Citifinancial, Inc., Equifax notified Suzanne that it would not remove these two items. At trial, Equifax admitted that under its "verified victim policy," it should have automatically removed these Citifinancial items at Suzanne's request, but it failed to do so in violation of its own written procedures.

Two months later, on May 9, 2005, Suzanne again wrote to Equifax, still disputing the two Citifinancial accounts, and now also contesting two Washington Mutual accounts that Equifax had previously deleted but had mistakenly restored to Suzanne's report. When Equifax attempted to correct these mistakes, it exacerbated matters further by generating a second credit file bearing Shovana Sloan's name but containing Suzanne's social security number. Compounding this mistake, on May 23, 2005, Equifax sent a letter to Suzanne's house addressed to Shovana Sloan, warning Shovana that *she* was possibly the victim of identity theft and offering to sell her a service to monitor her credit file. Then, on June 7, 2005, Equifax sent copies of *both* credit reports to Suzanne; notably, both credit reports still contained the disputed Citifinancial accounts.

The stress of these problems weighed on Suzanne and significantly contributed to the deterioration of her marriage to Tracey. . . . In May 2005, the credit situation forced Tracey, a high school teacher, to abandon his plans to take a sabbatical during which he had hoped to develop land for modular homes with his father. The Sloanes frequently fought during the day and slept in separate rooms at night. . . . Also, during this period, Suzanne was frequently unable to sleep at night, and as her insomnia worsened, she found herself nodding off while driving home from work in the evening. Even after the couple took a vacation to reconcile in August 2005, when they returned home, they were greeted with the denial of a line of credit from Wachovia Bank. . . .

On November 4, 2005 — following twenty-one months of struggle to correct her credit report — Suzanne filed this action against Equifax, Trans Union, LLC, Experian Information Solutions, Inc., and Citifinancial, alleging violations of the FCRA. After settling a separate suit against Prince William Hospital and the personnel company that placed Shovana Sloan in the hospital's accounting department, Suzanne settled her claims in this action against Experian, Trans Union, and Citifinancial. Equifax, however, refused to settle. Thus, the case proceeded to trial with Equifax the sole remaining defendant. The jury returned a verdict against Equifax, awarding Suzanne $106,000 for economic loss and $245,000 for mental anguish, humiliation, and emotional distress.

Equifax moved for judgment as a matter of law and for a new trial or remittitur on the jury's award of damages for emotional distress. The district court denied Equifax's post-trial motions and then, without permitting Equifax to submit an opposition to Suzanne's request for attorney's fees, ordered Equifax to pay $181,083 in attorney's fees. This appeal followed. . . .

In this case, the jury specifically found, via a special verdict, that Suzanne proved by a preponderance of the evidence that Equifax violated the FCRA by negligently: (1) failing to follow reasonable procedures designed to assure maximum accuracy on her consumer credit report; (2) failing to conduct a reasonable investigation to determine whether disputed information in her credit report was inaccurate; (3) failing to delete information from the report that it found after reinvestigation to be inaccurate, incomplete, or unverified; and (4) reinserting information into her credit file that it had previously deleted. On appeal, Equifax does not challenge the jury's findings that Suzanne proved that it violated the FCRA in all of these respects.

The FCRA provides a private cause of action for those damaged by violations of the statute. *See* 15 U.S.C.A. §§ 1681n, 1681o. A successful plaintiff can recover both actual and punitive damages for willful violations of the FCRA, *id.* § 1681n(a), and actual damages for negligent violations, *id.* § 1681o(a). Actual damages may include not only economic damages, but also damages for humiliation and mental distress. The statute also provides that a successful plaintiff suing under the FCRA may recover reasonable attorney's fees. 15 U.S.C.A. §§ 1681n(a)(3), 1681o(a)(2). . . .

Equifax first argues that because Suzanne assertedly suffered a single, indivisible injury, she should not recover any damages from Equifax or, alternatively, her recovery should be reduced to take account of her prior settlements with other defendants. According to Equifax, the prior settlements have fully, or almost fully, compensated Suzanne for all of her injuries.

Equifax relies on the "one satisfaction rule" to support its argument. *See Chisholm v. UHP Projects, Inc.,* 205 F.3d 731, 737 (4th Cir. 2000) ("[T]his equitable doctrine operates to reduce a plaintiff's recovery from the nonsettling defendant to prevent the plaintiff from recovering twice from the same assessment of liability."). But, in the case at hand, we cannot find, as a matter of law, that Suzanne has suffered from a "single, indivisible harm" that has already been redressed by other parties. . . .

To the contrary, Suzanne provided credible evidence that her emotional and economic damages resulted from separate acts by separate parties. She did not attempt to hold any of the credit reporting agencies responsible for damages arising from either the identity theft itself or the initial inaccuracies that the theft generated in her credit reports. Moreover, although some of Suzanne's interactions with Equifax overlapped with exchanges with other credit reporting agencies, her encounters with Equifax both predate and postdate these other exchanges. . . .

Further, during the period when Suzanne attempted to correct the mistakes made by all three agencies, each agency produced reports with different inaccuracies, and each agency either corrected or exacerbated these mistakes independently of the others. Thus, even during this period, the inaccuracies in Equifax's credit reports caused Suzanne discrete injuries independent of those caused by the other credit reporting agencies.

For all of these reasons, we reject Equifax's argument that Suzanne has suffered from a single, indivisible injury or has been doubly compensated as a consequence of her prior settlements.

Equifax next argues that the evidence does not support any award for economic losses. Equifax claims that only speculation and conjecture support such an award, and so the district court erred in denying Equifax's motion for judgment as to this award.

We disagree. The evidence at trial in this case clearly demonstrates that on numerous occasions Suzanne attempted to secure lines of credit from a variety of financial institutions, only to be either denied outright or offered credit on less advantageous terms that she might have received absent Equifax's improper conduct. At times, these financial institutions consulted credit reports from other agencies, but at other times these institutions relied exclusively on the erroneous credit information provided by Equifax. Based on these incidents, we find that there is a legally sufficient evidentiary basis for a reasonable jury to have found that Equifax's conduct resulted in economic losses for Suzanne. Therefore, the district court did not err in denying Equifax's motion regarding this award.

Additionally, Equifax asserts that the district court erred in refusing to order remittitur of the mental anguish, humiliation, and emotional distress damages award to no more than $25,000. Equifax contends that the jury's award of $245,000 is inconsistent with awards in similar cases and is disproportionate to any actual injury proved at trial. Suzanne, by contrast, contends that the evidence provides more than adequate support for the jury's award. To resolve this question, we set forth the relevant governing principles, apply these principles to the evidence before the jury, and compare the evidence and emotional distress award in Suzanne's case with the evidence and award in all assertedly relevant cases. . . .

We begin with Federal Rule of Civil Procedure 59(a), which provides that if a court concludes that a jury award of compensatory damages is excessive, it may order a new trial nisi remittitur. . . . A district court abuses its discretion only by upholding an award of damages when "the jury's verdict is against the weight of the evidence or based on evidence which is false."

In this case, the district court found that the jury's emotional distress award was "not an unreasonable conclusion from this evidence." The court noted that the jury could base its award on Equifax's specific actions, as distinct from those of the other credit reporting agencies, and that Equifax's actions directly led to the mounting frustration and distress that Suzanne felt for almost two years. As one example of Equifax's specific actions, the court recalled the letter that Equifax sent to Suzanne, many months after she had notified Equifax of the identity theft, bearing the name of the identity thief and warning the thief, not Suzanne, that the thief's personal information was in peril. . . .

Moreover, Equifax does not deny that Suzanne suffered emotional distress. Nor does Equifax contend that Suzanne failed to produce sufficient evidence to sustain some award for this injury. Rather, Equifax simply proposes replacing the jury's number with one of its own invention — offering $25,000 in place of $245,000. Yet when asked at oral argument to explain the basis for the proposed remittitur, Equifax's counsel could offer no legal or factual basis for this amount, conceding that the number had been taken "out of the air." Not only is such an unprincipled approach intrinsically unsound, but it also directly contravenes the Seventh Amendment, which precludes an appellate court from replacing an award of compensatory damages with one of the court's own choosing. In short, the issue before us is neither whether Suzanne offered sufficient evidence at trial to sustain an award for emotional distress nor whether we believe that Equifax's "out of the air" $25,000 represents a fair estimate of those damages, but whether the jury's award is *excessive* in light of evidence presented at trial.

Our previous cases establish the type of evidence required to support an award for emotional damages. We have warned that "[n]ot only is emotional distress fraught with vagueness and speculation, it is easily susceptible to fictitious and trivial claims." *Price v. City of Charlotte,* 93 F.3d 1241, 1250 (4th Cir. 1996). For this reason, although specifically recognizing that a plaintiff's testimony can provide sufficient evidence to support an emotional distress award, we have required a plaintiff to "reasonably and sufficiently explain the circumstances of [the] injury and not resort to mere conclusory statements." Thus, we have distinguished between plaintiff testimony that amounts only to "conclusory statements" and plaintiff testimony that "sufficiently articulate[s]" true "demonstrable emotional distress."

In *Knussman v. Maryland,* 272 F.3d 625 (4th Cir. 2001), we summarized the factors properly considered in determining the potential excessiveness of an award for emotional distress. They include the factual context in which the emotional distress arose; evidence corroborating the testimony of the plaintiff; the nexus between the conduct of the defendant and the emotional distress; the degree of such mental distress; mitigating circumstances, if any; physical injuries suffered due to the emotional distress; medical attention resulting from the emotional duress; psychiatric or psychological treatment; and the loss of income, if any.

In the present case, Suzanne offered considerable objective verification of her emotional distress, chronic anxiety, and frustration during the twenty-one months that she attempted to correct Equifax's errors. First, her repeated denials of credit and continuous problems with Equifax furnish an objective and inherently reasonable "factual context" for her resulting claims of emotional distress. Suzanne also corroborated her account in two ways. She offered "sufficiently articulated" descriptions of her protracted anxiety through detailed testimony of specific events and the humiliation and anger she experienced as a result of each occurrence. She also provided evidence that the distress was apparent to others, particularly her family; Tracey, for instance, described in detail his wife's ongoing struggles with Equifax and the emotional toll these events took upon her. In addition, substantial trial evidence attested to the direct "nexus" between Equifax's violations of the FCRA and Suzanne's emotional distress. Furthermore, Suzanne's emotional distress manifested itself in terms of physical symptoms, particularly insomnia. . . .

Reviewing this evidence in light of the appropriate factors already set forth, we conclude that substantial, if not overwhelming, objective evidence supports an emotional distress award. Equifax ignores much of this evidence, however, and insists that an award of $245,000 is "inconsistent with awards in other similar cases." But Equifax relies on cases which are in fact not very "similar" to the case at hand and so provide little assistance in assessing the amount of the emotional distress award here. . . .

As Equifax's authorities indicate, finding helpful precedent for comparison here is not a simple task. The recent emergence of identity theft and the rapid growth of the credit-reporting industry present a unique dilemma without clear precedent. When Congress enacted the FCRA in 1970, it recognized the vital role that credit-reporting agencies had assumed within the burgeoning culture of American consumerism. Since the mid-1980s, the introduction of computerized information technology and data-warehousing has led to the national consolidation of the credit-reporting industry into the "Big Three" — Equifax, Experian, and Trans Union — and rendered credit reporting an integral part of our most ordinary consumer transactions. According to recent data, each of these national credit-reporting agencies has perhaps 1.5 billion credit accounts held by approximately 190 million individuals. Each receives more than two billion items of information every month, and together these three agencies issue approximately two million consumer credit reports each day.

Against this backdrop, identity theft has emerged over the last decade as one of the fastest growing white-collar crimes in the United States. . . . Given the rapid emergence of identity theft in the last decade, it comes as no surprise that past precedent fails to fully reflect the unfortunate current reality. . . .

A survey of the other, more recent FCRA cases that involve requests for remittitur of emotional distress awards suggests that approved awards more typically range between $20,000 and $75,000.

This handful of cases, while helpful, differs from the case at hand. For, unlike the plaintiffs in those cases, Suzanne did not suffer from isolated or accidental reporting errors. Rather, as a victim of identity theft, she suffered the systematic manipulation of her personal information, which, despite her best efforts, Equifax failed to correct over a protracted period of time. Of course, Equifax bore no responsibility for the initial theft, but the FCRA makes the company responsible for taking reasonable steps to correct Suzanne's credit report once she brought the theft to the company's attention; this Equifax utterly failed to do. A reasonable jury could conclude that Equifax's repeated errors engendered more emotional distress than that found in these other FCRA cases.

We also believe that some guidance can be gained from case law concerning defamation. Prior to the enactment of the FCRA, defamation was one of several common-law actions used by plaintiffs in response to the dissemination of inaccurate credit information.[20] These common-law causes of action parallel those offered under the FCRA in that they typically involve a defendant found liable for propagating inaccurate information about the plaintiff, and the effects, while unquestionably harmful, are difficult to translate into monetary terms. . . .

---

[20] A provision of the FCRA bars consumers from bringing actions "in the nature of defamation, invasion of privacy, or negligence" in certain specified contexts, except as those causes of action arise under sections 1681n and 1681o of the FCRA. 15 U.S.C.A. § 1681h(e).

[C]ourts frequently sustain emotional distress awards in the range of $250,000 in defamation cases.

We do not believe the evidence presented here permits an award of this magnitude because, after all, this case does not involve actual defamation. Moreover, Suzanne presented almost no evidence at trial to suggest that Equifax's violations of the FCRA resulted in harm to her reputation, and it appears that few people beyond Suzanne's family and potential creditors knew of her disastrous credit file. We therefore believe that the maximum award supported by the evidence here must be significantly less than these defamation awards. But, considering the extensive corroboration offered at trial concerning the many months of emotional distress, mental anguish, and humiliation suffered by Suzanne, we believe that the evidence does support an award in the maximum amount of $150,000. We recognize that even this amount is appreciably more than that awarded for emotional distress in most other FCRA cases. But, as explained earlier, the case at hand differs significantly from those cases. A $150,000 award reflects those differences—the repeated violations of the FCRA found by the jury in its special verdict, the number of errors contained in Equifax's credit reports, and the protracted length of time during which Equifax failed to correct Suzanne's credit file. Accordingly, we reduce the emotional distress award to $150,000 and grant a new trial nisi remittitur at Suzanne's option. . . .

[The court vacated the district court's grant of attorney's fees in the amount of $181,083 because the district court failed to allow Equifax to submit a written opposition to Sloane's motion for attorney's fees. The case was remanded to allow Equifax to file its opposition.]

NOTES & QUESTIONS

1. *Damages.* Was the remittitur to $150,000 appropriate? Why should damage awards be limited based on the damage awards in other cases? As the court noted, they involve very different facts than the case at bar.

   Also recall the court's statement that "this case does not involve actual defamation. . . . Suzanne presented almost no evidence at trial to suggest that Equifax's violations of the FCRA resulted in harm to her reputation, and it appears that few people beyond Suzanne's family and potential creditors knew of her disastrous credit file." Why doesn't this case involve "harm to her reputation"? Don't reports on people's creditworthiness affect their financial reputations, that is, their ability to pay back their debts, their trustworthiness and dependability?

2. *The Harm of Identity Theft.* When assessing the damages Sloane suffered from her identity theft ordeal, how much of the harm was caused by Equifax's actions? Purportedly, the entire incident of identity theft caused her marital discord, insomnia, and emotional distress. Yet, the identity theft did involve, after all, not only Equifax, but the identity thief, creditors, and other credit reporting agencies. Are the damages assessed to Equifax proportionate to Equifax's contribution to Sloane's ordeal? Or should Equifax be viewed as

the "least cost avoider," the party who can internalize the costs of preventing this harm at the least overall cost?

B. COMMERCIAL ENTITIES AND PERSONAL DATA

Thus far, this chapter has examined the use of personal information within the financial sector. This part examines the use of personal information by commercial entities and how the law has attempted different ways to regulate in this area.

1. GOVERNANCE BY TORT

DWYER V. AMERICAN EXPRESS CO.

652 N.E.2d 1351 (Ill. App. 1995)

BUCKLEY, J. Plaintiffs, American Express cardholders, appeal the circuit court's dismissal of their claims for invasion of privacy and consumer fraud against defendants, American Express Company, American Express Credit Corporation, and American Express Travel Related Services Company, for their practice of renting information regarding cardholder spending habits.

On May 13, 1992, the New York Attorney General released a press statement describing an agreement it had entered into with defendants. The following day, newspapers reported defendants' actions which gave rise to this agreement. According to the news articles, defendants categorize and rank their cardholders into six tiers based on spending habits and then rent this information to participating merchants as part of a targeted joint-marketing and sales program. For example, a cardholder may be characterized as "Rodeo Drive Chic" or "Value Oriented." In order to characterize its cardholders, defendants analyze where they shop and how much they spend, and also consider behavioral characteristics and spending histories. Defendants then offer to create a list of cardholders who would most likely shop in a particular store and rent that list to the merchant.

Defendants also offer to create lists which target cardholders who purchase specific types of items, such as fine jewelry. The merchants using the defendants' service can also target shoppers in categories such as mail-order apparel buyers, home-improvement shoppers, electronics shoppers, luxury lodgers, card members with children, skiers, frequent business travelers, resort users, Asian/European travelers, luxury European car owners, or recent movers. Finally, defendants offer joint-marketing ventures to merchants who generate substantial sales through the American Express card. Defendants mail special promotions devised by the merchants to its cardholders and share the profits generated by these advertisements. . . .

Plaintiffs have alleged that defendants' practices constitute an invasion of their privacy [in particular, a violation of the intrusion upon seclusion tort]. . . .

. . . [There are] four elements [to intrusion upon seclusion] which must be alleged in order to state a cause of action: (1) an unauthorized intrusion or prying into the plaintiff's seclusion; (2) an intrusion which is offensive or objectionable to a reasonable man; (3) the matter upon which the intrusion occurs is private; and (4) the intrusion causes anguish and suffering. . . .

Plaintiffs' allegations fail to satisfy the first element, an unauthorized intrusion or prying into the plaintiffs' seclusion. The alleged wrongful actions involve the defendants' practice of renting lists that they have compiled from information contained in their own records. By using the American Express card, a cardholder is voluntarily, and necessarily, giving information to defendants that, if analyzed, will reveal a cardholder's spending habits and shopping preferences. . . .

Plaintiffs claim that because defendants rented lists based on this compiled information, this case involves the disclosure of private financial information and most closely resembles cases involving intrusion into private financial dealings, such as bank account transactions. Plaintiffs cite several cases in which courts have recognized the right to privacy surrounding financial transactions.

However, we find that this case more closely resembles the sale of magazine subscription lists, which was at issue in *Shibley v. Time, Inc.* In *Shibley*, the plaintiffs claimed that the defendant's practice of selling and renting magazine subscription lists without the subscribers' prior consent "constitut[ed] an invasion of privacy because it amount[ed] to a sale of individual 'personality profiles,' which subjects the subscribers to solicitations from direct mail advertisers." The plaintiffs also claimed that the lists amounted to a tortious appropriation of their names and "personality profiles." . . .

The *Shibley* court found that an Ohio statute, which permitted the sale of names and addresses of registrants of motor vehicles, indicated that the defendant's activity was not an invasion of privacy. . . .

Defendants rent names and addresses after they create a list of cardholders who have certain shopping tendencies; they are not disclosing financial information about particular cardholders. These lists are being used solely for the purpose of determining what type of advertising should be sent to whom. We also note that the Illinois Vehicle Code authorizes the Secretary of State to sell lists of names and addresses of licensed drivers and registered motor-vehicle owners. Thus, we hold that the alleged actions here do not constitute an unreasonable intrusion into the seclusion of another. We so hold without expressing a view as to the appellate court conflict regarding the recognition of this cause of action.

Considering plaintiffs' appropriation claim, the elements of the tort are: an appropriation, without consent, of one's name or likeness for another's use or benefit. This branch of the privacy doctrine is designed to protect a person from having his name or image used for commercial purposes without consent. According to the Restatement, the purpose of this tort is to protect the "interest of the individual in the exclusive use of his own identity, in so far as it is represented by his name or likeness." Illustrations of this tort provided by the Restatement include the publication of a person's photograph without consent in an advertisement; operating a corporation named after a prominent public figure without the person's consent; impersonating a man to obtain information regarding the affairs of the man's wife; and filing a lawsuit in the name of another without the other's consent.

Plaintiffs claim that defendants appropriate information about cardholders' personalities, including their names and perceived lifestyles, without their consent. Defendants argue that their practice does not adversely affect the interest of a cardholder in the "exclusive use of his own identity," using the language of the Restatement. Defendants also argue that the cardholders' names lack value and that the lists that defendants create are valuable because "they identify a useful aggregate of potential customers to whom offers may be sent.". . .

To counter defendants' argument, plaintiffs point out that the tort of appropriation is not limited to strictly commercial situations.

Nonetheless, we again follow the reasoning in *Shibley* and find that plaintiffs have not stated a claim for tortious appropriation because they have failed to allege the first element. Undeniably, each cardholder's name is valuable to defendants. The more names included on a list, the more that list will be worth. However, a single, random cardholder's name has little or no intrinsic value to defendants (or a merchant). Rather, an individual name has value only when it is associated with one of defendants' lists. Defendants create value by categorizing and aggregating these names. Furthermore, defendants' practices do not deprive any of the cardholders of any value their individual names may possess. . . .

NOTES & QUESTIONS

1. **Shibley v. Time.** In *Shibley v. Time, Inc.,* 341 N.E.2d 337 (Ohio Ct. App. 1975), the plaintiff sued the publishers of a number of magazines for selling subscription lists to direct mail advertising businesses. The plaintiff sued under the public disclosure tort and the appropriation tort. Despite the fact that the purchasers of the lists can learn about the plaintiff's lifestyle from the data, the court dismissed the plaintiff's public disclosure action. The court found that the sale of the lists did not "cause mental suffering, shame or humiliation to a person of ordinary sensibilities." The court also rejected the plaintiff's argument that by selling the lists, the defendants were appropriating his name and likeness because the tort of appropriation is available only in those "situations where the plaintiff's name or likeness is displayed to the public to indicate that the plaintiff indorses the defendant's product or business."

    According to *Shibley* and *Dwyer*, why does the public disclosure tort fail to provide a remedy for the disclosure of personal information to other companies? Why does the tort of intrusion upon seclusion fail? Why does the tort of appropriation fail? More generally, can tort law adequately remedy the privacy problems created by profiling and databases?[21]

---

[21] For an interesting argument about how the tort of breach of confidentiality might provide a weak but potential solution to the problem, see Jessica Litman, *Information Privacy/Information Property*, 52 Stan. L. Rev. 1283 (2000). For a discussion of the use of the tort of appropriation, see Andrew J. McClurg, *A Thousand Words Are Worth a Picture: A Privacy Tort Response to Consumer Data Profiling*, 98 Nw. U. L. Rev. 63 (2003).

2. *A Fair Information Practices Tort?* Sarah Ludington recommends that a new tort should be developed in the common law, one that "would impose on data traders a duty to use Fair Information Practices (based on the principles of notice, choice, access, and security)." Why the common law rather than legislation? Ludington argues:

> [B]ecause it is now clear that industry lobbying has succeeded while self-regulation has failed, and that legislatures have either failed to act or provided solutions that inadequately address the injuries, individuals must — indeed, should — look to the judiciary to help resolve the misuse of personal information.[22]

Would the use of the common law to regulate the collection and use of personal data be effective or appropriate? What would be the strengths and weaknesses of such a regulatory approach?

3. *Defining the Harm.* What is the harm of commercial entities collecting and using personal information? One might contend that the kind of information that companies collect about individuals is not very sensitive or intimate. How much is a person harmed by sharing data that she prefers Coke to Pepsi or Puffs to Kleenex? Is there a significant privacy problem in revealing that a person has purchased tennis products, designer sunglasses, orange juice, or other things? One might view the harm as so minimal as to be trivial.

Does information about a person's consumption patterns reveal something about that person's identity? Stan Karas argues that "consumption patterns may identify one as a liberal, moderate Republican, radical feminist or born-again Christian. . . . For some individuals, consumption is no longer a way of expressing identity but is synonymous with identity. . . . [T]he identity of many subcultures is directly related to distinctive patterns of consumption. One need only think of the personal styles of punk rockers, hip-hoppers, or Harley-fetishizing bikers."[23]

According to Jerry Kang, data collection and compiling is a form of surveillance that inhibits individual freedom and choice: "[I]nformation collection in cyberspace is more like surveillance than like casual observation." He notes that "surveillance leads to self-censorship. This is true even when the observable information would not be otherwise misused or disclosed."[24]

Daniel Solove contends that the problem of computer databases does not stem from surveillance. He argues that numerous theorists describe the problem in terms of the metaphor of Big Brother, the ruthless totalitarian government in George Orwell's *1984*, which constantly monitors its citizens. Solove contends that the Big Brother metaphor fails to adequately conceptualize the problem:

> A large portion of our personal information involves facts that we are not embarrassed about: our financial information, race, marital status, hobbies,

---

[22] Sarah Ludington, *Reining in the Data Traders: A Tort for the Misuse of Personal Information*, 66 Md. L. Rev. 140, 172-73 (2007).

[23] Stan Karas, *Privacy, Identity, Databases*, 52 Am. U. L. Rev. 393, 438-39 (2002).

[24] Jerry Kang, *Information Privacy in Cyberspace Transactions*, 50 Stan. L. Rev. 1193 (1998).

occupation, and the like. Most people surf the web without wandering into its dark corners. The vast majority of the information collected about us concerns relatively innocuous details. The surveillance model does not explain why the recording of this non-taboo information poses a problem.[25]

In contrast, Solove proposes that data collection and processing is most aptly captured by Franz Kafka's *The Trial*, where the protagonist (Joseph K.) is arrested by officials from a clandestine court system but is not informed of the reason for his arrest. From what little he manages to learn about the court system, which operates largely in secret, Joseph K. discovers that a vast bureaucratic court has examined his life and assembled a dossier on him. His records, however, are "inaccessible," and K.'s life gradually becomes taken over by his frustrating quest for answers:

> *The Trial* captures the sense of helplessness, frustration, and vulnerability one experiences when a large bureaucratic organization has control over a vast dossier of details about one's life. At any time, something could happen to Joseph K.; decisions are made based on his data, and Joseph K. has no say, no knowledge, and no ability to fight back. He is completely at the mercy of the bureaucratic process. . . .
>
> The problem with databases emerges from subjecting personal information to the bureaucratic process with little intelligent control or limitation, resulting in a lack of meaningful participation in decisions about our information. . . .
>
> Under this view, the problem with databases and the practices currently associated with them is that they disempower people. They make people vulnerable by stripping them of control over their personal information. There is no diabolical motive or secret plan for domination; rather, there is a web of thoughtless decisions made by low-level bureaucrats, standardized policies, rigid routines, and a way of relating to individuals and their information that often becomes indifferent to their welfare.[26]

Joel Reidenberg points out that the lack of protection of information privacy will "destroy anonymity" and take away people's "freedom to choose the terms of personal information disclosure."[27] According to Paul Schwartz, the lack of privacy protection can threaten to expose not just information about what people purchase, but also information about their communication and consumption of ideas:

> In the absence of strong rules for information privacy, Americans will hesitate to engage in cyberspace activities—including those that are most likely to promote democratic self-rule. . . . Current polls already indicate an aversion on the part of some people to engage even in basic commercial activities on the Internet. Yet, deliberative democracy requires more than shoppers; it demands speakers and listeners. But who will speak or listen when this

---

[25] Daniel J. Solove, *Privacy and Power: Computer Databases and Metaphors for Information Privacy*, 53 Stan. L. Rev. 1393 (2001).

[26] *Id.*

[27] Joel R. Reidenberg, *Setting Standards for Fair Information Practice in the U.S. Private Sector*, 80 Iowa L. Rev. 497 (1995).

behavior leaves finely-grained data trails in a fashion that is difficult to understand or anticipate?[28]

4. *Is Privacy Still Possible?* Is privacy still possible in an Information Age? Scott McNealy, CEO of Sun Microsystems, Inc., once remarked: "You already have zero privacy. Get over it." Should we eulogize the death of privacy and move on? Or is it possible to protect privacy in modern times? Consider David Brin:

> . . . [I]t is already far too late to prevent the invasion of cameras and databases. The *djinn* cannot be crammed back into its bottle. No matter how many laws are passed, it will prove quite impossible to legislate away the new surveillance tools and databases. They are here to stay.
>
> Light *is* going to shine into nearly every corner of our lives. . . .
>
> If neo-Western civilization has one great trick in its repertoire, a technique more responsible than any other for its success, that trick is *accountability*. Especially the knack — which no other culture ever mastered — of making accountability apply to the mighty. . . .
>
> Kevin Kelly, executive editor of *Wired* magazine, expressed the same idea with the gritty clarity of information-age journalism: "The answer to the whole privacy question is more knowledge. More knowledge about who's watching you. More knowledge about the information that flows between us — particularly the meta-information about who knows what and where it's going."
>
> In other words, we may not be able to eliminate the intrusive glare shining on citizens of the next century, but the glare just might be rendered harmless through the application of more light aimed in the other direction.[29]

Is greater transparency the solution to the increasing threats to privacy?

REMSBURG V. DOCUSEARCH, INC.

816 A.2d 1001 (N.H. 2003)

DALIANIS, J. . . . [Liam Youens contacted Docusearch and purchased the birth date of Amy Lynn Boyer for a fee. He again contacted Docusearch and placed an order for Boyer's SSN. Docusearch obtained Boyer's SSN from a credit reporting agency and provided it to Youens. Youens then asked for Boyer's employment address. Docusearch hired a subcontractor, Michele Gambino, who obtained it by making a "pretext" phone call to Boyer. Gambino lied about her identity and the purpose of the call, and she obtained the address from Boyer. The address was then given to Youens. Shortly thereafter, Youens went to Boyer's workplace and shot and killed her and then killed himself.]

All persons have a duty to exercise reasonable care not to subject others to an unreasonable risk of harm. Whether a defendant's conduct creates a risk of harm to others sufficiently foreseeable to charge the defendant with a duty to avoid such conduct is a question of law, because "the existence of a duty does not arise

---

[28] Paul M. Schwartz, *Privacy and Democracy in Cyberspace,* 52 Vand. L. Rev. 1609, 1651 (1999).

[29] David Brin, *The Transparent Society* 8-23 (1998).

solely from the relationship between the parties, but also from the need for protection against reasonably foreseeable harm." Thus, in some cases, a party's actions give rise to a duty. Parties owe a duty to those third parties foreseeably endangered by their conduct with respect to those risks whose likelihood and magnitude make the conduct unreasonably dangerous.

In situations in which the harm is caused by criminal misconduct, however, determining whether a duty exists is complicated by the competing rule "that a private citizen has no general duty to protect others from the criminal attacks of third parties." This rule is grounded in the fundamental unfairness of holding private citizens responsible for the unanticipated criminal acts of third parties, because "[u]nder all ordinary and normal circumstances, in the absence of any reason to expect the contrary, the actor may reasonably proceed upon the assumption that others will obey the law."

In certain limited circumstances, however, we have recognized that there are exceptions to the general rule where a duty to exercise reasonable care will arise. We have held that such a duty may arise because: (1) a special relationship exists; (2) special circumstances exist; or (3) the duty has been voluntarily assumed. The special circumstances exception includes situations where there is "an especial temptation and opportunity for criminal misconduct brought about by the defendant." This exception follows from the rule that a party who realizes or should realize that his conduct has created a condition which involves an unreasonable risk of harm to another has a duty to exercise reasonable care to prevent the risk from occurring. The exact occurrence or precise injuries need not have been foreseeable. Rather, where the defendant's conduct has created an unreasonable risk of criminal misconduct, a duty is owed to those foreseeably endangered.

Thus, if a private investigator or information broker's (hereinafter "investigator" collectively) disclosure of information to a client creates a foreseeable risk of criminal misconduct against the third person whose information was disclosed, the investigator owes a duty to exercise reasonable care not to subject the third person to an unreasonable risk of harm. In determining whether the risk of criminal misconduct is foreseeable to an investigator, we examine two risks of information disclosure implicated by this case: stalking and identity theft.

It is undisputed that stalkers, in seeking to locate and track a victim, sometimes use an investigator to obtain personal information about the victims.

Public concern about stalking has compelled all fifty States to pass some form of legislation criminalizing stalking. Approximately one million women and 371,000 men are stalked annually in the United States. Stalking is a crime that causes serious psychological harm to the victims, and often results in the victim experiencing post-traumatic stress disorder, anxiety, sleeplessness, and sometimes, suicidal ideations.

Identity theft, *i.e.*, the use of one person's identity by another, is an increasingly common risk associated with the disclosure of personal information, such as a SSN. A person's SSN has attained the status of a quasi-universal personal identification number. At the same time, however, a person's privacy interest in his or her SSN is recognized by state and federal statutes. . . .

Like the consequences of stalking, the consequences of identity theft can be severe. . . . Victims of identity theft risk the destruction of their good credit histories. This often destroys a victim's ability to obtain credit from any source and may, in some cases, render the victim unemployable or even cause the victim to be incarcerated.

The threats posed by stalking and identity theft lead us to conclude that the risk of criminal misconduct is sufficiently foreseeable so that an investigator has a duty to exercise reasonable care in disclosing a third person's personal information to a client. And we so hold. This is especially true when, as in this case, the investigator does not know the client or the client's purpose in seeking the information. . . .

[The plaintiff also brought an action for intrusion upon seclusion.] A tort action based upon an intrusion upon seclusion must relate to something secret, secluded or private pertaining to the plaintiff. Moreover, liability exists only if the defendant's conduct was such that the defendant should have realized that it would be offensive to persons of ordinary sensibilities.

In addressing whether a person's SSN is something secret, secluded or private, we must determine whether a person has a reasonable expectation of privacy in the number. . . . As noted above, a person's interest in maintaining the privacy of his or her SSN has been recognized by numerous federal and state statutes. As a result, the entities to which this information is disclosed and their employees are bound by legal, and, perhaps, contractual constraints to hold SSNs in confidence to ensure that they remain private. Thus, while a SSN must be disclosed in certain circumstances, a person may reasonably expect that the number will remain private.

Whether the intrusion would be offensive to persons of ordinary sensibilities is ordinarily a question for the fact-finder and only becomes a question of law if reasonable persons can draw only one conclusion from the evidence. The evidence underlying the certified question is insufficient to draw any such conclusion here, and we therefore must leave this question to the fact-finder. In making this determination, the fact-finder should consider "the degree of intrusion, the context, conduct and circumstances surrounding the intrusion as well as the intruder's motives and objectives, the setting into which he intrudes, and the expectations of those whose privacy is invaded." Accordingly, a person whose SSN is obtained by an investigator from a credit reporting agency without the person's knowledge or permission may have a cause of action for intrusion upon seclusion for damages caused by the sale of the SSN, but must prove that the intrusion was such that it would have been offensive to a person of ordinary sensibilities.

We next address whether a person has a cause of action for intrusion upon seclusion where an investigator obtains the person's work address by using a pretextual phone call. We must first establish whether a work address is something secret, secluded or private about the plaintiff.

In most cases, a person works in a public place. "On the public street, or in any other public place, [a person] has no legal right to be alone." . . . Thus, where a person's work address is readily observable by members of the public, the address cannot be private and no intrusion upon seclusion action can be maintained.

[Additionally, the plaintiff brought a cause of action for appropriation.] "One who appropriates to his own use or benefit the name or likeness of another is subject to liability to the other for invasion of his privacy." *Restatement (Second) of Torts* § 652E.

. . . Appropriation is not actionable if the person's name or likeness is published for "purposes other than taking advantage of [the person's] reputation, prestige or other value" associated with the person. Thus, appropriation occurs most often when the person's name or likeness is used to advertise the defendant's product or when the defendant impersonates the person for gain.

An investigator who sells personal information sells the information for the value of the information itself, not to take advantage of the person's reputation or prestige. The investigator does not capitalize upon the goodwill value associated with the information but rather upon the client's willingness to pay for the information. In other words, the benefit derived from the sale in no way relates to the social or commercial standing of the person whose information is sold. Thus, a person whose personal information is sold does not have a cause of action for appropriation against the investigator who sold the information. . . .

NOTES & QUESTIONS

1. *The Scope of the Duty.* The court concludes that Docusearch has a duty to people "foreseeably endangered" by its disclosure of personal information. Is this too broad a duty to impose on those who collect and disseminate personal data? What could Docusearch have done to avoid being negligent in this case? Suppose Jill tells Jack the address of Roe. Jack goes to Roe's house and kills her. Based on *Remsburg*, can Jill be liable?
2. *Tort Liability and the First Amendment.* Does liability for Docusearch implicate the First Amendment?

2. GOVERNANCE BY CONTRACT AND PROMISES

(a) Privacy Policies

Privacy policies are statements made by companies about their practices regarding personal information. Increasingly, companies on the Internet are posting privacy policies, and statutes such as the Gramm-Leach-Bliley Act require certain types of companies (financial institutions, insurance companies, and brokerage companies) to maintain privacy policies.

One of the common provisions of many privacy policies is an "opt-out" provision. An opt-out provision establishes a default rule that the company can use or disclose personal information in the ways it desires so long as the consumer does not indicate otherwise. The consumer must take affirmative steps, such as checking a box, calling the company, or writing a letter, to express her desire to opt out of a particular information use or disclosure. In contrast, an "opt-in" provision establishes a default rule that the company cannot use or disclose personal information without first obtaining the express consent of the individual.

JEFF SOVERN, *OPTING IN, OPTING OUT, OR NO OPTIONS AT ALL: THE FIGHT FOR CONTROL OF PERSONAL INFORMATION*
74 Wash. L. Rev. 1033 (1999)

. . . [F]ew consumers understand how much of their personal information is for sale, although they may have a general idea that there is a trade in personal data and that the specifics about that trade are kept from them. . . .

. . . [C]onsumers cannot protect their personal information when they are unaware of how it is being used by others. . . .

The second reason consumers have not acted to protect their privacy, notwithstanding surveys that suggest considerable consumer concern with confidentiality, has to do with how difficult it is to opt out. . . .

. . . Even if consumers can obtain the information needed to opt out, the cost in time and money of communicating and negotiating with all the relevant information gatherers may be substantial. . . .

Companies may not be eager to offer opt-outs because they may rationally conclude that they will incur costs when consumers opt out, while receiving few offsetting benefits. When consumers exercise the option of having their names deleted, mailing lists shrink and presumably become less valuable. . . .

Because of these added costs, companies might decide that while they must offer an opt-out plan, they do not want consumers to take advantage of it. . . . [C]ompanies that offer opt-outs have an incentive to increase the transaction costs incurred by consumers who opt out. . . .

Companies can increase consumers' transaction costs in opting out in a number of ways. A brochure titled "Privacy Notice," which my local cable company included with its bill, provides an example. This Privacy Notice discussed, among other things, how cable subscribers could write to the company to ask that the company not sell their names and other information to third parties. There are at least four reasons why this particular notice may not be effective in eliciting a response from consumers troubled by the sale of their names to others.

First, the Privacy Notice may be obscured by other information included in the mailing. . . .

The second reason why consumers may not respond to the Privacy Notice is its length. The brochure is four pages long and contains 17 paragraphs, 36 sentences, and 1062 words. . . .

Some companies have gone in the other direction, providing so little information in such vague terms that consumers are unable to discern what they are being told. . . .

A third reason why the Privacy Notice may not be effective stems from its prose. Notwithstanding the Plain Language Law in my home state, computer analysis of the text found it extremely difficult, requiring more than a college education for comprehension. By comparison, a similar analysis of this Article found that it required a lower reading level than that of the Privacy Notice.

Fourth, the Privacy Notice may be ineffective because it does not provide an easy or convenient mechanism for opting out. For example, the Privacy Notice invites consumers who object to the sale of their personal information to write to the cable company in a separate letter. By contrast, cable subscribers desiring to add a new premium channel can do so over the telephone, speaking either to a person or tapping buttons on their telephone, depending on their preference. The more difficult the opt-out process, the less likely consumers are to avail themselves of it. . . .

A third explanation for the failure of consumers to opt out as often as their survey answers might suggest is the consumers themselves. Extensive literature on consumer complaint behavior makes clear that many consumers who are distressed by merchant conduct cannot bring themselves to tell the merchant about it. This inability to communicate might translate into failure by consumers to add their names to opt-out lists. . . .

[Sovern suggests that an opt-in system would be more preferable than an opt-out system.]

One benefit of an opt-in system is that it minimizes transaction costs. While some transaction costs are inevitable in any system in which consumers can opt out or opt in, strategic-behavior transaction costs, at least, can be avoided by using a system which discourages parties from generating such costs. The current system encourages businesses to inflate strategic-behavior costs to increase their own gains, albeit at the expense of consumers and the total surplus from exchange. An opt-in system would encourage businesses to reduce strategic-behavior costs without giving consumers an incentive to increase these costs. Instead of an opt-out situation in which merchants are obligated to provide a message they do not wish consumers to receive, an opt-in regime would harness merchants' efforts in providing a message they want the consumer to receive. . . .

An opt-in system thus increases the likelihood that consumers will choose according to their preferences rather than choosing according to the default. . . .

An opt-in system also increases the prospect that direct mailing would be tailored to what consumers wish to receive, thus benefiting consumers who want to receive some, but not all, solicitations. . . .

The sale of information is troublesome in part because it creates externalities, or costs borne by others. Externalities are created when a person engages in an activity that imposes costs on others but is not required to take those costs into account when deciding whether to pursue the activity. The feelings experienced by consumers whose information is sold and used against their wishes constitute just such externalities. An opt-in system — or an opt-out system in which consumers who object to the trade in their personal information have a genuine opportunity to opt out — can shift costs and thereby "internalize" this externality. To put it another way, consumers could bar the sale of their information unless businesses paid them an amount they deemed adequate, thereby requiring businesses selling personal information to incur a cost otherwise borne by consumers. . . .

A regulated opt-out system is less likely than an opt-in system to solve the problem. Opt-out systems do not give businesses the incentive to minimize consumer transaction costs. Consequently, firms might respond to such regulation by generating formal, legalistic notices that consumers would likely ignore. An opt-out system might thus create only the illusion of a cure.

Accordingly, an opt-in system is preferable, chiefly because it eliminates the incentive firms have to engage in strategic behavior and thus inflate consumer transaction costs. An opt-in system would permit consumers who wish to protect their privacy to do so without incurring transaction costs. Consumers who permit the use of their personal information should also be able to realize their wish easily. Indeed, because firms profit from the use of consumer information, firms would have an incentive to make it as easy as possible for consumers to consent to the use of their personal information. . . . An opt-in system, therefore, seems to offer the best hope of accommodating consumer preferences while minimizing transaction costs. . . .

MICHAEL E. STATEN & FRED H. CATE, THE IMPACT OF OPT-IN PRIVACY RULES ON RETAIL MARKETS: A CASE STUDY OF MBNA

52 Duke L.J. 745, 750-51, 766, 770-74, 776 (2003)

To illustrate the costs of moving to an opt-in system, we examine MBNA Corporation, a financial institution that offers consumers a variety of loan and insurance products (primarily credit cards), takes deposits, but operates entirely without a branch network. Incorporated in 1981 and publicly traded since 1991, the company has compiled a stunning growth record in just two decades. As of the end of 2000, the company provided credit cards and other loan products to 51 million consumers, had $89 billion of loans outstanding, and serviced 15 percent of all Visa/MasterCard credit card balances outstanding in the United States.

MBNA's ability to access and use information about potential and existing customers is largely responsible for it becoming the second largest credit card issuer in the United States in less than twenty years. To appreciate the critical role that the sharing of information has played in MBNA's remarkable history, one need only reflect on the challenge of acquiring 51 million customers with no brick-and-mortar stores or branches. Like firms in a variety of businesses, but especially financial services, MBNA harnessed information technology as the engine for establishing and building customer relationships without ever physically meeting its customers. By using direct mail, telephone and, most recently, Internet contacts, the company has reached out to new prospects throughout the population, regardless of where they live, with offers tailored to their individual interests. . . .

At the core of its marketing and targeting strategies is the proposition that consumers who share a common institutional bond or experience will have an affinity for using a card that lets them demonstrate their affiliation each time they use it to pay for a purchase. The affinity for the institution raises the probability that a prospect will be converted to a customer. Equally important, the institution or organization usually maintains a list of members on which MBNA can focus its marketing efforts. Following this "affinity group" marketing strategy, MBNA designs a card product tailored to members of a particular group, negotiates a financial arrangement with the organization for the exclusive rights to market an affinity card to its members, and uses the member list as a source of potential names to contact via direct mail or telemarketing. . . .

Design of new affinity cards is an ongoing process. In 2000 alone, MBNA acquired the endorsements of 459 new groups, including the United States Tennis

Association, the Atlanta Braves, National Audubon Society, barnesand-noble.com, and the Thurgood Marshall Scholarship Fund.

Although targeting prospects through affinity groups has proven to be a clever strategy, not every group member is offered a card product. The key to the company's profitability and earnings growth, especially given the rapid growth in the size of the customer base, has been in screening the prospects from each affinity group to identify those likely to be quality customers. Given that MBNA's fundamental business is lending money via an unsecured credit card with a revolving line of credit attached, the company wants to put the card in the hands of customers who will use it, but who will not default on their balances. Consequently, MBNA uses information to screen prospects both before it makes card offers (the targeting process) and after it receives applications (the underwriting process). . . .

How large a drag does an "explicit-consent" system impose on economic efficiency? According to the U.S. Postal Service, 52 percent of unsolicited mail in this country is never read. If that figure translates to opt-in requests, then more than half of all consumers in an opt-in system would lose the benefits or services that could result from the use of personal information because the mandatory request for consent would never receive their attention. Moreover, even if an unsolicited offer is read, experience with company-specific and industry-wide opt-out lists demonstrates that less than 10 percent of the U.S. population ever opts out of a mailing list — often the figure is less than 3 percent. Indeed, the difficulty (and cost) of obtaining a response of any sort from consumers is the primary drawback of an opt-in approach. . . .

MBNA's core product is the affinity card tailored for and marketed to each of more than 4,700 affinity groups. . . . [T]he foundation of MBNA's affinity strategy is access to the member lists of each of its affinity organizations. This marketing partnership with thousands of member organizations nationwide makes MBNA unique among major credit card issuers and accounts for much of the company's superior financial performance and reputation for outstanding customer service. However, in the absence of an explicit joint-marketing exception in an opt-in law, a third-party opt-in regime could effectively end MBNA's unique direct marketing approach by sharply limiting an organization's ability to share its member list. . . .

Like all major credit card issuers, MBNA uses personal information to increase the chance that its credit card offer will reach an interested and qualified customer. This process greatly reduces the number of solicitations that must be sent to achieve a given target volume of new accounts, thereby reducing the cost of account acquisition. It also reduces the volume of junk mail in the form of card offers sent to consumers who are not qualified. Third-party or affiliate opt-in systems would eliminate MBNA's access to a significant portion of the information that it currently uses to identify which individuals on the member lists it receives would be good prospects for a given credit card or other product. A blanket opt-in system applicable to marketing activities would impose similar limits.

The MBNA direct mail marketing operations obtain and consider about 800 million consumer "leads" during the course of a year. The vast majority of these leads are names that appear on affinity group member lists (e.g., university alumni groups and professional associations), or names of consumers who are customers of institutions that have endorsed MBNA's credit card product. Because this is an annual figure, many names appear more than once because the individuals are on more than one list acquired during the course of a year, or may be considered in conjunction with a specific group's marketing campaign several times during the year. The most creditworthy names among them may receive multiple solicitations during the year.

MBNA does not wish to mail to all names on the list. Not all are equally likely to respond to a solicitation, nor will all meet the credit underwriting standards for a particular card product. In 2000, the MBNA direct marketing budget supported approximately 400 million mailings of card offers. The challenge to the company in managing the acquisition of new accounts is to cull the "lead list" of 800 million prospect names to identify and target the 400 million direct mail solicitations to consumers who are most likely to become new cardholders. Generally speaking, MBNA has developed a set of targeting criteria such that names reaching the final mailing list of 400 million: (1) are most likely to respond to the offer and the use of the credit card, and (2) are most likely to meet MBNA's creditworthiness standards for the card.

MBNA prepares hundreds of distinct solicitations throughout the year for its various affinity groups. As part of the targeting process for each new solicitation, the prospect list is scrubbed via comparison to a series of "suppression files" that the company maintains and routinely updates. These files pull information about either individuals or addresses from a variety of internal and external data sources. A few examples of the specific criteria illustrate the process.

[The authors describe how MBNA has proprietary response models to help it determine which customers are most likely to respond to its offer. It uses credit history information to find individuals who are likely to repay, but, at the same time, do not have "extraordinary creditworthiness" and are, hence, likely to be frequently solicited by card issuers and unlikely to respond to an MBNA offer.]

The bottom line from the culling process is that approximately 40 percent of the eight hundred million names are suppressed. The initial lead list is typically reduced by an additional 10 percent through a combination of eliminating duplicate records, suppressing undeliverable addresses, and dropping customer names that appear on various "do not mail" lists that record customer preferences not to be solicited. . . . The approximately four hundred million names remaining on the lead list receive targeted direct mail offers with the endorsement of the affinity group to which they belong. . . .

MBNA's proprietary response models indicate that its use of information in these three categories to cull likely prospects accounts for approximately a 19 percent reduction in names from the annual prospect list. In other words, by targeting offers under current rules, about 150 million names on the prospect list during the course of a typical annual solicitation cycle do not receive solicitations, because the direct mail piece would otherwise reach a consumer who was either not interested or not qualified for the card product. . . .

[Under an opt-in approach,] approximately 550 million names would remain, instead of 400 million under the current rules. Lacking the information necessary to further distinguish good prospects from poor prospects, the company's targeting efficiency would be impaired.

MBNA would have two choices. It could increase its direct mail volume to send solicitations to all 550 million names remaining on the prospect list after the culling process, or it could arbitrarily remove 150 million names from the list after the culling process so that its direct mail volume remained unchanged at 400 million. Under either scenario, approximately 27 percent of the solicitations (150 million of 550 million) would go to consumers who were less interested in, and/or less qualified for, the offer, and who would have been dropped from the target list had MBNA been allowed to access and use the information on which its presently relies under current privacy rules. . . .

Although MBNA's actual response rate and cost per account booked is proprietary, we can illustrate the impact of the decline by utilizing the credit card industry average response rate to direct mail solicitations for 2000, which was 0.6 percent. For every 100 million solicitations mailed to individuals under the opt-in scenario, only 492 thousand new accounts would be booked, as compared to 600 thousand if the offers were targeted under existing rules, an 18 percent reduction in new accounts for the same expenditure on direct mail solicitations. Of course, the higher cost per account booked is borne not only by MBNA, but by MBNA's customers as well, in the form of higher prices, reduced benefits, diminished service, and higher acceptance standards for new credit products.

But, the negative impact does not stop there. Regardless of whether MBNA's response to opt-in is to mail more solicitations or mail the same number to a less-targeted prospect list, under either scenario, the recipient group of four hundred million individuals will — on average — be more risky and less profitable than MBNA's target group reached under the current rules. As a result, MBNA's delinquency and charge-off rates will rise, relative to its current experience, thereby imposing additional costs that will be passed along to all of MBNA's customers. Card usage will also be affected by booking cardholders who are less likely to use the card.

NOTES & QUESTIONS

1. *Opt out vs. Opt in.* Do you agree with Sovern that an opt-in policy is more efficient than an opt-out policy? Do you think that an opt-in policy is feasible? Are the views of Staten and Cate convincing on this score? Do you think opt out or opt in should be required by law?

2. *Internalizing Costs.* Staten and Cate claim that MBNA's business model will be threatened by opt in. This business model relies in part, however, on sending out 400 million of mostly unwanted solicitations for credit in order to receive a 0.6 percent response rate. In other words, this model views as an externality the added cost of sorting through mail for 99.4 percent of those individuals solicited. Should MBNA be obliged to internalize these costs?

(b) Contract Law

A privacy policy can be thought of as a type of contract, though the terms are typically dictated by the company and are non-negotiable. Consider the following advice of Scott Killingsworth to the drafters of website privacy policies:

Considering enforcement leads to the question: what is the legal effect of a privacy policy? As between the website and the user, a privacy policy bears all of the earmarks of a contract, but perhaps one enforceable only at the option of the user. It is no stretch to regard the policy as an offer to treat information in specified ways, inviting the user's acceptance, evidenced by using the site or submitting the information. The website's promise and the user's use of the site and submission of personal data are each sufficient consideration to support a contractual obligation. Under this analysis, users would have the right to sue and seek all available remedies for breach of the privacy policy, without the need for private rights of action under such regulatory statutes as the FTC Act.[30]

Privacy policies can also be viewed simply as notices that warn consumers about the use of their personal information. Assuming that these notices are subject to change as business practices evolve, how effective are privacy policies as a means to protect privacy?

IN RE NORTHWEST AIRLINES PRIVACY LITIGATION

2004 WL 1278459 (D. Minn. 2004) (not reported in F. Supp. 2d)

MAGNUSON, J. . . . Plaintiffs are customers of Defendant Northwest Airlines, Inc. ("Northwest"). After September 11, 2001, the National Aeronautical and Space Administration ("NASA") requested that Northwest provide NASA with certain passenger information in order to assist NASA in studying ways to increase airline security. Northwest supplied NASA with passenger name records ("PNRs"), which are electronic records of passenger information. PNRs contain information such as a passenger's name, flight number, credit card data, hotel reservation, car rental, and any traveling companions.

Plaintiffs contend that Northwest's actions constitute violations of the Electronic Communications Privacy Act ("ECPA"), 18 U.S.C. § 2701 *et seq.*, the Fair Credit Reporting Act ("FCRA"), 15 U.S.C. § 1681, and Minnesota's Deceptive Trade Practices Act ("DTPA"), Minn. Stat. § 325D.44, and also constitute invasion of privacy, trespass to property, negligent misrepresentation, breach of contract, and breach of express warranties. The basis for most of Plaintiffs' claims is that Northwest's website contained a privacy policy that stated that Northwest would not share customers' information except as necessary to make customers' travel arrangements. Plaintiffs contend that Northwest's provision of PNRs to NASA violated Northwest's privacy policy, giving rise to the legal claims noted above.

Northwest has now moved to dismiss the Amended Consolidated Class Action Complaint (hereinafter "Amended Complaint"). . . .

The ECPA prohibits a person or entity from

(1) intentionally access[ing] without authorization a facility through which an electronic communication service is provided; or

(2) intentionally exceeds an authorization to access that facility; and thereby obtains, alters, or prevents authorized access to a wire or electronic

---

[30] Scott Killingsworth, *Minding Your Own Business: Privacy Policies in Principle and in Practice*, 7 J. Intell. Prop. L. 57, 91-92 (1999).

communication while it is in electronic storage in such system shall be punished. 18 U.S.C. § 2701(a).

Plaintiffs argue that Northwest's access to its own electronic communications service is limited by its privacy policy, and that Northwest's provision of PNRs to NASA violated that policy and thus constituted unauthorized access to the "facility through which an electronic communication service is provided" within the meaning of this section. Plaintiffs also allege that Northwest violated § 2702 of the ECPA, which states that "a person or entity providing an electronic communications service to the public shall not knowingly divulge to any person or entity the contents of a communication while in electronic storage by that service." 18 U.S.C. § 2702(a)(1). Northwest argues first that it cannot violate § 2702 because it is not a "person or entity providing an electronic communications service to the public." . . .

Defining electronic communications service to include online merchants or service providers like Northwest stretches the ECPA too far. Northwest is not an internet service provider. . . .

Similarly, Northwest's conduct as outlined in the Amended Complaint does not constitute a violation of § 2701. Plaintiffs' claim is that Northwest improperly disclosed the information in PNRs to NASA. Section 2701 does not prohibit improper disclosure of information. Rather, this section prohibits improper access to an electronic communications service provider or the information contained on that service provider. . . .

Finally, Northwest argues that Plaintiffs' remaining claims fail to state a claim on which relief can be granted. These claims are: trespass to property, intrusion upon seclusion, breach of contract, and breach of express warranties.

To state a claim for trespass to property, Plaintiffs must demonstrate that they owned or possessed property, that Northwest wrongfully took that property, and that Plaintiffs were damaged by the wrongful taking. Plaintiffs contend that the information contained in the PNRs was Plaintiffs' property and that, by providing that information to NASA, Northwest wrongfully took that property.

As a matter of law, the PNRs were not Plaintiffs' property. Plaintiffs voluntarily provided some information that was included in the PNRs. It may be that the information Plaintiffs provided to Northwest was Plaintiffs' property. However, when that information was compiled and combined with other information to form a PNR, the PNR itself became Northwest's property. Northwest cannot wrongfully take its own property. Thus, Plaintiffs' claim for trespass fails. . . .

Intrusion upon seclusion exists when someone "intentionally intrudes, physically or otherwise, upon the solitude or seclusion of another or his private affairs or concerns . . . if the intrusion would be highly offensive to a reasonable person." . . . In this instance, Plaintiffs voluntarily provided their personal information to Northwest. Moreover, although Northwest had a privacy policy for information included on the website, Plaintiffs do not contend that they actually read the privacy policy prior to providing Northwest with their personal information. Thus, Plaintiffs' expectation of privacy was low. Further, the disclosure here was not to the public at large, but rather was to a government agency in the wake of a terrorist attack that called into question the security of the nation's transportation system. Northwest's motives in disclosing the information cannot be questioned. Taking into account all of the factors listed above, the Court finds as a matter of law that the disclosure of Plaintiffs' personal information would not be highly offensive to a reasonable person and that Plaintiffs have failed to state a claim for intrusion upon seclusion. . . .

Northwest contends that the privacy policy on Northwest's website does not, as a matter of law, constitute a unilateral contract, the breach of which entitles Plaintiffs to damages. Northwest also argues that, even if the privacy policy constituted a contract or express warranty, Plaintiffs' contract and warranty claims fail because Plaintiffs have failed to plead any contract damages. . . .

Plaintiffs' rely on the following statement from Northwest's website as the basis for their contract and warranty claims:

> When you reserve or purchase travel services through Northwest Airlines nwa.com Reservations, we provide only the relevant information required by the car rental agency, hotel, or other involved third party to ensure the successful fulfillment of your travel arrangements. . . .

The usual rule in contract cases is that "general statements of policy are not contractual." . . .

The privacy statement on Northwest's website did not constitute a unilateral contract. The language used vests discretion in Northwest to determine when the information is "relevant" and which "third parties" might need that information. Moreover, absent an allegation that Plaintiffs actually read the privacy policy, not merely the general allegation that Plaintiffs "relied on" the policy, Plaintiffs have failed to allege an essential element of a contract claim: that the alleged "offer" was accepted by Plaintiffs. Plaintiffs' contract and warranty claims fail as a matter of law.

Even if the privacy policy was sufficiently definite and Plaintiffs had alleged that they read the policy before giving their information to Northwest, it is likely that Plaintiffs' contract and warranty claims would fail as a matter of law. Defendants point out that Plaintiffs have failed to allege any contractual damages arising out of the alleged breach. . . .

[The case is dismissed.]

NOTES & QUESTIONS

1. ***Breach of Contract.*** In *Dyer v. Northwest Airlines Corp.*, 334 F. Supp. 2d 1196 (D.N.D. 2004), another action involving Northwest Airlines' disclosure of passenger records to the government, the court reached a similar conclusion on the plaintiffs' breach of contract claim:

> To sustain a breach of contract claim, the Plaintiffs must demonstrate (1) the existence of a contract; (2) breach of the contract; and (3) damages which flow from the breach. . . .
> . . . [T]he Court finds the Plaintiffs' breach of contract claim fails as a matter of law. First, broad statements of company policy do not generally give rise to contract claims. . . . Second, nowhere in the complaint are the Plaintiffs alleged to have ever logged onto Northwest Airlines' website and accessed, read, understood, actually relied upon, or otherwise considered Northwest

Airlines' privacy policy. Finally, even if the privacy policy was sufficiently definite and the Plaintiffs had alleged they did read the policy prior to providing personal information to Northwest Airlines, the Plaintiffs have failed to allege any contractual damages arising out of the alleged breach.

2. ***Damages.*** In *In re Jet Blue Airways Corp. Privacy Litigation*, 379 F. Supp. 2d 299 (E.D.N.Y. 2005), a group of plaintiffs sued Jet Blue Airlines for breach of contract for sharing passenger records with the government. The court granted Jet Blue's motion to dismiss:

> An action for breach of contract under New York law requires proof of four elements: (1) the existence of a contract, (2) performance of the contract by one party, (3) breach by the other party, and (4) damages. . . .
>
> JetBlue . . . argues that plaintiffs have failed to meet their pleading requirement with respect to damages, citing an absence of any facts in the Amended Complaint to support this element of the claim. Plaintiffs' sole allegation on the element of contract damages consists of the statement that JetBlue's breach of the company privacy policy injured plaintiffs and members of the class and that JetBlue is therefore liable for "actual damages in an amount to be determined at trial." . . . At oral argument, when pressed to identify the "injuries" or damages referred to in the Amended Complaint, counsel for plaintiffs stated that the "contract damage could be the loss of privacy," acknowledging that loss of privacy "may" be a contract damage. It is apparent based on the briefing and oral argument held in this case that the sparseness of the damages allegations is a direct result of plaintiffs' inability to plead or prove any actual contract damages. As plaintiffs' counsel concedes, the only damage that can be read into the present complaint is a loss of privacy. At least one recent case has specifically held that this is not a damage available in a breach of contract action. *See Trikas v. Universal Card Services Corp.,* 351 F. Supp. 2d 37 (E.D.N.Y. 2005). This holding naturally follows from the well-settled principle that "recovery in contract, unlike recovery in tort, allows only for economic losses flowing directly from the breach."
>
> Plaintiffs allege that in a second amended complaint, they could assert as a contract damage the loss of the economic value of their information, but while that claim sounds in economic loss, the argument ignores the nature of the contract asserted. . . . [T]he "purpose of contract damages is to put a plaintiff in the same economic position he or she would have occupied had the contract been fully performed." Plaintiffs may well have expected that in return for providing their personal information to JetBlue and paying the purchase price, they would obtain a ticket for air travel and the promise that their personal information would be safeguarded consistent with the terms of the privacy policy. They had no reason to expect that they would be compensated for the "value" of their personal information. In addition, there is absolutely no support for the proposition that the personal information of an individual JetBlue passenger had any value for which that passenger could have expected to be compensated. . . . There is likewise no support for the proposition that an individual passenger's personal information has or had any compensable value in the economy at large.

If you were the plaintiffs' attorney, how would you go about establishing the plaintiffs' injury? Is there any cognizable harm when an airline violates its privacy policy by providing passenger information to the government?

3. *Promissory Estoppel.* According to the Restatement (Second) of Contracts § 90:

> A promise which the promisor should reasonably expect to induce action or forbearance on the part of the promisee or a third person and which does induce such action or forbearance is binding if injustice can be avoided only by enforcement of the promise. The remedy granted for breach may be limited as justice requires.

If website privacy policies are not deemed to be contracts, can they be enforced under the promissory estoppel doctrine?

4. *Breach of Confidentiality Tort.* Would the plaintiffs have a cause of action based on the breach of confidentiality tort?

5. *Enforcing Privacy Policies as Contracts Against Consumers.* Suppose privacy policies were enforceable as contracts. Would this be beneficial to consumers? It might not be, Allyson Haynes argues:

> [T]here is a distinct possibility that as website operators grow savvier with respect to the law, they will respond to the lack of substantive privacy protection (and lack of consumer awareness) by including in privacy policies terms that are not favorable to consumers.

On the flip side of consumers seeking to enforce privacy policies as contracts, companies might also desire to hold customers to be contractually bound to the companies' privacy policies. Would a privacy policy be enforceable as a contract against the customer? Haynes contends:

> [P]articularly in cases where consumers are deemed to have assented to privacy policies by virtue of their presence on the site or by giving information without affirmatively clicking acceptance, the consumer has a good argument that he or she did not assent to the privacy policy, preventing the formation of a binding contract, and preventing the website from enforcing any of its terms against the consumer.[31]

6. *Promises of Anonymity.* In *Saffold v. Plain Dealer Publishing Co.,* a state court judge (Shirley Strickland Saffold) sued the Cleveland Plain Dealer for stating that comments posted on the newspaper's website under the screen name "lawmiss" originated from a computer used by the judge and her daughter. Some of these comments related to cases before Judge Saffold. Judge Saffold claimed that the newspaper's disclosure of the identity of "lawmiss" violated its website's privacy policy, which stated that "personally identifiable information is protected." Moreover, the user agreement that was part of the registration process to create an account on the website incorporated the privacy policy. The case was settled before any judicial

---

[31] Allyson W. Haynes, *Online Privacy Policies: Contracting Away Control Over Personal Information?*, 111 Penn. St. L. Rev. 587, 612, 618 (2007).

decision was issued. Suppose, however, the litigation had proceeded. Would Judge Saffold have a claim for breach of contract or promissory estoppel?

7. *Website Communities and Promissory Estoppel.* Consider Woodrow Hartzog:

> Suppose a person improperly provides others with access to a friend's Facebook profile. Suppose a member of a dating website copies another's dating profile and discloses the information to the general public. Or suppose a member of an online support community for recovering alcoholics reveals the names and other personal information of other members. Should members of an online community be able to expect and legally enforce the confidentiality of their data? . . .
>
> I contend that the law can ensure confidentiality for members of online communities through promissory estoppel. . . .
>
> One of the immediate difficulties with using promissory estoppel is that members of online communities have not made agreements between each other. They have merely agreed to the terms of use of the website and community. Suppose Member A of an online community discloses the private information of Member B. Would Member B be able to sue Member A for promissory estoppel even though Member A never made a direct promise to Member B?
>
> In order to allow all users within the community the ability to rely on promises of confidentiality, I propose application of either the third-party beneficiary doctrine or the concept of dual agency effectuated through a website's terms of use. Although the implementation of promissory estoppel in this context would be challenging, I conclude that the promissory estoppel theory for confidential disclosure could have positive practical effects and advance both privacy and free speech objectives.[32]

What are the pros and cons of Hartzog's proposal? Should members of online communities have any obligations to each other?

8. *Are Website Privacy Settings Part of a Contract?* Woodrow Hartzog contends that website privacy settings and other design features should be considered as part of the contract between the website and the user:

> When courts seek to determine a website user's privacy expectations and the website's promises to that user, they almost invariably look to the terms of use agreement or to the privacy policy. They rarely look to the privacy settings or other elements of a website where users specify their privacy preferences. These settings and elements are typically not considered to be part of any contract or promise to the user. Yet studies have shown that few users actually read or rely upon terms of service or privacy policies. In contrast, users regularly take advantage of and rely upon privacy settings. . . . [T]o the extent website design is incorporated into or consistent with a website's terms of use, or to the extent website design induces reliance, courts should consider these design features as enforceable promises.[33]

Facebook and other social media websites, for example, have privacy settings that allow users to establish how broadly their information will be

---

[32] Woodrow Hartzog, *Promises and Privacy: Promissory Estoppel and Confidential Disclosure in Online Communities*, 82 Temp. L. Rev. 891, 893-96 (2009).

[33] Woodrow Hartzog, *Website Design as Contract,* 60 Am. U. L. Rev. __ (2011).

shared. If Facebook were to expose a person's information more broadly than he set it in his privacy settings, could that be the basis of a contract or promissory estoppel lawsuit? What other design elements might be considered to be part of a website's contract or promise with a user?

9. ***Contract and Morality.*** In Canada, Gabrielle Nagy sued her cellphone company, Rogers Communications, for breach of contract when it incorporated her cell phone bill into the family phone bill. The result was that her husband discovered that she was frequently calling another man. Nagy eventually confessed to her husband that she was having an affair, and they divorced. Consider David Hoffman:

> I think the breach of contract lawsuit, if filed in an American court applying fairly ordinary domestic contract principles, would be a loser. . . .
>
> The common law generally dislikes punishing breach with liability or damages when the inevitable consequence of performance is to motivate socially wrongful conduct, and nonperformance to retard it. . . .
>
> What about cases where A and B contract not to disclose some fact X, and the nondisclosure will create harm for innocent third parties. These contracts are often enforced (every confidentiality clause probably shelters some fact with the potential for third party harm). But the degree to which the nonbreaching party can recover ought to turn on what's being kept secret: if the secret is particularly socially harmful (oozing toxic sludge!) we might believe that the hiding, non-breaching, party doesn't get to recover for breach. Thus, you sometimes see cases where fraud-revealing employees are protected from consequences of nondisclosure agreements by (effectively) common law whistleblower doctrines.
>
> Where the third-party harm *relates to marriage*, the law appears to be more categorical. Public policy concerns about contracting and third party harm are strongest in agreements touching on issues of family life and infidelity.[34]

Is Hoffman correct that such a breach of contract case would lose under American law? Should courts choose which contracts to enforce based on morality? If a company breaches a contract and reveals that a person is doing something immoral, should that breach go unremedied?

(c) FTC Enforcement

Beyond private law actions such as contract and promissory estoppel, the promises that companies make regarding their privacy practices can be enforced by the government through public law. Private law actions are initiated on behalf of harmed individuals, who can obtain monetary or other redress for their injuries. In contrast, public law actions are initiated by government agencies or officials, and they typically involve fines and penalties.

In 1995, Congress and privacy experts first asked the Federal Trade Commission (FTC) to become involved with consumer privacy issues.[35] Since

---

[34] David Hoffman, *Contracts and Privacy,* Concurring Opinions (June 21, 2010), http://www.concurringopinions.com/archives/2010/06/contracts-and-privacy.html.

[35] Letter from EPIC Director Marc Rotenberg to FTC Commissioner Christine Varney, Dec. 14, 1995.

1998, the FTC has maintained the position that the use or dissemination of personal information in a manner contrary to a posted privacy policy is a deceptive practice under the FTC Act, 15 U.S.C. § 45. The Act prohibits "unfair or deceptive acts or practices in or affecting commerce." An "unfair or deceptive" act or practice is one that "causes or is likely to cause substantial injury to consumers which is not reasonably avoidable by consumers themselves and not outweighed by countervailing benefits to consumers or to competition." § 45(n).

The FTC does not have jurisdiction over all companies. Exempt from the FTC's jurisdiction are many types of financial institutions, airlines, telecommunications carriers, and other types of entities. § 45(a)(2). The Act authorizes the FTC to bring civil actions for penalties up to $10,000 for a knowing violation of the Act. § 45(m)(1)(A). Further, the FTC can obtain injunctive remedies. § 53. The Act does not provide for private causes of action; only the FTC can enforce the Act. Since it began enforcing the Act for breaches of privacy policies in 1998, the FTC has brought a number of actions, most of which have settled. Some of these enforcement cases concern companies not keeping their privacy promises.

IN THE MATTER OF GOOGLE INC.

2011 WL 1321658 (F.T.C. 2011)

---

3. Google is a technology company best known for its web-based search engine, which provides free search results to consumers. Google also provides various free web products to consumers, including its widely used web-based email service, Gmail, which has been available since April 2004. . . .

6. Respondent has disseminated or caused to be disseminated statements to consumers on its website regarding its privacy practices, including but not limited to:

a. From approximately October 2004 until October 2010, the following statement in the Gmail Privacy Policy about Google's use of consumer information provided through Gmail:

> Gmail stores, processes and maintains your messages, contact lists and other data related to your account in order to provide the service to you.

b. From approximately October 2005 until October 2010, the following statement in Google's Privacy Policy regarding consumers' choices about the uses of their personal information in all of Google's products, including Gmail:

> When you sign up for a particular service that requires registration, we ask you to provide personal information. If we use this information in a manner different than the purpose for which it was collected, then we will ask for your consent prior to such use.

RESPONDENT'S LAUNCH OF GOOGLE BUZZ

7. On February 9, 2010, Google launched a social networking service called Google Buzz ("Google Buzz" or "Buzz") within the Gmail product. Google Buzz is a platform that allows users to share updates, comments, photos, videos, and other information through posts or "buzzes" made either publicly or privately to individuals or groups of users. Google used the information of consumers who signed up for Gmail, including first and last name and email contacts, to populate the social network. Without prior notice or the opportunity to consent, Gmail users were, in many instances, automatically set up with "followers" (people following the user). In addition, after enrolling in Buzz, Gmail users were automatically set up to "follow" other users.

8. On the day Buzz was launched, Gmail users who signed into their accounts were taken to a welcome screen that announced the new service and highlighted features such as: "No set up needed — You're already following the people you email and chat with the most in Gmail." Gmail users had to elect one of two options to proceed to their inboxes: "Sweet! Check out Buzz" or "Nah, go to my inbox." . . .

a. If a Gmail user selected "Nah, go to my inbox" from the initial Buzz screen, that user's information was nonetheless shared in a number of ways:

i. The user could be "followed" by other Gmail users who had enrolled in Buzz.

ii. If the user had previously created a public Google profile, the user could appear on the public Google profiles of people who had enrolled in Buzz and were following the user.

iii. A Buzz link would appear in the list of links on the user's Gmail page. If the user clicked on the that link, he or she would be taken to the Buzz welcome screen and automatically enrolled in Buzz, without any disclosure of that fact and without any further action on the user's part. . .
.

b. Regardless of whether they chose "Sweet! Check out Buzz" or "Nah, go to my inbox," Gmail users had an option to click a "Turn off Buzz" link, contained in small type at the bottom of the Gmail home page after login. Clicking that link removed the Buzz tab from the user's Gmail page. Gmail users who had clicked "Sweet! Check out Buzz" or had clicked on the Buzz link in Gmail, then later clicked the "Turn off Buzz" link, nonetheless continued to appear as a "follower" on the Google profiles and Google Buzz pages of the people whom they emailed the most. In addition, on each such profile, a "follow" link was placed next to the Gmail user's name, so other individuals could begin following the user.

9. The setup process for Gmail users who enrolled in Buzz did not adequately communicate that certain previously private information would be shared publicly by default. Further, the controls that would allow the user to change the defaults were confusing and difficult to find.

10. Certain personal information of Gmail users was shared without consumers' permission through the Google Buzz social network. . . .

11. In response to the launch of Google Buzz, many users complained about the automatic generation of lists of followers and people to follow from email

contact lists that included in some cases: individuals against whom they had obtained restraining orders; abusive ex-husbands; clients of mental health professionals; clients of attorneys; children; and recruiters they had emailed regarding job leads. Further, because of the default settings and the complex and multi-step nature of respondent's disclosures described in paragraph 9, consumers were confused about what information was made public through Buzz and complained about the potential disclosure of private email addresses.

12. Following widespread public criticism and thousands of consumer complaints, Google made certain changes to the Buzz service. Among other things, Google: (1) gave users the ability to effectively disable or turn off Buzz; (2) switched from setting up Gmail users with an automatic list of people to follow to suggesting a list of people to follow for users to approve; (3) made the process for editing lists of followers and people to follow clearer and more easily accessible; (4) made it possible for users to block any follower, regardless of whether that follower had a public profile; (5) made the option not to show lists of followers on a user's public profile more prominent; (6) discontinued the feature that automatically connected to information from other websites, such as Picasa and Google Reader; and (7) fixed the @ reply function so that private email addresses of users would not be made public.

13. As set forth in paragraph 6(a), respondent has represented, expressly or by implication, that it used, and would use, information from consumers signing up for Gmail only for the purpose of providing them with a web-based email service.

14. In truth and in fact, as described in paragraphs 7-11, respondent did not use information from consumers signing up for Gmail only for the purpose of providing them with a web-based email service. Instead, Google used this information to populate its new social networking service. Therefore, the representations set forth in paragraph 13 were, and are, false or misleading and constitute a deceptive act or practice.

15. As set forth in paragraph 6(b), respondent has represented, expressly or by implication, that it would seek consumers' consent to use information they provided for a purpose other than that for which it was collected.

16. In truth and in fact, as described in paragraphs 7-11, respondent did not seek consumers' consent before using the information they provided in connection with Gmail for the Google Buzz social networking product. Therefore, the representations set forth in paragraph 15 were, and are, false or misleading and constitute a deceptive act or practice.

17. As set forth in paragraph 8, by offering the option "Nah, go to my inbox," as well as the option to "Turn off Buzz," respondent has represented, expressly or by implication, that consumers who clicked on these options would not be enrolled in Buzz.

18. In truth and in fact, . . . consumers who clicked on these options were enrolled in certain features of Buzz. Therefore, the representations set forth in paragraph 17 were, and are, false and misleading and constitute a deceptive act or practice.

19. As set forth in paragraph 9, respondent represented, expressly or by implication, through the Buzz enrollment screens and statements such as "How do you want to appear to others?" that consumers would be able to exercise

control over what information would be made public through their Google public profile. Respondent failed to disclose, or failed to disclose adequately, that in most instances the contacts with whom users emailed and chatted the most would become public by default and that user information submitted through other Google products would be automatically broadcast through Buzz. These facts would be material to consumers in their enrolment in and use of the Google Buzz service. Therefore, respondent's failure to adequately disclose these facts, in light of the representations made, was, and is, a deceptive act or practice.

U.S.-EU SAFE HARBOR FRAMEWORK

20. The U.S.-EU Safe Harbor Framework provides a method for U.S. companies to transfer personal data outside of the European Union ("EU") that is consistent with the requirements of the European Union Data Protection Directive ("Directive"). The Directive sets forth EU requirements for privacy and the protection of personal data. Among other things, it requires EU Member States to implement legislation that prohibits the transfer of personal data outside the EU, with exceptions, unless the European Commission ("EC") has made a determination that the recipient jurisdiction's laws ensure the protection of such personal data. This determination is commonly referred to as meeting the EU's "adequacy" standard.

21. To satisfy the EU's adequacy standard for certain commercial transfers, the U.S. Department of Commerce ("Commerce") and the EC negotiated the U.S.-EU Safe Harbor Framework, which went into effect in 2000. The Safe Harbor is a voluntary framework that allows U.S. companies to transfer personal data lawfully from the EU to the U.S. To join the Safe Harbor, a company must self-certify to Commerce that it complies with seven principles and related requirements that have been deemed to meet the EU's adequacy standard. [Among the Safe Harbor privacy principles are "notice" and "choice."]

23. From October 2005 until the present, Google has maintained a current self-certification to Commerce and has appeared on the list of Safe Harbor companies on the Commerce website. Prior to the launch of the Buzz social networking product, Google transferred data collected from Gmail users in Europe to the United States for processing. . . .

25. In truth and in fact, as described in paragraph 7, respondent did not adhere to the US Safe Harbor Privacy Principles of Notice and Choice. In particular, respondent did not give Gmail users notice before using the information collected for Gmail for a purpose other than that for which it was originally collected. Respondent also did not give Gmail users choice about using their information for a purpose that was incompatible with the purpose for which it was originally collected. Therefore, the representations [that Google made about following the Safe Harbor principles] were, and are, false or misleading and constitute a deceptive act or practice. . . .

ORDER

I. IT IS ORDERED that respondent, in or affecting commerce, shall not misrepresent in any manner, expressly or by implication:

A. the extent to which respondent maintains and protects the privacy and confidentiality of any covered information, including, but not limited to, misrepresentations related to: (1) the purposes for which it collects and uses covered information, and (2) the extent to which consumers may exercise control over the collection, use, or disclosure of covered information.

B. the extent to which respondent is a member of, adheres to, complies with, is certified by, is endorsed by, or otherwise participates in any privacy, security, or any other compliance program sponsored by the government or any other entity, including, but not limited to, the U.S.-EU Safe Harbor Framework.

II. IT IS FURTHER ORDERED that respondent, prior to any new or additional sharing by respondent of the Google user's identified information with any third party, that: 1) is a change from stated sharing practices in effect at the time respondent collected such information, and 2) results from any change, addition, or enhancement to a product or service by respondent, in or affecting commerce, shall:

A. Separate and apart from any final "end user license agreement," "privacy policy," "terms of use" page, or similar document, clearly and prominently disclose: (1) that the Google user's information will be disclosed to one or more third parties, (2) the identity or specific categories of such third parties, and (3) the purpose(s) for respondent's sharing; and

B. Obtain express affirmative consent from the Google user to such sharing.

III. IT IS FURTHER ORDERED that respondent, in or affecting commerce, shall, no later than the date of service of this order, establish and implement, and thereafter maintain, a comprehensive privacy program that is reasonably designed to: (1) address privacy risks related to the development and management of new and existing products and services for consumers, and (2) protect the privacy and confidentiality of covered information. Such program, the content and implementation of which must be documented in writing, shall contain privacy controls and procedures appropriate to respondent's size and complexity, the nature and scope of respondent's activities, and the sensitivity of the covered information . . . .

IV. IT IS FURTHER ORDERED that, in connection with its compliance with Part III of this order, respondent shall obtain initial and biennial assessments and reports ("Assessments") from a qualified, objective, independent third-party professional, who uses procedures and standards generally accepted in the profession. . . . The reporting period for the Assessments shall cover: (1) the first one hundred and eighty (180) days after service of the order for the initial Assessment, and (2) each two (2) year period thereafter for twenty (20) years after service of the order for the biennial Assessments. . . .

IX. This order will terminate twenty (20) years from the date of its issuance, or twenty (20) years from the most recent date that the United States or the Commission files a complaint (with or without an accompanying consent decree) in federal court alleging any violation of the order, whichever comes later. . . .

NOTES & QUESTIONS

1. *Broken Promises, Deception, and the US-EU Safe Harbor.* Like other "broken promise" privacy cases, the FTC charged Google with breaking its own representations that it would provide certain kinds of privacy practices or protections. Google promised that Gmail would process data related to the account to provide the service. It stated that if it used information in any of its services that required registration in a different manner than the purpose for which it was collected, the company would obtain consent from the user. The FTC alleged that Google's launch of Google Buzz violated these promises and it was therefore engaged in a deceptive act or practice under the FTC Act.

   Beyond its status as a "broken promise" FTC action, the *Google* settlement represents the first time that the FTC enforced the US-EU Safe Harbor Arrangement. See Chapter 9 for more coverage of the Safe Harbor Arrangement. Google's failure to provide notice and consent as it had promised when it self-certified for the Safe Harbor was deemed a deceptive act or practice.

   Note as well that Google, at least arguably, engaged in self-correction of its mistakes in the launch of Buzz. Nonetheless, the deceptive act or practice had taken place, and the FTC launched its investigation. In the settlement, the FTC did not require Google to pay any monetary damages, but did have Google agree to end any misrepresentations of its privacy practices, to provide greater transparency about its practices involving sharing of information, and to develop "a comprehensive privacy program." This was the first time that the FTC has ordered the development of a comprehensive privacy program. What should such a program entail? How is it to be evaluated? Also note that the FTC settlement order lasts for 20 years. This is the common duration of FTC settlement orders for privacy violations. Is such a long duration necessary?

2. *Unfairness, Deception, and Retroactive Changes.* The FTC has also found some data practices to be unfair under the FTC Act. The FTC Act classifies a trade practice as unfair if it "causes or is likely to cause substantial injury to consumers which is not reasonably avoidable by consumers themselves and is not outweighed by countervailing benefits to consumers or competition." 15 U.S.C. § 45(n). Actions of a company can be both deceptive and unfair.

   For example, Gateway Learning Corp. collected personal information from its consumers pursuant to a privacy policy stating that it would not sell, rent, or loan personal information to third parties unless people consented. It also promised that if it changed its privacy policy, it would give consumers the opportunity to "opt out" of having their data shared.

   Subsequently, Gateway altered its privacy policy to allow the renting of personal information to third parties without informing customers and obtaining their explicit consent. The FTC filed a complaint alleging that this practice was an unfair and deceptive act. *See In re Gateway Learning Corp.,* No. C-4120 (Sept. 10, 2004). According to the FTC, Gateway's retroactive application of a materially changed privacy policy to information that it had previously collected constituted an unfair practice. The FTC also charged that

Gateway's failure to inform consumers of its changes to its privacy policies, despite its promises to do so, constituted a deceptive practice. Gateway settled with the FTC, agreeing that it would "not misrepresent ... [t]he manner in which [it] will collect, use, or disclose personal information." It also agreed to pay $4,608, which was the amount it earned from renting the information.

Suppose a company puts the following line in its privacy policy: "Please be aware that we may change this policy at any time." Would this allow for the retroactive application of a revised policy? Or is there an argument that even with a statement such as this one, the revised policy could not be applied retroactively?

3. ***Transparency.*** The FTC is also beginning to develop elements of a broader approach to privacy based on a "transparency" approach. Its policing of privacy notices and enforcement of adequate security already move in this direction. More broadly, however, the agency has begun to develop substantive notices of disclosure beyond its "broken promises" approach.

Thus, in an enforcement action against Sears, which was settled in 2009, the FTC alleged that Sears had engaged in an unfair practice by failing to adequately disclose the extent of its tracking of customers who were paid to use a program that would record their Internet browsing. *In re Sears Holdings Management Corporation*, No. 082 3099 (Sept. 9, 2009). Sears had invited website users to "participate in exciting, engaging, and on-going interactions—always on your terms and always by your choice." The FTC acted even though Sears had provided users with a long license agreement that, albeit with obscure language, arguably informed users of the tracking. The FTC charged that Sears's failure to provide adequate disclosure of the scope of the data collection was a deceptive act. Its settlement order required Sears to destroy all data collected and to provide clear and prominent disclosure of "the types of data the [software] will monitor, record, or transmit" before the software is installed and apart from the user license agreement.

The FTC's enforcement of transparency continued in 2010 with a settlement against EchoMetrix. *Federal Trade Commission v. EchoMetrix, Inc.*, Civ. No. CV10-5516 (E.D.N.Y. Nov. 30, 2010). In that case, "parental controls" software led to the secret collection of data about children's computer activity and the feeding of the resulting database to marketers. The FTC's theory of the case was that the disclosure of the tracking at stake in the case was inadequate.

4. ***Privacy Promises and Bankruptcy:*** **Toysmart** *and* **Amazon.com.** In *FTC v. Toysmart.com, LLC*, Civ. Action No. 00-11341-RGS (July 21, 2000), an Internet toy retailer, Toysmart.com, went bankrupt in 2000. One of the company's most important assets was its database of personal information — it had a customer list with over 200,000 individual names. This list included addresses, names and ages of children, purchasing information, and a toy wish list. Toysmart was a member of TRUSTe, an e-commerce industry privacy protection organization that establishes rules for privacy policies and permits companies that follow them to display TRUSTe's privacy seal. Toysmart had

agreed to follow TRUSTe's guidelines and had displayed the TRUSTe seal on its website.

In its privacy policy, Toysmart promised: "Personal information voluntarily submitted by visitors to our site, such as name, address, billing information and shopping preferences, is never shared with a third party. All information obtained by toysmart.com is used only to personalize your experience online." To pay back creditors, Toysmart attempted to sell its database of personal information.

The FTC filed a complaint objecting to this practice and argued that such a sale, in light of Toysmart's promises never to sell its customer's personal information, would be a deceptive practice. The FTC approved a settlement by a 3–2 vote restricting how Toysmart could sell its database. The settlement states that:

> The Debtor shall only assign or sell its Customer Information as part of the sale of its Goodwill and only to a Qualified Buyer approved by the Bankruptcy Court. In the process of approving any sale of the Customer Information, the Bankruptcy Court shall require that the Qualified Buyer agree to and comply with the terms of this Stipulation.
>
> The Qualified Buyer shall treat Customer Information in accordance with the terms of the Privacy Statement and shall be responsible for any violation by it following the date of purchase. Among other things, the Qualified Buyer shall use Customer Information only to fulfill customer orders and to personalize customers' experience on the Web site, and shall not disclose, sell or transfer Customer Information to any Third Party.
>
> If the Qualified Buyer materially changes the Privacy Statement, prior notice will be posted on the Web site. Any such material change in policy shall apply only to information collected following the change in policy. The Customer Information shall be governed by the Privacy Statement, unless the consumer provides affirmative consent ("opt-in") to the previously collected information being governed by the new policy. . . .

Is this settlement adequate to resolve the problems raised by the FTC in its complaint? As a postscript, one should note that the settlement attracted the support of Toysmart's creditors, since it would allow the sale of the database to certain purchasers, and hence could be used to pay back the creditors. However, in August 2000, Judge Carol Kenner of the U.S. Bankruptcy Court rejected the settlement because there were currently no offers on the table to buy the database, and it would hurt the creditors to restrict the sale to certain types of purchasers without first having a potential buyer. In February 2001, Judge Kenner agreed to let Toysmart sell its customer database to Disney, the primary shareholder, for $50,000. Disney agreed, as part of the deal, to destroy the list.

The Toysmart bankruptcy also led Amazon.com, the Internet's largest retailer, to change its privacy policy. Prior to the Toysmart case, Amazon's privacy policy provided:

> Amazon.com does not sell, trade, or rent your personal information to others. We may choose to do so in the future with trustworthy third parties, but you can tell us not to by sending a blank e-mail message to never@amazon.com.

In its new policy, Amazon.com stated:

> Information about our customers is an important part of our business, and we are not in the business of selling it to others. We share customer information only with the subsidiaries Amazon.com, Inc., controls and as described below. . . .
>
> As we continue to develop our business, we might sell or buy stores or assets. In such transactions, customer information generally is one of the transferred business assets. Also, in the unlikely event that Amazon.com, Inc., or substantially all of its assets are acquired, customer information will of course be one of the transferred assets. . . .

Amazon.com's new policy was criticized by some privacy organizations. One of the criticisms was that the policy did not provide an opt-out right. Suppose Amazon.com went bankrupt and decided to sell all of its customer data. Can it sell data supplied by consumers under the old policy? Can the new policy apply retroactively?

5. ***Bankruptcy: Property Rights vs. Contract Rights.*** Edward Janger proposes that a property rights regime (as opposed to the contractual rights of a privacy policy) will best protect the privacy of personal data when companies possessing such data go bankrupt:

> Property rules are viewed as reflecting undivided entitlements. They allocate, as Carol Rose puts it, the "whole meatball" to the "owner." Liability rules, by contrast are viewed as dividing an entitlement between two parties. One party holds the right, but the other party is given the option to take the right and compensate the right holder for the deprivation (to breach and pay damages). . . .
>
> Propertization has some crucial benefits, but it also has some serious costs. Both the bankruptcy and non-bankruptcy treatment of privacy policies turn on whether a privacy policy creates a right enforceable only through civil damages, or a right with the status of property. If bankruptcy courts treat privacy policies solely as contract obligations [the liability rule], the debtor will be free to breach (or reject) the contract in bankruptcy. Any damage claim will be treated as a prepetition claim, paid, if at all, at a significant discount. Consumer expectations (contractual or otherwise) of privacy are likely to be defeated. By contrast, if personal information is deemed property subject to an encumbrance, then the property interest must be respected, or to use the bankruptcy term, "adequately protected."

In other words, Janger contends that giving individuals property rights in their personal data will provide more protection than giving individuals contract rights in the event a company goes bankrupt.[36]

6. ***Customer Databases as Collateral.*** Xuan-Thao Nguyen points out that companies are using their customer databases as collateral for loans, since these databases are one of their most significant assets:

> Whether intentional or unintentional, many Internet companies ignore their own privacy policy statements when the companies pledge their customer

---

[36] Edward J. Janger, *Muddy Property: Generating and Protecting Information Privacy Norms in Bankruptcy*, 44 Wm. & Mary L. Rev. 1801 (2002).

database as collateral in secured financing schemes. This practice renders on-line privacy statements misleading because the statements are silent on collateralization of the company's assets. . . .

The secured party can use the consumer database in its business or sell the consumer database to others. The collateralization of the consumer database and its end result may contradict the debtor's consumer privacy statement declaring that the debtor does not sell or lease the consumer information to others. Though there is no direct sale of the consumer database to the secured party, the effect of the collateralization of the consumer database is the same: the consumer database is in the hands of third parties with unfettered control and rights. Essentially, the collateralization of consumer databases violates the privacy policies publicized on debtors' Web sites.[37]

7. *The FTC as an Enforcer of Privacy: An Assessment.* In 2000, Steven Hetcher assessed the FTC's behavior in enforcing privacy in these terms:

> By the Agency's lights, its promotion of the fair practice principles should satisfy privacy advocates, as the fair information practice principles are derived from pre-existing norms of the advocacy community. Public interest advocates contend to the contrary, however, that privacy policies ill serve their aspirational privacy norms. They argue that privacy policies are typically not read by website users. They are written in legalese such that even if people read them, they will not understand them. Hence, they do not provide notice and thus cannot lead to consent. In addition, there is evidence that many sites do not adhere to their own policies. The policies are subject to change when companies merge, such that one company's policy is likely to go unheeded. Finally, very few privacy policies guarantee security or enforcement. Thus, the provision of a privacy policy by a website does not automatically promote the fair practice principles.
>
> Despite these problems, the FTC has strongly endorsed privacy policies. This raises a puzzle as to why the Agency should do so, given the severe criticism privacy policies have received. Why, for instance, is the FTC not coming out in support of the creation of a new agency to oversee privacy protection? . . .
>
> There is a public choice answer as to why the Agency has promoted privacy policies, despite their problems (and despite the fact that they do not appear to promote the interests of any industry groups whose favor the FTC might be seeking). It is through privacy policies that the FTC is gaining jurisdiction over the commercial Internet. Jurisdiction is power. In other words, the FTC acts as if it has a plan to migrate its activities to the Internet, and privacy policies have been at the core of this plan. . . .[38]

After the writings by Hetcher, however, the FTC developed an additional role — the agency began to enforce standards of data security. Does this role fit in with Hetcher's analysis ("through privacy policies . . . the FTC is gaining jurisdiction over the commercial Internet")?

---

[37] Xuan-Thao N. Nguyen, *Collateralizing Privacy,* 78 Tul. L. Rev. 553, 571, 590 (2004).

[38] Steven Hetcher, *The FTC as Internet Privacy Norm Entrepreneur,* 53 Vand. L. Rev. 2041 (2000). *See also* Steven Hetcher, *Norms in a Wired World* (2004); Steven Hetcher, *Changing the Social Meaning of Privacy in Cyberspace,* 15 Harv. J.L. & Tech. 149 (2001); Steven A. Hetcher, *Norm Proselytizers Create a Privacy Entitlement in Cyberspace,* 16 Berkeley Tech. L.J. 877 (2001).

8. *Apps.* Increasingly, users of various websites, software, and mobile devices are using applications (called "apps") developed by third parties. These apps add special features and functions and are quite popular. Many app developers are small companies or individuals without the normal cadre of lawyers, privacy officers, and other experts. At the same time, many apps gather a lot of personal information. In 2011, the Future of Privacy Forum (FPF), a privacy think tank, examined the top paid apps for mobile devices (such as the iPhone, Android, and Blackberry). FPF found that 22 out of 30 did not have a privacy policy.

In *United States v. W3 Innovations, LLC,* No. CV-11-03958-PSG (Aug. 12, 2011), W3 Innovations (doing business as Broken Thumbs Apps) developed gaming apps for the iPhone and iPod. Several of these apps involved children's games. These apps were downloaded more than 50,000 times. The apps gathered children's personal information and allowed children to post information to the public. In violation of the Children's Online Privacy Protection Act (COPPA), some of the apps failed to have a privacy policy and failed to obtain parental consent before collecting and disclosing the personal information of children under age 13. The case settled, with W3 agreeing to pay $50,000 and to delete all information collected in violation of COPPA.

Suppose an app developer does not collect data from children under age 13, which means it would not fall under COPPA's jurisdiction. Further, suppose the app developer lacks a privacy policy. Would the FTC have any grounds to bring an action against this app developer?

9. *State Deceptive Trade Practices Acts.* In addition to the FTC Act, which is enforced exclusively by the FTC, every state has some form of deceptive trade practices act of its own. Many of these statutes not only enable a state attorney general to bring actions but also provide a private cause of action to consumers. Several of these laws have provisions for statutory minimum damages, punitive damages, and attorneys' fees. *See, e.g.,* Cal. Civ. Code § 1780(a)(4) (punitive damages); Conn. Gen. Stat. § 42-110g(a) (punitive damages); Mich. Comp. Laws § 445.911(2) (minimum damages); N.Y. Gen. Bus. Law § 349(h) (minimum damages). In interpreting these state laws, many state courts have been heavily influenced by FTC Act jurisprudence. However, as Jeff Sovern notes, many states "have been more generous to consumers than has the FTC," and "even if the FTC concludes that practices pass muster under the FTC Act, it is still at least theoretically possible for a state to find the practices deceptive under their own legislation." Thus, Sovern concludes, "information practices that are currently in widespread use may indeed violate state little FTC Acts. Marketers should think carefully about whether they wish to alter their practices."[39]

---

[39] Jeff Sovern, *Protecting Privacy with Deceptive Trade Practices Legislation*, 69 Fordham L. Rev. 1305, 1352-53, 1357 (2001).

3. GOVERNANCE BY SELF-REGULATION

Pure Self-Regulation. Some commentators contend that the best solution to data collection and use is to allow companies to regulate themselves. Fred Cate points out that self-regulation is "more flexible and more sensitive to specific contexts and therefore allow[s] individuals to determine a more tailored balance between information uses and privacy than privacy laws do."[40]

Eric Goldman argues:

Relatively few consumers have bought privacy management tools, such as software to browse anonymously and manage Internet cookies and e-mail. Many vendors are now migrating away from consumer-centric business models. So, although consumers can take technological control over their own situation, few consumers do.

Plus, as most online marketers know, people will "sell" their personal data incredibly cheaply. As Internet pundit Esther Dyson has said: "You do a survey, and consumers say they are very concerned about their privacy. Then you offer them a discount on a book, and they'll tell you everything." Indeed, a recent Jupiter report said that 82% of respondents would give personal information to new shopping sites to enter a $100 sweepstakes.

Clearly consumers' stated privacy concerns diverge from what consumers do. Two theories might explain the divergence.

First, asking consumers what they care about reveals only whether they value privacy. That's half the equation. Of more interest is how much consumers will pay — in time or money — for the corresponding benefits. For now the cost-benefit ratio is tilted too high for consumers to spend much time or money on privacy.

Second, consumers don't have uniform interests. Regarding online privacy, consumers can be segmented into two groups: activists, who actively protect their online privacy, and apathetics, who do little or nothing to protect themselves. The activists are very vocal but appear to be a tiny market segment.

Using consumer segmentation, the analytical defect of broad-based online privacy regulations becomes apparent. The activists, by definition, take care of themselves. They demand privacy protections from businesses and, if they don't get it, use technology to protect themselves or take their business elsewhere.

In contrast, mainstream consumers don't change their behavior based on online privacy concerns. If these people won't take even minimal steps to protect themselves, why should government regulation do it for them?

Further, online businesses will invest in privacy when it's profitable. . . . When companies believed that few consumers would change their behavior if they were offered greater privacy, those companies did nothing or put into place privacy policies that disabused consumers of privacy expectations. Of course, if companies later discovered that they were losing business because customers wanted more privacy, they would increase their privacy initiatives.

Consumer behavior will tell companies what level of privacy to provide. Let the market continue unimpeded rather than chase phantom consumer fears through unnecessary regulation.[41]

---

[40] Fred H. Cate, *Privacy in Perspective* 26 (2001); *see also* Fred H. Cate, *Privacy in the Information Age* (1997).

[41] Eric Goldman, *The Privacy Hoax,* Forbes (Oct. 14, 2002), available at http://www.ericgoldman.org/Articles/privacyhoax.htm.

In contrast, Peter Swire contends that privacy legislation need not be antithetical to business interests. According to Swire, privacy legislation should be viewed as similar to the "trustwrap" that Johnson & Johnson placed around bottles of Tylenol after a scare involving cyanide poisoning of the pain reliever.[42] Swire believes that "privacy legislation targeted at online practices" would provide the kind of safety to allow consumers to engage in cyberspace activities with confidence.

Default Rules. In contrast to a pure self-regulatory approach, in which personal information belongs to whatever entity happens to obtain it, Jerry Kang argues that a default rule that individuals retain control over information they surrender during Internet transactions is more efficient than a default rule where companies can use the data as they see fit. According to Kang, the latter default rule would create two inefficiencies for individuals in attempting to bargain around the rule:

> . . . First, [the individual] would face substantial research costs to determine what information is being collected and how it is being used. That is because individuals today are largely clueless about how personal information is processed through cyberspace. Transacting parties and transaction facilitators do not generally provide adequate, relevant notice about what information will be collected and how it will be used. What is worse, consumer ignorance is sometimes fostered by deceptive practices.
>
> Second, the individual would run into a collective action problem. Realistically, the information collector — the "firm" — would not entertain one person's idiosyncratic request to purchase back personal information because the costs of administering such an individually tailored program would be prohibitive. This explains the popular use of form contracts, even in cyberspace, that cannot be varied much, if at all. Therefore, to make it worth the firm's while, the individual would have to band together with like-minded individuals to renegotiate the privacy terms of the underlying transaction. These individuals would suffer the collective action costs of locating each other, coming to some mutual agreement and strategy, proposing an offer to the information collector and negotiating with it — all the while discouraging free riders. . . .

Therefore, Kang argues, the appropriate default is to give control of information to the individual:

> With this default, if the firm valued personal data more than the individual, then the firm would have to buy permission to process the data in functionally unnecessary ways. Note, however, two critical differences in contracting around this default. First, unlike the individual who had to find out what information is being collected and how it is being used, the collector need not bear such research costs since it already knows what its information practices are. Second, the collector does not confront collective action problems. It need not seek out other like-minded firms and reach consensus before coming to the individual with a request. This is because an individual would gladly entertain an individualized, even idiosyncratic, offer to purchase personal information. In addition, there will be no general "holdout" problem because one individual's

---

[42] Peter P. Swire, *Trustwrap: the Importance of Legal Rules to Electronic Commerce and Internet Privacy*, 54 Hastings L.J. 847 (2003).

refusal to sell personal information to the collector will not generally destroy the value of personal information purchased from others.[43]

Would Kang's approach serve as a dramatic change for the self-regulatory approach? Couldn't companies regularly bargain around Kang's default rule in order to obtain control of the data from individuals? Does assigning the initial entitlement make a practical difference?

Flexible Regulation. Some commentators contend that a middle ground can be found between traditional legal regulation and self-regulation. Dennis Hirsch argues that environmental law suggests ways to regulate privacy that are flexible and that mix legal regulation with self-regulation:

> Over the past forty years, environmental law has been at the epicenter of an intense and productive debate about the most effective way to regulate. Initial environmental laws took the form of prescriptive, uniform standards that have come to be known as "command-and-control" regulation. These methods, while effective in some settings, proved costly and controversial. In the decades that followed, governments, academics, environmental and business groups, and others poured tremendous resources into figuring out how to improve upon these methods. This work has produced a "second generation" of environmental regulation. . . .
>
> Second generation initiatives encourage the regulated parties themselves to choose the means by which they will achieve environmental performance goals. That is what defines them and distinguishes them from first generation regulations under which the agency has the primary decisionmaking power over pollution control methods. This difference tends to make second generation strategies more cost-effective and adaptable than command-and-control rules. The proliferation of second generation strategies has led some to identify the environmental field as having "some of the most innovative regulatory instruments in all of American law."
>
> Privacy regulation today finds itself in a debate similar to the one that the environmental field has been engaged in for years. On the one hand, there is a growing sense that the digital age is causing unprecedented damage to privacy and that action must be taken immediately to mitigate these injuries. On the other, a chorus of voices warns against the dangers of imposing intrusive and costly regulation on the emerging business sectors of the information economy. Missing thus far from the dialogue is any significant discussion of the more flexible "second generation" regulatory strategies that might be able to bridge this gap. It took environmental law decades to arrive at these alternatives. The privacy field could capitalize on this experience by looking to these environmental policies as models for privacy regulation.[44]

Is the analogy of privacy law to environmental law an apt one? To what extent are the privacy statutes discussed in this book thus far command-and-control rules versus flexible rules? Is Hirsch calling less for self-regulation than for industry input into the form and content of rules?

---

[43] Jerry Kang, *Information Privacy in Cyberspace Transactions*, 50 Stan. L. Rev. 1193, 1253-54, 1257 (1998).

[44] Dennis D. Hirsch, *Protecting the Inner Environment: What Privacy Regulation Can Learn from Environmental Law*, 41 Ga. L. Rev. 1, 8-10 (2006).

Regulation by the Chief Privacy Officer. Over the last two decades, there has been a significant rise of "privacy professionals." The association for such individuals — the International Association of Privacy Professionals (IAPP) — has grown at rates from 30 percent to 40 percent. As Kenneth Bamberger and Deirdre Mulligan note, "[C]orporate privacy management in the United States has undergone a profound transformation."[45] Based on a series of interviews with leading chief privacy officers (CPOs), Bamberger and Mulligan present an account of "privacy on the ground." In their view, these firms, driven by the leadership of CPOs, adopted a dynamic approach to privacy issues. The approach "stressed the importance of integrating practices into corporate decisionmaking that would prevent the violation of consumer expectations." The respondent CPOs also emphasized the importance of developing "company law," by which they meant "consistent and coordinated firm-specific global privacy policies intended to ensure that a firm both complies with the requirements of all relevant jurisdictions and acts concordantly when dealing with additional business issues not governed by any particular regulation."

To what extent can CPOs predict changing "consumer expectations" as technology develops? Is this shorthand another way of identifying a metric for avoiding harm to the corporation from consumers who are angry or disappointed about the organization's data practices?

Regulation by Technology. As part of the self-governance, technology can assist companies as well as consumers in making privacy choices. Privacy on the Internet can be protected by another form of regulatory mechanism — technology. According to Joel Reidenberg, "law and government regulation are not the only source of rule-making. Technological capabilities and system design choices impose rules on participants."[46] Reidenberg calls such forms of technological governance "Lex Informatica."

In the privacy context, Privacy Enhancing Technologies (PETs) have received much attention from scholars and the privacy policy community. Herbert Burkert describes PETs as "technical and organizational concepts that aim at protecting personal identity. These concepts usually involve encryption in the form digital signatures, blind signature or digital pseudonyms."[47]

Ann Cavoukian, the Information and Privacy Commissioner of Ontario, Canada, has coined the term "privacy by design," a related concept to PETs. According to Cavoukian, "*Privacy by Design* refers to the philosophy and approach of embedding privacy into the design, operation and management of information technologies and systems, across the entire information life cycle."[48]

---

[45] Kenneth A. Bamberger & Deirdre K. Mulligan, *Privacy on the Books and on the Ground*, 63 Stan. L. Rev. 247, 251 (2011).

[46] Joel Reidenberg, *Lex Informatica: The Formulation of Information Policy Rules Through Technology*, 76 Tex. L. Rev. 553 (1998).

[47] Herbert Burkert, *Privacy-Enhancing Technologies: Typology, Critique, Vision*, in *Technology and Privacy: The New Landscape* 123, 125, 128 (Philip E. Agre & Marc Rotenberg, eds., 1997).

[48] Ann Cavoukian, *Privacy by Design Resolution* (2010), http://www.ipc.on.ca/site_documents/pbd-resolution.pdf.

Ira Rubinstein has developed a useful taxonomy of PETs as either "substitute PETs" or "complementary PETs."[49] In his definition, "[s]ubstitute PETs seek to protect privacy by ensuring that little or no personal data is collected in the first place, thereby making legal protections superfluous." As an example, Rubinstein points to client-centric architecture, such as the Tor network, that prevents or minimizes the collection of personal data by permitting anonymous browsing. He also notes that in "practice, many substitute PETs are more theoretical than practical" with few being widely deployed.

In contrast, complementary PETs are designed to implement legislative privacy principles or related legal requirements. Here, Rubinstein draws a further distinction and identifies two types of complementary PETs. First, there are "privacy-friendly PETs," which give people more control over their personal data through improved notice and consent mechanisms, browser management tools, and dashboard interfaces. Second, "privacy-preserving PETs" resemble substitute PETs in that they rely on technology to limit data collection while also complementing legal requirements. Rubinstein's examples of this final category are privacy-preserving data-mining and privacy-preserving targeted advertising. He concludes by arguing that "the market incentives for substitute PETs are feeble" and that "regulatory incentives may still be necessary to overcome the reluctance of private firms to increase their investments in PETs, especially in the face of limited consumer demand, competing business needs, and a weak economy."

Additionally, Rubinstein contrasts PETs with privacy by design. Whereas most PETs are "added-on to existing systems, sometimes as an afterthought by designers and sometimes by privacy-sensitive end-users," privacy by design is a systematic approach to developing any product or service "that embeds privacy into the underlying specifications or architecture." Although this approach has great potential, Rubinstein suggests that in order for privacy by design to achieve greater success than PETs, governments will have to clarify what it means for companies to "build in" privacy from the outset rather than "bolt it on" at the end and create regulatory incentives that will spur broader adoption.

4. GOVERNANCE BY PROPERTY

A number of commentators propose that privacy can be protected by restructuring the property rights that people have in personal information. For example, according to Richard Murphy, personal information "like all information, is property." He goes on to conclude:

> . . . [I]n many instances, privacy rules are in fact implied contractual terms. To the extent that information is generated through a voluntary transaction, imposing nondisclosure obligations on the recipient of the information may be the best approach for certain categories of information. The value that information has ex post is of secondary importance; the primary question is what is the efficient contractual rule. Common-law courts are increasingly willing to impose an implied contractual rule of nondisclosure for many categories of

---

[49] Ira S. Rubinstein, *Regulating Privacy by Design*, 26 Berkeley Tech. L.J. __ (forthcoming 2011).

transactions, including those with attorneys, medical providers, bankers, and accountants. Many statutes can also be seen in this light — that is, as default rules of privacy. And an argument can be made for the efficiency of a privacy default rule in the generic transaction between a merchant and a consumer.[50]

Lawrence Lessig also contends that privacy should be protected with property rights. He notes that "[p]rivacy now is protected through liability rules — if you invade someone's privacy, they can sue you and you must then pay." A "liability regime allows a taking, and payment later." In contrast, a property regime gives "control, and power, to the person holding the property right." Lessig argues: "When you have a property right, before someone takes your property they must negotiate with you about how much it is worth."[51]

Other commentators critique the translation of privacy into a form of property right that can be bartered and sold. For example, Katrin Schatz Byford argues that viewing "privacy as an item of trade . . . values privacy only to the extent it is considered to be of personal worth by the individual who claims it." She further contends: "Such a perspective plainly conflicts with the notion that privacy is a collective value and that privacy intrusions at the individual level necessarily have broader social implications because they affect access to social power and stifle public participation."[52]

Consider Pamela Samuelson's argument as to why property rights are inadequate to protect privacy:

> . . . Achieving information privacy goals through a property rights system may be difficult for reasons other than market complexities. Chief among them is the difficulty with alienability of personal information. It is a common, if not ubiquitous, characteristic of property rights systems that when the owner of a property right sells her interest to another person, that buyer can freely transfer to third parties whatever interest the buyer acquired from her initial seller. Free alienability works very well in the market for automobiles and land, but it is far from clear that it will work well for information privacy. . . . Collectors of data may prefer a default rule allowing them to freely transfer personal data to whomever they wish on whatever terms they can negotiate with their future buyers. However, individuals concerned with information privacy will generally want a default rule prohibiting retransfer of the data unless separate permission is negotiated. They will also want any future recipient to bind itself to the same constraints that the initial purchaser of the data may have agreed to as a condition of sale. Information privacy goals may not be achievable unless the default rule of the new property rights regime limits transferability. . . .
>
> . . . From a civil liberties perspective, propertizing personal information as a way of achieving information privacy goals may seem an anathema. Not only might it be viewed as an unnecessary and possibly dangerous way to achieve information privacy goals, it might be considered morally obnoxious. If

---

[50] Richard S. Murphy, *Property Rights in Personal Information: An Economic Defense of Privacy*, 84 Geo. L.J. 2381, 2416-17 (1996).

[51] Lawrence Lessig, *Code and Other Laws of Cyberspace* (1999).

[52] Katrin Schatz Byford, *Privacy in Cyberspace: Constructing a Model of Privacy for the Electronic Communications Environment*, 24 Rutgers Computer & Tech. L.J. 1 (1998). For an argument about the problems of commodifying certain goods and of viewing all human conduct in light of the market metaphor, see Margaret Jane Radin, *Contested Commodities* (1996).

information privacy is a civil liberty, it may make no more sense to propertize personal data than to commodify voting rights. . . .[53]

Daniel Solove also counsels against protecting privacy as a form of property right because the "market approach has difficulty assigning the proper value to personal information":

> . . . [T]he aggregation problem severely complicates the valuation process. An individual may give out bits of information in different contexts, each transfer appearing innocuous. However, the information can be aggregated and could prove to be invasive of the private life when combined with other information. It is the totality of information about a person and how it is used that poses the greatest threat to privacy. As Julie Cohen notes, "[a] comprehensive collection of data about an individual is vastly more than the sum of its parts." From the standpoint of each particular information transaction, individuals will not have enough facts to make a truly informed decision. The potential future uses of that information are too vast and unknown to enable individuals to make the appropriate valuation. . . .
>
> [Property rights] cannot work effectively in a situation where the power relationship and information distribution between individuals and public and private bureaucracies is so greatly unbalanced. In other words, the problem with market solutions is not merely that it is difficult to commodify information (which it is), but also that a regime of default rules alone (consisting of property rights in information and contractual defaults) will not enable fair and equitable market transactions in personal information. . . .[54]

In contrast to these skeptics, Paul Schwartz develops a model of propertized personal data that would help fashion a market for data trade that would respect individual privacy and help maintain a democratic order. Schwartz calls for "limitations on an individual's right to alienate personal information; default rules that force disclosure of the terms of trade; a right of exit for participants in the market; the establishment of damages to deter market abuses; and institutions to police the personal information market and punish privacy violations." In his judgment, a key element of this model is its approach of "hybrid inalienability" in which a law allows individuals to share their personal information, but also places limitations on future use of the information. Schwartz explains:

> This hybrid consists of a use-transferability restriction plus an opt-in default. In practice, it would permit the transfer for an initial category of use of personal data, but only if the customer is granted an opportunity to block further transfer or use by unaffiliated entities. Any further use or transfer would require the customer to opt in — that is, it would be prohibited unless the customer affirmatively agrees to it.
>
> As an initial example concerning compensated telemarketing, a successful pitch for Star Trek memorabilia would justify the use of personal data by the telemarketing company and the transfer of it both to process the order and for other related purposes. Any outside use or unrelated transfers of this information would, however, require obtaining further permission from the individual. Note

---

[53] Pamela Samuelson, *Privacy as Intellectual Property?*, 52 Stan. L. Rev. 1125, 1137-47 (2000).

[54] Daniel J. Solove, *Privacy and Power: Computer Databases and Metaphors for Information Privacy*, 53 Stan. L. Rev. 1393 (2001).

that this restriction limits the alienability of individuals' personal information by preventing them from granting one-stop permission for all use or transfer of their information. A data processor's desire to carry out further transfers thus obligates the processor to supply additional information and provides another chance for the individual to bargain with the data collector. . . .

To ensure that the opt-in default leads to meaningful disclosure of additional information, however, two additional elements are needed. First, the government must have a significant role in regulating the way that notice of privacy practices is provided. As noted above, a critical issue will be the "frame" in which information about data processing is presented. . . .

Second, meaningful disclosure requires addressing what Henry Hansmann and Reinier Kraakman term "verification problems." Their scholarship points to the critical condition that third parties must be able to verify that a given piece of personal information has in fact been propertized and then identify the specific rules that apply to it. As they explain, "[a] verification rule sets out the conditions under which a given right in a given asset will run with the asset." In the context of propertized personal information, the requirement for verification creates a role for nonpersonal metadata, a tag or kind of barcode, to provide necessary background information and notice.[55]

Finally, consider what Warren and Brandeis said about privacy as a property claim:

> The aim of [copyright] statutes is to secure to the author, composer, or artist the entire profits arising from publication. . . .
> But where the value of the production is found not in the right to take the profits arising from publication, but in the peace of mind or the relief afforded by the ability to prevent any publication at all, it is difficult to regard the right as one of property, in the common acceptation of that term.[56]

5. GOVERNANCE BY STATUTORY REGULATION

Numerous statutes are directly and potentially applicable to the collection, use, and transfer of personal information by commercial entities. Congress's approach is best described as "sectoral," as each statute is narrowly tailored to particular types of businesses and services. The opposite of sectoral in this context is omnibus, and the United States lacks such a comprehensive statute regulating the private sector's collection and use of personal information. Such omnibus statutes are standard in much of the rest of the world. All member nations of the European Union have enacted omnibus information privacy laws.

In the United States, sectoral laws also do not regulate all commercial entities in their collection and use of personal information. Thus far, federal statutes regulate three basic areas: (a) entertainment records (video and cable television); (b) Internet use and electronic communications; and (c) marketing (telemarketing

---

[55] Paul M. Schwartz, *Property, Privacy and Personal Data*, 117 Harv. L. Rev. 2055, 2056, 2098-99 (2004). *See also* Vera Bergelson, *It's Personal But Is It Mine? Toward Property Rights in Personal Information*, 37 U.C. Davis L. Rev. 379 (2003) (although a collector may have rights in individuals' personal information, a property approach would correctly subordinate these rights to the rights of the individuals).

[56] Samuel Warren & Louis Brandeis, *The Right to Privacy*, 4 Harv. L. Rev. 193 (1890).

and spam). As you examine the existing statutes, think about the kinds of commercial entities that the law does not currently regulate. Consider whether these entities should be regulated. Also consider whether one omnibus privacy law can adequately apply to all commercial entities. Would the differences between types of commercial entities make a one-size-fits-all privacy law impractical?

The sectoral statutes embody the Fair Information Practices originally developed by HEW and incorporated into the Privacy Act. However, not all statutes embody all of the Fair Information Practices. As you study each statute, examine which of the Fair Information Practices are required by each statute and which are not.

(a) Entertainment Records

THE VIDEO PRIVACY PROTECTION ACT

Incensed when a reporter obtained a list of videos that Supreme Court Justice Nominee Robert Bork and his family had rented from a video store, Congress passed the Video Privacy Protection Act (VPPA) of 1988, Pub. L. No. 100-618. The VPPA is also known as the "Bork Bill."

What Is a Video Tape? Who Is a Video Tape Service Provider? The VPPA is written in technology-neutral terms. It defines a "video tape service provider" as "any person engaged in the business, in or affecting interstate or foreign commerce, of rental, sale, or delivery of prerecorded video cassette tapes or similar audio visual materials. . . ." § 2710(a)(4). This statutory language allows the VPPA to extend to DVDs (as opposed to video cassette tapes) and should also cover online delivery of movies and other content.

Restrictions on Disclosure. The VPPA prohibits videotape service providers from knowingly disclosing personal information, such as titles of videocassettes rented or purchased, without the individual's written consent. The VPPA creates a private cause of action when a videotape service provider "knowingly discloses . . . personally identifiable information concerning any consumer of such provider." 18 U.S.C. § 2710(b)(1).

Destruction of Records. The VPPA requires that records of personal information be destroyed as soon as practicable. § 2710(e).

Exceptions. The VPPA contains several exceptions, permitting videotape providers to disclose "to any person if the disclosure is incident to the ordinary course of business of the video tape service provider." § 2710(b)(2)(E).

The statute provides that "the subject matter of such materials may be disclosed if the disclosure is for the exclusive use of marketing goods and services directly to the consumer." § 2710(b)(2)(D)(ii). Videotape service providers can disclose the names and addresses of consumers if the consumer has been given the right to opt out, and the disclosure does not identify information about the videos the consumer rents. § 2710(b)(2)(D).

The statute also permits disclosure to the consumer, § 2710(b)(2)(A); disclosure with the informed written consent of the consumer, § 2710(b)(2)(B); disclosure to a law enforcement agency pursuant to a warrant or subpoena, § 2710(b)(2)(C); and disclosure for civil discovery if there is notice and an opportunity to object, § 2710(b)(2).

Preemption. VPPA does not block states from enacting statutes that are more protective of privacy. § 2710(f).

Enforcement. The VPPA's private right of action permits recovery of actual damages and provides for liquidated damages in the amount of $2,500. The Act also authorizes recovery for punitive damages, attorneys' fees, and enables equitable and injunctive relief. § 2710(c). The VPPA also includes a statutory exclusionary rule that prevents the admission into evidence of any information obtained in violation of the statute. § 2710(d).

DIRKES V. BOROUGH OF RUNNEMEDE

936 F. Supp. 235 (D.N.J. 1996)

BROTMAN, J. Presently before this Court is a motion for summary judgment brought by the Borough of Runnemede, the Borough of Runnemede Police Department, and Lieutenant Emil Busko. . . .

The present action arises from the investigation of and disciplinary action taken against Plaintiff Chester Dirkes, formerly an officer with the Department. On May 24, 1990, in the course of an investigation into a citizen's death, Plaintiff Dirkes allegedly removed pornographic magazines and videotapes from the decedent's apartment. Based on this allegation, the Camden County Grand Jury returned a one count indictment for misconduct in office against him on May 29, 1991. As a result of the indictment, on May 30, 1991, the Department issued a disciplinary notice to Plaintiff Dirkes and suspended him without pay and benefits. Plaintiff Dirkes' trial commenced on April 20, 1992 and on May 5, 1992, he was acquitted of the sole charge against him.

Following the acquittal, the Borough retained special counsel and resumed its internal affairs investigation against Plaintiff Dirkes. The Department assigned Lt. Busko to investigate the matter. On or about May 7, 1992, Lt. Busko obtained the names and rental dates of certain pornographic videotapes previously rented by Plaintiff Dirkes and his wife, co-plaintiff Marie Dirkes. Lt. Busko received this information from an employee of Videos To Go, the store from which Plaintiffs apparently regularly rent or buy video tapes for their private use. In seeking to obtain this information, Lt. Busko failed to secure a warrant, a subpoena or a court order. He simply requested and received the information from an employee of Videos to Go without question.

The internal affairs memorandum listing the video tape rental information was distributed to the Borough's special counsel, who in turn distributed it in connection with Plaintiff Dirkes' disciplinary hearing and in a proceeding before the Superior Court of New Jersey, Camden County.

On or about March 19, 1993, Plaintiffs filed their complaint with this Court alleging that Defendants violated the provisions of the Videotape Privacy Protection Act of 1988, as codified at 18 U.S.C. § 2710 (the "Act"), as well as Plaintiffs' common law privacy rights. . . . Subsequently, the video information was received into evidence at Plaintiff Dirkes' disciplinary hearing. As a result of that hearing, the Department terminated Plaintiff Dirkes from his employment. . . .

Defendants have moved for summary judgment on Count I of Plaintiffs' complaint, which asserts a violation of the Videotape Privacy Protection Act. . . .

Section 2710(c) of the Act provides broadly that "[a]ny person aggrieved by any act of a person in violation of [§ 2710] may bring a civil action" in an appropriate U.S. District Court. The Act can be violated in one or all of three ways. First, a "video tape service provider" violates § 2710(b) of the Act by disclosing "personally identifiable information" regarding a customer unless the person to whom the disclosure is made or the disclosure itself falls into one of six categories. 18 U.S.C. § 2710(b). Second, § 2710(d) of the Act is violated when personally identifiable information obtained in any manner other than as narrowly provided by the Act is "received in evidence" in almost any adversarial proceeding. 18 U.S.C. § 2710(d). Third, a person subject to the Act violates § 2710(e) by failing to timely destroy a customer's personally identifiable information. 18 U.S.C. § 2710(e). Upon finding any of these violations, a court may, but need not, award a range of relief including actual damages, punitive damages, attorneys' fees, or "such other . . . equitable relief as the Court may determine to be appropriate." 18 U.S.C. § 2710(c).

Because it is undisputed that subsections (b) and (d) have been violated in the instant matter, § 2710(c) authorizes the Plaintiffs to bring a suit. Videos to Go, the video tape service provider in this matter, violated subsection (b) of the Act by disclosing Plaintiffs' video rental information to Lt. Busko. It is undisputed that this disclosure does not fall into one of the six permissible disclosure exceptions delineated in subsection (b)(2) of the Act. A second violation of the Act occurred when Plaintiffs' personally identifiable information was received into evidence at Plaintiff Dirkes' disciplinary hearing. 18 U.S.C. § 2710(d).

Having found that there have been two violations of the Act, the Court must now determine whether Lt. Busko, the Department, or the Borough are proper defendants. As noted earlier, subsection (c) provides that "[a]ny person aggrieved by any act of a person in violation of [§ 2710] may bring a civil action." 18 U.S.C. § 2710(c). While it broadly provides relief for violations of § 2710, this subsection does not delineate those parties against whom an action may be instituted. 18 U.S.C. § 2710(c). In support of its current summary judgment motion, the Defendants argue collectively that they cannot be held liable under the Act because their actions did not violate the Act. For example, only the actions of a video tape service provider can cause a violation of § 2710(b). Because the Defendants are not video tape service providers as that term is defined under the Act, they argue that they cannot be held responsible under the Act.

This Court must reject the Defendants' narrow reading of the statute. Again, the plain language of the Act does not delineate those parties against whom an action under this Act may be maintained. Taking the Defendants' argument to its logical extension, this omission would prevent plaintiffs from bringing a cause of action against anyone. Such an absurd result must be rejected. The clear intent of the Act is to prevent the disclosure of private information. As established by its legislative history, the Act enables consumers "to maintain control over personal information divulged and generated in exchange for receiving services from video tape service providers." S. Rep. No. 100-599, at 8 (1988). This purpose is furthered by allowing parties, like these Plaintiffs, to bring suit against those individuals who have come to possess (and who could disseminate) the private information in flagrant violation of the purposes of the Act. While it need not identify all potential categories of defendants in this opinion, the Court finds that those parties who are in possession of personally identifiable information as a direct result of an improper release of such information are subject to suit under the Act. Because it is undisputed that Lt. Busko, the Department, and the Borough all possess the information as a direct result of a violation of the Act, each is a proper defendant.

Furthermore, the Supreme Court in *Local 28 of Sheet Metal Workers v. E.E.O.C.*, 478 U.S. 421 (1986), reinforced the principle that remedial statutes should be construed broadly. *Local 28* involved a violation of Title VII, a statute designed to address employment discrimination. Upon examining the legislative history of Title VII, the Court determined that "Congress reaffirmed the breadth of the [district] court's remedial powers under § 706(g) by adding language authorizing courts to order 'any other equitable relief as the court deems appropriate.'" This added language is identical to that used in subsection (c)(2)(D) of the Videotape Privacy Protection Act. 18 U.S.C. § 2710(c). It is evident throughout the *Local 28* opinion that the Supreme Court intended to give effect to the legislators' intent to provide as broad remedial powers as possible to the district courts to eliminate the effects of illegal discrimination. This Court will exercise the same broad powers to give effect to the intent of Videotape Privacy Protection Act's U.S. Senate sponsors. The importance of maintaining the privacy of an individual's personally identifiable information mandates that people who obtain such information from a violation of the Act be held as proper defendants to prevent the further disclosure of the information. . . .

For the reasons set forth above, the Court will deny Defendants' motion for summary judgment. . . .

DANIEL V. CANTELL
375 F.3d 377 (6th Cir. 2004)

CUDAHY, J. The plaintiff, Alden Joe Daniel, Jr. (Daniel) was charged with and eventually pleaded guilty to the sexual molestation of three underage girls. Allegedly, part of his *modus operandi* was showing pornographic movies to the underage girls. . . . Therefore, as part of the criminal investigation into his conduct, law enforcement officials sought and were able to obtain his video rental records. . . .

Daniel brings this suit against (1) various police officers, attorneys, and the parents of one of Daniel's victims, as well as (2) the employees and owners of two video stores where Daniel rented pornographic videos. There is no dispute that the defendants making up this second category are proper parties under the Act. The only question which we must answer is whether the defendants not associated with the video stores are proper parties under the Act. We believe that based on the plain language of the Act, this first group of defendants are *not* proper parties. . . .

Section (b) provides that "[a] *video tape service provider* who knowingly discloses, to any person, personally identifiable information concerning any consumer of such provider shall be liable to the aggrieved person for the relief provided in subsection (d)." 18 U.S.C. § 2710(b)(1) (emphasis added). Therefore, under the plain language of the statute, only a "video tape service provider" (VTSP) can be liable. The term VTSP is defined by the statute to mean "any person, engaged in the business, in or affecting interstate or foreign commerce, of rental, sale, or delivery of prerecorded video cassette tapes or similar audio video materials, or any person or other entity to whom a disclosure is made under subparagraph (D) or (E) of subsection (b)(2), but only with respect to the information contained in the disclosure." *Id.* at § 2710(a)(4). Daniel does not allege that the defendants in question are engaged in the business of rental, sale or delivery of prerecorded video cassette tapes. Therefore, the defendants may only be VTSPs if personal information was disclosed to them under subparagraph (D) or (E) of subsection (b)(2).

Subparagraph (D) applies "if the disclosure is solely the names and addresses of consumers." *Id.* at § 2710(b)(2)(D). Moreover, disclosure under subparagraph (D) must be "for the exclusive use of marketing goods and services directly to the consumer." *Id.* at § 2710(b)(2)(D)(ii). For instance, if a video store provided the names and addresses of its patrons to a movie magazine publisher, the publisher would be considered a VTSP, but only with respect to the information contained in the disclosure. No disclosure in this case was made under subparagraph (D). The information provided was not limited to Daniel's name and address. Instead, the disclosure was of Daniel's history of renting pornographic videotapes and included the specific titles of those videos. Additionally, the disclosure was not for marketing purposes but for purposes of a criminal investigation. Therefore, subparagraph (D) is inapplicable in this case.

Daniel properly does not argue that the disclosure falls within subparagraph (E). . . . Subparagraph (E) applies only to disclosures made "incident to the ordinary course of business" of the VTSP. *Id.* at § 2710(b)(2)(E). The term "ordinary course of business" is "narrowly defined" in the statute to mean "only debt collection activities, order fulfillment, request processing, and the transfer of ownership." *Id.* at § 2710(a)(2) . . . In sum, because Daniel has presented no evidence suggesting that a disclosure was made under subparagraph (D) or (E) in this case, the non-video store defendants are not VTSPs under the Act and therefore, are not proper parties to this litigation.

Daniel argues, however, that any person, not just a VTSP, can be liable under the Act based on *Dirkes v. Borough of Runnemede,* 936 F. Supp. 235 (D.N.J. 1996). *Dirkes* did reach this conclusion but only by misreading the Act. The court in *Dirkes* was focused on language in the Act stating that "[a]ny person aggrieved by any act of *a person* in violation of this section may bring a civil action in the United States district court." 18 U.S.C. § 2710(c)(1) (emphasis added). Because the statute states that a suit can be based upon an act of "a person" rather than an act of "a VTSP," *Dirkes* found that any person can be liable under the Act. *Dirkes*, however, ignored the rest of the sentence. A lawsuit under the Act must be based on an "act of a person *in violation of this section.* . . ." 18 U.S.C. § 2710(c)(1) (emphasis added). The statute makes it clear that only a VTSP can be in violation of section 2710(b). *See* § 2710(b)(1) ("A video tape service provider who knowingly discloses . . . personally identifiable information . . . shall be liable. . . ."). Moreover, if any person could be liable under the Act, there would be no need for the Act to define a VTSP in the first place. More tellingly, if any person could be liable under the Act, there is no reason that the definition of a VTSP would be limited to "any person . . . to whom a disclosure is made under subparagraph (D) or (E) of subsection (b)(2)." *Dirkes* would have us ignore this limitation and find that any person can be liable under the Act whether or not a disclosure was made to him under subparagraph (D) or (E). We avoid interpretations of a statute which would render portions of it superfluous.

The court in *Dirkes* found otherwise because the "clear intent of the Act," as demonstrated by its legislative history, "is to prevent the disclosure of private information." Where the plain language of a statute is clear, however, we do not consult the legislative history. . . . In any case, our interpretation of the statute — that only a VTSP can be liable under § 2710(b) — does not conflict with Congress' purpose in adopting the Act. One can "prevent the disclosure of private information" simply by cutting off disclosure at its source, i.e., the VTSP. Just because Congress' goal was to prevent the disclosure of private information, does not mean that Congress intended the implementation of every conceivable method of preventing disclosures. Printing all personal information in hieroglyphics instead of English would also help prevent the disclosure of such information. However, nothing in the legislative history suggests that Congress was encouraging hieroglyphics and, similarly, nothing suggests that Congress intended that anyone other than VTSPs would be liable under the Act. In sum, the Act is clear that only a VTSP can be liable under § 2710(b). Because the non-video store defendants do not fit within the definition of a VTSP, they are not proper parties.

NOTES & QUESTIONS

1. ***To Whom Does VPPA Apply?*** The key question in *Dirkes* and *Daniel* is whether the VPPA *only* regulates videotape service providers. The *Daniel* court answered this question affirmatively; the *Dirkes* court would apply the VPPA to additional parties, including law enforcement officers. Which interpretation of the statutory language do you find most convincing? Would policy reasons support a broader or narrower application of the statute?

2. ***Facebook, Beacon, Blockbuster, and a VPPA Violation?*** In April 2008, Cathryn Elain Harris filed a lawsuit against Blockbuster Video (a video tape service provider) and Facebook claiming violations of the VPPA. The complaint objected to Blockbuster reporting its customers' activities to Facebook through the Beacon program.

Facebook introduced Beacon in November 2007; under it, partner companies shared information with Facebook about Facebook user activity that took place on their websites. Initially, this information became part of one's Facebook profile unless the user opted out. After consumer protest, Facebook changed its policy to require that a Facebook user would have to opt in to Beacon before information was disclosed on her Facebook page. It is not clear, however, whether opting out of Beacon stops partner companies from sharing information with Facebook.

The Harris complaint alleges that Blockbuster's website is still reporting a user's activities back to Facebook, whether or not the consumer opts out of having the information associated with her Facebook profile. Does the Blockbuster-Beacon-Facebook behavior, if as alleged, violate the VPPA? If so, what measure of damages should be used?

THE CABLE COMMUNICATIONS POLICY ACT

In 1984, Congress passed the Cable Communications Policy Act (CCPA or "Cable Act"), Pub. L. No. 98-549. The Act applies to cable operators and service providers. 47 U.S.C. § 551(a)(1).

Notice and Access. The Cable Act requires cable service providers to notify subscribers (in a written privacy policy) of the nature and uses of personal information collected. § 551(a)(1). Subscribers must have access to their personal data held by cable operators. § 551(d).

Limitations on Data Collection. Cable operators "shall not use the cable system to collect personally identifiable information concerning any subscriber without the prior written or electronic consent of the subscriber concerned." § 551(b)(1).

Limitations on Data Disclosure. Cable operators cannot disclose personally identifiable information about any subscriber without the subscriber's consent:

[A] cable operator shall not disclose personally identifiable information concerning any subscriber without the prior written or electronic consent of the subscriber concerned and shall take such actions as are necessary to prevent unauthorized access to such information by a person other than the subscriber or cable operator. § 551(c)(1).

However, cable operators can disclose personal data under certain circumstances, such as when necessary for a "legitimate business activity" or pursuant to a court order if the subscriber is notified. Cable operators may disclose subscriber names and addresses if "the cable operator has provided the subscriber the opportunity to prohibit or limit such disclosure." § 551(c)(2).

Data Destruction. Cable operators must destroy personal data if the information is no longer necessary for the purpose for which it was collected. § 551(e).

Government Access to Cable Information. Pursuant to § 551(h):

> A governmental entity may obtain personally identifiable information concerning a cable subscriber pursuant to a court order only if, in the court proceeding relevant to such court order —
>
> > (1) such entity offers clear and convincing evidence that the subject of the information is reasonably suspected of engaging in criminal activity and that the information sought would be material evidence in the case; and
> > (2) the subject of the information is afforded the opportunity to appear and contest such entity's claim.

Note that a court order to obtain cable records requires "clear and convincing evidence," a standard higher than probable cause. There is no exclusionary rule for information obtained in violation of the Cable Act.

Enforcement. The Cable Act provides for a private cause of action and actual damages, with a minimum of $1,000 or $100 for each day of the violation, whichever is higher. The plaintiff can collect any actual damages that are more than the statutory minimum. Further, the Cable Act provides for punitive damages and attorneys' fees. § 551(f).

Cable Internet Service. Section 211 of the USA PATRIOT Act amended the Cable Act, 47 U.S.C. § 551(c)(2)(D), to provide disclosure to a government entity under federal wiretap law when the government seeks information from cable companies except that "such disclosure shall not include records revealing cable subscriber selection of video programming from a cable operator." This provision of the PATRIOT Act will not sunset.

New Cable Services and Products? In March 2011, the *Wall Street Journal* reported on the testing by cable companies of new systems that are designed to show households highly targeted ads.[57] The goal is to "emulate the sophisticated tracking widely used on people's personal computers with new technology that reaches the living room." In one test of Cablevision's technology, for example, the U.S. Army used it to target four different recruitment ads to different categories of viewers. In many of these systems, companies generally seek to remove personal data, including names, before data is sent to third party companies who match ads to households. Does such a practice comport with the Cable Act?

(b) Internet Use and Electronic Communications

CHILDREN'S ONLINE PRIVACY PROTECTION ACT

Passed in 1998, the Children's Online Privacy Protection Act (COPPA), Pub. L. No. 106-170, 15 U.S.C. §§ 6501–6506, regulates the collection and use of children's information by Internet websites. COPPA applies to "an operator of a

---

[57] Jessica E. Vascellaro, *TV's Next Wave: Tuning into You*, Wall St. J., Mar. 7, 2011.

website or online service directed to children, or any operator that has actual knowledge that it is collecting personal information from a child." 15 U.S.C. § 6502(a)(1). COPPA only applies to websites that collect personal information from children under age 13. § 6502(1).

Notice. Children's websites must post privacy policies, describing "what information is collected from children by the operator, how the operator uses such information, and the operator's disclosure practices for such information." § 6502(b)(1)(A)(i).

Consent. Children's websites must "obtain verifiable parental consent for the collection, use or disclosure of personal information from children." § 6502(b)(1)(A)(ii). Websites cannot condition child's participation in a game or receipt of a prize on the disclosure of more personal information than is necessary to participate in that activity. § 6502(b)(1)(C). When information is not maintained in retrievable form, then consent is not required. § 6502(b)(2).

Right to Restrict Uses of Information. If parent requests it, the operator must provide to the parent a description of the "specific types of personal information collected," the right to "refuse to permit the operator's further use or maintenance in retrievable form, or future online collection, of personal information from that child," and the right to "obtain any personal information collected from the child." § 6502(b)(1)(B).

Enforcement. Violations of COPPA are "treated as a violation of a rule defining an unfair or deceptive act or practice" under 15 U.S.C. § 57a(a)(1)(B). Thus, the FTC enforces the law and can impose fines. There is no private cause of action for violations of COPPA.

States can bring civil actions for violations of COPPA in the interests of its citizens to obtain injunctions and damages. § 6504.

Preemption. COPPA preempts state law. § 6502(d).

Safe Harbor. If an operator follows self-regulatory guidelines issued by marketing or online industry groups that are approved by the FTC, then the COPPA requirements will be deemed satisfied. § 6503.

Should COPPA be extended to apply to everyone, not just children? Should there be a private cause of action under COPPA? Note that COPPA only applies when a website has "actual knowledge" that a user is under 13 or operates a website specifically targeted to children. Is this too limiting? Would a rule dispensing with the "actual knowledge" requirement be feasible?[58]

FTC Enforcement Actions. The FTC has engaged in several enforcement actions pursuant to COPPA. These cases have resulted in settlements

---

[58] For more information about COPPA, see Dorothy A. Hertzel, Note, *Don't Talk to Strangers: An Analysis of Government and Industry Efforts to Protect Child's Privacy Online*, 52 Fed. Comm. L.J. 429 (2000).

simultaneously with the filing of complaints. Heavy penalties have been assessed as part of some of the settlements. In 2011, the FTC received its largest civil settlement yet under COPPA. Playdom, an operator of online virtual worlds, agreed to pay $3 million to settle FTC charges that it had violated COPPA. The company was alleged to have illegally collected and disclosed personal information from hundreds of thousands of children under age 13 without their parents' prior consent.

In its complaint, the FTC stated that Playdom violated its stated privacy policy by collecting children's personal information and also enabled children to publicly disclose this information through their personal profile pages and in community forums at its websites. The company also did not take necessary steps "to provide parents with a direct notice of [its] information practices prior to collecting, using, or disclosing children's personal information" and to collect "verifiable consent from parents." The FTC tallied no fewer than 1.2 million instances of the company's collection, use, and/or disclosure of personal information in violation of COPPA.

As a further example, the FTC announced a settlement in 2006 with Xanga.com, which included a $1 million civil penalty. The complaint charges that Xanga.com, a social networking website, had actual knowledge of its collection of disclosure of children's personal information. The Xanga website stated that children under 13 could not join its social network, but it allowed visitors to create Xanga accounts even if they provided a birth date indicating that they were younger than that age. Moreover, Xanga did not provide parents with access to and control over their children's information, and did not notify the parents of children who joined the site of its information practices. Finally, the FTC found that Xanga had created 1.7 million accounts for users who submitted age information that indicated they were younger than 13 years old.

In addition, the FTC has fined operators of websites in situations where they lacked actual knowledge that they were collecting information of someone who was under 13. Thus, the FTC found a violation of COPPA when a website was directed to children and provided a pull-down menu for the year of birth that did not include any of the last 12 years.[59]

In 2011, in *United States v. W3 Innovations, LLC,* No. CV-11-03958-PSG (Aug. 12, 2011), the FTC settled an action against a developer of children's gaming apps for the iPhone and iPod. W3 Innovations (doing business as Broken Thumbs Apps) failed to have a privacy policy or to obtain parental consent before collecting and disclosing children's personal data. Under the settlement, W3 was fined $50,000 and ordered to delete all information collected in violation of COPPA.

Assessing COPPA. Consider the following critique of COPPA by Anita Allen:

> Not all parents welcome the veto power COPPA confers. New power has meant new responsibility. The statute forces parents who would otherwise be content to give their children free rein over their computers to get involved in

[59] United States v. Lisa Frank, No. 01-CV-1516 (E.D. Va. 2001), Complaint at ¶ 15, at http://www.ftc.gov/os/2001/10/lfcmp.pdf.

children's use of Internet sites that are geared toward children and collect personal information. . . .

Prohibiting voluntary disclosures by children lacking parental consent in situations in which they and their parents may be indifferent to privacy losses and resentful of government intervention, COPPA is among the most paternalistic and authoritarian of the federal privacy statutes thus far.[60]

More recently, Allen has wondered whether young adults might also need paternalistic laws.[61] At the same time, she concedes, "Sharing data is the way of the contemporary world. There is no chance the United States government will intervene in a strict censorship mode to curb radical forms of self-disclosure online." On a pessimistic note, Allen also notes:

[COPPA] could be viewed as part of a nation's formative educational project: the young are to be taught the value of privacy by imposing privacy protection rules limiting their choices until they are old enough to choose responsibly. But it will be difficult for children to get the message that privacy is a duty of self-care if they closely observe the actual behavior of teens and young adults. Everyone under the age of forty seems to be freely sharing personal facts, ideas, fantasies, and revealing images of themselves all the time.

Is COPPA doomed by a decline of modesty about self-revelation on the Internet? What role, if any, should the law play in nudging or coercing people to protect their own privacy?

ELECTRONIC COMMUNICATIONS PRIVACY ACT

In several cases, plaintiffs have attempted to use the Electronic Communications Privacy Act (ECPA) to prevent certain kinds of information collection, use, and disclosure by commercial entities. Recall from Chapter 3 that EPCA consists of three acts: (1) the Wiretap Act, 18 U.S.C. §§ 2510–2522, which regulates the interception of communications; (2) the Stored Communications Act (SCA), 18 U.S.C. §§ 2701–2711, which regulates communications in storage and ISP subscriber records; and (3) the Pen Register Act, 18 U.S.C. §§ 3121–3127, which regulates the use of pen register and trap and trace devices. The attempts to use ECPA to regulate commercial entities using personal information primarily seek to use the Wiretap Act or the SCA.

IN RE PHARMATRAK, INC. PRIVACY LITIGATION
220 F. Supp. 2d 4 (D. Mass. 2002)

TAURO, J. Plaintiffs . . . bring this consolidated action against Pharmatrak, Inc. and several pharmaceutical companies. . . .

Plaintiffs allege that Defendants "secretly intercepted and accessed Internet users' electronic communications with various health-related and medical-related

---

[60] Anita L. Allen, *Minor Distractions: Children, Privacy and E-Commerce*, 38 Hous. L. Rev. 751, 752-53, 768-69, 775-76 (2001).

[61] Anita L. Allen, *Unpopular Privacy* 190-94 (2011).

Internet Web sites and secretly accessed their computer hard drives in order to collect private information about their Web browsing habits [and] confidential health information without their knowledge, authorization, or consent." Plaintiffs contend that the Pharmaceutical Defendants conspired with Plaintiff Pharmatrak to "collect and share this wrongfully obtained personal and sensitive information." This activity was allegedly accomplished through the use of "web bugs," "persistent cookies," and other devices.

The Pharmaceutical Defendants hired Defendant Pharmatrak to monitor their corporate web sites and provide monthly analysis of web site traffic. . . . Pharmatrak specifically represented to the Pharmaceutical Defendants that these products did not collect "personally identifiable information." Even though the Pharmaceutical Defendants may not have known precisely how Pharmatrak's software worked, Plaintiffs readily admit that "the Pharmaceutical Defendants did authorize Pharmatrak's presence upon their Web sites."

Pharmatrak's system operated through the use of HTML programming, JavaScript programming, cookies, and "web bugs." Each of the Pharmaceutical Defendants' web pages were programmed with Pharmatrak code, which allowed Pharmatrak to monitor web site activity. When a computer browser requested information from a Pharmaceutical Defendant's web page, the web page would send the requested information to the user, and the site's programming code would instruct the user's browser to contact Pharmatrak's web server and retrieve a "clear GIF" from it. A clear GIF is a one pixel-by-one pixel or two pixels-by-two pixels graphic image, and is sometimes called a web bug or a "pixel tag." The purpose of a clear GIF was to cause the user's computer browser to communicate directly with Pharmatrak's web server. . . .

Having caused the user's Internet browser to contact Pharmatrak, Pharmatrak then sent a cookie back to the browser. A cookie is an electronic file "attached" to a user's computer by a computer server. Plaintiffs concede that "[c]ookies generally perform many convenient and innocuous functions." Commonly, cookies are used to store users' preferences and other information, which allows users to easily access and utilize personalized services on the web or to maintain an online "shopping cart." Cookies also allow web sites to differentiate between users as they visit by assigning each individual browser a unique, randomly generated numeric or alphanumeric identifier. If an individual browser had already visited the "Pharmatrak-enabled" website, Pharmatrak would recognize the previously placed cookie and could therefore differentiate between a repeat visit and an initial visit. . . .

Plaintiffs allege that the JavaApplet used by Pharmatrak allowed Pharmatrak to monitor the length of time that a particular user viewed one of the Pharmaceutical Defendants' web pages. Plaintiffs also allege that the JavaScript programming allowed Pharmatrak to "intercept the full URL of the tracked Web page visited by the user," as well as "the full URL of the Web page visited by the Internet user *immediately prior* to the user's visit to the Pharmatrak-coded Web page. This prior Web page address is known as a 'referrer URL.'" According to Plaintiffs, Pharmatrak used JavaScript "to extract referring URLs from the client's history, thereby bypassing any security or privacy mechanisms put in place to control the flow of potentially sensitive data." The JavaScript and JavaApplet, therefore, also caused users' computer browsers to communicate with Pharmatrak's server while they intentionally communicated with the Pharmaceutical Defendants' servers.

The examination of Pharmatrak's logs "identified hundreds of people by name." . . . Plaintiffs claim that Pharmatrak collected information which included: names, addresses, telephone numbers, dates of birth, sex, insurance status, medical conditions, education levels, and occupations. Pharmatrak also collected data about email communications, including user names, email addresses, and subject lines from emails. . . .

In sum, Plaintiffs argue that "Pharmatrak's technology permits defendants to collect extensive, detailed information about plaintiffs and Class members." In addition to the personal information discussed above, the information collected allegedly included "Web sites the Internet users were at prior to the time they went to the Pharmaceutical Defendants' Web sites, questions they asked and typed in at those prior sites, information they entered while at the Pharmaceutical Defendants' web sites, and the types of computers they were using."

Title I of the Electronic Communication Privacy Act of 1986 ("ECPA"), Interception of Electronic Communications ("The Wiretap Act"), provides that:

> Except as otherwise specifically provided in this chapter[,] any person who —
> (a) intentionally intercepts, endeavors to intercept, or procures any other person
> to intercept, any wire, oral, or electronic communication . . . shall be punished as
> provided in subsection (4) or shall be subject to suit as provided in subsection
> (5). 18 U.S.C. § 2511(1)(a).

This criminal statute provides for a private right of action, and is subject the following statutory exception:

> (d) It shall not be unlawful under this chapter for a person not acting under color
> of law to intercept a wire, oral, or electronic communication where such person
> is a party to the communication or where one of the parties to the
> communication has given prior consent to such interception unless such
> communication is intercepted for the purpose of committing any criminal or
> tortious act. 18 U.S.C. § 2511(2)(d).

Plaintiffs argue that Defendants intentionally "intercepted plaintiffs' or Class members' electronic communications with the Web sites they visited without plaintiffs' or the Class' [sic] knowledge, authorization, or consent. . . ."

Plaintiffs claim that "Pharmatrak intercepted plaintiffs' transmission of their personal information to the Pharmaceutical Defendants' Web sites without the express or implied consent of either plaintiffs or the Pharmaceutical Defendants." Despite the fact that the Pharmaceutical Defendants may have consented to Pharmatrak's assembly of anonymous, aggregate information, Plaintiffs insist that the web sites never consented to Pharmatrak's collection of personally identifiable information. Absent this specific consent, Plaintiffs argue, the Wiretap Act's statutory exception simply does not apply. . . .

In the present case, Plaintiffs concede that the Pharmaceutical Defendants consented to the placement of code for Pharmatrak's . . . service on their web sites. . . . [C]onsent precludes a claim under the Wiretap Act. The Pharmaceutical companies contracted with Pharmatrak, and authorized Pharmatrak to communicate with any users who contacted the Pharmaceutical Web sites. . . . It is sufficient that the Pharmaceutical Defendants were parties to communications with Plaintiffs and consented to the monitoring service provided by Defendant Pharmatrak.

Plaintiffs are also unable to demonstrate that Defendants acted with a tortious purpose. Plaintiffs have produced no evidence "either (1) that the primary motivation, or (2) that a determinative factor in the actor [Pharmatrak's] motivation for intercepting the conversation was to commit a criminal [or] tortious . . . act." Without a showing of the requisite *mens rea,* Plaintiffs cannot succeed on their claim under the Wiretap Act. . . .

Title II of the ECPA, also known as the "Stored Wire and Electronic Communications and Transactional Records Act," "aims to prevent hackers from obtaining, altering, or destroying certain stored electronic communications." The statute provides:

> [W]hoever — (1) intentionally accesses without authorization a facility through which an electronic communication service is provided; or (2) intentionally exceeds an authorization to access that facility; and thereby obtains, alters, or prevents authorized access to a wire or electronic communication while it is in electronic storage in such system shall be punished as provided by subsection (b) of this section. 18 U.S.C. § 2701(a).

Plaintiffs acknowledge that § 2701 was primarily designed to provide a cause of action against computer hackers, and argue that "Defendants' conduct of accessing data in plaintiffs' computers, including the content of plaintiffs' e-mails, constitutes electronic trespassing and falls squarely within the ambit of Section 2701."

Defendants disagree, and claim that they are entitled to summary judgment on at least two separate grounds: (1) Plaintiffs' computers are not facilities which provide electronic communications services, an essential element of § 2701; and (2) any alleged access to "communications" was authorized.

Defendants are correct that an individual Plaintiff's personal computer is not a "facility through which an electronic communication service is provided" for the purposes of § 2701. Plaintiffs find it noteworthy that "[p]ersonal computers provide consumers with the opportunity to access the Internet and send or receive electronic communications," and that "[w]ithout personal computers, most consumers would not be able to access the Internet or electronic communications." Fair enough, but without a telephone, most consumers would not be able to access telephone lines, and without televisions, most consumers would not be able to access cable television. Just as telephones and televisions are necessary devices by which consumers access particular services, personal computers are necessary devices by which consumers connect to the Internet. While it is possible for modern computers to perform server-like functions, there is no evidence that any of the Plaintiffs used their computers in this way. While computers and telephones certainly provide services in the general sense of the word, that is not enough for the purposes of the ECPA. The relevant *service* is Internet access, and the service is provided through ISPs or other servers, not though Plaintiffs' PCs.

Even if the court were to assume that Plaintiffs' computers are "facilities" under § 2701, any access to stored communications was authorized and, thus,

Defendants' conduct falls under the exception from liability created by § 2701(c)(2). . . . [T]he Pharmaceutical Defendants are "users" under the ECPA. . . . As users, the Pharmaceutical Defendants could consent to Pharmatrak's interception of Plaintiffs' communications. . . .

In addition, the ECPA does not prohibit Pharmatrak's actions with regard to the placing of cookies on Plaintiffs' computers. Section § 2701 seeks to target communications which are in "electronic storage" incident to their transmission. . . . "Title II only protects electronic communications stored 'for a limited time' in the 'middle' of a transmission, i.e. when an electronic communication service temporarily stores a communication while waiting to store it." Even if such cookies were covered by the ECPA, Pharmatrak created and sent the cookies, and thus any accessing of the cookies by Pharmatrak at a later date would certainly be "authorized." Because Pharmatrak's cookies fall outside the scope of § 2701, Plaintiffs' claim under that section must fail. . . .

NOTES & QUESTIONS

1. *Postscript.* On appeal, the First Circuit let stand the district court's holding dismissing the plaintiff's Stored Communications Act claim. *In re Pharmatrak, Inc. Privacy Litigation,* 392 F.3d 9 (1st Cir. 2003). As for the Wiretap Act claim, the court reversed. To prove a violation of the Wiretap Act, the court stated, the plaintiff must prove that "a defendant (1) intentionally (2) intercepted, endeavored to intercept or procured another person to intercept or endeavor to intercept (3) the contents of (4) an electronic communication (5) using a device." The court concluded that the "district court made an error of law . . . as to what constitutes consent." The court reasoned that the "client pharmaceutical companies did not give the requisite consent. The pharmaceutical clients sought and received assurances from Pharmatrak that its . . . service did not and could not collect personally identifiable information. . . . Nor did the users consent." The court remanded as to whether the interception had been intentional.

   Note that there was no consent here because Pharmatrak didn't adequately inform its pharmaceutical clients. Suppose that Pharmatrak told its pharmaceutical clients that it was gathering personal information, but that Pharmatrak did not inform the individual users of the pharmaceutical websites. Would the consent exception apply under these circumstances?

   On remand, the district court concluded that the interception was not intentional, and that at most, Pharmatrak had negligently gathered the personal data. Accordingly, the Wiretap Act claim was again dismissed. *In re Pharmatrak, Inc. Privacy Litigation,* 292 F. Supp. 2d 263 (D. Mass. 2003).

2. *Does ECPA Prohibit Cookies?* When a person interacts with a website, the site can record certain information about the person, such as what parts of the website the user visited, what the user clicked on, and how long the user spent reading different parts of the website. This information is called "clickstream data."

Websites use "cookies" to identify particular users.[62] A cookie is a small text file that is downloaded into the user's computer when a user accesses a web page. The text in a cookie, which is often encoded, usually includes an identification number and several other data elements, such as the website and the expiration date. The cookie lets a website know that a particular user has returned. The website can then access any information it collected about that individual on her previous visits to the website. Cookies can also be used to track users as they visit multiple websites.

In *In re Doubleclick Inc. Privacy Litigation*, 154 F. Supp. 2d 497 (S.D.N.Y. 2001), a group of plaintiffs challenged DoubleClick's use of cookies under the Stored Communications Act (SCA) and Wiretap Act. In 2001, DoubleClick was the leading company providing online advertising. DoubleClick helps advertisers distribute advertisements to websites based on information about specific web surfers. When a person visits a DoubleClick-affiliated website, DoubleClick places a cookie on that person's computer. As the person visits other sites that use DoubleClick, it builds a profile of that person's web surfing activity. DoubleClick then can target ads to specific people based on their profile. For example, suppose a news website uses DoubleClick. A person visits the news website. The website checks with DoubleClick to see if DoubleClick recognizes the person. If the person's computer has a DoubleClick cookie, DoubleClick then looks up the profile associated with the cookie and sends the website advertisements tailored to that person's interests. Suppose Person A likes tennis and Person B likes golf. When Person A goes to the news website, a banner ad for tennis might appear. When Person B visits the same site, a banner ad for golf might appear.

The plaintiffs in the *DoubleClick* case raised an SCA claim and a Wiretap Act claim. Regarding the SCA claim, the Act provides:

> [W]hoever (1) intentionally accesses without authorization a facility through which an electronic information service is provided; or (2) intentionally exceeds an authorization to access that facility; and thereby obtains . . . access to a wire or electronic communication while it is in electronic storage in such system shall be punished. . . . 18 U.S.C. § 2701(a).

Although the court ultimately concluded that the SCA did not apply, its reasoning was very controversial. The court first held that an individual's computer, when connected to the Internet, was a "facility through which an electronic information service is provided." This means that when DoubleClick accessed cookies on people's computers, it was "intentionally access[ing] without authorization a facility through which an electronic information service is provided." However, the consent exception to this provision of the SCA is that "users" may authorize access "with respect to a communication of or intended for that user." § 2701(c). The individuals whose computers were accessed were obviously users, and they did not consent. But the websites that the users visited that used DoubleClick cookies

---

[62] For a discussion of the *DoubleClick* case, see Tal Zarsky, *Cookie Viewers and the Undermining of Data-Mining: A Critical Review of the DoubleClick Settlement*, 2002 Stan. Tech. L. Rev. 1.

were also "users" in the court's interpretation, and they consented. Only one party needs to consent for the SCA consent exception to apply.

Moreover, the court noted that the SCA only applies to "temporary, intermediate storage of a wire or electronic communication," § 2510(17), and that DoubleClick's cookies were not "temporary" because they exist on people's hard drives for a virtually infinite time period.

Commentators argue that the court's application of the SCA is wrong because a "facility" refers to an Internet Service Provider, not an individual computer. Indeed, this was the conclusion of *In re Pharmatrak.* Consider Orin Kerr:

> [T]he Stored Communications Act regulates the privacy of Internet account holders at ISPs and other servers; the law was enacted to create by statute a set of Fourth Amendment-like set of rights in stored records held by ISPs. The theory of the *Doubleclick* plaintiffs turned this framework on its head, as it attempted to apply a law designed to give account holders privacy rights in information held at third-party ISPs to home PCs interacting with websites.[63]

Regarding the Wiretap Act claim, DoubleClick conceded, for the purposes of summary judgment, that it had "intercepted" electronic communications. Orin Kerr also takes issue with this concession:

> [T]he Wiretap Act prohibits a third-party from intercepting in real-time the contents of communications between two parties unless one of the two parties consents. This law had no applicability to Doubleclick's cookies, as the cookies did not intercept any contents and did not intercept anything in real-time. The cookies merely registered data sent to it from Doubleclick's servers.[64]

DoubleClick argued that even if it intercepted electronic communications, the consent exception applied, since one party (the websites using DoubleClick) consented. The court agreed. The consent exception, however, does not apply if even with consent the "communication is intercepted for the purpose of committing any criminal or tortious act." 18 U.S.C. § 2511(2)(d). The court concluded: "DoubleClick's purpose has plainly not been to perpetuate torts on millions of Internet users, but to make money by providing a valued service to commercial Web sites."

3. Web Bugs. Beyond cookies, another device for collecting people's data is called a "web bug." As one court describes it, web bugs (or "action tags") are very tiny pixels on a website that can record how a person navigates around the Internet. Unlike a cookie, which can be accepted or declined by a user, a web bug is a very small graphic file that is secretly downloaded to the user's computer. Web bugs enable the website to monitor a person's keystrokes and cursor movement. Web bugs can also be placed in e-mail messages that use HTML, or HyperText Markup Language. E-mail using HTML enables users to see graphics in an e-mail. A web bug in an e-mail message can detect

---

[63] Orin S. Kerr, *Lifting the "Fog" of Internet Surveillance: How a Suppression Remedy Would Change Computer Crime Law*, 54 Hastings L.J. 805, 831 (2003).

[64] *Id.* at 831.

whether the e-mail was read and to whom it was forwarded. According to computer security expert Richard M. Smith, a web bug can gather the IP address of the computer that fetched the web bug; the URL of the page that the web bug is located on; the URL of the web bug image; the time the web bug was viewed; the type of browser that fetched the web bug image; and a previously set cookie value. Is the use of a web bug a violation of federal electronic surveillance law?

DYER V. NORTHWEST AIRLINES CORP.

334 F. Supp. 2d 1196 (D.N.D. 2004)

HOVLAND, C.J. . . . Following September 11, 2001, the National Aeronautical and Space Administration ("NASA") requested system-wide passenger data from Northwest Airlines for a three-month period in order to conduct research for use in airline security studies. Northwest Airlines complied and, unbeknownst to its customers, provided NASA with the names, addresses, credit card numbers, and travel itineraries of persons who had flown on Northwest Airlines between July and December 2001.

The discovery of Northwest Airlines' disclosure of its customers' personal information triggered a wave of litigation. Eight class actions — seven in Minnesota and one in Tennessee — were filed in federal court prior to March 19, 2004. The seven Minnesota actions were later consolidated into a master file.

[In this case, t]he complaint alleges that Northwest Airlines' unauthorized disclosure of customers' personal information constituted a violation of the Electronic Communications Privacy Act ("ECPA"), 18 U.S.C. §§ 2702(a)(1) and (a)(3). . . .

The Electronic Communications Privacy Act (ECPA) provides in relevant part that, with certain exceptions, a person or entity providing either an electronic communication service or remote computing service to the public shall not:

- knowingly divulge to any person or entity the contents of a communication while in electronic storage by that service (18 U.S.C. § 2702(a)(1)); and

- knowingly divulge a record or other information pertaining to a subscriber to or customer of such service . . . to any governmental entity (18 U.S.C. § 2702(a)(3)).

In its complaint, the Plaintiffs asserted claims under both 18 U.S.C. §§ 2702(a)(1) and (a)(3) of the ECPA. The plaintiffs have conceded no claim exists under 18 U.S.C. § 2702(a)(1). Consequently, the Court's focus will be directed at the Plaintiffs' ability to sustain a claim against Northwest Airlines under 18 U.S.C. § 2702(a)(3). To sustain a claim under 18 U.S.C. § 2702(a)(3), the Plaintiffs must establish that Northwest Airlines provides either electronic communication services or remote computing services. It is clear that Northwest Airlines provides neither.

The ECPA defines "electronic communication service" as "any service which provides the users thereof the ability to send or receive wire or electronic communications." 18 U.S.C. § 2510(15). In construing this definition, courts have distinguished those entities that sell access to the internet from those that sell goods or services on the internet. 18 U.S.C. § 2702(a)(3) prescribes the conduct only of a "provider of a remote computing service or electronic communication service to the public." A provider under the ECPA is commonly referred to as an internet service provider or ISP. There is no factual allegation that Northwest Airlines, an airline that sells airline tickets on its website, provides internet services.

Courts have concluded that "electronic communication service" encompasses internet service providers as well as telecommunications companies whose lines carry internet traffic, but does not encompass businesses selling traditional products or services online. See *In re DoubleClick Inc. Privacy Litig.,* 154 F. Supp. 2d 497 (S.D.N.Y. 2001). . . .

The distinction is critical in this case. Northwest Airlines is not an electronic communications service provider as contemplated by the ECPA. Instead, Northwest Airlines sells its products and services over the internet as opposed to access to the internet itself. The ECPA definition of "electronic communications service" clearly includes internet service providers such as America Online, as well as telecommunications companies whose cables and phone lines carry internet traffic. However, businesses offering their traditional products and services online through a website are not providing an "electronic communication service." As a result, Northwest Airlines falls outside the scope of 18 U.S.C. § 2702 and the ECPA claim fails as a matter of law. The facts as pled do not give rise to liability under the ECPA. 18 U.S.C. § 2702(a) does not prohibit or even address the dissemination of business records of passenger flights and information as described in the complaint. Instead, the focus of 18 U.S.C. § 2702(a) is on "communications" being stored by the communications service provider for the purpose of subsequent transmission or for backup purposes.

[The plaintiffs also raised a claim under the Minnesota Deceptive Trade Practices Act. The court held that the claim was barred by the federal Airline Deregulation Act, which preempts state regulation of "a price, route, or service of an airline carrier." 49 U.S.C. § 4173(b)(1).]

NOTES & QUESTIONS

1. *ISPs vs. Non-ISPs.* In this case, Northwest Airlines violated its privacy policy by disclosing its customer records to the government. Suppose Northwest Airlines had been an ISP like AOL or Earthlink. Would it have been liable under the Stored Communications Act?

2. *Other Remedies.* What other potential remedies might the plaintiffs have in this case? The plaintiffs brought an action for breach of contract, which was discussed earlier in this chapter in the section on privacy policies. Besides breach of contract, can you think of any other causes of action that might be brought?

COMPUTER FRAUD AND ABUSE ACT

The Computer Fraud and Abuse Act (CFAA) of 1984, 18 U.S.C. § 1030, provides criminal and civil penalties for unauthorized access to computers. Originally passed in 1984, the statue was amended updated throughout the 1990s. Several states have similar statutes regarding the misuse of computers. As Orin Kerr notes:

> While no two statutes are identical, all share the common trigger of "access without authorization" or "unauthorized access" to computers, sometimes in tandem with its close cousin, "exceeding authorized access" to computers.[65]

Scope. The CFAA applies to all "protected computer[s]." A "protected computer" is any computer used in interstate commerce or communication. Whereas the Stored Communications Act of ECPA appears to apply only to ISPs, the CFAA applies to both ISPs and individual computers.

Criminal Penalties. The CFAA creates seven crimes. Among these, it imposes criminal penalties when a person or entity "intentionally accesses a computer without authorization or exceeds authorized access, and thereby obtains . . . information from any protected computer." § 1030(a)(2)(c). It criminalizes unauthorized access to "any nonpublic computer of a department or agency of the United States." § 1030(a)(3). The CFAA also criminalizes unauthorized access to computers "knowingly with intent to defraud" and the obtaining of "anything of value, unless the object of the fraud and the thing obtained consists only of the use of the computer and the value of such use is not more than $5,000 in any 1-year period." § 1030(a)(4). Yet another crime created by the CFAA prohibits knowingly transmitting "a program, information, code, or command" or "intentionally access[ing] a protected computer without authorization" that causes damage to a protected computer. § 1030(5)(A)(i). Punishments range from fines to imprisonment for up to 20 years depending upon the provision violated.

Damage. The term "damage" means "any impairment to the integrity or availability of data, a program, a system, or information." § 1030(e). In many provisions in the CFAA, the damage must exceed $5,000 in a one-year period.

Civil Remedies. "Any person who suffers damage or loss by reason of a violation of this section may maintain a civil action against the violator to obtain compensatory damages or injunctive relief or other equitable relief." § 1030(g). "Damage" must cause a "loss aggregating at least $5,000 in value during any 1-year period to one or more individuals." § 1030(e).

---

[65] Orin S. Kerr, *Cybercrime's Scope: Interpreting "Access" and "Authorization" in Computer Misuse Statutes*, 78 N.Y.U. L. Rev. 1596, 1615 (2003).

Exceeding Authorized Access. Many provisions in the CFAA can be violated not just by unauthorized access, but also when one "exceeds authorized access." To exceed authorized access means "to access a computer with authorization and to use such access to obtain or alter information in the computer that the accesser is not entitled so to obtain and alter." § 1030(e)(6).

CREATIVE COMPUTING V. GETLOADED.COM LLC

386 F.3d 930 (9th Cir. 2004)

KLEINFELD, J. Truck drivers and trucking companies try to avoid dead heading. "Deadheading" means having to drive a truck, ordinarily on a return trip, without a revenue-producing load. If the truck is moving, truck drivers and their companies want it to be carrying revenue-producing freight. In the past, truckers and shippers used blackboards to match up trips and loads. Eventually television screens were used instead of blackboards, but the matching was still inefficient. Better information on where the trucks and the loads are — and quick, easy access to that information — benefits shippers, carriers, and consumers.

Creative Computing developed a successful Internet site, truckstop.com, which it calls "The Internet Truckstop," to match loads with trucks. The site is very easy to use. It has a feature called "radius search" that lets a truck driver in, say, Middletown, Connecticut, with some space in his truck, find within seconds all available loads in whatever mileage radius he likes (and of course lets a shipper post a load so that a trucker with space can find it). The site was created so early in Internet history and worked so well that it came to dominate the load-board industry.

Getloaded decided to compete, but not honestly. After Getloaded set up a load-matching site, it wanted to get a bigger piece of Creative's market. Creative wanted to prevent that, so it prohibited access to its site by competing loadmatching services. The Getloaded officers thought trucking companies would probably use the same login names and passwords on truckstop.com as they did on getloaded.com. Getloaded's president, Patrick Hull, used the login name and password of a Getloaded subscriber, in effect impersonating the trucking company, to sneak into truckstop.com. Getloaded's vice-president, Ken Hammond, accomplished the same thing by registering a defunct company, RFT Trucking, as a truckstop.com subscriber. These tricks enabled them to see all of the information available to Creative's bona fide customers.

Getloaded's officers also hacked into the code Creative used to operate its website. Microsoft had distributed a patch to prevent a hack it had discovered, but Creative Computing had not yet installed the patch on truckstop.com. Getloaded's president and vice-president hacked into Creative Computing's website through the back door that this patch would have locked. Once in, they examined the source code for the tremendously valuable radius-search feature. . . .

Getloaded argues that no action could lie under the Computer Fraud and Abuse Act because it requires a $5,000 floor for damages from each unauthorized access, and that Creative Computing submitted no evidence that would enable a jury to find that the floor was reached on any single unauthorized access. . . .

The briefs dispute which version of the statute we should apply — the one in effect when Getloaded committed the wrongs, or the one in effect when the case went to trial (which is still in effect). The old version of the statute made an exception to the fraudulent access provision if "the value of such use [unauthorized access to a protected computer] is not more than $5,000 in any 1-year period."[66] The new version, in effect now and during trial, says "loss . . . during any 1-year period . . . aggregating at least $5,000 in value."[67] These provisions are materially identical.

The old version of the statute defined "damage" as "any impairment to the integrity or availability of data, a program, a system, or information" that caused the loss of at least $5,000. It had no separate definition of "loss." The new version defines "damage" the same way, but adds a definition of loss. "Loss" is defined in the new version as "any reasonable cost to any victim, including the cost of responding to an offense, conducting a damage assessment, and restoring the data . . . and any revenue lost, cost incurred, or other consequential damages incurred because of interruption of service."

For purposes of this case, we need not decide which version of the Act applies, because Getloaded loses either way. Neither version of the statute supports a construction that would require proof of $5,000 of damage or loss from a single unauthorized access. The syntax makes it clear that in both versions, the $5,000 floor applies to how much damage or loss there is to the victim over a one-year period, not from a particular intrusion. Getloaded argues that "impairment" is singular, so the floor has to be met by a single intrusion. The premise does not lead to the conclusion. The statute (both the earlier and the current versions) says "damage" means "any impairment to the integrity or availability of data [etc.] . . . that causes loss aggregating at least $5,000." Multiple intrusions can cause a single impairment, and multiple corruptions of data can be described as a single "impairment" to the data. The statute does not say that an "impairment" has to result from a single intrusion, or has to be a single corrupted byte. A court construing a statute attributes a rational purpose to Congress. Getloaded's construction would attribute obvious futility to Congress rather than rationality, because a hacker could evade the statute by setting up thousands of $4,999 (or millions of $4.99) intrusions. As the First Circuit pointed out in the analogous circumstance of physical impairment, so narrow a construction of the $5,000 impairment requirement would merely "reward sophisticated intruders." The damage floor in the Computer Fraud and Abuse Act contains no "single act" requirement.

---

[66] 18 U.S.C. § 1030(a)(4) (2001) ("[Whoever] knowingly and with intent to defraud, accesses a protected computer without authorization, or exceeds authorized access, and by means of such conduct furthers the intended fraud and obtains anything of value, unless the object of the fraud and the thing obtained consists only of the use of the computer and the value of such use is not more than $5,000 in any 1-year period.").

[67] 18 U.S.C. § 1030(a)(5)(B)(i) ("[Whoever caused] loss to 1 or more persons during any 1-year period (and, for purposes of an investigation, prosecution, or other proceeding brought by the United States only, loss resulting from a related course of conduct affecting 1 or more other protected computers) aggregating at least $5,000 in value.").

NOTES & QUESTIONS

1. **DoubleClick, Pharmatrak,** *and the CFAA.* In both the *DoubleClick* and *Pharmatrak* cases, the plaintiffs brought CFAA claims. In both cases, the plaintiffs lost. In *In re Doubleclick Inc. Privacy Litigation*, 154 F. Supp. 2d 497 (S.D.N.Y. 2001), the plaintiffs contended that collectively they suffered more than $5,000 in damages, but the court held that the plaintiffs could not add up their damages. Damages could only be combined "for a single act" against "a particular computer." Since the plaintiffs' CFAA claims concerned multiple acts against many different computers, they could not be aggregated to reach the $5,000 threshold. In *In re Pharmatrak, Inc. Privacy Litigation*, 220 F. Supp. 2d 4 (D. Mass. 2002), the court concluded:

   > Plaintiffs do not allege that their computers were physically damaged in any way, or that they suffered any damage resulting from the repair or replacement of their computer systems. . . .
   >
   > Plaintiffs have not shown any evidence whatsoever that Defendants have caused them at least $5,000 of damage or loss. . . . Any damage or loss under the CFAA may be aggregated across victims and across time, but only for a single act. Because Plaintiffs have not shown any facts that demonstrate damage or loss of over $5,000 for any single act of the Defendants, [the CFAA claim is dismissed].

2. *Spyware.* Spyware is a new kind of computer program that raises significant threats to privacy. Paul Schwartz distinguishes "spyware" from "adware" in terms of the notice provided to the user. He also explains how these programs come about through the linking of personal computers via the Internet: "Spyware draws on computer resources to create a network that can be used for numerous purposes, including collecting personal and nonpersonal information from computers and delivering adware or targeted advertisements to individuals surfing the Web. Adware is sometimes, but not always, delivered as part of spyware; the definitional line between the two depends on whether the computer user receives adequate notice of the program's installation."[68] Would the CFAA apply to a company that secretly installs spyware in a person's computer that transmits her personal data back to the company without her awareness? Would the Wiretap Act apply?

3. *State Spyware Statutes.* The state of Utah became the first state to pass legislation to regulate spyware. The original Spyware Control Act, Utah Code Ann. §§ 13-40-101 *et seq.*, prohibited the installation of spyware on another person's computer, limited the display of certain types of advertising, created a private right of action, and empowered the Utah Division of Consumer Protection to collect complaints. WhenU, an advertising network, challenged the Act in 2004, arguing that it violated the Commerce Clause of the U.S. Constitution, and it obtained a preliminary injunction against the statute. A revised bill was signed by the Utah governor on March 17, 2005. The revised Act defines "spyware" as "software on a computer of a user who resides in

---

[68] Paul M. Schwartz, *Property, Privacy, and Personal Data*, 117 Harv. L. Rev. 2055 (2004).

this state that . . . collects information about an Internet website at the time the Internet website is being viewed in this state, unless the Internet website is the Internet website of the person who provides the software; and . . . uses the information . . . contemporaneously to display pop-up advertising on the computer."

Following Utah's lead, California enacted a spyware bill, which was signed by Governor Arnold Schwarzenegger on September 28, 2004. The Consumer Protection Against Computer Spyware Act, SB 1426, prohibits a person from causing computer software to be installed on a computer and using the software to (1) take control of the computer; (2) modify certain settings relating to the computer's access to the Internet; (3) collect, through intentionally deceptive means, personally identifiable information; (4) prevent, without authorization, the authorized user's reasonable efforts to block the installation of or disable software; (5) intentionally misrepresent that the software will be uninstalled or disabled by the authorized user's action; or (6) through intentionally deceptive means, remove, disable, or render, inoperative security, anti-spyware, or antivirus software installed on the computer.

UNITED STATES V. DREW

259 F.R.D. 449 (C.D. Cal. 2009)

WU, J. This case raises the issue of whether (and/or when will) violations of an Internet website's terms of service constitute a crime under the Computer Fraud and Abuse Act ("CFAA"), 18 U.S.C. § 1030. . . .

In the Indictment, Drew was charged with one count of conspiracy in violation of 18 U.S.C. § 371 and three counts of violating a felony portion of the CFAA, *i.e.,* 18 U.S.C. §§ 1030(a)(2)(C) and 1030(c)(2)(B)(ii), which prohibit accessing a computer without authorization or in excess of authorization and obtaining information from a protected computer where the conduct involves an interstate or foreign communication and the offense is committed in furtherance of a crime or tortious act.

The Indictment included, *inter alia,* the following allegations (not all of which were established by the evidence at trial). Drew, a resident of O'Fallon, Missouri, entered into a conspiracy in which its members agreed to intentionally access a computer used in interstate commerce without (and/or in excess of) authorization in order to obtain information for the purpose of committing the tortious act of intentional infliction of emotional distress upon "M.T.M.," subsequently identified as Megan Meier ("Megan"). Megan was a 13 year old girl living in O'Fallon who had been a classmate of Drew's daughter Sarah. Pursuant to the conspiracy, on or about September 20, 2006, the conspirators registered and set up a profile for a fictitious 16 year old male juvenile named "Josh Evans" on the www. My Space. com website ("MySpace"), and posted a photograph of a boy without that boy's knowledge or consent. Such conduct violated My Space's terms of service. The conspirators contacted Megan through the MySpace network (on which she had her own profile) using the Josh Evans pseudonym and began to flirt with her over a number of days. On or about October 7, 2006, the conspirators had "Josh" inform Megan that he was moving away. On or about October 16, 2006, the conspirators had "Josh" tell Megan that he no longer liked her and that "the world would be a better place without her in it." Later on that same day, after learning that Megan had killed herself, Drew caused the Josh Evans MySpace account to be deleted.

At the trial, after consultation between counsel and the Court, the jury was instructed that, if they unanimously decided that they were not convinced beyond a reasonable doubt as to the Defendant's guilt as to the felony CFAA violations of 18 U.S.C. §§ 1030(a)(2)(C) and 1030(c)(2)(B)(ii), they could then consider whether the Defendant was guilty of the "lesser included" misdemeanor CFAA violation of 18 U.S.C. §§ 1030(a)(2)(C) and 1030(c)(2)(A). [The jury found Drew not guilty of the felony CFAA violations and guilty of the misdemeanor CFAA violation. Drew made a motion for judgment of acquittal under Fed. R. Crim. P. 29(c).]

As Jae Sung (Vice President of Customer Care at MySpace) testified at trial, MySpace is a "social networking" website where members can create "profiles" and interact with other members. . . .

In 2006, to become a member, one had to go to the sign-up section of the MySpace website and register by filling in personal information (such as name, email address, date of birth, country/state/postal code, and gender) and creating a password. In addition, the individual had to check on the box indicating that "You agree to the MySpace Terms of Service and Privacy Policy." The terms of service did not appear on the same registration page that contained this "check box" for users to confirm their agreement to those provisions. . . . A person could become a MySpace member without ever reading or otherwise becoming aware of the provisions and conditions of the MySpace terms of service [MSTOS] by merely clicking on the "check box" and then the "Sign Up" button without first accessing the "Terms" section.

The MSTOS prohibited the posting of a wide range of content on the website including (but not limited to) material that: a) "is potentially offensive and promotes racism, bigotry, hatred or physical harm of any kind against any group or individual"; b) "harasses or advocates harassment of another person"; c) "solicits personal information from anyone under 18"; d) "provides information that you know is false or misleading or promotes illegal activities or conduct that is abusive, threatening, obscene, defamatory or libelous"; e) "includes a photograph of another person that you have posted without that person's consent"; f) "involves commercial activities and/or sales without our prior written consent"; g) "contains restricted or password only access pages or hidden pages or images"; or h) "provides any phone numbers, street addresses, last names, URLs or email addresses. . . ."

[In 2006, the CFAA (18 U.S.C. § 1030) punished a person who "intentionally accesses a computer without authorization or exceeds authorized access, and thereby obtains . . . information from any protected computer."]

As used in the CFAA, the term "computer" "includes any data storage facility or communication facility directly related to or operating in conjunction with such device. . . ." 18 U.S.C. § 1030(e)(1). The term "protected computer" "means a computer—(A) exclusively for the use of a financial institution or the

United States Government . . . ; or (B) which is used in interstate or foreign commerce or communication. . . ." *Id.* § 1030(e)(2). The term "exceeds authorized access" means "to access a computer with authorization and to use such access to obtain or alter information in the computer that the accesser is not entitled so to obtain or alter . . . ." *Id.* § 1030(e)(6).

In addition to providing criminal penalties for computer fraud and abuse, the CFAA also states that "[A]ny person who suffers damage or loss by reason of a violation of this section may maintain a civil action against the violator to obtain compensatory damages and injunctive relief or other equitable relief." 18 U.S.C. § 1030(g). Because of the availability of civil remedies, much of the law as to the meaning and scope of the CFAA has been developed in the context of civil cases.

During the relevant time period herein, the misdemeanor 18 U.S.C. § 1030(a)(2)(C) crime consisted of the following three elements:

First, the defendant intentionally [accessed without authorization] [exceeded authorized access of] a computer;

Second, the defendant's access of the computer involved an interstate or foreign communication; and

Third, by [accessing without authorization] [exceeding authorized access to] a computer, the defendant obtained information from a computer . . . [used in interstate or foreign commerce or communication] . . . .

As to the term "without authorization," the courts that have considered the phrase have taken a number of different approaches in their analysis. . . . [W]here the relationship between the parties is contractual in nature or resembles such a relationship, access has been held to be unauthorized where there has been an ostensible breach of contract. . . .

Within the breach of contract approach, most courts that have considered the issue have held that a conscious violation of a website's terms of service/use will render the access unauthorized and/or cause it to exceed authorization. *See, e.g., Southwest Airlines Co. v. Farechase, Inc.,* 318 F. Supp. 2d 435, 439-40 (N.D. Tex. 2004); *Nat'l Health Care Disc., Inc.,* 174 F. Supp. 2d at 899; *Register.com, Inc. v. Verio, Inc.,* 126 F. Supp. 2d 238, 247-51 (S.D.N.Y. 2000), *aff'd,* 356 F.3d 393 (2d Cir. 2004); *Am. Online, Inc. v. LCGM, Inc.,* 46 F. Supp. 2d 444, 450 (E.D. Va. 1998); *see also EF Cultural Travel BV v. Zefer Corp.,* 318 F.3d 58, 62-63 (1st Cir. 2003) ("A lack of authorization could be established by an explicit statement on the website restricting access. . . . [W]e think that the public website provider can easily spell out explicitly what is forbidden. . . ."). . . .

In this particular case, as conceded by the Government, the only basis for finding that Drew intentionally accessed MySpace's computer/servers without authorization and/or in excess of authorization was her and/or her co-conspirator's violations of the MSTOS by deliberately creating the false Josh Evans profile, posting a photograph of a juvenile without his permission and pretending to be a sixteen year old O'Fallon resident for the purpose of communicating with Megan. Therefore, if conscious violations of the My Space terms of service were not sufficient to satisfy the first element of the CFAA misdemeanor violation as per 18 U.S.C. §§ 1030(a)(2)(C) and 1030(b)(2)(A), Drew's Rule 29(c) motion would have to be granted on that basis alone. However, this Court concludes that an intentional breach of the MSTOS can potentially constitute accessing the MySpace computer/server without authorization and/or in excess of authorization under the statute. . . .

Justice Holmes observed that, as to criminal statutes, there is a "fair warning" requirement. . . .

The void-for-vagueness doctrine has two prongs: 1) a definitional/notice sufficiency requirement and, more importantly, 2) a guideline setting element to govern law enforcement. In *Kolender v. Lawson,* 461 U.S. 352 (1983), the Court explained that:

> As generally stated, the void-for-vagueness doctrine requires that a penal statute define the criminal offense with sufficient definiteness that ordinary people can understand what conduct is prohibited and in a manner that does not encourage arbitrary and discriminatory enforcement. . . .

To avoid contravening the void-for-vagueness doctrine, the criminal statute must contain "relatively clear guidelines as to prohibited conduct" and provide "objective criteria" to evaluate whether a crime has been committed. . . .

The pivotal issue herein is whether basing a CFAA misdemeanor violation as per 18 U.S.C. §§ 1030(a)(2)(C) and 1030(c)(2)(A) upon the conscious violation of a website's terms of service runs afoul of the void-for-vagueness doctrine. This Court concludes that it does primarily because of the absence of minimal guidelines to govern law enforcement, but also because of actual notice deficiencies. . . .

First, an initial inquiry is whether the statute, as it is written, provides sufficient notice. Here, the language of section 1030(a)(2)(C) does not explicitly state (nor does it implicitly suggest) that the CFAA has "criminalized breaches of contract" in the context of website terms of service. Normally, breaches of contract are not the subject of criminal prosecution. Thus, while "ordinary people" might expect to be exposed to civil liabilities for violating a contractual provision, they would not expect criminal penalties. . . .

Second, if a website's terms of service controls what is "authorized" and what is "exceeding authorization" — which in turn governs whether an individual's accessing information or services on the website is criminal or not, section 1030(a)(2)(C) would be unacceptably vague because it is unclear whether any or all violations of terms of service will render the access unauthorized, or whether only certain ones will. . . .

Third, by utilizing violations of the terms of service as the basis for the section 1030(a)(2)(C) crime, that approach makes the website owner — in essence — the party who ultimately defines the criminal conduct. This will lead to further vagueness problems. The owner's description of a term of service might itself be so vague as to make the visitor or member reasonably unsure of what the term of service covers. . . .

Fourth, because terms of service are essentially a contractual means for setting the scope of authorized access, a level of indefiniteness arises from the necessary application of contract law in general and/or other contractual requirements within the applicable terms of service to any criminal prosecution. . . .

Treating a violation of a website's terms of service, without more, to be sufficient to constitute "intentionally access[ing] a computer without authorization or exceed[ing] authorized access" would result in transforming section 1030(a)(2)(C) into an overwhelmingly overbroad enactment that would convert a multitude of otherwise innocent Internet users into misdemeanant criminals. . . .

One need only look to the MSTOS terms of service to see the expansive and elaborate scope of such provisions whose breach engenders the potential for criminal prosecution. Obvious examples of such breadth would include: 1) the lonely-heart who submits intentionally inaccurate data about his or her age, height and/or physical appearance, which contravenes the MSTOS prohibition against providing "information that you know is false or misleading"; 2) the student who posts candid photographs of classmates without their permission, which breaches the MSTOS provision covering "a photograph of another person that you have posted without that person's consent"; and/or 3) the exasperated parent who sends out a group message to neighborhood friends entreating them to purchase his or her daughter's girl scout cookies, which transgresses the MSTOS rule against "advertising to, or solicitation of, any Member to buy or sell any products or services through the Services." However, one need not consider hypotheticals to demonstrate the problem. In this case, Megan (who was then 13 years old) had her own profile on MySpace, which was in clear violation of the MSTOS which requires that users be "14 years of age or older." No one would seriously suggest that Megan's conduct was criminal or should be subject to criminal prosecution. . . .

In sum, if any conscious breach of a website's terms of service is held to be sufficient by itself to constitute intentionally accessing a computer without authorization or in excess of authorization, the result will be that section 1030(a)(2)(C) becomes a law "that affords too much discretion to the police and too little notice to citizens who wish to use the [Internet]."

NOTES & QUESTIONS

1. *The Implications of* **Drew.** Is the prosecutor's theory consistent with the CFAA's purpose? Suppose the court in *Drew* had reached the opposite conclusion. What effect would criminal liability for violating a website's terms of service have for people who use the Internet?
2. *Is the CFAA Unconstitutionally Vague?* The *Drew* court's holding is narrow, concluding only that the application of the CFAA to website terms of service violations would be unconstitutionally vague. More broadly, is the CFAA unconstitutionally vague on its face?

(c) Marketing

TELEPHONE CONSUMER PROTECTIONS ACT

The Telephone Consumer Protections Act (TCPA) of 1991, Pub. L. No. 102-243, 47 U.S.C. § 227, permits individuals to sue a telemarketer in small claims court for an actual loss or up to $500 (whichever is greater), for each call received after requesting to be placed on its "Do Not Call" list:

A person who has received more than one telephone call within any 12-month period by or on behalf of the same entity in violation of the regulations prescribed under this subsection may, if otherwise permitted by the laws or rules of a court of a State bring in an appropriate court of that State [an action for an injunction and to recover actual damages or $500 for each violation]. § 227(c)(5).

Telemarketers can offer as an affirmative defense that they established "reasonable practices and procedures to effectively prevent telephone solicitations in violation of the regulations prescribed under this subsection." § 227(c)(5). If telemarketer has acted "willfully or knowingly," then damages are trebled. § 227(c)(5).

The TCPA prohibits telemarketers from calling residences and using prerecorded messages without the consent of the called party. 47 U.S.C. § 227(b)(1)(B). The TCPA prohibits the use of a fax, computer, or other device to send an unsolicited advertisement to a fax machine. § 227(b)(1)(C). The Act also requires the FCC to promulgate rules to "protect residential telephone subscribers' privacy rights and to avoid receiving telephone solicitations to which they object." § 227(c)(1). In addition, the FCC is authorized to require that a "single national database" be established of a "list of telephone numbers of residential subscribers who object to receiving telephone solicitations." § 227(c)(3). It is within the discretion of the FCC to determine whether such a database is necessary or feasible.

States may initiate actions against telemarketers "engaging in a pattern or practice of telephone calls or other transmissions to residents of that State" in violation of the TCPA. § 227(f)(1).

In *Destination Ventures, Ltd. v. FCC,* 46 F.3d 54 (9th Cir. 1995), Destination Ventures challenged a provision of the TCPA banning unsolicited faxes that contained advertisements on First Amendment grounds. The court upheld the ban because it was designed to prevent shifting advertising costs to consumers, who would be forced to pay for the toner and paper to receive the ads.

As a continuation of the "Do Not Call" list, a discussion is now emerging about "Do Not Track" (DNT) protection for the Internet. The idea of DNT turns on the use of an "opt-out header" in a Web browser.[69] The FTC has told Congress that it supports giving consumers a DNT option to give them a simple and easy way to control the fashion in which companies track them online.

In contrast to "Do Not Call," considerable complexity exists around the concept of "tracking" on the Internet. The Center for Democracy and Technology (CDT) has defined tracking "as the collection and correlation of data about the Internet activities of a particular user, computer or device, over time and across non-commonly branded websites, for any purpose other than fraud prevention or compliance with law enforcement requests."[70] Thus, CDT considers behavioral advertising as "tracking."

---

[69] For more on the technology behind this policy proposal, see *Do Not Track*, at http://www.donottrack.us/.

[70] CDT, *What Does "Do Not Track" Mean?* (Jan. 31, 2011). For an approach that is largely in agreement with the CDT, see Electronic Frontier Foundation, *What Does the "Track" in "Do Not Track" Mean?* (Feb. 19, 2011).

CDT also argues that any "actively shared" data, such as information that data users provide in social networking profiles and Web forums or by registering for various accounts, should not fall within Do Not Track prohibitions.

Consider Omer Tene and Jules Polonetsky:

> The FTC put forth the following criteria to assess industry responses: DNT should be universal, that is, a single opt-out should cover all would-be trackers; easy to find, understand, and use; persistent, meaning that opt-out choices do not "vanish"; effective and enforceable, covering all tracking technologies; and controlling not only use of data but also their collection.[71] As discussed, the FTC has not yet taken a position on whether any legislation or rulemaking is necessary for DNT. It is clear, however, that regardless of the regulatory approach chosen, industry collaboration will remain key since the system will only work if websites and ad intermediaries respect users' preferences. . . .
>
> The debate raging around online behavioral tracking generally and DNT in particular is a smoke screen for a discussion that all parties hesitate to hold around deeper values and social norms. Which is more important — efficiency or privacy; law enforcement or individual rights; reputation or freedom of speech? Policymakers must engage with the underlying normative question: is online behavioral tracking a societal good, funding the virtue of the online economy and bringing users more relevant, personalized content and services; or is it an evil scheme for businesses to enrich themselves on account of ignorant users and for governments to create a foundation for pervasive surveillance? Policymakers cannot continue to sidestep these questions in the hope that "users will decide" for themselves.[72]

CAN-SPAM ACT

In 2003, Congress enacted the Controlling the Assault of Non-Solicited Pornography and Marketing (CAN-SPAM) Act, Pub. L. No. 108-187, 15 U.S.C. §§ 7701 *et seq.*, to address the problem of spam. Spam is a term to describe unsolicited commercial e-mail sent to individuals to advertise products and services.[73] Companies that send unsolicited e-mail are referred to as spammers. Spam is often mailed out in bulk to large lists of e-mail addresses. A recent practice has been to insert hidden HTML tags (also known as "pixel tags") into spam. This enables the sender of the e-mail to detect whether the e-mail was opened. It can also inform the sender about whether the e-mail message was forwarded, to what e-mail address it was forwarded, and sometimes, even comments added by a user when forwarding the e-mail. This only works if the recipient has an HTML-enabled e-mail reader rather than a text-only reader. HTML e-mail is e-mail that contains pictures and images rather than simply plain text. The practice has become known as a "web bug."

---

[71] Ed Felten, FTC Perspective, W3C Workshop on Web Tracking and User Privacy, Apr. 28-29, 2011, http://www.w3.org/2011/track-privacy/slides/Felten.pdf.

[72] Omer Tene & Jules Polonetsky, *To Track or "Do Not Track": Advancing Transparency and Individual Control in Online Behavioral Advertising* 29, 34 (work-in-progress 2011), available at http://www.futureofprivacy.org/tracking/.

[73] For more information on spam, see David E. Sorkin, *Technical and Legal Approaches to Unsolicited Electronic Mail*, 35 U.S.F. L. Rev. 325, 336 (2001).

Applicability. The CAN-SPAM Act applies to commercial e-mail, which it defines as a "message with the primary purpose of which is the commercial advertisement or promotion of a commercial product or service."

Prohibitions. The Act prohibits the knowing sending of commercial messages with the intent to deceive or mislead recipients.

Opt Out. The CAN-SPAM Act also requires that a valid opt-out option be made available to e-mail recipients. To make opt out possible, the Act requires senders of commercial e-mail to contain a return address "clearly and conspicuously displayed." Finally, it creates civil and criminal penalties for violations of its provisions. For example, the law allows the DOJ to seek criminal penalties, including imprisonment, for commercial e-mailers who engage in activities such as using a computer to relay or retransmit multiple commercial e-mail messages to receive or mislead recipients or an Internet access service about the message's origin and falsifying header information in multiple e-mail messages and initiate the transmission of these messages.

Assessing the Act. A year after enactment of CAN-SPAM, media accounts faulted the law as ineffective. Indeed, reports stressed the increase in spam during this time. According to one anti-spam vendor, 67 percent of all e-mail was spam in February 2004, and 75 percent in November 2004. Some spammers employed new tactics after the passage of the Act, such as using "zombie networks," which involve hijacking computers with Trojan horse programs. Anti-spam activists faulted CAN-SPAM for preempting tougher state laws, failing to provide a private right of action, and providing an opt-out option instead of an opt in.

State Anti-Spam Laws. At least 20 states have anti-spam statutes. For example, Cal. Bus. & Professions Code § 17538.4 mandates that senders of spam include in the text of their e-mails a way through which recipients can request to receive no further e-mails. The sender must remove the person from its list. A provider of an e-mail service located within the state of California can request that spammers stop sending spam through its equipment. If the spammer continues to send e-mail, it can be liable for $50 per message up to a maximum of $25,000 per day. *See* § 17538.45.

A Critique of Anti-Spam Legislation. Consumers don't always dislike marketing messages. As Eric Goldman reminds us, "consumers want marketing when it creates personal benefits for them, and marketing also can have spillover benefits that improve social welfare." Goldman is worried that current legal regulation will block the kinds of filters that will improve the ability of consumers to manage information and receive information that will advance their interests. He points to anti-adware laws in Utah and Alaska as especially problematic; these statutes "prohibit client-side software from displaying pop-up ads triggered by the consumer's use of a third party trademark or domain name — even if the consumer has fully consented to the software." For Goldman, these statutes are flawed because they try to "ban or restrict matchmaking technologies." The ideal filter would be a "mind-reading wonder" that "could costlessly — but accurately — read consumers' minds, infer their expressed and latent preferences without the consumer bearing any disclosure costs, and act on the inferred preferences to screen out unwanted content and proactively seek out wanted content." Goldman is confident that such filtering technology is not only possible, but "inevitable — perhaps imminently."[74] What kind of regulatory approach would encourage development and adoption of Goldman's favored filters while also blocking existing SPAM technology? Will surrendering more privacy help better target marketing and thus clear out our inboxes of unwanted spam?

Spam and Speech. Is spam a form of speech, protected by the First Amendment? In *Cyber Promotions, Inc. v. America Online, Inc.,* 948 F. Supp. 436 (E.D. Pa. 1996), Cyber Promotions, Inc. sought a declaratory judgment that America Online (AOL) was prohibited under the First Amendment from denying it the ability to send AOL customers unsolicited e-mail. The court rejected Cyber Promotion's argument because of a lack of state action: "AOL is a private online company that is not owned in whole or part by the government." Today, the Internet is increasingly becoming a major medium of communication. Prior to modern communications media, individuals could express their views in traditional "public fora" — parks and street corners. These public fora are no longer the central place for public discourse. Perhaps the Internet is the modern public forum, the place where individuals come to speak and express their views. If this is the case, is it preferable for access to the Internet to be controlled by private entities?

(d) State Statutory Regulation

Many states have passed legislation regulating business records and databases. Many state statutes have stronger protections of privacy than federal statutes. In particular, California has passed a series of strong privacy protections, and it is probably safe to generalize that California has the strongest privacy law in the United States.[75]

Office of Privacy Protection. In 2000, California created an Office of Privacy Protection. "The office's purpose shall be protecting the privacy of individuals' personal information in a manner consistent with the California Constitution by identifying consumer problems in the privacy area and facilitating development of fair information practices." Cal. Bus. & Prof. Code §§ 350–352. The office also is authorized to make recommendations to organizations about privacy policies and practices.

In its report of activity highlights for the fiscal year July 2006–June 2007, the Office of Privacy Protection noted that it responded to 4,777 calls and e-mails.

---

[74] Eric Goldman, *A Cosean Analysis of Marketing*, 2006 Wis. L. Rev. 1151, 1154-55, 1202, 1211-12.

[75] The California Office of Privacy Protection maintains a comprehensive summary of California's privacy statutes: http://www.privacy.ca.gov/lawenforcement/laws.htm.

The largest amount of contacts concerned identity theft (53 percent), with the next categories being business practices and privacy laws (14 percent) and online databases (8 percent).[76] The office also noted its implementation of "a train-the-trainers strategy." It provided training in assisting victims of identity theft to community organizations, and in basic privacy awareness to state information security officers. It also developed a law enforcement manual on investigation and prosecution of identity theft for use in law enforcement classes.

Destruction of Consumer Records. Pursuant to Cal. Civ. Code § 1798.81:

> A business shall take all reasonable steps to destroy, or arrange for the destruction of a customer's records within its custody or control containing personal information which is no longer to be retained by the business by (1) shredding, (2) erasing, or (3) otherwise modifying the personal information in those records to make it unreadable or undecipherable through any means.

"Shine the Light" Law. In 2003, California passed SB27, codified at Cal. Civ. Code § 1798.83. This statute allows consumers to obtain from businesses information about the personal data that the businesses disclosed to third parties for direct marketing purposes. People can find out what kinds of personal information were provided to third parties for their direct marketing purposes as well as the "names and addresses of all of the third parties that received personal information from the business." § 1798.83(1). The law applies to businesses with 20 or more employees. § 1798(c)(1). It does not apply to financial institutions. Companies with privacy policies that allow people to opt out of the sharing of their data with third parties are exempt. § 1798(c)(2).

(e) The Concept of Personally Identifiable Information (PII)

PII is one of the most central concepts in privacy regulation. It defines the scope and boundaries of a large range of privacy statutes and regulations. Federal statutes that turn on this distinction include the Children's Online Privacy Protection Act, the Gramm-Leach-Bliley Act, the HITECH Act, and the Video Privacy Protection Act. Moreover, state statutes that rely on PII as a jurisdictional trigger include California's Song-Beverly Credit Card Act and the many data security breach notification laws. These laws all share the same basic assumption—that in the absence of PII, there is no privacy harm. Thus, privacy regulation focuses on the collection, use, and disclosure of PII and leaves non-PII unregulated.

Given PII's importance, it is surprising that information privacy law in the United States lacks a uniform definition of the term. Computer science has also shown that the very concept of PII is far from straightforward. Increasingly, technologists can take information that appears on its face to be non-identifiable and turn it into identifiable data. Instead of defining PII in a coherent and consistent manner, privacy law offers multiple competing definitions, each with some significant problems and limitations.

---

[76] See Office of Privacy Protection, at http://www.privacy.ca.gov/.

Approaches to PII. There are three predominant approaches to defining PII in various laws and regulations: (1) the "tautological" approach, (2) the "non-public" approach, and (3) the "specific-types" approach.[77] These approaches are also made either as a rule or standard. A standard is an open-ended decision-making yardstick, and a rule, its counterpart, is a harder-edged decision-making tool.

The tautological approach defines PII as any information that identifies a person. The Video Privacy Protection Act (VPPA) demonstrates this model. The VPPA, which safeguards the privacy of video sales and rentals, simply defines "personally identifiable information" as "information which identifies a person." One problem with this approach is that it simply states that PII is PII without providing guidance about how to identify PII.

A second approach toward defining PII focuses on non-public information. The Gramm-Leach-Bliley Act (GLB Act) epitomizes this approach by defining "personally identifiable financial information" as "nonpublic personal information." The statute fails to define "nonpublic," but presumably this term means information not found within the public domain. The non-public approach, however, does not map onto whether the information is in fact identifiable.

The third approach is to list specific types of data that constitute PII. In the context of the specific-types approach, if the information falls into an enumerated group, it becomes a kind of statutory "per se" PII. The federal Children's Online Privacy Protection Act (COPPA) of 1998 illustrates this approach. COPPA states that personal information is "individually identifiable information about an individual collected online" that includes a number of elements beginning with "first and last name," and continuing through a physical address, Social Security number, telephone number, and e-mail address. Its definition of PII also includes "any other identifier that the [Federal Trade Commission (FTC)] determines permits the physical or online contacting of a specific individual." A limitation with the specific-types approach is that it can fail to respond to new technology, which is capable of transforming the kinds of data that are PII. .

PINEDA V. WILLIAMS-SONOMA STORES

246 P.3d 162 (2011)

MORENO, J. The Song–Beverly Credit Card Act of 1971 (Credit Card Act) (Civ. Code, § 1747 *et seq.*) is "designed to promote consumer protection." *Florez v. Linens 'N Things, Inc.*, 108 Cal. App. 4th 447, 450, (2003). One of its provisions, section 1747.08, prohibits businesses from requesting that cardholders provide "personal identification information" during credit card transactions, and then recording that information.

Plaintiff sued defendant retailer, asserting a violation of the Credit Card Act. Plaintiff alleges that while she was paying for a purchase with her credit card in one of defendant's stores, the cashier asked plaintiff for her ZIP code. Believing it necessary to complete the transaction, plaintiff provided the requested

---

[77] Paul Schwartz & Daniel Solove, *The PII Problem: Privacy and a New Concept of Personally Identifiable Information*, 86 N.Y.U. L. Rev. __ (forthcoming 2011).

information and the cashier recorded it. Plaintiff further alleges that defendant subsequently used her name and ZIP code to locate her home address.

We are now asked to resolve whether section 1747.08 is violated when a business requests and records a customer's ZIP code during a credit card transaction. In light of the statute's plain language, protective purpose, and legislative history, we conclude a ZIP code constitutes "personal identification information" as that phrase is used in section 1747.08. Thus, requesting and recording a cardholder's ZIP code, without more, violates the Credit Card Act. We therefore reverse the contrary judgment of the Court of Appeal and remand for further proceedings consistent with our decision. . . .

Plaintiff visited one of [defendant Williams-Sonoma's] California stores and selected an item for purchase. She then went to the cashier to pay for the item with her credit card. The cashier asked plaintiff for her ZIP code and, believing she was required to provide the requested information to complete the transaction, plaintiff provided it. The cashier entered plaintiff's ZIP code into the electronic cash register and then completed the transaction. At the end of the transaction, defendant had plaintiff's credit card number, name, and ZIP code recorded in its database.

Defendant subsequently used customized computer software to perform reverse searches from databases that contain millions of names, e-mail addresses, telephone numbers, and street addresses, and that are indexed in a manner resembling a reverse telephone book. The software matched plaintiff's name and ZIP code with plaintiff's previously undisclosed address, giving defendant the information, which it now maintains in its own database. Defendant uses its database to market products to customers and may also sell the information it has compiled to other businesses. . . .

Section 1747.08, subdivision (a) provides, in pertinent part, "[N]o person, firm, partnership, association, or corporation that accepts credit cards for the transaction of business shall . . . : (2) Request, or require as a condition to accepting the credit card as payment in full or in part for goods or services, the cardholder to provide *personal identification information,* which the person, firm, partnership, association, or corporation accepting the credit card writes, causes to be written, or otherwise records upon the credit card transaction form or otherwise. Subdivision (b) defines personal identification information as "information concerning the cardholder, other than information set forth on the credit card, and including, but not limited to, the cardholder's address and telephone number." Because we must accept as true plaintiff's allegation that defendant requested and then recorded her ZIP code, the outcome of this case hinges on whether a cardholder's ZIP code, without more, constitutes personal identification information within the meaning of section 1747.08. We hold that it does.

Subdivision (b) defines personal identification information as "information *concerning* the cardholder . . . including, but not limited to, the cardholder's address and telephone number" (italics added). "Concerning" is a broad term meaning "pertaining to; regarding; having relation to; [or] respecting. . . ." (Webster's New Internat. Dict. (2d ed. 1941) p. 552.) A cardholder's ZIP code, which refers to the area where a cardholder works or lives is certainly information that pertains to or regards the cardholder.

In nonetheless concluding the Legislature did not intend for a ZIP code, without more, to constitute personal identification information, the Court of Appeal pointed to the enumerated examples of such information in subdivision (b), i.e., "the cardholder's address and telephone number." . . . [T]he Court of Appeal reasoned that an address and telephone number are "specific in nature regarding an individual." By contrast, the court continued, a ZIP code pertains to the *group* of individuals who live within the ZIP code. Thus, the Court of Appeal concluded, a ZIP code, without more, is unlike the other terms specifically identified in subdivision (b).

There are several problems with this reasoning. First, a ZIP code is readily understood to be part of an address; when one addresses a letter to another person, a ZIP code is always included. The question then is whether the Legislature, by providing that "personal identification information" includes "the cardholder's address" intended to include components of the address. The answer must be yes. Otherwise, a business could ask not just for a cardholder's ZIP code, but also for the cardholder's street and city in addition to the ZIP code, so long as it did not also ask for the house number. Such a construction would render the statute's protections hollow. Thus, the word "address" in the statute should be construed as encompassing not only a complete address, but also its components.

Second, the court's conclusion rests upon the assumption that a complete address and telephone number, unlike a ZIP code, are specific to an individual. That this assumption holds true in all, or even most, instances is doubtful. In the case of a cardholder's home address, for example, the information may pertain to a group of individuals living in the same household. Similarly, a home telephone number might well refer to more than one individual. The problem is even more evident in the case of a cardholder's *work* address or telephone number—such information could easily pertain to tens, hundreds, or even thousands of individuals. Of course, section 1747.08 explicitly provides that a cardholder's address and telephone number constitute personal identification information; that such information *might also* pertain to individuals other than the cardholder is immaterial. Similarly, that a cardholder's ZIP code pertains to individuals in addition to the cardholder does not render it dissimilar to an address or telephone number.

More significantly, the Court of Appeal ignores another reasonable interpretation of what the enumerated terms in section 1747.08, subdivision (b) have in common, that is, they both constitute information unnecessary to the sales transaction that, alone or together with other data such as a cardholder's name or credit card number, can be used for the retailer's business purposes. Under this reading, a cardholder's ZIP code is similar to his or her address or telephone number, in that a ZIP code is both unnecessary to the transaction and can be used, together with the cardholder's name, to locate his or her full address. The retailer can then, as plaintiff alleges defendant has done here, use the accumulated information for its own purposes or sell the information to other businesses.

There are several reasons to prefer this latter, broader interpretation over the one adopted by the Court of Appeal. The Court of Appeal's interpretation, by contrast, would permit retailers to obtain indirectly what they are clearly prohibited from obtaining directly, "end-running" the statute's clear purpose.

This is so because information that can be permissibly obtained under the Court of Appeal's construction could easily be used to locate the cardholder's complete address or telephone number. Such an interpretation would vitiate the statute's effectiveness. . . .

[T]he legislative history of section 1747.08 offers additional evidence that plaintiff's construction is the correct one. . . .

Thus, in light of the statutory language, as well as the legislative history and evident purpose of the statute, we hold that personal identification information, as that term is used in section 1747.08, includes a cardholder's ZIP code.

NOTES & QUESTIONS

1. **Pineda *and the "Specific Types" Approach to PII.*** The California Supreme Court reversed the lower courts in *Pineda*, but did so on the narrowest possible grounds. It analyzed the statutory language and legislative history, and found that both supported a legislative intent to include a zip code as part of the "cardholder's address." In other words, that statutory category included "not only a complete address, but its components."

   In a sense, the California Supreme Court in *Pineda* only tweaked a subcategory within the specific-types approach to defining PII. It did not reach the broader conclusion that the Song-Beverly Act reflected a policy to prevent retailers from collecting "identification" indices that would permit a definitive linkage between a customer and her address. In fact, the law can be read simply as a prohibition on merchants collecting information that is specific enough to allow the unique identification of a person. Although as many as tens of thousands of people might share a zip code, it was precisely the piece of information, when added to a person's name, which permitted linkage of the customer to a wealth of PII about her.

2. ***Behavioral Marketing and PII.*** The burgeoning practice of behavioral marketing, which is also sometimes termed "targeted marketing," involves examining the behavioral patterns of consumers to target advertisements to them. In this technique, companies generally do not track individuals through use of their names. Instead they utilize software to build personal profiles that exclude this item but that contain a wealth of details about the individual. Typically, these firms associate these personal profiles with a single alphanumerical code placed on an individual's computer. These codes are used to decide which advertisements people see as well as the kinds of products that are offered to them.

   While advertising networks may not know a person's name, identification of individuals is nonetheless possible in many cases. For example, enough pieces of information linked to a single person, even in the absence of a name, Social Security number, or financial information, will permit identification of the individual. Nonetheless, online companies have attempted to short-circuit the discussion of privacy harms and necessary legal reforms by simply asserting that they do not collect PII.

3. *Ohm on the PII Problem.* In the view of Paul Ohm, privacy law must abandon its reliance on PII and find a new regulatory paradigm.[78] He argues that the concept of PII is unworkable and unfixable. He points to new re-identification research that has demonstrated that de-identified records can be re-identified "with astonishing ease." This occurs because there is already so much data available about individuals that is linked to their identity. To re-identify records, one can simply try to match the information in the records to other available data about an identified person. For example, Netflix, a popular online movie rental service, made a supposedly de-identified database of ratings publicly available as part of a contest to improve the predictive capabilities of its movie recommending software. Two researchers, Arvind Narayanan and Vitaly Shmatikov, found a way to link this data with the movie ratings that some participating individuals gave to films in the Internet Movie Database (IMDb), a popular website with information and ratings about movies.[79] They did this by matching the data to individuals' public movie ratings on IMDb.[80]

Because data can be so readily linked to a person's identity, Ohm contends that the "list of potential PII will never stop growing until it includes everything." Ohm proposes that regulators abandon PII and instead "prevent privacy harm by squeezing and reducing the flow of information in society, even though in doing so they may need to sacrifice, at least a little, important counter values like innovation, free speech, and security." He would replace the current reliance on PII as a gatekeeper for privacy law with a cost-benefit analysis for *all* data processing and data collection of any kind. Ohm proposes that privacy regulation "should weigh the benefits of unfettered information flow against the cost of privacy harms." He proposes a minimum floor of safe handling of data for every data processor in the United States plus even stricter practices to be imposed on the entities that he terms "large entropy reducers." Ohm writes:

> Large entropy reducers are entities that amass massive databases containing so many links between so many disparate kinds of information that they represent a significant part of the database of ruin, even if they delete from their databases all particularly sensitive and directly linkable information. We can justify treating these entities differently using the language of duty and fault. Because large entropy reducers serve as one-stop shops for adversaries trying to link people to ruinous facts, they owe their data subjects a heightened duty of care. When a large entropy reducer loses control of its massive database, it causes much more harm than an entity holding much less data.

---

[78] Paul Ohm, *Broken Promises of Privacy*, 57 UCLA L. Rev. 1701 (2010).

[79] Arvind Narayanan & Vitaly Shmatikov, *Robust De-Anonymization of Large Sparse Datasets*, 2008 IEEE Symp. on Security and Privacy 111 (Feb. 5, 2008), available at http://arxiv.org/PS_cache/cs/pdf/0610/0610105v2.pdf.

[80] Narayanan & Shmatikov concede that the results did not "imply anything about the percentage of IMDb users who can be identified in the Netflix Prize dataset." *Id.* For an insightful technical analysis of the limits of the Netflix study and how it is has been misunderstood, see Jane Yakowitz, *Tragedy of the Data Commons*, 25 Harv. J.L. & Tech. __ (forthcoming 2011).

More specifically, Ohm identifies as "large entropy reducers" companies such as the credit reporting agencies (i.e., Equifax), data brokers (i.e., LexisNexis), and Internet search engines (i.e., Google). Do you think that a specific set of regulations should be devoted to companies such as the ones Ohm identifies?

4. ***Schwartz and Solove Propose PII 2.0.*** In contrast to Ohm, Paul Schwartz and Daniel Solove contend that information privacy law needs a concept of PII.[81] Without such a concept, information privacy law will be a boundless area—it will grow to regulate all information use. At the same time, Schwartz and Solove also propose that PII must be reconceptualized if privacy law is to remain effective in the future.

In their concept of PII 2.0, they propose three different regulatory categories, each of which would be treated differently. Schwartz and Solove write:

> Rather than a hard "on-off" switch, this approach allows legal safeguards for both identified and identifiable information, ones that permit tailored FIPs built around the different levels of risk to individuals. In our model of PII 2.0, information refers to (1) an identified, (2) identifiable, or (3) non-identifiable person. The continuum runs from actually being identified to no risk of identification, and our three categories divide up this spectrum and provide three different regimes of regulation. Because these categories do not have hard boundaries and are fluid, we define them in terms of standards.
>
> Information refers to an *identified* person when it singles out a specific individual from others. Put differently, a person has been identified when her identity is ascertained. There is general international agreement about the content of this category, albeit not of the implications of being placed in it. For example, in the U.S., the General Accounting Office, Office of Management and Budget, and National Institute of Standards and Technology associate this concept with information that distinguishes or traces a specific individual's identity.[82] In Europe, the Article 29 Group states that a person is identified "when, within a group of persons, he or she is 'distinguished' from all other members of the group."[83]
>
> In the middle of the risk continuum, information refers to an *identifiable* individual when a specific identification, while possible, is not a significantly probable event. In other words, an individual is identifiable when there is some non-remote possibility of future identification. The risk level is moderate to low. This information should be treated differently than an important sub-category of nominally identifiable information, where a linkage to a specific person has not yet been made, but where such a connection is more likely. . . . [S]uch nominally identifiable data should be treated the same as identified data.

---

[81] Paul Schwartz & Daniel Solove, *The PII Problem: Privacy and a New Concept of Personally Identifiable Information*, 86 N.Y.U. L. Rev. __ (2011).

[82] National Institute of Standards and Technology, *Guide to Protecting the Confidentiality of Personally Identifiable Information* (PII) 2–1 (2010); General Accounting Office, *Privacy: Alternatives Exist for Enhancing Protection of Personally Identifiable Information* (May 2008); Office of Management & Budget, *Memorandum 07-16, Safeguarding Against and Responding to the Breach of Personally Identifiable Information* (2007).

[83] Article 29 Data Protection Working Party, *Opinion 4/2007 on the Concept of Personal Data* 12 (June, 20, 2007).

At the other end of the risk continuum, *non-identifiable* information carries only a remote risk of identification. Such data cannot be said to be relatable to a person taking account of the means reasonably likely to be used for identification. In certain kinds of data sets, for example, the original sample is so large that other information will not enable the identification of individuals.

Schwartz and Solove argue that re-identification is a risk rather than a certainty, and the law should be based upon the degree of risk. That risk, however, is changing, because the ability to transform non-PII into identified information depends in part on the amount of personal data about people that is available — the more data, the easier it is to find a match. The risk also depends upon technology, which is changing. How should privacy regulation deal with this evolving landscape? Does PII 2.0 adequately address this problem?

5. ***Risks in De-identified Data?*** For Jane Yakowitz, the key question is "how much marginal risk does a public research database create in comparison to the background risks we already endure?"[84] Yakowitz assesses this marginal risk from data-sharing involving de-identified data as "trivially small." She reaches this conclusion by arguing that actual "adversaries" who will seek to de-identify are scarce, in part because of "lower hanging fruit," such as consumer databases that can be purchased, compared to anonymized databases. Yakowitz also points out that re-identifying subjects in anonymized databases is far from easy, but requires statistical expertise, and that "large repeat players" who share anonymized databases do not make "rookie mistakes."

A white paper by Ann Cavoukian, the Information and Privacy Commissioner of Ontario, Canada, and Khaled El Emam has argued along similar lines.[85] In their view, despite "a residual risk of re-identification, in the vast majority of cases, de-identification will protect the privacy of individuals, as long as additional safeguards are in place." In their four-step process, the re-identification risk exposure of a data disclosure depends upon: "the re-identification probability; the mitigating controls that are in place; the motives and capacity of the data recipient to re-identify the data; and the extent to which an inappropriate disclosure would be an invasion of privacy."

Data security breach laws also rely on definitions of PII. We examine this area of law in the next section.

---

[84] Jane Yakowitz, *Tragedy of the Data Commons*, 25 Harv. J.L. & Tech. __ (2011).

[85] Ann Cavoukian & Khaled El Emam, *Dispelling the Myths Surrounding De-Identification: Anonymization Remains a Strong Tool for Protecting Privacy* (Information and Privacy Commissioner of Ontario, June 2011).

C. DATA SECURITY

1. INTRODUCTION

The Database Industry. The database industry consists of companies that compile, analyze, and trade personal data. These companies are known as data brokers. Journalist Robert O'Harrow, Jr., describes several of the large database companies in detail. For example, Acxiom is "a billion-dollar player in the data industry, with details about nearly every adult in the United States." Acxiom provides information to marketers for profiling consumers, manages credit records, sells data for background checks, and provides data to government agencies. According to O'Harrow:

> It's not just names, ages, addresses, and telephone numbers. The computers in [Acxiom's] rooms also hold billions of records about marital status and families and ages of children. They track individuals' estimated incomes, the value of their homes, the make and price of their cars. They maintain unlisted phone numbers and details about people's occupations, religions, and ethnicities. They sometimes know what some people read, what they order over the phone and online, and where they go on vacation. . . .
>
> When someone makes a toll-free call to a client of Acxiom to inquire about clothing or to buy some shoes, information about who the caller is and where he or she lives pops up on a screen. . . . Using TeleSource, the agent can often find out the kind of home the caller lives in, the type of cars the people in the household drive, whether they exercise.

Another major database company is ChoicePoint, which was formed in 1997 as a spin-off from the credit reporting agency Equifax. O'Harrow observes: "ChoicePoint has a total of about 17 billion online public records, a figure that grows by more than 40,000 every day. . . . All told, the company has more than 250 terabytes of data regarding the lives of about 220 million adults."[86]

LexisNexis is another of the large data broker companies. It is commonly known for its legal research services, but it also processes personal information.

In addition to these large data brokers are numerous companies that compile, analyze, and sell data for marketing purposes. Daniel Solove describes some of these companies:

> The most powerful database builders construct information empires, sometimes with information on more than half of the American population. For example, Donnelly Marketing Information Services of New Jersey keeps track of 125 million people. Wiland Services has constructed a database containing over 1,000 elements, from demographic information to behavioral data, on over 215 million people.[87]

---

[86] Robert O'Harrow, Jr., *No Place to Hide* 34, 37-50, 145 (2005). For more background, see Chris Jay Hoofnagle, *Big Brother's Little Helpers: How ChoicePoint and Other Commercial Data Brokers Collect and Package Your Data for Law Enforcement*, 29 N.C. J Int'l L. & Commercial Reg. 595, 602-03 (2004).

[87] Daniel J. Solove, *The Digital Person: Technology and Privacy in the Information Age* 20 (2004).

Data Security Breaches. Several of the largest database companies have had significant security breaches. In 2003, Acxiom had two security breaches. In the first, a person "took the names, credit card numbers, Social Security numbers, addresses, and other details about an estimated 20 million people." In the second, hackers from Florida improperly gained access to Acxiom's records over a period of a few months.[88] In 2005, LexisNexis announced that unauthorized individuals had improperly accessed personal information on about 32,000 people from its Accurint database, which is part of Seisint that LexisNexis acquired in 2004.

The security breach that garnered the most attention, however, involved ChoicePoint. In 2005, ChoicePoint sent over 30,000 letters to California residents announcing that it had suffered a major security breach. It did so because of California's data security notification law, S.B. 1386, codified at Cal. Civ. Code § 1798.82(a), which required individual notification when a security breach involved people's data. At the time, California was the only state with such a law.

The security breach occurred because an identity theft crime ring set up fake businesses and then signed up to receive ChoicePoint's data. As a result, personal information, including names, addresses, and SSNs of over 145,000 people, were improperly accessed. Over 700 of these individuals were victimized by some form of identity theft.

The fraud was discovered in October 2004 by ChoicePoint, but victims were not notified until February 2005 to avoid impeding the law enforcement investigation. When news of the breach was announced, it sparked considerable public attention. After angry statements by many state attorneys general and a public outcry, ChoicePoint decided to voluntarily notify all individuals affected by the breach, not just Californians.

Subsequent to the ChoicePoint incident, there has been no shortage of other security breaches. Today, data security breaches continue to be announced on a frequent basis. In response, Congress initiated several hearings and bills to examine the database industry and address information privacy and identity theft issues. Bills with various information privacy protections were proposed and passed in many states. Moreover, very shortly after the ChoicePoint security breach, states began to enact data security breach notification laws. Today, 46 states, the District of Columbia, and the Virgin Islands now have enacted such statutes.

2. DATA SECURITY BREACH NOTIFICATION STATUTES

California was the first state to require companies that maintain personal information to notify individuals in the event of a security breach where personal information is leaked or improperly accessed. Pursuant to SB 1386, codified at Cal. Civ. Code § 1798.82(a):

Any person or business that conducts business in California, and that owns or licenses computerized data that includes personal information, shall disclose any

---

[88] O'Harrow, *supra,* at 71-72.

breach of the security of the system following discovery or notification of the breach in the security of the data to any resident of California whose unencrypted personal information was, or is reasonably believed to have been, acquired by an unauthorized person. The disclosure shall be made in the most expedient time possible and without unreasonable delay, consistent with the legitimate needs of law enforcement. . . .

The California security breach notice provision received national attention after the ChoicePoint data security breach in 2005. Afterwards, almost all states enacted data breach notification laws. These statutes require governmental agencies and/or private companies to disclose security breaches involving personal information.[89] These laws vary according to the following criteria: (1) the entities that the law covers; (2) the law's trigger for notification; (3) any exceptions to the law's notification requirement; (4) the party to whom disclosure is required under the law; (5) whether there is a substantive requirement for data security; and (6) the presence or absence of a private right of action.[90]

Most states follow the California approach and rely on the "acquisition" standard for breach notification. These states generally require notification whenever there is a reasonable likelihood that an unauthorized party has "acquired" person information. A minority of states have adopted a higher standard. These states consider whether there is a reasonable likelihood of "misuse" of the information, or "material risk" of harm to the person. The idea is that a breach letter should not be sent to the affected public unless there is a more significant likelihood of harm. Similarly, only a minority of the statutes provide a private right of action for individuals whose information has been breached, or create a substantive duty to take reasonable steps to safeguard data. Typically, these statutes provide open-ended, general standards, such as a requirement to provide "reasonable security procedures and practices appropriate to the nature of the information." In California, such standards are supplemented by nonbinding, albeit more specific, recommendations from the Office of Privacy Protection.

As noted, most states rely on the same basic trigger for notification: a reasonable belief of "acquisition" of the leaked data. A minority of states require the likelihood of outside "misuse" of the information. More generally, breach notification letters may lose their effectiveness if consumers become dulled by frequent cautions about harms that never materialize. In this sense, Fred Cate writes "if the California law were adopted nationally, like the boy who cried wolf, the flood of notices would soon teach consumers to ignore them. When real danger threatened, who would listen?"[91]

The HITECH Act of 2009 amended the Health Insurance Portability and Accountability Act (HIPAA) regulations to create the first federal data security breach notification requirement. A breach consists of an unauthorized disclosure of "unsecured" (unencrypted) health information. Individuals must be notified

---

[89] National Conference of State Legislatures, State Security Breach Notifications Laws, http://www.ncsl.org/programs/lis/cip/priv/breachlaws.htm (last visited July 16, 2008. For an analysis of data security breach laws, see Paul Schwartz & Edward Janger, *Notification of Data Security Breaches*, 105 Mich. L. Rev. 913, 924-25 (2007).

[90] For a chart examining these laws, state by state, see Daniel J. Solove & Paul M. Schwartz, *Privacy Law Fundamentals* 136-38 (2011).

[91] *See, e.g.,* Fred H. Cate, *Another Notice Isn't an Answer*, USA Today, Feb. 27, 2005, at 14A.

"without reasonable delay" — and no later than 60 days after discovering the breach.

What kind of breach notification statute would be optimal? Schwartz and Janger contend that notification letters to people whose data was leaked play an important role. Within organizations, notification letters have the potential to (1) create a credible threat of negative costs or other punishments for the firm, (2) improve information flows within the firm, and (3) strengthen the position of the data security and privacy officers at the company. Moreover, breach notification letters can play an important role outside the breached organization. Mandated breach disclosure can trigger legislative and other regulatory activity. Schwartz and Janger argue:

> As information about data security breaches and industry practices becomes public, the public, media, and legislators learn about the kinds of errors that lead to data breaches and the types of mistakes that companies make. This situation creates an opportunity for legislators to suggest new regulations and for governmental agencies to provide pressure as to the appropriate content of existing legal standards.[92]

Schwartz and Janger propose that the critical need is for a "coordinated response architecture," which would include a "coordinated response agent" (CRA) to help tailor notice content and supervise the decision whether to give notice. Notification to the consumer would follow upon a reasonable likelihood of "misuse" of notification-triggering information, and notification to the CRA would require the lower standard of a reasonable likelihood of "unauthorized access." The CRA will help coordinate actions that companies take after a breach, tailor the content of the notification in light of the nature of the data breach, and help prepare comparative statistical information regarding data security events.

3. CIVIL LIABILITY

PISCIOTTA V. OLD NATIONAL BANCORP
499 F.3d 629 (7th Cir. 2007)

RIPPLE, J. Plaintiffs Luciano Pisciotta and Daniel Mills brought this action on behalf of a putative class of customers and potential customers of Old National Bancorp ("ONB"). They alleged that, through its website, ONB had solicited personal information from applicants for banking services, but had failed to secure it adequately. As a result, a third-party computer "hacker" was able to obtain access to the confidential information of tens of thousands of ONB site users. The plaintiffs sought damages for the harm that they claim to have suffered because of the security breach; specifically, they requested compensation for past and future credit monitoring services that they have obtained in response to the compromise of their personal data through ONB's website. ONB answered the allegations and then moved for judgment on the pleadings under Rule 12(c).

---

[92] Schwartz & Janger, *Data Security, supra,* at 956.

The district court granted ONB's motion and dismissed the case. The plaintiffs timely appeal. For the reasons set forth in this opinion, we affirm the judgment of the district court. . . .

ONB operates a marketing website on which individuals seeking banking services can complete online applications for accounts, loans and other ONB banking services. The applications differ depending on the service requested, but some forms require the customer or potential customer's name, address, social security number, driver's license number, date of birth, mother's maiden name and credit card or other financial account numbers. In 2002 and 2004, respectively, Mr. Pisciotta and Mr. Mills accessed this website and entered personal information in connection with their applications for ONB banking services.

In 2005, NCR, a hosting facility that maintains ONB's website, notified ONB of a security breach. ONB then sent written notice to its customers. The results of the investigation that followed have been filed under seal in this court; for present purposes, it will suffice to note that the scope and manner of access suggests that the intrusion was sophisticated, intentional and malicious.

Mr. Pisciotta and Mr. Mills, on behalf of a putative class of other ONB website users, brought this action in the United States District Court for the Southern District of Indiana. They named ONB and NCR as defendants and asserted negligence claims against both defendants as well as breach of implied contract claims by ONB and breach of contract by NCR. The plaintiffs alleged that:

> [b]y failing to adequately protect [their] personal confidential information, [ONB and NCR] caused Plaintiffs and other similarly situated past and present customers to suffer substantial potential economic damages and emotional distress and worry that third parties will use [the plaintiffs'] confidential personal information to cause them economic harm, or sell their confidential information to others who will in turn cause them economic harm.

In pleading their damages, the plaintiffs stated that they and others in the putative class "have incurred expenses in order to prevent their confidential personal information from being used and will continue to incur expenses in the future." Significantly, the plaintiffs did not allege any *completed direct* financial loss to their accounts as a result of the breach. Nor did they claim that they or any other member of the putative class *already had been* the victim of identity theft as a result of the breach. The plaintiffs requested "[c]ompensation for all economic and emotional damages suffered as a result of the Defendants' acts which were negligent, in breach of implied contract or in breach of contract," and "[a]ny and all other legal and/or equitable relief to which Plaintiffs . . . are entitled, including establishing an economic monitoring procedure to insure [sic] prompt notice to Plaintiffs . . . of any attempt to use their confidential personal information stolen from the Defendants." . . .

As we have noted, in reaching the conclusion that dismissal was appropriate, the district court in this case relied on several cases from other district courts throughout the Country. Many of those cases have concluded that the federal courts lack jurisdiction because plaintiffs whose data has been compromised, but not yet misused, have not suffered an injury-in-fact sufficient to confer Article III standing. We are not persuaded by the reasoning of these cases. As many of our sister circuits have noted, the injury-in-fact requirement can be satisfied by a threat of future harm or by an act which harms the plaintiff only by increasing the risk of future harm that the plaintiff would have otherwise faced, absent the defendant's actions. We concur in this view. Once the plaintiffs' allegations establish at least this level of injury, the fact that the plaintiffs anticipate that some greater potential harm might follow the defendant's act does not affect the standing inquiry. . . .

The principal claims in this case are based on a negligence theory. The elements of a negligence claim under Indiana law are: "(1) a duty owed to plaintiff by defendant, (2) breach of duty by allowing conduct to fall below the applicable standard of care, and (3) a *compensable injury* proximately caused by defendant's breach of duty." The plaintiffs' complaint also alleges that ONB has breached an implied contract. Compensable damages are an element of a breach of contract cause of action as well.

As this case comes to us, both the negligence and the contractual issues can be resolved, and the judgment of the district court affirmed, *if* the district court was correct in its determination that Indiana law would not permit recovery for credit monitoring costs incurred by the plaintiffs. . . . We must determine whether Indiana would consider that the harm caused by identity information exposure, coupled with the attendant costs to guard against identity theft, constitutes an existing *compensable injury and consequent damages* required to state a claim for negligence or for breach of contract. Neither the parties' efforts nor our own have identified any Indiana precedent addressing this issue. Nor have we located the decision of any court (other than the district court in this case) that examines Indiana law in this context. We are charged with predicting, nevertheless, how we think the Supreme Court of Indiana would decide this issue. . . .

We begin our inquiry with the Indiana authority most closely addressed to the issue before us. On March 21, 2006, the Indiana legislature enacted a statute that applies to certain database security breaches. Specifically, the statute creates certain duties when a database in which personal data, electronically stored by private entities or state agencies, potentially has been accessed by unauthorized third parties. I.C. § 24-4.9 *et seq.* The statute took effect on July 1, 2006, after the particular incident involved in this case; neither party contends that the statute is directly applicable to the present dispute. We nevertheless find this enactment by the Indiana legislature instructive in our evaluation of the probable approach of the Supreme Court of Indiana to the allegations in the present case.

The provisions of the statute applicable to private entities storing personal information require only that a database owner *disclose* a security breach to potentially affected consumers; they do not require the database owner to take any other affirmative act in the wake of a breach. If the database owner fails to comply with the only affirmative duty imposed by the statute — the duty to disclose — the statute provides for enforcement *only* by the Attorney General of Indiana. It creates no private right of action against the database owner by an affected customer. It imposes no duty to compensate affected individuals for inconvenience or potential harm to credit that may follow. . . .

The plaintiffs maintain that the statute is evidence that the Indiana legislature believes that an individual has suffered a compensable injury at the moment his personal information is exposed because of a security breach. We cannot accept this view. Had the Indiana legislature intended that a cause of action should be available against a database owner for failing to protect adequately personal information, we believe that it would have made some more definite statement of that intent. Moreover, given the novelty of the legal questions posed by information exposure and theft, it is unlikely that the legislature intended to sanction the development of common law tort remedies that would apply to the same factual circumstances addressed by the statute. The narrowness of the defined duties imposed, combined with state-enforced penalties as the exclusive remedy, strongly suggest that Indiana law would not recognize the costs of credit monitoring that the plaintiffs seek to recover in this case as compensable damages.

The plaintiffs further submit that cases decided by the Indiana courts in analogous areas of the law instruct that they suffered an immediate injury when their information was accessed by unauthorized third parties. Specifically, the plaintiffs claim that Indiana law acknowledges special duties on the part of banks to prevent the disclosure of the personal information of their customers; they further claim that Indiana courts have recognized explicitly the significant harm that may result from a failure to prevent such a loss. . . . [One of these cases concerned disclosure to law enforcement that a bank account had been "marked for repossession"; the other, a creditor who was told that the plaintiff's bank account had insufficient funds to cover checks written.]

Whatever these cases say about the relationship of banks and customers in Indiana, they are of marginal assistance to us in determining whether the present plaintiffs are entitled to the remedy they seek as a matter of Indiana law. The reputational injuries suffered by the plaintiffs in [the previous Indiana cases] were direct and immediate; the plaintiffs sought to be compensated for that harm, rather than to be reimbursed for their efforts to guard against some future, anticipated harm. We therefore do not believe that the factual circumstances of the cases relied on by the plaintiffs are sufficiently analogous to the circumstances that we confront in the present case to instruct us on the probable course that the Supreme Court of Indiana would take if faced with the present question.

Although not raised by the parties, we separately note that in the somewhat analogous context of toxic tort liability, the Supreme Court of Indiana has suggested that compensable damage requires more than an exposure to a future potential harm. Specifically, in *AlliedSignal, Inc. v. Ott,* 785 N.E.2d 1068 (Ind. 2003), the Supreme Court of Indiana held that no cause of action accrues, despite incremental physical changes following asbestos exposure, until a plaintiff reasonably could have been diagnosed with an actual exposure-related illness or disease. . . . [E]xposure alone does not give rise to a legally cognizable injury.

Although some courts have allowed medical monitoring damages to be recovered or have created a special cause of action for medical monitoring under similar circumstances, *see Badillo v. American Brands, Inc.,* 16 P.3d 435 (Nev. 2001) (citing cases interpreting the law of seventeen states to allow medical monitoring in some form), no authority from Indiana is among them. Indeed, its recent holding in *AlliedSignal* indicates a contrary approach. To the extent the decision of the Supreme Court of Indiana in that matter provides us with guidance on the likely approach that court would adopt with respect to the information exposure injury in this case, we think it supports the view that no cause of action for credit monitoring is available.

Finally, without Indiana guidance directly on point, we next examine the reasoning of other courts applying the law of other jurisdictions to the question posed by this case. *Allstate Ins. Co.,* 392 F.3d at 952. In this respect, several district courts, applying the laws of other jurisdictions, have rejected similar claims on their merits. In addition to those cases in which the district court held that the plaintiff lacked standing, a series of cases has rejected information security claims on their merits. Most have concluded that the plaintiffs have not been injured in a manner the governing substantive law will recognize.

Although some of these cases involve different types of information losses, all of the cases rely on the same basic premise: Without more than allegations of increased risk of future identity theft, the plaintiffs have not suffered a harm that the law is prepared to remedy. Plaintiffs have not come forward with a single case or statute, from any jurisdiction, authorizing the kind of action they now ask this federal court, sitting in diversity, to recognize as a valid theory of recovery under Indiana law. We decline to adopt a "substantive innovation" in state law, or "to invent what would be a truly novel tort claim" on behalf of the state, absent some authority to suggest that the approval of the Supreme Court of Indiana is forthcoming.

In sum, all of the interpretive tools of which we routinely make use in our attempt to determine the content of state law point us to the conclusion that the Supreme Court of Indiana would not allow the plaintiffs' claim to proceed.

NOTES & QUESTIONS

1. ***Private Rights of Action?*** In *Pisciotta*, the court decides that the Indiana legislature did not create "a cause of action against the database owner for failing to protect adequately personal information." As an example of a statute with such a private right of action, California enacted AB 1950 in 2004, a year after passing SB 1386, its data breach notification law. AB 1950 provides: "A business that owns or licenses personal information about a California resident . . . [to] implement and maintain reasonable security procedures and practices appropriate to the nature of the information, to protect the personal information from unauthorized access, destruction, use, modification, or disclosure." Cal. Civ. Code § 1798.81(b). California law also provides a private right of action in its unfair competition law (which generally permits a private party to bring a lawsuit against any business practice otherwise forbidden by law) and in its breach notification law, § 1798.84 (which provides for a right of action for any "customer injured by a violation of this title"). What is the promise and peril of a private right of action for an organization's failure to maintain reasonable data security?

2. ***Tort Negligence for Data Security Breaches.*** In tort law, under a general negligence theory, litigants might sue a company after a data security incident and seek to collect damages. Thus far, however, class action lawsuits

following data breaches have been notably unsuccessful. Among other problems, claimants are facing trouble convincing courts that the data processing entities owe a duty to the individuals whose data are leaked, or that damages can be inferred from the simple fact of a data breach. For example, a South Carolina court declared in 2003 that "[t]he relationship, if any, between credit card issuers and potential victims of identity theft is far too attenuated to rise to the level of a duty between them." *Huggins v. Citibank*, 585 S.E.2d 275 (S.C. 2003).

3. ***Proving Harm from Data Security Breaches.*** Suppose a person has been notified that her personal information has been improperly accessed, but she has not yet suffered from identity theft. Should she be entitled to any form of compensation? Has she suffered an injury? One might argue that being made more vulnerable to future harm has made her worse off than before. The individual might live with greater unease knowing that she is less secure. On the other hand, no identity theft has occurred, and it may never occur. How should the law address this situation? Recognize a harm? If so, how should damages be assessed?

In *Forbes v. Wells Fargo Bank, N.A.*, 420 F. Supp. 2d 1018 (D. Minn. 2006), a contractor for Wells Fargo Bank had computers stolen containing unencrypted data about customers, such as names, addresses, Social Security numbers, and account numbers. A group of customers sued for breach of contract, breach of fiduciary duty, and negligence. The court, however, dismissed the case:

> Plaintiffs allege that Wells Fargo negligently allowed Regulus to keep customers' private information without adequate security. To establish a negligence claim, a plaintiff must prove that (1) the defendant owed plaintiff a duty of care, (2) the defendant breached that duty, (3) the plaintiff sustained damage and (4) the breach of the duty proximately caused the damage. A plaintiff may recover damages for an increased risk of harm in the future if such risk results from a present injury and indicates a reasonably certain future harm. Alone, however, "the threat of future harm, not yet realized, will not satisfy the damage requirement."
>
> Plaintiffs contend that the time and money they have spent monitoring their credit suffices to establish damages. However, a plaintiff can only recover for loss of time in terms of earning capacity or wages. Plaintiffs have failed to cite any Minnesota authority to the contrary. Moreover, they overlook the fact that their expenditure of time and money was not the result of any present injury, but rather the anticipation of future injury that has not materialized. In other words, the plaintiffs' injuries are solely the result of a perceived risk of future harm. Plaintiffs have shown no present injury or reasonably certain future injury to support damages for any alleged increased risk of harm. For these reasons, plaintiffs have failed to establish the essential element of damages. Therefore, summary judgment in favor of defendant on plaintiffs' negligence claim is warranted.
>
> Plaintiffs also bring a claim for breach of contract against Wells Fargo. To establish their claim, plaintiffs must show that they were damaged by the alleged breach. *See Jensen v. Duluth Area YMCA*, 688 N.W.2d 574, 578-79 (Minn. App. 2004). For all of the reasons discussed above, plaintiffs have

failed to establish damages. Therefore, summary judgment in favor of defendant on plaintiffs' breach of contract claim is warranted.

Also consider *In re Hannaford Bros. Co. Customer Data Security Breach Litigation*, 4 A.3d 492 (Me. 2010). Customers of a store whose payment data was stolen sued, claiming "that time and effort expended to avoid or remediate harm from fraudulent charges was a cognizable loss." The court disagreed:

> Our case law . . . does not recognize the expenditure of time and effort alone as a harm. The plaintiffs contend that because their time and effort represented reasonable efforts to avoid reasonably foreseeable harm, it is compensable. However, we do not attach such significance to mitigation efforts. . . . Unless the plaintiffs' loss of time reflects a corresponding loss of earnings or earning opportunities, it is not a cognizable injury under Maine law of negligence.

Why aren't expenditures to reduce risks of future harm created by another recoverable? Suppose a company leaks a toxic chemical, causing a person to have an increased risk of cancer. The person sees a doctor and gets a prescription for a drug that will reduce the likelihood that the chemical will cause cancer. Would the expenses of seeing the doctor and purchasing the drug be recoverable? Is this hypothetical analogous to a data security breach?

Although most courts conclude that data security breaches that do not lead to an incident of identity theft or fraud do not give rise to cognizable injuries sufficient for standing, a few courts have departed from this trend. *Pisciotta* is one of them. Although the plaintiffs ultimately lost, the court concluded that the plaintiff at least had standing because "the injury-in-fact requirement can be satisfied by a threat of future harm or by an act which harms the plaintiff only by increasing the risk of future harm that the plaintiff would have otherwise faced, absent the defendant's actions." Likewise, in *Krottner v. Starbucks Corp.*, 628 F.3d 1139 (9th Cir. 2010), the court concluded that increased vulnerability to identity theft could give rise to standing:

> If a plaintiff faces "a credible threat of harm," and that harm is "both real and immediate, not conjectural or hypothetical," the plaintiff has met the injury-in-fact requirement for standing under Article III. Here, Plaintiffs–Appellants have alleged a credible threat of real and immediate harm stemming from the theft of a laptop containing their unencrypted personal data. Were Plaintiffs–Appellants' allegations more conjectural or hypothetical—for example, if no laptop had been stolen, and Plaintiffs had sued based on the risk that it would be stolen at some point in the future—we would find the threat far less credible. On these facts, however, Plaintiffs–Appellants have sufficiently alleged an injury-in-fact for purposes of Article III standing.

4. *The Nature of Privacy Harms.* Ryan Calo has proposed a theory for how privacy harms should be understood:

> [T]he vast majority of privacy harms fall into just two categories — one subjective, the other objective. The subjective category of privacy harm is the perception of unwanted observation. This category describes unwelcome mental states — anxiety, for instance, or embarrassment — that accompany the belief that one is or will be watched or monitored. . . .

The objective category of privacy harm is the unanticipated or coerced use of information concerning a person against that person. These are negative, external actions justified by reference to personal information. Examples include the unanticipated sale of a user's contact information that results in spam and the leaking of classified information that exposes an undercover intelligence agent.

How does Calo's theory apply to data security breaches? Consider his analysis:

> As an initial matter, data breaches register as subjective privacy harms. When a consumer receives a notice in the mail telling her that her personal information has leaked out into the open, she experiences the exact sort of apprehension and feeling of vulnerability the first category of privacy harm is concerned about. That is, she believes that there has been or could be unwanted sensing of her private information. The same is true, to a lesser degree, when any of us read about a data breach — we feel less secure in our privacy overall.
>
> But what if there is a data breach or other increased risk of adverse consequence and the "victim" never knows about it? Then there has been neither subjective nor objective privacy harm, unless or until the information is used. Worse still, it would appear on this analysis that breach notification is a net evil in that it creates (subjective) privacy harm where there would be none.
>
> Here I disagree with this premise. A risk of privacy harm is no more a privacy harm than a chance of a burn is a burn. They are conceptually distinct: one is the thing itself, the other the likelihood of that thing. A feeling of greater vulnerability can constitute privacy harm, just as the apprehension of battery can constitute a distinct tort. But there is no assault or battery without the elements of apprehension or unwanted contact. . . .
>
> Similarly, it does not disparage the seriousness of a data breach, nor the inconvenience of having to protect against identity theft, to deny that any objective privacy harm has yet occurred. If anything, clarifying the nature of the harm at risk should help us protect against that harm actually occurring by selecting the appropriate remedy. The goal of some rules is to deter specific harms, for instance; others exist to empower the vulnerable or hinder the powerful in an effort to make harm less likely. Data breach notification laws fulfill both functions, even if they are technically the "but for" cause of one category of privacy harm.[93]

5. *Class Actions.* Many of the lawsuits in the wake of data security breaches are class actions. Although many have been dismissed because courts do not recognize a harm from a mere data leak without more direct proof of injuries to plaintiffs, others have ended in multi-million dollar settlements. Defendants may choose to settle, among other reasons, due to the high expense of litigation.

Do these class actions serving a valuable purpose? The attorneys receive a large award for attorney's fees, and class members rarely get significant benefits from the settlement. One might view class actions for data security

---

[93] M. Ryan Calo, *The Boundaries of Privacy Harm,* 86 Ind. L.J. 1131, 1133, 1256-57 (2011).

breaches as a kind of opportunistic extortion of settlement money. On the other hand, class actions provide a strong incentive for companies to be careful with personal data and take measures to avoid data security breaches. The attorney's fees serve as an incentive for spurring lawyers to bring and litigate the case — a reward for serving as a kind of "private attorney general." If not class action litigation, is there a more appropriate mechanism to deter data security breaches?

6. *Strict Liability for Data Security Breaches?* Danielle Citron argues for strict liability for harms caused by data breaches. Computer databases of personal information, Citron contends, are akin to the water reservoirs of the early Industrial Age:

> The dynamics of the early Industrial Age, a time of great potential and peril, parallel those at the advent of the Information Age. Then, as now, technological change brought enormous wealth and comfort to society. Industry thrived as a result of machines powered by water reservoirs. But when the dams holding those reservoirs failed, the escaping water caused massive property and personal damage different from the interpersonal harms of the previous century. *Rylands v. Fletcher* provided the Industrial Age's strict-liability response to the accidents caused by the valuable reservoirs' escaping water. The history of *Rylands's* reception in Britain and the United States reflects the tension between that era's desire for economic growth and its concern for security from industrial hazards.
>
> Computer databases are this century's reservoirs. . . . Much as water reservoirs drove the Industrial Age, computer databases fuel the Internet economy of our Information Age.

Citron argues that a strict liability regime is preferable to negligence tort liability:

> The rapidly changing nature of information technologies may create uncertainty as to what a negligence regime entails. . . .
>
> Due to the rapidly changing threats to information security, database operators will likely be uncertain as to what constitutes optimal care. Cyber-intruders employ increasingly innovative techniques to bypass security measures and steal personal data, thereby requiring an ever-changing information-security response to new threats, vulnerabilities, and technologies. . . .
>
> A negligence regime will fail to address the significant leaks that will occur despite database operators' exercise of due care over personal data. Security breaches are an inevitable byproduct of collecting sensitive personal information in computer databases. No amount of due care will prevent significant amounts of sensitive data from escaping into the hands of cyber-criminals. Such data leaks constitute the predictable residual risks of information reservoirs.
>
> Consequently, negligence will not efficiently manage the residual risks of hazardous databases. Negligence would neither induce database operators to change their activity level nor discourage marginal actors from collecting sensitive information because such operators need not pay for the accident costs of their residual risk.
>
> The high levels of residual risk suggest treating cyber-reservoirs as ultrahazardous activities — those with significant social utility and significant

risk — that warrant strict liability. As Judge Richard Posner has explained, ultrahazardous activities often involve something "new" that society has "little experience" securing, where neither the injurer nor victim can prevent the accident by taking greater care. This characterized water reservoirs in nineteenth-century England. Strict liability creates an incentive for actors engaging in ultrahazardous activities to "cut back on the scale of the activity . . . to slow its spread while more is learned about conducting it safely."

Classifying database collection as an ultrahazardous activity is a logical extension of Posner's analysis. Just as no clear safety standard governing the building and maintenance of water reservoirs had emerged in the 1850s, a stable set of information-security practices has not yet materialized today. . . .

In this analysis, strict liability has the potential to encourage a change in activity level respecting the storage of sensitive personal information, unless and until more information allows operators to better assess optimal precaution levels and to respond to the persistent problem of residual risk. Because strict liability would force database operators to internalize the full costs of their activities, marginally productive database operators might refrain from maintaining cyber-reservoirs of personal data. Strict liability also may decrease the collection of ultrasensitive data among those who are at greatest risk of security breaches. Moreover, as insurance markets develop in this emerging area, database operators that continue collecting sensitive information will be better positioned to assess the cost of residual risk and the extent to which they can spread the cost of such risk onto consumers.[94]

Are you convinced by the analogy between the database industry and reservoirs? Will strict liability lead to the correct level of investment in security by companies? Could it lead to over-investment in data security?

7. *Assessing the Federal Approach to Data Security.* As discussed above, after the ChoicePoint data security breach in 2005 — along with the numerous other breaches that followed — a majority of states have now passed data security breach legislation. Despite several proposed bills, the federal government has yet to pass a comprehensive data security law. However, some existing federal privacy laws protect data security in the context of particular industries. Consider Andrea Matwyshyn:

The current approach to information security, exemplified by statutes such as COPPA, HIPAA, and GLBA, attempts to regulate information security by creating legal "clusters" of entities based on the type of business they transact, the types of data they control, and that data's permitted and nonpermitted uses. In other words, the current regulatory approach has singled out a few points in the system for the creation of information security enclaves. . . .

The current approach ignores the fundamental tenet of security that a system is only as strong as its weakest links, not its strongest points. . . . It will not prove adequate to only ensure that a few points or clusters in the system are particularly well-secured. . . .

The biggest economic losses arise not out of illegal leveraging of these protected categories of data; rather, losses arise out of stolen personally

---

[94] Danielle Keats Citron, *Reservoirs of Danger: The Evolution of Public and Private Law at the Dawn of the Information Age,* 80 S. Cal. L. Rev. 241, 243-44, 263-67 (2007).

identifiable information, such as credit card data and social security numbers, which are warehoused frequently by entities that are not regulated by COPPA, HIPAA or GLBA. Therefore, creating enclaves of superior data security for data related to children online, some financial information, and some health data will not alleviate the weak information security in other parts of the system and will not substantially diminish information crime. . . . [95]

4. FTC REGULATION

The FTC has acted on numerous occasions to penalize merchants that fail to take reasonable measures to protect customer data. In a typical data security complaint, the FTC argues that the firm's data-handling practices constituted unfair acts or practices in violation of Section 5 of the Federal Trade Commission Act. In settling its enforcement actions, the FTC has required both general and specific pledges of reasonable data security.

The most dramatic of these FTC enforcement actions involved ChoicePoint. In settling the FTC charges, ChoicePoint agreed in January 2006 to pay $10 million in civil penalties and $5 million into a consumer redress fund.[96] The $10 million fine is the largest civil penalty in the FTC's history. ChoicePoint also promised changes to its business and improvements to its security practices.

The stipulated final judgment bars the company from furnishing consumer reports to customers without a permissible purpose and requires it to establish reasonable procedures to ensure that it will provide consumer reports only to those with a permissible purpose. One requirement placed on ChoicePoint is to verify the identity of businesses that apply to receive consumer reports by auditing subscribers' use of consumer reports and by making site visits to certain of its customers.

Finally, the settlement obligated ChoicePoint to establish and maintain a comprehensive information security program and to submit this program for two decades to outside independent audits. It agreed to "establish and implement, and thereafter maintain, a comprehensive information security program that is reasonably designed to protect the security, confidentiality, and integrity of personal information collected from or about consumers." In maintaining this "comprehensive information security program," ChoicePoint promised to engage in risk assessments and to design and implement regular testing of the effectiveness of its security program's key controls, systems, and procedures. It also agreed to obtain an initial and then biennial outside assessment of its data security safeguards from an independent third-party professional. The FTC has reached significant settlements in other data security cases as well. Consider the FTC's settlement in *In the Matter of Reed Elsevier, Inc. and Seisint* below.

---

[95] Andrea M. Matwyshyn, *Material Vulnerabilities: Data Privacy, Corporate Information Security, and Securities Regulation*, 3 Berkeley Bus. L.J. 129, 169-70 (2005).

[96] News Release, FTC, ChoicePoint *Settles Data Security Breach Charges* (Jan. 26, 2006), at http://www.ftc.gov/opa/2006/01/choicepoint.htm.

IN THE MATTER OF REED ELSEVIER, INC. AND SEISINT
2008 WL 903806 (F.T.C. 2008)

[Reed Elsevier acquired Seisint in September 2004 and operated it as a wholly owned subsidiary within LexisNexis, more widely known for providing legal information. Seisint collected and sold information about consumers, and did so under the trade name of "Accurint." According to the FTC's complaint, Seisint used its information "to locate assets and people, authenticate identities, and verify credentials." It also sold products about consumers to "insurance companies, debt collectors, employers, landlords, law firms, and law enforcement and other government agencies." In order to sell these products, Reed Elsevier and Seisint collected and aggregated information about millions of consumers from public and nonpublic sources.

The FTC alleged that in its security practices, Reed Elsevier and Seisint failed to provide "reasonable and appropriate security to prevent authorized access" to sensitive consumer information. It argued, "In particular, respondents failed to establish or implement reasonable policies and procedures governing the creation and authentication of user credentials for authorized customers. . . ." Among other flawed practices, the FTC pointed to the companies' failure to establish or enforce rules that would make it difficult to guess user credentials. It permitted their customers to use the same word as both password and user ID. In addition, it allowed the sharing of user credentials among multiple users at a single customer firm, which lowered the likely detection of unauthorized services. It also failed to mandate periodic changes of user credentials and did not implement simple, readily available defenses against common network attacks.

The consequences of the shortcomings in security practices at Reed Elsevier and Seisint were dramatic. In its complaint, the FTC stated:

> On multiple occasions since January 2003, attackers exploited respondent Seisint's user ID and password structures to obtain without authorization the user credentials of legitimate Accurint customers. The attackers then used these credentials to make thousands of unauthorized searches for consumer information in Accurint databases. These attacks disclosed sensitive information about several hundred thousand consumers, including, in many instances, names, current and prior addresses, dates of birth, and Social Security numbers. Although some of these attacks occurred before respondent REI acquired respondent Seisint, they continued for at least 9 months after the acquisition, during which time respondent Seisint was operating under the control of respondent REI. Since March 2005, respondent REI through LexisNexis has notified over 316,000 consumers that the attacks disclosed sensitive information about them that could be used to conduct identity theft.

These incidents also led to new credit accounts being opened in the name of customers.

On March 27, 2008, the FTC announced a settlement with Reed Elsevier and its Seisint subsidiary.]

AGREEMENT CONTAINING CONSENT ORDER

The Federal Trade Commission has conducted an investigation of certain acts and practices of Reed Elsevier Inc. and Seisint, Inc. ("proposed respondents"). Proposed respondents, having been represented by counsel, are willing to enter into an agreement containing a consent order resolving the allegations contained in the attached draft complaint. . . .

ORDER

For purposes of this order, the following definitions shall apply:

1. Unless otherwise specified, "respondents" shall mean Reed Elsevier Inc., its successors and assigns, officers, agents, representatives, and employees, and Seisint, Inc., and its successors and assigns, officers, agents, representatives, and employees.

2. "Personal information" shall mean individually identifiable information from or about a consumer including, but not limited to: (a) a first and last name; (b) a home or other physical address, including street name and name of city or town; (c) an email address or other online contact information, such as an instant messaging user identifier or a screen name that reveals a consumer's email address; (d) a telephone number; (e) a Social Security number; (f) a date of birth; (g) a driver's license number; (h) credit and/or debit card information, including but not limited to card number and expiration date and transaction detail data; (i) a persistent identifier, such as a customer number held in a "cookie" or processor serial number, that is combined with other available data that identifies a consumer; or (j) any other information from or about a consumer that is combined with (a) through (i) above.

3. "Information product or service" shall mean each product, service, or other means by which respondents individually or collectively provide direct or indirect access to personal information from or about consumers that is comprised in whole or part of nonpublic information; *provided, however*, that this term shall not include information products or services that: (a) provide access solely to personal information that is publicly available information, or (b) permit customers to upload or otherwise supply, organize, manage, or retrieve information that is under the customer's control.

4. "Publicly available information" shall mean information that respondents have a reasonable basis to believe is lawfully made available to the general public from: (a) Federal, State, or local government records, (b) widely distributed media, or (c) disclosures to the general public that are required to be made by Federal, State, or local law. Respondents shall have a reasonable basis to believe information is lawfully made available to the general public if respondents have taken reasonable steps to determine: (a) that the information is of the type that is available to the general public, and (b) whether an individual can direct that the information not be made available to the general public and, if so, that the individual has not done so.

I.

IT IS ORDERED that each respondent, directly or through any corporation, subsidiary, division, or other device, in connection with the advertising, marketing, promotion, offering for sale, or sale of personal information collected from or about consumers made available through any information product or service of LexisNexis ("the information"), in or affecting commerce, shall, no later than the date of service of this order, establish and implement, and thereafter maintain, a comprehensive information security program that is reasonably designed to protect the security, confidentiality, and integrity of the information. Such program, the content and implementation of which must be fully documented in writing, shall contain administrative, technical, and physical safeguards appropriate to each respondent's size and complexity, the nature and scope of each respondent's activities, and the sensitivity of the information, including:

A. the designation of an employee or employees to coordinate and be accountable for the information security program.

B. the identification of material internal and external risks to the security, confidentiality, and integrity of the information that could result in the unauthorized disclosure, misuse, loss, alteration, destruction, or other compromise of the information, and assessment of the sufficiency of any safeguards in place to control these risks. At a minimum, this risk assessment should include consideration of risks in each area of relevant operation, including, but not limited to: (1) employee training and management; (2) information systems, including network and software design, information processing, storage, transmission, and disposal; and (3) prevention, detection, and response to attacks, intrusions, or other systems failures.

C. the design and implementation of reasonable safeguards to control the risks identified through risk assessment, and regular testing or monitoring of the effectiveness of the safeguards' key controls, systems, and procedures.

D. the development and use of reasonable steps to select and retain service providers capable of appropriately safeguarding personal information they receive from respondent, and requiring service providers by contract to implement and maintain appropriate safeguards; *provided, however*, that this subparagraph shall not apply to personal information about a consumer that respondent provides to a government agency or lawful information supplier when the agency or supplier already possesses the information and uses it only to retrieve, and supply to respondent, additional personal information about the consumer.

E. the evaluation and adjustment of respondent's information security program in light of the results of the testing and monitoring required by subparagraph C, any material changes to respondent's operations or business arrangements, or any other circumstances that respondent knows or has reason to know may have a material impact on the effectiveness of its information security program.

II.

IT IS FURTHER ORDERED that, in connection with its compliance with Paragraph I of this order, each respondent shall obtain initial and biennial assessments and reports ("Assessments") from a qualified, objective, independent third-party professional, who uses procedures and standards generally accepted in the profession. The reporting period for the Assessments shall cover: (1) the first one hundred and eighty (180) days after service of the order for the initial Assessment, and (2) each two (2) year period thereafter for twenty (20) years after service of the order for the biennial Assessments. Each Assessment shall:

A. set forth the specific administrative, technical, and physical safeguards that respondent has implemented and maintained during the reporting period;

B. explain how such safeguards are appropriate to respondent's size and complexity, the nature and scope of respondent's activities, and the sensitivity of the personal information collected from or about consumers;

C. explain how the safeguards that have been implemented meet or exceed the protections required by Paragraph I of this order; and

D. certify that respondent's security program is operating with sufficient effectiveness to provide reasonable assurance that the security, confidentiality, and integrity of personal information is protected and has so operated throughout the reporting period.

Each Assessment shall be prepared and completed within sixty (60) days after the end of the reporting period to which the Assessment applies by a person qualified as a Certified Information System Security Professional (CISSP) or as a Certified Information Systems Auditor (CISA); a person holding Global Information Assurance Certification (GIAC) from the SysAdmin, Audit, Network, Security (SANS) Institute; or a similarly qualified person or organization. . . .

VII.

This order will terminate twenty (20) years from the date of its issuance, or twenty (20) years from the most recent date that the United States or the Federal Trade Commission files a complaint (with or without an accompanying consent decree) in federal court alleging any violation of the order, whichever comes later. . . .

NOTES & QUESTIONS

1. *The Terms of Settlement.* This settlement illustrates the FTC's classic approach in its data security settlements of imposing long-term requirements for an information security program. Do you think that the settlement terms in *Reed Elsevier* are appropriate? Does the FTC strike the correct balance in providing some flexibility to the companies in deciding the content of a reasonable security program?

2. *Damages:* **Reed Elsevier** *vs.* **ChoicePoint.** Unlike other companies with whom the FTC has settled claims, Reed Elsevier and Seisint avoided paying fines. Should the FTC have sought to negotiate the payment of damages in *Reed Elsevier*? In its *ChoicePoint* settlement, discussed above, the FTC negotiated a payment of $10 million in civil penalties and $5 million for civil redress. It found that ChoicePoint violated the FCRA by furnishing credit histories to subscribers without a permissible purpose and violated the FTC Act by making false and misleading statements about its privacy practices. One possible difference in the FTC's ability to obtain damages in *ChoicePoint*

concerned the company's FCRA violations. The FTC in its *ChoicePoint* complaint sought monetary civil penalties for each separate violation of the FCRA. A violation of FCRA, according to the FTC, occurred each time ChoicePoint (1) furnished a consumer report to a person without a permissible purpose for it, (2) failed to make a reasonable effort to verify the identity of the prospective user, or (3) furnished a consumer report to any person when it had reasonable grounds for believing the report would not be used for a FCRA permissible purpose. Is there a similar way to create a framework for assessing damages in *Reed Elsevier*?

3. *Data Leaks:* **Eli Lilly.** In *FTC v. Eli Lilly*, No. 012-3214, the FTC charged Eli Lilly, a pharmaceutical company, with disclosing people's health data that it collected through its Prozac.com website. Prozac is a drug used for treating depression. Lilly offered customers an e-mail service that would send them e-mail messages to remind them to take or refill their medication. In June 2001, the company sent e-mail messages to all 669 users of the reminder service announcing that the service was terminated. However, this message contained the e-mail addresses of all subscribers in the "To" line of the message. The FTC alleged that the company's privacy policy promising confidentiality was deceptive because the company failed to establish adequate security protections for its consumers' data. Specifically, the FTC complaint alleged that Eli Lilly failed to

> provide appropriate training for its employees regarding consumer privacy and information security; provide appropriate oversight and assistance for the employee who sent out the e-mail, who had no prior experience in creating, testing, or implementing the computer program used; and implement appropriate checks and controls on the process, such as reviewing the computer program with experienced personnel and pretesting the program internally before sending out the e-mail.

In January 2002, Eli Lilly settled. The settlement requires Eli Lilly to establish a new security program. It must designate personnel to oversee the program, identify and address various security risks, and conduct an annual review of the security program. FTC Commissioners voted 5–0 to approve the settlement.

Consider the settlements in the cases described above. Do you think that these settlements are adequate to redress the rights of the individuals affected?

4. **Microsoft Passport** *and* **Guess:** *Proactive FTC Enforcement?* Microsoft launched Microsoft.NET Passport, an online authentication service. Passport allowed consumers to use a single username and password to access multiple websites. The goal of Passport was to serve as a universal sign-on service, eliminating the need to sign on to each website separately. A related service, Wallet, permitted users to submit credit card and billing information in order to make purchases at multiple websites without having to reenter the information on each site.

The FTC initiated an investigation of the Passport services following a July 2001 complaint from a coalition of consumer groups. In the petition to the

FTC, the privacy groups raised questions about the collection, use, and disclosure of personal information that Passport would make possible, and asserted that Microsoft's representations about the security of the system were both unfair and deceptive. In its privacy policy, Microsoft promised that ".NET Passport is protected by powerful online security technology and a strict privacy policy." Further, Microsoft stated: "Your .NET Passport information is stored on secure .NET Passport servers that are protected in controlled facilities."

On August 8, 2002, the FTC found that Microsoft had violated § 5 of the FTC Act and announced a proposed settlement with the company. *See In the Matter of Microsoft Corp.,* No. 012-3240. The Commission found that Microsoft falsely represented that (1) it employs reasonable and appropriate measures under the circumstances to maintain and protect the privacy and confidentiality of consumers' personal information collected through its Passport and Wallet services; (2) purchases made with Passport Wallet are generally safer or more secure than purchases made at the same site without Passport Wallet when, in fact, most consumers received identical security at those sites regardless of whether they used Passport Wallet to complete their transactions; (3) Passport did not collect any personally identifiable information other than that described in its privacy policy when, in fact, Passport collected and held, for a limited time, a personally identifiable sign-in history for each user; and (4) the Kids Passport program provided parents control over what information participating websites could collect from their children.

Under the terms of the proposed consent order, Microsoft may not make any misrepresentations, expressly or by implication, of any of its information practices. Microsoft is further obligated to establish a "comprehensive information security program," and conduct an annual audit to assess the security practices. Microsoft is also required to make available to the FTC for a period of five years all documents relating to security practices as well as compliance with the orders. The order remains in place for 20 years.

The FTC took a similar approach in *In re Guess.com, Inc.,* No. 022-3260 (July 30, 2003). Guess, a clothing company, had promised that all personal information "including . . . credit card information and sign-in password, are stored in an unreadable, encrypted format at all times." This assertion of company policy was false, and the FTC initiated an action even before data was leaked or improperly accessed. The case was eventually settled.

In both *Microsoft* and *Guess,* the FTC brought an action before any data security breach had occurred. Is this a form of proactive enforcement? Suppose a company merely makes a general promise to "keep customer data secure." The FTC believes that the company is not providing adequate security and brings an action. How should the adequacy of a company's security practices be evaluated, especially in cases in which privacy policies are vague about the precise security measures taken?

5. ***The Gramm-Leach-Bliley Act and the FTC.*** Consider the following observation by Daniel Solove:

> [O]ne problem with the FTC's jurisdiction is that it is triggered when a company breaches its own privacy policy. But what if a company doesn't make explicit promises about security? One hopeful development is the Gramm-Leach-Bliley (GLB) Act. The GLB Act requires a number of agencies that regulate financial institutions to promulgate "administrative, technical, and physical safeguards for personal information." In other words, financial institutions must adopt a security system for their data, and the minimum specifications of this system are to be defined by government agencies. . . .[97]

Solove argues that the security practices of many financial institutions are quite lax, as such institutions often provide access to accounts if a person merely supplies her Social Security number. Based on the GLB Act, could the FTC use its enforcement powers to curtail such practices?

D. FIRST AMENDMENT LIMITATIONS ON PRIVACY REGULATION

Although the First Amendment protects privacy, privacy restrictions can come into conflict with the First Amendment. In particular, many privacy statutes regulate the disclosure of true information. The cases in this section explore the extent to which the First Amendment limits the privacy statutes. Before turning to the cases, some background about basic First Amendment jurisprudence is necessary. The cases in this section often focus on commercial speech, and the Court analyzes commercial speech differently than other forms of expression.

First Amendment Protection of Commercial Speech. For a while, the Court considered commercial speech as a category of expression that is not accorded First Amendment protection. However, in *Virginia State Board of Pharmacy v. Virginia Citizens Consumer Council, Inc.,* 425 U.S. 748 (1976), the Court held that commercial speech deserves constitutional protection. However, the Court held that commercial speech has a lower value than regular categories of speech and therefore is entitled to a lesser protection. *Ohralik v. Ohio State Bar Ass'n,* 436 U.S. 447 (1978).

Defining Commercial Speech. What is "commercial speech"? The Court has defined it as speech that "proposes a commercial transaction," *Virginia State Board,* 425 U.S. 748 (1976), and as "expression related solely to the economic interests of the speaker and its audience." *Central Hudson Gas & Electric Corp. v. Public Service Comm'n of New York,* 447 U.S. 557 (1980). The Court later held that neither of these are necessary requirements to define commercial speech; both are factors to be considered in determining whether speech is commercial. *See Bolger v. Youngs Drug Products Corp.,* 463 U.S. 60 (1983).

---

[97] Daniel J. Solove, *The Digital Person: Technology and Privacy in the Information Age* 107-08 (2004).

The **Central Hudson** *Test.* In *Central Hudson,* 447 U.S. 557 (1980), the Court established a four-part test for analyzing the constitutionality of restrictions on commercial speech:

> At the outset, we must determine whether the expression is protected by the First Amendment. For commercial speech to come within that provision, it at least must concern lawful activity and not be misleading. Next, we ask whether the asserted governmental interest is substantial. If both inquiries yield positive answers, we must determine whether the regulation directly advances the governmental interest asserted, and whether it is not more extensive than is necessary to serve that interest.

In *Board of Trustees of State University of New York v. Fox,* 492 U.S. 469 (1989), the Court revised the last part of the *Central Hudson* test — that speech "not [be] more extensive than is necessary to serve [the governmental] interest" — to a requirement that there be a "fit between the legislature's ends and the means chosen to accomplish the ends, . . . a fit that is not necessarily perfect, but reasonable."

In *Cincinnati v. Discovery Network, Inc.,* 507 U.S. 410 (1993), the Court, applying the commercial speech test in *Central Hudson* and *Fox,* struck down an ordinance that banned news racks with "commercial handbills." The ordinance did not apply to news racks for newspapers. The Court concluded that the ban was not a "reasonable fit" with the city's interest in aesthetics. Moreover, the Court concluded that the ordinance was not content-neutral. The Court held that Cincinnati "has enacted a sweeping ban on the use of newsracks that distribute 'commercial handbills,' but not 'newspapers.' Under the city's newsrack policy, whether any particular newsrack falls within the ban is determined by the content of the publication resting inside that newsrack. Thus, by any commonsense understanding of the term, the ban in this case is 'content based.' . . . [B]ecause the ban is predicated on the content of the publications distributed by the subject newsracks, it is not a valid time, place, or manner restriction on protected speech."

ROWAN V. UNITED STATES POST OFFICE DEPARTMENT

397 U.S. 728 (1970)

[A federal statute permitted individuals to require that entities sending unwanted mailings remove the individuals' names from their mailing lists and cease to send future mailings. A group of organizations challenged the statute on First Amendment grounds.]

BURGER, C.J. . . . The essence of appellants' argument is that the statute violates their constitutional right to communicate. . . . Without doubt the public postal system is an indispensable adjunct of every civilized society and communication is imperative to a healthy social order. But the right of every person "to be let alone" must be placed in the scales with the right of others to communicate.

In today's complex society we are inescapably captive audiences for many purposes, but a sufficient measure of individual autonomy must survive to permit every householder to exercise control over unwanted mail. To make the householder the exclusive and final judge of what will cross his threshold undoubtedly has the effect of impeding the flow of ideas, information, and arguments that, ideally, he should receive and consider. Today's merchandising methods, the plethora of mass mailings subsidized by low postal rates, and the growth of the sale of large mailing lists as an industry in itself have changed the mailman from a carrier of primarily private communications, as he was in a more leisurely day, and have made him an adjunct of the mass mailer who sends unsolicited and often unwanted mail into every home. It places no strain on the doctrine of judicial notice to observe that whether measured by pieces or pounds, Everyman's mail today is made up overwhelmingly of material he did not seek from persons he does not know. And all too often it is matter he finds offensive. . . .

The Court has traditionally respected the right of a householder to bar, by order or notice, solicitors, hawkers, and peddlers from his property. In this case the mailer's right to communicate is circumscribed only by an affirmative act of the addressee giving notice that he wishes no further mailings from that mailer.

To hold less would tend to license a form of trespass and would make hardly more sense than to say that a radio or television viewer may not twist the dial to cut off an offensive or boring communication and thus bar its entering his home. Nothing in the Constitution compels us to listen to or view any unwanted communication, whatever its merit; we see no basis for according the printed word or pictures a different or more preferred status because they are sent by mail. The ancient concept that "a man's home is his castle" into which "not even the king may enter" has lost none of its vitality, and none of the recognized exceptions includes any right to communicate offensively with another. . . .

If this prohibition operates to impede the flow of even valid ideas, the answer is that no one has a right to press even "good" ideas on an unwilling recipient. That we are often "captives" outside the sanctuary of the home and subject to objectionable speech and other sound does not mean we must be captives everywhere. The asserted right of a mailer, we repeat, stops at the outer boundary of every person's domain. . . .

Mainstream Marketing Services, Inc. v. Federal Trade Commission

358 F.3d 1228 (10th Cir. 2004)

EBEL, J. . . . In 2003, two federal agencies—the Federal Trade Commission (FTC) and the Federal Communications Commission (FCC) — promulgated rules that together created the national do-not-call registry *See* 16 C.F.R. § 310.4(b)(1)(iii)(B) (FTC rule); 47 C.F.R. § 64.1200(c)(2) (FCC rule). The national do-not-call registry is a list containing the personal telephone numbers of telephone subscribers who have voluntarily indicated that they do not wish to receive unsolicited calls from commercial telemarketers. Commercial telemarketers are generally prohibited from calling phone numbers that have been placed on the do-not-call registry, and they must pay an annual fee to access the numbers on the registry so that they can delete those numbers from their telephone solicitation lists. So far, consumers have registered more than 50 million phone numbers on the national do-not-call registry.

The national do-not-call registry's restrictions apply only to telemarketing calls made by or on behalf of sellers of goods or services, and not to charitable or political fundraising calls. Additionally, a seller may call consumers who have signed up for the national registry if it has an established business relationship with the consumer or if the consumer has given that seller express written permission to call. Telemarketers generally have three months from the date on which a consumer signs up for the registry to remove the consumer's phone number from their call lists. Consumer registrations remain valid for five years, and phone numbers that are disconnected or reassigned will be periodically removed from the registry.

The national do-not-call registry is the product of a regulatory effort dating back to 1991 aimed at protecting the privacy rights of consumers and curbing the risk of telemarketing abuse. In the Telephone Consumer Protection Act of 1991 ("TCPA") — under which the FCC enacted its do-not-call rules — Congress found that for many consumers telemarketing sales calls constitute an intrusive invasion of privacy. . . . The TCPA therefore authorized the FCC to establish a national database of consumers who object to receiving "telephone solicitations," which the act defined as commercial sales calls. . . .

The national do-not-call registry's telemarketing restrictions apply only to commercial speech. Like most commercial speech regulations, the do-not-call rules draw a line between commercial and non-commercial speech on the basis of content. In reviewing commercial speech regulations, we apply the *Central Hudson* test. *Central Hudson Gas & Elec. Corp. v. Pub. Serv. Comm'n of N.Y.,* 447 U.S. 557 (1980).

Central Hudson established a three-part test governing First Amendment challenges to regulations restricting non-misleading commercial speech that relates to lawful activity. First, the government must assert a substantial interest to be achieved by the regulation. Second, the regulation must directly advance that governmental interest, meaning that it must do more than provide "only ineffective or remote support for the government's purpose." Third, although the regulation need not be the least restrictive measure available, it must be narrowly tailored not to restrict more speech than necessary. Together, these final two factors require that there be a reasonable fit between the government's objectives and the means it chooses to accomplish those ends. . . .

The government asserts that the do-not-call regulations are justified by its interests in 1) protecting the privacy of individuals in their homes, and 2) protecting consumers against the risk of fraudulent and abusive solicitation. Both of these justifications are undisputedly substantial governmental interests.

In *Rowan v. United States Post Office Dep't,* the Supreme Court upheld the right of a homeowner to restrict material that could be mailed to his or her house. The Court emphasized the importance of individual privacy, particularly in the context of the home, stating that "the ancient concept that 'a man's home is his castle' into which 'not even the king may enter' has lost none of its vitality." In *Frisby v. Schultz,* the Court [held] . . .

One important aspect of residential privacy is protection of the unwilling listener. . . . [A] special benefit of the privacy all citizens enjoy within their own walls, which the State may legislate to protect, is an ability to avoid intrusions. Thus, we have repeatedly held that individuals are not required to welcome unwanted speech into their own homes and that the government may protect this freedom.

A reasonable fit exists between the do-not-call rules and the government's privacy and consumer protection interests if the regulation directly advances those interests and is narrowly tailored. . . .

These criteria are plainly established in this case. The do-not-call registry directly advances the government's interests by effectively blocking a significant number of the calls that cause the problems the government sought to redress. It is narrowly tailored because its opt-in character ensures that it does not inhibit any speech directed at the home of a willing listener.

The telemarketers assert that the do-not-call registry is unconstitutionally underinclusive because it does not apply to charitable and political callers. First Amendment challenges based on underinclusiveness face an uphill battle in the commercial speech context. As a general rule, the First Amendment does not require that the government regulate all aspects of a problem before it can make progress on any front. . . . The underinclusiveness of a commercial speech regulation is relevant only if it renders the regulatory framework so irrational that it fails materially to advance the aims that it was purportedly designed to further. . .

As discussed above, the national do-not-call registry is designed to reduce intrusions into personal privacy and the risk of telemarketing fraud and abuse that accompany unwanted telephone solicitation. The registry directly advances those goals. So far, more than 50 million telephone numbers have been registered on the do-not-call list, and the do-not-call regulations protect these households from receiving most unwanted telemarketing calls. According to the telemarketers' own estimate, 2.64 telemarketing calls per week — or more than 137 calls annually — were directed at an average consumer before the do-not-call list came into effect. *Cf.* 68 Fed. Reg. at 44152 (discussing the five-fold increase in the total number of telemarketing calls between 1991 and 2003). Accordingly, absent the do-not-call registry, telemarketers would call those consumers who have already signed up for the registry an estimated total of 6.85 *billion* times each year.

To be sure, the do-not-call list will not block all of these calls. Nevertheless, it will prohibit a substantial number of them, making it difficult to fathom how the registry could be called an "ineffective" means of stopping invasive or abusive calls, or a regulation that "furnish[es] only speculative or marginal support" for the government's interests. . . .

Finally, the type of unsolicited calls that the do-not-call list does prohibit—commercial sales calls — is the type that Congress, the FTC and the FCC have all determined to be most to blame for the problems the government is seeking to redress. According to the legislative history accompanying the TCPA, "[c]omplaint statistics show that unwanted commercial calls are a far bigger problem than unsolicited calls from political or charitable organizations." H.R. Rep. No. 102-317, at 16 (1991). Additionally, the FTC has found that commercial callers are more likely than non-commercial callers to engage in deceptive and abusive practices. . . . The speech regulated by the do-not-call list is therefore the speech most likely to cause the problems the government sought to alleviate in enacting that list, further demonstrating that the regulation directly advances the government's interests. . . .

Although the least restrictive means test is not the test to be used in the commercial speech context, commercial speech regulations do at least have to be "narrowly tailored" and provide a "reasonable fit" between the problem and the solution. Whether or not there are "numerous and obvious less-burdensome alternatives" is a relevant consideration in our narrow tailoring analysis. . . . We hold that the national do-not-call registry is narrowly tailored because it does not over-regulate protected speech; rather, it restricts only calls that are targeted at unwilling recipients. . . .

The Supreme Court has repeatedly held that speech restrictions based on private choice (i.e., an opt-in feature) are less restrictive than laws that prohibit speech directly. In *Rowan,* for example, the Court approved a law under which an individual could require a mailer to stop all future mailings if he or she received advertisements that he or she believed to be erotically arousing or sexually provocative. Although it was the government that empowered individuals to avoid materials they considered provocative, the Court emphasized that the mailer's right to communicate was circumscribed only by an affirmative act of a householder. . . .

Like the do-not-mail regulation approved in *Rowan,* the national do-not-call registry does not itself prohibit any speech. Instead, it merely "permits a citizen to erect a wall . . . that no advertiser may penetrate without his acquiescence." *See Rowan,* 397 U.S. at 738. Almost by definition, the do-not-call regulations only block calls that would constitute unwanted intrusions into the privacy of consumers who have signed up for the list. . . .

NOTES & QUESTIONS

1. *The Do Not Call List and* **Rowan.** To what extent is this case controlled by *Rowan*? Does the Do Not Call (DNC) list go beyond the statute in *Rowan*?
2. *Charitable and Political Calls.* The DNC list permits calls based on charitable or political purposes. There is no way to block such calls. Suppose that Congress decided that all calls could be included. Would a charity or political group have a First Amendment ground to overturn the DNC list?

U.S. WEST, INC. V. FEDERAL COMMUNICATIONS COMMISSION
182 F.3d 1224 (10th Cir. 1999)

TACHA, J. . . . U.S. West, Inc. petitions for review of a Federal Communication Commission ("FCC") order restricting the use and disclosure of and access to customer proprietary network information ("CPNI"). *See* 63 Fed. Reg. 20,326 (1998) ("CPNI Order"). [U.S. West argues that FCC regulations, implementing 47 U.S.C. § 222, among other things, violate the First Amendment. These regulations require telecommunications companies to ask consumers for approval (to "opt-in") before they can use a customer's personal information for marketing purposes.] . . .

The dispute in this case involves regulations the FCC promulgated to implement provisions of 47 U.S.C. § 222, which was enacted as part of the Telecommunications Act of 1996. Section 222, entitled "Privacy of customer information," states generally that "[e]very telecommunications carrier has a duty to protect the confidentiality of proprietary information of, and relating to . . . customers." To effectuate that duty, § 222 places restrictions on the use, disclosure of, and access to certain customer information. At issue here are the FCC's regulations clarifying the privacy requirements for CPNI. The central provision of § 222 dealing with CPNI is § 222(c)(1), which states:

> Except as required by law or with the approval of the customer, a telecommunications carrier that receives or obtains customer proprietary network information by virtue of its provision of a telecommunications service shall only use, disclose, or permit access to individually identifiable customer proprietary network information in its provision of (A) the telecommunication service from which such information is derived, or (B) services necessary to, or used in, the provision of such telecommunications service, including the publishing of directories.

Section 222(d) provides three additional exceptions to the CPNI privacy requirements. [These exceptions permit the companies to use and disclose CPNI for billing purposes, to prevent fraud, and to provide services to the consumer if the consumer approves of the use of such information to provide the service. Any other uses or disclosures of CPNI not specifically permitted by § 222 require the consumer's consent. The regulations adopted by the CPNI Order implementing § 222 divides telecommunications services into three categories: (1) local, (2) long-distance, and (3) mobile or cellular. A telecommunications carrier can use or disclose CPNI to market products within one of these service categories if the customer already subscribes to that category of service. Carriers can't use or disclose CPNI to market categories of service to which the customer does not subscribe unless first obtaining the customer's consent. The regulations also prohibit using CPNI without consent to market other services such as voice mail or Internet access, to track customers that call competitors, or to try to regain the business of customers that switch carriers.] . . .

The regulations also describe the means by which a carrier must obtain customer approval. Section 222(c)(1) did not elaborate as to what form that approval should take. The FCC decided to require an "opt-in" approach, in which a carrier must obtain prior express approval from a customer through written, oral, or electronic means before using the customer's CPNI. The government acknowledged that the means of approval could have taken numerous other forms, including an "opt-out" approach, in which approval would be inferred from the customer-carrier relationship unless the customer specifically requested that his or her CPNI be restricted. . . .

Petitioner argues that the CPNI regulations interpreting 47 U.S.C. § 222 violate the First Amendment. . . .

Because petitioner's targeted speech to its customers is for the purpose of soliciting those customers to purchase more or different telecommunications services, it "does no more than propose a commercial transaction." Consequently, the targeted speech in this case fits soundly within the definition of commercial speech. It is well established that nonmisleading commercial speech regarding a lawful activity is a form of protected speech under the First Amendment, although it is generally afforded less protection than noncommercial speech. The parties do not dispute that the commercial speech based on CPNI is truthful and nonmisleading. Therefore, the CPNI regulations implicate the First Amendment by restricting protected commercial speech. . . .

We analyze whether a government restriction on commercial speech violates the First Amendment under the four-part framework set forth in *Central Hudson* [*Gas & Elec. Corp. v. Public Serv. Comm'n of N.Y.*, 477 U.S. 557 (1980)]. First, we must conduct a threshold inquiry regarding whether the commercial speech concerns lawful activity and is not misleading. If these requirements are not met, the government may freely regulate the speech. If this threshold requirement is met, the government may restrict the speech only if it proves: "(1) it has a substantial state interest in regulating the speech, (2) the regulation directly and materially advances that interest, and (3) the regulation is no more extensive than necessary to serve the interest." As noted above, no one disputes that the commercial speech based on CPNI is truthful and nonmisleading. We therefore proceed directly to whether the government has satisfied its burden under the remaining three prongs of the *Central Hudson* test. . . .

The respondents argue that the FCC's CPNI regulations advance two substantial state interests: protecting customer privacy and promoting competition. While, in the abstract, these may constitute legitimate and substantial interests, we have concerns about the proffered justifications in the context of this case. . . .

. . . Although we agree that privacy may rise to the level of a substantial state interest, the government cannot satisfy the second prong of the *Central Hudson* test by merely asserting a broad interest in privacy. It must specify the particular notion of privacy and interest served. Moreover, privacy is not an absolute good because it imposes real costs on society. Therefore, the specific privacy interest must be substantial, demonstrating that the state has considered the proper balancing of the benefits and harms of privacy. In sum, privacy may only constitute a substantial state interest if the government specifically articulates and properly justifies it.

In the context of a speech restriction imposed to protect privacy by keeping certain information confidential, the government must show that the dissemination of the information desired to be kept private would inflict specific and significant harm on individuals, such as undue embarrassment or ridicule, intimidation or harassment, or misappropriation of sensitive personal information for the purposes of assuming another's identity. Although we may feel uncomfortable knowing that our personal information is circulating in the world, we live in an open society where information may usually pass freely. A general level of discomfort from knowing that people can readily access information about us does not necessarily rise to the level of a substantial state interest under *Central Hudson* for it is not based on an identified harm.

Neither Congress nor the FCC explicitly stated what "privacy" harm § 222 seeks to protect against. The CPNI Order notes that "CPNI includes information that is extremely personal to customers . . . such as to whom, where, and when a customer places a call, as well as the types of service offerings to which the customer subscribes," and it summarily finds "call destinations and other details about a call . . . may be equally or more sensitive [than the content of the calls]." The government never states it directly, but we infer from this thin justification that disclosure of CPNI information could prove embarrassing to some and that the government seeks to combat this potential harm. . . .

Under the next prong of *Central Hudson,* the government must "demonstrate that the harms it recites are real and that its restriction will in fact alleviate them to a material degree.". . . On the record before us, the government fails to meet its burden.

The government presents no evidence showing the harm to either privacy or competition is real. Instead, the government relies on speculation that harm to privacy and competition for new services will result if carriers use CPNI. . . . While protecting against disclosure of sensitive and potentially embarrassing personal information may be important in the abstract, we have no indication of how it may occur in reality with respect to CPNI. Indeed, we do not even have indication that the disclosure might actually occur. The government presents no evidence regarding how and to whom carriers would disclose CPNI. . . . [T]he government has not explained how or why a carrier would disclose CPNI to outside parties, especially when the government claims CPNI is information that would give one firm a competitive advantage over another. This leaves us unsure exactly who would potentially receive the sensitive information. . . .

In order for a regulation to satisfy this final *Central Hudson* prong, there must be a fit between the legislature's means and its desired objective. . . .

. . . [O]n this record, the FCC's failure to adequately consider an obvious and substantially less restrictive alternative, an opt-out strategy, indicates that it did not narrowly tailor the CPNI regulations regarding customer approval. . . .

The respondents merely speculate that there are a substantial number of individuals who feel strongly about their privacy, yet would not bother to opt-out if given notice and the opportunity to do so. Such speculation hardly reflects the careful calculation of costs and benefits that our commercial speech jurisprudence requires. . . .

In sum, even assuming that respondents met the prior two prongs of *Central Hudson,* we conclude that based on the record before us, the agency has failed to satisfy its burden of showing that the customer approval regulations restrict no more speech than necessary to serve the asserted state interests. Consequently, we find that the CPNI regulations interpreting the customer approval requirement of 47 U.S.C. § 222(c) violate the First Amendment.

BRISCOE, J. dissenting. . . . After reviewing the CPNI Order and the administrative record, I am convinced the FCC's interpretation of § 222, more specifically its selection of the opt-in method for obtaining customer approval, is entirely reasonable. Indeed, the CPNI Order makes a strong case that, of the two options seriously considered by the FCC, the opt-in method is the only one that legitimately forwards Congress' goal of ensuring that customers give informed consent for use of their individually identifiable CPNI. . . .

. . . U.S. West suggests the CPNI Order unduly limits its ability to engage in commercial speech with its existing customers regarding new products and services it may offer. . . .

The problem with U.S. West's arguments is they are more appropriately aimed at the restrictions and requirements outlined in § 222 rather than the approval method adopted in the CPNI Order. As outlined above, it is the statute, not the CPNI Order, that prohibits a carrier from using, disclosing, or permitting access to individually identifiable CPNI without first obtaining informed consent from its customers. Yet U.S. West has not challenged the constitutionality of § 222, and this is not the proper forum for addressing such a challenge even if it was raised. . . .

The majority, focusing at this point on the CPNI Order rather than the statute, concludes the FCC failed to adequately consider the opt-out method, which the majority characterizes as "an obvious and substantially less restrictive alternative" than the opt-in method. Notably, however, the majority fails to explain why, in its view, the opt-out method is substantially less restrictive. Presumably, the majority is relying on the fact that the opt-out method typically results in a higher "approval" rate than the opt-in method. Were mere "approval" percentages the only factor relevant to our discussion, the majority would perhaps be correct. As the FCC persuasively concluded in the CPNI Order, however, the opt-out method simply does not comply with § 222's requirement of informed consent. In particular, the opt-out method, unlike the opt-in method, does not guarantee that a customer will make an informed decision about usage of his or her individually identifiable CPNI. To the contrary, the opt-out method creates the very real possibility of "uninformed" customer approval. In the end, I reiterate my point that the opt-in method selected by the FCC is the only method of obtaining approval that serves the governmental interests at issue while simultaneously complying with the express requirement of the statute (i.e., obtaining informed customer consent). . . .

In conclusion, I view U.S. West's petition for review as little more than a run-of-the-mill attack on an agency order "clothed by ingenious argument in the garb" of First Amendment issues. . . .

NOTES & QUESTIONS

1. *The Aftermath of* **U.S. West:** *The FCC and the D.C. Circuit.* The FCC responded to the *U.S. West* decision at length in its 2007 CPNI Order and largely rejected its holdings. FCC Report and Order, 07-22 (April 2, 2007). The one change that it made was to modify its 1998 Order at issue in *U.S. West* so that opt-in consent would be required only with respect to a carrier's sharing of customer information with third-party marketers.

The FCC also declared that the Tenth Circuit in *U.S. West* had based its decision "on a different record than the one compiled here" and in particular on premises that were no longer valid. First, the FCC reasoned, there was now ample evidence of disclosure of CPNI and the adverse effects it could have on customers. Second, there was now substantial evidence that an opt-out strategy would not adequately protect customer privacy "because most customers either do not read or do not understand carriers' opt-out notices." The FCC also stated that requiring opt-in consent from customers before sharing CPNI with joint venture partners and independent contractors for marketing purposes would pass First Amendment scrutiny.

The D.C. Circuit upheld the FCC's 2007 Report and Order. *National Cable and Telecommunications Association*, 555 F.3d 996 (D.C. Cir. 2009). It found that the government had a "substantial" interest, under the *Central Hudson* test, in "protecting the privacy of consumer credit information." In its analysis of the second part of the *Central Hudson* test, the D.C. Circuit found that the Commission's 2007 Order "directly advances" the government's interest:

> [C]ommon sense supports the Commission's determination that the risk of unauthorized disclosure of customer information increases with the number of entities possessing it. The Commission therefore reasonably concluded that an opt-in consent requirement directly and materially advanced the interests in protecting customer privacy and in ensuring customer control over the information.

Finally, the court found that under *Central Hudson*'s final requirement the 2007 Report and Order easily met the standard of a regulation proportionate to the government's interest. The court reasoned that the difference between opt in and opt out is only a marginal one in the relative degree of burden on First Amendment interests. The D.C. Circuit found that the "Commission carefully considered the differences between the two regulatory approaches, and the evidence supports the Commission's decision to prefer opt-in consent."

If the *U.S. West* court were to examine the FCC's 2007 Report and Order, would it likely agree or disagree with the D.C. Circuit?

2. *Is Opt In Narrowly Tailored?* Is the opt-in system involved in *U.S. West* more restrictive than the do-not-mail list in *Rowan* or the DNC list in *Mainstream Marketing*? Is the privacy interest in *U.S. West* different than in *Rowan* and *Mainstream Marketing*?

3. *Personal Information: Property, Contract, and Speech.* Consider the following critique of *U.S. West* by Julie Cohen:

> The law affords numerous instances of regulation of the exchange of information as property or product. Securities markets, which operate entirely by means of information exchange, are subject to extensive regulation, and hardly anybody thinks that securities laws and regulations should be subjected to heightened or strict First Amendment scrutiny. Laws prohibiting patent, copyright, and trademark infringement, and forbidding the misappropriation of trade secrets, have as their fundamental purpose (and their undisputed effect) the restriction of information flows. The securities and intellectual property laws, moreover, are expressly content-based, and thus illustrate that (as several leading First Amendment scholars acknowledge) this characterization doesn't always matter. Finally, federal computer crime laws

punish certain uses of information for reasons entirely unrelated to their communicative aspects. . . .

The accumulation, use, and market exchange of personally-identified data don't fit neatly into any recognized category of "commercial speech" . . . because in the ways that matter, these activities aren't really "speech" at all. Although regulation directed at these acts may impose some indirect burden on direct-to-consumer communication, that isn't the primary objective of data privacy regulation. This suggests that, at most, data privacy regulation should be subject to the intermediate scrutiny applied to indirect speech regulation.[98]

4. ***Is Opt In Too Expensive?*** Michael Staten and Fred Cate have defended the *U.S. West* decision by noting the results of the testing of an opt-in system by U.S. West:

> In 1997, U.S. West (now Qwest Communications), one of the largest telecommunications companies in the United States, conducted one of the few affirmative consent trials for which results are publicly available. In that trial, the company sought permission from its customers to utilize information about their calling patterns (e.g., volume of calls, time and duration of calls, etc.) to market new services to them. The direct mail appeal for permission received a positive response rate between 5 and 11 percent for residential customers (depending upon the size of a companion incentive offered by the company). Residential customers opted in at a rate of 28 percent when called about the service.
>
> When U.S. West was actually communicating in person with the consumers, the positive response rate was three to six times higher than when it relied on consumers reading and responding to mail. But even with telemarketing, the task of reaching a customer is daunting. U.S. West determined that it required an average of 4.8 calls to each consumer household before they reached an adult who could grant consent. In one-third of households called, U.S. West never reached the customer, despite repeated attempts. In any case, many U.S. West customers received more calls than would have been the case in an opt-out system, and despite repeated contact attempts, one-third of their customers missed opportunities to receive new products and services. The approximately $20 cost per positive response in the telemarketing test and $29 to $34 cost per positive response in the direct mail test led the company to conclude that opt-in was not a viable business model because it was too costly, too difficult, and too time intensive.[99]

Robert Gellman, however, generally disputes the findings of industry studies about the costs of privacy protective measures. With regard to opt-in cost assessments, Gellman argues that industry studies often fail "to consider other ways [beyond direct mail and telemarketing] that business and charities can solicit individuals to replace any losses from opt-in requirements. Newspaper, Internet, radio, and television advertising may be effective substitutes for direct mail. There are other ways to approach individuals

---

[98] Julie E. Cohen, *Examined Lives: Informational Privacy and the Subject as Object*, 52 Stan. L. Rev. 1373, 1416-18, 1421 (2000).

[99] Michael E. Staten & Fred H. Cate, *The Impact of Opt-In Privacy Rules on Retail Credit Markets: A Case Study of MBNA*, 52 Duke L.J. 745, 767-68 (2003).

without the compilation of detailed personal dossiers. None of the alternatives is adequately considered."[100]

5. *Is Commercial Transaction Information Different from Other Speech?* Courts analyzing First Amendment challenges to regulation of data about commercial transactions have typically viewed the dissemination and use of such data as commercial speech, and they have applied the *Central Hudson* test. This test is less protective than regular First Amendment protection. Solveig Singleton contends that data about commercial transactions should be considered regular speech, not commercial speech:

> Is commercial tracking essentially different from gossip? . . .
>
> Gossip and other informal personal contacts serve an important function in advanced economies. In Nineteenth Century America, entrepreneurs would increase their sales by acquiring information about their customers. Customers relied on their neighborhood banker, whom they knew since childhood, to grant them credit. They would return again and again to the same stores for personalized service. . . .
>
> [E]conomic actors must develop new mechanisms of relaying information to each other about fraud, trust, and behavior of potential customers. Towards the end of the Nineteenth Century and throughout the Twentieth Century, formal credit reporting began to evolve out of gossip networks. . . .
>
> The equivalence of gossip and consumer databases suggests that there is no need to treat the evolution of databases as a crisis. Those who argue for a new legal regime for privacy, however, view new uses of information as having crossed an "invisible line" between permissible gossip and violative information collection. While the use of new technology to collect information may make people uneasy, is there any reason to suppose that any harm that might result will amount to greater harm than the harm that could come from being a victim of vicious gossip?[101]

Singleton goes on to contend that information collected by businesses in databases is less pernicious than gossip because few people have access to it and it is "likely to be much more accurate than gossip." Is the information in computer databases merely gossip on a more systemic scale? Compare how the First Amendment regulates gossip with how it regulates commercial speech.

6. *The Value of Privacy.* What is the value of protecting the privacy of consumer information maintained by telecommunications companies? Is it more important than the economic benefits that the telecommunications companies gain by using that information for marketing? How should policymakers go about answering such questions? Consider James Nehf:

> The choice of utilitarian reasoning — often reduced to cost-benefit analysis ("CBA") in policy debates — fixes the outcome in favor of the side that can more easily quantify results. In privacy debates, this generally favors the side

---

[100] Robert Gellman, *Privacy, Consumers, and Costs: How the Lack of Privacy Costs Consumers and Why Business Studies of Privacy Costs Are Biased and Incomplete* (March 2002), at http://www.epic.org/reports/dmfprivacy.html.

[101] Solveig Singleton, *Privacy Versus the First Amendment: A Skeptical Approach*, 11 Fordham Intell. Prop. Media & Ent. L.J. 97, 126-32 (2000).

arguing for more data collection and sharing. Although CBA can mean different things in various contexts, the term here means a strategy for making choices in which quantifiable weights are given to competing alternatives. . . .

We should openly acknowledge that non-economic values are legitimate in privacy debates, just as they have been recognized in other areas of fundamental importance. Decisions about the societal acceptance of disabled citizens, the codification of collective bargaining rights for workers, and the adoption of fair trial procedures for the accused did not depend entirely, or even primarily, on CBA outcomes. Difficulties in quantifying costs and benefits do not present insurmountable obstacles when policymakers address matters of basic human dignity. The protection of personal data should be viewed in a similar way, and CBA should play a smaller role in privacy debates. . . .

A similar phenomenon is at work in the formulation of public policy. Policymakers are often asked to compare incomparable alternatives. . . .

By converting all values to money, the incomparability problem is lessened, but only if we accept the legitimacy of money as the covering value. In the privacy debate, the legitimacy of monetizing individual privacy preferences is highly suspect. Benefits are often personal, emotional, intangible, and not readily quantifiable. Preferences on privacy matters are generally muddled, incoherent, and ill-informed. If privacy preferences are real but not sufficiently coherent to form a sound basis for valuation, any attempt to place a monetary value on them loses meaning. The choice of CBA as the model for justifying decisions fixes the end, because the chosen covering value will usually result in a decision favoring data proliferation over data protection. . . .

People make choices between seemingly incomparable things all the time, and they can do so rationally. A person is not acting irrationally by preferring a perceived notable value over an incomparable nominal value, even if she cannot state a normative theory to explain why the decision is right. A similar phenomenon may be seen in the formulation of public policy. Notable values may be preferred over nominal ones in the enactment of laws and the implementation of policies even if policymakers cannot explain why one alternative is better than the other. Moreover, by observing a number of such decisions over time, we may begin to see a pattern develop and covering values emerge that can serve as guides to later decisions that are closer to the margin.[102]

TRANS UNION CORP. v. FEDERAL TRADE COMMISSION

245 F.3d 809 (D.C. Cir. 2001)

TATEL, J. . . . . Petitioner Trans Union sells two types of products. First, as a credit reporting agency, it compiles credit reports about individual consumers from credit information it collects from banks, credit card companies, and other lenders. It then sells these credit reports to lenders, employers, and insurance companies. Trans Union receives credit information from lenders in the form of "tradelines." A tradeline typically includes a customer's name, address, date

---

[102] James P. Nehf, *Incomparability and the Passive Virtues of Ad Hoc Privacy Policy*, 76 U. Colo. L. Rev. 1, 29-36, 42 (2005).

of birth, telephone number, Social Security number, account type, opening date of account, credit limit, account status, and payment history. Trans Union receives 1.4 to 1.6 billion records per month. The company's credit database contains information on 190 million adults.

Trans Union's second set of products — those at issue in this case — are known as target marketing products. These consist of lists of names and addresses of individuals who meet specific criteria such as possession of an auto loan, a department store credit card, or two or more mortgages. Marketers purchase these lists, then contact the individuals by mail or telephone to offer them goods and services. To create its target marketing lists, Trans Union maintains a database known as MasterFile, a subset of its consumer credit database. MasterFile consists of information about every consumer in the company's credit database who has (A) at least two tradelines with activity during the previous six months, or (B) one tradeline with activity during the previous six months plus an address confirmed by an outside source. The company compiles target marketing lists by extracting from MasterFile the names and addresses of individuals with characteristics chosen by list purchasers. For example, a department store might buy a list of all individuals in a particular area code who have both a mortgage and a credit card with a $10,000 limit. Although target marketing lists contain only names and addresses, purchasers know that every person on a list has the characteristics they requested because Trans Union uses those characteristics as criteria for culling individual files from its database. Purchasers also know that every individual on a target marketing list satisfies the criteria for inclusion in MasterFile.

The Fair Credit Reporting Act of 1970 ("FCRA"), 15 U.S.C. §§ 1681, 1681a-1681u, regulates consumer reporting agencies like Trans Union, imposing various obligations to protect the privacy and accuracy of credit information. The Federal Trade Commission, acting pursuant to its authority to enforce the FCRA, *see* 15 U.S.C. § 1681s(a), determined that Trans Union's target marketing lists were "consumer reports" subject to the Act's limitations. [The FTC concluded that targeted marketing was not an authorized use of consumer reports under the FCRA and ordered Trans Union to halt its sale of the lists.] . . .

. . . [Trans Union challenges the FTC's application of the FCRA as violative of the First Amendment.] Banning the sale of target marketing lists, the company says, amounts to a restriction on its speech subject to strict scrutiny. Again, Trans Union misunderstands our standard of review. In *Dun & Bradstreet, Inc. v. Greenmoss Builders, Inc.,* 472 U.S. 749 (1985), the Supreme Court held that a consumer reporting agency's credit report warranted reduced constitutional protection because it concerned "no public issue." "The protection to be accorded a particular credit report," the Court explained, "depends on whether the report's 'content, form, and context' indicate that it concerns a public matter." Like the credit report in *Dun & Bradstreet,* which the Supreme Court found "was speech solely in the interest of the speaker and its specific business audience," the information about individual consumers and their credit performance communicated by Trans Union target marketing lists is solely of interest to the company and its business customers and relates to no matter of public concern. Trans Union target marketing lists thus warrant "reduced constitutional protection."

We turn then to the specifics of Trans Union's First Amendment argument. The company first claims that neither the FCRA nor the Commission's Order advances a substantial government interest. The "Congressional findings and statement of purpose" at the beginning of the FCRA state: "There is a need to insure that consumer reporting agencies exercise their grave responsibilities with . . . respect for the consumer's right to privacy." 15 U.S.C. § 1681 (a)(4). Contrary to the company's assertions, we have no doubt that this interest — protecting the privacy of consumer credit information — is substantial.

Trans Union next argues that Congress should have chosen a "less burdensome alternative," i.e., allowing consumer reporting agencies to sell credit information as long as they notify consumers and give them the ability to "opt out." Because the FCRA is not subject to strict First Amendment scrutiny, however, Congress had no obligation to choose the least restrictive means of accomplishing its goal.

Finally, Trans Union argues that the FCRA is underinclusive because it applies only to consumer reporting agencies and not to other companies that sell consumer information. But given consumer reporting agencies' unique "access to a broad range of continually-updated, detailed information about millions of consumers' personal credit histories," we think it not at all inappropriate for Congress to have singled out consumer reporting agencies for regulation. . . .

NOTES & QUESTIONS

1. **U.S. West *vs.* Trans Union.** Compare *U.S. West* with *Trans Union*. Are these cases consistent with each other? Which case's reasoning strikes you as more persuasive?

2. **Trans Union II.** In *Trans Union v. FTC*, 295 F.3d 42 (D.C. Cir. 2002) (*Trans Union II*), Trans Union sued to enjoin regulations promulgated pursuant to the Gramm-Leach-Bliley (GLB) Act, alleging, among other things, that they violated the First Amendment. Trans Union argued that these regulations would prevent it from selling credit headers, which consist of a consumer's name, address, Social Security number, and phone number. Trans Union contended that the sale of credit headers is commercial speech. The court concluded that Trans Union's First Amendment arguments were "foreclosed" by its earlier opinion in *Trans Union v. FTC*, which resolved that "the government interest in 'protecting the privacy of consumer credit information' 'is substantial.'"

3. *Free Speech and the Fair Information Practices.* Recall the discussion of the Fair Information Practices from Chapter 6. The Fair Information Practices provide certain limitations on the uses and disclosure of personal information. Eugene Volokh contends:

> I am especially worried about the normative power of the notion that the government has a compelling interest in creating "codes of fair information practices" restricting true statements made by nongovernmental speakers. The protection of free speech generally rests on an assumption that it's not for the government to decide which speech is "fair" and which isn't; the unfairnesses,

excesses, and bad taste of speakers are something that current First Amendment principles generally require us to tolerate. Once people grow to accept and even like government restrictions on one kind of supposedly "unfair" communication of facts, it may become much easier for people to accept "codes of fair reporting," "codes of fair debate," "codes of fair filmmaking," "codes of fair political criticism," and the like. . . .[103]

Consider Paul Schwartz, who contends that free discourse is promoted by the protection of privacy:

> When the government requires fair information practices for the private sector, has it created a right to stop people from speaking about you? As an initial point, I emphasize that the majority of the core fair information practices do not involve the government preventing disclosure of personal information. [The fair information practices generally require: (1) the creation of a statutory fabric that defines obligations with respect to the use of personal information; (2) the maintenance of processing systems that are understandable to the concerned individual (transparency); (3) the assignment of limited procedural and substantive rights to the individual; and (4) the establishment of effective oversight of data use, whether through individual litigation (self-help), a government role (external oversight), or some combination of these approaches.] . . . [F]air information practices one, two, and four regulate the business practices of private entities without silencing their speech. No prevention of speech about anyone takes place, for example, when the Fair Credit Reporting Act of 1970 requires that certain information be given to a consumer when an "investigative consumer report" is prepared about her.
>
> These nonsilencing fair information practices are akin to a broad range of other measures that regulate information use in the private sector and do not abridge the freedom of speech under any interpretation of the First Amendment. The First Amendment does not prevent the government from requiring product labels on food products or the use of "plain English" by publicly traded companies in reports sent to their investors or Form 10-Ks filed with the Securities and Exchange Commission. Nor does the First Amendment forbid privacy laws such as the Children's Online Privacy Protection Act, which assigns parents a right of access to their children's online data profiles. The ultimate merit of these laws depends on their specific context and precise details, but such experimentation by the State should be viewed as noncontroversial on free speech grounds.
>
> Nevertheless, one subset of fair information practices does correspond to Volokh's idea of information privacy as the right to stop people from speaking about you. . . . [S]o long as [laws protecting personal information disclosure] are viewpoint neutral, these laws are a necessary element of safeguarding free communication in our democratic society. . . .
>
> . . . [A] democratic order depends on both an underlying personal capacity for self-governance and the participation of individuals in community and democratic self-rule. Privacy law thus has an important role in protecting individual self-determination and democratic deliberation. By providing access to one's personal data, information about how it will be processed, and other fair information practices, the law seeks to structure the terms on which

---

[103] Eugene Volokh, *Freedom of Speech and Information Privacy: The Troubling Implications of a Right to Stop People from Speaking About You*, 52 Stan. L. Rev. 1049, 1090 (2000).

individuals confront the information demands of the community, private bureaucratic entities, and the State. Attention to these issues by the legal order is essential to the health of a democracy, which ultimately depends on individual communicative competence.[104]

SORRELL V. IMS HEALTH, INC.

131 S. Ct. 2653 (2011)

KENNEDY, J. Vermont law restricts the sale, disclosure, and use of pharmacy records that reveal the prescribing practices of individual doctors. Vt. Stat. Ann., Tit. 18, § 4631. Subject to certain exceptions, the information may not be sold, disclosed by pharmacies for marketing purposes, or used for marketing by pharmaceutical manufacturers. Vermont argues that its prohibitions safeguard medical privacy and diminish the likelihood that marketing will lead to prescription decisions not in the best interests of patients or the State. It can be assumed that these interests are significant. Speech in aid of pharmaceutical marketing, however, is a form of expression protected by the Free Speech Clause of the First Amendment. As a consequence, Vermont's statute must be subjected to heightened judicial scrutiny. The law cannot satisfy that standard. . . .

Pharmaceutical manufacturers promote their drugs to doctors through a process called "detailing." This often involves a scheduled visit to a doctor's office to persuade the doctor to prescribe a particular pharmaceutical. Detailers bring drug samples as well as medical studies that explain the "details" and potential advantages of various prescription drugs. Interested physicians listen, ask questions, and receive followup data. Salespersons can be more effective when they know the background and purchasing preferences of their clientele, and pharmaceutical salespersons are no exception. Knowledge of a physician's prescription practices—called "prescriber-identifying information"—enables a detailer better to ascertain which doctors are likely to be interested in a particular drug and how best to present a particular sales message. Detailing is an expensive undertaking, so pharmaceutical companies most often use it to promote high-profit brand-name drugs protected by patent. Once a brand-name drug's patent expires, less expensive bioequivalent generic alternatives are manufactured and sold.

Pharmacies, as a matter of business routine and federal law, receive prescriber-identifying information when processing prescriptions. Many pharmacies sell this information to "data miners," firms that analyze prescriber-identifying information and produce reports on prescriber behavior. Data miners lease these reports to pharmaceutical manufacturers subject to nondisclosure agreements. Detailers, who represent the manufacturers, then use the reports to refine their marketing tactics and increase sales.

In 2007, Vermont enacted the Prescription Confidentiality Law. The measure is also referred to as Act 80. It has several components. The central provision of the present case is § 4631(d).

---

[104] Paul M. Schwartz, *Free Speech vs. Information Privacy: Eugene Volokh's First Amendment Jurisprudence*, 52 Stan. L. Rev. 1559 (2000).

"A health insurer, a self-insured employer, an electronic transmission intermediary, a pharmacy, or other similar entity shall not sell, license, or exchange for value regulated records containing prescriber-identifiable information, nor permit the use of regulated records containing prescriber-identifiable information for marketing or promoting a prescription drug, unless the prescriber consents . . . . Pharmaceutical manufacturers and pharmaceutical marketers shall not use prescriber-identifiable information for marketing or promoting a prescription drug unless the prescriber consents. . . ."

The quoted provision has three component parts. The provision begins by prohibiting pharmacies, health insurers, and similar entities from selling prescriber-identifying information, absent the prescriber's consent. . . . The provision then goes on to prohibit pharmacies, health insurers, and similar entities from allowing prescriber-identifying information to be used for marketing, unless the prescriber consents. This prohibition in effect bars pharmacies from disclosing the information for marketing purposes. Finally, the provision's second sentence bars pharmaceutical manufacturers and pharmaceutical marketers from using prescriber-identifying information for marketing, again absent the prescriber's consent. The Vermont attorney general may pursue civil remedies against violators. § 4631(f). . . .

On its face, Vermont's law enacts content- and speaker-based restrictions on the sale, disclosure, and use of prescriber-identifying information. The provision first forbids sale subject to exceptions based in large part on the content of a purchaser's speech. For example, those who wish to engage in certain "educational communications," § 4631(e)(4), may purchase the information. The measure then bars any disclosure when recipient speakers will use the information for marketing. Finally, the provision's second sentence prohibits pharmaceutical manufacturers from using the information for marketing. The statute thus disfavors marketing, that is, speech with a particular content. More than that, the statute disfavors specific speakers, namely pharmaceutical manufacturers. As a result of these content- and speaker-based rules, detailers cannot obtain prescriber-identifying information, even though the information may be purchased or acquired by other speakers with diverse purposes and viewpoints. . . . For example, it appears that Vermont could supply academic organizations with prescriber-identifying information to use in countering the messages of brand-name pharmaceutical manufacturers and in promoting the prescription of generic drugs. But § 4631(d) leaves detailers no means of purchasing, acquiring, or using prescriber-identifying information. The law on its face burdens disfavored speech by disfavored speakers. . . .

Act 80 is designed to impose a specific, content-based burden on protected expression. It follows that heightened judicial scrutiny is warranted. . . . Vermont's law does not simply have an effect on speech, but is directed at certain content and is aimed at particular speakers. The Constitution "does not enact Mr. Herbert Spencer's Social Statics." *Lochner v. New York*, 198 U.S. 45 (1905) (Holmes, J., dissenting). It does enact the First Amendment.

This Court has held that the creation and dissemination of information are speech within the meaning of the First Amendment. *See, e.g., Bartnicki* ("[I]f the acts of 'disclosing' and 'publishing' information do not constitute speech, it is hard to imagine what does fall within that category, as distinct from the category of expressive conduct"). Facts, after all, are the beginning point for much of the speech that is most essential to advance human knowledge and to conduct human affairs. There is thus a strong argument that prescriber-identifying information is speech for First Amendment purposes.

The State asks for an exception to the rule that information is speech, but there is no need to consider that request in this case. The State has imposed content- and speaker-based restrictions on the availability and use of prescriber-identifying information. So long as they do not engage in marketing, many speakers can obtain and use the information. But detailers cannot. Vermont's statute could be compared with a law prohibiting trade magazines from purchasing or using ink. As a consequence, this case can be resolved even assuming, as the State argues, that prescriber-identifying information is a mere commodity. . . .

The State's asserted justifications for § 4631(d) come under two general headings. First, the State contends that its law is necessary to protect medical privacy, including physician confidentiality, avoidance of harassment, and the integrity of the doctor-patient relationship. Second, the State argues that § 4631(d) is integral to the achievement of policy objectives—namely, improved public health and reduced healthcare costs. Neither justification withstands scrutiny.

Vermont argues that its physicians have a "reasonable expectation" that their prescriber-identifying information "will not be used for purposes other than . . . filling and processing" prescriptions. It may be assumed that, for many reasons, physicians have an interest in keeping their prescription decisions confidential. But § 4631(d) is not drawn to serve that interest. Under Vermont's law, pharmacies may share prescriber-identifying information with anyone for any reason save one: They must not allow the information to be used for marketing. . . .

Perhaps the State could have addressed physician confidentiality through "a more coherent policy." *Greater New Orleans Broadcasting*, [527 U.S. 173, 195 (1999)]. For instance, the State might have advanced its asserted privacy interest by allowing the information's sale or disclosure in only a few narrow and well-justified circumstances. *See, e.g.*, Health Insurance Portability and Accountability Act of 1996, 42 U.S.C. § 1320d–2; 45 CFR pts. 160 and 164. A statute of that type would present quite a different case than the one presented here. But the State did not enact a statute with that purpose or design. Instead, Vermont made prescriber-identifying information available to an almost limitless audience. The explicit structure of the statute allows the information to be studied and used by all but a narrow class of disfavored speakers. Given the information's widespread availability and many permissible uses, the State's asserted interest in physician confidentiality does not justify the burden that § 4631(d) places on protected expression.

. . . Section 4631(d) may offer a limited degree of privacy, but only on terms favorable to the speech the State prefers. Cf. *Rowan* (sustaining a law that allowed private parties to make "unfettered," "unlimited," and "unreviewable" choices regarding their own privacy). This is not to say that all privacy measures must avoid content-based rules. Here, however, the State has conditioned privacy on acceptance of a content-based rule that is not drawn to serve the State's asserted interest. To obtain the limited privacy allowed by § 4631(d), Vermont physicians are forced to acquiesce in the State's goal of burdening disfavored speech by disfavored speakers.

The State also contends that § 4631(d) protects doctors from "harassing sales behaviors." It is doubtful that concern for "a few" physicians who may have "felt coerced and harassed" by pharmaceutical marketers can sustain a broad content-based rule like § 4631(d). Many are those who must endure speech they do not like, but that is a necessary cost of freedom. In any event the State offers no explanation why remedies other than content-based rules would be inadequate. Physicians can, and often do, simply decline to meet with detailers, including detailers who use prescriber-identifying information. Doctors who wish to forgo detailing altogether are free to give "No Solicitation" or "No Detailing" instructions to their office managers or to receptionists at their places of work. . . .

Vermont argues that detailers' use of prescriber-identifying information undermines the doctor-patient relationship by allowing detailers to influence treatment decisions. . . . But the State does not explain why detailers' use of prescriber-identifying information is more likely to prompt these objections than many other uses permitted by § 4631(d). In any event, this asserted interest is contrary to basic First Amendment principles. . . . If pharmaceutical marketing affects treatment decisions, it does so because doctors find it persuasive. Absent circumstances far from those presented here, the fear that speech might persuade provides no lawful basis for quieting it.

The State contends that § 4631(d) advances important public policy goals by lowering the costs of medical services and promoting public health. If prescriber-identifying information were available for use by detailers, the State contends, then detailing would be effective in promoting brand-name drugs that are more expensive and less safe than generic alternatives. . . . While Vermont's stated policy goals may be proper, § 4631(d) does not advance them in a permissible way. . . . The State seeks to achieve its policy objectives through the indirect means of restraining certain speech by certain speakers—that is, by diminishing detailers' ability to influence prescription decisions. Those who seek to censor or burden free expression often assert that disfavored speech has adverse effects. But the "fear that people would make bad decisions if given truthful information" cannot justify content-based burdens on speech. . . .

It is true that content-based restrictions on protected expression are sometimes permissible, and that principle applies to commercial speech. . . . Here, however, Vermont has not shown that its law has a neutral justification.

The State nowhere contends that detailing is false or misleading within the meaning of this Court's First Amendment precedents. Nor does the State argue that the provision challenged here will prevent false or misleading speech. The State's interest in burdening the speech of detailers instead turns on nothing more than a difference of opinion. . . .

The capacity of technology to find and publish personal information, including records required by the government, presents serious and unresolved issues with respect to personal privacy and the dignity it seeks to secure. In considering how to protect those interests, however, the State cannot engage in content-based discrimination to advance its own side of a debate.

If Vermont's statute provided that prescriber-identifying information could not be sold or disclosed except in narrow circumstances then the State might have a stronger position. Here, however, the State gives possessors of the information broad discretion and wide latitude in disclosing the information, while at the same time restricting the information's use by some speakers and for some purposes, even while the State itself can use the information to counter the speech it seeks to suppress. Privacy is a concept too integral to the person and a right too essential to freedom to allow its manipulation to support just those ideas the government prefers. . . .

The State has burdened a form of protected expression that it found too persuasive. At the same time, the State has left unburdened those speakers whose messages are in accord with its own views. This the State cannot do. . . .

BREYER, J., joined by GINSBURG, J. and KAGAN, J., dissenting. The Vermont statute before us adversely affects expression in one, and only one, way. It deprives pharmaceutical and data-mining companies of data, collected pursuant to the government's regulatory mandate, that could help pharmaceutical companies create better sales messages. In my view, this effect on expression is inextricably related to a lawful governmental effort to regulate a commercial enterprise. The First Amendment does not require courts to apply a special "heightened" standard of review when reviewing such an effort. And, in any event, the statute meets the First Amendment standard this Court has previously applied when the government seeks to regulate commercial speech. For any or all of these reasons, the Court should uphold the statute as constitutional. . . .

In this case I would ask whether Vermont's regulatory provisions work harm to First Amendment interests that is disproportionate to their furtherance of legitimate regulatory objectives. . . .

[O]ur cases make clear that the First Amendment offers considerably less protection to the maintenance of a free marketplace for goods and services. And they also reflect the democratic importance of permitting an elected government to implement through effective programs policy choices for which the people's elected representatives have voted. . . .

Vermont's statute neither forbids nor requires anyone to say anything, to engage in any form of symbolic speech, or to endorse any particular point of view, whether ideological or related to the sale of a product. . . . Further, the statute's requirements form part of a traditional, comprehensive regulatory regime. The pharmaceutical drug industry has been heavily regulated at least since 1906. Longstanding statutes and regulations require pharmaceutical companies to engage in complex drug testing to ensure that their drugs are both "safe" and "effective." 21 U.S.C. §§ 355(b)(1), 355(d). Only then can the drugs be marketed, at which point drug companies are subject to the FDA's exhaustive regulation of the content of drug labels and the manner in which drugs can be advertised and sold.

Finally, Vermont's statute is directed toward information that exists only by virtue of government regulation. Under federal law, certain drugs can be dispensed only by a pharmacist operating under the orders of a medical practitioner. 21 U.S.C. § 355(b). Vermont regulates the qualifications, the fitness, and the practices of pharmacists themselves, and requires pharmacies to maintain a "patient record system" that, among other things, tracks who prescribed which drugs. But for these regulations, pharmacies would have no way to know who had told customers to buy which drugs (as is the case when a doctor tells a patient to take a daily dose of aspirin).

Regulators will often find it necessary to create tailored restrictions on the use of information subject to their regulatory jurisdiction. A car dealership that obtains credit scores for customers who want car loans can be prohibited from using credit data to search for new customers. *See* 15 U.S.C. § 1681b; *cf. Trans Union Corp. v. FTC,* 245 F.3d 809, *reh'g denied,* 267 F.3d 1138 (D.C. Cir. 2001). Medical specialists who obtain medical records for their existing patients cannot purchase those records in order to identify new patients. *See* 45 CFR § 164.508(a)(3). Or, speaking hypothetically, a public utilities commission that directs local gas distributors to gather usage information for individual customers might permit the distributors to share the data with researchers (trying to lower energy costs) but forbid sales of the data to appliance manufacturers seeking to sell gas stoves. . . . Thus, it is not surprising that, until today, this Court has *never* found that the First Amendment prohibits the government from restricting the use of information gathered pursuant to a regulatory mandate—whether the information rests in government files or has remained in the hands of the private firms that gathered it.

In short, the case law in this area reflects the need to ensure that the First Amendment protects the "marketplace of ideas," thereby facilitating the democratic creation of sound government policies without improperly hampering the ability of government to introduce an agenda, to implement its policies, and to favor them to the exclusion of contrary policies. To apply "heightened" scrutiny when the regulation of commercial activities (which often involve speech) is at issue is unnecessarily to undercut the latter constitutional goal. The majority's view of this case presents that risk. . . .

Moreover, given the sheer quantity of regulatory initiatives that touch upon commercial messages, the Court's vision of its reviewing task threatens to return us to a happily bygone era when judges scrutinized legislation for its interference with economic liberty. History shows that the power was much abused and resulted in the constitutionalization of economic theories preferred by individual jurists. *See Lochner v. New York,* 198 U.S. 45 (1905) (Holmes, J., dissenting). . . .

The statute threatens only modest harm to commercial speech. I agree that it withholds from pharmaceutical companies information that would help those entities create a more effective selling message. But I cannot agree with the majority that the harm also involves unjustified discrimination in that it permits "pharmacies" to "share prescriber-identifying information with anyone for any reason" (but marketing). Whatever the First Amendment relevance of such discrimination, there is no evidence that it exists in Vermont. The record contains no evidence that prescriber-identifying data is widely disseminated. . . .

The legitimate state interests that the statute serves are "substantial." *Central Hudson,* 447 U.S., at 564. . . . The protection of public health falls within the traditional scope of a State's police powers. The fact that the Court normally exempts the regulation of "misleading" and "deceptive" information even from the rigors of its "intermediate" commercial speech scrutiny testifies to the importance of securing "unbiased information," as does the fact that the FDA sets forth as a federal regulatory goal the need to ensure a "fair balance" of information about marketed drugs. As major payers in the health care system, health care spending is also of crucial state interest. And this Court has affirmed the importance of maintaining "privacy" as an important public policy goal—even in respect to information already disclosed to the public for particular purposes (but not others). *See Department of Justice v. Reporters Comm. for Freedom of Press,* 489 U.S. 749 (1989); *see also* Solove, *A Taxonomy of Privacy,* 154 U. Pa. L. Rev. 477, 520–522 (2006); *cf. NASA v. Nelson,* 131 S. Ct. 746 (2011) (discussing privacy interests in nondisclosure). . . .

The record also adequately supports the State's privacy objective. Regulatory rules in Vermont make clear that the confidentiality of an individual doctor's prescribing practices remains the norm. Exceptions to this norm are comparatively few.

. . . The prohibition against pharmaceutical firms using this prescriber-identifying information works no more than modest First Amendment harm; the prohibition is justified by the need to ensure unbiased sales presentations, prevent unnecessarily high drug costs, and protect the privacy of prescribing physicians. There is no obvious equally effective, more limited alternative. . . .

In sum, I believe that the statute before us satisfies the "intermediate" standards this Court has applied to restrictions on commercial speech. *A fortiori* it satisfies less demanding standards that are more appropriately applied in this kind of commercial regulatory case—a case where the government seeks typical regulatory ends (lower drug prices, more balanced sales messages) through the use of ordinary regulatory means (limiting the commercial use of data gathered pursuant to a regulatory mandate). The speech-related consequences here are indirect, incidental, and entirely commercial. . . .

Regardless, whether we apply an ordinary commercial speech standard or a less demanding standard, I believe Vermont's law is consistent with the First Amendment. And with respect, I dissent.

NOTES & QUESTIONS

1. *The Impact of* **Sorrell.** The Supreme Court takes an expansive view of commercial speech, which encompasses the sale and use of personal data. What kind of impact will this case likely have on other privacy laws regulating the trade of personal data? Does *Sorrell* affect *Mainstream Marketing Services, Inc. v. FTC* (excerpted above)? Does it affect the *Trans Union* cases (excerpted and discussed above)? What likely impact, if any, will it have?

2. *Narrow vs. Broad Laws.* Ironically, the Court's decision to strike down the law was based in part on how narrowly the law restricted the use or disclosure of personal data. How would you redraft the law to address the Court's concerns?

3. *HIPAA.* The *Sorrell* Court characterizes HIPAA as a law "allowing the information's sale or disclosure in only a few narrow and well-justified circumstances." Is this an accurate characterization of HIPAA? If HIPAA's

restrictions pass muster, then can *Sorrell* be read as a narrow holding that applies only to laws that single out one particular use or one particular group of speakers?

4. ***Is Information Speech?*** Is the collection, use, and/or transfer of personal information a form of speech? Or is it merely trade in property?

Eugene Volokh contends that such information processing constitutes speech:

> Many . . . databases — for instance, credit history databases or criminal record databases — are used by people to help them decide whom it is safe to deal with and who is likely to cheat them. Other databases, which contain less incriminating information, such as a person's shopping patterns . . . [contain] data [that] is of direct daily life interest to its recipients, since it helps them find out with whom they should do business.[105]

Further, Volokh contends: "[I]t is no less speech when a credit bureau sends credit information to a business. The owners and managers of a credit bureau are communicating information to decisionmakers, such as loan officers, at the recipient business."[106]

Daniel Solove recognizes that some forms of database information transfer and use can constitute speech:

> There are no easy analytic distinctions as to what is or is not "speech." The "essence" of information is neither a good, nor is it speech, for information can be used in ways that make it akin to either one. It is the *use* of the information that determines what information is, not anything inherent in the information itself. If I sell you a book, I have engaged in a commercial transaction. I sold the book as a good. However, the book is also expressing something. Even though books are sold as goods, the government cannot pass a law restricting the topics of what books can be sold. . . .
>
> Volokh appears to view all information dissemination that is communicative as speech. Under Volokh's view, therefore, most forms of information dissemination would be entitled to equal First Amendment protection. . . .
>
> However, Volokh's view would lead to severe conflicts with much modern regulation. Full First Amendment protection would apply to statements about a company's earnings and other information regulated by the SEC, insider trading, quid pro quo sexual harassment, fraudulent statements, perjury, bribery, blackmail, extortion, conspiracy, and so on. One could neatly exclude these examples from the category of speech, eliminating the necessity for First Amendment analysis. Although this seems the easiest approach, it is conceptually sloppy or even dishonest absent a meaningful way to argue that these examples do not involve communication. I contend that these examples of highly regulated forms of communication have not received the full rigor of standard First Amendment analysis because of policy considerations. Categorizing them as nonspeech conceals these policy considerations under the façade of an analytical distinction that thus far has not been persuasively articulated.

---

[105] Volokh, *Freedom of Speech, supra,* at 1093-94.
[106] *Id.* at 1083-84.

> I am not eschewing all attempts at categorization between speech and nonspeech. To do so would make the First Amendment applicable to virtually anything that is expressive or communicative. Still, the distinction as currently constituted hides its ideological character. . . .

> Dealing with privacy issues by categorizing personal information as nonspeech is undesirable because it cloaks the real normative reasons for why society wants to permit greater regulation of certain communicative activity. Rather than focusing on distinguishing between speech and nonspeech, the determination about what forms of information to regulate should center on policy considerations. These policy considerations should turn on the uses of the information rather than on notions about the inherent nature of the information.[107]

Solove goes on to argue that although transfers of personal information may be speech, they are of lower value than other forms of free speech, such as political speech. He contends that whereas speech of public concern is of high value, speech of private concern is given a lower constitutional value, and hence less stringent scrutiny, as is commercial speech and other lower-value categories of speech.

Neil Richards, however, contends that "most privacy regulation that interrupts information flows in the context of an express or implied commercial relationship is neither 'speech' within the current meaning of the First Amendment, nor should it be viewed as such." He criticizes Schwartz and Solove because "they grant too much ground to the First Amendment critique, and may ultimately prove to be underprotective of privacy interests, particularly in the database context." Richards finds Solove's contextual balancing approach too messy to "provide meaningfully increased protection for privacy in the courts." Richards argues instead for a categorical solution and contends that much regulation of speech in the commercial context should be seen as falling entirely outside the scope of the heightened First Amendment scrutiny:

> This might be the case because the speech is threatening, obscene, or libelous, and thus part of the "established" categories of "unprotected speech." But it might also be the case because the speech is an insider trading tip, . . . an offer to create a monopoly in restraint of trade, or a breach of the attorney-client privilege. In either case, the speech would be outside the scope of the First Amendment and could be regulated as long as a rational basis existed for so doing. . . .

> [I]nformation disclosure rules that are the product of generally applicable laws fall outside the scope of the First Amendment. Where information is received by an entity in violation of some other legal rule — whether breach of contract, trespass, theft, or fraud — the First Amendment creates no barrier to the government's ability to prevent and punish disclosure. This is the case even if the information is newsworthy or otherwise of public concern. . . .

> From a First Amendment perspective, no such equivalently important social function [as dissemination of information by the press] . . . is played by database companies engaged in the trade of personal data. Indeed, a general

---

[107] Daniel J. Solove, *The Virtues of Knowing Less: Justifying Privacy Protections Against Disclosure,* 53 Duke L.J. 967, 979-80 (2003).

law regulating the commercial trade in personal data by database, profiling, and marketing companies is far removed from the core speech protected by the First Amendment, and is much more like the "speech" outside the boundaries of heightened review.

Richards goes on to equate the First Amendment critique of privacy regulation to *Lochnerism,* where the Supreme Court in *Lochner v. New York,* 198 U.S. 45 (1905), struck down a statute regulating the hours bakers could work per week based on "freedom of contract." *Lochner* was, and remains, highly criticized for being an impediment to New Deal legislation by an activist ideological Court. Richards notes:

> [T]here are some fairly strong parallels between the traditional conception of *Lochner* and the First Amendment critique of data privacy legislation. Both theories are judicial responses to calls for legal regulation of the economic and social dislocations caused by rapid technological change. *Lochnerism* addressed a major socio-technological problem of the industrial age — the power differential between individuals and businesses in industrial working conditions, while the First Amendment critique is addressed to a major socio-technological problem of our information age — the power differential between individuals and businesses over information in the electronic environment. Both theories place a libertarian gloss upon the Constitution, interpreting it to mandate either "freedom of contract" or "freedom of information." Both theories seek to place certain forms of economic regulation beyond the power of legislatures to enact. And both theories are eagerly supported by business interests keen to immunize themselves from regulation under the aegis of Constitutional doctrine. To the extent that the First Amendment critique is similar to the traditional view of *Lochner,* then, its elevation of an economic right to first-order constitutional magnitude seems similarly dubious.[108]

E. GOVERNMENT ACCESS TO PRIVATE SECTOR RECORDS

1. INFORMATION GATHERING WITHOUT SEARCH WARRANTS

(a) Subpoenas

A subpoena is an order to obtain testimony or documents. Numerous statutes authorize federal agencies to issue subpoenas. In *Doe v. Ashcroft,* 334 F. Supp. 2d 471 (S.D.N.Y. 2004), the court explained:

> For example, the Internal Revenue Service (IRS) may issue subpoenas to investigate possible violations of the tax code, and the Securities Exchange Commission (SEC) may issue subpoenas to investigate possible violations of the securities laws. More obscure examples include the Secretary of Agriculture's power to issue subpoenas in investigating and enforcing laws related to honey

---

[108] Neil Richards, *Reconciling Data Privacy and the First Amendment,* 52 UCLA L. Rev. 1149, 1169, 1180, 1172-73, 1206, 1212-13 (2005).

research, and the Secretary of Commerce's power to issue subpoenas in investigating and enforcing halibut fishing laws. . . .

Where an agency seeks a court order to enforce a subpoena against a resisting subpoena recipient, courts will enforce the subpoena as long as: (1) the agency's investigation is being conducted pursuant to a legitimate purpose, (2) the inquiry is relevant to that purpose, (3) the information is not already within the agency's possession, and (4) the proper procedures have been followed. The Second Circuit has described these standards as "minimal." Even if an administrative subpoena meets these initial criteria to be enforceable, its recipient may nevertheless affirmatively challenge the subpoena on other grounds, such as an allegation that it was issued with an improper purpose or that the information sought is privileged.

In contrast to an administrative subpoena, an ordinary subpoena may be issued in civil or criminal cases. For criminal cases, the government may obtain a subpoena from the clerk of court. Subpoenas are not issued directly by judges. Instead, "[t]he clerk must issue a blank subpoena — signed and sealed — to the party requesting it, and that party must fill in the blanks before the subpoena is served." Fed. R. Crim. P. 17(a). Failure to comply with a subpoena can lead to contempt of court sanctions. A subpoena can broadly compel the production of various documents and items:

> A subpoena may order the witness to produce any books, papers, documents, data, or other objects the subpoena designates. The court may direct the witness to produce the designated items in court before trial or before they are to be offered in evidence. When the items arrive, the court may permit the parties and their attorneys to inspect all or part of them. Fed. R. Crim. P. 17(c)(1).

If the party served with the subpoena has an objection, she may bring a motion to quash or modify the subpoena. "[T]he court may quash or modify the subpoena if compliance would be unreasonable or oppressive." Fed. R. Crim. P. 17(c)(2). As *Doe v. Ashcroft,* 334 F. Supp. 2d 471 (S.D.N.Y. 2004) explains:

> The reasonableness of a subpoena depends on the context. For example, to survive a motion to quash, a subpoena issued in connection with a criminal trial "must make a reasonably specific request for information that would be both relevant and admissible at trial." By contrast, a grand jury subpoena is generally enforced as long as there is a "reasonable possibility that the category of materials the Government seeks will produce information relevant to the general subject of the grand jury's investigation." Considering the grand jury's broad investigatory power and minimal court supervision, it is accurate to observe, as the Second Circuit did long ago, that "[b]asically the grand jury is a law enforcement agency."

When do subpoenas violate the Fourth or Fifth Amendments? Subpoenas can compel the production of documents with incriminating information. Recall that in *Boyd v. United States,* 116 U.S. 616 (1886), the Supreme Court concluded that the government was barred from obtaining a person's papers or documents via a subpoena. However, the Court reversed course in *Hale v. Henkel,* 201 U.S. 43 (1906), when it concluded that the administrative state depended upon the government's ability to subpoena business documents. The Court made a "clear distinction . . . between an individual and a corporation."

Later on, in *Couch v. United States,* 409 U.S. 322 (1973), the Court held that tax records could be subpoenaed without violating the Fourth or Fifth Amendments: "[In a] situation where obligations of disclosure exist and under a system largely dependent upon honest self-reporting even to survive . . . [people] cannot reasonably claim, either for Fourth or Fifth Amendment purposes, an expectation of protected privacy or confidentiality." Then, in *Fisher v. United States,* 425 U.S. 391 (1976), the Court expanded its holding in *Couch* to encompass the disclosure not just of corporate documents or tax records but of nearly all private papers. Christopher Slobogin notes that this was an alteration in the Court's jurisprudence because the Court had long maintained a distinction between corporate records and personal papers. Later cases cut back on the breadth of *Fisher,* holding that the act of a party producing a document can constitute a Fifth Amendment violation. *See, e.g., United States v. Hubbell,* 530 U.S. 27 (2000).[109] However, as Christopher Slobogin notes, the "lion's share of subpoenas that seek personal papers . . . are directed at third parties." In the next section, consider the Court's approach to the applicability of the Fourth Amendment to information held by third parties.

GONZALES V. GOOGLE

234 F.R.D. 674 (N.D. Cal. 2006)

[The government sought information for its use in *ACLU v. Gonzales,* No. 98-CV-5591, pending in the Eastern District of Pennsylvania. That case involved a challenge by the ACLU to the Children's Online Privacy Protection Act (COPPA). Google was not a party to that case, but the government subpoenaed from Google: (1) URL samples: "[a]ll URL's that are available to be located to a query on your company's search engine as of July 31, 2005" and (2) search queries: "[a]ll queries that have been entered on your company's search engine between June 1, 2005 and July 31, 2005 inclusive." Subsequently, the government narrowed its URL sample demand to 50,000 URLs and it narrowed its search query demand to all queries during a one-week period rather than the two-month period mentioned above. Google still raised a challenge, and the government again narrowed its search query request for only 5,000 entries from Google's query log. It continued to seek a sample of 50,000 URLs from Google's search index. Under Federal Rule of Civil Procedure 26, a subpoena sought must be "reasonably calculated to lead to admissible evidence." It may be quashed if the "burden or expense of the proposed discovery outweighs its likely benefit."]

WARE, J. . . . . As narrowed by negotiations with Google and through the course of this Miscellaneous Action, the Government now seeks a sample of 50,000 URLs from Google's search index. In determining whether the information sought is reasonably calculated to lead to admissible evidence, the party seeking the information must first provide the Court with its plans for the requested information. The Government's disclosure of its plans for the

---

[109] For an excellent history of the Supreme Court's jurisprudence regarding subpoenas, see Christopher Slobogin, *Subpoenas and Privacy,* 53 DePaul L. Rev. 805 (2005).

sample of URLs is incomplete. The actual methodology disclosed in the Government's papers as to the search index sample is, in its entirety, as follows: "A human being will browse a random sample of 5,000-10,000 URLs from Google's index and categorize those sites by content" and from this information, the Government intends to "estimate . . . the aggregate properties of the websites that search engines have indexed." The Government's disclosure only describes its methodology for a study to categorize the URLs in Google's search index, and does not disclose a study regarding the effectiveness of filtering software. Absent any explanation of how the "aggregate properties" of material on the Internet is germane to the underlying litigation, the Government's disclosure as to its planned categorization study is not particularly helpful in determining whether the sample of Google's search index sought is reasonably calculated to lead to admissible evidence in the underlying litigation.

Based on the Government's statement that this information is to act as a "test set for the study" and a general statement that the purpose of the study is to "evaluate the effectiveness of content filtering software," the Court is able to envision a study whereby a sample of 50,000 URLs from the Google search index may be reasonably calculated to lead to admissible evidence on measuring the effectiveness of filtering software. In such a study, the Court imagines, the URLs would be categorized, run through the filtering software, and the effectiveness of the filtering software ascertained as to the various categories of URLs. The Government does not even provide this rudimentary level of general detail as to what it intends to do with the sample of URLs to evaluate the effectiveness of filtering software, and at the hearing neither confirmed nor denied the Court's speculations about the study. In fact, the Government seems to indicate that such a study is not what it has in mind: "[t]he government seeks this information *only* to perform a study, in the aggregate, of trends on the Internet" (emphasis added), with no explanation of how an aggregate study of Internet trends would be reasonably calculated to lead to admissible evidence in the underlying suit where the efficacy of filtering software is at issue. . . .

Given the broad definition of relevance in Rule 26, and the current narrow scope of the subpoena, despite the vagueness with which the Government has disclosed its study, the Court gives the Government the benefit of the doubt. The Court finds that 50,000 URLs randomly selected from Google's data base for use in a scientific study of the effectiveness of filters is relevant to the issues in the case of *ACLU v. Gonzales.*[110]

In its original subpoena the Government sought a listing of the text of all search queries entered by Google users over a two month period. As defined in the Government's subpoena, "queries" include only the text of the search string entered by a user, and not "any additional information that may be associated with such a text string that would identify the person who entered the text string into the search engine, or the computer from which the text string was entered." The Government has narrowed its request so that it now seeks only a sample of

---

[110] To the extent that the Government is gathering this information for some other purpose than to run the sample of Google's search index through various filters to determine the efficacy of those filters, the Court would take a different view of the relevance of the information. For example, the Court would not find the information relevant if it is being sought just to characterize the nature of the URL's in Google's database.

5,000 such queries from Google's query log. The Government discloses its plans for the query log information as follows: "A random sample of approximately 1,000 Google queries from a one-week period will be run through the Google search engine. A human being will browse the top URLs returned by each search and categorize the sites by content." . . .

Google also argues that it will be unduly burdened by loss of user trust if forced to produce its users' queries to the Government. Google claims that its success is attributed in large part to the volume of its users and these users may be attracted to its search engine because of the privacy and anonymity of the service. According to Google, even a perception that Google is acquiescing to the Government's demands to release its query log would harm Google's business by deterring some searches by some users.

Google's own privacy statement indicates that Google users could not reasonably expect Google to guard the query log from disclosure to the Government. . . . Google's privacy policy does not represent to users that it keeps confidential any information other than "personal information." Neither Google's URLs nor the text of search strings with "personal information" redacted, are reasonably "personal information" under Google's stated privacy policy. Google's privacy policy indicates that it has not suggested to its users that non-"personal information" such as that sought by the Government is kept confidential.

However, even if an expectation by Google users that Google would prevent disclosure to the Government of its users' search queries is not entirely reasonable, the statistic cited by Dr. Stark that over a quarter of all Internet searches are for pornography indicates that at least some of Google's users expect some sort of privacy in their searches. The expectation of privacy by some Google users may not be reasonable, but may nonetheless have an appreciable impact on the way in which Google is perceived, and consequently the frequency with which users use Google. Such an expectation does not rise to the level of an absolute privilege, but does indicate that there is a potential burden as to Google's loss of goodwill if Google is forced to disclose search queries to the Government.

Rule 45(c)(3)(B) provides additional protections where a subpoena seeks trade secret or confidential commercial information from a nonparty. . . . Because Google still continues to claim information about its entire search index and entire query log as confidential, the Court will presume that the requested information, as a small sample of proprietary information, may be somewhat commercially sensitive, albeit not independently commercially sensitive. Successive disclosures, whether in this lawsuit or pursuant to subsequent civil subpoenas, in the aggregate could yield confidential commercial information about Google's search index or query log. . . .

What the Government has not demonstrated, however, is a substantial need for *both* the information contained in the sample of URLs and sample of search query text. Furthermore, even if the information requested is not a trade secret, a district court may in its discretion limit discovery on a finding that "the discovery sought is unreasonably cumulative or duplicative, or is obtainable from some other source that is more convenient, less burdensome, or less expensive." Rule 26(b)(2)(i).

Faced with duplicative discovery, and with the Government not expressing a preference as to which source of the test set of URLs it prefers, this Court exercises its discretion pursuant to Rule 26(b)(2) and determines that the marginal burden of loss of trust by Google's users based on Google's disclosure of its users' search queries to the Government outweighs the duplicative disclosure's likely benefit to the Government's study. Accordingly, the Court grants the Government's motion to compel only as to the sample of 50,000 URLs from Google's search index.

The Court raises, sua sponte, its concerns about the privacy of Google's users apart from Google's business goodwill argument. . . .

Although the Government has only requested the text strings entered, basic identifiable information may be found in the text strings when users search for personal information such as their social security numbers or credit card numbers through Google in order to determine whether such information is available on the Internet. The Court is also aware of so-called "vanity searches," where a user queries his or her own name perhaps with other information. . . . This concern, combined with the prevalence of Internet searches for sexually explicit material — generally not information that anyone wishes to reveal publicly — gives this Court pause as to whether the search queries themselves may constitute potentially sensitive information.

The Court also recognizes that there may a difference between a private litigant receiving potentially sensitive information and having this information be produced to the Government pursuant to civil subpoena. . . . Even though counsel for the Government assured the Court that the information received will only be used for the present litigation, it is conceivable that the Government may have an obligation to pursue information received for unrelated litigation purposes under certain circumstances regardless of the restrictiveness of a protective order. The Court expressed this concern at oral argument as to queries such as "bomb placement white house," but queries such as "communist berkeley parade route protest war" may also raise similar concerns. In the end, the Court need not express an opinion on this issue because the Government's motion is granted only as to the sample of URLs and not as to the log of search queries.

The Court also refrains from expressing an opinion on the applicability of the Electronic Communications Privacy Act. . . . The Court only notes that the ECPA does not bar the Government's request for sample of 50,000 URLs from Google's index though civil subpoena.

NOTES & QUESTIONS

1. *URL Samples vs. Search Queries.* The sought-after subpoena in *Gonzales v. Google* concerned information about both URL samples and search queries. What decision did the district court reach for each type of data? Are there different privacy implications for governmental access to the two kinds of information?

2. *Can People Be Identified from Anonymous Search Data?* An incident involving AOL proved that individuals can be identified based on their search queries. In August 2006, AOL revealed that it had released to researchers

about 20 million search queries made by over 650,000 users of its search engine. Although AOL had substituted numerical IDs for the subscribers' actual user names, the personal identity of the user could be found based on the search queries. The *New York Times* demonstrated as much by tracking down AOL user No. 4417749; it linked this person's data trail to a 62-year old widow who lived in Lilburn, Georgia, and admitted to the reporter, "Those are my searches."[111]

(b) Financial Information and the Third Party Doctrine

THE BANK SECRECY ACT

The Bank Secrecy Act, Pub. L. No. 91-508, was enacted by Congress in 1970. The Act requires the retention of bank records and creation of reports that would be useful in criminal, tax, or regulatory investigations or proceedings. The Bank Secrecy Act was passed because of worry that shifting from paper to computer records would make white collar law enforcement more complicated.[112] The Act requires that federally insured banks record the identities of account holders as well as copies of each check, draft, or other financial instrument. Not all records and financial instruments must be maintained; only those that the Secretary of the Treasury designates as having a "high degree of usefulness." 12 U.S.C. § 1829b. Further, the Act authorizes the Secretary of the Treasury to promulgate regulations for the reporting of domestic financial transactions. 31 U.S.C. § 1081. The regulations require that a report be made for every deposit, withdrawal, or other transfer of currency exceeding $10,000. *See* 31 C.F.R. § 103.22. For transactions exceeding $5,000 into or out of the United States, the amount, the date of receipt, the form of financial instrument, and the person who received it must be reported. *See* 31 C.F.R. §§ 103.23, 103.25.

CALIFORNIA BANKERS ASSOCIATION V. SHULTZ

416 U.S. 21 (1974)

[A group of bankers as well as depositors challenged the Bank Secrecy Act as a violation of the First, Fourth, and Fifth Amendments. The Court held that the Act did not violate the Fourth Amendment. First, the Court held that the bankers did not possess Fourth Amendment rights in the information because "corporations can claim no equality with individuals in the enjoyment of a right to privacy." Second, as to the Fourth Amendment rights of the individual depositors, the Court concluded that they lacked standing to pursue their claims.]

REHNQUIST, J. . . . The complaint filed in the District Court by the ACLU and the depositors contains no allegation by any of the individual depositors that they were engaged in the type of $10,000 domestic currency transaction which

---

[111] Michael Barbaro & Tom Zeller, Jr., A Face is Exposed for AOL Searcher No. 4417749, N.Y. Times, Aug. 9, 2006.
[112] H. Jeff Smith, *Managing Privacy* 24 (1994).

would necessitate that their bank report it to the Government. . . . [W]e simply cannot assume that the mere fact that one is a depositor in a bank means that he has engaged or will engage in a transaction involving more than $10,000 in currency, which is the only type of domestic transaction which the Secretary's regulations require that the banks report. That being so, the depositor plaintiffs lack standing to challenge the domestic reporting regulations, since they do not show that their transactions are required to be reported. . . .

We therefore hold that the Fourth Amendment claims of the depositor plaintiffs may not be considered on the record before us. Nor do we think that the California Bankers Association or the Security National Bank can vicariously assert such Fourth Amendment claims on behalf of bank customers in general. . .

[The Court also rejected a Fifth Amendment challenge to the Act as well as a First Amendment challenge. With regard to the First Amendment challenge, the Court concluded that the "threat to any First Amendment rights of the ACLU or its members from the mere existence of the records in the hands of the bank is a good deal more remote than the threat assertedly posed by the Army's system of compilation and distribution of information which we declined to adjudicate in *Laird v. Tatum*, 408 U.S. 1 (1972)."]

DOUGLAS, J. dissenting. . . . One's reading habits furnish telltale clues to those who are bent on bending us to one point of view. What one buys at the hardware and retail stores may furnish clues to potential uses of wires, soap powders, and the like used by criminals. A mandatory recording of all telephone conversations would be better than the recording of checks under the Bank Secrecy Act, if Big Brother is to have his way. The records of checks — now available to the investigators — are highly useful. In a sense a person is defined by the checks he writes. By examining them the agents get to know his doctors, lawyers, creditors, political allies, social connections, religious affiliation, educational interests, the papers and magazines he reads, and so on ad infinitum. These are all tied to one's social security number; and now that we have the data banks, these other items will enrich that storehouse and make it possible for a bureaucrat — by pushing one button — to get in an instant the names of the 190 million Americans who are subversives or potential and likely candidates.

It is, I submit, sheer nonsense to agree with the Secretary that all bank records of every citizen "have a high degree of usefulness in criminal, tax, or regulatory investigations or proceedings." That is unadulterated nonsense unless we are to assume that every citizen is a crook, an assumption I cannot make.

Since the banking transactions of an individual give a fairly accurate account of his religion, ideology, opinions, and interests, a regulation impounding them and making them automatically available to all federal investigative agencies is a sledge-hammer approach to a problem that only a delicate scalpel can manage. Where fundamental personal rights are involved — as is true when as here the Government gets large access to one's beliefs, ideas, politics, religion, cultural concerns, and the like — the Act should be "narrowly drawn" to meet the precise evil. Bank accounts at times harbor criminal plans. But we only rush with the crowd when we vent on our banks and their customers the devastating and leveling requirements of the present Act. I am not yet ready to agree that

America is so possessed with evil that we must level all constitutional barriers to give our civil authorities the tools to catch criminals. . . .

UNITED STATES V. MILLER
425 U.S. 435 (1976)

POWELL, J. . . . [A]gents from the Treasury Department's Alcohol, Tobacco and Firearms Bureau presented grand jury subpoenas issued in blank by the clerk of the District Court, and completed by the United States Attorney's office, to the presidents of the Citizens & Southern National Bank of Warner Robins and the Bank of Byron, where respondent maintained accounts. The subpoenas required the two presidents to appear on January 24, 1973, and to produce [all records of loans as well as savings and checking accounts in the name of Mitch Miller]. . . .

The banks did not advise respondent that the subpoenas had been served but ordered their employees to make the records available and to provide copies of any documents the agents desired. . . .

The grand jury met on February 12, 1973, 19 days after the return date on the subpoenas. Respondent and four others were indicted. . . . The record does not indicate whether any of the bank records were in fact presented to the grand jury. They were used in the investigation and provided "one or two" investigatory leads. Copies of the checks also were introduced at trial to establish the overt acts [in a conspiracy in which the defendants were charged].

In his motion to suppress, denied by the District Court, respondent contended that the bank documents were illegally seized. It was urged that the subpoenas were defective because they were issued by the United States Attorney rather than a court, no return was made to a court, and the subpoenas were returnable on a date when the grand jury was not in session. The Court of Appeals reversed. Citing the prohibition in *Boyd v. United States*, 116 U.S. 616, 622 (1886), against "compulsory production of a man's private papers to establish a criminal charge against him," the court held that the Government had improperly circumvented *Boyd*'s protections of respondent's Fourth Amendment right against "unreasonable searches and seizures" by "first requiring a third party bank to copy all of its depositors' personal checks and then, with an improper invocation of legal process, calling upon the bank to allow inspection and reproduction of those copies." . . . The subpoenas issued here were found not to constitute adequate "legal process." The fact that the bank officers cooperated voluntarily was found to be irrelevant, for "he whose rights are threatened by the improper disclosure here was a bank depositor, not a bank official." . . .

We find that there was no intrusion into any area in which respondent had a protected Fourth Amendment interest and that the District Court therefore correctly denied respondent's motion to suppress. . . .

On their face, the documents subpoenaed here are not respondent's "private papers." Unlike the claimant in *Boyd* [*v. United States*], respondent can assert neither ownership nor possession. Instead, these are the business records of the banks. Respondent argues, however, that the Bank Secrecy Act introduces a factor that makes the subpoena in this case the functional equivalent of a search and seizure of the depositor's "private papers." We have held, in *California*

Bankers Ass'n v. Shultz, that the mere maintenance of records pursuant to the requirements of the Act "invade(s) no Fourth Amendment right of any depositor." But respondent contends that the combination of the recordkeeping requirements of the Act and the issuance of a subpoena to obtain those records permits the Government to circumvent the requirements of the Fourth Amendment by allowing it to obtain a depositor's private records without complying with the legal requirements that would be applicable had it proceeded against him directly. Therefore, we must address the question whether the compulsion embodied in the Bank Secrecy Act as exercised in this case creates a Fourth Amendment interest in the depositor where none existed before. This question was expressly reserved in *California Bankers Ass'n.*

Respondent urges that he has a Fourth Amendment interest in the records kept by the banks because they are merely copies of personal records that were made available to the banks for a limited purpose and in which he has a reasonable expectation of privacy. He relies on this Court's statement in *Katz v. United States*, 389 U.S. 347, 353 (1967), that "we have . . . departed from the narrow view" that "'property interests control the right of the Government to search and seize,'" and that a "search and seizure" become unreasonable when the Government's activities violate "the privacy upon which (a person) justifiably relie[s]." But in *Katz* the Court also stressed that "[w]hat a person knowingly exposes to the public . . . is not a subject of Fourth Amendment protection." We must examine the nature of the particular documents sought to be protected in order to determine whether there is a legitimate "expectation of privacy" concerning their contents.

Even if we direct our attention to the original checks and deposit slips, rather than to the microfilm copies actually viewed and obtained by means of the subpoena, we perceive no legitimate "expectation of privacy" in their contents. The checks are not confidential communications but negotiable instruments to be used in commercial transactions. All of the documents obtained, including financial statements and deposit slips, contain only information voluntarily conveyed to the banks and exposed to their employees in the ordinary course of business. The lack of any legitimate expectation of privacy concerning the information kept in bank records was assumed by Congress in enacting the Bank Secrecy Act, the expressed purpose of which is to require records to be maintained because they "have a high degree of usefulness in criminal tax, and regulatory investigations and proceedings." 12 U.S.C. § 1829b(a)(1).

The depositor takes the risk, in revealing his affairs to another, that the information will be conveyed by that person to the Government. This Court has held repeatedly that the Fourth Amendment does not prohibit the obtaining of information revealed to a third party and conveyed by him to Government authorities, even if the information is revealed on the assumption that it will be used only for a limited purpose and the confidence placed in the third party will not be betrayed.

This analysis is not changed by the mandate of the Bank Secrecy Act that records of depositors' transactions be maintained by banks. In *California Bankers Ass'n v. Shultz,* we rejected the contention that banks, when keeping records of their depositors' transactions pursuant to the Act, are acting solely as agents of the Government. But, even if the banks could be said to have been acting solely as Government agents in transcribing the necessary information and complying without protest with the requirements of the subpoenas, there would be no intrusion upon the depositors' Fourth Amendment rights. . . .

Since no Fourth Amendment interests of the depositor are implicated here, this case is governed by the general rule that the issuance of a subpoena to a third party to obtain the records of that party does not violate the rights of a defendant, even if a criminal prosecution is contemplated at the time of the subpoena is issued. Under these principles, it was firmly settled, before the passage of the Bank Secrecy Act, that an Internal Revenue Service summons directed to a third-party bank does not violate the Fourth Amendment rights of a depositor under investigation.

Many banks traditionally kept permanent records of their depositors' accounts, although not all banks did so and the practice was declining in recent years. By requiring that such records be kept by all banks, the Bank Secrecy Act is not a novel means designed to circumvent established Fourth Amendment rights. It is merely an attempt to facilitate the use of a proper and long-standing law enforcement technique by insuring that records are available when they are needed.

We hold that the District Court correctly denied respondent's motion to suppress, since he possessed no Fourth Amendment interest that could be vindicated by a challenge to the subpoenas. . . .

BRENNAN, J. dissenting. . . . The pertinent phrasing of the Fourth Amendment "The right of the people to be secure in their persons, houses, papers, and effects, against unreasonable searches and seizures, shall not be violated" is virtually in haec verba as Art. I, § 19, of the California Constitution "The right of the people to be secure in their persons, houses, papers, and effects, against unreasonable seizures and searches, shall not be violated." The California Supreme Court has reached a conclusion under Art. I, § 13, in the same factual situation, contrary to that reached by the Court today under the Fourth Amendment. I dissent because in my view the California Supreme Court correctly interpreted the relevant constitutional language. . . .

Addressing the threshold question whether the accused's right of privacy was invaded, and relying on part on the decision of the Court of Appeals in this case, Mr. Justice Mosk stated in his excellent opinion for a unanimous court:

> It cannot be gainsaid that the customer of a bank expects that the documents, such as checks, which he transmits to the bank in the course of his business operations, will remain private, and that such an expectation is reasonable. The prosecution concedes as much, although it asserts that this expectation is not constitutionally cognizable. Representatives of several banks testified at the suppression hearing that information in their possession regarding a customer's account is deemed by them to be confidential.
>
> In the present case, although the record establishes that copies of petitioner's bank statements rather than of his checks were provided to the officer, the distinction is not significant with relation to petitioner's expectation of privacy. That the bank alters the form in which it records the information transmitted to it by the depositor to show the receipt and disbursement of money on a bank statement does not diminish the depositor's anticipation of privacy in the matters

which he confides to the bank. A bank customer's reasonable expectation is that, absent compulsion by legal process, the matters he reveals to the bank will be utilized by the bank only for internal banking purposes. Thus, we hold petitioner had a reasonable expectation that the bank would maintain the confidentiality of those papers which originated with him in check form and of the bank statements into which a record of those same checks had been transformed pursuant to internal bank practice. . . .

The underlying dilemma in this and related cases is that the bank, a detached and disinterested entity, relinquished the records voluntarily. But that circumstance should not be crucial. For all practical purposes, the disclosure by individuals or business firms of their financial affairs to a bank is not entirely volitional, since it is impossible to participate in the economic life of contemporary society without maintaining a bank account. In the course of such dealings, a depositor reveals many aspects of his personal affairs, opinions, habits and associations. Indeed, the totality of bank records provides a virtual current biography. While we are concerned in the present case only with bank statements, the logical extension of the contention that the bank's ownership of records permits free access to them by any police officer extends far beyond such statements to checks, savings, bonds, loan applications, loan guarantees, and all papers which the customer has supplied to the bank to facilitate the conduct of his financial affairs upon the reasonable assumption that the information would remain confidential. To permit a police officer access to these records merely upon his request, without any judicial control as to relevancy or other traditional requirements of legal process, and to allow the evidence to be used in any subsequent criminal prosecution against a defendant, opens the door to a vast and unlimited range of very real abuses of police power.

Cases are legion that condemn violent searches and invasions of an individual's right to the privacy of his dwelling. The imposition upon privacy, although perhaps not so dramatic, may be equally devastating when other methods are employed. Development of photocopying machines, electronic computers and other sophisticated instruments have accelerated the ability of government to intrude into areas which a person normally chooses to exclude from prying eyes and inquisitive minds. Consequently judicial interpretations of the reach of the constitutional protection of individual privacy must keep pace with the perils created by these new devices. . . .

NOTES & QUESTIONS

1. *The Right to Financial Privacy Act.* Two years after *Miller*, in 1978, Congress passed the Right to Financial Privacy Act (RFPA), Pub. L. No. 95-630, which partially filled the void left by *Miller*. The RFPA prevents banks and other financial institutions from disclosing a person's financial information to the government unless the records are disclosed pursuant to subpoena or search warrant. *See* 29 U.S.C. §§ 3401–3422.

2. *State Law.* As discussed throughout this book, many states have rejected the Supreme Court's interpretations of the Fourth Amendment, opting to provide additional protections. In 2004, a New Jersey court rejected the reasoning of *Miller*:

> The discomfort in finding a stranger pouring over one's checkbook, deposit slips and cancelled checks is equal to seeing someone sifting through his or

her garbage, or reviewing a list of dialed telephone numbers called from home, like telephones, are an extension of one's desk or home office. Indeed, as in the case of the telephone, technological advances in the form of personal computers with access to the internet and electronic banking services have made those services available to the homes of its depositors. Bank records kept at home could not be seized in the absence of a duly issued search warrant based upon probable cause and they should not be vulnerable to viewing, copying, seizure or retrieval simply because they are readily available at a bank.

Finally, the fact that financial affairs are memorialized in written records of banks or maintained in their electronic data systems to which, as part of its legitimate business, a bank's employees have access, does not suggest that persons have any sense that their private and personal traits and affairs are less confidential when they deal with their bank than when they make telephone calls or put out their garbage. The repose of confidence in a bank goes beyond entrustment of money, but extends to the expectation that financial affairs are confidential except as may be reasonable and necessary to conduct customary bank business. *State v. McAllister*, 840 A.2d 967 (2004).

3. *Pen Registers and* **Smith v. Maryland.** Recall the Court's reasoning in *Smith v. Maryland* (Chapter 3), where the Court held that the Fourth Amendment was inapplicable to pen registers of phone numbers. How does the Court's rationale in *Smith* compare to that in *Miller*?

4. *The Implications of the Third Party Doctrine.* Daniel Solove contends that *Miller* and *Smith* pose a substantial threat to privacy in the modern world given the dramatic extent to which third parties hold personal information:

> In the Information Age, an increasing amount of personal information is contained in records maintained by private sector entities, Internet Service Providers, phone companies, cable companies, merchants, bookstores, websites, hotels, landlords and employers. Many private sector entities are beginning to aggregate the information in these records to create extensive digital dossiers.
>
> The data in these digital dossiers increasingly flows from the private sector to the government, particularly for law enforcement use. . . . Detailed records of an individual's reading materials, purchases, magazines, diseases and ailments, and website activity, enable the government to assemble a profile of an individual's finances, health, psychology, beliefs, politics, interests, and lifestyle. This data can unveil a person's anonymous speech, groups and personal associations.
>
> The increasing amount of personal information flowing to the government poses significant problems with far-reaching social effects. Inadequately constrained government information gathering can lead to at least three types of harms. First, it can result in the slow creep toward a totalitarian state. Second, it can chill democratic activities and interfere with individual self-determination. Third, it can lead to the danger of harms arising in bureaucratic settings. Individuals, especially in times of crisis, are vulnerable to abuse from government misuse of personal information. Once government entities have collected personal information, there are few regulations in how it can be used and how long it can be kept. The bureaucratic nature of modern law enforcement institutions can enable sweeping searches, the misuse of personal

data, improper exercises of discretion, unjustified interrogation, arrests, roundups of disfavored individuals, and discriminatory profiling.[113]

Because of the third party doctrine in *Miller* and *Smith*, the Fourth Amendment fails to limit the government from gathering personal information maintained by businesses. *Miller* and *Smith* were decided in the 1970s. Should they be reconsidered in light of the extensive computerized records maintained today? What would be the consequences of overruling *Miller* and *Smith*?

(c) The USA PATRIOT Act § 215

Section 215 of the USA PATRIOT Act adds a new § 501 to the Foreign Intelligence Surveillance Act (FISA):

> (a)(1) The Director of the Federal Bureau of Investigation or a designee of the Director (whose rank shall be no lower than Assistant Special Agent in Charge) may make an application for an order requiring the production of any tangible things (including books, records, papers, documents, and other items) for an investigation to protect against international terrorism or clandestine intelligence activities, provided that such investigation of a United States person is not conducted solely upon the basis of activities protected by the first amendment to the Constitution.
>
> (2) An investigation conducted under this section shall —
> (A) be conducted under guidelines approved by the Attorney General under Executive Order 12333 (or a successor order); and
> (B) not be conducted of a United States person solely upon the basis of activities protected by the first amendment to the Constitution of the United States.

Applications for court orders shall be made to a judge and "shall specify that the records are sought for an authorized investigation" and "to protect against international terrorism or clandestine intelligence activities." § 501(b). This section also has a gag order:

> (d) No person shall disclose to any other person (other than those persons necessary to produce the tangible things under this section) that the Federal Bureau of Investigation has sought or obtained tangible things under this section. § 501(d).

The American Library Association (ALA) led a spirited campaign against § 215. It issued a resolution stating, in part, that

> the American Library Association encourages all librarians, library administrators, library governing bodies, and library advocates to educate their users, staff, and communities about the process for compliance with the USA PATRIOT Act and other related measures and about the dangers to individual privacy and the confidentiality of library records resulting from those measures.

---

[113] Daniel J. Solove, *Digital Dossiers and the Dissipation of Fourth Amendment Privacy*, 75 S. Cal. L. Rev. 1083, 1084-86 (2002).

In 2003, Attorney General John Ashcroft stated that § 215 had never been used to access library records. He further stated: "The fact is, with just 11,000 FBI agents and over a billion visitors to America's libraries each year, the Department of Justice has neither the staffing, the time nor the inclination to monitor the reading habits of Americans. . . . No offense to the American Library Association, but we just don't care." In 2005, the ALA revealed the results of a survey of librarians indicating a minimum of 137 formal law enforcement inquiries to library officials since 9/11, 49 of which were by federal officials and the remainder by state and local officials. The study did not indicate whether any of these were pursuant to § 215.

(d) National Security Letters

Provisions in several laws permit the FBI to obtain personal information from third parties merely by making a written request in cases involving national security. No court order is required. These requests are called "National Security Letters" (NSLs).

The Stored Communications Act. ECPA's Stored Communications Act contains an NSL provision, 18 U.S.C. § 2709. This provision allows the FBI to compel communications companies (ISPs, telephone companies) to release customer records when the FBI makes a particular certification. Before the USA PATRIOT Act, the FBI had to certify that the records were "relevant to an authorized foreign counterintelligence investigation" and that "there are specific and articulable facts giving reason to believe that the person or entity to whom the information sought pertains is a foreign power or an agent of a foreign power as defined in section 101 of the Foreign Intelligence Surveillance Act of 1978 (50 U.S.C. 1801)."

Section 505 of the USA PATRIOT Act amended the National Security Letters provision of ECPA by altering what must be certified. The existing requirements regarding counterintelligence and specific and articulable facts that the target was an agent of a foreign power were deleted. The FBI now needs to certify that the records are "relevant to an authorized investigation to protect against terrorism or clandestine intelligence activities, provided that such an investigation of a United States person is not conducted solely on the basis of activities protected by the first amendment to the Constitution of the United States." 18 U.S.C. § 2709.

This provision also has a gag order:

> No wire or electronic communication service provider, or officer, employee, or agent thereof, shall disclose to any person that the Federal Bureau of Investigation has sought or obtained access to information or records under this section. § 2709(c).

Unlike § 215, Ashcroft made no statement about § 505.[114]

---

[114] Mark Sidel, *More Secure, Less Free?: Antiterrorism Policy and Civil Liberties After September 11*, at 14 (2004).

The Right to Financial Privacy Act. The Right to Financial Privacy Act (RFPA) also contains an NSL provision. As amended by the Patriot Act, this provision states that the FBI can obtain an individual's financial records if it "certifies in writing to the financial institution that such records are sought for foreign counter intelligence purposes to protect against international terrorism or clandestine intelligence activities, provided that such an investigation of a United States person is not conducted solely upon the basis of activities protected by the first amendment to the Constitution of the United States." 12 U.S.C. § 3414(a)(5)(A). As with the Stored Communications Act NSL provision, the RFPA NSL provision contains a "gag" rule prohibiting the financial institution from disclosing the fact it received the NSL. § 3414(a)(5)(D).

The Fair Credit Reporting Act. Likewise, the Fair Credit Reporting Act provides for NSLs. Pursuant to a written FBI request, consumer reporting agencies "shall furnish to the Federal Bureau of Investigation the names and addresses of all financial institutions . . . at which a customer maintains or has maintained an account." 15 U.S.C. § 1681u(a). Consumer reporting agencies must also furnish "identifying information respecting a consumer, limited to name, address, former addresses, places of employment, or former places of employment." 15 U.S.C. § 1681u(b). To obtain a full consumer report, however, the FBI must obtain a court order ex parte. 15 U.S.C. § 1681u(c). Like the other NSL provisions, the FCRA NSL provisions restrict NSLs for investigations based "solely" upon First Amendment activities. The FCRA NSL also has a "gag" rule. 15 U.S.C. § 1681u(d).

The USA PATRIOT Reauthorization Act. In the USA PATRIOT Reauthorization Act of 2005, Congress made several amendments that affected NSLs. It explicitly provided for judicial review of NSLs. It also required a detailed examination by the DOJ's Inspector General "of the effectiveness and use, including any improper or illegal use" of NSLs. This kind of audit proved its value in March 2006 when the Inspector General issued its review of the FBI's use of NSLs. First, the Inspector General found a dramatic underreporting of NSLs. Indeed, the total number of NSL requests between 2003 and 2005 totaled at least 143,074. Of these NSLs requests, as the Inspector General found, "[t]he overwhelming majority . . . sought telephone toll billing records information, subscriber information (telephone or e-mail) or electronic communication transaction records under the ECPA NSL statute."[115]

The Inspector General also carried out a limited audit of investigative case files, and found that 22 percent of them contained at least one violation of investigative guidelines or procedures that was not reported to any of the relevant internal authorities at the FBI. Finally, the Inspector General also found over 700 instances in which the FBI obtained telephone records and subscriber information from telephone companies based on the use of a so-called "exigent letter" authority. This authority, absent from the statute, was invented by the FBI's Counterterrorism Division. Having devised this new power, the FBI did not set

---

[115] Office of the Inspector General, *A Review of the Federal Bureau of Investigations Use of National Security Letters* x-xiv (Mar. 2007).

limits on its use, or track how it was employed. Witnesses told the Inspector General that many of these letters "were not issued in exigent circumstances, and the FBI was unable to determine which letters were sent in emergency circumstances due to inadequate recordkeeping." Indeed, "in most instances, there was no documentation associating the requests with pending national security investigations."[116]

NSL Litigation. In *Doe v. Ashcroft*, 334 F. Supp. 2d 471 (S.D.N.Y. 2004), a federal district court invalidated 18 U.S.C. § 2709 (*Doe I*). It found that § 2709 violated the Fourth Amendment because, at least as applied, it barred or at least substantially deterred a judicial challenge to an NSL request. It did so by prohibiting an NSL recipient from revealing the existence of an NSL inquiry. The court also found that the "all inclusive sweep" of § 2709 violated the First Amendment as a prior-restraint and content-based restriction on sweep that was subject to strict scrutiny review. Additionally, the court found that in some instances the use of an NSL might infringe upon people's First Amendment rights. For example, suppose that the FBI uses an NSL to find out the identity of an anonymous speaker on the Internet. Does the First Amendment limit using an NSL in this manner? Does the First Amendment restriction on the NSL provisions, which prohibits NSLs for investigations based "solely" upon First Amendment activities, adequately address these potential First Amendment problems?

Shortly after *Doe I,* another district court invalidated 18 U.S.C. § 2709(c), which prevented a recipient of an NSL to disclose information about the government's action. *Doe v. Gonzales*, 386 F. Supp. 2d 66, 82 (D. Conn. 2005) (*Doe II*).

While appeals in *Doe I* and *Doe II* were pending, Congress enacted the USA PATRIOT Reauthorization Act of 2005, which made several changes to § 2709 and added several provisions concerning judicial review of NSLs, which were codified at 18 U.S.C. § 3511. Following enactment of these provisions, plaintiffs challenged the amended nondisclosure provisions of §§ 2709(c) and 3511. The same district court that issued the *Doe I* opinion then found §§ 2709(c) and 3511(b) to be facially unconstitutional. *Doe v. Gonzales*, 500 F. Supp. 2d 379 (S.D.N.Y. 2007) (*Doe III*).

The newly enacted § 3511 provided for judicial review of NSLs. As a result, the *Doe III* plaintiffs did not challenge it on Fourth Amendment grounds as in *Doe I*. Instead, they argued, and the court agreed, that the nondisclosure provisions of § 2709(c) remained an unconstitutional prior restraint and content-based restriction on speech. The court also concluded that § 3511(b) was unconstitutional under the First Amendment and the doctrine of separation of powers. Among its conclusions, the court noted that Congress in amending § 2709(c) allowed the FBI to certify on a case-by-case basis whether nondisclosure was necessary. Yet, this narrowing of the statute to reduce the possibility of unnecessary limitation of speech also means that the FBI could conceivably engage in viewpoint discrimination. As a consequence, the amended

---

[116] *Id.* at xxxviii, xxxiv.

statute was a content-based restriction as well as a prior restraint on speech and, therefore, subject to strict scrutiny.

The Second Circuit modified the district court's opinion. In *Doe v. Mukasey*, 549 F.3d 861 (2008), the court found that the challenged statutes did not comply with the First Amendment, although not to the extent that the district court found. It also concluded that the lower court's ordered relief was too broad. The Second Circuit began by construing § 2709(c) to permit a nondisclosure requirement only when senior FBI officials certify that disclosure may result in an enumerated harm that is related to "an authorized investigation to protect against international terrorism or clandestine intelligence activities." It also interpreted § 3511(b)(2) and (b)(3) as placing the burden on the Government "to show that a good reason exists to expect that disclosure of receipt of an NSL will risk an enumerated harm." Additionally, it held the relevant subsections unconstitutional to the extent that they would impose a nondisclosure requirement without placing the burden on the government to initiate judicial review of that obligation, and to the extent that judicial review would treat "a government official's certification that disclosure may endanger the national security of the United States or interfere with diplomatic relations . . . as conclusive."

2. INFORMATION GATHERING WITH SEARCH WARRANTS

Under the Fourth Amendment, a search warrant may be issued if there is probable cause to believe that there is incriminating evidence in the place to be searched. This is not limited to places owned or occupied by the criminal suspect. In certain instances, incriminating documents or things may be possessed by an innocent party. What if that innocent party is a journalist or news entity, and the search implicates First Amendment rights? Consider the following case:

ZURCHER V. THE STANFORD DAILY
436 U.S. 547 (1978)

[A demonstration at the Stanford University Hospital turned violent when police tried to force demonstrators to leave. A group of demonstrators attacked and injured nine police officers. The officers were able to identify only two of the assailants. The *Stanford Daily*, a student newspaper, published articles and photographs about the incident. The District Attorney obtained a search warrant to search the *Daily*'s offices for negatives, film, and pictures about the incident. After the search, the *Daily* brought suit under 42 U.S.C. § 1983, alleging that the search was unconstitutional.]

WHITE, J. . . . The issue here is how the Fourth Amendment is to be construed and applied to the "third party" search, the recurring situation where state authorities have probable cause to believe that fruits, instrumentalities, or other evidence of crime is located on identified property but do not then have probable cause to believe that the owner or possessor of the property is himself implicated in the crime that has occurred or is occurring. . . .

Under existing law, valid warrants may be issued to search *any* property, whether or not occupied by a third party, at which there is probable cause to believe that fruits, instrumentalities, or evidence of a crime will be found. Nothing on the face of the Amendment suggests that a third-party search warrant should not normally issue. . . .

As the Fourth Amendment has been construed and applied by this Court, "when the State's reason to believe incriminating evidence will be found becomes sufficiently great, the invasion of privacy becomes justified and a warrant to search and seize will issue." . . .

As we understand the structure and language of the Fourth Amendment and our cases expounding it, valid warrants to search property may be issued when it is satisfactorily demonstrated to the magistrate that fruits, instrumentalities, or evidence of crime is located on the premises. The Fourth Amendment has itself struck the balance between privacy and public need, and there is no occasion or justification for a court to revise the Amendment and strike a new balance by denying the search warrant in the circumstances present here and by insisting that the investigation proceed by subpoena *duces tecum*, whether on the theory that the latter is a less intrusive alternative or otherwise. . . .

[The *Daily* argues] that searches of newspaper offices for evidence of crime reasonably believed to be on the premises will seriously threaten the ability of the press to gather, analyze, and disseminate news. This is said to be true for several reasons: First, searches will be physically disruptive to such an extent that timely publication will be impeded. Second, confidential sources of information will dry up, and the press will also lose opportunities to cover various events because of fears of the participants that press files will be readily available to the authorities. Third, reporters will be deterred from recording and preserving their recollections for future use if such information is subject to seizure. Fourth, the processing of news and its dissemination will be chilled by the prospects that searches will disclose internal editorial deliberations. Fifth, the press will resort to self-censorship to conceal its possession of information of potential interest to the police.

It is true that the struggle from which the Fourth Amendment emerged "is largely a history of conflict between the Crown and the press," and that in issuing warrants and determining the reasonableness of a search, state and federal magistrates should be aware that "unrestricted power of search and seizure could also be an instrument for stifling liberty of expression." Where the materials sought to be seized may be protected by the First Amendment, the requirements of the Fourth Amendment must be applied with "scrupulous exactitude." . . . Where presumptively protected materials are sought to be seized, the warrant requirement should be administered to leave as little as possible to the discretion or whim of the officer in the field. . . .

Aware of the long struggle between Crown and press and desiring to curb unjustified official intrusions, the Framers took the enormously important step of subjecting searches to the test of reasonableness and to the general rule requiring search warrants issued by neutral magistrates. They nevertheless did not forbid warrants where the press was involved, did not require special showings that subpoenas would be impractical, and did not insist that the owner of the place to be searched, if connected with the press, must be shown to be implicated in the offense being investigated. Further, the prior cases do no more than insist that the courts apply the warrant requirements with particular exactitude when First Amendment interests would be endangered by the search. As we see it, no more than this is required where the warrant requested is for the seizure of criminal evidence reasonably believed to be on the premises occupied by a newspaper. Properly administered, the preconditions for a warrant — probable cause, specificity with respect to the place to be searched and the things to be seized, and overall reasonableness — should afford sufficient protection against the harms that are assertedly threatened by warrants for searching newspaper offices. . . .

STEWART, J. joined by MARSHALL, J. dissenting. It seems to me self-evident that police searches of newspaper offices burden the freedom of the press. The most immediate and obvious First Amendment injury caused by such a visitation by the police is physical disruption of the operation of the newspaper. Policemen occupying a newsroom and searching it thoroughly for what may be an extended period of time will inevitably interrupt its normal operations, and thus impair or even temporarily prevent the processes of newsgathering, writing, editing, and publishing. By contrast, a subpoena would afford the newspaper itself an opportunity to locate whatever material might be requested and produce it.

But there is another and more serious burden on a free press imposed by an unannounced police search of a newspaper office: the possibility of disclosure of information received from confidential sources, or of the identity of the sources themselves. . . .

It requires no blind leap of faith to understand that a person who gives information to a journalist only on condition that his identity will not be revealed will be less likely to give that information if he knows that, despite the journalist's assurance his identity may in fact be disclosed. And it cannot be denied that confidential information may be exposed to the eyes of police officers who execute a search warrant by rummaging through the files, cabinets, desks, and wastebaskets of a newsroom. Since the indisputable effect of such searches will thus be to prevent a newsman from being able to promise confidentiality to his potential sources, it seems obvious to me that a journalist's access to information, and thus the public's will thereby be impaired.

NOTES & QUESTIONS

1. ***Searches Implicating the First Amendment.*** In certain circumstances, a search may implicate the First Amendment, as it did in *Zurcher*. Suppose the police desire to search a bookstore's records to determine who purchased a particular book. The police obtain a valid warrant. However, First Amendment rights may be implicated, as such searches might chill people's ability to read. Would the government have to, in addition to securing a warrant, satisfy First Amendment scrutiny? For one court's answer, see *Tattered Cover v. City of Thornton* in Chapter 5.

2. ***Subpoenas vs. Warrants.*** In certain ways, subpoenas can be more protective of privacy than warrants. The person served with the subpoena can produce the requested documents herself rather than having government officials

physically enter the person's office or dwelling to conduct the search. Further, the person can challenge the subpoena in court prior to complying; with a search warrant, judicial authorization is granted ex parte, and the warrant is most often challenged only after it is executed. On the other hand, subpoenas can be obtained without any requirement of particularized suspicion or probable cause. The role for judicial oversight is rather minimal.

PRIVACY PROTECTION ACT

In 1980, Congress responded to *Zurcher* by passing the Privacy Protection Act (PPA), Pub. L. No. 96-440, 94 Stat. 1879, codified at 42 U.S.C. § 2000aa.

Work Product. Pursuant to the PPA:

> Notwithstanding any other law, it shall be unlawful for a government officer or employee, in connection with the investigation or prosecution of a criminal offense, to search for or seize any work product materials possessed by a person reasonably believed to have a purpose to disseminate to the public a newspaper, book, broadcast, or other similar form of public communication, in or affecting interstate or foreign commerce. . . . § 2000aa(a).

However, if "there is probable cause to believe that the person possessing such materials has committed or is committing the criminal offense to which the materials relate," then such materials may be searched or seized. The "criminal offense" cannot consist of the mere receipt, possession, or communication of the materials (except if it involves national defense data, classified information, or child pornography). § 2000aa(a)(1). The materials may be searched or seized if "there is reason to believe that the immediate seizure of such materials is necessary to prevent the death of, or serious bodily injury to, a human being." § 2000aa(a)(2).

Other Documents. The PPA also restricts the search or seizure of "documentary materials, other than work product materials, possessed by a person in connection with a purpose to disseminate to the public a newspaper, book, broadcast, or other similar form of public communication." § 2000aa(b). This provision has the same exceptions as the work product provision, with additional exceptions permitting search or seizure when there is reason to believe that the documents will be destroyed or concealed.

Subpoenas. The effect of the PPA is to require law enforcement officials to obtain a subpoena in order to obtain such information. Unlike search warrants, subpoenas permit the party subject to them to challenge them in court before having to comply. Further, instead of law enforcement officials searching through offices or records, the persons served with the subpoena must produce the documents themselves.

INDEX